D0185003

THE REVELS PLAYS

Former Editors
Clifford Leech 1958–71
F. David Hoeniger 1970–85

General Editors
E. A. J. Honigmann, J. R. Mulryne,
David Bevington and Eugene M. Waith

EDWARD THE SECOND

This latest and most valuable addition to the 'Revels Plays' series provides the most complete and detailed edition of *Edward II* ever published.

The introduction contains a fresh analysis of the first quarto (including new evidence of its original dating) and a reconsideration of the play's complex relation to the Shakespearean histories that preceded and followed it. Charles Forker offers a fascinating and far-reaching discussion of Marlowe's use of sources, and presents a new argument for the drama's five-act structure. He delves into the conflicting and controversial opinions concerning the genre and sexual politics of the play, and also includes the fullest record of the stage history ever assembled.

With meticulous scholarship, Forker has collated some forty-six editions (including the important, rare, and usually ignored editions of Broughton and Oxberry in 1818). The appendices provide substantive variants from the Broughton and Oxberry texts as well as generous extracts from the sources. This edition will stand as the definitive scholarly text for Marlowe's most provocative play for years to come.

Charles R. Forker is Professor of English at Indiana University.

Introduction, critical apparatus, etc.,
© Charles R. Forker 1994

Published by
Manchester University Press
Oxford Road, Manchester M13 9PL, UK
and Room 400, 175 Fifth Avenue, New York,
NY 10010, USA

Distributed exclusively in the USA and Canada by
St. Martin's Press, Inc., 175 Fifth Avenue,
New York, NY 10010, USA

ISBN 0 7190 3089 7 *paperback*

British Library Cataloguing-in-Publication Data
A catalogue record for this book is available from
the British Library

Library of Congress Cataloging-in-Publication Data
Marlowe, Christopher, 1564–1593.
   [Edward the Second]
   Edward II / Christopher Marlowe; edited by Charles R. Forker.
      p.   cm. — (The Revels plays)
   Includes bibliographical references and index.
   ISBN 0-7190-1536-7
   1. Edward II, King of England, 1284–1327—Drama.   I. Forker, Charles
R.   II. Title.   III. Series.
PR2665.A2F67   1994
822'.3—dc20   93-28184
                                                                                    CIP

Paperback edition published 1995

Typeset by Best-set Typesetter Ltd., Hong Kong

Printed in Great Britain by
Biddles Ltd, Guildford and King's Lynn

Contents

General Editors' Preface

The series known as the Revels Plays was conceived by Clifford Leech. The idea for the series emerged in his mind, as he explained in his preface to the first of the Revels Plays in 1958, from the success of the New Arden Shakespeare. The aim of the new group of texts was 'to apply to Shakespeare's predecessors, contemporaries and successors the methods that are now used in Shakespeare editing'. The plays chosen were to include well known works from the early Tudor period to about 1700, as well as others less familiar but of literary and theatrical merit: 'the plays included,' Leech wrote, 'should be such as to deserve and indeed demand performance.' We owe it to Clifford Leech that the idea became reality. He set the high standards of the series, ensuring that editors of individual volumes produced work of lasting merit, equally useful for teachers and students, theatre directors and actors. Clifford Leech remained General Editor until 1971, and was succeeded by F. David Hoeniger, who retired in 1985.

The Revels Plays are now under the direction of four General Editors, E. A. J. Honigmann, J. R. Mulryne, David Bevington and E. M. Waith. The publishers, originally Methuen, are now Manchester University Press. Despite these changes, the format and essential character of the series will continue, and it is hoped that its editorial standards will be maintained. Except for some work in progress, the General Editors intend, in expanding the series, to concentrate for the immediate future on plays from the period 1558–1642, and may include a small number of non-dramatic works of interest to students of drama. Some slight changes have been forced by considerations of cost. For example, in editions from 1978, notes to the introduction are placed together at the end, not at the foot of the page. Collation and commentary notes will continue, however, to appear on the relevant pages.

The text of each Revels play, in accordance with established practice in the series, is edited afresh from the original text of best authority (in a few instances, texts), but spelling and punctuation are modernised and speech headings are silently made consistent. Elisions in the original are also silently regularised, except where metre would be affected by the change; since 1968 the '-ed' form is used for non-syllabic terminations in past tenses and past participles ('-'d' earlier), and '-èd' for syllabic ('-ed' earlier). The editor emends, as distinct from modernises, his original only in instances where error is patent, or at least very probable, and correction persuasive. Act divisions are given only if they appear in the original or if the structure of the play clearly points to them. Those act and scene divisions not found in the original are provided unobtrusively in small type and in square brackets. Square brackets are also used for any other additions to or changes in the stage directions of the original.

Revels Plays do not provide a variorum collation, but only those variants which require the critical attention of serious textual students. All departures of substance from 'copy-text' are listed, including any relineation and those changes in punctuation which involve to any degree a decision between alternative interpretations; but not such accidentals as turned letters, nor necessarily additions to stage directions whose editorial nature is already made clear by the use of brackets. Press corrections in the 'copy-text' are likewise included. Of later emendations of the text, only those are given which as alternative readings still deserve attention.

One of the hallmarks of the Revels Plays is the thoroughness of their annotations. Besides explaining the meaning of difficult words and passages, the editor provides comments on customs or usage, text or stage-business—indeed, on anything he judges pertinent and helpful. Each volume contains a Glossarial Index to the Commentary, in which particular attention is drawn to meanings for words not listed in *O.E.D.*

The Introduction to a Revels play assesses the authority of the 'copy-text' on which it is based, and discusses the editorial methods employed in dealing with it; the editor also considers his play's date and (where relevant) sources, together with its place in the work of the author and in the theatre of its time. Stage history is offered, and in the case of a play by an author not previously represented in the series a brief biography is given.

It is our hope that plays edited in this fashion will promote further scholarly and theatrical investigation of one of the richest periods in theatrical history.

E. A. J. HONIGMANN

J. R. MULRYNE

DAVID BEVINGTON

E. M. WAITH

Preface

In preparing this edition I have been unusually fortunate in the various kinds of assistance I have received from friends, colleagues, and other scholars. My general editor, Eugene M. Waith of Yale University (a distinguished expert on *Edward II* in his own right), has not only been unfailingly supportive but has also saved me from several blunders as well as offering constructive advice at nearly every stage. His encouragement, patience, and attention to detail have been exemplary. My greatest debt is to him. Thomas L. Berger of St Lawrence University read a draft of my discussion of the text and with his usual meticulousness offered a number of useful suggestions. I must also thank David Riggs of Stanford University, who generously sent me some preliminary notes of his own on textual aspects of *Edward II*. G. K. Hunter of Yale University kindly read a draft of my section on the date. L. A. Beaurline gave invaluable assistance by securing for me a microfilm of the rare Broughton edition of 1818, a copy of which is housed in his own University library at the University of Virginia. In several stimulating discussions with G. R. Proudfoot of King's College, London, I was the beneficiary of illuminating insights on the problematic staging of Edward's murder in V.v. I must also acknowledge the services of F. David Hoeniger of the University of Toronto, who passed on some valuable manuscript notes on *Edward II* (made many years ago by his late colleague, Millar Maclure) to which frequent reference is made in my own running commentary. In collecting information for the stage history of the play I have profited richly from the assistance of Niky Rathbone of the Birmingham Shakespeare Library (who made available press clippings of several British productions), and also from that of Inga-Stina Ewbank of the University of Leeds and her student, Rima Hakim (whose recent thesis on the modern staging of Marlowe's plays in England has proved especially informative). Michael Jamieson of the University of Sussex, an inveterate theatregoer with a superb memory, read my draft of the stage history with a knowledgeable eye, in some cases supplying crucial details that I had ignorantly omitted and in others offering helpful clarification. Timothy Long and Ian Thomson, good colleagues at Indiana University, served as valued consultants on Marlowe's use of classical allusion and myth and on several of the Latin quotations embedded in the 1587 edition of Holinshed—Marlowe's major source. For still other favours and advice on particular points I am indebted to N. W. Bawcutt of the University of Liverpool, to Joseph Candido of the University of Arkansas, to Joseph A. Porter of Duke University, to George Walton Williams, also of Duke, to John W. Velz of the University of Texas, to Susan Cerasano of Colgate University, and to Trevor Lloyd of the University of Toronto. Last, I must thank my copy-editor, John Banks, not only for his sharp eyes but also for excellent suggestions, especially in regard to glosses in the commentary. All serious editions of Renaissance plays are in some sense co-operative ventures. This one, clearly, is no exception.

Indiana University, 1993   CHARLES R. FORKER

Works referred to

EDITIONS COLLATED

Q (1594) *The troublesome raigne . . . of Edward the second.* . . . London: William Iones, 1594 [octavo].

Q2 (1598) *The troublesome raigne . . . of Edward the second.* . . . London: Richard Bradocke, 1598 [quarto].

Q3 (1612) *The troublesome raigne . . . of Edward the second.* . . . London: Roger Barnes, 1612 [quarto].

Q4 (1622) *The troublesome raigne . . . of Edward the second.* . . . London: Henry Bell, 1622 [quarto].

Dodsley[1] (1744) *A Select Collection of Old Plays*, ed. Robert Dodsley. 12 vols. London: R. Dodsley, 1744 (Vol. II).

Dodsley[2] (1780) *A Select Collection of Old Plays*, ed. Robert Dodsley. 12 vols. London: J. Dodsley, 1870 (Vol. II).

Scott (1810) *The Ancient British Drama*, [ed. Sir Walter Scott?]. 3 vols. London: William Miller, 1810 (Vol. I).

Broughton (1818) *Edward the Second*, [ed. James Broughton], sold by J. Chappell, Jr. London: F. Marshall, 1818.

Oxberry (1818) *Edward the Second*, ed. William Oxberry. London: W. Simpkin & R. Marshall, 1818.

Dodsley[3] (1825) *A Select Collection of Old Plays*, ed. J. P. Collier. 12 vols. London: Septimus Prowett, 1825–27 (Vol. II).

Robinson (1826) *The Works of Christopher Marlowe*, [ed. George Robinson]. 3 vols. London: William Pickering, 1826 (Vol. II).

Dyce[1] (1850) *The Works of Christopher Marlowe*, ed. Alexander Dyce. 3 vols. London: William Pickering, 1850 (Vol. II).

Dyce[2] (1858) *The Works of Christopher Marlowe*, ed. Alexander Dyce. Rev. ed. London: E. Moxon, 1858.

Cunningham (1870) *The Works of Christopher Marlowe*, ed. Francis Cunningham. London: Albert J. Crocker Bros., 1870.

Keltie (1870) *The Works of the British Dramatists*, ed. John S. Keltie. Edinburgh: William P. Nimmo, 1870.

Wagner (1871) *Christopher Marlowe's Tragedy of Edward the Second*, ed. Wilhelm Wagner. Hamburg: Boyes & Geisler, 1871.

Fleay (1877) *Marlow's Tragedy of Edward the Second*, ed. F. G. Fleay. London: William Colllins, 1877.

Tancock (1879) *Edward the Second*, ed. Osborne William Tancock. Oxford: Clarendon Press, 1879.

Bullen (1885) *The Works of Christopher Marlowe*, ed. A. H. Bullen. 3 vols. London: John C. Nimmo, 1885 (Vol. II).

Pinkerton (1885) *The Dramatic Works of Christopher Marlowe*, ed. Percy E. Pinkerton (The Canterbury Poets). New York: J. Pott & Co., 1885.

Ellis (1887) *Christopher Marlowe,* ed. Havelock Ellis (Mermaid ed.). London: Vizetelly & Co., 1887.

McLaughlin (1894) *Edward the Second,* ed. Edward T. McLaughlin. New York: Henry Holt & Co., 1894.

Verity (1896) *Edward the Second,* ed. A. W. Verity (The Temple Dramatists). London: J. M. Dent, 1896.

Thomas (1909) *Christopher Marlowe: Plays,* intro. Edward Thomas (Everyman's Library). London: J. M. Dent, 1909; rev. ed. with introduction by M. R. Ridley, 1955.

Brooke (1910) *The Works of Christopher Marlowe,* ed. C. F. Tucker Brooke. London: Oxford University Press, 1910.

Neilson (1911) *The Chief Elizabethan Dramatists Excluding Shakespeare,* ed. William Allen Neilson. Cambridge, Mass.: Riverside Press, 1911.

Briggs (1914) *Marlowe's 'Edward II,'* ed. William Dinsmore Briggs. London: David Nutt, 1914.

Greg (1926) *Edward the Second,* ed. W. W. Greg (The Malone Society). Oxford: Oxford University Press, 1926 [for 1925].

Oliphant (1929) *Shakespeare and His Fellow Dramatists,* ed. E. H. C. Oliphant. 2 vols. New York: Prentice-Hall, 1929 (Vol. I).

Brooke–Paradise (1933) *English Drama, 1580–1642,* ed. C. F. Tucker Brooke and N. B. Paradise. Lexington, Mass.: D. C. Heath, 1933.

Charlton–Waller (1933) *Edward II,* ed. H. B. Charlton and R. D. Waller, 1933 (rev. F. N. Lees, 1955). London: Methuen, 1955.

Spencer (1933) *Elizabethan Plays Written by Shakespeare's Friends, Colleagues, Rivals, and Successors,* ed. Hazleton Spencer. Boston: D. C. Heath, 1933.

Baskervill (1934) *Elizabethan and Stuart Plays,* ed. C. R. Baskervill, V. B. Heltzel, and A. H. Nethercot (rev. 1971). New York: Holt, Rinehart & Winston, 1934.

Parks–Beatty (1935) *The English Drama: An Anthology 900–1642,* ed. Edd Winfield Parks and Richmond Croom Beatty. New York: W. W. Norton, 1935.

Lunt (1939) *Edward the Second,* ed. R. G. Lunt. London: Blackie & Son, 1939.

World's Classics (1939) *The Plays of Christopher Marlowe* (The World's Classics). London: Oxford University Press, H. Milford, 1939.

Hampden (1940) *Christopher Marlowe: Three Plays,* ed. John Hampden (Nelson's Classics). London: Thomas Nelson & Sons, 1940.

Morpurgo (1949) *Edward the Second,* ed. J. E. Morpurgo. London: Falcon Educational Books, 1949.

Kirschbaum (1962) *The Plays of Christopher Marlowe,* ed. Leo Kirschbaum. Cleveland: World Publishing Co., 1962.

Ribner (1963) *The Complete Plays of Christopher Marlowe,* ed. Irving Ribner. New York: Odyssey Press, 1963.

Gill[1] (1967) *Edward II,* ed. Roma Gill. London: Oxford University Press, 1967.

Merchant (1967) *Edward the Second,* ed. W. Moelwyn Merchant (New Mermaid ed.). London: Ernest Benn, 1967.

Steane (1969) *Christopher Marlowe: The Complete Plays,* ed. J. B. Steane. Harmondsworth: Penguin Books, 1969.

Gill[2] (1971) *The Plays of Christopher Marlowe*, ed. Roma Gill. London: Oxford University Press, 1971.

Fraser–Rabkin (1976) *Drama of the English Renaissance*, ed. Russell A. Fraser and Norman Rabkin. 2 vols. New York: Macmillan, 1976 (Vol. I).

Pendry–Maxwell (1976) *Christopher Marlowe: Complete Plays and Poems*, ed. E. D. Pendry and J. C. Maxwell (Everyman's Library). London: Dent, 1976.

Bowers (1981) *The Complete Works of Christopher Marlowe*, ed. Fredson Bowers. 2nd ed. Cambridge: Cambridge University Press, 1981 (Vol. II).

OTHER TEXTUAL MATERIALS CONSULTED

Q2MS. Manuscript transcript in Dyce's copy of Q2 (1598), Victoria and Albert Museum, London; (6209).

Broughton MS. James Broughton's annotations in the British Library copy of Robinson's ed. (1826); (11771 d).

Collier MS. J. P. Collier's annotations in the British Library copy of Dyce[1] (1850); (11771 bbb 6).

Brereton J. Le Gay Brereton, 'Marlowe: Some Textual Notes,' *M.L.R.*, 6 (1911), 94–96.

WORKS OF REFERENCE

Abbott E. A. Abbott, *A Shakespearian Grammar* (London, 1879). Numbers refer to sections.

Arber Edward Arber. ed., *A Transcript of the Registers of the Company of Stationers of London, 1554–1640*, 5 vols. (London, 1875–94).

Bakeless John Bakeless, *The Tragicall History of Christopher Marlowe*, 2 vols. (Cambridge, Mass., 1942).

Bentley Gerald Eades Bentley, *The Jacobean and Caroline Stage*, 7 vols. (Oxford, 1941–68).

Bibliography W. W. Greg, ed., *A Bibliography of the English Printed Drama to the Restoration*, 4 vols. (London, 1939–59).

Brooks Harold F. Brooks, 'Marlowe and Early Shakespeare,' in Brian Morris, ed., *Mermaid Critical Commentaries: Christopher Marlowe* (London, 1968), pp. 65–94.

Campbell Lily B. Campbell, ed., *The Mirror for Magistrates, Edited from Original Texts in the Huntington Library* (Cambridge, 1938).

Chambers E. K. Chambers, *The Elizabethan Stage*, 4 vols. (Oxford, 1923).

Deats[1] Sara Munson Deats, 'Myth and Metamorphosis in Marlowe's *Edward II*,' *Texas Studies in Literature and Language*, 22.3 (fall 1980), 304–321.

Deats[2] Sara Munson Deats, '*Edward II*: A Study in Androgyny,' *Ball State University Forum*, 22.1 (1981), 30–41.

Dent R. W. Dent, *Shakespeare's Proverbial Language: An Index* (Berkeley, 1981).

Geckle George L. Geckle, *Text and Performance: 'Tamburlaine' and 'Edward II'* (Atlantic Highlands, 1988).

Hakim   Rima Hakim, 'Marlowe on the English Stage, 1588–1988: A Stage History of Three Marlowe Plays, *Dr. Faustus*, *Edward II*, and *The Jew of Malta*' (University of Leeds thesis, 1990).

Henslowe   R. A. Foakes and R. T. Rickert, eds., *Henslowe's Diary* (Cambridge, 1961).

Jenkins   Elizabeth Jenkins, *Elizabeth the Great* (New York, 1959).

Leech   Clifford Leech, 'Marlowe's *Edward II*: Power and Suffering,' *Critical Quarterly*, 1 (1959), 181–196.

Levin   Harry Levin, *The Overreacher: A Study of Christopher Marlowe* (Cambridge, Mass., 1952).

Muir   Kenneth Muir, 'The Chronology of Marlowe's Plays,' *Proceedings of the Leeds Philosophical and Literary Society*, 5 (1938–43), 345–356.

O.E.D.   *Oxford English Dictionary*.

Pistotnik   Vesna Pistotnik, 'Marlowe in Performance: Professional Productions on the British Stage, 1960–1982' (University of Birmingham thesis, 1983).

Smith   Bruce R. Smith, *Homosexual Desire in Shakespeare's England: A Cultural Poetics* (Chicago, 1991).

Sunesen   Bent Sunesen, 'Marlowe and the Dumb Show,' *E.S.*, 35 (1954), 241–253.

Tilley   M. P. Tilley, *A Dictionary of the Proverbs in England in the Sixteenth and Seventeenth Centuries* (Ann Arbor, 1950).

PERIODICALS

E.L.H.   *English Literary History.*
E.S.   *English Studies.*
J.E.G.P.   *Journal of English and Germanic Philology.*
M.L.N.   *Modern Language Notes.*
M.L.R.   *Modern Language Review.*
N.&Q.   *Notes and Queries.*
P.M.L.A.   *Publications of the Modern Language Association.*
P.Q.   *Philological Quarterly.*
R.O.R.D.   *Research Opportunities in Renaissance Drama.*
S.B.   *Studies in Bibliography.*
S.P.   *Studies in Philology.*
T.L.S.   *Times Literary Supplement.*
T.D.R.   *Tulane Drama Review.*

TEXTS

Alphonsus, King of Aragon   J. Churton Collins, ed., *The Plays and Poems of Robert Greene*, 2 vols. (Oxford, 1905), Vol. I.

Annals   John Stowe, *The Annales of England* (London, 1592).

Arden of Faversham   M. L. Wine, ed., Anon., *The Tragedy of Master Arden of Faversham* (London, 1973).

Battle of Alcazar   John Yoklavich, ed., George Peele, *The Battle of Alcazar*, in C. T. Prouty, gen. ed., *The Life and Works of George Peele*, 3 vols. (New Haven, 1952–70), Vol. II.

Book of Common Prayer   John E. Booty, ed., *The Book of Common Prayer,
1559: The Elizabethan Prayer Book* (Charlottesville, 1976).

Browne   Geoffrey Keynes, ed., *The Works of Sir Thomas Browne*, 4 vols.
(London, 1964).

Bussy D'Ambois   Nicholas Brooke, ed., George Chapman, *Bussy D'Ambois*
(London, 1964).

Contention   *The First part of the Contention betwixt the two famous Houses of
Yorke and Lancaster*, in Herbert Farjeon, ed., *The Complete Works of
Shakespeare*, 4 vols. (London, 1953), Vol. II.

Cornelia   Frederick S. Boas, ed., *The Works of Thomas Kyd* (Oxford, 1955).

Dido   H. J. Oliver, ed., Christopher Marlowe, *'Dido Queen of Carthage' and
'The Massacre at Paris'* (London, 1968).

Doctor Faustus   John D. Jump, ed., Christopher Marlowe, *Doctor Faustus*
(Cambridge, Mass., 1962).

Drayton   J. William Hebel, ed., *The Works of Michael Drayton*, 5 vols.
(Oxford, 1961).

Edward I   Frank S. Hook, ed., George Peele, *Edward I*, in C. T. Prouty,
gen. ed., *The Life and Works of George Peele*, 3 vols. (New Haven,
1952–70), Vol. II.

Edward II   This edition unless otherwise specified.

Edward III   Fred Lapides, ed., Anon., *The Raigne of King Edward the
Third: A Critical, Old-Spelling Edition* (New York, 1980).

Fabyan   Robert Fabyan, *The Chronicle of Fabian . . . continued . . . to thende
of Queen Mary*, 2 vols. (London, 1559), Vol. II.

Fair Em   Standish Henning, ed., Anon., *Fair Em: A Critical Edition* (New
York, 1980).

First Part of Jeronimo   Frederick S. Boas, ed., *The Works of Thomas Kyd*
(Oxford, 1955).

Grafton   Richard Grafton, *The Chronicle at large and meere History of the
affayres of Englande*, 2 vols. (London, 1569), Vol. II.

H.&S.   C. H. Herford and P. and E. Simpson, eds., *Ben Jonson*, 11 vols.
(Oxford, 1925–52).

Hero and Leander   Millar Maclure, ed., Christopher Marlowe, *The Poems*
(London, 1968).

Holinshed   Raphael Holinshed, *et al.*, *The Chronicles of England, Scotland,
and Ireland*, 2nd ed., 3 vols. in 2 (London, 1587), Vol. III.

James IV   Norman Sanders, ed., Robert Greene, *The Scottish History of
James the Fourth* (London, 1970).

Jeronimo   See *First Part of Jeronimo*.

Jew of Malta   N. W. Bawcutt, ed., Christopher Marlowe, *The Jew of Malta*
(Manchester, 1978).

Lucan's First Book   Millar Maclure, ed., Christopher Marlowe, *The Poems*
(London, 1968).

Lust's Dominion   Fredson Bowers, ed., *The Dramatic Works of Thomas
Dekker*, 4 vols. (Cambridge, 1953–61), Vol. IV.

Massacre at Paris   H. J. Oliver, ed., Christopher Marlowe, *'Dido Queen of
Carthage' and 'The Massacre at Paris'* (London, 1968).

Milton   John T. Shawcross, ed., *The Complete Poetry of John Milton*, rev.
ed. (New York, 1963).

Mirror for Magistrates *The Last part of the Mirour for Magistrates* (London, 1578).

Nashe Ronald B. McKerrow, ed., *The Works of Thomas Nashe*, 5 vols. (Oxford, 1958).

Ovid's Elegies Millar Maclure, ed., Christopher Marlowe, *The Poems* (London, 1968).

Peele David H. Horne, ed., *Minor Works of George Peele*, in C. T. Prouty, gen. ed., *The Life and Works of George Peele*, 3 vols. (New Haven, 1952–70), Vol. I.

Ralph Roister Doister Clarence Griffin Child, ed., Nicholas Udall, *Ralph Roister Doister* (Boston, 1912).

Soliman and Perseda Frederick S. Boas, ed., *The Works of Thomas Kyd* (Oxford, 1955).

Spanish Tragedy Philip Edwards, ed., Thomas Kyd, *The Spanish Tragedy* (London, 1959).

Spenser J. C. Smith and E. de Selincourt, eds., *The Poetical Works of Edmund Spenser* (London, 1912).

Stowe John Stowe, *The Chronicles of England from Brute unto this present yeare* (London, 1580).

Sylvester Susan Synder, ed., Joshua Sylvester, trans., *The Divine Weeks and Works of Guillaume de Saluste Sieur de Bartas*, 2 vols. (Oxford, 1979).

1 and 2 Tamburlaine J. S. Cunningham, ed., Christopher Marlowe, *Tamburlaine the Great* (Manchester, 1981).

1 and 2 Troublesome Reign Anon., *The Troublesome Raigne of King John*, in Geoffrey Bullough, ed., *Narrative and Dramatic Sources of Shakespeare*, 8 vols. (London, 1957–75), Vol. IV.

True Tragedy *The true Tragedie of Richard Duke of Yorke*, in Herbert Farjeon, ed., *The Complete Works of Shakespeare*, 4 vols. (London, 1953), Vol. II.

Webster F. L. Lucas, ed., *The Complete Works of John Webster*, 4 vols. (London, 1927).

White Devil John Russell Brown, ed., John Webster, *The White Devil*, 2nd ed. (London, 1966).

Whore of Babylon Fredson Bowers, ed., *The Dramatic Works of Thomas Dekker*, 4 vols. (Cambridge, 1953–61), Vol. II.

Woodstock A. P. Rossiter, ed., Anon., *Woodstock: A Moral History* (London, 1946).

Wounds of Civil War Joseph W. Houppert, ed., Thomas Lodge, *The Wounds of Civil War* (Lincoln, 1969).

Titles of Shakespeare's plays and poems are abbreviated as in C. T. Onions, *A Shakespeare Glossary*, rev. ed. (Oxford, 1986). Quotations and line numbers of Shakespeare are taken from *The Complete Works of Shakespeare*, ed. David Bevington, 3rd ed. (Glenview, Ill., 1980). Bevington's American spelling, however, has been silently altered to conform with British usage.

Introduction

Our only authoritative text for *Edward II* is the quarto-form octavo of 1594 made up in fours of half sheets cut from double-size paper and referred to throughout this edition as Q. As we learn from its title page, it was printed for the publisher and bookseller William Jones, to whom the text was entered in the Stationers' Register on 6 July 1593, five weeks after Marlowe's murder.[1] Q collates A–M4, the text proper commencing on A2 and ending on M3; the title occupies the first page of the A gathering, A1^v being blank, while the final leaf of the M gathering (M4 and M4^v) is missing and, like M3^v, was presumably also blank. The book is clearly printed and presents relatively few bibliographical or textual problems. Only two copies of this rare volume are known—one formerly housed in the Landesbibliothek of Cassel, Germany, but now lost as a casualty of World War II, the other in the Zentralbibliothek of Zürich, Switzerland. Sir Walter Greg, working from photostats, collated both copies for his Malone Society edition of *Edward II* in 1925–26 and found them to be identical except for the outer forme of sheet H, which, in the Zürich copy, reveals seven minor printing-house corrections (six of them affecting punctuation only) not present in the Cassel copy.[2]

Three subsequent quartos (Q2–4) appeared in 1598, 1612, and 1622, each having been printed from its immediate predecessor. None of these later editions, it follows, can possess independent authority, but all are of some interest for the occasional clarifications or hypothetical corrections that they introduce, even when these seem to be mistaken. The three reprints all expand Q's title ('The troublesome / raigne and lamentable death of / Edward *the second, King of* / England: with the tragicall / *fall of proud* Mortimer') by adding 'And also the life and death of *Peirs Gaueston,* / *the great Earle of* Cornewall, *and mighty* / fauorite of king *Edward* the second . . .'). The title pages of Q2–4 repeat in substance, though not in exact wording, the statement on Q's title page that the play 'was sundrie times publiquely acted / *in the honourable citie of London, by the* / right honourable the Earle of Pem- / *brooke his seruants*,' but a second

1

issue of Q4 (1622), obviously referring to a stage revival, altered this to read: 'As it was publikely Acted by the late Queenes / *Maiesties Seruants* [i.e., Queen Anne's Men] *at the* Red Bull / *in S*. Iohns *streete*.' The second quarto, like the first, was published by William Jones, who held the initial copyright; the third and fourth quartos were printed for Roger Barnes and Henry Bell, respectively, to whom, in succession, the copyright passed on 16 December 1611 and 17 April 1617. John Haviland and John Wright Senior acquired the copyright on 4 September 1638 through transfer from Henry and Moses Bell, but the new owners appear to have published no fresh edition.[3]

Although four quartos of *Edward II* survive, speculation about a possible fifth quarto earlier than the 1594 edition continues to crop up. This discussion is based upon an imperfect copy of Q2 (1598), once owned by Alexander Dyce and now in the Victoria and Albert Museum, London (designated Q2MS. in the present edition). In this copy the missing first two leaves—the title and the opening of the play (consisting of a head-title, two lines of stage directions, and the first seventy lines of dialogue)—have been replaced in an early (probably seventeenth-century) hand; the date is given as 1593, which agrees suggestively with that of the Stationers' Register entry mentioned above.[4] Dyce, who knew nothing of the 1594 quarto (which in his time had not yet been discovered) believed that the quarto of 1598 was either a re-issue of a quarto dated 1593 for which a new title page had been prepared, or that a distinct edition of 1593 had been lost and that the 1598 quarto represented the first reprinting. We know now that the scribe could not have been copying from the edition of 1598 or from its two later derivatives. The handwritten title page agrees with that of the 1594 quarto in omitting the reference to Gaveston and in the phrasing of the statement about performance; moreover, the head-title on the second manuscript leaf ('The troublesome Raigne & Lamentable death of Edward the second King of England with the tragicall fall of proude Mortimer') follows that of the 1594 edition, a head-title which the three later quartos dropped. In addition, there are three variants in which the manuscript and the 1594 text are congruent but that depart from Q2–4.[5] C. F. Tucker Brooke, followed by H. B. Charlton and R. D. Waller, argued, however, that the scribe had before him not a copy of Q (1594) but a lost *editio princeps* of 1593, the year of Marlowe's death. Greg also entertained this possibility seriously. Brooke based his case on several points: (1) of fifteen substantive variants recorded between Q and the manuscript he judged the manuscript to be superior in three readings and inferior in six, the remaining six being of indifferent preferability;[6] (2) he noted that the manuscript title page abbreviates the author's name more drastically than Q ('Chri. Mar.' as against 'Chri. Marlow'); and (3) he drew attention to the 'surprising' gap in time between the Stationers' Register entry of 6 July 1593 and the publication of 1594, a period of 'nine months or more' according to the Elizabethan calendar.[7]

It is probably safe to say that if we could account for the date of 1593 on the manuscript title page and the hiatus between the 1593 Stationers' Register entry and the appearance of the 1594 quarto, little doubt about the latter's having been the first edition would ever have arisen. Fredson Bowers brings strong evidence to bear against the theory that the manuscript represents a transcription of a separate 1593 quarto[8]—evidence with which, in the main, I agree. What follows here, then, is a summary of Bowers's major points to which I have added observations of my own.

First, the three readings of the manuscript (*thine*, *dinner*, and *Syluan*) that Brooke adduced as preferable to their counterparts in Q (*thy* [1.i.9], *dinner time* [1.i.31], and *Siluian* [1.i.57]) make for a weak case: *thine* and *Syluan* are little more than normalizations of spelling, while *dinner* probably represents a lame attempt to improve the metre of a speech that is metrically anomalous throughout and can best be read as a compositorial mis-setting of prose.[9] The alleged superiority of the manuscript for these readings is therefore highly questionable.

Second, if Q is thought to be a reprint of a lost 1593 edition, its three doubtful 'corruptions' must be weighed against the more numerous readings of the manuscript that are manifestly—sometimes even nonsensically—inferior to those of Q, especially *Its* (for *As*), *bakt* (for *Rakt*), *eate* (for *dart*), *gasing* (for *grazing*), and *by* (for *hard by*) at 1.i.20, 21, 40, 58, and 65. Charlton and Waller hypothesized that these clear mistakes were faithful transcriptions of the lost quarto, originally 'made by a printer working hastily from manuscript to catch a public still excited by Marlowe's death';[10] but, as Bowers points out, such errors by a hypothetical 1593 compositor must be considered in the larger context of the sixteen substantive variants that distinguish the manuscript text from that of the 1594 quarto. If Q corrupted a supposed 1593 quarto in only three places, but corrected it unmistakably in six other places, while making

additional alterations of an indifferent kind in at least some of the
remaining seven cases (since it would be unreasonable to assign *every*
indifferent change to the scribe alone)—all within the short run of
two printed pages, logic would compel us to conclude, through a
process of extrapolation, that the compositor who set the hypothetical 1593 text was so inaccurate that he made, on average, one
substantive error for every ten lines. Such frequent blundering, if
not unprecedented, would be most unusual, and nothing about
the generally reliable 1594 quarto suggests that its compositor (or
compositors) had to contend with anything like so bad a copy-text.
The scribe's interest, after all, would presumably be limited to
the mere replacement of two missing leaves of a defective book in
his own or someone else's library. The inferior variants of the
manuscript are thus more readily explicable as a combination of
careless errors and misguided 'improvements' on the part of someone who was transcribing the 1594 text than as readings that already
antedated his efforts.

This hypothesis might seem to fit even the shortened form of
the author's name on the manuscript title page, for it is easier to
suppose, *prima facie*, that a scribe might lazily abbreviate 'Marlow'
to 'Mar' than that a printer, wishing to capitalize on the playwright's
notoriety for a previously unpublished drama, would risk the possibility that a truncated surname might go unrecognized by his
prospective readers. Indeed, the printers of the third and fourth
quartos removed the last scintilla of doubt as to the author's identity
(if any existed) by spelling out 'Christopher Marlow' in full. And
it may be relevant to note that except for the early editions of
Tamburlaine (which omit the dramatist's name entirely) and the
undated first edition of *Ovid's Elegies* (which anounces the poet as
'C. M.'), none of Marlowe's works printed before 1604 (when *Doctor
Faustus* first appeared) fails to give the family name in full.[11] But
such reasoning must be met with the greatest scepticism, for we
know that all ten of the early editions of *Faustus* similarly curtail
Marlowe's name on their title pages—three times as 'Ch. Marl.'
(1604, 1609, 1611) and seven times as 'Ch. Mar.' (1616, 1619, 1620,
1624, 1628, 1631, 1663); obviously the abbreviated name of Q2MS.
is not unique.

Even if we accept the arguments presented so far against the
existence of a separate edition of 1593, however, we are nevertheless
left with the question of how a copyist could misread 1594 as '1593'
on the title page of Q, a change that is virtually impossible to explain

as the result of either inattention or deliberate falsification. Fortunately a close examination of the Zürich copy suggests a likely answer—namely that the book may originally have existed in two states, first with a 1593 title page that was either altered to 1594 while sheet A was still in press or cancelled and then replaced by a freshly set title page with 1594 as its date of imprint. The evidence for this probablility is physical. The title leaf (A1) is plainly not conjugate with the rest of the gathering, although the separation could be the result of wear since no stub from a cancellandum is evident: the entire book has been resewn, as is obvious from the presence of an earlier set of holes near the centre seam, and the first gathering (sheet A) has been repaired and attached to a modern fly leaf whose right stub extends across the opening. The differing positions of the vertical chainlines on A1 and A2, however, would seem to point to a cancel.[12] Changes in the date of imprint while plays were still in press—usually through the simple expedient of altering a numeral in the standing type—were fairly common. This was the case, for instance, with Wilmot's *Tancred and Gismund* (1591–92), with Q2 of Shakespeare's *Hamlet* (1604–05), with Chapman's *Bussy D'Ambois* (1607–08), with Tourneur's(?) *Revenger's Tragedy* (1607–08), with Tourneur's *Atheist's Tragedy* (1611–12), with Q4 of Dekker's *1 Honest Whore* (1615–16), with Q3 of Beaumont and Fletcher's *Elder Brother* (1650–51), with Massinger's *City Madam* (1658–59), and with several other plays.[13] If a lost copy of Q identical to the Zürich or Cassel copy in all respects but its title page were to lie behind the Dyce transcription, we could make sense of the handwritten date in Q2MS. and perhaps also of the early entry in the Stationers' Register.[14] Most of the plays whose dates of imprint were altered during the course of printing seem to have been in press around the end of the New Style year, i.e., during October, November, or December. If Q had been printed, say, in November or December of 1593, we would be considering a delay of some five or six months after registration with the Company of Stationers—a period that could hardly be regarded as abnormal enough to be significant. A 1593 variant of Q (as against an independent edition of that date) might also account for the abbreviated form of the dramatist's name, for the printer could well have decided to expand 'Mar' to 'Marlow' for greater clarity at the same time that he was making his book look newer by postdating it.

Third, an analysis of the process by which Q was printed supports the hypothesis that the book was indeed a first, as opposed to a second, edition. Although no printer is named on the title page (A1) or in the colophon (M3), we may confidently identify him as Robert Robinson on the basis of three ornaments and an ornamental capital that appear in Q and in other books known to have been printed by Robinson during the period 1594–96.[15] Robert Ford Welsh, to whom we owe this identification, also assembled evidence to throw light on the compositorial procedure and method of presswork that Robinson employed[16]—evidence upon which Bowers was able to enlarge. Reasoning (1) from repeating patterns of type shortages (especially the substitution of italic for roman capitals and vice versa—patterns that move contiguously from page to page across inner and outer formes, (2) from recurrences of specific pieces of type along with the revelatory intervals that separate such recurrences, and (3) from the corresponding positions of identifiable running-titles in each forme on successive sheets, Bowers confirms Welsh's three principal judgements: first, that Q was printed on a single press with the use of two skeleton-formes (for imposing the outer and inner forme of each sheet); second, that the text was set seriatim beginning with sheet B and continuing in regular sequence to sheet M; and, third, that sheet A, consisting of the title page and the first six pages of the play, was the last to be composed and machined, after the type for sheet L (the previous sheet but one to go through the press) had been distributed. The certain identification of individual pieces of type in an Elizabethan book can be treacherous and deceptive, especially when only a single copy exists and when comparisons must necessarily rely on photographic reproductions; but if Welsh's findings can be trusted (and my examination of the Zürich original appears to confirm him), it would seem likely that Robinson (or someone in his shop) was typesetting from manuscript rather than from a previous quarto. As Bowers observes, a printer who was resetting an earlier book verbatim and literatim, perhaps even page for page,[17] would have little reason to worry about new or changed front-matter arriving at the last minute, and so would probably feel no need to protect himself against such contingencies by casting off the first six pages of text and delaying the composing of sheet A until the rest of the book had been processed. In addition, if the printer had been using a quarto as copy, he might well have found it more convenient to set the entire volume by formes rather than seriatim, since, in large part, the guesswork about lengths and pagination would have already been done for him by the previous printer.

It should be noted also that simple reprints sometimes compress the text being reset so as to save paper. Q2, for instance, reduces Q's forty-eight leaves to thirty-eight. The 1594 quarto contains a good deal of unnecessary white space, particularly in sheets A, K, L, and M. Had Q been set from a previously printed text (as was the case with Q2), the printer could have eliminated numerous gaps and open places, thus saving as much as an entire sheet. It will appear, too, that the wastage in sheet A, although not as obvious as in later sheets, is consistent with the inference of Welsh and Bowers that the first pages of the text were cast off, the compositor having presumably made an overgenerous allowance for the opening of his manuscript.

Bowers differs from Welsh in detecting the presence of not one but two compositors in Q, arguing that X, the more experienced of the pair, set the first part of the book (sheets A to E), while Y, his less expert assistant, continued with the second part (sheets F to M). This contention rests upon several kinds of evidence: (1) on the fact that the third leaves of sheets A–E are consistently signed, while the corresponding leaves of sheets F–M remain unsigned; (2) on the alleged preference in X's stint for the spelling *France* (over *Fraunce*) and for the exclamation *Ah* (over *A*); (3) on the tendency of Y to make more errors in lineation than X (twenty-two as against seven instances); and (4) on the greater accuracy of X than Y as indicated by the need to make substantive emendations in Y's section of the text more than twice as often as in X's (seventeen times as compared with eight by Bowers's computation).

In assessing this evidence it is necessary first to correct Bowers's account of the spelling preferences. Bowers reports that X prefers *France* to *Fraunce* by a ratio of four to two; but in fact there are eight, not six, occurrences of the word in the first five sheets with a ratio of five to three.[18] In Y's stint (sheets F–M) the word occurs twenty-three times (not thirteen as Bowers would have it), the preference for *Fraunce* over *France* adding up to twenty-one instances to two, rather than the alleged twelve instances to one. *Ah* is invariably the spelling in sheets A–E as Bowers correctly notices, but the word occurs eight times, not six; in sheets F–M the exclamation occurs sixteen times (not fourteen), and the preference for *A* (nine times) over *Ah* (seven times) is much less decisive than Bowers's incorrect ratio of nine to five would suggest. To reinterpret the corrected word-count then, pooling the total incidences of *France/Fraunce* and *Ah/A* in Q and limiting ourselves for the

moment to the consideration of these features alone, it would not be
wholly implausible to posit for the entire volume a single compositor
whose preference for *Fraunce* over *France* was at a ratio of twenty-
four to seven, and whose favouring of *Ah* over *A* numbered fifteen to
nine. Perhaps in this connection one should mention the negative
evidence that several familiar tests for determining a division between compositors (preferences for such spellings as *we/wee, do/doe,
go/goe, doth/dooth, here/heere*, and the like, as well as counting the
number of unpunctuated line endings per page) have proved un-
productive. Also, the argument for two compositors requires us to
accept that compositor *X*, having finished sheets B–E and having
turned over the completion of the book (sheets F–M) to *Y*, resumed
the typesetting for sheet A, the last to be composed. Whether such a
division of labour would be efficient or likely is at least questionable.

On the other side of the issue, however, the spellings *parle* (on A4,
I.i.125) and *parled* (on C4, I.iv.320) versus *parley* (on F3, II.vi.14
and F4^v, III.i.71), assuming that all four are variants of the same
disyllabic verb, might seem to corroborate the theory of two compositors.[19] While Bowers seems to me to exaggerate the greater
inaccuracy and tendency to mislineation of the later pages of Q—or
at least to magnify the significance of these factors—the striking
difference between the signed and unsigned third leaves in the two
parts of the text remains suggestive. On balance, however, I regard
the case for two compositors as yet to be demonstrated.

If Q was printed from manuscript, as now seems most probable,
what was the nature of the underlying copy? Greg speculated that
the book was set 'from a playhouse manuscript' that 'had undergone
some kind of revision for the stage'[20]—an opinion, as Bowers notes,
that less cautious commentators have transformed into the notion
that the manuscript was the actual promptbook. The text, as we
have it, does indeed imply connections to the process of stage production, but it can hardly have been the promptbook itself. Discussion of certain of Q's problems should make the matter clearer.

Dyce long ago drew attention to the misnaming of the Earl of
Arundel as Matrevis in the stage directions and speech prefixes of
three different scenes (II.v, III.i, and IV.iii)—an obvious indication
that the same actor doubled in both roles since Arundel and Matrevis
never appear onstage together but appear under their correct names
at other points in the play. That this sustained misidentification is
authorial rather than scribal appears from the dialogue, which in two
places allows Arundel to be incorrectly addressed as 'lord *Matre.*'

and '*Matre.*' (III.i.89, 92). Marlowe probably had a specific actor in mind for both parts as he was writing, or at least conceived of the two roles as suitable for a single actor, and, since metre was relatively unaffected, mistakenly wrote 'Matrevis' when he meant Arundel. Clearly a prompter would have had to correct this mistake in his marked copy as the tragedy was being prepared for the stage.

Greg pointed out a few additional anomalies and ambiguities of identification, at least some of which would probably have required further clarification in a promptbook. Q designates the Archbishop of Canterbury simply as '*Bishop*' in the stage directions and speech prefixes of I.ii, I.iv, and presumably V.iv, where he is needed again for the coronation of Edward III.[21] The mistake in title is odd for a poet born, raised, and educated in the shadow of Canterbury Cathedral, and especially for the recipient of a Cambridge scholarship endowed by Archbishop Parker; but the term '*Bishop*' (without specification of diocese) is also used in V.i, where the Bishop of Winchester, who retrieves the crown after Edward's abdication, is apparently meant. Again the intention to double roles might explain the ambiguity, for none of the three bishops in the play (Coventry, Canterbury, and Winchester) ever appears in the company of his fellow prelates. Marlowe or a later annotator, then, could perhaps have been using '*Bishop*' generically for an actor who would play more than one episcopal part. A similar explanation could apply to the naming of the various messengers in the text. The Post from Scotland (at II.ii.110.1) and the Herald from the Barons (at III.i.150.1) are properly distinguished in the stage directions that affect them, but both are named '*Messenger*' in speech prefixes, while a third 'Messenger' (at V.ii.22.1) is so called in both his stage direction and prefix, and the Post from France (at IV.iii.44.1) retains the designation '*Poaste*' in his prefix. The confusion in regard to messengers seems to bear the earmarks of someone other than the author who was contemplating a production in which minor characters with a similar function might efficiently be played by a single member of the same cast.

The 1594 text presents two additional evidences of annotation for staging on both of which Greg commented. The first is the garbled conflation of Pembroke's and Edward's speeches at II.ii.81–82: '*Pen.* Heere here King: conuey hence *Gaueston*, thaile murder him.' It is fairly clear that the printer has mistakenly absorbed Edward's speech prefix ('*King*') into Pembroke's line, thus making one speech of two. But as Greg shrewdly notes, both the prefix and the punctuation

adopted are anomalous—'King' followed by a colon instead of 'Edw'
followed by a full stop. The inference is that Edward's speech was
probably added to the manuscript marginally 'by a different hand or
at least on a different occasion'.[22] The second clue, discussed by
both Greg and Bowers, is the incorrectly marked entrance at v.i.
111.1 of Sir Thomas Berkeley (consistently called 'Bartley' in Q and
on two occasions 'Lord *Bartley*' and 'The lord of *Bartley*' [v.ii.30,
34]). Q also assigns the speech immediately after the wrong entrance
to '*Bartley*' (v.i.112), which may represent a misunderstood expan-
sion of '*B*' (for '*Bishop*' [*of Winchester*]), the usual emendation
adopted by modern editors. Berkeley should enter sixteen lines later
at v.i.127.1, when Edward greets him by name and is eager to learn
the contents of a letter he carries, but Q leaves the correct entrance
unspecified. As Greg explains, 'It would seem that a stage warning
was marked in the copy' several lines before Berkeley's entry, 'and
that this warning was expanded into a stage direction on the one
hand, and on the other substituted for the prefix to the Bishop's
words "My Lord". . . .' Greg continues, 'Berkeley's proper entry . . .
was either originally left unmarked or else the direction was omitted
by the printer as duplicating' the earlier one.[23] Once more it is
obvious that the uncorrected text as it stood in the printer's copy
could not have been performed by actors, and yet it seems clear that
some sort of intervention with a view to future staging must have
occurred after the author's manuscript (or a copy thereof) had come
into the possession of the theatre.

Further difficulties arise in the staging of v.ii, in which the Bishop
of Winchester delivers Edward's crown to Mortimer and the queen,
arriving at the same moment apparently that a 'Messenger,' acting
independently, brings letters from Killingworth. Q marks neither
entrance nor exit for the bishop, and his sudden brief appearance
and unceremonious departure are curiously abrupt. His chief function is ostensibly to confirm Edward's official resignation by presenting both the crown and the signed instrument of abdication, but he
also reports on Berkeley's lenient treatment of the king and on
Kent's plot to free him—information that could have been conveyed
less problematically through the letters that the Messenger has
just delivered. Not implausibly, Bowers speculates that, as it was
originally conceived, the scene omitted the bishop altogether but
that it was later decided, 'not necessarily by Marlowe,' to show the
return of the crown to London onstage and that the reviser adapted
Mortimer's reading of a communiqué from one of his spies by

making it into a speech for Winchester without deleting the now
superfluous messenger.[24] If this is what occurred, it would fit the
hypothesis that the printer's copy was not a promptbook but a
manuscript that had undergone some incomplete preparations for
staging.

Apart from the numerous unmarked entrances and exits in addition to those that have already been mentioned (a good many of
which would certainly have had to be specified in a promptbook), Q
abounds in descriptive and Latin stage directions neither of which
features are characteristic of theatrical manuscripts but are usually
taken as hallmarks of authorial copy. Examples of the first class are
'*Enter* Gauestone *reading on a letter that was brought him from the king*'
(I.i.0.1–2), '*Enter king Edward moorning*' (I.iv.303.1), '*Enter Gaueston
moorning, and the earle of Penbrookes men*' (II.vi.0.1), '*Enter* Hugh
Spencer *an old man, father to the yong* Spencer, *with his trunchion, and
soldiers*' (III.i.31.1–2), '*Edward kneeles, and saith*' (III.i.128), '*Enter
the King, Baldock, and Spencer the sonne, flying about the stage*'
(IV.v.0.1–2), '*Enter the king, Leiscester, with a Bishop for the crowne*'
(V.i.0.1–2), '*Enter the yong Prince, and the Earle of Kent talking
with him*' (V.ii.72.3–4), '*They hale Edmund away, and carie him
to be beheaded*' (V.iv.105.1–2), and '*Then Gurney stabs Lightborne*'
(V.v.116.1). In the second group we may note such Latin directions
as '*Exeunt Nobiles*' (I.i.132.1, I.iv.93.1, II.ii.198.1), '*Enter Nobiles*'
(I.iv.0.1), '*Manent* Mortimers' (I.iv.384.1), '*Manent Pembrooke, Mat.
Gauest. & Penbrookes men, foure souldiers*' (II.v.96.2–3), '*Exit cum
seruis Pen.*' (II.v.108.1), '*Exeunt ambo*' (II.v.109.1), '*Manet Iames
cum caeteris*' (II.vi.17.2), '*Enter the Barons . . . cum caeteris*' (III.ii.10.1–
2), '*Manent Isabell and Mortimer*' (V.ii.72.2), and '*Manent Edmund
and the souldiers*' (V.iii.62.2) as well as the speech prefixes '*Spen. pa.*'
and *Spen. filius*' (III.i.32, 36, 43; see also III.ii.77.1) to distinguish
the older and younger Spencers when they are first introduced.
These features also support the hypothesis that Robinson's manuscript was indeed Marlowe's fair copy (or a scribal transcript of this)
sold to Pembroke's Men by the playwright and annotated in such a
way as partially to guide a future copyist in the preparation of a
promptbook.

The manuscript appears to have contained no division into acts
and scenes, the absence of which persisted in all editions until the
anonymous editor of the so-called Chappell text (now identified as
James Broughton) introduced them in 1818.[25] The later editor
George Robinson, apparently ignorant of his predecessor's work,

redivided the play in 1826 with less satisfactory results, and modern
editors until Bowers (who drew belated attention to the merits of the
totally ignored Broughton text) have generally followed Robinson.
With some modifications the present edition restores the dramatically logical shape of *Edward II* as discerned by Broughton, the
Chappell editor. The five-act structure that his text discloses and
that Bowers further refined will now, it is hoped, become the standard one in references to, and in editions of, the tragedy. My
modernization of the text conforms to the general practice of the
Revels series, particularly as articulated by the general editors in the
most recent Marlowe volume, *Tamburlaine the Great*, ed. J. S.
Cunningham (1981). In the matter of orthography, however, I have
been guided for the most part by the rationale of Stanley Wells
in *Modernizing Shakespeare's Spelling* (Oxford: Clarendon Press,
1979). Thus, except in special cases, I have not hesitated to mod-
ernize aggressively, 'Bristow' becoming 'Bristol,' 'Circes' 'Circe,'
'mushrump' 'mushroom,' 'shipwrack' 'shipwreck,' 'porpintine'
'porcupine,' 'renowme' 'renown,' and the like.

The action of *Edward II* involves complex and sometimes ambiguous stage movements; accordingly, with theatrical directors as well
as students in mind, I have tried to clarify what actually happens
onstage, sometimes more explicitly than most previous editors have
thought necessary but always crediting the first editor to add a
particular stage direction, whether I have adopted it verbatim or in
substance only. As is usual in modern editions, I have enclosed all
directions not in Q in square brackets—a practice extended even to
translated stage directions, although the Latin originals appear below
in the textual notes. In cases where such directions present a mixture
of translation and interpolation, distinguishing what is authorial
from what is not by the use of square brackets becomes too cumber-
some and misleading. My textual notes of course record these
details.

Marlowe's lineation in *Edward II* (which is more irregular than
that of Shakespeare's chronicle plays) is frequently debatable, a
fact that emerges insistently to anyone who has collated the major
nineteenth- and twentieth-century editions. In several places it is
difficult to decide whether Marlowe's generally smooth blank verse
is temporarily interrupted by prose or dissolves into much rougher
verse; and there are a number of hypermetrical lines that may be
either rationalized as hexameters or broken up into two lines—a full
pentameter introduced by, or followed by, a single-footed line with a

caesura between, as in 'Spencer, / Ah sweet Spencer, thus then must we part?' (IV.vii.72–73) or 'And bear the king's to Mortimer, our lord. / Away!' (V.v.118–119). Sometimes bursts of rapid dialogue make it hard to know whether two or three brief speeches make up a single line of rough verse or whether the play momentarily lapses into prose. Total consistency in such cases being impossible, I have judged each occurrence separately on the basis of context, keeping in mind also Tucker Brooke's useful study of Marlowe's versification made many years ago;[26] but I am aware that decisions different from mine can, and probably will, be defended.

Although the Revels series does not attempt to present full historical collations, I have been somewhat more generous in recording rejected readings from the Broughton and Oxberry texts (see especially Appendix A to which most of these have been relegated) than might at first seem justified. My reasons are two: first, both appear to have been conceived as acting editions and may possibly reflect a lost tradition (or traditions) of actual performance; second, the Broughton text is extremely rare (I know of only two surviving copies, both in the United States), and I have found Bowers's list of variants from it as well as from Oxberry to be somewhat unreliable. Both Broughton and Oxberry published in 1818. Bowers was uncertain which came first but thought the Chappell editor (Broughton) might have influenced Oxberry to some extent; Bawcutt, who discovered Broughton's identity, brings strong evidence to suggest that although the latter's edition preceded Oxberry's by a month or so, there was 'no connection at all between [Broughton's] work and Oxberry's.'[27] For readings in which the two agree, however, my textual notes cite both editors in alphabetical order without implication of priority.

Any modern editor of Marlowe must be heavily indebted to the pioneering work of Dyce, whose edition of 1850, revised in 1858, has directly or indirectly influenced all his successors. In the matter of annotation, especially for historical background, Tancock's edition of 1879 has been almost equally influential. Among the twentieth-century editions that I have found most helpful I must mention those by William Dinsmore Briggs (for citations of Holinshed and for verbal parallels), by E. H. C. Oliphant (particularly for its treatment of stage action), by Charlton and Waller (especially for their commentary), by Kirschbaum (again for matters of staging), by Ribner, Merchant, Gill, Pendry, and Maxwell (for their intelligent and responsible handling of the text), and of course by Bowers (who has conducted the most expert and rigorous analysis of Q as well as of the manuscript that must have lain behind it).

2 DATE

Edward II is notoriously difficult to date with precision. The obvious *terminus ad quem* is, of course, Marlowe's death on 30 May 1593, a little over a month before the play was registered for publication (6 July 1593). As we know from the title page of Q, it was acted in London by Pembroke's Servants—a troupe of which there is no record at all before the last three months of 1592, although an earlier unrecorded existence of the company (particularly if its principal activities were in the provinces) remains a possibility. Pembroke's Men were in London briefly during the Christmas season of 1592 –93, for they acted at court on St Stephen's Day (26 December) and again on the Feast of the Epiphany (6 January).[28] A brief theatrical season seems to have been possible at this period, for Henslowe records some twenty-nine performances between 29 December and 1 February.[29] Just prior to this Pembroke's Men may have been playing at Leicester (performances in London had been restrained from 23 June 1592 until Michaelmas on account of civil disorders and the danger of plague);[30] in June and July of 1593 the actors were again in the provinces but, by August, were bankrupt and had to sell their costumes and probably also their play scripts because two items from their repertory besides *Edward II* came into the possession of the booksellers shortly thereafter.[31] It seems unlikely therefore that Marlowe's tragedy could have been staged in London before December of 1592, although it might conceivably have been played on provincial stages earlier than this. There is also the possibility—a mere speculation—that *Edward II* might have been written originally for actors under a different patron, performed in London under his auspices, and then transferred to Pembroke's Men at a later date; if so, the silence of the records is not easy to explain. Plague closed the London theatres during almost the whole of 1593—from late January or early February until the following December. If *The Massacre at Paris* (performed as a new play in January 1593) followed *Edward II* in order of composition, as is generally agreed, Marlowe's English chronicle history could hardly have been written later than 1592.

Further narrowing down of the date must depend on the relation of *Edward II* to other plays of the period that have been thought to influence or to have been influenced by it. This is slippery ground. Almost all scholars agree that *2* and *3 Henry VI* must antedate *Edward II* since Marlowe clearly echoes both plays; and others, including the present writer, believe that Marlowe was indebted both verbally and conceptually to the entire sequence of Shakespearean histories from *1 Henry VI* through *Richard III* (see the section below on the creative interrelationship between Marlowe and Shakespeare). The year 1591 is the usual date assigned to Parts II and III of *Henry VI*, and some scholars (including the New Arden editor) place *Richard III* in 1591 as well.[32] Also *Edward II* may borrow from the anonymous *Troublesome Reign of King John* (published in 1591) and almost certainly does borrow from Peele's *Edward I* (c. 1590–91).[33]

Such unmemorable but hardly accidental phrases as 'God of Kings' (*T.R., Part I*, l. 1057; *Edward II*, IV.vi.19), 'feele the crowne' (*T.R., Part I*, l. 1663; *Edward II*, v.i.82), 'new elected King' (*T.R., Part II*, l. 189; *Edward II*, v.i.78), 'dying heart' (*T.R., Part II*, l. 972; *Edward II*, IV.vii.43), and 'tymes advantage' (*T.R., Part II*, l. 976; *Edward II*, IV.ii.18) occur in both *The Troublesome Reign* and *Edward II*; but a few even more unmistakable parallels appear as well:

(1) That see the teares distilling from mine eyes. . . .

    (*T.R., Part I*, l. 136)

  And let these tears, distilling from mine eyes. . . .

    (*Edward II*, v.vi.100)

(2) Proud, and disturber of thy Countreyes peace. . . .

    (*T.R., Part I*, l. 1059)

  Thou proud disturber of thy country's peace. . . .

    (*Edward II*, II.v.9)

(3) Was ever King as I opprest with cares?

    (*T.R., Part II*, l. 225)

  Was ever king thus overruled as I?

    (*Edward II*, I.iv.38)

(4) My soule doth fleete, worlds vanities farewell.

    (*T.R., Part II*, l. 767)

  Spencer, I see our souls are fleeted hence. . . .

    (*Edward II*, IV.vii.105)[34]

For none of these parallels is the direction of the borrowing conclusive, but if, as many think, the anonymous play was on the boards around 1587–88 (the period of the Armada and *Tamburlaine*), the anonymous author presumably would have been composing too early to make use of *Edward II*.[35] Peele's *Edward I*, although not entered in the Stationers' Register until 8 October 1593, was probably written 1590–91, and, because it contains a clear allusion to a defence pact among England, Scotland, Denmark, and France against Spain, could not be earlier than May or June of 1590. Charlton and Waller list the most obvious verbal parallels between it and *Edward II*, showing convincingly that in two cases at least the borrowed language is more natural or more vital to Peele's context than to Marlowe's.[36] Even if we suppose that *The Troublesome Reign* followed rather than preceded *Edward II* (a possibility that its numerous echoes of other plays forces us to consider), Marlowe's apparent indebtedness to Peele makes 1590 a reasonable working *terminus a quo*.

If we acknowledge in addition that *Arden of Faversham* (which was registered with the Stationers 3 April 1592) and *Soliman and Perseda* (registered 20 November 1592) are both indebted verbally to Marlowe's play (as Charlton and Waller reasonably assume),[37] 1591 or early 1592, virtually of necessity, becomes the date for the composition of Marlowe's tragedy. The likelihood of the earlier of these dates gains support from the close relationship between Marlowe and Kyd. *Soliman and Perseda* is probably by Kyd, and *Arden of Faversham* may be by him. We know that the two dramatists were sharing a room around May 1591—a likely time for Kyd to have read a draft or part of a draft of *Edward II*—and that after this Kyd avoided Marlowe's company. Kenneth Muir, who believes that the rooming arrangements may well explain Kyd's echoing of *Edward II*, goes on to argue that even if *Arden of Faversham* and *Soliman and Perseda* are not by Kyd, the borrowings from *Edward II* necessarily push the date of Marlowe's play back to at least the autumn of 1591, because there would have to be time for the source drama to have been performed, for the borrowers to incorporate phrases and lines from it into their own works, for these dramas in turn to be staged, and then finally for them to be sold for publication—a sequence that would require some months. That all the plays mentioned here are verbally interrelated can scarcely be denied, but their proximity to each other in date and the ambiguous direction of the borrrowing in some cases make their exact chronology impossible to establish with certainty. The year 1591 emerges as the likeliest date of *Edward II*, but, theoretically, the play could have been written as late as early 1592.[38] What we can deduce from metrical tests about the troubled chronology of Marlowe's canon would seem to consist with 1591 as the putative date of composition.[39]

3   THE PLAY AND ITS SHAKESPEAREAN RELATIVES

It is a commonplace of scholarship that Marlowe's influence upon Shakespeare, particularly in the early years of the latter's career, was both profound and pervasive—perhaps even more so than that of Kyd (whose imprint can be discerned in *Titus Andronicus* and *Hamlet*) or of Lyly (to whom the early comedies obviously owe much). For years editors have pointed to Shakespeare's tribute to Marlowe (with its accompanying quotation from *Hero and Leander*) in *As You Like It* ('Dead shepherd, now I find thy saw of might, / "Who ever lov'd that lov'd not at first sight?"' [III.v.81–82])[40] and to Pistol's parody of Tamburlaine in *2 Henry IV* ('Shall pack-horses / And hollow pamper'd jades of Asia, / Which cannot go but thirty mile a day, / Compare with Caesars, and with Cannibals...?' [II.iv.162–165]).[41] We have long been aware, of course, of how much Shakespeare must have learned from his shorter-lived contemporary in plays such as *Richard III* (which takes over from *Tamburlaine* the strategy of a single dominant character)[42] and *The Merchant of Venice* (which in Shylock complicates and deepens a stereotype from *The Jew of Malta*)[43] and *Macbeth* (which dramatizes the psychology of damnation in ways that recall *Doctor Faustus*). It is accepted, also, that *Hero and Leander* must have set the fashion for erotic mythological narrative that Shakespeare took up in *Venus and Adonis*,[44] in addition to which Marlowe has frequently been suggested as the rival poet to whose 'proud full sail of...great verse' Sonnet 86 alludes. What is less widely recognized, although we have become increasingly cognizant of it in recent times,[45] is the almost equally formative impress of Shakespeare upon Marlowe.

Peter Alexander opened the door to this last perception in his ground-breaking work on the first historical tetralogy (*Shakespeare's 'Henry VI' and 'Richard III'* [Cambridge, 1929]) in which he showed that *The First Part of the Contention betwixt the Two Famous Houses of York and Lancaster* (1594) and *The True Tragedy of Richard, Duke of York* (1595) are bad quartos and, in the main, pirated versions of *2* and *3 Henry VI*.[46] Alexander's work in conjunction with that of Charlton and Waller (who first proposed that *Edward II* borrowed from Shakespeare's earliest histories) and of A. P. Rossiter (who argued that Marlowe's tragedy levied upon *Woodstock*, which in turn had echoed *2 Henry VI*)[47] allowed us to date Shakespeare's originals about 1590–91—earlier, that is, than Marlowe's *Edward II*, which had previously been assumed by most scholars to mark the beginning of the chronicle history as a dignified, coherent dramatic genre. It follows then, as F. P. Wilson pointed out, that except for morality interludes such as Skelton's *Magnyfycence* (1519) and Bale's *Kynge Johan* (originally composed before 1536, revised in 1538, and rewritten in 1561) the crude, anonymous *Famous Victories of Henry V* (1586?) with its manifest debt to the traditions of the jest-book is the only historical drama in English that can reliably be established as earlier than Shakespeare's trilogy.[48] Wilson also endorsed the argument for the priority of *2* and *3 Henry VI* to Marlowe's play by underlining Rossiter's convincing point that 'the two passages in Part II and the one in Part III which resemble passages in *Edward II* were . . . suggested to Shakespeare by the chronicles for the reigns of Henry VI and Edward IV, whereas there are no corresponding passages in the chronicles of Edward II's reign which might have suggested these passages to Marlowe.'[49] Harold Brooks argues in similar fashion that Marlowe's characterization of Mortimer, unhistorically styled Protector, is partly based upon incidents and behaviour that have no counterparts in the chronicles but must derive from the Protectors of *2* and *3 Henry VI* (Duke Humphrey and York) and of *Richard III* (Richard of Gloucester).[50] Although the exact chronology of Marlowe's plays and of Shakespeare's early works remains a vexed problem depending on incomplete knowledge of the acting companies involved, the shaky evidence of parallel passages, speculative inferences about stylistic habits, and a miscellany of baffling variables,[51] a certain scholarly consensus may be said to have emerged.

Most informed opinion now holds that Marlowe's popular *Tamburlaine* and *The Jew of Malta* stimulated Shakespeare's dramatic and prosodic imagination in the late 1580s when these plays were first staged, and that the four dramas of the Henry VI–Richard III sequence, plays that display unquestionable features of Marlovian style and characterization, followed in rapid succession during 1590–91.[52] *Edward II*, probably written in 1591–92, then took up the Shakespearean fashion of adapting materials from Holinshed and other historical sources to the stage, echoing the first tetralogy in the process and abetted also by dramas such as Peele's *Edward I* (1591), which Marlowe's play likewise echoes, and anonymous pieces such as *Jack Straw* (1590–91), *The Troublesome Reign of King John* (1590–91), and *Woodstock* (1591–93), the last two of which probably antedate but may postdate Marlowe's tragedy.[53] *The Contention* and *The True Tragedy*, perhaps assembled hastily from memory by actors for performance in the provinces, clearly came after *Edward II* but incorporated (unconsciously?) a few verbal scraps from Marlowe that were probably absent from *2* and *3 Henry VI* in their original form. Marlowe's play, after all, had been acted by Pembroke's Men, the same company with which the two mutilated texts of the *Henry VI* plays are associated. Then Shakespeare's *Richard II* (1594–95), a second tragedy about the deposition of a weak king dominated by flatterers, obviously imitated the analogous Marlowe play not only in its choice of subject but also in its structural design, nevertheless emerging as a drama wholly different in tone and emotional effect from its predecessor. Despite other similarities, Shakespeare in *Richard II* seems to have depended comparatively little on Marlowe's chronicle play for verbal or imagistic details, but there are demonstrable verbal links between *Edward II* and the plays of the first tetralogy as well as between Marlowe's tragedy and Kyd's (?) *Soliman and Perseda* (1592?), Lodge's *Wounds of Civil War* (1588?), Nashe's *Summer's Last Will and Testament* (1592–93), and the anonymous *Arden of Faversham* (1592).[54] In addition to *Richard II*, *Romeo and Juliet* contains a clear reminiscence of *Edward II* in Juliet's lines, 'Gallop apace, you fiery-footed steeds, / Towards Phoebus' lodging!' (III.ii.1–2), an echo, apparently, of Edward's anticipation of meeting enemy forces: 'Gallop apace bright Phoebus through the sky...' (IV.iii.66). And Hamlet's famous reference to death as 'The undiscover'd country from whose bourn / No traveller returns' (*Ham.*, III.i.80–81) may have taken its inception from Mortimer's parting words as he is led off to execution, 'as a traveller / Go[ing] to discover countries yet unknown' (*Edward II*, v.vi.64–65).

Marlowe's chronicle history may thus be claimed to occupy a pivotal position in the putative sequence outlined above—a centrality that becomes even more obvious when we note the close verbal connections (borrowings, imitations, imperfect recollections, possible interpolations, and the like) that have been shown to exist between *Edward II* and the first Shakespearean tetralogy (in both the Folio and corrupt texts) as well as between it and other histories such as *Edward I*, *Woodstock*, and *The Troublesome Reign*. It may be more than fortuitous, for instance, that the descriptive title, *The Troublesome Raigne of John King of England, with the discoverie of*

King Richard Cordelions Base Sonne (vulgarly named, The Bastard Fawconbridge): also the death of King John at Swinstead Abbey, is suspiciously similar in form and phrasing to that of the first edition of Marlowe's play: *The troublesome raigne and lamentable death of Edward the second, King of England: with the tragicall fall of proud Mortimer.* If Marlowe's tragedy was the receiver of artistic stimuli from Shakespeare as well as a stimulus upon him, we have a fascinating case of theatrical and stylistic interchange between the two dramatists that suggests something approaching symbiosis. That Marlowe's play is so obviously distinct from its Shakespearean precedessors and successors tells us something, perhaps, about the anxiety of influence or even the growing confidence on both sides of the relationship. But the points of contact are worth considering in greater detail than has generally been attempted. This, though in necessarily tentative and provisional outline, is the purpose of the following discussion. As a starting point I shall invoke a few of the more illustrative verbal and situational parallels, but I hope that these in turn will direct our attention to larger matters of characterization, form, theme, and overall concept. In the end, perhaps, we may gain a clearer idea of how, between them, Shakespeare and Marlowe established, and then experimented with, the chronicle history as an exciting new genre on the English stage.

Going back to the first phase of these alternating pressures, we may inquire what Shakespeare learned from Marlowe in composing the early tetralogy. Certainly there is the appeal of the 'mighty line' with its impressive freight of cosmic imagery and 'high astounding terms' (*1 Tamburlaine,* Pro., 5)—an influence readily apparent in the opening lines of *1 Henry VI*:

> Hung be the heavens with black, yield day to night!
> Comets, importing change of times and states,
> Brandish your crystal tresses in the sky
> And with them scourge the bad revolting stars
> That have consented unto Henry's death—. . . .
>
> (I.i.1–5)

The theatre that served Marlowe as the 'tragic glass' in which to reflect the career of aspiring Tamburlaine could serve Shakespeare equally well for ambitious overreachers such as the Duke of York and his son, Richard III, to say nothing of heroic soldiers like Talbot. But Tamburlaine's obsession with the mystique of crowns and his lyrical exaltation over the symbolism of royal power was

clearly transmissible as well. The feeling of 'bloody and insatiate
Tamburlaine,' who deprives Cosroe of his throne out of the sheer
'thirst of reign and sweetness of a crown' (*1 Tamburlaine*, II.vii.11–
12), is recognizable in young Richard of Gloucester's speech, 'How
sweet a thing it is to wear a crown, / Within whose circuit is Elysium
/ And all that poets feign of bliss and joy' (*3H6*, I.ii.29–31). Later
Richard embroiders the same sentiment:

> I'll make my heaven to dream upon the crown,
> And, whiles I live, t' account this world but hell,
> Until my mis-shap'd trunk that bears this head
> Be round impaled with a glorious crown.
>
> (*3H6*, III.ii.168–171)

As his catching up of the words 'bliss' and 'sweet' in the first
example would indicate, Shakespeare must surely have recalled in
these passages Tamburlaine's similar restlessness, his upward thrust
for 'That perfect bliss and sole felicity, / The sweet fruition of an
earthly crown' (*1 Tamburlaine*, II.vii.28–29).

Yet how unlike Tamburlaine, 'Of stature tall, and straightly
fashionèd' (*1 Tamburlaine*, II.i.7), is crook-back Dick. Some of the
dauntless self-confidence remains, but, in conceiving Richard III,
Shakespeare has wedded the *virtù* of the Scythian shepherd to the
Machiavellian diabolism of such figures as Barabas and perhaps also
(if *Titus Andronicus* is an earlier play) of his own Aaron, the Moor.
Gloucester's gleeful fantasy of wickedness also has a Marlovian ring:

> Why, I can smile, and murder whiles I smile,
> And cry 'Content' to that which grieves my heart,
> And wet my cheeks with artificial tears,
> And frame my face to all occasions.
> . . .
> I can add colours to the chameleon,
> Change shapes with Proteus for advantages,
> And set the murderous Machiavel to school.
> Can I do this, and cannot get a crown?
>
> (*3H6*, III.ii.182–194)

Indeed, as more than one critic has noticed, this soliloquy may hark
back to the figure of Machiavel, who had introduced Marlowe's *Jew
of Malta*:

> I count religion but a childish toy,
> And hold there is no sin but ignorance.
> Birds of the air will tell of murders past?

I am ashamed to hear such fooleries!
Many will talk of title to a crown:
What right had Caesar to the empery?
Might first made kings, and laws were then most sure
When like the Draco's they were writ in blood.

(Pro., 14–21)

And the contemptuous attitude of Shakespeare's royal Antichrist is also of a piece with Barabas's advice to Ithamore:

First, be thou void of these affections,
Compassion, love, vain hope, and heartless fear;
Be moved at nothing, see thou pity none,
But to thyself smile when the Christians moan.

(*Jew of Malta*, II.iii.171–174)

As he plans the murder of the princes, for example, Richard III announces flatly, 'Tear-falling pity dwells not in this eye' (*R3*, IV.ii.65).

As Brooke has pointed out, Queen Margaret's warning to Buckingham about his treacherous master ('take heed of yonder dog. / Look when he fawns, he bites . . .' [*R3*, I.iii.288–289]) appropriates Barabas's boast, 'We Jews can fawn like spaniels when we please, / And when we grin, we bite . . .' (*Jew of Malta*, II.iii.20–21). Given Shakespeare's obvious indebtedness to *The Jew* in *3 Henry VI* and *Richard III*, it may not be too fanciful to lay a bit of the phantasmagoric imagery of Clarence's dream to Marlovian inspiration. Barabas's delight in 'heap[ing] pearl like pebble-stones,' in 'Bags of fiery opals, sapphires, amethysts, / Jacinths, hard topaz, grass-green emeralds, / Beauteous rubies, sparkling diamonds, / And seld-seen costly stones of so great price' (*Jew of Malta*, I.i.23–28), seems to reappear, much more eerily, in the doomed duke's vision of sunken treasure:

Wedges of gold, great anchors, heaps of pearl,
Inestimable stones, unvalued jewels,
All scatt'red in the bottom of the sea.
Some lay in dead men's skulls; and, in the holes
Where eyes did once inhabit, there were crept,
As 'twere in scorn of eyes, reflecting gems,
That woo'd the slimy bottom of the deep. . . .

(*R3*, I.iv.26–32)[55]

Interestingly in this comparison, the sheer pleasure of wealth in its tactile and visual aspects captures Marlowe's poetic imagination, whereas Shakespeare, while still invoking a sense of material beauty, transforms the imagery symbolically—almost emblematically—to associate it with death and thus to give it a moral and metaphysical significance absent from Marlowe's context.

Finally Shakespeare probably absorbed from Marlowe the idea of 'the scourge of God,' repeatedly stressed in *Tamburlaine* (especially in Part II), although the concept was familiar and already available to the dramatist in several of his historical sources. Pucelle in *1 Henry VI* announces that she is 'Assign'd . . . to be the English scourge' (I.ii.129), and in the same play Talbot is called 'the scourge of France' (II.iii.15) and her 'bloody scourge' (IV.ii.16). In *2 Henry VI* York refers to Margaret as 'England's bloody scourge' (V.i.118), and, as Hammond observes, the notion fundamentally informs the characterization of the tyrant in *Richard III*, who is conceived as 'hell's black intelligencer' (IV.iv.71), an agent for sending lesser sinners such as Clarence, Hastings, Rivers, Vaughan, and Grey to their deserved ends, but whose own destruction at the hands of Richmond, God's 'captain' (V.iii.108), takes place under divine sanction.[56]

Although it is dangerous to generalize about the effect of such Marlovian touches upon Shakespeare's early histories, one tendency does appear to stand out—namely that the borrowing, whether conscious or not, goes well beyond the merely incidental and phrasal. And the fresh contexts into which Shakespeare assimilates Marlovian ideas and images seem always to be significantly different from Marlowe's. The Henry VI–Richard III tetralogy was planned on an altogether more comprehensive scale and rests on a more coherent moral and humanistic base than the Marlowe plays that preceded it. There is a curious absence of metaphysical design in both *Tamburlaine* and *The Jew of Malta*, as though Marlowe were excited by the sheer grandeur and strength of the one protagonist and by the evil energy of the other, by their emotional appeal as astonishing natural forces. Neither the psychology of the characters nor their function in a morally intelligible universe is of primary importance. In contrast Shakespeare presents Richard III—a compound, in some sense, of elements from both Tamburlaine and Barabas—as a tyrant-Machiavel whose rise and fall dramatizes the final phase of a national myth (shaped by Hall's chronicle) with political, social, and religious implications that radiate beyond its own centre. And despite its colour and brilliancy, Marlowe's imagery seems harder, more metallic, less given to particularity, and less revelatory of character than does Shakespeare's. The first tetralogy already organizes political conflicts and personality clashes with a grasp of human complexity far in advance of the dramaturgical powers of the early Marlowe.

That Marlowe in *Edward II* was indebted to Shakespeare's first histories is now generally taken as proved. Charlton and Waller in their edition of the tragedy list at least eight indubitable parallels of language or idea, together with others that, although more tenuous, are also strongly suggestive of Shakespearean origin. Thus, for instance, Marlowe borrows Queen Margaret's charge about the Duchess of Gloucester's extravagance ('She bears a duke's revenue on her back' [*2H6*, I.iii.80]) for Mortimer's hostility to Gaveston: 'He wears a lord's revénue on his back' (*Edward II*, I.iv.406). Similarly Margaret, scoffing at her husband's weakness in military affairs, announces that 'Stern Falconbridge commands the narrow seas' (*3H6*, I.i.239), a line that Marlowe (with a change of subject) reassigns to Mortimer, who in like manner is rebuking the passiveness of Edward: 'The haughty Dane commands the narrow seas' (II.ii.167). In both *3 Henry VI* (v.ii.11–12) and *Richard III* (I.iii.263) cedar trees and eagles are linked as twin symbols of hierarchical priority. Marlowe picks up the Shakespearean association and applies it to the emblem on Mortimer's shield, an emblem intended, of course, to insult Gaveston as a social inferior: 'A lofty cedar tree fair flourishing, / On whose top branches kingly eagles [i.e., the barons] perch . . .' (*Edward II*, II.ii.16–17). In *1 Henry VI* Duke Humphrey scoffs at Winchester's preference for a weak king, 'an effeminate prince, / Whom, like *a schoolboy*, you may *overawe*' (I.i.35–36; emphasis added). A related image appears in the next play: when the enemies of Humphrey have succeeded in disempowering him as Protector and Henry claims regal authority in his own right, Margaret crows, 'I see no reason why a king of years / Should be to be protected *like a child*' (*2H6*, II.iii.28–29; emphasis added).[57] Marlowe catches up these ideas (with a suggestion of phrasing from both examples) in Baldock's flattery to King Edward at a moment of similar self-assertion, after the barons have captured Gaveston:

> This haught resolve becomes your majesty,
> Not to be tied to their affection
> As though your highness were *a schoolboy* still,
> And must be *awed* and governed *like a child*.
>
> (*Edward II*, III.i.28–31; emphasis added)

As for the vulnerability of children in a world of savage political aggression, Marlowe again seems to take his cue from Shakespeare. Isabella is anxious for the safety of her son, the future Edward III: 'Ah boy, this towardness makes thy mother fear / Thou art not marked to many days on earth' (*Edward II*, III.i.79–80). This seems to have been suggested by Gloucester's mordant asides in the presence of the boy king, Edward V, in *Richard III*: 'So wise so young, they say, do never live long,' and 'Short summers lightly have a forward spring' (III.i.79, 94). As Brooks warily reminds us, we are dealing here with proverbial ideas—part of the common linguistic currency of the period; but the two contexts are so strikingly alike, both foreshadowing the early death of royal children, that the link between them is most unlikely to have been fortuitous. A question arises as to the dramatic function of the Marlowe appropriation, since the prophecy about Edward III's early demise, unlike its counterpart in Shakespeare's play, turns out to be untrue. But of course it prepares us for the rapid maturation of the prince, and also for the ironic scene at the end of the play when the complicity of the queen in Edward II's murder is made public and she, not her son, is the one in need of protection.[58] In *Edward II* Prince Edward defends Kent, his uncle, against Mortimer, who is eager to separate the boy from a 'false' influence (V.ii.103) sympathetic to the persecuted king. This tension between the innocence of a child and Machiavellian realpolitik could also have come from *Richard III*, in which another Prince Edward defends his uncle and cousin against Gloucester's claim that they were 'false friends' (III.i.15–16); like Lord Rivers (the uncle in *Richard III*), Marlowe's Kent is also beheaded.

Shakespeare obviously made much of the *de casibus* motif and its traditional association with Fortune's wheel. When Edward IV is forcibly dispossessed of the crown by Warwick in *3 Henry VI*, he manages a conventional expression of stoic defiance just before he is led offstage under guard: 'Though fortune's malice overthrow my state, / My mind exceeds the compass of her wheel' (IV.iii.46–47). The downward revolution of the wheel turns out in this instance to be temporary, for Edward regains the crown later in the play; but the hubris of his boast implies that his earthly days are already numbered. Again Marlowe appears to imitate Shakespeare when he makes Mortimer utter a similar line as he too is being led captive from the stage: 'Mortimer's hope surmounts his fortune far' (*Edward II*, III.ii.75). Once more the defeat is temporary and again it carries

within it the seeds of greater disaster for the speaker, a point that
Marlowe reinforces in Mortimer's exit speech before execution:

> Base Fortune, now I see that in thy wheel
> There is a point to which, when men aspire,
> They tumble headlong down. That point I touched,
> And, seeing there was no place to mount up higher,
> Why should I grieve at my declining fall?

(v.vi.58–62)

Such moralizing carries all the more force since only a few scenes
earlier, when he was arranging to exacerbate King Edward's misery,
the same speaker had boasted, 'Mortimer . . . now makes Fortune's
wheel turn as he please' (v.ii.51–52).

Marlowe of course would have had no need to consult Shakespeare
for the commonplace of Fortune's wheel, available to him in *A
Mirror for Magistrates* and a hundred other places; indeed he had
used the concept effectively himself in *Tamburlaine*.[59] But the first
tetralogy (especially in its final two plays, of which Marlowe clearly
made use in other ways) embodies the tradition more dramatically
than other likely sources, and here he could have appreciated its
structural and theatrical possibilities more prominently utilized than
elsewhere. Two separate speeches in *Edward II* that echo the scene
of Henry VI's murder would seem to confirm this influence. In
Shakespeare's play Richard of Gloucester, having just stabbed the
defenceless king, sarcastically juxtaposes the high ambitions of the
House of Lancaster with its ignominious fall: 'What, will the *aspiring*
blood of *Lancaster* / Sink in the ground? I thought it would have
mounted' (*3H6*, v.vi.61–62; emphasis added). Marlowe must have
remembered part of this utterance in composing Edward II's threat
to one of his refractory barons: 'Frownst thou thereat, *aspiring
Lancaster*? / The sword shall plane the furrows of thy brows . . .'
(*Edward II*, I.i.92–93; emphasis added); another fragment of the
Shakespearean speech surfaces later in Marlowe's play when the
captured king, ironically foreshadowing his own death, compares
himself to a lion who, 'highly scorning that the lowly earth / Should
drink his blood, *mounts* up into the air' (v.i.13–14; emphasis added).
In both plays we have the same combination—blood sinking into the
ground associated with mounting up and with violence upon the
person of a king.

Shakespeare's histories seem also to have suggested a few vivid
strokes of characterization to Marlowe. The most remarkable of

these, as Brooks has shown,[60] is Mortimer's feigned reluctance to accept the office of Lord Protector while along the way, in good Machiavellian fashion, he arranges to have power foisted upon him:

> They thrust upon me the protectorship
> And sue to me for that that I desire.
> While at the council table, grave enough,
> And not unlike a bashful Puritan,
> First I complain of imbecility [i.e., weakness],
> Saying it is *onus quam gravissimum*,
> Till being interrupted by my friends,
> *Suscepi* that *provinciam*, as they term it,
> And to conclude, I am Protector now.

> > (*Edward II*, v.iv.54–62)

The Mortimer presented to us in this speech (there is no precedent for these traits in the chronicles) is strikingly like the comically sanctimonious Gloucester who, assisted by Catesby and Buckingham, manipulates a pre-assembled group of Londoners into pressing the crown upon him. Richard appears '*aloft, between two Bishops*'—as 'a holy man,' prayer book in hand, acting out an exaggerated display of 'devotion and right Christian zeal' (*R3*, III.vii.94–103). Hypocritically urging his 'poverty of spirit' and his 'many . . . defects' (III.vii.159–160), protesting his 'unfit[ness] for state and majesty' (III.vii.205) and alleging that the acceptance of such a weight is 'against my conscience and my soul' (III.vii.226), Richard, 'play[ing] the maid's part' (III.vii.51), enacts precisely the 'bashful Puritan' to whom Mortimer cynically likens himself.[61] How better to diabolize Mortimer at the end of *Edward II* than to make him describe himself for the nonce as though he were a pupil of Shakespeare's arch-hypocrite?

Marlowe adds a searing touch of pathos to Edward's tattered degradation in his sewer-prison—as well as a piercing irony—by having the exhausted and terrified king recall his wooing days. With a hint of self-mockery he says to Lightborn, 'Tell Isabel, the queen, I looked not thus / When for her sake I ran at tilt in France / And there unhorsed the Duke of Cleremont' (*Edward II*, v.v.67–69). Given Edward's rejection of his wife in favour of male favourites and his characteristic lack of chivalry elsewhere, this reminiscence of a heterosexual courtship comes somewhat unexpectedly; but it has the effect of engaging our sympathies more deeply than ever by reminding us not only of a lost gaiety and splendour but also of the queen's vindictive complicity in her husband's present wretchedness. Again, nothing in Holinshed could suggest such a detail, and it undoubtedly comes from a scene in *2 Henry VI* in which an equally unfeeling French queen (Margaret of Anjou) recalls her own proxy wooing by Suffolk, the man who has now become her adulterous lover. Margaret feels only contempt for her monkish spouse and, soon after her arrival in England, voices her preference for the more glamorous figure who has sued for her hand in the king's name while promoting his own libidinous interest:

> I tell thee, Pole, when in the city Tours
> Thou ran'st a-tilt in honour of my love
> And stol'st away the ladies' hearts of France,
> I thought King Henry had resembled thee
> In courage, courtship, and proportion;
> But all his mind is bent to holiness,
> To number Ave-Maries on his beads;
> His champions are the prophets and apostles,
> His weapons holy saws of sacred writ,
> His study is his tilt-yard, and his loves
> Are brazen images of canonized saints.

(I.iii.50–60)

Although Shakespeare's context is quite different, scorn rather than pathos being the principal effect of Margaret's speech, we should notice that weak kings, victimized in each case by an unfaithful queen in league with a power-thirsty nobleman, make up the background situation in both plays.

Perhaps Marlowe remembered the ominous lines of Suffolk that conclude the first drama in Shakespeare's series ('Margaret shall now be Queen, and rule the King; / But I will rule both her, the King, and realm' [*1H6*, v.v.107–108]); for after Gaveston and the Spencers have been taken from him, Edward too is ruled by a flint-hearted queen (Isabella), who in turn has become the pawn of a political schemer (Mortimer). The latter's words in soliloquy ('The prince I rule, the queen do I command . . .' [v.iv.46]) clearly recall Suffolk's. Certainly the two queens have points of similarity: Marlowe's Isabella, for instance, coldly consents to the murder of her husband under Mortimer's domination, just as Shakespeare's Margaret, for equally political reasons and with Suffolk at her side, counsels the elimination of Duke Humphrey. Moreover the policy meeting in which Margaret, Suffolk, and their allies discuss the best means of liquidating Humphrey (*2H6*, III.i) could have prompted Marlowe's similar scene in which Isabella persuades Mortimer to agree to

Gaveston's recall from banishment—the better to 'greet his lordship with a poniard' (*Edward II*, I.iv.266). In this episode Mortimer speaks of a hypothetical situation that might provide 'some colour' (I.iv.279), or justification, for rising in arms against the king; in the corresponding Shakespearean scene Winchester suggests that the conspirators against Duke Humphrey 'want a colour for his death' (III.i.236). Both queens, too, are warlike, being actively engaged in military campaigns.

Holinshed records that the Earl of Lancaster was so contemptuous of Edward II that he 'greeuously and vndutifullie reproched him, without respect had to his roiall estate' (p. 328). Marlowe gives this detail dramatic vitality by having Lancaster and Mortimer Junior openly taunt the young monarch for his weakness, folly, and unkingly policies:

> *Lancaster*. Look for rebellion, look to be deposed.
>   Thy garrisons are beaten out of France,
>   And, lame and poor, lie groaning at the gates;
>   The wild O'Neil, with swarms of Irish kerns,
>   Lives uncontrolled within the English pale;
>   Unto the walls of York the Scots made road
>   And unresisted drave away rich spoils.
> *Mortimer Junior*. The haughty Dane commands the narrow seas,
>   While in the harbour ride thy ships unrigged.
> *Lancaster*. What foreign prince sends thee ambassadors?
> *Mortimer Junior*. Who loves thee but a sort of flatterers?
>
>   (*Edward II*, II.ii.160–170)

It is not unlikely, however, that, in addition to Holinshed, Marlowe may have been stimulated by the similar scene of *3 Henry VI* in which Warwick browbeats Edward IV, whom he has just reduced to the rank of Duke of York in his anger at being betrayed in his recent embassy to arrange Edward's marriage to the Lady Bona:

> Alas, how should you govern any kingdom,
> That know not how to use ambassadors,
> Nor how to be contented with one wife,
> Nor how to use your brothers brotherly,
> Nor how to study for the people's welfare,
> Nor how to shroud yourself from enemies?
> . . .
>   Henry now shall wear the English crown,
>   And be true king indeed, thou but the shadow.
>
>   (IV.iii.35–40, 49–50)

The probability of influence here is perhaps all the greater in that the omitted part of the speech just quoted contains Edward's words, already cited above, on his mind's exceeding the compass of Fortune's wheel. And, as has also been noted earlier, Mortimer's line, 'The haughty Dane commands the narrow seas,' echoes Margaret's scornful words to King Henry ('Stern Falconbridge commands the narrow seas') from a similar context in the same play. Nor can one help noticing the image of Edward IV as the 'shadow' king. Edward II's most elegiac lines, 'But what are kings when regiment is gone / But perfect shadows in a sunshine day?' (*Edward II*, v.i.26–27), movingly invert the traditional association of kingship with the sun in a way that might also have been prompted by this episode.[62]

Different as they are in other respects, we might hesitantly suggest a tenuous link between the conceptions of the two King Edwards addressed so disrespectfully in these quotations. Both monarchs are portrayed as sensualists, their judgement clouded by sexual attachments (the widow Grey and Mistress Shore in Shakespeare, Gaveston and Spencer Junior in Marlowe), and both too are characterized by stubbornness of will. Edward IV seems just as ready to imperil his crown by insisting on an upstart queen (Elizabeth) as Edward II is willing to risk his throne by refusing to give up Gaveston. Lancaster at one point compares Gaveston to Helen of Troy, 'the Greekish strumpet,' who has caused 'many valiant knights' to risk their lives in 'bloody wars' (II.v.15–16). The whole climate of sexual politics, in fact—an emphasis almost wholly absent from Marlowe's sources—was to be found repeatedly in the Shakespearean tetralogy. If Marlowe borrowed this concept from Shakespeare (for it pervades the entire series from Talbot's encounter with the Countess of Auvergne to Richard III's attempt to marry Elizabeth of York), he clearly gave it a uniquely macabre twist, for sexual domination (Gaveston's over Edward, Mortimer's over Isabella, Lightborn's over his royal victim) becomes a controlling metaphor in Marlowe's tragedy for the force of self-destruction. And the anal penetration with a fiery spit that constitutes the play's painful climax makes a far bleaker statement about the intersection of sex and politics than Shakespeare ever saw fit to dramatize.

None the less, the very savagery of Edward's murder could have been linked in Marlowe's mind with the almost equally brutal scene of York's ritual killing in *3 Henry VI*. Here the victim is made to stand upon a molehill, mocked for his kingly pretensions, crowned with paper, and given a napkin wet with the blood of his slaughtered son. The entire episode, as has often been observed, is conceived to evoke overtones of the Crucifixion and probably owes something to the biblical cycle plays of the late Middle Ages that survived in some localities into the period of Shakespeare's boyhood.[63] A major point of Shakespeare's scene is the animalistic degradation of a royal figure. When Marlowe came to do something similar, to stage the degradation of Edward II, he turned to Stowe's *Chronicles of England* (1580) for a human interest and a pathos not available in either Holinshed's or Grafton's chronicles. It was here that he found the detail of Edward's being shaved in puddle water—a detail that underscores the theme of humiliation, for the shaving was apparently undertaken not merely to make the king unrecognizable but also to violate his royal dignity, his symbolic manhood, as signified by the beard.[64] Marlowe chose not to make use of Stowe's description of how King Edward was crowned with hay, scoffed at and mocked as a would-be king, and then 'set on a Molehill' (p. 356) to be barbered; but he could hardly have failed to associate the mole-hill scene in Stowe with its counterpart in Shakespeare's play, es-ecially since he was already drawing upon the latter independently for suggestions of characterization and speech. It is therefore inter-esting to speculate whether York's memorable epithet for Margaret, a 'tiger's heart wrapt in a woman's hide' (*3H6*, I.iv.137), might have conditioned Edward's images of his enemies—'Inhuman creatures, nursed with tiger's milk' in whose 'embracements' one would find less 'safety' than 'in a tiger's jaws' (*Edward II*, v.i.71, 116–117). Another verbal link between the two suffering characters may show up in Edward's self-pitying gesture of sending a tear-drenched handkerchief to his queen: 'If with the sight thereof she be not moved, / Return it back and *dip it in my blood*' (*Edward II*, v.i.119–120; emphasis added). Conceivably Marlowe recalled the lines of York in Shakespeare's play:

This cloth thou *dip'dst in blood* of my sweet boy,
And I with tears do wash the blood away.
Keep thou the napkin, and go boast of this;
    [*Gives back the bloodstained cloth.*]
And if thou tell'st the heavy story right,
Upon my soul, the hearers will shed tears.
Yea even my foes will shed fast-falling tears
And say, 'Alas, it was a piteous deed!'
          (*3H6*, I.iv.157–163; emphasis added)

Shakespeare of course used the molehill violence in *3 Henry VI* partly as a structural device, for it effectively sets up the contrast with the play's later molehill scene—that in which King Henry

retreats from the Battle of Towton to contemplate the attractions of
the pastoral life and during which the blind killing of fathers by sons
and sons by fathers is emblematized with such schematic irony.
The characterization of the king as a would-be contemplative more
attached to a spiritual 'crown . . . call'd content' (III.i.64) than to the
'polish'd perturbation' (2H4, IV.v.22) pursued so relentlessly by
figures like York, Edward IV, and Richard of Gloucester also makes
a brief appearance in Edward II. Marlowe gives us no emblematic
molehill—in Shakespeare the double-edged symbol of lowliness and
futile ambition; but he does show us King Edward at Neath Abbey,
disguised apparently as a monk,[65] laying his head in the abbot's lap
in a childlike gesture of exquisite vulnerability. The same kind of
escapist fantasy that characterizes Henry's reverie on the molehill
actuates Edward in the monastery: 'Father, this life contemplative is
heaven— / O that I might this life in quiet lead!' (IV.vii.20–21). And
the purpose of the contemplative motif is the same in both plays
also—to heighten the contrast between civilized calm, reason, and a
settled order on the one hand and the chaos of civil butchery on the
other. Indeed, it is hard not to think that 'holy Harry of Lancaster,'
Shakespeare's least regal monarch, had set a precedent for the
dramatization of unkingly weakness that Marlowe, whether consciously or not, was to exploit in the figure of Edward of Carnarvon.
Naivety and softness of inclination are stressed in both characters:
Margaret, for example, sneers at a husband 'Too full of childish pity'
(2H6, III.i.225), and Clifford rebukes his 'too much lenity' (3H6,
II.ii.9), while Edward, with imperfect self-understanding, asks, 'Yet
how have I transgressed / Unless it be with too much clemency?'
(v.i.122–123).

Shakespeare's early cycle even suggests parallels with Marlowe's
play in the treatment of a subordinate character such as Kent, who,
like Clarence, defects to the enemies of his royal brother and then,
plagued by guilt, returns to family loyalty. Kent rebukes himself in
soliloquy:

> Vile wretch, and why hast thou, of all unkind,
> Borne arms *against thy brother and thy king*?
>
> (*Edward II*, IV.vi.5–6; emphasis added)

These lines, particularly the second, seem to imitate a similar
Shakespearean speech in which Clarence justifies his desertion of
Warwick and his reversion to the support of Edward IV:

> Why, trowest thou, Warwick,
> That Clarence is so harsh, so blunt, unnatural,
> To bend the fatal instruments of war
> *Against his brother and his lawful king?*
>
> (*3H6*, v.i.85–88; emphasis added)

Enough has been said, I trust, to suggest that Shakespeare's early histories must be regarded, at least in principle, as the progenitors of Marlowe's only attempt at an English chronicle play—a history, that is, not based on foreign subjects such as *Tamburlaine* or *The Masssacre at Paris*. Marlowe was clearly experimenting with a genre that Shakespeare had already evolved, a genre that necessitated compressions of time; rearrangements, simplifications, and imaginative expansions of episodes; and additions to the crowded matter of Holinshed. In choosing to dramatize the reign of Edward II, Marlowe was continuing to deal with the same kind of politics that Shakespeare had confronted in the troubled reigns of Henry VI, Edward IV, and Richard III—with extremes of power and weakness, with treachery, aggression, carnage, and contested thrones, with child kings and their protectors (both good and evil), with sexual partners and self-serving advisers who dominate or corrupt those in authority, with the ignoring of wise counsel, and with destructive foreign policies in conjunction with the chaos of civil war at home. All this required a diffusion of interest and the use of multiple characters rather than the concentration on a single commanding figure that had been typical of Marlowe's earlier dramas. The beheading of political enemies occurs with accelerating frequency in the work of both playwrights (York's head is ironically to 'overlook the town of York' [*3H6*, I.iv.180] as Warwick's is similarly to 'overlook' those of his fellow rebels [*Edward II*, III.ii.55]), and Shakespeare's series exposes us to a succession of murders of helpless royal victims, often in prison—Duke Humphrey, York, Henry VI, Clarence, Richard III's nephews—that might be thought to provide models for the atrocities of Lightborn.[66] Coronations, sometimes shown onstage, succeed deaths or falls from power in the tetralogy, and Marlowe follows Shakespeare here as well. When Edward IV is proclaimed king, Montgomery throws down his gauntlet as the official champion (*3H6*, IV.vii.75); in similar fashion an unnamed champion ceremonially defends Edward III at his accession (*Edward II*, v.iv.73–76). Marlowe obviously had much to learn from his fellow dramatist's example. Douglas Cole has suggested, for instance, that the 'closest analogue' to Edward's emotional suffering when the king must part from Gaveston at the time of his banishment occurs in *2 Henry VI* when 'the banished Suffolk bids a sorrowful farewell to the faithless Queen' (III.ii);[67] later in the same play, Queen Margaret weeps over the head of her decapitated paramour—an action that could well have prompted Mortimer's cruel speech in which he imagines Edward 'bestow[ing] / His tears' on the severed head of Gaveston (II.v.50–51).

What is perhaps more important than any of the hints, verbal or otherwise, that Marlowe may have taken from Shakespeare is the total difference of ethos and philosophic perspective that *Edward II* projects. One clue to this difference lies in the absence of any action in Marlowe's play that requires the use of the upper stage. The explanation here, of course, may lie simply in the physical arrangements of the particular theatre for which *Edward II* was written; but the apparently missing 'above' (repeatedly used in the Shakespeare histories) implies an altered metaphysic—or perhaps a more profound scepticism about inherited religious categories than Shakespeare normally expresses. Shakespeare's placing of scenes occasionally seems to reflect a remnant of the old medieval-allegorical concept of stage space, as, for instance, when the Duchess of Gloucester and Hume, a priest, observe from their position 'aloft' while the conjurer Bolingbroke and his confederates raise from the trap a 'fiend,' who then 'Descend[s] to darkness' (*2H6*, I.iv.9, 40–41), or when the saintly King Henry VI, who is reading a book of devotions, meets his violent death ironically '*on the walls*'—on high, as it were—just after he moralizes bitterly on his murderer's true identity as a 'good devil' (*3H6*, V.vi.1–4). Hall's providential concept of historical process—of the sins of the fathers being visited on the sons, for instance, of national transgressions to be expiated by future generations, of England as a place of gardens reflecting natural law as in Spenser and Hooker, of royalty as quintessentially mystical, gets scant or no emphasis in Marlowe. Despite the brutality from which Shakespeare refuses to shrink, Marlowe's universe continues to look morally darker and psychologically more tormented. It is a world in which consistency and predictability of attitude or behaviour seem alien—as comes out in the radical changes and inexplicably sudden shifts that seem to govern the actions of Isabella, Mortimer, Kent, and even the protagonist himself. Finally Marlowe's focus is both narrower and more realistic than Shakespeare's. There is an element of petty spite and nastiness in Marlowe's drama that makes the hostilities of the Shakespearean tetralogy seem almost heroic by contrast. We have little sense of past or future reigns in *Edward II*, nothing, that is, of the Shakespearean longer view of time; and Marlowe also limits us to a more constricted social spectrum. Nor do we get anything in *Edward II* like the emblematic moralism of the contrasting pairs of fathers and sons divided only by their allegiance to the warring factions of a single family (*3 Henry VI*), nor anything like the didactic murderers of Clarence, who stage a semi-allegorical debate between the visitings of conscience and determined thuggery (*Richard III*).

If Marlowe felt the impress of Shakespeare in *Edward II*, this patently did not prevent his becoming a pressure (even after his death) in the opposite direction. Borrowings from Marlowe in the reported texts of *2* and *3 Henry VI*, however, were almost certainly more accidental than deliberate. *The Contention*, as Alexander has shown,[68] provides a convincing example. Here the pirate (an actor who had played in both *2 Henry VI* and *Edward II*?) seems to have recalled a passage from Marlowe's play and embedded it by mistake in the Shakespearean scene he was attempting to reconstruct. Lancaster's catalogue of national calamities, flung accusingly at Edward II, includes the lines (quoted above in another context): 'The wild O'Neil, with swarms of Irish kerns, / Lives uncontrolled within the English pale' (*Edward II*, II.ii.163–164). Nothing like this appears in the Folio text of *2 Henry VI*, but *The Contention* does contain a bloated version of the speech: 'The wilde Onele my Lords, is up in Armes, / With troupes of Irish Kernes that uncontrold, / Doth plant themselves within the English pale' (*Contention*, pp. 698–699).[69] It may be indicative that O'Neil is an unhistorical fiction in both contexts, although members of this family were active in Ireland during Edward II's reign and the name would be well known to Elizabethan audiences. Perhaps Marlowe's tragedy contributed also to the staging of the cobbled-up play. In the good text of *2 Henry VI* Duke Humphrey's murder occurs discreetly offstage whereas the reported text, perhaps bidding for greater sensationalism, actually shows it. The stage direction in *The Contention* reads: 'Then the Curtaines being drawne, Duke *Humphrey* is discovered in his bed, and two men lying on his brest and smothering him in his bed' (p. 700). Since bits of *Edward II* seem to have invaded this text in other places,[70] it is at least possible that the reconstructors, undoubtedly theatre men, were recording a visual effect based partly on the even more horrific overpowering of Marlowe's title character, where the victim is similarly held down on his bed. Could it be that Marlowe's scene had proved too gruesomely popular with audiences not to be emulated? Also *The Contention*, unlike the Folio text of *2 Henry VI*, makes it obvious that King Henry publicly seats his newly arrived wife beside him on the throne ('Lovely Queene *Margaret* sit down by my side' [p. 668]), even though he has had to give away Anjou and Maine as the unpopular price of the alliance. Again the staging here could have been prompted by the scene of Marlowe's tragedy in which Edward similarly seats his recently returned favourite by his side: 'What, are you moved that Gaveston sits here?' (*Edward II*, I.iv.8). In both cases the sharing of the throne with a foreigner symbolizes ominous weakness and dependency.

It is hardly necessary to dwell at length on the obvious debt that Shakespeare owed to *Edward II* in the most lyrical of his histories— *Richard II*. Lamb wrote long ago that 'The reluctant pangs of abdicating Royalty in *Edward* furnished hints which Shakespeare scarce improved in his *Richard the Second*,'[71] and everyone has noticed that the two plays are similarly structured, audiences being alienated by the wilful irresponsibility of the title figure in the early scenes and then gradually drawn into sympathy with him as he loses first his crown and then his life. The minions of the king are executed in both plays, and both end with funeral rites in which the hearse or coffin of the slain monarch is borne in procession. Other parallels are obvious enough. Shakespeare, very nearly at least, seems to take over Marlowe's exclusion of comedy[72] as well as the emphasis on sorrowful parting—although, unlike Marlowe, he uses this latter to underscore the king's devotion to his queen rather than to favourites such as Gaveston and Spencer. Shakespeare makes much of the paradox of a monarch who is theoretically absolute, yet constrained by lesser mortals—a king who 'must': 'What must the King do now? Must he submit? . . . Must he be depos'd? / The King shall be contented' (*R2*, III.iii.143–145). Suggestions for such frustration may have come from Marlowe's Edward, who expresses similar sentiments: 'Am I a king and must be overruled?' (I.i.134); 'I see I must, and therefore am content' (I.iv.85); 'Must! 'Tis somewhat hard when kings must go' (IV.vii.83); 'But tell me, must I now resign my crown . . . ?' (V.i.36); 'But what the heavens appoint I must obey. / Here, take my crown—the life of Edward too' (V.i.56–57); 'And needs I must resign my wishèd crown' (V.i.70).

Shakespeare's insight that Richard's very identity is symbolically bound up with his crown also has a precedent in Marlowe's character, who in his torment finds no comfort 'But that I feel the crown upon my head,' and therefore begs to 'wear it yet a while' (v.i.82–83). Richard II is also shown as physically attached to the crown, holding on to it tenaciously in the bucket-and-well speech. Richard's elaborate meditation in prison, where a multitude 'of still-breeding thoughts' (R2, v.v.8) peoples his consciousness, may have been suggested by Edward's 'strange despairing thoughts, / Which thoughts are martyrèd with endless torments' (Edward II, v.i.79–80). Nor is it impossible that for the language in which Richard's queen rebukes her husband's passivity Shakespeare again drew upon Marlowe's play:

> The lion dying thrusteth forth his paw,
> And wounds the earth, if nothing else, with rage
> To be o'erpow'r'd; and wilt thou, pupil-like,
> Take the correction, mildly kiss the rod,
> And fawn on rage with base humility,
> Which art a lion and a king of beasts?
>
> (R2, v.i.29–34)

Of course the lion-king and schoolboy metaphors are not uncommon, but in combination they suggest a possible indebtedness to two different passages from Edward II—one in which the king inveighs against his barons ('shall the crowing of these cockerels / Affright a lion? Edward, unfold thy paws . . .' [II.ii.202–203]) and the other, already mentioned above, in which Baldock urges the king to assert himself and so resist being treated like 'a schoolboy' who 'must be awed and governed like a child' (III.i.30–31).

Comparison of the two dramas has tended, justly enough, to stress differences rather than similarities.[73] Shakespeare's play, unlike Marlowe's, is almost wholly devoid of violence, and the one physical assault that does occur (Richard's murder) rouses the king to an act of heroic resistance that contrasts markedly with Edward's helpless abjection. Richard II employs the language and tone of ritual in conjunction with the visual formalism of pageantry. The theme of divine right and of the sacredness of royalty imparts to the central figure and to the ethos that surrounds him what Coleridge called an 'attention to decorum and high feeling of the kingly dignity,'[74] all of which helps to associate the deposition less with political necessities than with sacrilege and its attendant guilt. His tyrannies set aside, the verbal fancy and theatrical self-indulgence of Richard complicate our response to his sacramental claims, but the play nevertheless

enacts a martyrdom, however partially self-induced—a 'passion' that
makes the comparisons to Christ and Pilate something more than
childish or absurd hyperboles. Shakespeare's tragedy is rooted in a
love of country that reveals itself in numerous ways, not least in the
stylizations of the quasi-allegorical garden scene and in Gaunt's
speech on England as 'This other-Eden, demi-paradise' (II.i.42).
A profoundly national, almost mythic, grief lies at the heart of
the play—a grief of which the principal voice is the refined but lang-
ourous eloquence of its suffering monarch. All of this is Shakespeare's
doing. Certainly nothing of it was to be found in Marlowe's more
brutish and less luxuriantly worded effort.

Nevertheless it may be appropriate to conclude this survey of
uneasy creative interchanges by drawing attention to two passages
in *Richard II* that seem to bespeak the continuing presence of
Marlowe's dramaturgy in the consciousness or half-consciousness of
his rival. Although both have been noticed in the past, neither
has seemed to deserve much critical attention. The first concerns
Bolingbroke's illegal condemnation of Bushy and Green—an early
indication of how ruthless, and therefore how ambitious, the usurper
(despite his diplomatic posture to Richard in a later scene) is capable
of being. The doomed men remain silent, doubtless recognizing the
futility of defending themselves, but among the charges levelled at
them we find one that rings particularly hollow:

> You have in manner with your sinful hours
> Made a divorce betwixt his queen and him,
> Broke the possession of a royal bed,
> And stain'd the beauty of a fair queen's cheeks
> With tears drawn from her eyes by your foul wrongs.

(III.i.11–15)

The implication of homosexual attachments between the king and
his flatterers—attachments that have brought grief to the queen and
wrecked her marriage—has no historical validity and obviously
contradicts the impression of devoted fidelity between Richard and
his consort that Shakespeare is at pains to build up throughout the
play. Holinshed does mention the sexual immorality of Richard's
court ('there reigned abundantlie the filthie sinne of leacherie and
fornication, with abhominable adulterie, speciallie in the king, but
most cheefelie in the prelacie' [p. 508])[75] but is nowhere specific
about homoeroticism. The anonymous *Woodstock* is equally vague on
the point. The obvious source would seem to be *Edward II*, in

which the sexual relationship between Edward and Gaveston is not only unmistakable but also produces grief and jealousy in Isabella. Shakespeare probably recalled her hostile words to Gaveston:

> thou corrupts my lord,
> And art a bawd to his affections. . . .
> . . .
> Villain, 'tis thou that robb'st me of my lord.
>
> (*Edward II*, I.iv.150–160)[76]

But why did Shakespeare introduce this apparently groundless charge into his own play? Probably, I would suggest, he saw it as a subtle means of undermining our respect for Bolingbroke at a point in the action where he needed to begin manipulating audience sympathies in the direction of Richard. The words convey expediency and underhandedness in the speaker, who is shown to behave in the episode like a military dictator presiding at a show trial of expendable dissidents.

The second probable debt to Marlowe occurs in the famous 'mirror speech' of the deposition scene when Richard gazes narcissistically into the glass that not only gratifies his vanity but also symbolizes the painful acknowledgement of his folly. The shattering of the mirror is both a theatricalization of his grief and an emblem of his self-destruction, a way of coping with the unbridgeable divide between the divinity that hedges kings and the 'nothing' to which his flawed reign as a mortal has now reduced him. As nearly every editor observes, the rhetoric here echoes the equally memorable address to Helen of Troy in *Doctor Faustus* ('Was this the face that launch'd a thousand ships / And burnt the topless towers of Ilium?' [xviii.99–100]):

> Was this face the face
> That every day under his household roof
> Did keep ten thousand men? Was this the face
> That, like the sun, did make beholders wink?
> Is this the face which fac'd so many follies,
> And was at last out-fac'd by Bolingbroke?
> A brittle glory shineth in this face—
> As brittle as the glory is the face,
> [*Dashes the looking-glass against the ground.*]
> For there it is, crack'd in an hundred shivers.
>
> (*R2*, IV.i.282–290)

For Elizabethans who could recall the context of Marlowe's great speech, this echo would be rich in dramatic irony, for of course

Helen was not only the supreme icon of beauty and sensual desire but also the source of Troy's ruin and therefore a tragic emblem of civilization destroyed.[77] Also, in Marlowe's play, the image of Helen that Faustus confronts is probably a succuba; hence she becomes an agent of damnation whom he himself has asked Mephistophilis to summon and in whose embrace he desires to obliterate his pain. Faustus, like Richard, has courted his own destruction. Marlowe's passage, then, complicates and enriches Shakespeare's by enlarging its context, by extending and deepening its tragic implications. The tension between appearance and reality, already present in the mirror situation, takes on a fresh and more cosmic dimension.

Nor does Shakespeare seem entirely to have abandoned a consciousness of *Edward II* in this scene, however divergent from Edward's character Richard's behaviour at this point may appear to be. Possibly he recalled Lancaster's scornful comparison of Gaveston to 'the Greekish strumpet' who 'trained to arms / And bloody wars so many valiant knights' (*Edward II*, II.v.15–16), but there may also be a subtler connection. After the smashing of the glass, Bolingbroke comments on the essential unreality of Richard's posturing and Richard cleverly answers him:

> *Bolingbroke.* The shadow of your sorrow hath destroy'd
>   The shadow of your face.
> *King Richard.*   Say that again.
> The shadow of my sorrow? Ha! Let's see.
> 'Tis very true, my grief lies all within;
> And these external manners of laments
> Are merely shadows to the unseen grief
> That swells with silence in the tortur'd soul.
> There lies the substance. . . .

> (IV.i.293–300)

The verbal agility and quickness of mind that Richard's response displays here could scarcely contrast more starkly with the intellectually limited personality of his counterpart in Marlowe. Yet this dialogue, exploring, as it does, opposing attitudes to the significance of shadows in a context of self-pity and lost kingship, could well have grown out of Edward's most familiar and affecting lines:

> But what are kings when regiment is gone
> But perfect shadows in a sunshine day?

> (*Edward II*, V.i.26–27)

And, as we have seen, this is a speech that Marlowe in his turn could have derived from the image of the 'shadow' king (Edward IV) in *3*

Henry VI. If so, the pedigree of Richard II's lines may extend
through Marlowe back to an earlier Shakespearean play. But to
speculate on the blood lines of individual images in a drama as fluid
and absorptive as that of Marlowe and Shakespeare may be to
consider too curiously.[78] It seems safe to conclude at any rate that
even after the creator of Tamburlaine, Edward II, and Doctor
Faustus had ceased to make plays, his poetic shadow continued to
hover, sometimes creatively, sometimes disturbingly, over his rival
and successor.

4 THE TREATMENT OF SOURCES

Marlowe's primary source for *Edward II* (like Shakespeare's for
his histories) was Raphael Holinshed's *Chronicles of England, Scotland, and Ireland*. Whether the dramatist used the 1577 or 1587
edition of this book cannot be settled with assurance, but his eight
references to 'Killingworth' Castle, the consistent spelling of one of
Edward's prisons in the 1587 Holinshed (whereas the 1577 text
invariably prints 'Kenilworth'),[79] would seem to suggest that (again
like Shakespeare) he consulted the second edition. Additional support for this conclusion may lie in several passages added to the later
version, a text edited and considerably augmented seven years after
Holinshed's death (mainly by Abraham Fleming).[80] The first of the
additions to be considered comments on the extraordinary ardor of
the king's devotion to Gaveston—an ardor that Marlowe certainly
stresses, though without the chronicler's moralism:

> A wonderfull matter that the king should be so inchanted with the said
> earle, and so addict himselfe, or rather fix his hart vpon a man of such a
> corrupt humor . . . but the lesse maruell it is that the king bare him such a
> feruant affection, and set his hart vpon him, considering that

> ——vetus autorum sententia, mores
> Quod similes, simile & studium sunt fomes amoris,
> Sic vanus vanum, studiosus sic studiosum
> Diligit, & socios adeunt animalia coetus.

> [. . . it is a commonplace of philosophers that similar character and
> similar interests are the tinder of love. An empty person loves an empty
> one and a serious person a serious one, just as animals seek the company
> of their kind.][81]

Strong emotional attachment between the king and his Gascon friend
is already present in the first edition of the chronicle, but the added
passage, by giving the relationship a psychological *raison d'être*,

has the effect of making it more prominent and significant. Also Mortimer Senior's line about the king's infatuation, 'Is it not strange that he is thus bewitched?" (*Edward II*, I.ii.55), sounds as though it might have been partly suggested, despite the absence of verbal echoing, by the similar idea that appeared for the first time in the fuller text of the source: 'A wonderfull matter that the king should be so inchanted. . . .'[82]

A second passage, also interpolated by Fleming into the 1587 edition, underlines Gaveston's arrogance towards his aristocratic enemies; the minion was 'so scornefull and contemptuous a merchant, as in respect of himselfe (bicause he was in the princes fauour) esteemed the Nobles of the land as men of such inferioritie, as that in comparison of him they deserued no little iot or mite of honour' (p. 321). This too agrees with Marlowe's emphasis in the play, which in several ways dramatizes Gaveston's contempt for the established peers and, contrary to the earlier text of the chronicle, makes a point of his 'base and obscure' (I.i.100) or 'peasant' (I.ii.30, I.iv.7, 14, 218) origins, he being 'hardly . . . a gentleman by birth' (I.iv.29), 'a night-grown mushroom' (I.iv.284), 'basely born' (I. iv.402), a 'slave' (II.v.19), and a 'base groom' (II.v.70). Fleming's word 'merchant' seems to carry overtones of a commoner's—even a parvenu's—bloodline in addition to its suggestion of Gaveston's vulgar opportunism and profit motive.

In a third addition Fleming expands Holinshed's 1577 report that Edward dealt leniently with the rebellious Earl of Lancaster in 1321 by giving him a chance to return to obedience and live in friendship: 'Wherein though he did [no] more than stood with the dignitie of his roiall title, in somuch as he had the earles life at his commandement, yet for that he tollerated such insolencie of behauiour, as was vnseemelie to be shewed against the person of his prince, the kings clemencie and patience is highlie therein to be commended; though his forbearing and seeking means of quietnesse did neuer a whit amend the malignant mind of the earle . . .' (p. 328). Marlowe might well have had this passage in mind when he made Edward in the abdication scene protest, 'Yet how have I transgressed / Unless it be with too much clemency?' (v.i.122–123).[83] Obviously the use here of the chronicle's word 'clemencie,' common though it is, strengthens this likelihood.

A fourth interpolation by Fleming moralizes Queen Isabella's disloyalty to her husband in the context of her attempt to mislead him while she tarried at the court of France:

A lamentable case, that such diuision should be betweene a king and his queene, being lawfullie married, and hauing issue of their bodies, which ought to haue made that their copulation [was] more comfortable: but (alas) what will not a woman be drawne and allured vnto, if by euill counsell she be once assaulted? And what will she leaue vndoone, though neuer so inconuenient to those that should be most deere vnto hir, so hir owne fansie and will be satisfied? And how hardlie is she reuoked from proceeding in an euill action, if she haue once taken a taste of the same? (p. 336)

Marlowe, who almost from the start of his tragedy hints at Isabella's wilful and devious tendencies and, at the end, confirms her implacability (Edward says that her 'eyes, being turned to steel, / Will sooner sparkle fire than shed a tear' [v.i.104–105]), may possibly have been stimulated by these remarks. Fleming's pious condemnation comes closer than any other passage in Holinshed to implying sexual jealousy as a factor in her make-up, a jealousy that lies at the heart of Marlowe's conception. Moreover the playwright points up the 'euill counsell' (chiefly Mortimer's) that lies behind the behaviour of 'the subtle queen' (III.ii.88)—especially after her return to England, as for instance in Kent's statement that 'Mortimer / And Isabel do kiss while they conspire; / And yet she bears a face of love [to her husband], forsooth' (IV.vi.12–14), and in Mortimer's advice to his female partner, 'Be ruled by me, and we will rule the realm' (v.ii.5). Later in the chronicle Fleming also implicates the queen directly in the plans for Edward's murder: 'she with the rest of her confederats had (no doubt) laid the plot of their deuise for [the king's] dispatch, though by painted words she pretended a kind of remorse to him in this his distresse, & would seeme to be faultless in the sight of the world . . .' (p. 341). The 1577 text of Holinshed, which omits these words, portrays Isabella as somewhat more passive. In Marlowe, the queen prompts her fellow conspirator to do away with her husband ('But Mortimer, as long as he survives, / What safety rests for us, or for my son?'), and the dialogue that immediately follows (especially since it seems to echo Fleming's word 'dispatch') looks as though it also might be indebted to the same interpolation:

> *Mortimer Junior.* Speak, shall he presently be dispatched and die?
> *Isabella.* I would he were, so it were not by my means.

> (v.ii.44–45)

Cumulatively, then, the evidence points to the second edition of Holinshed as Marlowe's source. But such an inference, based for the most part on the subjectivities of characterization rather than on verifiable fact, must remain speculative. The truth is that none of the features of the 1587 Holinshed is distinctive enough, especially considering the other chronicles that Marlowe read, to establish it rather than the 1577 text as indubitably the version that lay open before him as he wrote.

Holinshed's crowded account of Edward II's twenty-year reign (1307–27) taken together with the relevant parts of the reigns that preceded and followed—Edward I's with its description of the youthful irresponsibility of Gaveston and his royal playmate as well as its mention of the betrothal of the Prince of Wales to the daughter of the French king, Edward III's with its record of the aftermath of his father's deposition and murder—makes up a clotted and oppressively dispiriting chain of personal, political, and military catastrophes that would seem to offer but meagre attraction to a playwright. That Marlowe was able to select, compress, rearrange, simplify, and shape these inchoate materials so powerfully, freely inventing when it suited him, tells us much about his skill as a dramatist as well as providing clues to his bleak concept of history and to his tragic view of human suffering and cruelty.

Modern historians tend to divide the reign of Edward II into three phases.[84] The first (1307–11) was dominated by the king's dispute with his barons over the unprecedented influence and privilege of Gaveston and characterized by demands occasioned thereby for administrative, judicial, and financial reforms—essentially for the greater sharing of rule with an oligarchically minded nobility. The second phase (1311–22), a logical outgrowth of the first, began with the proclamation of the Ordinances, a formal set of Parliamentary restrictions upon the royal prerogative, followed rapidly by the capture and execution of the favourite at the hands of the king's powerful enemies. The death of Gaveston and the continuing struggle between Edward and the Lords Ordainers set the pattern of politics for the next decade, a pattern for which civil war is hardly too extreme a term. Thomas, Earl of Lancaster, a kinsman of Edward who commanded his own private army and who held title to four other earldoms besides the one by which he was known, became the major focus of opposition to the king; and his defeat in 1322 at the Battle of Boroughbridge, followed by his execution for treason (together with that of many supporters) and by the repeal of the Ordinances, left the sovereign and his party, to which the elder and the younger Despenser had already made themselves useful, in a position of temporary control. The final phase (1322–27) was defined by the burgeoning ambitions of the Despensers, who virtually directed national policy after the fall of Lancaster. Their greed and high-handedness generated widespread resistance, which finally crystallized in an alliance between the disaffected queen and Sir Roger Mortimer, a Marcher Lord and the master of Wigmore, who appears to have become her paramour in France. She had been sent, followed by her son (the future Edward III), on a diplomatic mission to her brother, Charles IV (the issue concerned England's hereditary suzerainship of Ponthieu and Aquitaine), and was refusing to return home until her husband should curb the power of the Despensers; Mortimer, having daringly escaped from the Tower of London, where he had been imprisoned even before Boroughbridge for traitorous opposition to the king (and to the territorial acquisitiveness of the Despensers in Wales), was already in enforced exile across the channel. It was the queen's invasion of England in 1326, supported by Mortimer and soldiers supplied by the Count of Hainault in Flanders, that brought the Despensers to their death, drove Edward II from his throne, and finally established Mortimer and the queen as rulers of England (officially she was regent) under the titular authority of the new boy king. But only in 1330—three years into the reign of Edward III—did the backlash of retribution against the invaders take effect—in the arraignment and execution of Mortimer for Edward II's murder (among other crimes) and in the sequestration of Queen Isabella for life (with, however, a comfortable annual allowance).

This outline, which contains the essential action of Marlowe's tragedy, can of course be disinterred from Holinshed's depressing year-by-year sequence of details—from his welter of names, places, natural calamities, foreign and domestic battles, executions, diplomatic affairs, contents of letters and legal documents, and shifting alliances; indeed the concept of Edward's reign as dramaturgically viable may already be implicit in the theatrical metaphors that inform a couple of the Latin quotations (added by Fleming to embellish the 1587 text)[85] and in Holinshed's summary reference to 'the pitifull tragedie of this kings time' (p. 342). But to read the chronicle with a view to its stage possibilities is to encounter many trees rather than a forest. The emotional power and unity of effect that *Edward II* conveys to modern readers and playgoers must be explained in terms of the imaginative process by which Marlowe transformed the cluttered narrative of Holinshed into an eloquent

drama of character and ideas—a tragedy built upon the politics of
weakness, of naked aggression, of wilful selfishness, of savagery, of
miscalculation, of sexual rejection and magnetism, and of civil chaos,
which nevertheless preserves a firm and intelligible structure.

The most obvious aspect of Marlowe's procedure is the quantity
of matter excluded from the play. As Holinshed makes obvious,
Edward II from the moment of his accession presided over a nation
in more or less perpetual turmoil with Scotland, Ireland, and France
as well as with shifting coalitions among its own feudal nobility. The
young king, who as Prince of Wales had already participated with
his father in campaigns against the Scots, continued to fight battles
in the north during much of his reign. Most were disastrous for both
his country and his popularity, not only because of the ruinous
devastation but also because the foreign conflict became dangerously
entangled with internal disputes between the king and his rebel
barons. By the start of Edward III's reign English hegemony over
the Scots had dwindled to the point where Mortimer was forced
to conclude a humiliating peace granting that nation virtual independence. At one point in Marlowe's drama Edward praises the
senior Mortimer for his 'great achievements in our foreign war,'
appointing him (in a marked departure from the chronicle) 'general
of the levied troops / That now are ready to assail the Scots' (I.iv.
359–362); but almost nothing of the complicated military struggle
gets into the play. Only two of the famous battles, Bannockburn and
Boroughbridge, are included—the first merely through allusions to
the effeminate finery of the English soldiers and a 'jig' mocking their
defeat (II.ii.181–194), the second dramatized as a nameless encounter (actually an amalgamation of the two separate engagements
of Burton-on-Trent and Boroughbridge) which establishes Edward
II ironically as a temporary victor over his own disloyal nobles
(III.ii).

Significantly, Marlowe associates both battles closely with Gaveston,
who had already been beheaded before either contest was fought:
Bannockburn (1314) becomes a disaster of the favourite's causing
(the civilian victims 'curs[e] the name of . . . Gaveston' [II.ii.180],
who in the play is unhistorically still alive); and Boroughbridge
(1322) is treated not only as a failed attempt by Lancaster and his
adherents to rid Edward of the Spencers but also as vengeance on
the king's part 'for the murder of [his] dearest friend . . . Good
Pierce of Gaveston' (III.ii.42–44). On this latter point the dramatist
follows his source, which sums up the victory at Boroughbridge

in these words: 'Thus the king seemed to be reuenged of the displeasure doone to him by the earle of Lancaster, for the beheading
of . . . Cornewall, whom he so deerelie loued, and bicause . . .
Lancaster was the cheefe occasioner of his death, the king neuer
loued him entirelie after' (p. 331). Marlowe gives us a sense of
Scottish warfare on the margins of the action by inventing the
episode of the elder Mortimer's being 'taken prisoner by the Scots'
(II.ii.114), by alluding to one of the Scottish invasions that penetrated as far south as York (II.ii.165), and by having Lancaster
refer to the burnt houses and slaughtered families of the 'northern
borderers' (II.ii.178–179). But Robert Bruce (the Scottish leader)
and Edward Bruce (his equally active brother who fought the English
in Ireland and Wales) go entirely unmentioned. So too do many
other incidents connected with the northern war such as the English
attempt to rescue Stirling, the king's narrow escape to York, the
eventual loss of Berwick, Lancaster's refusal to defend Durham
when the foreigners attacked it, the Pope's excommunication of
Scotland, the treason of the Earl of Carlisle, and the remarkable
'white battle,' so called because it was fought against the Scots by
clerics organized under the Archbishop of York.

Marlowe's tragedy scants Edward II's affairs in Ireland even more
drastically than those in Scotland. We hear nothing, for instance, of
the Scottish assault upon that nation or of Sir John Birmingham's
momentous achievement there—the slaying of Edward Bruce.
Instead the dramatist is content merely to invent the unhistorical
reference to the 'wild O'Neil,' who supposedly occupies 'the English
pale' with 'swarms of Irish kerns' (II.ii.163–164), and to mention
Ireland as the venue of Gaveston's exile and as the intended refuge of
King Edward in flight from the forces of Mortimer and the queen.

The playwright is equally vague about the Anglo-French difficulties that beset his protagonist. He omits all reference to Edward's
betrothal and marriage, probably because Philip the Fair's daughter
was a girl of only sixteen when she became Queen of England in
1308 and, owing to the compression of historical time, must appear
onstage with Prince Edward, her teenage son, as early as III.i. Our
single insight into the king's first relationship with his wife comes,
pathetically enough, in the murder scene, where the tatterdemalion
victim in a totally fictional detail recalls his courtship: 'Tell Isabel,
the queen, I looked not thus / When for her sake I ran at tilt in
France / And there unhorsed the Duke of Cleremont' (V.v.67–69).
The play almost wholly ignores England's tenuous authority over its

continental territories, particularly Gascony and Guienne. According to Holinshed, Edward's failure to do homage in person offended Charles IV, and armed hostilities between the two kings broke out when the English seneschal in Guienne attacked a frontier town in the Agenais that had been newly fortified by the French—the crisis that in history originally prompted Isabella's embassy to Paris. The King of France did at one point nullify Edward's title to his French possessions, and Guienne, ineptly defended by Edmund, Earl of Kent, fell temporarily to superior forces under Charles de Valois, uncle to the French monarch, who forced the English to sue for peace; the French also seized English castles in Aquitaine. But Marlowe's sole appropriation of this material is an invented report (originating from an invented character, Levune) that the King of France 'Hath seizèd Normandy into his hands' because Edward has been 'slack in homage' (III.i.63–64).[86] Normandy, of course, was not at issue during the twenty years of Edward II's rule.

The English king's several visits to France earlier in his reign for the purpose of doing homage and for the coronation of Philip V (one of the three brothers of Isabella to assume the French crown) are omitted for the same reason as the territorial conflicts—because they would only complicate the action unprofitably and detract from the desired emphasis on intense personal relationships. Even the politics of Isabella's military opposition to her husband and of her quest for foreign allies is greatly simplified in the play, for Marlowe combines the historically separate journeys of the queen and her son to the French court, totally omitting the role of Walter Stapleton, Bishop of Exeter, who escorted the young prince and returned to England to warn of the queen's actions when he discovered them to be treasonous. Also (with even greater licence) he unites the unrelated episodes of Mortimer's escape from the Tower and Kent's departure for France as an emissary of King Edward.

Holinshed gives no inkling of Kent's disloyalty to his half brother until Edmund suddenly appears without explanation as one of the party of invaders with Isabella, Mortimer, and Sir John of Hainault. Marlowe also reverses the order of Mortimer's escape (1323) and Isabella's journey to Paris (1325) so that Kent, unhistorically banished and outraged by the wholesale executions of the nobles after Boroughbridge, can give as his motive for the collaborative voyage with Mortimer a desire to 'cheer the wrongèd queen, / And certify what Edward's looseness is' (IV.i.6–7). In addition, Marlowe has Isabella deciding on her own initiative to visit France so that she may 'complain' to her brother 'How Gaveston hath robbed [her] of [Edward's] love' (II.iv.66–67), although later, to be sure, her husband does send her to 'parley with the King of France' (III.i.71); in Holinshed, initially at least, she goes to Paris only as an agent of her husband—'to confirme' a 'treatie of peace' (p. 336)—and complains of her ill treatment in England only after she has been abroad for some time. Again, obviously, Marlowe's colouring of Isabella's motive personalizes her mission and consequently has the effect of augmenting the aggressive and independent side of her character. Also omitted from the tragedy is the escape of Sir Robert Walkfare from Corfe Castle; Holinshed relates how this 'craftie and subtill' traitor, having murdered the constable of his prison, 'got ouer to the queene into France' (p. 337), thus lending impetus to a daily increasing stream of English defectors to her cause, and even managed to seduce Humphrey de Bohun, Earl of Hereford (an active nobleman whom Marlowe entirely ignores), to the rebel party.

Regarding the domestic affairs of Edward's reign as related by Holinshed, Marlowe's omissions and simplifications are perhaps even more radical than those involving foreign policy. Except for the Prince of Wales and Kent, all the king's children and siblings are excised from the narrative, as is (surprisingly) the marriage of the younger Spencer to the sister of Gaveston's widow. In Holinshed, this alliance with the family of the Earl of Gloucester helps reinforce the parallel between the earlier and the later favourites, a parallel important to Marlowe's design. The famous Ordinances are also notable for their absence in the play, but since Holinshed barely mentions these by name, their omission is scarcely to be wondered at. Marlowe follows his chief authority in making the baronial opposition to the king rest almost wholly upon his refusal to shed his corrupt and corrupting advisers. Apart from Edward's quarrel with his nobles, the two most dramatic incidents of the reign, both highlighted by Holinshed, were probably the suppression of the Knights Templar in 1308 and the claim of the impostor John Ponderham (or Poidras) to be the rightful king in 1318. Marlowe excludes both from the tragedy.

Edward II, following the lead of his more ruthless father-in-law in France, seized the lands and treasure of the religious order on a single day throughout the realm, although, unlike Philip IV, he stopped short of torturing confessions out of the Templars and burning them at the stake. Enrichment of his exchequer was obviously Edward's motive, but the pretext, according to Holinshed,

was that the Knights were suspected of heresy—'of hainous crimes
& great enormities by them practised, contrarie to the articles of the
christian faith' (p. 319). Despite the chronicler's discreet refusal to
be specific, it was widely understood that the charges against the
Templars included sodomy. Marlowe's conception of his title figure
involves the combination of administrative weakness with homosexual infatuation. Clearly, to have dramatized the episode of the
Templars, apart from further crowding an already crowded story,
would have made the king seem too aggressive early in his reign and
might, in addition, have risked the inappropriate impression of a
homophobic streak in Edward's personality.

Holinshed's quasi-humorous tale of Ponderham, who in certain
ways recalls Jack Cade, concerns the son of an tanner of Exeter who
claimed that as an infant he had been stolen from the royal cradle
and secretly replaced by a commoner who grew up to be Edward II.
Stubbornly wedded to his delusion, the impostor was speedily arrested and hanged for treason, finally confessing before his death
that he had been prompted by a diabolical spirit 'in likenesse of
a cat' (p. 324). Obviously this incident also would have comported
badly with Marlowe's image of a king who, by means of his own
passivity, neglect, and folly, had actually fostered treason and dyn-
astic upheaval in England rather than efficiently crushing it. Moreover,
social commentary (particularly from the perspective of the lower
citizenry) and dark comedy of the kind that Shakespeare exploited in
2 Henry VI were aspects of the earlier chronicle plays that Marlowe
chose pointedly to reject. In any case the folk-tale romanticism of the
Ponderham affair, however factual it may have been, would work
against the gritty realism that marks the handling of politics in
Marlowe's drama.

Patently it was necessary to streamline the events surrounding the
historically separate ascendancies of Gaveston and the Spencers, at
the same time making the king's later attachment to Hugh Junior a
kind of replication of, and substitute for, the earlier relationship to
Piers. Marlowe ties the two phases of Edward's emotional life more
closely together by imagining the younger Spencer and Baldock early
in the play as servants of the Gloucester household and dependent
for their advancement upon the 'liberal Earl of Cornwall' (II.i.10).
Moreover, as a result of Marlowe's compression, the Spencers
already enjoy high favour in the drama before Edward has been
apprised of Gaveston's death. Historically, of course, the Spencers
had little connection with either the Earl of Gloucester or Gaveston.

To be sure (as already mentioned) the younger Spencer was married to Eleanor de Clare, a sister of the Margaret de Clare to whom Gaveston is betrothed in the play, but the union occurred only after the latter's execution. And although Marlowe's Edward creates Spencer Junior 'Earl of Gloucester' (III.i.146), the dramatist seems to have been misled by Holinshed, who at first mentions only Spencer's aspiration to 'haue enioied the whole earledome of Glocester' (p. 327), and who later refers to the favourite incorrectly (p. 338) as though he had finally obtained the peerage by right of inheritance (see the note on III.i.146). The historical Spencer Junior was Earl neither of Wiltshire nor of Gloucester—the titles successively conferred upon him in the play—although he sometimes seems to have been designated unofficially by the latter style (as in Holinshed) because he got the better of his brothers-in-law, Sir Hugh Audley and Sir Roger Damory, who through marriage were fellow heirs with him of the Gloucester properties; Marlowe, of course, entirely passes over Audley, Damory, and the jockeying for wealth and status among the Gloucester in-laws. The elder Spencer remained loyal to the king throughout the period of Gaveston's prominence, but his son, Hugh Junior, had originally been one of the Lords Ordainers opposed to Edward's personal rule, and Holinshed notes that 'the king bare no good will at all to him at the first, though afterwards through the prudent policie, and diligent industrie of the man, he quicklie crept into his fauour, and that further than those that preferred him could haue wished' (p. 321). In the play Edward is introduced to both Spencers as strangers, whom he instantly and gratefully accepts as friends and supporters.

Marlowe collapses the successive banishments of Gaveston to Ireland and Flanders into a single event, and although the nobles threaten Edward for dependency upon the 'pernicious' Spencers (III.i.165) and demand that he remove them, their disinheritance, exile, and repeal from banishment, as recounted by Holinshed, are omitted altogether. So, too, are the barons' vengeful plundering and despoiling of the Spencer estates, which Holinshed describes in considerable detail. The effect, then, is to reduce the complicated and disparate careers of Edward's favourites over a period of many years to a unitary impression of parallel rises and falls within the briefest possible time span and to present both as experiences of intense personal fulfilment to the king followed by profound loss. Marlowe deliberately debases the Spencers in social rank as he debases Gaveston, the better to emphasize Edward's wilful disregard of duty to his class and his 'unnatural' (IV.i.8) violation of aristocratic tradition; both younger men are sneered at as 'upstarts' (I.iv.41, 422; III.i.165; III.ii.21). Obviously such changes provide the arrogant nobles with a better pretext for hating the minions. Historically, all three favourites came from gentry. Holinshed mentions Gaveston as 'an esquire of Gascoine' (p. 313)—that is, the scion of a knightly house; and the Spencers descended from minor nobility, as the chronicle plainly implies. Holinshed carefully avoids explicit mention of a sexual relationship between the king and either Gaveston or the younger Spencer, although he probably hints at such a concept by referring to the former as 'a lewd and wanton person' (p. 313) who led the king 'into most heinous vices,' 'voluptuous pleasure,' 'riotous excesse,' and 'filthie and dishonorable exercises' (p. 318), and to the Spencers as 'men of corrupt and most wicked liuing' (p. 321). By unambiguously eroticizing Holinshed's account of Edward's personal attachments and by widening the social gap between the king and his favourites, Marlowe forges an unmistakable link between the politics of class and of sexuality, indeed making the two elements conceptually and dramatically indivisible.[87]

Still other changes and omissions from Holinshed are worth remarking. Gilbert de Clare, ninth Earl of Gloucester (the son of Edward II's brother-in-law), was the most important casualty at Bannockburn, as the chronicle suggests; indeed it was the earl's untimely fate that occasioned the infighting, mentioned above, among the husbands (including Spencer Junior) of the three surviving sisters, nieces to the king. Not specifying a cause of death, Marlowe brings Gloucester's demise forward in time to the early period of Gaveston's prosperity (II.i.2), thereby giving Baldock and Spencer Junior a reason for transferring their hopes for promotion to a new and even more influential master, and also because it suits the playwright's focus on personal feelings to obfuscate and deemphasize military details. Warwick, whom Holinshed describes reverentially as 'a man of great counsell and skilfull prouidence' (p. 323), died in his bed, according to the chronicle, some six years before Boroughbridge; Marlowe, deliberately darkening the character, keeps the treacherous kidnapper of Gaveston alive so that he can be captured with Lancaster and suffer a traitor's death with the other rebels as part of Edward's vengeance for the murder of his friend.

The Mortimers, of whom we hear nothing in Holinshed until several years after Gaveston's beheading, are also introduced early by

Marlowe; indeed the dramatist makes the younger Mortimer share
with Lancaster the leadership of the rebel party, mainly of course to
endow him with a dramatic prominence at the beginning of the play
that will balance and make credible his dominant role at the end.
And much of the special malignancy to Edward that Holinshed
attributes to Lancaster is transferred by Marlowe to Mortimer
Junior. In Holinshed the Mortimers surrender without resistance to
Edward at Shrewsbury in an action earlier than the armed engagement at Boroughbridge, and the king in consequence spares their
lives by sending them to the Tower. In the play Mortimer (the
uncle), as noted already, is unhistorically held for ransom by the
Scots and so disappears permanently from the action—one of the
few loose threads in Marlowe's carefully wrought fabric, although
we quickly forget about him, overshadowed as he is by his more
important nephew. Marlowe, of course, includes the junior Mortimer
with Warwick, Lancaster, and Kent among the captives taken at
Boroughbridge, but sentences him to prison (somewhat incredibly
perhaps) rather than to the block, not only because he is following
his historical authority in respect of the lighter punishment but
because Mortimer must later escape to play the part of chief male
antagonist to Edward in the falling action. Although the dramatist
does not trouble to justify Edward's exceptional treatment of the
younger Mortimer in the context of his merciless slaughter of his
other enemies, the necessary sparing of life at this point may be
regarded as yet another (and ironically fatal) miscalculation on the
king's part—a further example of political ineptitude and even
perhaps a manifestation in a new key of Edward's characteristic self-
destructiveness.

Holinshed gives no hint of a sexual liaison between Mortimer and
the queen until very late in his account, not even mentioning the
two together until their political alliance in France the year before
Edward's murder; and the chronicler suggests the element of lust
only when he comes to describe Mortimer's fall in the following
reign: 'But whosoeuer was glad or sorie for the trouble of the said
earle [i.e., Mortimer Junior, recently created Earl of March], suerlie
the queene mother tooke it most heauilie aboue all other, as she that
loued him more (as the fame went) than stood well with hir honour.
For as some write, she was found to be with child by him' (p. 349).
Also the charges against Mortimer at his attainder, according to
Holinshed, contain the statement that he 'had beene more priuie
with queene Isabell the kings mother, than stood either with Gods

law, or the kings pleasure' (p. 349). In Marlowe's play the queen is
already intimate enough with 'gentle Mortimer' in her opening
speech (I.ii.47) to complain to him jealously of Edward's dotage
upon Gaveston; and by the fourth scene of the play, her rival for the
king's love is already insinuating that a parallel adultery exists:

> *Edward.* Fawn not on me, French strumpet; get thee gone.
> *Isabella.* On whom but on my husband should I fawn?
> *Gaveston.* On Mortimer; with whom, ungentle queen—
>   I say no more; judge you the rest, my lord.

>   (I.iv.145–148)

At this point, certainly, Isabella is innocent of Gaveston's accusation,
and in fact reacts with astonishing forbearance to her husband's
heartless provocations. Later in this scene, however, the queen
draws Mortimer aside for a private conference, choosing him specifically to be her intercessor to the other nobles: 'as thou lovest and
tend'rest me, / Be thou my advocate unto these peers' (I.iv.211–
212). And here apparently she sugggests to him that, by recalling
Gaveston from banishment, he can position the favourite more
effectively for assassination; she refers suggestively to 'reasons of
such weight / As thou wilt soon subscribe to his repeal' (I.iv.226–
227).[88] Marlowe may intend here (by dramatizing her unexpected
success in altering Mortimer's resolution) to hint already at the
beginnings of a sexual attraction. The queen of course continues to
protest devotion to the king, and even exclaims without obvious
hypocrisy, 'O how a kiss revives poor Isabel!' (I.iv.332), when
Edward later rewards her with an embrace for helping to get his
friend back. For his part, Edward persists in suspecting her of being
Mortimer's 'lover' (II.iv.14), apparently using groundless suspicion
as an excuse for loving Gaveston. But by the time Mortimer is ready
to depart for Scarborough in pursuit of the hated minion, Isabella
seems to have despaired of retaining her husband's love and can say
revealingly to the man who will become a replacement for Edward in
her emotional life, 'So well hast thou deserved, sweet Mortimer, / As
Isabel could live with thee for ever' (II.iv.59–60). By the middle of
Act II, then, and well before Gaveston's capture, Marlowe has
carefully laid the foundations of the queen's future relationship with
her paramour—a relationship that grows increasingly vicious in
its effects and that gradually alienates sympathy. Isabella enters
Holinshed's narrative in a politically significant way only in 1325,
when she is sent to France as ambassadress of her husband.

Marlowe magnifies the outrageous rudeness of the king and Gaveston to the Bishop of Coventry not only by adding public humiliation and physical assault to the episode (Holinshed speaks only of the prelate's lands and wealth being confiscated), but also by withholding from the audience the particular circumstances that originally motivated the churchman's hostility to the favourite. The chronicle explains that in 1305 Edward I had 'put his sonne prince Edward in prison, bicause that he had riotouslie broken the parke of Walter Langton [i.e., Coventry]' and that 'bicause the prince had doone this deed by the procurement of . . . Gauaston . . . , the king banished him the realme, least the prince, who delighted much in his companie, might by his euill and wanton counsell fall to euill and naughtie rule' (p. 313). Marlowe's omission of this background, even though the bishop is accused of being 'the only cause of [Gaveston's first] exile' (1.i.178), augments our impression of Edward's arbitrary and unkingly rule as well as our sense of the brutishness that informs the reign generally. In addition, Marlowe's invented detail of stripping the bishop of his vestments and of 'christen[ing] him anew' in 'channel' or ditch water (1.i.187) serves effectively as an ironic prolepsis of Edward's own humiliation near the end of the drama when Matrevis and Gurney violate the king's person by shaving him in 'channel water' (v.iii.27).

The playwright also entirely passes over events in connection with the defection of Lord Badlesmere (spelled Badelismere in Holinshed) to the enemy barons and the fall of his castle in Kent to a royalist military expedition. Holinshed relates how the queen, returning from a religious pilgrimage to Canterbury, was refused the hospitality of Leeds Castle near Maidstone by Lady Badlesmere in the absence of her rebel husband, and how Edward quickly avenged this insult to royalty by besieging the fortress in person, supported by a sizeable army and a contingent of loyal nobles including Kent, Pembroke, and Arundel. When the castle surrendered, Lady Badlesmere was sent to the Tower and a dozen or so of her garrison were summarily hanged; Lord Badlesmere, who was away from home at the time of these events, was executed later with other traitors in the aftermath of Boroughbridge. Since in this instance Edward had crushed the opposition out of loyalty to Isabella, Marlowe could hardly dramatize the episode without wrecking his carefully constructed image of estrangement between the king and his spouse. Also the circumstances of the royal couple's presence in Kent—a devotional journey to the shrine of St Thomas à Becket—would jar with the self-absorbed and amorous psychology of both characters as Marlowe conceives them. By the same token Marlowe omits all mention of the sexual infidelities of Lancaster, which would tend to weaken the contrast between Edward's adulterous liaison with Gaveston and his hardboiled cousin's disapproval of the king's 'wanton humour' (I.iv.199). Holinshed notes that Lancaster (like Edward) 'fauoured not his wife, but liued in spouse-breach, defiling a great number of damosels and gentlewomen' (p. 331). According to the chronicle, both Edward and Lancaster after their deaths attracted the religious devotion of many, who, superstitiously venerating their remains, conferred a kind of unofficial canonization upon them for supposed miracles. Marlowe, whose ethos in the tragedy is notably secular and sceptical, obviously had no use for such details, which would have introduced a strain of religiosity—even of sentimentality—entirely alien to his purposes.

Again, consistent with his intensification of the king's personal sufferings, Marlowe greatly simplifies Holinshed's account of the civil chaos consequent upon the queen's invasion. The rioting in the streets of London, which involved the liberation of prisoners from the Tower, is entirely suppressed with, of course, the lynching of John Marshall (a follower of the younger Spencer) and of Bishop Stapleton, who was seized at the door of St Paul's, decapitated in Cheapside with two of his servants, and his head 'set on a pole for a spectacle' (p. 338). Marlowe's double reference to letting rebel heads 'preach upon poles' (I.i.117; III.i.20) may nevertheless owe something to this description, however indirectly.

Holinshed's detailed account of the several riots at the monastic town of Bury St Edmunds after the accession of Edward III also receives no mention in the play for the obvious reason that Marlowe eliminates the time gap in which the disturbances occurred—that is, the hiatus in history between Edward II's murder and the execution of Mortimer, who in Marlowe's version of the story bears chief responsibility for the regicide. Marlowe may, however, have noticed an interesting detail in Holinshed's report of anarchic assaults upon the abbey, for the narrator mentions at one point that the abbot was forcibly abducted from his manor, shaved by his captors to prevent his being recognized, 'secretlie conueied . . . to London' where he was removed 'from street to street vnknowne,' and ultimately transported to the Duchy of Brabant in the Low Countries, where 'they kept him for a time in much penurie, thraldome and miserie' (p. 346). This account is so clearly parallel in certain ways to the treatment of the king in Marlowe's tragedy that it is tempting to regard it as a secondary source or, more properly, an influence on the dramatization of Edward's captivity. Holinshed says nothing about the monarch's being shaved; Stowe (as will be documented below) is the dramatist's principal authority for this episode. But the shaving and stealthy moving about of the abbot could well have reinforced the concept in Marlowe's mind.

Also in conformity with the radical compression of time at the end of the play, Marlowe sends Kent to his death while Edward II, whom the repentant earl has futilely tried to rescue, still lives. In Holinshed Kent is beheaded several years after the king's murder, having been found guilty of plotting 'to restore [his brother] to the crowne' because he believed a rumour of 'one Thomas Dunhed, a frier,' who 'affirmed for certeine' that Edward had secretly survived his ill treatment at Berkeley Castle (p. 348). The boy king's attempt to save his uncle from execution (not in Holinshed) is Marlowe's own idea, buttressed probably, as noted earlier, by the similar attitude of young Edward V towards his doomed uncles in Shakespeare's *Richard III*.

For good practical and dramatic reasons Marlowe simplifies Holinshed's account of Edward's capture, abdication, and murder, as well as of the destruction of his adherents. Although Arundel was executed by the queen's forces at the same time as Spencer Junior, Marlowe suppresses this detail, probably because the death of so uncertain a supporter of the king, by broadening the political effects of Edward's defeat, would blunt our sense of his personal sorrow at the loss of Spencer and Baldock. (Arundel, a hater of Gaveston, had formerly been of the rebel party but had changed sides on the occasion of his son's marrying a daughter of the Spencer family.) Baldock was spared execution after capture because of his status as a cleric and, according to Holinshed, died miserably in Newgate Prison. Marlowe sends him to the scaffold with the younger Spencer so as to intensify the grief of both Edward and the favourites themselves at their final parting, and also to magnify the force of vengeance meted out by Mortimer and the queen. Simon de Reading, the marshal of Edward II's household, who was captured at the Abbey of Neath with Baldock, Spencer Junior, and the king, is omitted altogether from the play for the same reason that Arundel's fate is excluded. Reading, according to the chronicle, 'had vsed the queene very vncourteouslie, giuing hir manie reprochfull words, which now were remembered' at his fall (p. 340); this report sounds a note that Marlowe would obviously wish to avoid in a scene of which pathos rather than spite is the desired effect.

In Holinshed the most detestable enemy of King Edward is Adam Orleton, Bishop of Hereford, who not only composes the riddling, unpunctuated letter directing the king's murderers, but who, conniving with the queen, exacerbates the prisoner's misery and then attempts to conceal his villainy by having Gurney and Matrevis banished. Marlowe eliminates Orleton entirely by making Mortimer responsible for sending the equivocal message and by having him refer mysteriously to an unnamed 'friend' (v.iv.6) as the actual author. The play suggests, in short, that Mortimer himself has secretly commissioned the letter. And in a further and revelatory departure from the source the dramatist also excludes Isabella from the specifics of the murder plot, although he leaves little doubt as to her general complicity. In the 1587 version of the chronicle, as pointed out above, she becomes an active participant. Holinshed gives no indication that Mortimer has been the cause of Edward's death until he is charged with this and other enormities some years after the fact. Moreover, although Holinshed is perfectly clear about the treason itself, his listing of the crimes for which Mortimer was executed fails to square precisely with the man's earlier actions as they have been presented in the chronicle. A notable feature of Marlowe's characterization in *Edward II* is his purposeful beclouding of motive and his delight in complicating responses by causing figures onstage to behave with puzzling inconsistency. In the case of Mortimer, at least, and possibly of Kent as well, the dramatist may have picked up hints for this technique from Holinshed, who in compiling material from various sources, often fails to reconcile contradictory redactions and traditions. In the early acts of the play Mortimer comes off as typical of the nobles who openly resist Edward and who can plausibly claim an interest in the public welfare; by Act V he has undergone a kind of demonization, Marlowe by then having endowed him with the ruthless ingenuity of the stage Machiavel and having invented the diabolical Lightborn as a grotesque extension of his cruelty and menace.

The dramatist also intensifies Mortimer's villainy by increasing the horror and physical misery of Edward's fate. Holinshed says that Edward was 'lodged . . . in a chamber ouer a foule filthie dungeon, full of dead carrion' with the object of poisoning him by means of 'the abhominable stinch' (p. 341). Marlowe, adding 'foul excrements' (v.iii.26) to the stench, plus thirst and starvation, places the king *in* the dungeon rather than above it, 'in a vault up to the knees in water, / To which the channels of the castle run' (v.v.2–3), 'the sink / Wherein the filth of all the castle falls' (v.v.55–56). And he exacerbates the torture still further by imposing sleeplessness, perpetual fear, numbness from cold, and the nerve-shattering noise of an incessant drum. Obviously the play degrades human—let alone royal—dignity well beyond the warrant of history.

The tragedian also alters the business of Edward's formal deposition—not only by simplifying the deputation to Killingworth but also by changing Edward's response. Holinshed reports that two separate groups approached the imprisoned king—first the bishops of Winchester and Lincoln with the Earl of Leicester to persuade him to yield the crown, then a larger group of nobles, clergy, and citizens (twenty-four in all) to witness his actual renunciation. And he notes that although the king at first 'was brought into a maruelous agonie' and 'inwardlie grieued,' he finally submitted, acknowledging 'that he was fallen into this miserie through his owne offenses, and therefore he was contented patientlie to suffer it,' also giving the lords 'most heartie thanks, that they had so forgotten their receiued iniuries' as to allow his son to succeed him (pp. 340–341). Marlowe combines the separate delegations, reducing them to two persons— the Bishop of Winchester and Sir William Trussel, the speaker of Parliament (who in fact remained in London). He also removes from Edward nearly all traces of moral self-recognition and dignity of bearing. Although the king commends himself to his son, 'bid[d-ing] him rule / Better than I' (v.i.121–122), the playwright allows Edward in the same breath to ask rhetorically, 'Yet how have I transgressed / Unless it be with too much clemency?' (v.i.122– 123),[89] and also to speak blindly of his 'guiltless life' (v.i.73) and 'innocent hands' (v.i.98). Marlowe chooses rather to emphasize the 'maruelous agonie' of which Holinshed speaks by laying stress on the king's frustrated will, on his 'outrageous passions . . . of rancour and disdain' (v.i.19–20), and on the impotent rage that reaches its climax in the 'poor revenge' (v.i.141) of his tearing Mortimer's signature on the directive relieving Leicester of his post as guardian. The more violent passions—self-pity, unreasoning anger, and personal hurt—rather than moral growth or sacramental desecration become the focus of Marlowe's handling of the deposition, so that the effect is mainly to emphasize power dominating weakness and the turbulent emotions thereby generated. The broader issues of ethical and civil order, let alone the theological foundations of monarchy as an institution, go deliberately unprobed so as to narrow the field of vision and to intensify the experience of individual human pain.

Marlowe intentionally minimizes the baleful economic aspects of Edward's reign as Holinshed reports them—again because these would tend to deflect attention from the semi-private and emotional relationships in which he is chiefly interested. The king's unpopular tax policies, which worked considerable hardship, rate but a single allusion—in Edward's willingness to let the younger Mortimer use 'the broad seal / To gather' funds for the ransom of his uncle (II.ii.146–147), an abuse that Lancaster in the following line lays to the wicked counsel of Gaveston. The minion in his opening soliloquy refers dismissively to 'the multitude' as 'sparks / Raked up in embers of their poverty' (I.i.20–21), but our only exposure to the common people in Marlowe's play occurs with the three nameless 'Poor Men' (I.i.24.1) who approach Gaveston for employment in the opening scene and with the emblematic Mower, an obvious personification of death, who betrays the king to his captors at the abbey in Neath. Lightborn, as his name suggests, is more devil than man and, in any case, is included for his shocking monstrosity, not his representativeness. These figures are symbolic, even quasi-allegorical, and offer no vision of life from the perspective of the general populace.

In the acrimonious episode in which the nobles rebuke the king to his face, we get a momentary glimpse of popular unrest—of the 'murmuring commons' and those who resent the 'prodigal gifts' to Gaveston that have 'drawn [Edward's] treasure dry' (II.ii.157–159). We also learn fleetingly of discontented subjects in France, 'lame and poor' as a result of war, who 'lie groaning at the gates' of cities (II.ii.162), and of 'Libels . . . cast against [the king] in the street' (II.ii.176). Edward is at first afraid to commit the insubordinate younger Mortimer to the Tower because 'the people love him well' (II.ii.234). But Marlowe ignores most of the costly ruination that the civil war and private feuds occasioned, as well as the murrains, floods, windstorms, and other disasters that devastated crops and livestock, raising the prices of commodities alarmingly and causing famines and widespread lawlessness. Wishing to preserve a certain sympathy for both Gaveston and the Spencers as well as for the king, Marlowe also plays down the shameless profiteering and exploitation that often characterize their behaviour in Holinshed. He carefully omits, for instance, the detail of Gaveston's expropriation from the royal jewel-house of a valuable table with trestles of gold, thought to have belonged originally to King Arthur, which that lord arranged to convey to his estates in Gascony. We hear almost nothing of the grasping, self-aggrandizing land manoeuvres of the Spencers or, apart from the treatment of Coventry, of Edward's own seizure of property—of his confiscating the queen's estates, for instance (and also Prince Edward's), when the lady refused to obey her husband by returning promptly from France. It is clear from Holinshed's account that Edward's reckless and irresponsible rule amounted, in several respects at least, to tyranny, for the many mischiefs of which he was the cause 'happened not onlie to him, but to the whole state of the realme' (p. 342). Although Lancaster complains early in the play that Edward and his minion 'tyrannize upon the Church' (I.ii.3), Marlowe allows the word 'tyrant' to be applied directly only once to his protagonist (by the defiant Warwick just before his execution [III.ii.57]), whereas the king himself uses it twice—and with undeniable justice—to describe the cruelty of Mortimer (IV.vii.92; v.iii.36).[90] The stress on Mortimer's tyranny is but one symptom of the altered balance of sympathies that Marlowe imposes upon his material, thereby altering also the nature of our moral response to the characters and events dramatized.

One further point about Marlowe's purposeful omissions may be mentioned—namely his suppression of cosmological or planetary omens of the kind to which Shakespeare was occasionally attracted. Holinshed notes the appearance of 'a blasing starre or comet' in 1315, which he interprets as a prophecy of the 'dearth and death' soon to follow (p. 323). After Edward's short-lived victory at Boroughbridge in 1322, the chronicle records that 'the sunne appeared to mans sight in colour like to bloud, and so continued six houres' (p. 332), an apparent warning of further misfortunes in prospect (although the writer omits to specify examples). Again in 1330, shortly before Mortimer's fall, Holinshed reports an eclipse of the sun accompanied by bad weather—excessive rain and wind that ruined the harvest that year. Characteristically, Holinshed, like Shakespeare, views disturbances in nature as prophetic of disaster. This is not Marlowe's way in *Edward II*, a play in which the dramatist confines his sphere of action—even symbolic action—to human agency, resisting implications of supernatural or otherwordly causation. As Clifford Leech has observed, 'There are few references to cosmic powers' in the play,[91] and when Spencer Junior resigns himself to execution by stoically acknowledging 'the angry heavens' as the force that brings him down, Edward disagrees: 'The gentle

heavens have not to do in this' (IV.vii.74–76). Marlowe seems stead-
fastly to reject the conventional moralizing of the chronicle, especially of Fleming, as well as the metaphysical order that Holinshed
wished to discern in the events he was narrating.

Marlowe was not content to rely upon a single source. We know
that, in addition to Holinshed, he read Robert Fabyan's *Chronicle . . .
continued . . . to thende of Queene Mary* (1559), because the Scottish
'jig' (II.ii.187–194), recited by Lancaster to mock Edward II's defeat
at Bannockburn, appears here rather than in the later account. Also
Fabyan, unlike Holinshed and in accordance with Marlowe, lays
prime responsibility for Edward's murder on Mortimer, by whose
'meanes' 'the said Edward . . . was miserably slayne' (p. 194). Little
else in Fabyan, however, captured the dramatist's imagination.
Even more than Holinshed, Fabyan emphasizes Edward's 'greate
remors of conscience' (p. 174) for his misrule in respect of the
Spencers, adding that during his imprisonment the king 'tooke
greate repentaunce of hys former life, and made a lamentable com-
plainte, for that he had so greuously offended God . . .' (p. 185). As
we have seen, Marlowe rejects as too moralistic and sentimental the
concept of a seriously repentant Edward II, nor does he mention the
king's literary compositions, supposedly inspired by intense self-
examination, to which Fabyan alludes. A further connection between Marlowe's play and Fabyan's chronicle is, however, just possible: this historian includes 'iustes' (i.e., knightly tournaments)
among the rich entertainments that were arranged for the young
Edward III, when, shortly after his accession, he did homage to the
King of France for the Duchy of Guienne (p. 197). Holinshed omits
these festivities, but their appearance in Fabyan could well have
suggested to Marlowe the effective detail of Edward's pathetic reminiscence in the dungeon about his having 'unhorsed the Duke of
Cleremont' at the 'tilt in France' (V.v.69–70).

John Stowe's *Chronicles of England from Brute unto this present
yeare* (1580), in subsequent editions retitled *The Annales of England*,
provided Marlowe with the account of Edward's being shaved in
puddle water—an incident that he probably associated, for reasons
already explained in an earlier section of this introduction, with the
humiliation of the Duke of York in *3 Henry VI*. As Charlton and
Waller explain, this story derives from the *Vita et Mors Edwardi
Secundi*, a manuscript owned and circulated by Stowe but not published until 1602, when William Camden included it in his collection
entitled *Anglica, Normannica, etc.*[92] Stowe incorporates from the *Vita*

et Mors the pathetic account of how the king insisted that he would have 'warme water' for the shaving, and then, 'that he might keepe his promise, he beganne to weepe and to shed teares plentifullye' (p. 356). It is typical of his tough-minded naturalism that Marlowe should fasten upon the violent and humiliating aspect of this incident, yet pass over the fanciful conceit of the king's tears.

Apart from the shaving episode, Stowe may have influenced Marlowe in a few additional respects. According to Holinshed (p. 318), Gaveston's marriage took place on 31 October 1307, i.e., before his banishment to Ireland, whereas Stowe places the marriage in 1309 after his return from exile (p. 328). Because of the play's order of events, Tancock believed Marlowe followed Stowe rather than Holinshed, but Briggs, noticing the distinction between betrothal and actual marriage, concludes, quite reasonably, 'that the two accounts fused in Marlowe's mind' (p. 130). In the context of Gaveston's unpopularity with the English, Stowe mentions that the minion was 'a straunger borne' (p. 326), a point that Marlowe underlines by having Mortimer Junior sneer at 'that peevish Frenchman' (I.ii.7) and again at 'That sly inveigling Frenchman' (I.ii.57). Technically, of course, Gaveston had always been a subject of the crown in the sense that Gascony, his birthplace, was officially under English authority and control. Stowe also notes that Edward expressed the wish that Gaveston could succeed him on the throne, 'calling him brother' (p. 327); Marlowe's king seems to accord his companion similar status when he scolds the barons for their emblematic insults 'Against the Earl of Cornwall and my brother' (II.ii.35). Stowe writes that the younger Spencer was 'in body very comely' (p. 332), a detail that may have influenced Marlowe inasmuch as the dramatist suggests a closer physical relationship between this character and the king than seems warranted by Holinshed. Stowe also designates Spencer Junior early in the reign as official 'Treasurer' (p. 328), a title that Marlowe conceivably reflects in Mortimer's charge that Edward's 'flatterers' had 'havoc[ked] England's wealth and treasury' (IV.iv.25–26; but see Commentary note) and in Rice ap Howell's statement that the elder Spencer likewise had 'Revelled in England's wealth and treasury' (IV.vi.52).

Two additional works may have affected Marlowe's drama— Thomas Churchyard's poem on 'The Two Mortimers,' probably read in the 1578 edition of *A Mirror for Magistrates*, and Richard Grafton's *Chronicle at large and meere History of the affayres of Englande* (1569). The *Mirror*, although necessarily general, portrays Mortimer as the chief malefactor in Edward II's murder: 'by his meanes syr Edward of Carnaruan / In Berckley Castel, most cruelly was slayne' (ll. 38–39).[93] This emphasis agrees with Marlowe (despite the involvement of accomplices in the drama), and, as we have seen, Holinshed ascribes the instigation of the villainy principally to Bishop Orelton. The *Mirror*, like the play, also highlights the adulterous relationship of Mortimer and the queen. It is worth observing in addition that Marlowe, also like the *Mirror*, makes prominent use of the topos of Fortune's wheel (v.ii.52; v.vi.58), although patently the dramatist had no need of a specific source for so commonplace an idea.

The chief evidence for Marlowe's having consulted Grafton lies in several details that agree better with Marlowe's play than do the rival historians available to him. One of these is Grafton's version of the queen's departure for France: according to this account, Isabella, feigning a pilgrimage to Canterbury, 'tooke hir way to Winchelsey, and in the night entred into a ship which before was prepared for her, and had with her, her eldest sonne Edwarde, and the Erle of Cane [i.e., Kent], and Sir Roger Mortymer, who a little before brake out of the Tower of London . . .' (p. 204).[94] Here Grafton collapses into a single journey four different trips to France—the queen's, the prince's, Kent's, and Mortimer's—that Holinshed clearly (and with greater accuracy) separated. Marlowe has the prince accompany his mother on one voyage, then combines Mortimer's escape with Kent's unhistorical banishment for a second crossing of the channel. It rather looks, therefore, as if these dramaturgical economies are indebted to Grafton.[95]

Also Grafton, like Marlowe (and even more explicitly than the *Mirror*), imputes the planning of King Edward's murder to Mortimer: a summary note in the margin says that 'Sir Roger Mortimer deuised the maner how king Edward should be put to death,' and the narrative proper adds that 'the aforesadye Sir Roger sent a letter vnto [Gurney and Matrevis], signifyeng howe and in what wise he should be' slain (p. 218). In Marlowe, of course, it is Lightborn who invents and keeps secret the grisly method of assassination, but the detail of Mortimer's authorizing letter would appear to come from Grafton. This chronicler's account of the murder itself is, if possible, even more terrible than Holinshed's: Gurney and Matrevis 'came priuely into [Edward's] Chamber, and their company with them, and layde a great Table vpon his belly, and with strength of men at all the foure corners pressed it downe vpon his body, wherewith the king awooke and beyng sore afrayde of death turned hys bodye, so that then he laye grouelyng' (p. 218); the description of his penetration with the spit follows, as in Holinshed. The groveling and fear of death in conjunction with waking from sleep—certainly significant effects of Marlowe's scene (but not directly mentioned by Holinshed)—again point to Grafton as a source.

Marlowe's handling of Kent's arrest and execution also bears the marks of Grafton's influence. Holinshed dispassionately records the legal charges against the earl but refrains from a political interpretation of his fall. Grafton, like Marlowe, not only shows more sympathy for the king's brother but sees the hand of Mortimer in his death: taking Froissart as his authority, Grafton notes 'how that the sayde Mortymer had caused the king [i.e., the young Edward III] to put to death his Vncle [i.e., Kent] without reasonable or iust cause, for all the realme accompted him for a noble and good man' (p. 222). This is strikingly similar to the situation that Marlowe dramatizes when Mortimer condemns Kent in the king's name but against his wishes. Finally, Grafton is the sole chronicler among those whom Marlowe seems to have read who says that Mortimer was decapitated: after being 'quartered,' his 'head [was] set on London Bridge' (p. 223). Obviously the severed head is symbolically necessary to Marlowe's final scene. According to Holinshed, however, Mortimer was hanged at Tyburn, and his 'bodie remained two daies and two nights on the gallowes' (p. 349), after which it was buried.

A few additional details may be tentatively adduced in support of Marlowe's use of Grafton. This chronicler specifically mentions 'adulterie' as being among the 'manifold vices' to which Gaveston 'brought the king by meane of his wanton condicions' (p. 194); Holinshed, Fabyan, and Stowe may be thought to imply a sexual relationship between Gaveston and the king but are not explicit about Edward's marital infidelity. Grafton goes into more circumstantial detail than the other historians about the bribing of the French so as to weaken Isabella's threat to her husband; Marlowe likewise gives the bribery considerable prominence. In Grafton the imprisoned king wishes for oblivion: 'I would to God I were deade, for then were I past all my trouble' (p. 217); these words could well lie behind the speech that Marlowe wrote for Edward at Neath, 'O might I never open these eyes again, / Never again lift up this drooping head' (IV.vii.41–42).

Finally, Grafton's description of the queen's reception by her brother in Paris might have suggested an effective detail of staging to

Marlowe. In the chronicle Isabella 'woulde haue kneeled downe two or three times at the feet of [Charles IV]: But the king would not suffer her, but helde her still by the right hande . . .'; after being assured of Charles's willingness to help her, the 'Queene then kneeled downe whether the king would or not. . . . The king then tooke hir vp in his armes . . .' (p. 205). A little later Grafton relates how the queen knelt again in supplication to Sir John of Hainault, to which that gentleman responded by taking 'her vp quickly in his armes' and saying, 'By the grace of God, the noble Queene of Englande shall not kneele to me' (p. 208). Could Marlowe have recalled these passages when he came to dramatize the reunion of Edward and Gaveston after their long separation? In the play King Edward (like the French king in Grafton), greets a person emotionally close to him but long absent by insisting that personal affection should override formality: 'Embrace me, Gaveston, as I do thee. / Why shouldst thou kneel? Knowest thou not who I am?' (I.i.140–141).

We must conclude, I believe, that the probability of Marlowe's having read Grafton, in addition to Holinshed, Fabyan, and Stowe, is substantial. Indeed a careful study of all the sources, whether known or merely putative, suggests that Marlowe approached his subject with exemplary thoughtfulness and attention to detail. But we learn almost as much from what he altered or neglected as from what he decided to incorporate into the densely woven fabric of *Edward II*.

5 DRAMATIC STRUCTURE AND CHARACTERIZATION

The episodic nature of Holinshed's account with its events spanning more than two decades presented Marlowe with a genuine structural challenge. Edward was only twenty-three and still unmarried when he began his reign by recalling Gaveston in 1307, the episode with which the dramatic action commences. The king was forty-three in 1327, the year of his murder, but his multiple troubles had prematurely aged him, so that Marlowe's character can credibly refer to himself in the final act as 'old Edward' (v.iii.23) and Kent can speak of his brother as 'agèd' (v.ii.119). Edward's son and successor (afterwards Edward III) was not born until 1312 and did not execute Mortimer, the action with which the play concludes, until 1330. Marlowe therefore faced the need to accelerate history precipitously so as to make the confusion and weakness of Edward's story dramatically compelling without sacrificing the psychological changes that inevitably accompany the full tragic effect. And since his protagonist was more fundamentally a victim than a doer, more importantly a receiver of the action than its energizing force, he needed to plot his drama in a manner that would allow reactive emotions to predominate without impeding the headlong rush of events. He also had to contend with a narrative in which rivalries and changing relationships among a variety of persons created the national and personal crises that defined Edward's reign. The title of the first edition already announced the play's interest as divided between the 'troublesome reign and lamentable death' of Edward and the 'tragical fall of proud Mortimer,' to which the second and subsequent quartos added 'the life and death of Piers Gaveston.'

As Eugene Waith has pointed out, the two kinds of moral pattern that Holinshed and the *Mirror for Magistrates* (which in fact included the fall of Mortimer)[96] invited Marlowe to invoke were those that either emphasized the bad consequences of evil counsellors for a king and his country, or pointed to the instability of Fortune and the folly of trusting in earthly powers.[97] But, as Waith goes on to observe, although Marlowe imported both traditions into his play (Isabella moralizes pithily upon 'Misgoverned kings' [IV.iv.9] just as Mortimer speaks more than once of 'Fortune's wheel' [v.ii.52; v.vi.58]), he also deployed the major events of the reign in such a way as to diffuse interest over a 'net of relationships between the King's chief friends and enemies' (p. 60). Within this network the unifying element is the continual 'crossing' and 'being crossed' of multiple characters whose lines of action intersect—characters who suffer galling frustration in the attempt to exercise their wills and who, in turn, frustrate the wills of others just as gallingly (p. 63). Waith's analysis implies, therefore, that the patterns of emotional intensity created by the conflicts between and within individuals reflect the overlapping of lines that results from Marlowe's condensation and layering of Holinshed's more linear and relaxed narrative.

Marlowe's text, as has been noted already, specifies no act divisions—a situation that has led to some disagreement about the formal shape of the play. Although the action implies a few time breaks of indeterminate length—a hiatus between Gaveston's departure for Ireland and his return; a short pause between the favourite's death and the king's receiving the bitter news; a brief gap between Mortimer's escape and his reaching the queen in France; a slightly

longer break between Isabella's departure for Hainault and her
armed arrival in England; a series of implied intervals separating the
king's escape to Neath, his capture, imprisonment, and murder, and
the recoil of Mortimer's downfall—Marlowe conveys the impression
of virtually uninterrupted action. Waith sees Marlowe's design as
essentially tripartite. According to this view, the first block fills what
is usually designated as Act I (centred on the banishment and recall
of Gaveston), an action that leaves King Edward vis à vis his barons
in the same position as his situation at the opening, although it
has defined the clash of wills that will affect everything to follow.
The second block occupies the tumultuous up-and-down struggle
that culminates in the king's capture and final separation from his
favourites, thus marking the moment of tragic irreversibility (Acts
II, III, and IV of modern editions). The final block dramatizes the
hero's confinement, torture, and death (Act V), which provides
the satisfactions of closure by fulfilling the tragic destiny of the
protagonist and punishing his murderers. Although such a division
is attractive in its neatness and logic, it is also possible to discern in
Marlowe's arrangement the more traditional architecture of the five-
act tragedy.

Act I, opening with its immediate focus on Gaveston and his
unique emotional hold upon the king, establishes Edward and his
lover as having created between them a private world of their own—
a world set apart from, and even against, the general needs and
concerns of the realm. Gaveston expresses contempt for both the
common people (symbolized by the poor men who sue to him for
employment) and the 'lordly peers' (1.i.18) to whom he does not
intend to stoop. By the time he and the king abuse the Bishop
of Coventry later in the scene, the play has already dramatized
Gaveston's overriding influence as a threat to all three estates—
the commons, the nobles, and the church—and shown the king,
politically speaking, to be a cypher. The first scene also fixes the
younger Mortimer in our minds as the most fiery and menacing of
the antagonistic barons. The following episode introduces the long-
suffering queen, whose brutal rejection by her husband causes her to
air her grief to Edward's principal enemy. The nobles' insistence
that the favourite be banished raises the prospect of 'civil mutinies,'
but Isabella, preferring to 'endure a melancholy life' (1.ii.65–66)
rather than see her beloved confronted by open war, acts as a brake
upon the baronial opposition. Tension rises higher as Edward, having already showered undeserved honours upon his friend, sym-

bolically makes him his consort by allowing him to share the throne. This reckless violation of protocol produces an instant reaction: swords are drawn in the royal presence, Gaveston is seized, and Edward forced against his will to sign the document of exile. The king and his friend part tearfully, after which Edward reviles his wife and threatens her with permanent separation from him unless she intervenes to have her rival recalled. Isabella succeeds in this painful task but in the process allies herself with Mortimer more closely than before, at the same time betraying a hint of that capacity for guile and ruthlessness that will emerge in her character more fully later on. With Gaveston's recall, with Edward's reconciliation or 'second marriage' (I.iv.334) to Isabella, and with new rewards for the barons, including Mortimer's promotion to be 'Lord Marshal of the realm' (I.iv.355), the act concludes on a note of tenuous and obviously hollow peace.

It is clear that the deepest kinds of conflict have been merely papered over and that worse troubles are in store. This first movement of the play, then, presents us with a characteristic oscillation between elation and unhappiness, or rather with brief moments of joy, already hedged about with misery and defiance, that promise defeat and failure ahead. The act is centred on irrascible confrontations or eruptions of hostility (Gaveston and the peers, Gaveston and Coventry, the king and the barons, Canterbury and the king, Edward and the queen) punctuated by more reflective, lyrical, and private moments (Gaveston's description of the hedonistic entertainments planned for the king, Edward's ecstatic reunion with his friend, Isabella's anguished lamentation as the discarded wife, Edward's soliloquy of resentment at the necessity of banishing his favourite, his speech of mourning after the forced departure). It also sets up an unstable triangle of intense desire and its frustration involving three of the pivotal figures—Gaveston, the king, and Isabella; and in addition it prepares us for the formation of a second such triangle, incipiently present in the unfolding relationship of Mortimer, the queen, and Edward.

The second act develops the pattern already implied by its predecessor. Although Gaveston's downfall has already been forecast by the formidable powers arrayed against him, Marlowe now introduces Spencer Junior, the sycophantic figure who will replace the first minion, together with his cynical associate, Baldock. The arc of Spencer's rise to power begins before Gaveston's star has begun to set, but the timing, at least in retrospect, is ominous and ironic.

Also the playwright further complicates the pattern of emotional triangulation already articulated by bringing in Margaret de Clare, the lady who will marry Gaveston and, at least by implication, will have to compete with Edward for her husband's affections just as Isabella has had to compete with Gaveston. Margaret's eager anticipation of her fiancé's return from exile is prelusory to that expressed by Edward in the scene that immediately follows, and the love letter that she reads aloud ('I will not long be from thee, though I die' [II.i.62]) recalls Gaveston's love letter from the king with which the play had opened; it even echoes the passionate verb that Gaveston had used in his exultant expectancy—'The king, upon whose bosom let me die . . .' (I.i.14). The rebel peers, who insult Edward by devising cryptic emblems on their shields to threaten Gaveston, now thwart the king once more in his amorous fixation; and when the returning earl arrives, Edward's moment of rapture is cut short by Mortimer, who actually thrusts at Gaveston and wounds him, a marked escalation of the previous hostility. Then as threats of death and vengeance are being hurled extravagantly from both sides, news comes of the capture of Mortimer's uncle, which fuels the barons' rage more hotly still and provokes their stinging assault upon the king for *all* his disastrous policies at home and abroad, including the humiliation of Bannockburn. Kent's defection to the rebels (after his brother has spurned his warnings) marks the seriousness of the crisis, and Edward's separation from Gaveston as the two fly in different directions from their common enemies signals the beginning of the end of their homoerotic affair and the clear ascendancy of the barons. Mortimer, in pursuit of Gaveston, also separates himself from Isabella, who now looks toward France; but not before she has attached herself more closely than before to her extramarital supporter (it is she who betrays Gaveston's whereabouts to the barons) and has nearly abandoned hope of Edward's love.

These events lead naturally to Gaveston's capture at Scarborough— the turning point of the act and an action that balances Mortimer's loss of his uncle in Scotland. Significantly, Lancaster compares the hated favourite to Helen of Troy, 'the Greekish strumpet' (II.v.15) who caused such epic loss of life. But Marlowe prolongs tension by means of the negotiations to allow the prisoner a final tryst with the king before his execution, at the same time ameliorating our assessment of the man by allowing an apparently genuine devotion to his sovereign to modify our earlier impression of opportunistic self-interest. Warwick's treachery weights the balance of sympathies still

more heavily toward Edward and his friend, while depriving the
rebel cause of most of its claim to high-minded or disinterested
reform. The act ends with Gaveston's being haled to the block,
his final utterance a cry of futile protest: 'Treacherous earl! Shall I
not see the king?' (II.vi.15). The moment is one that foreshadows
Edward II's own tragedy, conveys a sense of personal frustration and
defeat more irrevocably than before, and prepares us for a fresh
intensification of pain, vengeance, and civil chaos once the reaction
sets in. Act II therefore marks a lower point in Edward's decline
than we have witnessed as yet, but it also completes a cycle of
personal disaster that had been in prospect from the start.

Act III, the shortest of the play, is also the most condensed and
crowded, spanning, as it does, the fourteen years between Gaveston's
capture in 1312 and the bribing of the French in 1326 (designed
to thwart the queen in her plan to enlist aid from her brother against
Edward). We meet the young prince for the first time in a way that
prepares us initially for his dominance by Isabella and Mortimer,
and ultimately for his dominance over them. In this act, too, Marlowe
adds the element of physical separation to the emotional alienation
that has steadily been developing between the king and his spouse.
The movement opens with the protagonist's anguished waiting for
news of Gaveston (as he had waited for the man himself near the
beginning of the previous act). Since we already know what Edward
only fears—that the Gascon nobleman has indeed been executed—
the effect is one of suspenseful irony. Meanwhile the younger Spencer
stiffens his master to fresh defiance of the rebels and is raised to an
earldom, even as Gaveston had been similarly raised in Act I. Only
after the king has welcomed Spencer's father to the loyalists and dispatched his wife and son to deal with nagging problems in France,
does he receive from Arundel the report of Gaveston's murder. This
triggers Edward's terrible vow of revenge, solemnized by kneeling,
and impels him instantly to confer upon the new favourite Gaveston's
former post of Lord Chamberlain as well as a second earldom
(Gloucester). When a herald arrives from the barons to demand that
the younger Spencer be exiled, Edward ostentatiously embraces his
friend to demonstrate that already he has become a second Gaveston.
(Marlowe, incidentally, adds the embrace, conspicuously missing
from Holinshed, to suggest a physical component in the new relationship and to reinforce the parallel with the dead lover, whom
Edward had similarly embraced in Act I.) Now armed battle, to
which the conflicts have steadily been building, erupts—battle dra-

matized first as a retreat by the king's forces and then a successful rally in which the rebels are overwhelmed and taken captive. Edward's triumph over the barons at Boroughbridge, the climax of the act, marks a brief parenthesis of royal power and kingly energy, thus defining the highest pitch of his fortunes. For the moment vindictive rage has concentrated the king's resistance and made it an effective weapon against his enemies.

But the unrestrained slaughter and wild vengeance that Edward exacts only produce more chaos: he speaks wildly of reducing 'England's civil towns' to 'huge heaps of stones' (III.ii.31) and beheads Warwick and Lancaster while foolishly sparing Mortimer, the figure who appears to have led them. Impulsively, he also banishes Kent, the earl whose loyalty is vital and whose support had held on longer than that of the other captives. With a certain cruel symmetry the heads of the traitors pay for the beheading of Gaveston in the previous act, but retributive passion rather than considered justice dominates the stage. And the final episode of Levune's being sent to corrupt 'the lords of France' so that they will withhold support from Isabella sounds a note of realpolitik that tends, by mere juxtaposition, to besmirch whatever honour Edward has won in defeating his disloyal vassals. To the policy of bribing the French, Spencer Junior applies the myth of Danaë (III.ii.81–85), who was seduced by Jove in the form of a golden shower. The allusion suggests a disquieting link between sexual and monetary forms of persuasion; and attentive listeners may recognize here the strategic echo of a passage from the previous act in which Edward had compared his longing for Gaveston to the unfulfilled lovers of Danaë—lovers frustrated because the lady was locked away from them in a tower (II.ii.53–56). Thus Marlowe conveys the impression of taint even at the brief moment of Edward II's heroic success. But unlike the previous acts, this central section of the play, stuffed as it is with activity, contains almost no pauses for reflection or lyrical expostulation.

Act IV begins with Kent's testing the favourable winds that will send his ship to France to join the queen, an action that glances backward to the similar business at the opening of II.ii when Edward remarked upon the wind that should speed Gaveston's arrival home from banishment. Kent's exile recalls that of Edward's favourite, and the speaker soliloquizes bitterly on his brother's 'unnatural' policy of punishing true 'friends' while 'cherish[ing] flatterers' (IV.i. 4–9). The unhistorical alliance at this point between Kent and

Mortimer, whose escape from the Tower we briefly witness, already bodes ill for the king. The scene in Paris, which adds Sir John of Hainault to the coalition forming about the queen and which shows us the arrival of Kent and Mortimer, builds still more pessimism about Edward's chances of survival; but Marlowe retards the drift towards Isabella's empowerment by emphasizing her despair at being denied the political support of Charles IV. The queen's double rejection by two kings, her husband and her brother, deepens our sense of her victimization and bitterness, thus helping to motivate her later fierceness; it therefore reinforces once more the relatedness of sex and politics. This episode also complicates our impression of the prince, who is characterized as a child unwilling to leave his 'gracious mother's side' (IV.ii.23) when the plan of moving to Hainault is broached, but who also is reluctant to be the standard bearer of the impending invasion as long as 'the king my father lives' (IV.ii.43). Against this background Edward's exultant confidence in his own strength—the announcement of the multiple executions of traitors throughout the land and of the failure of the queen to garner aid in France—sounds hubristic; and the reward offered for Mortimer's head (based on the false assumption that the rebel is still in England) makes the expression of triumph seem even more groundless. Marlowe intensifies the dramatic irony still further in Edward's rash speech beginning, 'Gallop apace bright Phoebus through the sky,' in which the king urges time forward to the moment when he can 'meet [the remaining] traitors in the field' (IV.iii.66–70).

Even in his overconfidence, Edward retires to Bristol, a strategy that implies weakness; and again he invokes favourable winds—this time not to return a minion to his embrace but, ironically, to bring back the vengeful queen who, under Mortimer's direction, will depose him. Immediately we see that the 'prosperous winds' (IV.iv.2) for which Edward hoped have indeed ensured her arrival, but she uses the occasion to greet her supporters with an effusive speech condemning her husband's misgovernment—a speech for which the hard-nosed Mortimer, shrewdly recognizing the dangers of too vocal an attack upon their lawful sovereign, chastens her: 'Nay madam, if you be a warrior, / Ye must not grow so passionate in speeches' (IV.iv.14–15). Already Marlowe is preparing us for the change in Mortimer from the outraged baron who opposed the king's flatterers to the calculating pragmatist and cold-hearted power-seeker who will play the role of overreaching villain in the denouement. A note of

deceptive calculation in the character has already been introduced
in the escape scene, where we learn that Mortimer has cleverly
administered a 'potion' (IV.i.14) to his guards. The patriotic speech
by which he arouses his forces in support of 'our country's cause'
(IV.iv.18) and Prince Edward's right suggests at least a hint of selfish
motivation, especially in his putting the 'wrongs and injuries . . .
done to us' before those done to the 'queen' and the 'land' (IV.iv.20–
21).

The remainder of the act quickly compasses the total captitulation
of the king's forces—Edward's flight from battle (albeit under protest), the triumph of the queen, the creation of the prince as titular
head of the realm, the arrest and execution of Spencer Senior, the
pursuit of Edward, Baldock, and the younger Spencer to Neath, and
finally their capture. The speed with which all this is presented
reinforces the familiar *de casibus* theme of unstable fortune and
makes Edward's earlier victory seem particularly short-lived. And
the beheading of the elder Spencer not only recapitulates the motif
of Gaveston's death but also initiates a whole chain of killings
(Spencer Junior's, Baldock's, Kent's, Edward II's, Lightborn's, and
finally Mortimer's) that balances the holocaust of Boroughbridge and
partly results from it. But Marlowe already turns our sympathies
toward Edward by revealing the guilt that plagues Kent (through the
latter's soliloquy) and by having him return once more to loyalty.
Kent functions in the drama as a barometer of moral feeling, and
his characterization of Mortimer and the queen as lustful and deadly
conspirators quickly confirms our suspicion of their doubtful sin-
cerity in IV.iv.[98] Given the Machiavellian realities that have now
prevailed, the repentant earl recognizes the necessity of fighting the
deceptive couple with dissembling of his own. The prince, too,
strengthens our impression of tyrannical forces now in the saddle
through his futile, unanswered question, 'Shall I not see the king my
father yet?' (IV.vi.61), an ironic echo of Gaveston's final utterance,
'Treacherous earl! Shall I not see the king!' (II.vi.15).

Marlowe ends this penultimate movement of the play with the
long scene at the monastery of Neath of which the primary effect is
pathos, and which one commentator has well described as possessing
a 'unique mixture of quiet and unrest.'[99] Appropriately the initial
note is one of human vulnerability. Edward with his two closest
friends, all three being disguised as monks, fears that the abbot will
betray them for money to their enemies; and we are reminded of
how the king had used similar bribes as a weapon against the queen

in France. Edward nevertheless endeavours to trust his protector, even laying his head in the abbot's lap like a frightened child seeking solace. This image of a monarch dependent upon a priest dramatically reverses that of the king triumphing over the beheading of his foes earlier in the act and shows, again in good *de casibus* fashion, how quickly pride can be humbled by fickle circumstance. Supplication to a cleric also dramatically inverts the earlier situation in which Edward had bullied the Bishop of Coventry. Royal pretension has been reduced to virtual nullity. Praise of the 'life contemplative,' which Edward now equates with 'heaven' (IV.vii.20), also marks an important shift in tone, expanding the focus on bitter political and personal strife to more philosophical and religious concerns, and thus preparing the context for a gradually more insistent awareness of mortality.

The motif of weather appears for the last time in Baldock's mention of the 'awkward winds and sore tempests' (IV.vii.34) that have prevented escape to Ireland. Then Rice ap Howell, Leicester, and their forces suddenly arrive to confirm the king's worst fears; they are accompanied significantly by the 'gloomy' Mower whom Spencer had suspected for his 'long look' in the 'mead below' (IV.vii.29–30) and who probably carries the symbolic scythe of the Grim Reaper. Marlowe intensifies compassion for the prisoners by having Leicester, the highest ranking of the arresting party, comment aside (like Kent at an earlier point) on the tyrannous Mortimer whose power stands behind the 'queen's commission' (IV.vii.49). And the abbot also is shocked by the affront to royalty: 'A king to bear these words and proud commands!' (IV.vii.71). Edward plangently laments his fate, 'O day! The last of all my bliss on earth, / Centre of all misfortune' (IV.vii.61–62)—a cry that seems designed by Marlowe to be heard as a variation on Gaveston's lament at the moment of his capture, 'O, must this day be period of my life, / Centre of all my bliss?' (II.vi.4–5).[100] Before Spencer and Baldock are led away to execution, they voice their devotion to the king even as Gaveston had done: 'O is he gone? Is noble Edward gone? / Parted from hence, never to see us more?' (IV.vii.100–101), and 'We are deprived the sunshine of our life' (IV.vii.106). For his part, Edward defines his very existence in terms of these attachments: 'Here, man, rip up this panting breast of mine, / And take my heart in rescue of my friends!' (IV.vii.66–67).

The act ends, then, in total defeat for the protagonist, isolating him first from his power as king and finally from those on whom he most closely depends. The throwing back of his monk's cowl to make obvious his royal identity effectively emblematizes this exposure. The separation from friends both recapitulates the loss of Gaveston and looks forward to the final suffering and degradation to be realized in Act V. As Baldock says so ruefully to his sovereign: 'Our lots are cast. I fear me, so is thine' (IV.vii.79). And Marlowe also continues the cynicism implied by the power of money, the final exit being marked by the Mower's request for the payment due him for his deadly service as an intelligencer.

Act V completes the inevitable pattern of the tragedy, first, by formalizing the protagonist's abdication and the installation of his successor, second, by tracing the progressive degradation and suffering of Edward to the point of death, and third, by dramatizing the swift recoil against Mortimer and the queen, thus restoring a kind of moral and emotional equilibrium. Marlowe structures this final movement of the play by means of a series of scenes that alternate between a focus on Edward as victim (in confinement) and on Mortimer as oppressor (at court). But he implies an ironic parallel as well, for the king, 'pent and mewed . . . in a prison,' soars 'up to heaven' in the 'dauntless' intensity of his desire to 'curb' his persecutor (V.i.15–21), just as Mortimer at an earlier point had defied the 'ragged stony walls' of the Tower to 'Immure' his resistance and fetter a 'virtue that aspires to heaven' (III.ii.72–73). The dramatist also returns to an antiphony between softer, more lyrical, more meditative strains on the one hand and harsher, more violent, more retributive sonorities on the other. At the climax of the king's murder the poet ironically combines the soothing and the terrifying to brilliant psychological effect.

Leicester's attempt to cheer Edward at Killingworth by inviting him to imagine that the castle were his 'court' (V.i.2) only provokes the prisoner to more 'outrageous passions . . . of rancour and disdain' (V.i.19–20), but as the king struggles with impotent fantasies and gestures of vengeance and with the frustration of having to relinquish his crown, to which he clings with the same obstinacy that had marked his adhesion to favourites, he also begins to accommodate himself to the loss of 'regiment' (V.i.26) and to the reality of death. Light (especially sunshine) and shadow are among the powerful images that convey this opposition in verbal terms, and Edward's need to retard the movement sweeping him downward, 'Stand still you watches of the element; / All times and seasons rest you at a stay, / That Edward may be still fair England's king' (V.i.66–68), contrasts wonderfully with his ebullient outburst of the previous act, 'Gallop apace bright Phoebus through the sky . . .' (IV.iii.66), when he could scarcely wait to engage the enemy in battle. Marlowe also sets up a splendid counterpoint in the deposition scene by having the king self-pityingly send his wife a tear-stained handkerchief, a gift that she reciprocates hypocritically in the following episode by sending him a jewel 'as witness of [her] love' (V.ii.71). The first stage in Edward's steadily worsening treatment is marked by his transference from the gentle care of Leicester, with whom Edward has been relatively comfortable, to that of Berkeley, whom he suspects of greater harshness.

The contrasting scene (V.ii) establishes Mortimer and the queen as unequivocally tyrannical and vicious, confirming the accusatory words of Kent in his soliloquy of repentance in IV.vi. Mortimer plans to make himself (unhistorically) Lord Protector over the prince, receives the instrument of abdication and the crown from the Bishop of Winchester, contemplates the neutralizing of Kent, and appoints Matrevis and Gurney as Edward's jailors to replace Berkeley, instructing them to conceal the whereabouts of the king by moving him from place to place in secret and to 'amplify his grief with bitter words' (V.ii.64). The scene ends with an ugly struggle between Kent and the queen for control of the boy king, which the earl loses, prompting him to attempt his brother's rescue in person. Isabella's public pretence of solicitude for her suffering husband, which Mortimer privately commends by whispering, 'Finely dissembled; do so still, sweet queen' (V.ii.73), balances Kent's earlier advice to himself: 'Dissemble or thou diest . . .' (IV.vi.12). Marlowe strengthens our sense of young Edward's loyalty to his father, at the same time dramatizing the boy's instinctive preference for Kent over Mortimer as a mentor.

When the focus shifts back again to Edward II, we see that his degradation under the control of Matrevis and Gurney is already under way. Matrevis claims that he and his partner are the king's 'friends,' but he solaces his prisoner with the cold comfort of a platitude: 'Men are ordained to live in misery' (V.iii.1–2). A new weariness enters Edward's voice as he is being shunted by night from one castle to another, and already he anticipates being killed by 'hateful Mortimer' (V.iii.5) and the queen. Despairingly he offers his blood in an extravagant image: 'unbowel straight this breast, / And give my heart to Isabel and him' (V.iii.10–11); here Marlowe seems deliberately to recall the similar outburst of the previous act in which

Edward had greeted Leicester (who had come to arrest him and his companion fugitives) with 'Here, man, rip up this panting breast . . . And take my heart in rescue of my friends!' (IV.vii.66–67). Now the details of Edward's imprisonment accumulate—the dreadful stench, the starvation, the thirst, the excremental filth—to which is added the humiliation of being shaved in puddle water, an ironic echo of the puddle 'christening' (I.i.187) to which the Bishop of Coventry had been subjected. Significantly Edward personalizes his martyrdom: 'O Gaveston, it is for thee that I am wronged; / For me, both thou and both the Spencers died' (v.iii.41–42); he wishes to see his own impending death as an act of sacrifice to their memories rather than as a punishment for wilful and incompetent rule. Kent's futile attempt at rescue follows. The royal brothers are not permitted to meet, but as the king's helpless defender contemplates his own inevitable execution, he moralizes in choric fashion on the violation of natural order that we are witnessing: 'O, miserable is that commonweal, where lords / Keep courts and kings are locked in prison!' (v.iii.63–64).

Back at court once more, we overhear Mortimer plotting Edward's murder by means of the equivocal letter. Marlowe continues to build sympathy for the victim by revealing the Lord Protector in the unambiguous villainy of his invincible presumption and Machiavellian ruthlessness: 'Feared am I more than loved . . .' (v.iv.50). We learn that the 'commons now begin to pity' Edward, and hear the overreaching politician ironically foreshadow his own downfall by his statement that 'The king must die, or Mortimer goes down' (v.iv.1–2). Mortimer's agent Lightborn, drawn (as Harry Levin points out) from the tradition of medieval stage devils,[101] heightens our expectation of horror by touting his ingenious professionalism as an assassin, nevertheless withholding the secret of the 'braver way' (v.iv.36) by which he intends to dispatch the king. After Lightborn has been dismissed to Berkeley Castle, unwittingly bearing his own death warrant as well as the authorization to murder Edward, Mortimer preens himself on his clever hypocrisy and total control over Isabella and her son, whose coronation follows immediately. Mortimer's excessive pride cries out for condign punishment. Then the ancient solemnity of the king's champion, who symbolically defends the young monarch's right against all challengers, produces a further ironic effect, because the boy's first attempt to use his fresh authority—by sparing the life of his uncle Kent—meets with dismissive refusal on the part of his controllers, who condescend to him as a child.

We reach the point of highest emotional intensity in the murder scene, the obvious climax of the tragedy, for here Marlowe maximizes the pity and terror of Edward's story and concentrates both in a uniquely powerful fashion. Psychological torment is wedded to physical suffering, and Edward's capacity for sheer endurance commands a certain respect. Unspeakable misery elicits a surprising fortitude in its formerly self-indulgent victim. Tension increases as Lightborn presents himself to Gurney and Matrevis, bidding them prepare the mysterious implements of destruction—the spit, the featherbed, and the table. What follows is an almost unendurable seduction of sorts in which the sadist toys quasi-sexually with his human object (who is invited to lie passively on a bed); the seducer uses a combination of techniques—feigned sympathy, soothing comfort, and transparent lies, beneath all of which menace is the motivating force. Delay heightens the terror both for the victim and for the audience. Edward, torn between physical exhaustion and paralyzing anxiety, between the desire for sleep (or oblivion) and the fear of violent death, wrestles with the contradiction between anticipated doom and a fantasy of hope. Futilely he attempts to resist his murderer by telling of the atrocities to which his royalty has been subjected; he pleads, he offers his last jewel, he reminisces pathetically, he falls into despair, he tries to pray, he succumbs briefly to unconsciousness, and finally accepts the inevitable consummation: 'O spare me! Or dispatch me in a trice!' (v.v.110). The childlike vulnerability and dread that Edward had revealed to the abbot at the end of Act IV becomes now the irreducible datum of his being. In his final moments he embodies all the extremities that cruelty and oppression are capable of inflicting upon body, mind, and spirit. And the visceral scream that accompanies the figurative sodomy of his mortal wound expresses, as words could not, the nightmare conjunction of sex, politics, and savagery that the drama as a whole has been exploring. Regicide, in itself shocking enough for Elizabethans, has been fused with rape; the grandeur of princely command has been degraded to the *ne plus ultra* of terror-stricken servility. Lightborn scarcely has a second to admire his handiwork before he is stabbed and his corpse disposed of as garbage 'in the moat' (v.v.118). The scene, which had begun with an image of the king 'up to the knees in water' (v.v.2), concludes fittingly with the same element.

Marlowe's final scene restores a kind of justice by allowing the child king to emerge from the domination of his handlers, to act as an adult, and, as such, to punish tyranny and avenge his father's

murder. The peripety is swift. Mortimer receives the report of
Matrevis, who already feels remorse for the king's death and who
predicts that Gurney, in guilty flight, will betray them both. Matrevis,
like his accomplice, is lucky to escape into exile with his life.
Mortimer, blinded by untrammelled power, continues to assert his
invincibility, whereas the queen, who has witnessed her son's grief at
the news of Edward's fate, already foresees her 'tragedy' (v.vi.23)
and that of her lover. Edward III, for the moment at least no longer
a puppet monarch, straightway interrogates, judges, and condemns
the murderer, while Mortimer pessimistically philosophizes upon
his fall in terms of Fortune's wheel but scornfully refuses to acknowledge guilt. Stoical acceptance of the unavoidable rather than
Christian humility defines his attitude, and in his denial of conventional moralism, he curiously resembles his victim. The queen,
by pleading for the life of her paramour, exposes her own wrongdo-
ing to scrutiny, and is sent (unhistorically) to the Tower to await
further trial. Marlowe leaves her ultimate punishment uncertain, but
perhaps she anticipates her fate in her exit line: 'Then come, sweet
death, and rid me of this grief' (v.vi.91). That Edward III has finally
become a king in deed as well as title emerges in his capacity to
override private feelings for his mother that might impel him to treat
her more leniently. The play ends with the formal obsequies of the
dead monarch to whose hearse the severed head of Mortimer is
offered up in tribute.

The emotional contours of Marlowe's tragedy, as the foregoing
analysis has tried to show, follow the layout of its complex, varied,
and even scattered materials as selected, arranged, and altered from
Holinshed. Nevertheless a fivefold structure, corresponding to the
act divisions of the present edition, emerges with some clarity.[102]
The initial four acts present two sequences of action, each of which
is defined by Edward's bitter strife with his enemies and by his
defiant, unswerving commitment to his friends. In each case a short-
term victory for the king, which occasions unjustified optimism and
a factitious sense of control, is followed by a cruel and devastating
defeat, ending in frustration, separation, the death of favourites, and
profound grief. The concluding act then brings the king himself to
a protracted ordeal of torture and death, depriving him of his
ultimately loyal brother, and also visiting retributive punishment
upon the traitors who have survived to usurp his power, imprison,
and destroy him. The final effect is tragic because it consummates a
long struggle of wills, loyalties, and passions that are recognized to

be inevitable as well as painfully destructive and self-consuming.

Marlowe's design, especially in its radical compression of historical time, has the effect of lending speed and dramatic momentum to the play; but it also creates problems of consistency in the characterization. Numerous commentators have complained of the rapidity with which Mortimer metamorphoses from a patriotic nobleman, sincerely if irascibly concerned for his country's wellbeing, into a wily usurper and power-obsessed Machiavel. The queen's shift from a Patient Griselda to a heartless conniver, adultress, and accesory to murder—the 'she-wolf of France' as she came to be known[103]—has occasioned even greater objection. Marlowe does his best to prepare us for these changes, however sudden they may appear in the pell-mell rush of unfolding action, and, in the case of Isabella, he handles the transformation more subtly than has often been acknowledged. But the impression of a puzzling doubleness remains. David Bevington plausibly suggests that much of the ambiguity we feel about the characters arises from the conflict between the historical facts of their behaviour, as Marlowe derived these from Holinshed, and the tendency to polarize good and evil semi-allegorically that he inherited from the traditions of the morality play; thus the combination 'engenders a dichotomy . . . between moral absolutes and psychological complexities.'[104] But if Marlowe was embarrassed, as Bevington implies, by the contradictory requirements of his raw material and the formative structures bequeathed to him by his native theatre, he seems to have made a virtue of necessity.

Mysterious dualities of conduct and attitude pervade nearly all the central figures of *Edward II*. Gaveston is arrogantly manipulative and ambitious when Edward recalls him from banishment at his accession but, facing death and having nothing more to gain, seems wholly and personally committed to the king. Even earlier, his response to Edward's commiseration, ' 'Tis something to be pitied of a king' (I.iv.130), seems to reflect sincere feeling, and Edward never doubts that his favourite 'loves [him] more than all the world' (I.iv.77). Spencer and Baldock are also presented as cynical climbers and hypocrites when we first meet them, but their loyalty to Edward is never afterwards in question, and their sorrow at losing a monarch who is also a friend appears even greater than the pain they feel at the prospect of execution. During a considerable part of the action the queen seems cruelly torn between unrequited passion for her husband and the need to destroy him. Kent also wavers between extremes of loyalty and disloyalty, risking his life in the service of both attitudes; and Prince Edward is characterized as both a pawn— a naif who would shun political involvement if he could—and a child in whom independent judgement and forceful leadership are already latent. Lightborn, too, contributes to our sense of dividedness, masking, as he does, the grotesque horror of his function under the guise of comforter and symbolic lover. Even Edward himself is seen to embody conflicting attributes: on the one hand, his effeminate passivity, childish self-indulgence, and wilful irresponsibility invite contempt, especially in a king; but on the other, his fierce assertiveness crushes enemies, and his unshakeable loyalty commands astonishing devotion from friends. Lancaster's flat assertion that 'In no respect can contraries be true' (I.iv.249) is clearly invalid for the most important figures of *Edward II*.

Marlowe, then, manages to convey a sense of deep-seated ambiguity at the heart of human personality, and, as one perceptive critic has noticed, he presents the complex relationship of Edward, Isabella, and Gaveston in such a way as to suggest the concept of androgyny: a certain feminine softness in Edward complements the streak of masculine hardness in Isabella, and the theoretically distinct roles of monarch and minion seem to be reversed, or at least confused, by Gaveston's sexual and psychological dominance over Edward.[105] If, then, Marlowe clarified and simplified the narrative of Holinshed, he did just the opposite in his conceptualization of character. As a consequence *Edward II* would seem to mark the highest point in Marlowe's dramatic career of emotional complexity subtly and powerfully rendered.

6 CRITICAL RECEPTION AND ASSESSMENT

With the possible exception of Ford's anomalously late *Perkin Warbeck*, *Edward II* remains our finest non-Shakespearean example of the English chronicle play as well as our first tragedy of intense personal suffering based on Holinshed. Its high place in dramatic and literary history has nevertheless taken time to establish. As early as 1781 Thomas Warton could speak of Marlowe's 'forgotten tragedy' even as he admired (while also bowdlerizing) Gaveston's speech on the erotic entertainments planned for Edward. Appreciation of *Edward II* as a serious work of art properly begins with Lamb, who, in addition to comparing the abdication scene favourably to its counterpart in *Richard II*, went on to praise 'the death-scene of Marlowe's king' as an episode that 'moves pity and terror beyond any scene ancient or modern with which I am acquainted.'[106] Several writers including Nathan Drake, James Broughton, Leigh Hunt, and the biographer of Edmund Kean (in 1817, 1818, 1844, and 1869 respectively) echoed Lamb's praise of the death-scene; and Swinburne (in 1875), also taking his cue from Lamb, asserted boldly that Marlowe's play is superior to *Richard II* in the characterization of all but the title figure, York, Norfolk, and Aumerle being 'ghosts, not men,' in comparison with Gaveston and Mortimer.[107] Broughton, expanding in 1830 upon the preface to his 1818 edition, declared *Edward II* to be 'by far the best of [the dramatatist's] plays,' and thought that the varied traits of the title character, both sympathetic and unsympathetic, were 'severally depicted with an adherence to nature and a boldness of colouring which impart the deepest interest. . . .'[108]

The eminent historian and drama critic A. W. Ward was perhaps the leading Victorian enthusiast; Ward admired the clear construction, the 'powerfully sustained' interest and varied characterization, particularly of the king, 'whose passionate love for his favourites is . . . traced to a generous motive' and who 'is not without courage and spirit in the face of danger.' Like Lamb, Ward praised the 'tragic power' of the king's death, its 'unutterable horror' being presented in such a way as to avoid arousing 'our sense of the loathsome' while preserving the victim's dignity and causing spectators to share the agony of suspense to which the doomed king is subjected. Havelock Ellis also regarded *Edward II* as 'the summit of [Marlowe's] art' in comparison to which Shakespeare's *Richard II* 'with its exuberant eloquence, its facile and diffuse poetry, is distinctly inferior' in structure and characterization.[109] A few commentators (such as H. N. Hudson in 1872) recognized that Marlowe's style in *Edward II* was admirably suited to its subject, the dialogue being 'generally . . . nervous, animated, and clear' and the versification 'mov[ing], throughout, with a freedom and variety' characteristic of Shakespeare. Dyce (in 1850) remarked the absence of 'turgidity' in the language, unusual in an early chronicle play, although he missed the poetic 'raptures' for which Marlowe was commonly read; and A. C. Bradley (in 1880) noticed that the 'stately monotone of *Tamburlaine* . . . gives place in *Edward II* to rhythms less suited to pure poetry, but far more rapid and flexible.'[110]

Negative responses to the play, however, continued to find expression throughout the nineteenth century. Oxberry, although he acknowledged the 'rich colouring of character,' censured Marlowe for a 'crowded' and 'barren plot,' for the absence of 'the sublime' and 'the beautiful,' and for the 'violation of all reality' that resulted from too radical a compression of historical time (pp. iii, xi). More surprising still is the undervaluation of the drama by Hazlitt in 1820, even though he judged it 'Marlowe's best play' by contemporary standards of composition and admired the king's 'heart-breaking distress' at the end: 'Edward II is drawn with historic truth, but without much dramatic effect. The management of the plot is feeble and desultory; little interest is excited in the various turns of fate; the characters are too worthless, have too little energy, and their punishment is, in general, too well deserved, to excite our commiseration; so that this play will bear, on the whole, but a distant comparison with Shakespear's Richard II in conduct, power, or effect.'[111] Writing in 1870, Edward Dowden was equally lukewarm: *Edward II* is 'free from the violence and extravagance of the [Marlowe] dramas that preceded it' as well as from the bombast; 'but, except in a few scenes, and notably the closing ones, it wants also the clear raptures, the high reaches of wit, the "brave translunary things" . . . which especially characterise Marlowe. The historical matter he is unable to handle as successfully as a subject of an imaginative or partly mythical kind . . . and accordingly . . . [the play], though containing a few splendid passages, is rather a series of scenes from the chronicles . . . than a drama.'[112]

Like Dowden, George Saintsbury believed that 'the limitations of a historical story impose[d] something like a restraining form on [Marlowe's] glowing imagination,' and James Russell Lowell in 1892 wrote similarly that the 'more orderly arrangement of scenes and acts' was purchased at the expense of a 'drag' on the dramatist's spontaneity.[113] Even those who admired Marlowe's powers of characterization tended to judge Isabella a dramatic failure: Ward (like many after him) thought the singular weakness of *Edward II* was the lack of any credible 'transition' between the queen's 'despairing attachment to the King' and her 'guilty love for Mortimer'; John Addington Symonds, making the same point in 1884, went so far as to asseverate that 'Marlowe never drew a woman's character,' perhaps echoing A. C. Bradley's earlier statement that 'there is not a female character in [any of Marlowe's] plays whom we remember with much interest.'[114] The very subject of the tragedy seemed to arouse thinly veiled expressions of homophobia: Hawkins, the biographer of Kean, spoke of 'the disgust . . . provoked by [Edward's] irresolution and effeminacy,' while an anonymous reviewer of Bullen's edition of Marlowe wrote in 1885 that 'as the chief character is one that we do not like to think of or know about, and there is not one noble scene or person in the play, it could not be great, nor could it hold a good place in our liking or our memory.'[115]

Serious analysis of *Edward II* as a play (as opposed to desultory comments on its poetry, characters, subject matter, and individual scenes) came only with the twentieth century. Even in our own era, however, the drama continues to generate controversy so that true consensus as to the nature and value of Marlowe's achievement remains elusive. Two interrelated problems seem to lie at the root of this disagreement. The first and older of the two questions is whether *Edward II* is dominantly a history play or a tragedy, that is, whether its primary focus is the ill fortune of a nation ruled by a weak and irresponsible monarch (who is contrasted at least by implication with both his heroic precedessor and successor), or whether the emphasis falls on the tragic predicament and personal suffering of a man who happens to be king, on the plight of a fallible human being trapped in a conflict between the satisfaction of his private desires and the constraints of his inherited role.

The second question, which has only been acknowledged in recent decades and discussed with candour more recently still, concerns Marlowe's attitude toward homosexual love—condemnatory, sympathetic, or some amalgam of the two—particularly when the objects of that love are royal minions whose special status places them at the heart of a king's emotional life, thereby allowing them to promulgate and administer policies ruinous to the welfare of the commonwealth. Marlowe's drama is clearly about the complex encounter between sexual passion and politics and (as frequently in the dramatist's work) about the clash of stubborn individual wills with the intensity of unfulfilled desire, dramatized now in a context of state where public stability and order as well as private happiness are at stake. *Edward II* is unique in English Renaissance drama for its non-satiric and humane portrayal of explicit homoerotic emotion. Its purely literary merits aside, therefore, the play becomes an important document in attempts to define Elizabethan attitudes toward sexuality, and more particularly (since Marlowe's dramas reflect the personality of their author in a way foreign, let us say, to the 'negative capability' of Shakespeare), in the assessment of the dramatist's own inner compulsions and sexual proclivities. For however wary we may be of reading authorial subjectivities into plays (normally the most objective of genres), it is surely more than fortuitous that homosexual themes and situtations also surface noticeably in *Dido*, *The Massacre at Paris*, and *Hero and Leander*, as well as more subtly and indirectly in *Tamburlaine* and *Doctor Faustus*;[116] nor should we forget Symonds's remark, quoted above, on Marlowe's inability—or disinclination—to portray women with much sympathy or depth. In the circumstances, therefore, *Edward II* becomes more than usually significant as a piece of evidence in the ongoing study of Marlowe's perennially discussed but puzzlingly obscure psyche.

We may take up the debate about kind first. In publishing his important edition of 1914, Briggs presented *Edward II* as the first drama to shape and integrate chronicle materials successfully for the stage and therefore as a progenitor of Shakespeare's work in the historical form. For Briggs Marlowe's work established the chronicle play as a genre; but he wrote before Alexander, Charlton–Waller, Rossiter, F. P. Wilson, Brooks, and others were fatally to undercut this position by showing that the *Henry VI* plays antedated Marlowe's drama. In any case it was Tillyard's influential book on the Shakespearean cycle in 1944 that set the prevailing style for definitions of the history play by stressing a long-range providential design in national affairs and by emphasizing conservative social and political concepts rooted in the principles of divine right and the great chain of being—criteria that *Edward II* clearly fails to satisfy. Tillyard argues that although *Edward II* 'does contain political reflection' on the themes of royal legitimacy and the punishment of usurpation, 'What animates the play is . . . Edward's personal obsession, his peculiar psychology, the humour and finally the great pathos of his situation. Marlowe shows no sense of national responsibility: he merely attaches two current political orthodoxies to a play concerned nominally but not essentially with historical matter.'[117]

Following Tillyard, most commentators in the 1950s, 1960s, and 1970s emphasized the private as opposed to the public side of the play. Clifford Leech says, for instance, that Marlowe 'cared only for what happened to the individual' and 'was interested in Edward, not as embodying a suffering England, but as a man . . . who had and lost power.' In a similar vein J. C. Maxwell writes that the 'historical process . . . has little interest for Marlowe,' who finds the task of 'selecting from the chronicle material . . . burdensome'; and he adds that the traditionally political 'problem of the king and his "favourites" . . . assumes a disproportionate and independent psychological interest.' For J. B. Steane, Marlowe's characters 'cast no shadows: the self is all there is,' 'England and the realm [being] sometimes mentioned, but . . . not emotionally or dramatically involved.' Wilbur Sanders, one of the harshest critics of *Edward II*, complains of the 'singular absence of any guiding and shaping intelligence behind the presentation of the historical material,' reproving Marlowe for his 'consistent subjugation of the political and the public to a very narrowly conceived pattern of personal conflict.' More sympathetically, Glynne Wickham and Wolfgang Clemen also comment on the dominance of personal over political elements in *Edward II*. The first terms it 'the true tragedy' in contrast to *Richard II*, 'the Chronicle play with tragic consequences'; the second also believes that Marlowe, unlike Shakespeare, was more interested in 'the finality' and 'brutal horror' of Edward's fate than in 'the "problem" posed by the murder of an anointed king.'[118]

Without denying Marlowe's stress on personal suffering and individualized character, however, several critics have continued to insist on the political implications of any play taken from the chronicle accounts of a failed reign and finally to reject an oversimple dichotomy between historical tragedy and the history play. As early as 1946 Paul H. Kocher drew attention to Holinshed's statement that the 'mischeefes' of King Edward's time 'happened not onlie to [the monarch himself], but also to the whole state of the realme,' because the king 'wanted iudgement and prudent discretion to make choise of sage and discreet councellors, receiuing those into his fauour, that abused the same to their priuate gaine and aduantage, not respecting the aduancement of the common-wealth . . . in so-much that by their couetous rapine, spoile, and immoderate ambition, the hearts of the common people & nobilitie were quite estranged from the dutifull loue and obedience which they ought to haue shewed to their souereigne . . .' (p. 342). As Kocher points out, Marlowe takes this formulation seriously, but he alters its emphasis significantly by modifying Holinshed's moralistic contrast between the mainly patriotic barons (before they rebel) and the wholly parasitic and manipulative Gaveston, so as to make the causes of national ruin appear more ambiguous and complex.

Marlowe divides and balances our sympathies so as to achieve a less conventional but more realistic depiction of political struggle. By showing that the favourites harbour sincere feelings for Edward, the dramatist is kinder to them than Holinshed; and he also complicates our reaction to Isabella by making her paradoxically both more of a victim of her husband's cruelty and more of an adulterous hypocrite and traitor than she is in the source. While Edward's weakness as a ruler acquires a psychological dimension absent from the chronicle, Marlowe's king nevertheless becomes more despotic and absolutist in his futile attempts to retain control. In addition the dramatist's unhistorical emphasis on Gaveston's low birth and his having Edward appeal to Elizabethan anti-Catholic prejudice (although more medieval religious attitudes also get into the play) introduce yet further complexities of political reponse. There is an undertow of democratic approval in hearing a commoner retort fearlessly to the voices of aristocratic insolence; and Edward defends Gaveston against baronial snobbery: 'Were he a peasant, being my minion, / I'll make the proudest of you stoop to him' (I.iv.30–31). Nor is it easy to side enthusiastically with peers (some of whose complaints are plainly justified), when to do so means also supporting prelates who take their authority from Rome (cf. I.iv.51–62) and who threaten to excommunicate Edward and give his subjects leave to rebel (as Pius V in Marlowe's lifetime had already done to Elizabeth I). Although spectators in Marlowe's audience would probably have been shocked by the loutish mauling of the Bishop of Coventry, they could also have responded with something like applause to Edward's later outburst after having been hard-pressed by Canterbury (unhistorically 'legate of the Pope'): 'Why should a king be subject to a priest?' (I.iv.96). And as David Bevington notices, we also get eruptions of a virulently anti-French animus (presumably ever popular with Elizabethan audiences) expressed on both sides of the conflict between Edward and his peers: Mortimer speaks of Gaveston as 'That sly inveigling Frenchman' (I.ii.57) while Edward calls the queen 'French strumpet' (I.iv.145). Clear lines of political sympathy and alienation are thus further blurred, for there is enough petty nastiness and vindictive carping to disfigure all the principals.[119]

Despite his use of emblematic figures such as the Mower and Lightborn (whom critics have often associated with the medieval Vice), Marlowe generally eschews the semi-allegorical, morality-play approach to the dramatization of history with its easily defined exemplars of good and evil. Even atrocity tends to be presented without overt moralizing in a mode of quasi-documentary detachment. Speaking of Edward's terrible death, for instance, Leech underscores the dramatist's unblinking realism: 'He was a man who speculated on, and brought alive to his mind, the furthest reaches of human power and human suffering and humiliation. These things, he saw, men could do and had done, could suffer and had suffered, and his wondering mind gave them dramatic shape.'[120]

As Kocher rightly observes, however, *Edward II* does enforce truths of state that any Renaissance student of government would readily endorse—namely that 'Power is dangerous' because 'only power can retain power,' and that a sovereign who would keep his throne 'must observe justice' and possess 'the elementary awareness that the nobles and the commons are political forces of prime importance.' As for implied limitations on royal power, there is some truth in Michel Poirier's idea that the play explores a tension between different traditions of kingship—that *Edward II* may be viewed as 'the story of a feudal monarch who attempts to govern as an absolute monarch and fails.' It should be noted, however, that the grounds of such attempted absolutism in Marlowe's thinking are apparently more humanist and secular (as in the case of the Medici autocrats) than divinely sanctioned or sacramental (as in the case of the Tudors).[121] James Voss indeed has analyzed the play as a dramatization of a many-sided conflict between 'opposing ways of life' represented initially by the values to which Edward and Gaveston on the one side and the barons on the other subscribe, a working out of fundamentally hostile but interlocking sociopolitical forces involving 'transformation in the distribution of state power and prestige, the weakening of the Church, the devaluation of the principle of birth, the desire for freedom from traditional restraints [in both monarchy and peerage], the difficulty of orienting oneself in a changing world, the omnipresence of political intrigue and deceptive forms of behavior, the destruction of traditional values, the absence of adequate models for comprehending reality—all phenomena more or less typical of [Marlowe's] age' which the dramatist skilfully integrates 'into a meaningful vision of history.'[122]

Irving Ribner, who approaches the question of genre with much good sense, also regards *Edward II* as essentially a chronicle play. He writes that although 'Marlowe is deeply concerned with the personal tragedy of Edward as a man' as well as with 'the parallel tragedy of Mortimer' with its more conventional *de casibus* orientation, 'it is impossible to separate [the major] characters from their historical roles. . . . Suffering humanity in this play is a suffering English king, with the ends of tragedy and those of history entirely fused, for Edward's sins are sins of government, the crisis he faces is a political one, and his disaster is not merely death but the loss of his crown and the ruin of his kingdom by civil war.'[123] Ribner shrewdly notes the complementary relationship between Edward and Mortimer in Marlowe's design, the political weaknesses of the one being mirrored in the political strength of the other; he also points out that such humane virtues as Edward may acquire in defeat are 'set off by Mortimer's corresponding loss' of public virtue as a treacherous regicide. One pessimistic and (in Christian terms) unorthodox implication of Marlowe's political vision, tempered at the end perhaps by our expectations for young Edward III, is that, in the case of princes, the successful wielding of power comports ill with generous feelings for others, whether expressed in romantic love or friendship. And yet 'the decline of Mortimer,' to quote Ribner again, illustrates also that 'ruthless self-sufficiency' is finally no more to be desired in the character of a ruler than the emotional dependency and wilful incompetence of Edward. The king's lack of Machiavellian *virtù* and Mortimer's overreaching embodiment of it lead equally to catastrophe. And in the absence of providence or even of the human acknowledgement of moral failing, we are left (despite the punishments for insurrection and treason) with a grim fatalism as regards the national destiny. In Ribner's terms, Marlowe 'come[s] to see the moving spirits of history not as prototypes of an impossible ideal, but as men who are themselves moulded by the pressure of events, who develop and change.'

Ribner agrees with Kocher, however, that, following Holinshed, Marlowe nevertheless embeds the lesson of prudent political relations in his dramatization of Edward II's fall. Kings must inspire trust and respect in their nobles (in a brief moment of reconciliation Isabel proclaims didactically, 'Now is the King of England rich and strong, / Having the love of his renownèd peers' [1.iv.365–366]). Kings must also *wish* to rule for the benefit and well ordering of their realms. Edward has no true interest in good government, caring chiefly for the power of the crown as a means to gratify private emotional needs, and however absolute in theory he may believe himself to be, is as ready to share this power with his lover (1.i.160–169) as he is reluctant to surrender it to enemies (v.i.59–74). Ribner's conclusion, then, has considerable merit: in this tragedy 'Marlowe accomplishes the political purposes of the Elizabethan historian, for while the play embodies no assurance that any human king can survive in an absolute state, the downfall of Edward is nevertheless explained in terms of his violation of political principles.'[124]

According to Levin, Marlowe's 'unique contribution' in *Edward II* 'was to bring the chronicle within the perspective of tragedy, to adapt the most public of forms to the most private of emotions' (p. 88). Douglas Cole develops and extends this insight by arguing that in destroying himself through his inordinate passion for corrupting favourites together with the self-absorption and isolation that these attachments bring, Edward also exposes both his family (through the estrangement of his wife and brother) and his country (through the alienation of his barons) to calamity. And Cole goes on to suggest that in Marlowe's tragic king the intensity of suffering has as much to do with the nature of the monarchical role as with the particular character flaws and sensibility of the man. For although there is no specific stress on the doctrine of divine right, the play does underline the poignancy of royal desecration in such lines as the abbot's 'My heart with pity earns to see this sight; / A king to bear these words and proud commands!' (IV.vii.70–71), in Kent's 'O, miserable is that commonweal, where lords / Keep courts and kings are locked in prison!' (v.iii.63–64), and in Edward's own 'They give me bread and water, being a king' (v.v.61). Marlowe capitalizes brilliantly on the dramatic ironies created by the huge gap between the inherent majesty of the crown and the feeble incapacity of its wearer, 'in the contrast between Edward's utter disregard of the meaning of kingship before his defeat, and the intolerable anxiety he experiences afterwards *because* of his kingship':

> What once could not engage his concern now cannot be forgotten, and again it is the sense of loss that provokes the sufferer's most grievous pain. Too late Edward becomes fully aware of what he was meant to be, and realization of the irreparable loss of his original status plunges him into a hell of grief. His inward hell is appropriately accompanied by an outward hell—the foul lake of sewage in which he is imprisoned becomes his Cocytus; the drumming of Matrevis and Gurney, and the fiery spit of Lightborn, become the infernal instruments of torture wielded by his tormentors.
>
> It is in part this hellish quality of his psychological and physical situation that makes Edward's suffering more akin to the suffering of Faustus than to that of any other Marlovian figure. . . . It is Edward's tragedy to be less than he was intended to be, rather than to fall in the attempt to be more than he could be. It is Edward's suffering to look back in agony at the lost chance, to yearn for the crown that he did not grace and can no longer bear. His hell is the hideous present tormented by the memory of the past. . . .[125]

Not surprisingly, critics who acknowledge the importance of homoeroticism in the tragedy have tended to divide between those

who regard Marlowe as fundamentally a moral and social conservative, an upholder of official orthodoxies, and those who regard him
as a politico-sexual subversive—between those who see Edward's
sexuality as a sin to be punished (or at least a weakness to be
deplored) and those who read the drama as a daring (though necessarily subterranean) contestation of homophobic repression and
barbarity. In an uncharacteristically early expression of sympathy for
Edward's sexual nature as the dramatist portrays him, Una Ellis-
Fermor in 1927 remarked the king's 'power of inspiring undying
affection in the men who come within the circle of his intimacy';
in consequence she argued that Marlowe converted what many
historians regarded 'as perversion' into 'a not unbeautiful love-story'
set 'against a dark background of storm and danger.' The intensity
of critical resistance to such a notion may partly be gauged by the
fact that Leonora Leet Brodwin's development *in extenso* of the
concept of romantic love in *Edward II* did not appear until some
three and a half decades after Ellis-Fermor's book.[126] To be sure,
as early as 1931, Mario Praz had related Marlowe's 'thirst for impossible things' to his presumed homosexuality—what Praz was
pleased to call his 'Ganymede complex'; and in 1946 William Empson
had already underscored the centrality of sexual deviance to Marlowe's play by noting in a review of Kocher's book that 'The obscene
torture' by which Edward is murdered constitutes 'an appalling
parody of the homosexual act.' He went on to observe significantly
that the dramatist, who often catered to the sadistic prejudices of his
public, would not necessarily have 'agreed with his audience that the
punishment was deserved.' In Empson's opinion, it was Marlowe's
way as a dramatist to erect 'absolutely opposed ideals' (the majesty of
divine judgement and the attraction of blasphemy, for instance, in
the case of *Doctor Faustus*)—presenting the 'unmentionable sin for
which the punishment was death' and for which the playwright
himself 'stood boastfully and defiantly in peril' of his life as both
a violation of acceptable order and a modish form of sceptical
irreverence and rebellion against authority.[127]

Sympathy for Edward's suffering notwithstanding, moralistic
condemnation of his 'abnormality' has continued to find voices. Bent
Sunesen, who interprets Gaveston's voluptuous evocation of the
Actaeon myth (1.i.60–69) as a kind of dumb show prefiguring the
sexual trespass and punishment of the king, refers to 'the unnatural
extravagance of Edward's infatuation' (p. 244), to his 'abdication of
manliness' (p. 245), and regards the avenging barons (the 'yelping

hounds' who hunt Actaeon to his death) as 'a necessary corrective of sin,' however 'hateful' (p. 246). Commenting on the explicit but theologically unsurprising cruelty of Edward's death, Merchant calls attention to the 'well-established tradition' in medieval literature and iconography of visualizing 'the tortures of the damned,' instancing Dante's 'very precise images of appropriate suffering' (p. xxi). Charles G. Masinton moralizes Edward's tragedy as a second fall: Gaveston, 'puffed up with pride,' is 'a snake in the bosom' of his royal patron, a 'betrayer of his friend' who becomes 'the Serpent in the Garden' and 'the living symbol of Edward's corruption as a homosexual'; exemplifying 'human decadence,' the relationship is no more than a 'travesty of love and friendship.' The interpretation of W. L. Godshalk follows similar lines. Godshalk regards the erotic bonding of Isabella and Mortimer and of Edward and Gaveston, both liaisons being 'immoral, adulterous, and unnatural,' as thematically parallel. Moreover 'Edward's homosexuality . . . reflects the "unnatural" state of the realm,' becoming 'a symbol of a more total inversion.'[128]

Adopting a more psychoanalytical approach, Constance Brown Kuriyama (who was strongly influenced by Irving Bieber's now obsolete concept of homosexuality as pathology) treats the character of Edward II as a study in 'sexual and emotional infantilism,' as the portrait of an essentially 'feminine' and 'passive' human being whose appalling punishment consummates a pattern of the *lex talionis*, the thrust and counterthrust of power politics being echoed in the numerous rhetorical and structural antitheses that mark the play's style and craftsmanship. Kuriyama also thinks that the mixture of condemnation and sympathy we are invited to feel for Edward, 'a protagonist who is apparently an incarnation and epitome of Marlowe's own "vices" and "weaknessess",' represents the dramatist's 'private attack on [his] own rigid superego, and on the harsh paternal authority reflected in it . . .'; for her, therefore, the drama becomes Marlowe's oblique strategy for working out interior conflicts between personal guilt and self-hatred on the one hand and the need for understanding and forgiveness on the other.[129] More enlightened critics who moralize Edward's sexual obsession as the triumph of lust over responsibility or disorderly passion over reason nevertheless reject the notion of talion (or like-for-like) punishment so judgementally insisted upon by Kuriyama. Judith Weil, for instance, argues that since Edward acquires a heightened awareness of his own royal identity in the course of suffering, Lightborn ironically 'punishes him by methods exactly appropriate to the man he was, but is no longer' so that the tragedy 'thoroughly transvalues the narrow, barbaric legalism which informs the old Actaeon story.' Stephen Greenblatt similarly turns the conventional moralistic reading on its head: 'in *Edward II* Marlowe uses the emblematic method of admonitory drama, but uses it to such devastating effect that the audience recoils from it in disgust.' The king's grisly execution may be 'iconographically "appropriate," but this very appropriateness can only be established *at the expense of* every complex, sympathetic human feeling evoked by the play.'[130]

On the left or revolutionary side of the sexual debate, commentary (most of it fairly recent) has stemmed from the new interest in the 'cultural poetics' of Renaissance literature and what writers see as the modalities of sociopolitical power struggle in Marlowe's age. More narrowly, it has tended to become involved with the effort to historicize ideologies of gender and sexual orientation that grow out of the theoretical concerns of feminist and gay–lesbian studies. At the heart of this discussion has been the work of Alan Bray whose ground-breaking book, *Homosexuality in Renaissance England* (London, 1982), although it contains no analysis of Marlowe's tragedy, advances what has all but become the new orthodoxy in considerations of same-sex eroticism—namely that homosexual identity (the adjective, after all, is a late nineteenth-century coinage) is a social construct contingent upon particular historical pressures and conditions rather than a constant of human nature; that what today we regard as a distinct type of gay individual, supported by a definable subculture of shared appetites and desires, would be unrecognizable to sixteenth-century dramatists and audiences, who regarded buggery not as a specialized temptation but as an expression of lust theoretically dangerous to all men; and that physical love-making between males, although officially demonized as a species of satanism and legally punishable by death, was in practice often ignored or went unprosecuted, not out of tolerance in the modern sense but out of a reluctance to confront or fully acknowledge the unspeakable horror of sodomy. It might be objected that such a position takes insufficient cognizance of recent psycho-biological researches, which suggest that sexual orientation, at least in part, may be genetically determined and therefore transhistorical. But several analysts emerging out of the gay rights movement nevertheless make an interesting case for the Marlowe of *Edward II* as a dramatist who subtly ironizes his subject matter, manipulating audience responses in such as way as to subvert the repressiveness of Elizabethan sexual dogma. And a few try to show that the play implicitly critiques the tyrannical program of officialdom which, by entangling sexual deviation in a larger web of 'unnatural' or criminal enormities such as blasphemy, heresy, atheism, papistry, and treason, legitimizes hatred and violence against the unacceptable 'other' and works upon the deviant elements of society so as to make them co-operate unconsciously in their own subjection.

Purvis Boyette was among the first to advance the interpretation of Marlowe's king as a martyr to sexual and emotional individualism. Noting the dramatist's refusal explicitly to diabolize Edward's sexual nature (Mortimer Senior gives an honorific list of classical precedents for homosexual attachments at I.iv.390–396), Boyette, without defending the king's incompetence or the exploitative selfishness of his favourites, argues that Marlowe presents the anal ravishment in a way that makes his protagonist 'the archetypal Victim, a scapegoat for the personal, cultural and social forces that have repudiated his essential humanity, his decline into flesh'; Marlowe's 'point is to deplore the violence necessary in political life—coercion, intrigue, wars—which finds its image in the sadistic rape by the assassin.' The murder scene thus 'generates a catharsis linking sexual orgasm and violence as they had never before been linked on the English stage,' enabling Marlowe to 'shatter a sexual taboo as he makes his audience party to the play's violence' and to strike 'a blow against the foundations of the status quo, by making them seem ugly.' The same idea is touched upon by Karen Cunningham, who connects the politically constructed theatricality of public executions in Renaissance England with Marlowe's dramatization of savage punishments: the dramatist 'makes absurd the notion of creating morality by killing subjects and debasing bodies.'[131] Ronald Huebert probes the sexual psychology of the title character by exploring 'Marlowe's characteristic fusion of defiance and desire.' Given society's tyrannical intolerance but also the hedging and evasion permitted to those of privilege, the sexual invert, Huebert believes, would necessarily 'think of himself as an outlaw, always living in defiance of the sacred and secular code'; and for such a man, desire 'would be by its very nature an act of defiance.' Danger, in others words, would enhance erotic excitement. Huebert sees Edward as the single-minded lover who is blindly and wilfully ready to ruin himself for the satisfaction

of his deepest need but who in the process of sharing his kingdom
with unworthy subordinates challenges the social and moral authority he is theoretically called upon to represent.[132]

Among the most balanced and astute contributions to our understanding of sexual politics in *Edward II* are discussions of the play
by Claude J. Summers and Bruce R. Smith. Both emphasize the
ambivalent response that Marlowe's dramatization of homoeroticism
is designed to evoke. Summers argues that the dramatist depicts 'a
solipsistic universe' in which the clash of egos, class struggle against
a background of hierarchical fluidity, an unstable or protean concept
of identity, and the breakdown of conventional values all conduce to
the questioning of 'social, political, and familial relationships':

> While Marlowe refuses to condemn homosexuality, he complicates the
> relationships of Edward and his lovers, presenting them ambiguously
> rather than merely sympathetically. The king's willful attachment to his
> lovers clearly accounts for his failure as a king and culminates in his grue-
> some murder, making him finally a martyr to his passion. But Edward's
> martyrdom encompasses more than his victimization as a lover or even his
> failure as a king. . . . In *Edward II*'s world of egotism and opportunism,
> value finally inheres only in self-realization, a process complicated by the
> tyranny of circumstance and the conflicts of identity. In the play, charac-
> ters are torn not merely between the private and public roles that they are
> called upon to play, but by a fundamental confusion of their social and real
> [i.e., psychic] identities. And it is in this insight that sex and politics
> intersect, for the king's tragedy is neither simply personal nor yet provi-
> dential. Ultimately, it is a tragedy of existential loneliness, in which the
> king's conflicting identities are reconciled only in his brutal murder.[133]

Smith analyzes the play in terms of how Marlowe, by playing
the interrelated problems of gender, social class, and individual
autonomy off against each other, complicates and ironizes the traditional relationship of master and minion, much satirized in the
sixteenth century and explicitly ascribed to Edward and Gaveston by
the contemptuous barons, who use the latter term pejoratively (cf.
1.i.132 and note in the Commentary). Although superficially Edward
and Gaveston might seem to fit the stereotyped roles of master and
minion 'with all the disparities in power that those roles imply'
(king versus commoner, dominant versus passive partner, masculine
versus feminine sensibility, sexual aggressor versus sexual receptor,
man versus boy), Marlowe meaningfully cuts athwart the expected
pattern. Gaveston after all is a grown man rather than the androgy-
nous adolescent or 'Ganymede' (I.iv.180) of the literary model—a

figure of whom Marlowe nevertheless keeps us aware through such images as the 'lovely boy in Dian's shape' (I.i.60) that the favourite envisions as a titillating element of his erotic theatre, and the beautiful lad Hylas (I.i.143) to whom Edward likens Gaveston when he casts himself rhetorically as the grief-stricken Hercules. Gaveston is also portrayed as an ambitious climber who flamboyantly exerts control over the king, sharing both his wealth and his authority, rather than a mere erotic playmate kept for idle diversion. Indeed Marlowe tends to invert the traditional master–minion hierarchy by making Edward childlike and emotionally dependent on his social inferior, clearly developing Holinshed's description of Gaveston as a 'a goodly gentleman and a stout, [who] would not once yeeld an inch' to his enemies (p. 319). Moreover the king's sexual passivity (Edward plays Hero to Gaveston's Leander in the latter's opening soliloquy) is grotesquely emblematized in his death by reaming, which reduces Edward to the catamite, the minion overmastered and penetrated by someone symbolically above him in the scale of political power (in this case Mortimer acting through his agent Lightborn). Since low birth rather than sexuality is felt to constitute Gaveston's most serious threat to privilege or status, and since on the other side the romantic feeling inherent in Edward's need for male bonding is felt to transcend conventional distinctions of blood (as in romances where love often rises above humble station to offer a 'fantasy-world of sexual freedom'), Marlowe cross-relates gender, sex roles, and social rank in *Edward II* to give us 'an eroticization of class difference.' Instead of accepting received didactic categories, therefore, 'we are allowed to see all sides of the situation: Gaveston's calculations, Edward's devotion, the lords' distress, England's needs as a kingdom.' Nevertheless, with the rise of Edward III and the punishment of the usurpers (which of course involves the violent termination of the other sexually irregular coupling in the plot), Marlowe returns us seemingly 'to principles of social order and sexual orthodoxy.' But the question of what is finally 'natural' and 'unnatural' (the latter word is applied in different contexts to the irresponsibility of Edward, to the rebellion of the nobles, and to the cruelty of Isabella) remains obscure; for what may be *sexually natural* for Edward causes behaviour that is *politically unnatural* for a monarch. And as Smith puts it, 'The straightforward world of rewards and punishments that Edward III sets up in the play's last scene can seem substantial only to someone who does not know the devious ways of erotic desire.' If, then, Marlowe portrays his protagonist as both the 'passion-crazed author of his own doom' and the 'victim of evil manipulators,' the play ends by showing us the tragic 'conflict, not of right against wrong, but of two irreconcilable rights against each other.' Marlowe's embedded dialectic between emotional self-fulfilment and patriotic duty, between identity as a lover and identity as a king, erects an impasse that only death can remove.[134]

The central truth about *Edward II* on which critics of whatever kidney can agree is the profound pessimism of its vision. As one critic phrases it, 'The characters finger their way along the edges of a metaphysical darkness, and collide in the confusion of their attitudes . . . .'[135] Some commentators, remembering the high esteem in which Elizabethans held the warrior king Edward III, interpret Marlowe's ending as a hesitant or perfunctory return to some measure of moral and political stability; others, emphasizing the visual symbolism of the funeral cortège with the severed head of Mortimer (at least partly an icon of private revenge) and the sense of fragile authority projected by a child king, take an even gloomier view of the concluding scene. For them the final judgements represent one further turn of Fortune's wheel—yet another shift in the continuing instability of power.[136] But as Clifford Leech truly remarks, Marlowe illustrates 'no theory . . . , no warning or program for reform, no overt affirmation of a faith in man' but only the brutal connections between suffering and power with their oblique suggestion that if any human being, let alone a king, can undergo such extreme degradation, man, for all his weakness, folly, and vulnerability, 'has much to fall from.'[137] Long ago M. M. Mahood perceived a pattern of erosion in Marlowe's plays from a humanistic celebration of energy and pride in life to its opposite—'from the visualising of death as the only unconquerable enemy [in the character of Tamburlaine] to the welcoming of it as a tardy friend' in the agony of Edward II: 'Come, death, and with thy fingers close my eyes, / Or, if I live, let me forget myself' (V.i.110–111).[138] In *Edward II* Marlowe dramatizes the link between sexuality and self-destruction without ever descending to self-pity, special pleading, or conventional sexual moralizing. We simply feel that the spacious kingdom which Edward inherits, in which he is doomed and in which he dooms himself, contracts spiritually—indeed humanly—to the wretched dark cell that seems to have awaited him from the outset. Sexual love and the inevitability of destruction are shown finally to be inseparably coupled. Murder in the symbolic form of sodomitic rape represents only the most extreme form of ruthlessness and ego assertion in a play that specializes in humiliation, tyranny, and victimization—forces always latent in Marlowe's portrayal of the sexual urge. But there is something in Edward that invites the fiery spit even as he fears it, and the monarch's conduct of his own affairs, as of his kingdom, is rooted in a curious intermingling of wilful assertion and abject dependency.

7 STAGE HISTORY

Edward II appears to have been a popular play when it was first performed, perhaps as early as 1591–93, for Q tells us that it was 'sundrie times' acted by Pembroke's Men in London and, as has already been suggested, may have been played in the provinces as well. Unfortunately we do not know at what theatre the play was mounted nor who played the title role, although it is doubtful that it was Edward Alleyn, Tamburlaine, Barabas, and Faustus being his only documentable roles in Marlowe's plays. It may have been presented at court.[139] Peele's poem *The Honour of the Garter* (1593) gives an account of Edward's murder (ll. 220–224) that seems to reflect the impact of Marlowe's dramatization; Drayton's *Piers Gaveston* (1593) and *Mortimeriados* (1596) as well as Jonson's unfinished tragedy, *The Fall of Mortimer* (1595–1637), might likewise be taken to indicate the popularity of a subject to which Marlowe had lent theatrical excitement. The printing of three quartos after the first (in 1598, 1612, and 1622) suggests continued interest in the play, an inference that is borne out by the statement in Q4 that it was revived at the Red Bull by Queen Anne's Servants, apparently at some point between 1609 and 1619.[140] After this, however, the tragedy disappears entirely from theatrical history until the early twentieth century. The 1818 texts of both James Broughton and William Oxberry (the latter a well-known actor and theatre manager) contain features that suggest stage performance; but no record of an early nineteenth-century revival survives. The closest we come is Edmund Kean's largely unsuccessful revival of *The Jew of Malta* at Drury Lane in 1818 in a text extensively altered to incorporate many borrowings from *Edward II*; Lightborn's catalogue of Italinate atrocities, for instance, was transferred to Ithamore, and in an effort to lend greater prominence to the love interest between Mathias and Abigail and to expand the Mathias–Lodowick rivalry, the reviser (Samson Penley) drew heavily upon the more emotional speeches of Edward, Gaveston, and Isabella.[141] Perhaps a staging of *Edward II* was contemplated during this period but rejected because of the unacceptability of the openly homosexual theme.

When Marlowe's tragedy finally reappeared on the boards, academic interest not surprisingly provided the impetus. In 1903 William Poel directed a pioneering production at the New Theatre, Oxford, on behalf of the University Extension Delegacy; sponsored by the Elizabethan Stage Society, it featured the young Harley Granville Barker in the title role. An anonymous reviewer for the London *Times* (11 August 1903), noting that the play had not been seen for nearly three hundred years, regarded Barker's efforts as 'scholarly and intelligent' but thought the actor, eliminating much of the majesty from Edward's fall, emphasized the pathetic at the expense of the tragic; and he wrote also that Madge Flynn presented Isabella throughout as 'lighthearted and shallow, incapable of any genuine feeling,' while Shakespeare Stewart, the Gaveston of the production, conceived his character 'too much in the vein of light comedy' (p. 8).[142] A somewhat more sympathetic commentator in the *Morning Post* (11 August 1903) praised Barker's characterization in the title role as a 'very subtle study in insolence, cowardice, and depravity.'[143] Robert Speaight reports that 'The text was treated with reasonable respect, although the current conventions of propriety robbed Gaveston of the last ten lines of his great speech: "I must have wanton poets, pleasant wits." '[144] Obviously the homosexuality had to be heavily muted and the horrors of the murder scene considerably softened—'rightly curtailed,' to quote the *Times* critic (p. 8). The political emphasis of Marlowe's original seems also to have been subdued, Mortimer's villainy being considerably mitigated.[145] A third newspaper reviewer remarked that in 'his careful study' Barker did 'not so much show physical suffering itself as the effect which intense physical suffering often produces on the mind.'[146] Poel chose him for the role because of his earlier success in the part of Richard II (also directed by Poel), but most critics seem to have compared his Marlovian performance unfavourably to his Shakespearean one. George Bernard Shaw went so far as to write to the actor that he would have 'advised [him] strongly not to wipe out Richard II by playing' *Edward II*, which has 'words & a turn for their music, but nothing to say': 'There is nothing in it—no possibility of success.'[147] Shaw's dismissive words, although characteristically extreme, show the resistance to Marlowe's tragedy as a stage vehicle that prevailed in the early decades of the century and that Poel, even with so talented a performer, could only partly overcome.

Two years later the distinguished actor-manager Frank Benson both directed and played the leading role in a radically abridged production of *Edward II* at Stratford-upon-Avon. According to the *Leamington Spa Courier* (5 May 1905) this fully professional staging, acted by Benson's Shakespearean Company, shrank the five acts of the original to a four-act play of only twelve scenes. It also sanitized Marlowe. The same reviewer noted approvingly that 'The death scene, revolting as we know it to have been in detail, was . . . robbed of its horrors,' but even so, the dripping head of Mortimer (carried in a basket) apparently upset the women in the audience.[148] Again the homoeroticism was suppressed: 'favourite,' 'foreigner,' and 'Frenchman' were the only terms applied to Gaveston, who was treated by 'the headstrong monarch' in a way that one reviewer considered 'generous and kingly' despite the political blindness entailed.[149] Critics also seem to have had difficulty with the mixed nature of Isabella's character even though Gertrude Scott, who played the role, contrived (in obvious violation of Marlowe's text) 'to show that [the queen] did not connive at her husband's death.'[150] Viewers enjoyed the poetry of the play and its delivery by Benson and his cohorts, praising the production for its seriousness and intelligence. But again the comparison of Marlowe's play to Shakespeare's *Richard II* proved damaging: the reviewer for the *Manchester Guardian* (29 April 1905) commended Benson's 'occasional moments of introspection' but felt there was nothing in the portrayal 'that quite took one's breath away, as there was in several passages of his [earlier] Richard.' Benson, he opined, did not so much 'revive' *Edward II* as enable 'collectors' to 'remember . . . it with gratitude.'[151] Marlowe's deliberate ambiguities of characterization continued to make stage presentation difficult for both actors and audiences while the politico-sexual implications of the play together with its uncompromising brutality would present almost insuperable problems to most middle-class and morally conservative sensibilities for many years to come.

The students of Birkbeck College at the University of London revived *Edward II* in December 1920;[152] then the Phoenix Society followed with a version of their own on 18–19 November 1923 at the Regent Theatre, London, directed by Allan Wade. In this latter the long-established theatre critic James Agate praised Duncan Yarrow (despite his being handicapped by severe laryngitis) for his portrayal of the king, agreeing with Lamb and Swinburne that Marlowe's play, at least in the treatment of deposition, compares favourably with Shakespeare's. Gwen Ffrangcon-Davies as the queen was singled

out for her beautiful verse-speaking, and the actors who played
the younger Mortimer and Warwick (Edmund Willard and Victor
Lewisohn respectively) were thought particularly effective. Ernest
Thesiger acted Gaveston as a foppish intellectual rather than as
an empty vessel of male charm.[153] Nevertheless, Ralph Wright,
reviewing for the *New Statesman* (24 November 1923), felt that the
production was a failure—mainly because the elocution (apart from
that of the Isabella) 'was on a far lower level than usual,' because the
actors did not sufficiently meet the inherent structural and charac-
terological challenges of the play, and because the Gaveston was
acted 'as if he were an affected and disreputable old lady' with *fin de
siècle* overtones of 'the *Yellow Book*' (p. 211). Clearly the production
still had to contend with widespread resistance to the representation
of a homosexual relationship on the public stage.

Meanwhile interest in *Edward II* had been rekindled on the continent. In 1922 Karel Hilar directed a 'highly modernistic performance at Prague . . . with stage sets designed by B. Feurstein.'[154]
Karl-Heinz Martin produced an arrangement of Marlowe's text in
his own German translation at Heinrich George's Berlin Schauspieler-
theater on 2 November 1923.[155] It is possible that this production
influenced Bertolt Brecht whose *Leben Eduards des Zweiten von
England (Nach Marlowe)* opened the next year at the Kammerspiel
in Munich on 19 March 1924 and was played subsequently in Berlin,
Hamburg, and Leipzig.[156] Brecht's play (a radical rewriting and
reconceptualization of Marlowe's original undertaken in collaboration
with Lion Feuchtwanger) relies partly on Alfred Walter Heymel's
German translation of the sixteenth-century tragedy (1912) but with
the intention of producing 'something like a caricature of Marlowe's
work.'[157] Some of the original speeches are duly transcribed but
mainly for parodic effect, and, overall, the verse is conspicuously
roughened. Using the techniques of expressionism, Brecht consciously
fragments, de-poeticizes, coarsens, and vulgarizes the Elizabethan
play so as to make it a vehicle for conveying bitter alienation,
political cynicism, cosmic absurdity, and even nihilism. Instead of
altering and compressing history for dramatic effect (like Marlowe),
Brecht deliberately falsifies and perverts historical fact, inventing
battles and dates in a way that almost totally repudiates historicity
while preserving its surface appearance. Isabella's name, for instance,
is unaccountably changed to Anne, Gaveston is called Danyell
('Danny' for short) rather than Piers, and the several bishops are
collapsed into the unhistorical *Arch*bishop of Winchester, a title with

which Brecht's abbot is ultimately rewarded. Events and characters are more ruthlessly pruned than even Marlowe dared to attempt; and the major figures have been thoroughly re-imagined—turned into animated attitudes almost. 'Eddie' (as the protagonist is glibly called) is made to embody sexual appetite and the elemental instinct for vengeance in quasi-heroic fashion as contrasted with a bookish and essentially disengaged Mortimer; comparing the enraged monarch to a 'tiger,' Brecht thus sets Nature in mortal combat with Reason. It is the king's treacherous double-crossing of the barons, not a political decision on their part, that brings Gaveston to his ungentlemanly death, and the favourite himself is transformed into an Irish butcher's son baffled by the sexual passion he arouses and too limited intellectually to take advantage of his privileges. The king stubbornly refuses to abdicate and is cynically betrayed by Baldock, finally being choked to death rather than anally spitted; the insatiate queen is reduced to incoherence and laughter at the meaninglessness of life.

Brecht's play intentionally distorts its original in the service of anti-humanistic ideology, but, possessing a certain brutal force, it has continued to hold the stage. The German text was performed for the first time in England in 1956 at the Palace Theatre, when the Berliner Ensemble visited London; the same company mounted the German play again in East Berlin during the season of 1974–75 in a production directed by Ekkehard Schall and Barbara Berg.[158] Eric Bentley made an English translation, staged in October 1965 by the Actor's Workshop in San Francisco, and the National Theatre acted another English version at the Old Vic, London, directed by Frank Dunlop (it opened 30 April 1968), using a text by William E. Smith and Ralph Manheim.[159] Students at the University of Toronto performed the play at the University College Playhouse under the direction of Paul Mulholland (19–27 March 1971).[160] Back in London in August 1975 the Bush Theatre Company played the Brecht drama in a tent on Shepherd's Bush Green and then at the Young Vic, later taking it on tour; and Rowland Rees directed still another production at the Roundhouse, London, in late February and early March 1982.[161] The Lion Theater Company, directed by Gene Nye, staged the Bentley translation in New York (6 May 1983) in an 'off off Broadway' production.[162] Brecht's drama proved historically significant in drawing fresh attention to Marlowe, and it shattered for ever the barrier of genteel conventionality that had previously made it impossible to deal frankly with homosexuality as a subject for the stage.

After the generally praised Phoenix Society production of 1923, Marlowe's chronicle play continued to attract student actors. In March 1926 the Marlowe Dramatic Society of Cambridge University performed *Edward II* in a production that was judged unacceptably amateurish by a reviewer for the *Spectator*.[163] In Oxted, England, the Holywell Players, directed by Kenneth Johnstone, performed *Edward II* with an anonymous cast at the Barn Theatre on 2 April 1928. Then on 10–11 February 1933 the Christ Church Players acted the play in the upper gallery of the college library in Oxford with magnificent costumes and Elizabethan music; John Izan was the director, Peter Glenville and Neil Hutchison respectively taking the parts of Edward and Gaveston. Both the acting and the physical arrangements drew high praise.[164] The National Broadcasting Company presented an American radio performance on 5 November 1939.[165] The next production of record took place at Barnard College (Columbia University, New York City) when an all-girl cast from the college dramatic society (Wigs and Cues), directed by José Ruben, acted the tragedy on 16–17 December 1943 at the Brinckerhoff Theater; a 'Miss Dana' played the title role and Jennifer Howard (the daughter of the American playwright Sidney Howard) took the part of Mortimer Junior.[166] This was apparently the earliest stage revival of Marlowe's play in the United States. Five years later another American academic production, directed by Wilson Lehr for the Theatre Workshop of the City College of New York with Sheppard Kerman in the lead, took place on 1 May 1948.[167] Then the Amateur Dramatic Club of Cambridge University mounted *Edward II* in December 1951 at the ADC Theatre, Cambridge, in a production directed by John Barton; Toby Robertson, who was to have a continuing relationship with the tragedy, played the king to Tony White's Gaveston. The reviewer for the London *Times* reported that Marlowe's play was 'remarkably well served by the actors,' and Michael L. Greenwald writes that the effort is 'still considered one of the most extraordinary productions ever seen at Cambridge.'[168]

On 1 September 1954 the Oxford University Dramatic Society, directed by Casper Wrede, put on a splendid amphitheatre performance of Marlowe's tragedy during the Edinburgh Festival in the great hall of George Heriot's School, Edinburgh, with a cast numbering more than forty; and the same year the French playwright and director Roger Planchon mounted the play (in a translation by Arthur Adamov) at the Théâtre de la Comédie in Lyons.

Planchon, who, like Brecht, was attracted by the opportunity to express leftist political ideas by using Marlowe as a base, completely reworked his original 1954 conception, freely adapting the chronicle play for a second production at the outdoor Roman Theatre in Orange, France (near Avignon), in July 1960; in August this version also played at Baalbek, Lebanon. Collaborating with Jacques Rosner, Planchon made still a third and more Marxist adaptation of *Edward II* for his company based at the Théâtre de la Cité de Villeurbanne (a working-class suburb of Lyons), which utilized elements of the Adamov text together with those of Brecht and was essentially a new play. Opening in 1961, it was later taken to Paris. Although lacking Marlowe's mighty line, difficult in any case to reproduce in French, Planchon's revised piece was rich in cinematographic poetry—colourful costumes, tableaux, black-outs, and close-up effects through special lighting. The Villeurbanne version, in which Jean Leuvrais played the title role, featured an offstage voice that commented on the action somewhat like a Greek chorus.[169] Meanwhile on 17 January 1955 the BBC Home Service had broadcast a radio production of Marlowe's text, abridged to ninety minutes, which garnered high praise. The distinguished Shakespearean actor Paul Scofield interpreted the part of the king, Richard Hurndall and Pamela Brown respectively taking the roles of Gaveston and Isabella.[170] The poetic strengths of the play, although these had traditionally been disparaged in comparison with such works as *Tamburlaine* and *Doctor Faustus*, were at last gaining their deserved recognition.

During the period 19–28 April 1956 a Theatre Workshop Company production of Marlowe's historical tragedy, directed by Joan Little-wood, could be seen at the Theatre Royal in Stratford-atte-Bowe (Stratford East). Littlewood, according to the reviewer for the London *Times* (20 April 1956), conceived the play as 'a sacrificial ritual' with overtones of Christ in which the protagonist was played (by Peter Smallwood) as 'a civilized butterfly broken under a political wheel' (p. 3); the performance was generally well received.[171] Later the same year (10–21 July) Eric Salmon's production of the play at Ludlow Castle was one of the features of the Ludlow Festival.[172] Then *Edward II* was revived in New York City on 11 February 1958 in a version adapted and abridged by Robert Kidd (the adapter played the leading role himself) at the Theatre de Lys, an off-Broadway location; the performing group was the American National Theatre and Academy (ANTA).[173] Toby Robertson (who had played King Edward in the 1951 ADC production at Cambridge) directed a new production for the Cambridge University Marlowe Society that opened at the Arts Theatre, Cambridge, and then moved on to the Open-Air Festival at Stratford-upon-Avon (near the Shakespeare Memorial Theatre), beginning 11 August 1958; later in the month it was transferred to the Lyric Theatre at Hammersmith, London. The young Derek Jacobi played the king and John Barton, the director of the 1951 production, enacted the younger Mortimer (both anonymously according to the custom of the Marlowe Society); but the production was highly regarded, especially by Clifford Leech, for its 'neutrality'—that is, for its refusal to push one line of interpretation at the expense of others, and for its bringing alive of the secondary characters in a complex study of the relation between 'power and suffering.'[174] Edward's homosexual attachment to Gaveston was presented candidly but with sympathy, and it was the king's inability to adjust his emotional needs to the requirements of public rule from which the tragic consequences flowed. This production, gorgeously apparelled in late medieval costumes and widely applauded by both theatre people and academics, finally established *Edward II* as a masterpiece for which there was no need to apologize. Since its multiple excellences have yet to be surpassed, many academic critics have understandably taken it as the artistic yardstick by which to measure subsequent efforts.

It was perhaps to be expected that in 1964, the quatercentenary of Marlowe's birth, a theatrical interest in his plays should quicken significantly. Accordingly, at least five different productions of *Edward II* were mounted. The most important of these was Clive Perry's robust, kaleidoscopically fast-paced presentation acted by the Phoenix Theatre Company—first at the Phoenix Theatre, Leicester (opening 30 April), and later at the New Arts Theatre, London (opening 1 July). Christopher Morley designed the set, which was also used for a concurrent production of *Richard II*. Richard Kay, who had taken the part of the boy king in Toby Robertson's 1958 production, played the title role aggressively to John Quentin's more passive Gaveston; the performances were uneven, but the now famous Anthony Hopkins (in the multiple roles of Lancaster, Gurney, and the Abbot) was singled out for special commendation. Unsubtle, rushed, and noisy speaking of the verse was a major complaint, but the strongly physical nature of the character relationships won approval.[175] The king, however, was not portrayed as effeminate (he and Gaveston never kissed), and his murder was represented offstage. Emphasis fell on the political rather than the personal aspects of the play's action. Other performances of *Edward II* the same year included one directed by Professor Glynne Wickham at the Theatre Royal in Bristol for the Bristol Old Vic Theatre School; a 'concert reading' directed by George Hamlin at the Loeb Theatre, Cambridge, Massachusetts, as part of the Harvard University Shakespeare–Marlowe festival with John Lithgow in the title role; another produced by Ruth Oppenheim and given by the Marlowe Society Drama Company of London (not to be confused with the organization of the same name at Cambridge) at the Commonwealth Institute in Kensington and later at Berkeley Castle in Gloucestershire (the historical site of Edward's murder); and still another acted by the Drama Department of the University of Manchester.[176]

More productions followed in the later 1960s. In January 1965 the Mountview Theatre Club of Crouch End, London, performed the play, to be followed the next year by the Birmingham Repertory Company who, under the direction of John Harrison, mounted a production at their home theatre that ran from 26 April to 11 July 1966; Henry Knowles acted the title role and Gary Watson played Gaveston. Theatrical self-consciousness and metadramatic experimentation marked Harrison's approach throughout: the performers, dressed in sombre rehearsal tights, sat in a semicircle of chairs, donning their costumes as needed and doubling roles in many instances without attempting to change their basic appearance. The suggestion clearly was that power politics is a mere game of role-playing.[177] In March 1966 members of the Royal Shakespeare Company, directed by Peter Hall, acted parts of *Edward II* (I.i, v.iii, v.v) at the Lyric Theatre in Hammersmith for a sequence in the spy film, *A Deadly Affair* (a cinematic adaptation of John Le Carré's novel *Call for the Dead*); David Warner took the name part.[178] The play was performed in Toronto in 1967 and 1969: Leon Major directed a production at the Hart House Theatre (University of Toronto) under the sponsorship of the Centre for the Study of Drama (20–28 January 1967); then the Theatre Toronto, a professional Canadian troupe under the direction of Clifford Williams, played the tragedy at the Royal Alexandra Theatre, Toronto (9–28 January 1969). This latter was agreed to be an unqualified disaster, not only because of undistinguished acting but also because of the ugliness of the set and the cheap, unsuitable costumes.[179]

The most celebrated production of the decade was obviously Toby

Robertson's Prospect Theatre Company staging of *Edward II* for the Edinburgh Festival of 1969 with Ian McKellen in the title role; the Assembly Hall of the Church of Scotland was the venue, McKellen also playing the parallel character in Shakespeare's *Richard II* (directed by Richard Cottrell) during the same season on alternate nights. This time Robertson seemed to emphasize the sexual and personal aspects of the character relationships, giving somewhat less prominence to the political side of the play than he had done in his 1958 production, although this effect was largely the result of the star's consciously exaggerated and histrionic approach to the leading part. In any event, much of the admired 'neutrality' of the earlier Robertson production was sacrificed. McKellen's performance proved so successful that the play later moved to the Mermaid Theatre, Puddle Dock, London (12 September–11 October); it also went on tour to Cambridge, Southampton, Cardiff, Leeds, and Birmingham after visiting Vienna and Bratislava. Subsequently it moved to the Piccadilly Theatre, London, where it was filmed (January 1970), and it was ultimately shown on television in both Britain and America—on 6 August over the BBC, and in the United States over various PBS stations in 1975 and 1977. George Geckle excerpts a variety of critical responses to this production (mostly favourable) in addition to printing the remarks of Robertson himself gathered from personal interviews in 1976 and 1982.[180] Some of the most interesting commentators noted how well Marlowe's play stood up to its Shakespearean successor in McKellen's nicely contrasted portrayal of the two kings, although the voices of those who thought that Shakespeare continued to outshine Marlowe could still be heard. The production was conspicuously freighted with stage business. McKellen played the king in the early acts (in a gold wig) as a young, sensuously appetitive hysteric—as a compound of frenetic gestures whom suffering finally transformed in the falling action into a passive, dessicated wreck of an old man; thus incessant motion gave way—in certain moments at least—to a kind of tragic inertness, insatiable hunger for bodily touching being the constant. Philip Hope-Wallace of the *Guardian* (29 August 1969) praised the actor for his effective combination of 'neurotic defiance,' 'unbiddable temper,' and 'deviant passion,' all conveyed with an eloquence suggestive of Gielgud's famous vocal powers (p. 6); but Harold Hobson in the *Sunday Times* (31 August 1969) missed the 'remnants of the beautiful and gallant prince who ran at tilt in France' (p. 25). Two intervals allowed McKellen to mark the protagonist's changes from lover

to warrior to exhausted shell by means of plausible physical trans-
formations. James Laurenson, managing to bring out both the
opportunistic and emotionally committed aspects of Edward's lover,
played Gaveston as a slack, casual, bare-chested, but virile fellow
calculated to generate loathing in Timothy West's hard and implacable Mortimer.

The Prospect *Edward II* was conceived after the lifting of theatrical
censorship in the United Kingdom and also after the decriminalization
of homosexual acts between consenting adults in private.[181] Perhaps
for this reason, physical homoeroticism was deliberately stressed,
Edward kissing Gaveston, Spencer, and Baldock full on the lips; this
emphasis was then carefully replicated in the murder scene where
Lightborn (played terrifyingly by Robert Eddison) first washed, then
kissed his victim before penetrating him with the heated iron, and,
after being stabbed, fell suggestively upon the corpse of the king.
The prominence of deviant sexuality, however, constituted more
than mere sensationalism; erotic exhibitionism was clearly intended
as part of the play's political statement—as a weapon that Edward
consciously used against the repressive power of his nobles. The set
and costumes were highly stylized and emblematic, involving various
compromises between medieval and modern, so as to stimulate a
certain alienation and also (by breaking the illusion of a specific
period) to suggest the fable's universality.[182]

Edward J. Feidner directed a well-received production of *Edward
II* at the Champlain Shakespeare Festival in Burlington, Vermont,
which opened 28 July 1970; Tony Wiles played the lead to Anthony
Passantino's Gaveston.[183] Ken Eulo directed a production of the play
at the tiny Courtyard Playhouse, New York City, for the Courtyard
Playhouse Foundation (23 October–22 November 1970) with Matt
Conley in the lead and Michael Crosby portraying Lightborn; the
cast numbered only twelve and the house, when full, only thirty.[184]
The Classic Stage Company, a repertory troupe under the artistic
direction of Christopher Martin, staged an 'off off Broadway' production of Marlowe's tragedy, its text considerably abridged, at the
Abbey Theatre in New York City in October 1974; Edith Oliver,
who reviewed it in the *New Yorker* (14 October 1974), judged the
acting 'clear and quite professional' but 'tame' (pp. 141–142); Clive
Barnes in his notice for the *New York Times* (1 October 1974)
was also generally appreciative, but thought Harlan Schneider as
the deposed monarch lacked panache and objected to a pointless
unMarlovian epilogue that traced the royal succession down to

Richard II—apparently in a directorial attempt to remind audiences of the connection to Shakespeare's better-known play about deposition (p. 35).[185] The most important American staging of Marlowe's tragedy during the decade was undoubtedly that done by John Houseman's Acting Company at the Harkness Theatre, New York (21 October–8 November 1975); this production, directed by Ellis Rabb with Norman Snow as the suffering king, toured extensively in the United States. The publicity announced it as 'the first full-scale American production' of *Edward II*, and Brendan Gill's enthusiastic review in the *New Yorker* pronounced it 'brilliant.'[186] Clive Barnes, writing in the *New York Times* (22 October 1975), thought Snow conveyed an 'air of compelling, even sinister glamour—the sense of a tinsel king with a toy heart,' also praising Peter Dvorsky for his 'odiously preening Gaveston' and Mary-Joan Negro for her strong characterization of Isabella; he also commended the 'stark simplicity of the production' with its 'sensitive sound score by Bob James' (p. 41); Walter Kerr, likewise commenting in the *New York Times* (2 November 1975), was pleased by the strong sense of 'ensemble' the Acting Company had developed for Marlowe's tragedy (sec. 2, p. 5).

Neil Harris staged a student performance of *Edward II* (by the Fletcher Players) at Marlowe's own college, Corpus Christi, Cambridge, in June 1977; the play (with Simon Griffith in the leading role) was mounted 'on a stark and simple stage in the Old Court' and 'greatly enhanced' by period costumes with touches of 'occasional anachronism.' Much was made of the Battle of Boroughbridge, realized with a violence dangerous to the actors, and Edward's murder, complete with 'horribly' glowing poker and terrible screams, 'was portrayed a trifle too convincingly for some.'[187] Then the following year Stephen MacDonald directed another Edinburgh Festival production by the Royal Lyceum Company in August and September at the Little Lyceum Theatre; Cordelia Oliver, the reviewer for the *Guardian* (29 September 1978), depreciated this latter as a performance 'of absolutely no subtlety with declamatory acting pretty well straight from stock'; Philip Franks played the lead 'as a totally ineffectual, petulant boy' who sprouted a 'wispy' moustache and beard in the later scenes but otherwise failed to mature. The murder with the spit, however, was 'cleverly done in a blaze of light' to the accompaniment of 'an electronic screech' (p. 10). Another significant innovation was the symbolic doubling of Gaveston and Lightborn by the same actor (William Lindsay)—an idea that at least two later productions were to appropriate. This device obviously underlined the self-destructive element in Edward's make-up and helped to suggest an important sado-masochistic link between his sexuality and his grostesquely sodomitic death.

Edward II continued to be variously performed in the 1980s. Richard Cottrell directed Robert O'Mahoney as the king in a Bristol Old Vic production at the New Vic Studio Theatre, Bristol (15 April–10 May 1980). According to the *Guardian* (25 April 1980), the 'same sparse style' was employed as that used in the 1969 McKellen revival; O'Mahoney played the title character like 'a nervy cat on a hot tin roof, a queen with his Queen,' while Clive Wood as Gaveston (who also doubled as Lightborn) supplied 'all the right tones of nonchalance and sexual cunning' (p. 7). A review in the *Times* (23 April 1980) noted that the whole play was 'a constant exercise in isolating' Isabella (played by Meg Davies) from both her husband and her lover, even the secondary female role of Lady Margaret being taken by a male actor. Sentenced to die, Mortimer bounded off the stage 'expectantly, very like Peter Pan,' eager for the ultimate adventure. Simple costumes and a metallic hexagonal set, likened by the same reviewer to 'a noisy hot-air vent' (p. 13), supplied a forbidding visual effect. The Brasenose Players, directed by Jonathan M. Critchley, put on *Edward II* in February 1981 at Oxford in the college hall 'with no set and a small but well-chosen cast'; Marc Polansky, who played the lead, headed a group of only seven players (six men and a woman) who doubled roles daringly. The following year the Oxford Theatre Group also performed the play.[188] A highly experimental production of Marlowe's tragedy with a cast of only six from the Compass Theatre Company opened at the Arts Centre, York, in late September 1983, afterwards going on tour for almost a year. One of their appearances was at the Gulbenkian Studio Theatre in Newcastle-upon-Tyne in March 1984. Directed by Neil Sissons, this effort featured a text reduced to ninety minutes of playing time (without an interval), a set and costumes in severe black and white, and an interpolated love song. Paul Rider acted the title role with (according to one reviewer) a 'see-saw monotony of mood'; Piers Storey portrayed all three of Edward's 'fatal lovers' (Gaveston, Spencer Junior, and Lightborn), thus not only continuing the tradition established by MacDonald's Edinburgh Festival production of 1978 and Cottrell's Bristol Old Vic version of 1980 but going them one better.[189] Still another university production, adapted by David Barnett and directed by Danny Moar, was mounted in the Fellows' Garden by the Clare Actors of Clare College, Cambridge, in 'May

Week' (actually June) of 1985; this 'went on tour . . . during the summer' to York, Oxford, and London, before finishing with a two-week run 'at the Edinburgh Festival in August.'[190]

Two additional mountings of *Edward II* filled out the decade: Nicholas Hytner's production in the round at the Royal Exchange Theatre in Manchester starring Ian McDiarmid in the title role (23 October–22 November 1986); and George Pothitos's Equity Showcase Theatre production in Toronto, which opened on 14 January 1987 with Brent Carver as the weakling king.[191] The former of these, which attracted great attention in the British press, was clearly the most important since Rabb's Acting Company production eleven years earlier. With a highly eclectic use of costumes and props (enveloping belted water-repellent greatcoats, puttees, army boots, a toy-like paper crown, crimson velvet cloaks splashed with dirt, and medieval armour), and with a circular stage at first covered with a black cloth and later transformed by the use of peat and onstage rain into a mud pit (the acting area was surrounded by a raised catwalk and surmounted by a gigantic hemisphere suggestive of the globe), this production aimed at an effect of harrowing disorientation, at the same time presenting what Grevel Lindop in the *Times Literary Supplement* (7 November 1986) referred to as a 'timeless parable' (p. 1248). The visual aspects were especially inventive. Gaveston's erotic entertainments for Edward (conjured up through imagery in Marlowe's original) were actually staged by means of 'a blasphemous Italianate dance-orgy' written and choreographed by Martin Duncan.[192] As the *Guardian* reviewer observed (25 October 1986), the stage represented both the decadent frivolity of a aesthete's 'circus' and the savage debasement of a 'bearpit' (p. 12). Many reviewers speculated about the horrific budget for laundry necessitated by the symbolic nightly wallowing in filth. McDiarmid portrayed Edward as 'a bitter mixture of naivety, tenderness, folly, and corruption,' boyish in certain gleeful moments, petulant and viciously ruthless in others. Overt homosexuality was uninhibited and hedonistic, the prone king publicly writhing atop Gaveston when the latter returned from banishment. But the barons, presented in the military scenes 'like a gang of loutish boys,' diverted sympathy increasingly to Edward;[193] in the opinion of one commentator, they behaved 'like an anti-gay freemasonry of Lancashire butchers.'[194] Loyalties born of amorous passion seemed to take an almost morally justified precedence over responsibility to the nation. Original details of stage business were striking—the offstage sound of an aeroplane engine when Gaveston arrived from exile, the disrespectful rolling up of the king in a red carpet that had been used to welcome his minion, the trussing up of Gaveston at his capture like a piece of meat, the betrayal of Edward in the garden of Neath Abbey (with overtones of Christ at Gethsemane), the emblematic substitution of the upturned throne in the murder scene for the table of Marlowe's text, the wrapping of the spit at its cooler end to suggest heat, and the lightning-swift but none the less lewd thrust between the king's exposed buttocks followed by an 'excruciatingly prolonged' shriek.[195] Lightborn (acted by Louis Hilyer) fell dead across his naked victim, thus consummating a love-death with the same symbolic image that had earlier been used in the 1969 Prospect staging. For the sake of symmetry Hytner introduced an untextual ritual establishing Edward I's funeral and his son's coronation to balance the later episodes of Edward III's accession ceremony and his father's obsequies. Most reviewers, like Paul Allen of the *New Statesman* (31 October 1986), were impressed with McDiarmid's 'extremely distinguished central performance' (p. 23), which tended to overshadow less brilliant characterizations by the other principals (Michael Grandage as Gaveston, Brid Brennan as Isabella, and Duncan Bell as the younger Mortimer).

The most highly publicized revival thus far in our decade was that of the Royal Shakespeare Company, directed by Gerard Murphy, which opened at the Swan Theatre, Stratford-upon-Avon, on 27 June 1990. Simon Russell Beale, an actor then known for comic roles (he played Thersites in the RSC's concurrent *Troilus and Cressida*), portrayed the title character as a mincing, unroyal, almost porcine sensualist ruled by sexual obsession and given to infantile rages and petulant narcisscism.[196] The barons, dressed malevolently in grim modern ties and collars under pseudo-Elizabethan doublets with puffed sleeves, were meant to suggest the kinship of homophobia to Nazi tyranny (Ciaran Hinds as Mortimer wore Hitler's signature forelock), while Edward, fondling a dazzlingly handsome Gaveston (Grant Thatcher) dressed first in studded black leather and later in the white and gold of an Elvis Presley outfit, presided over a court of almost 'pop' licentiousness. Prurient eroticism dominated the stage throughout—the three Poor Men of the opening suggestively stroking the minion from whose largesse they hoped to profit, the king toying with the hair of the catamite who nestled between the royal knees, Spencer and Baldock introduced as lovers in provocatively anachronistic underwear, a sex-starved Isabella (Katy Behean) being groped by Mortimer and later appearing as pregnant with his child, a bare-chested, Ortonesque Lightborn (George Anton) passionately embracing Edward before inserting the fatal spit in a way that involved the explicitness of full-front nudity. Murphy was at pains to insist that sexual need is the motive force that drives all politics whether this expresses itself as official repression or shameless orgy. (As in Hytner's Royal Exchange production, the king was treated to a homoerotic entertainment—in this case a trio of half naked male acrobats simulating anal intercourse.) The unMarlovian ghost of Gaveston, appearing before the climactic murder, reinforced the idea that Edward's death was both a retribution for, and a consummation of, his former passion. Writing in the *Guardian* (12 July 1990), Michael Billington described Beale's Edward as someone who at first 'assumes' that 'monarchy makes him immune from sanctions' and then in panic realizes 'his own vulnerability'; we watch 'the protective layers peeled off one by one until [the man] is at last reduced to stinking sack-clothed misery.' Although he praised Beale for 'a touching performance,' Billington also thought that Murphy's production was reductive, monotonously 'devalu[ing] Marlowe's play and smother[ing] its plangent lyricism in unrelieved sound and fury' (p. 24). Benedict Nightingale of the *Times* (11 July 1990) particularly admired the scene in which the king, stripped of any 'fineness, grandeur, or . . . dignity,' 'clutches for comfort at his murderer'; here Beale powerfully enacted 'an appalling unsentimental end to the tale of a man out of his emotional time and place' (p. 20). Many critics, however, thought that Murphy's insistence on voracious sexuality, amounting to a thematic overstatement, tended to deprive the central characters of their complexity and the play as a whole of its psychological, moral, and political subtlety.[197]

The most recent stagings of *Edward II* to date were mounted by the Mandrake Theatre Company at the Theatre Museum, Covent Garden (1 May–2 June 1991) and by the Yale Repertory Theatre in New Haven, Connecticut (12 March–11 April 1992). The London production, directed by Aaron Mullen with Zahim Albakri playing the lead, was somewhat misleadingly referred to in the company's advertising as a 'neglected classic.' The much more significant production in New Haven, directed by Stan Wojewodski, Jr (Dean of the Yale Drama School) and starring Byron Jennings and Thomas Gibson as Edward and Gaveston, restored a measure of royal dignity and classical restraint to Marlowe's drama, neither ignoring the homoeroticism nor sensationalizing it to the exclusion of political and philosophical themes. The opulent costuming (velvets, taffetas, embroidered silks punctuated by heavy gold crowns and dangling pendants worn near the heart) suggested the purple of wealth and power as well as the crimson of bloodshed. Most critics, like Malcolm Johnson of the *Hartford Courant*, admired Michael Yeargan's ingenious set—'a series of red staircases and puzzlelike platforms' that rose and fell like drawbridges, turning walls to floors and opening up bottomless chasms so as to physicalize Mortimer's 'musings on the turnings of fortune's wheel' while conveying a sense of private and public instability in a manner at once medieval and modern.[198] The same effect of continuity between a thirteenth- and a twentieth-century ambience was assisted by an eerie musical score that drew upon plainsong as well as more mechanical sounds such as buzzing and drum rolls. Jennings's portrayal of the title character, according to the same writer, was a 'fascinating and many-faceted triumph' while Gibson played Gaveston 'with superb cynical dash'; Cara Duff-MacCormick's Isabella, 'acted with clarion, regal command,' complemented Michael Gill's Mortimer, a 'smooth' Machiavellian who nevertheless spoke with 'some vocal strain.' Johnson commented also on the 'Asian stylization' of the actors' movements—'hieratic posings of the court' and 'half-seen comings and goings of figures on a catwalk high above the stage' for instance—which were almost 'abstract' without being 'dry or reserved.' In contrast to the Royal Shakespeare version of 1990, the Yale Repertory production treated Edward's murder in a way that mingled horror with a certain under-statement, so that audiences could experience the subtle progress of the king's movement from 'effete hauteur' in the early scenes 'to ringing, poignant pathos and regret' at the end. Jordan Schildcrout, writing for *The Yale Daily News Weekend Magazine* (27 March 1992), thought, however, that 'The impressionistic technique of using shadowy lighting and a hazy mirror to reflect the action [with the red-hot spit],' which took place beneath the stage level, 'robbed the scene of its stark cruelty and climactic gruesomeness' (p. 3).

Finally Derek Jarman's consciously sensational film (first shown in London in October 1991) must be mentioned. Despite its being generally faithful to Marlowe's language, this cinematic *Edward II* is a frankly polemical (and therefore controversial) work dedicated to the repeal of society's anti-gay laws. Apart from heavy cutting and considerable rearrangement of contexts, the major departure from the Elizabethan text occurs at the end when Isabella, rather than Mortimer, amorously commissions the handsome Lightborn (played by Kevin Collins) to murder Edward, and when the king's impaling is presented as a premonition after which Lightborn unexpectedly casts the red-hot poker into water and kisses the still unexecuted Edward to suggest the possibility (or fantasy?) of a happy ending. Although Edward II is apparently dead by the concluding frames, Jarman deliberately fosters ambiguity, blurring the line between illusion and reality and deconstructing chronological sequence for psychological effect. The young Edward III inherits his father's erotic interests and is shown listening to Tchaikovsky's 'Dance of the Sugar Plum Fairy' while wearing his mother's earrings, lipstick, and high-heeled shoes and dancing atop a cage in which the queen and Mortimer are imprisoned. In Jarman's interpretation King Edward's only offence is his sexual proclivity, the disastrous effects of his feeble rule being otherwise overlooked. The costuming is eclectic twentieth-century (military uniforms, strapless ball gowns, business suits, gym wear, police in riot gear, the street garb of gay activists), and the treatment of women unsparingly misogynist. At one point Isabella rids the court of Kent by savaging his neck in vampire fashion with her teeth. Steven Waddington plays the love-stricken but unregal king to Andrew Tiernan's unpleasantly bumptious Gaveston; Nigel Terry and Tilda Swinton are cast as the politically ambitious Mortimer and his adulterous paramour. The film employs a naturalistic, anti-rhetorical style of delivery and minimalist claustrophobic settings with touches of surrealism. Jarman sums up his approach in the foreword to a published script of his film: 'How to make a film of a gay love-affair and get it commissioned. Find a dusty old play and violate it.'[199]

It is clear that presentations of Marlowe's tragedy in our own century have run the gamut from prudish avoidance of the play's sexual content to an almost obsessive and exclusive embracement of it. Nor can it be accidental that two of the most important actors to play the title role (McKellen and Beale) are self-affirmingly gay. Emphasis has increasingly fallen on the more personal and sexual aspects of Edward's distressing story. But there have been occasional pauses for interpretations that honestly address the play's obvious concern with sexuality without destroying its integrity as historical tragedy in a more complex and comprehensive understanding of the term.

NOTES

1 'William Jones / Entred for his copie vnder th[e h]andes of Master Richard Judson and the Wardens. / A booke, Intituled *The troublesome Reign and Lamentable Death of Edward the Second, king of England, with the tragicall fall of proud Mortymer* ... vj^d W. [probably T. Woodcock]'; see Arber, II, 299.

2 These variants, taken from Greg's Malone Society reprint of Q, appear in the textual notes.

3 See Arber, II, 634; III, 473; III, 607; IV, 434. Greg also reproduces these entries in his edition (*Edward II*, p. v).

4 An inscription on the verso of the manuscript title page reads 'Mary Clarke her Book and Writing' and is dated 3 October 1751. As Greg points out, this hand is 'clearly not ... the same' as that of the transcript, 'which would appear to be about a century earlier' (*Edward II*, p. vii).

5 These are *horses* (Q, Q2MS.) versus *horse* (Q2–4) at 1.i.28; *Porpintine* or *Porpentine* (Q, Q2MS.) versus *Porcupine* (Q2–4) at 1.i.39; and *an antick* (Q, Q2MS.) versus *the antick* (Q2–4) at 1.i.59. See C. F. Tucker Brooke, 'On the Date of the First Edition of Marlowe's *Edward II*,' *M.L.N.*, 24 (1909), 72.

6 Confining himself to substantive changes in the manuscript version of the play text proper, Brooke counted 'fifteen variations from the edition of 1594' (ibid., p. 72). In fact there are sixteen substantive variants. Omitted from Brooke's list is *hard by* (Q) versus *by* (Q2MS.) at 1.i.65.

7 Ibid., p. 73. Brooke probably exaggerates the length of the period between the book's registration and its printing by assuming that printers invariably reckoned the new year as beginning on Lady Day (25 March), as in legal and court documents, rather than on 1 January. As Greg shows, practice varied greatly; see 'Old Style–New Style,' in J. C. Maxwell, ed., *W. W. Greg: Collected Papers* (Oxford: Clarendon Press, 1966), pp. 366–373. There is also evidence that printers sometimes dated their imprints for the year following that in which the printing actually occurred to make their product seem newer; see Greg, 'Old Style–New Style,' p. 372. Robert Robinson, the printer of Q (see note 15 below), sold copies of Robert Wilmot's *Tragedy of Tancred and Gismund* (printed by Thomas Scarlet), a book in which the date of imprint was altered from 1591 to 1592 'in the course of printing the preliminary sheet'; see Greg, *Bibliography*, I, 105.

8 See Bowers, 'Textual Introduction' to *Edward II*, in *Complete Works*, II, 3–12. This introduction, in part, absorbs an earlier article by Bowers: 'Was There a Lost 1593 Edition of Marlowe's *Edward II*?,' *S.B.*, 25 (1972), 143–148.

9 In his edition, however, Bowers treats this passage as verse; see *Complete Works*, II, 16.

10 Charlton–Waller, eds., *Edward II*, p. 4.

11 Even the initial publication of *Ovid's Elegies* (usually dated 1594–95), an octavo that also includes the *Epigrams* of Sir John Davies, contains the name 'C. Marlow' on the internal title of the section in which Marlowe's work begins (see sig. E1).

12 On A1 recto five vertical chainlines spaced approximately 2.2 centimetres

apart are visible, the fifth of which is located very close to the right edge of the page (a distance of .2 centimetres at most). On A2 recto only four chainlines are visible, the farthest to the right of which is 1.5 centimetres from the edge of the paper, a significantly greater distance than that of the analogous chainline on the preceding leaf. If A1 and A2 were originally conjugate at the top fold (as would be normal in quarto format) the chainline patterns of the two leaves should match up, as is approximately the case with the corresponding leaves of the later gatherings. The mismatch therefore constitutes strong evidence of a cancellans. Unfortunately the absence of watermarks on the two leaves deprives us of a corroborative test. Also the book has been closely cropped throughout so that chainlines are often out of parallel with the edges of the paper; in addition some shrinkage appears to have occurred. For these reasons the variation in chainline patterns, though certainly suggestive of nonconjugation, is probably less than conclusive.

13 We may add to the list given above the following dramas: *The Repentance of Mary Magdalene* (1566–67), Middleton's *A Trick to Catch the Old One* (1608–09; two separate issues with variant title pages, the later date being deduced from performance information contained thereon, make this case somewhat unparallel), F2 of Berkeley's *Lost Lady* (1638–39), Glapthorne's *Albertus Wallenstein* (1639–40), and Tatham's *Scotts Figgaries* (1652–53). For bibliographical details, see Greg's *Bibliography*, items 47, 104, 197, 204, 246, 253, 262, 293, 515, 534, 564, 711, and 788.

14 In Q the date of imprint (1594) appears not only on the title page but also in the colophon. The question therefore arises whether our hypothetical earlier state of Q had 1593 in the colophon as well as on the title—in other words whether the final leaf of the book (M3) is also a cancel—or whether the date on the title page was changed to make it agree with a colophon that had already been dated 1594. Unfortunately, the chainline test is not possible in this case because the normally conjugate leaf (M4) is missing from the gathering. The evidence that sheet A was printed after sheet M is discussed later in this section.

15 See Robert Ford Welsh, 'The Printer of the 1594 Octavo of Marlowe's *Edward II*,' *S.B.*, 17 (1964), 197–198. Welsh shows that Robinson's widow married Richard Bradock (the printer of Q2), to whom Robinson's stock of ornaments must have passed as a consequence of her remarriage. The change in ownership explains why two of the ornaments in Q reappear in Q2 despite the latter's having been typeset in a different shop. The printer of Q3 was probably William Jaggard. According to Greg, the printer of Q4 remains anonymous although 'the book may have come from the Eliot's Court Press'; see item 129 in Greg, *Bibliography*, I, 130.

16 See Welsh, 'The Printing of the Early Editions of Marlowe's Plays,' Duke University diss., 1964, pp. 59–72.

17 The compositor of Q3, for instance, sedulously followed his predecessor by reproducing the pagination and layout of Q2 almost exactly.

18 As Bowers points out, 'Fraunce' is probably Marlowe's own preferred spelling since it appears in the Collier Leaf manuscript of *The Massacre at Paris*; see Robert J. Fehrenbach, Lea Ann Boone, and Mario A. Di

Cesare, *A Concordance to the Plays, Poems, and Translations of Christopher Marlowe* (Ithaca, 1982), p. 409. In the total corpus of Marlowe, 'Fraunce' occurs thirty times, 'France' sixty times.

19 In all four instances the metre appears to require a disyllable (modernized in the present edition as *parley* or *parlied*); but the matter is not beyond dispute, for the *O.E.D.* lists *parle* not only as a variant of *parley* but also as a separate monosyllabic word. Marlowe may have used the two spellings indifferently: apart from *Edward II*, the verb *parle* occurs twice in *2 Tamburlaine* (1.i.11, 50) and once in *Hero and Leander* (I, 185), while *parly* occurs twice in *Doctor Faustus* (III.i.118, IV.ii.98). All the occurrences in Marlowe are disyllabic.

20 Greg, ed., *Edward II*, p. xii.

21 Q1 of Shakespeare's *2 Henry IV* (1600) also uses '*Bishop*' or '*Bish.*' as the speech prefix for Scroop, Archbishop of York; but no ambiguity is thereby created since the term '*Archbishop*' is used in stage directions and since Scroop is the only prelate in the play. In the Folio text of *Henry V* (1623) '*Bish.*' is again used as a speech prefix, apparently for the Bishop of Ely (1.ii.115), where the Archbishop of Canterbury (variously designated as '*B. Cant.*', '*B. Can.*', '*Bish. Cant.*', '*Bish. Can.*', and '*Cant.*') is also onstage; the other speech of the subordinate prelate in this scene, however, is clearly marked '*Bish. Ely*' (1.ii.166).

22 Greg, ed., *Edward II*, p. ix.

23 Ibid., pp. ix–x.

24 Bowers, ed., *Complete Works*, II, 100–101.

25 Fredson Bowers was the first editor to make use of the anonymous 'Chappell' edition of *Edward II* in his collations and textual apparatus (see *The Complete Works of Christopher Marlowe*, first ed. [Cambridge: Cambridge University Press, 1973], II, 1–119), and he reprinted his remarks without substantive change in his second edition of 1981. Bowers was apparently unaware, however, that N. W. Bawcutt in 1971 had conclusively identified the Chappell editor as James Broughton, a gentleman scholar with an absorbing interest in Marlowe despite his wish to remain anonymous. See Bawcutt, 'James Broughton's Edition of Marlowe's Plays,' *N.&Q.*, N.S. 18 (December 1971), 449–452.

26 Brooke, 'Marlowe's Versification and Style,' *S.P.*, 19 (1922), 186–205; see also Kenneth Muir, who in 'The Chronology of Marlowe's Plays,' *Proceedings of the Leeds Philosophical and Literary Society*, 5 (1938–43), 352, shows that the dramatist's verse became increasingly irregular.

27 Bawcutt, 'James Broughton's Edition of Marlowe's Plays,' p. 450; Bowers, ed., *Complete Works*, II, 12.

28 See Chambers, *Elizabethan Stage*, IV, 107.

29 See Foakes and Rickert, eds., *Henslowe's Diary*, pp. 19–20.

30 The date of the Leicester performances is somewhat uncertain; see Lees's discussion of the problem in Charlton–Waller, eds., *Edward II*, pp. 213–217. For the restraint of plays in 1592–93, see Chambers, *Elizabethan Stage*, IV, 311–314; also J. Leeds Barroll, Alexander Leggatt, Richard Hosley, and Alvin Kernan, eds., *The Revels History of Drama in English: Volume III, 1576–1613* (London, 1975), pp. 34–35.

31 Chambers, *Elizabethan Stage*, II, 128–129.

32 E. A. J. Honigmann points to a probable echo of *Richard III* in *The*

Troublesome Reign (printed 1591); see *Shakespeare's Impact on His Contemporaries* (Totowa, N.J., 1982), pp. 82–83, 132.

33 See Charlton–Waller, eds., *Edward II*, pp. 8–10.

34 Rupert Taylor lists these parallels, among others, in 'A Tentative Chronology of Marlowe's and Some Other Elizabethan Plays,' *P.M.L.A.*, 51 (1936), 644–647; Taylor, however, without giving reasons, accepts *The Troublesome Reign* as the later play. E. A. J. Honigmann agrees with Taylor on grounds that the anonymous playwright pilfered phrases and lines from many different dramatists, being 'essentially derivative, or parasitic' in compositional method; see *Shakespeare's Impact*, p. 81.

35 E. A. J. Honigmann, who believes that *The Troublesome Reign* is a bad quarto of *King John*, would date the anonymous play later than 1590, his date for the Shakespeare drama; see his New Arden edition of *King John* (London, 1954) as well as his *Shakespeare's Impact*, pp. 132–133. L. A. Beaurline in his edition of *King John* (Cambridge, 1990), concurs with Honigmann on the dating (p. 210).

36 Charlton–Waller, eds., *Edward II*, pp. 8–10; see also Muir, 'Chronology of Marlowe's Plays,' p. 348.

37 See the striking parallel passages listed by Charlton–Waller, pp. 17–19.

38 The case for 1591 rather than 1592 as the date of composition is further strengthened by the researches of Charles Nicholl, who presents evidence to show that Marlowe was in Flushing in the Netherlands 'in late 1591 or early 1592' and that by the end of January 1592 he was back in England to be interrogated by Lord Burghley on charges of counterfeiting money abroad. Marlowe had been arrested in the Low Countries and may also have been briefly in custody upon his forced return to London. See Nicholl, *The Reckoning: The Murder of Christopher Marlowe* (London, 1992), pp. 234–239; the quoted phrase appears on p. 236.

39 See Muir, 'Chronology,' p. 352.

40 *As You Like It* may contain another allusion to Marlowe: Touchstone remarks in response to Audrey's ignorance, 'When a man's verses cannot be understood, nor a man's good wit seconded with the forward child, understanding, it strikes a man more dead than a great reckoning in a little room' (III.iii.10–13). Here Shakespeare seems to be echoing *The Jew of Malta* ('Infinite riches in a little room' [I.i.37]) in conjunction with the circumstances of Marlowe's death by stabbing at a lodging house in Deptford on 30 May 1593. Also Sir Hugh Evans quotes, or rather misquotes, lines from Marlowe's popular lyric, 'Come live with me and be my love,' in *The Merry Wives of Windsor* (III.i.16–28). The standard early study of the Marlowe–Shakespeare relationship is A. W. Verity's *The Influence of Christopher Marlowe on Shakspere's Earlier Style* (Cambridge, 1886; rpt. Folcroft, Pa., 1969). For a more modern, political, and ideologically oriented discussion of the artistic interchange, see James Shapiro, *Rival Playwrights: Marlowe, Jonson, Shakespeare* (New York, 1991), pp. 75–132.

41 See *2 Tamburlaine*, IV.iii.1–2.

42 Of course the dominance of a single character over the dramatic action of a play is older than Marlowe (Preston's *Cambyses* comes to mind), but *Tamburlaine* obviously lent the technique an irresistible glamour and assurance that must have made it seem fresh, even novel.

43 M. C. Bradbrook comments on this relationship; see 'Shakespeare's Recollections of Marlowe,' in *Shakespeare's Styles: Essays in Honour of Kenneth Muir*, ed. Philip Edwards, Inga-Stina Ewbank, and G. K. Hunter (Cambridge, 1980), pp. 192–193. Shakespeare also quotes a line from Marlowe's translation of Ovid's *Elegies* ('The moon sleeps with Endymion every day'; I.xiii.43) in *The Merchant of Venice*: 'Peace, ho! The moon sleeps with Endymion' (v.i.109).

44 Nicholas Brooke writes suggestively on 'Marlowe as Provocative Agent in Shakespeare's Early Plays,' *Shakespeare Survey*, 14 (1961), 34–44; see also David Riggs, *Shakespeare's Heroical Histories: "Henry VI" and Its Literary Tradition* (Cambridge, Mass., 1971). Bradbrook, however, believes that the 'prime model of *Venus and Adonis* is not Marlowe, but [John] Clapham,' whose Latin poem *Narcissus* was published in 1591; 'the two Ovidian poems' by Marlowe and Shakespeare 'seem rather to be running parallel to each other, both deriving from Clapham.' See 'Shakespeare's Recollections of Marlowe,' pp. 197–198.

45 See especially F. P. Wilson, *Marlowe and the Early Shakespeare* (Oxford, 1953), pp. 104–131, and Harold F. Brooks, 'Marlowe and Early Shakespeare,' in Brian Morris, ed., *Mermaid Critical Commentaries: Christopher Marlowe* (New York, 1969), pp. 65–94.

46 Madeleine Doran, independently of Alexander, also argued for the reported nature of *The Contention* and *The True Tragedy* in *Henry VI Parts II and III: Their Relation to the Contention and the True Tragedy* (Iowa City: University of Iowa Studies, 1928). For a more recent discussion of the textual complexities of *The Contention* and *The True Tragedy*, see the sections on these plays by William L. Montgomery in Stanley Wells and Gary Taylor, eds., *William Shakespeare: A Textual Companion* (Oxford, 1987), pp. 175–208. Montgomery accepts the 'bad quarto' theory of these texts. Montgomery and Taylor discuss, but disagree with, the unpublished work of Steven Urkowitz, who has argued that *The True Tragedy* embodies an earlier conception of King Henry's character than that found in the Folio text (*3 Henry VI*). See also Urkowitz's 'Good News about "Bad" Quartos,' in Maurice Charney, ed., *'Bad' Shakespeare: Revaluations of the Shakespeare Canon* (Rutherford, N.J., 1988), pp. 197–199.

47 See note 53 below.

48 Thomas Legge's academic Latin tragedy, *Richardus Tertius* (1579–80), must also be included among the earliest history plays. Most scholars are agreed, however, that its influence on Shakespeare, if any, was indirect.

49 Wilson, *Marlowe and the Early Shakespeare*, p. 105. Wilson is paraphrasing Rossiter (see note 53 below).

50 Brooks, 'Marlowe and Early Shakespeare,' p. 72.

51 See Muir, 'Chronology,' pp. 345–356.

52 See, for instance, Clifford Leech, 'The Dramatists' Independence,' *R.O.R.D.*, 10 (1967), 18–19. Antony Hammond cogently summarizes the arguments for an early dating (1591) of *Richard III*; see his New Arden edition (London, 1981), pp. 54–61. Taylor and Wells, however, finding the alleged indebtedness of *Edward II* to *Richard III* 'unconvincing,' date Shakespeare's play 1592–93; see *William Shakespeare: A Textual Companion*, p. 116. The later date coincides with that

assigned the play by E. K. Chambers in *William Shakespeare: A Study of Facts and Problems* (Oxford, 1930), I, 270.

53 For the likely priority of *Edward I* to Marlowe's play, see Charlton–Waller, eds., *Edward II*, pp. 8–10. Wolfgang Keller believed that *Woodstock* depended on Marlowe (see '*Richard II, Erster Teil*, Ein Drama aus Shakespeares Zeit,' *Shakespeare Jahrbuch*, 35 [1899], 1–12), but Rossiter argues more cogently for the reverse order of composition in his standard edition of *Woodstock*, pp. 53–71; see also Lees's comments on Rossiter's position (Charlton–Waller, p. 219). Rupert Taylor lists numerous verbal parallels, some of them quite doubtful, between *The Troublesome Reign* and *Edward II* (see 'A Tentative Chronology of Marlowe's and Some Other Elizabethan Plays,' *P.M.L.A.*, 51 [1936], 643–688), concluding that 'the anonymous author was the borrower' (p. 648); but since *The Troublesome Reign* was printed in 1591, Marlowe's play (if it was a source) together with *The Massacre at Paris* (which also contains verbal links to the anonymous play) would have to be pushed back to unacceptably early dates. Indeed it seems more likely that Marlowe lifted phrases and other details from *The Troublesome Reign*, which probably preceded *Edward II*; Lees notes that Taylor 'offers no reasons' for his assertion, 'which runs counter to all received opinion' (Charlton–Waller, p. 220).

54 See Tucker Brooke, 'The Marlowe Canon,' *P.M.L.A.*, 27 (1922), 375–377; also Brooke, 'The Authorship of the Second and Third Parts of *King Henry VI*,' *Transactions of the Connecticut Academy of Arts and Sciences*, 17 (1912), 160–177; Taylor, 'A Tentative Chronology'; Charlton–Waller, pp. 17–27; Frederick S. Boas, *Christopher Marlowe: A Biographical and Critical Study* (Oxford, 1946), pp. 192–201.

55 F. P. Wilson contrasts these passages in *Marlowe and the Early Shakespeare*, pp. 122–123.

56 Hammond, ed., *Richard III*, p. 103. Interestingly, the motif reappears in *Edward II*, in which Mortimer Junior refers to the king as 'England's scourge' (III.ii.74); the phrasing here, similar to that employed by Shakespeare to characterize Queen Margaret, might indicate another of Marlowe's several imitations of *2 Henry VI* (see Charlton–Waller, pp. 10–17).

57 Shakespeare's source for these passages was Edward Hall's *Vnion of the Two Noble and Illustre Famelies of Lancastre and Yorke* (1548): '[Queen Margaret] determined with her self, to take vpon her the rule and regiment, bothe of the kyng and his kyngdome, & to depriue & evict out of al rule and aucthoritie, the said duke [Humphrey], then called the lord protector of the realme: least men should saie & report, that she had neither wit nor stomacke, whiche would permit & suffre her husband, beyng of perfect age & mans estate, like a yong scholer or innocent pupille, to be gouerned by the disposicion of another man' (fols. cl^v–clii).

58 See Brooks, 'Marlowe and Early Shakespeare,' pp. 75–76. Another of Richard III's wry witticisms could have influenced Marlowe. Just before his execution Gaveston asks Warwick, 'Treacherous earl! Shall I not see the king?' and is answered, '*The King of Heaven* perhaps, no other king' (*Edward II*, II.vi.15–16; emphasis added). This is a little like Richard's cheeky defence of having killed Henry VI: to Lady Anne's statement,

'O, he was gentle, mild, and virtuous!' Richard ripostes, 'The better for *the King of Heaven* that hath him' (*R3*, I.ii.104–105; emphasis added). The repeated phrase, however, does not appear to have originated with Shakespeare; it occurs also, for instance, in the anonymous *King Leir* (*c.* 1590), l. 1604 (see the edition by Geoffrey Bullough in *Narrative and Dramatic Sources of Shakespeare* [London, 1957–75], VII, 376).

59 Compare *1 Tamburlaine*: 'I hold the Fates bound fast in iron chains, / And with my hand turn Fortune's wheel about . . .' (I.ii.173–174).

60 Brooks, 'Marlowe and Early Shakespeare,' pp. 73–74.

61 Another of Marlowe's possible borrowings from this scene occurs in *Edward II* when the king, under house arrest at Killingworth, resists the entreaty of Sir William Trussel and the Bishop of Winchester to 'resign' his crown. At first he refuses, at which point the two commissioners from London are about to leave the stage. Then at the urging of Leicester ('Call them again, my lord, and speak them fair, / For if they go, the prince shall lose his right'), Edward relents: 'Call thou them back . . .' (v.i.91–93). Although Marlowe's context is directly opposite to Shakespeare's (the wily acquisition of the crown rather than anguished surrender of it), the author of *Richard III* employs suspiciously similar staging as well as similar language:

Catesby. Call them again, sweet prince, accept their suit.
   If you deny them, all the land will rue it.
Gloucester. Will you enforce me to a world of cares?
   Call them again. I am not made of stones. . . .

                                        (III.vii.221–224)

62 Marlowe could also have recalled the extended wordplay on 'shadow' and 'substance' in *1 Henry VI*: the Countess of Auvergne uses 'shadow' to refer to Talbot's portrait and 'substance' to mean his physical body; Talbot then wittily inverts the terms to distinguish his individual person (his 'shadow') from his army (his 'substance'). See *1H6*, II.iii.36–62. In the same play the French king, Charles VII, is also referred to as the 'shadow of himself' (v.iv.133) when he is forced to acknowledge Henry VI as his liege lord, thus becoming a mere 'viceroy' under him. In *Richard III* Queen Margaret gloats over Elizabeth after Edward IV's death as 'poor shadow, painted queen, / The presentation of but what I was . . .' (IV.iv.83–84). Antony Hammond suggests Gloucester's opening soliloquy in *Richard III* as a source: 'I . . . Have no delight to pass away the time, / Unless to see my shadow in the sun . . .' (I.i.24–26); see Hammond, ed., *Richard III*, p. 57. Hammond (pp. 57–61) also discusses other possible links between *Richard III* and *Edward II*.

63 See Harold C. Gardiner, S.J., *Mysteries' End: An Investigation of the Last Days of the Medieval Religious Stage*, Yale Studies in English, Vol. 103 (New Haven, 1946), pp. 65–93.

64 Brooks suggests that Shakespeare may have recalled Marlowe's episode with the puddle water in *The Comedy of Errors*, where Dr Pinch, like Edward II, also suffers a humiliating assault: a messenger reports that the doctor's 'beard they have sing'd off with brands of fire; / And ever, as it blaz'd, they threw on him / Great pails of puddled mire to quench the hair' (v.i.171–173). See 'Marlowe and Early Shakespeare,' pp. 78–79. For evidence that Shakespeare's comedy postdates *Edward II*, see R.

A. Foakes, ed., *The Comedy of Errors* (London, 1962), pp. xix–xx. Chambers dates the play 1592–93 (*William Shakespeare*, I, 270); Wells and Taylor date it 1594 (*William Shakespeare: A Textual Companion*, p. 116). Violation of manly dignity by means of assaulting the beard comes out again in *King Lear*, in which Regan, before the blinding of Gloucester, 'ignobly' 'pluck[s]' the helpless duke 'by the beard' (III. vii.36–37).

65 The monkish disguise comes from Peele's *Edward I*, which Marlowe echoes verbally at this point (*Edward I*, xxiii [l. 2519]; cf. *Edward II*, IV.vii.97); but the disguise of Henry VI (*3H6*, III.i.12), who, like Edward II, is seeking futilely to elude capture and who carries a '*prayer book*,' may well have contributed to Marlowe's episode in a secondary way.

66 As Hammond points out (pp. 58–59), Marlowe may have picked up a hint or two in his portrayal of Lightborn from the scenes of *Richard III* in which the murderers of Clarence appear. In commissioning the villains, Richard warns them that 'Clarence is well-spoken, and perhaps / May move your hearts to pity if you mark him,' to which the First Murderer responds, 'Tut, tut, my lord, we will not stand to prate . . .' (I.iii.347–349). A similar exchange occurs when Mortimer commissions Lightborn to murder Edward:

> *Mortimer Junior.* But at his looks, Lightborn, thou wilt relent.
> *Lightborn.* Relent? Ha, ha! I use much to relent.
>
> (v.iv.25–26)

Moreover Marlowe seems to echo here the scene of Shakespeare's play that immediately follows in which the murder itself occurs:

> *Clarence.*   Relent and save your souls.
>
> . . . .
>
> *First Murderer.* Relent? No. 'Tis cowardly and womanish.
> *Clarence.* Not to relent is beastly, savage, devilish.
>
> (I.iv.259–265)

67 Cole, *Suffering and Evil in the Plays of Christopher Marlowe* (Princeton, 1962), p. 165.

68 Alexander, *Shakespeare's 'Henry VI' and 'Richard III*,' pp. 93–94.

69 Farjeon's edition of *The Contention* and *The True Tragedy* (*The Complete Works of Shakespeare*, Vol. II) supplies no line numbering; quotations are therefore designated in the text parenthetically by page number.

70 Charlton–Waller list several verbal parallels between *The Contention* and *Edward II* (pp. 10–17). I add two others that they either underemphasize (1) or overlook (2):

> (1) Even to my death, for I have lived too long.
>
> (*Contention*, p. 689)
>
> Nay, to my death, for too long have I lived. . . .
>
> (*Edward II*, v.vi.82)
>
> (2) Then is he gone, is noble Gloster gone. . . .
>
> (*Contention*, p. 694)
>
> O is he gone? Is noble Edward gone?
>
> (*Edward II*, IV.vii.100)

71 Charles Lamb, *Specimens of English Dramatic Poets*, in E. V. Lucas, ed., *The Works of Charles and Mary Lamb*, 7 vols. (London, 1903–05), IV, 24.

72 Some critics have regarded the scene in which Aumerle's mother, the Duchess of York, begs Henry IV for her son's pardon as 'comic,' since the king remarks with a touch of levity that 'Our scene is alt'red from a serious thing, / And now chang'd to "The Beggar and the King"' (v.iii.79–80). There is indeed a humorous aspect to this episode, but its central issue, the life or death of a would-be traitor, can scarcely be considered comic in the usual sense of the term.

73 See, for instance, Glynne Wickham, 'Shakespeare's *King Richard II* and Marlowe's *King Edward II*,' in *Shakespeare's Dramatic Heritage* (London, 1969), pp. 165–179; also Wolfgang Clemen, 'Shakespeare and Marlowe,' in Clifford Leech and J. M. R. Margeson, eds., *Shakespeare 1971* (Toronto, 1972), pp. 123–132.

74 T. M. Raysor, ed., *Coleridge's Shakespearean Criticism*, 2 vols. (Cambridge, Mass., 1930), I, 144.

75 Bradbrook notes that in *Richard II* 'the homosexual element is so played down that Bushy, Bagot and Green seem almost irrelevant' ('Shakespeare's Recollections of Marlowe,' p. 196); but, apart from Bolingbroke's unsupported statement, no explicit homosexuality appears anywhere in the play. Actors and theatrical directors, however, perhaps with Marlowe's precedent in mind, have sometimes seized upon the opportunity to present Richard as dallying sexually with his favourites or at least to imply as much. John Gielgud in his 1929 characterization of Richard at the Old Vic and again at the Queen's Theatre in 1937 imparted a certain languid effeminacy to the role, and Michael Redgrave in his Stratford-upon-Avon performance of 1951 played the character (in the words of Sir Laurence Olivier) 'as an out-and-out pussy queer, with mincing gestures to match.' John Justin also exaggerated the king's supposed homosexual tendencies in his Old Vic portrayal of 1959. Ian McKellan acted both Edward II and Richard II on alternating nights in a Prospect Company offering of 1968–70, thus stressing the close relationship of the two protagonists. A French production of Shakespeare's play in 1970 at the Odéon-Théâtre de France with Patrice Chéreau in the lead emphasized homoeroticism in the monarch, and Ian Richardson in 1974 (at a Royal Shakespeare Company production at the Brooklyn Academy of Music) played Richard, to quote a New York critic, as 'a distasteful, flaming queen.' The BBC television production of 1978 starring Derek Jacobi (recorded on a Time-Life video cassette) showed the king relaxing with his minions in a state of semi-nakedness with obvious overtones of homosexuality. Finally, Zoe Caldwell's 1979 production of *Richard II* at Stratford, Ontario (with three different actors playing the title role on different evenings) also made much of the alleged homosexuality: at one point 'Richard took Aumerle's hand for comfort, and then Aumerle stealthily put his arm round Richard's waist. Richard also gently put a hand on Bushy's knee, while always keeping his distance from his Queen. . . .' See Malcolm Page, *Richard II: Text and Performance* (Atlantic Highlands, N.J., 1987), pp. 49, 70; also Josephine A. Roberts, *Richard II: An Annotated Bibliography* (New York, 1988), II, 376, 420, 444.

76 Also Isabella, about to depart for France, intends to complain to her brother 'How Gaveston hath robbed me of [Edward's] love' (ii.iv.67).

77 Marlowe's speech seems to have lodged in Shakespeare's consciousness,
   for the dramatist echoes it again in *Troilus and Cressida*: Troilus refers to
   Helen as 'a pearl / Whose price hath launch'd above a thousand ships'
   (II.ii.81–82).

78 Perhaps we should also recall here the Dauphin Lewis's elaborately
   Petrarchan sun–shadow wordplay in response to his father's offer of
   Blanch as a prospective bride:

   in her eye I find
   A wonder, or a wondrous miracle,
   The shadow of myself form'd in her eye,
   Which, being but the shadow of your son,
   Becomes a sun and makes your son a shadow.
   (*Jn*, II.i.496–500)

   But the context here is more romantic than political and has nothing to
   do with the loss of a crown. See also note 62 above.

79 Both spellings were current in the sixteenth century. Stowe, whose
   chronicle (in the 1580 edition) Marlowe also read, uses the two forms
   interchangeably. Fabyan and Grafton in their chronicles (the 1559 and
   1569 editions respectively) both have 'Kenelworth.' Shakespeare in *2
   Henry VI*, a play that influenced *Edward II* (see the discussion above),
   writes 'Killingworth' (IV.iv.39, 44).

80 See Stephen Booth, *The Book Called Holinshed's Chronicles: An Account
   of Its Inception, Purpose, Contributors, Contents, Publication, Revision,
   and Influence on William Shakespeare* (San Francisco, 1968), pp. 61–65.
   Booth summarizes the conclusions of two earlier scholars: Sarah C.
   Dodson, 'Abraham Fleming, Writer and Editor,' *University of Texas
   Studies in English*, 34 (1955), 51–66; and William E. Miller, 'Abraham
   Fleming: Editor of Shakespeare's Holinshed,' *Texas Studies in Literature
   and Language*, 1 (1959–60), 89–100.

81 Holinshed, *Chronicles* (1587), III, 320. Unless otherwise indicated, all
   subsequent quotations are from this edition and volume and are noted
   parenthetically by page number in the text. The translation of the Latin
   is my own.

82 John Stowe, however, reports the rumour that Gaveston's mother was a
   witch and that the Gascon favourite, presumably taught by her, had
   himself 'bewitched the king' (*Chronicles of England* [1580], p. 327).
   Unless otherwise specified, further quotations from Stowe are to this
   edition and noted parenthetically by page number in the text.

83 But see also note 89 below.

84 See, for example, Michael Prestwich, *The Three Edwards: War and State
   in England, 1272–1377* (London, 1980), p. 82.

85 See, for instance, pp. 318 and 321. For Fleming's additions of the
   'gratuitous' Latin tags and adages together with the moralizations that
   usually accompany them, see Booth, *The Book Called Holinshed's
   Chronicles*, p. 68.

86 Marlowe prepares the ground for this unhistorical defeat by having
   Mortimer announce at an earlier point, 'The King of France sets foot in
   Normandy' (II.ii.9).

87 The only chronicler who explicitly attributes homosexuality to the
   younger Spencer is Jean Froissart, who reports that at his execution Sir

Hugh's 'member and ... testicles were first cut off, because he was a heretic and a sodomite, even, it is said, with the King, and this was why the King had driven away the Queen on his suggestion'; see Geoffrey Brereton, ed. and trans., *Froissart Chronicles* (Baltimore, 1968), p. 44. Whether Marlowe knew Froissart in the original, however, is uncertain. Lord Berners, in his English translation of Froissart (published 1523–25), either suppresses this detail for reasons of tact or, more likely, was misread by the compositor who set his manuscript in type, for the 1523 text prints 'so demed' for 'sodomite'; see *The Chronicle of Froissart Translated Out of French by Sir John Bourchier, Lord Berners ... With an Introduction by William Paton Ker*, The Tudor Translations (London, 1901), XXVII, 38. Froissart of course was among the several chroniclers upon whom Holinshed drew.

88 Claude J. Summers was the first to notice the element of Machiavellian subtlty in Marlowe's characterization of the queen early in the play, and he shrewdly points out how her behaviour in I.iv 'adumbrate[s] her later attitude toward Edward' (p. 310) when she secretly advocates his murder, yet wishes to conceal her advocacy by letting Mortimer make the practical arrangements. See Summers, 'Isabella's Plea for Gaveston in Marlowe's *Edward II*,' *P.Q.*, 52 (April 1973), 308–310.

89 The mention of clemency may, however, be Marlowe's way of referring to the sparing of Mortimer's life after Boroughbridge—a 'transgression' on the king's part in the sense that leniency in this instance made possible the later treasons of Mortimer, including his alliance with the queen.

90 Edward speaks of himself as potentially 'cruel and ... tyrannous' to the rebel barons (II.ii.205), but only justly in response to what he regards as their treasonable behaviour.

91 Leech, 'Marlowe's *Edward II*: Power and Suffering,' pp. 192–193.

92 Charlton–Waller, eds., *Edward II*, p. 50; see also William Stubbs, ed., *Chronicles of the Reigns of Edward I and Edward II* (London, 1883), II, lvii–cix.

93 *The Last Part of the Mirour for Magistrates* (London, 1578), sig. B3; see also Campbell, ed., *The Mirror for Magistrates*, p. 84.

94 Grafton derived the story of the queen's feigned pilgrimage from Froissart, but there is nothing to suggest that Marlowe consulted the French chronicler.

95 Apart from his reliance on Grafton for the connection between Mortimer's escape and Kent's departure, Marlowe (in addition to Holinshed) may also have remembered Fabyan and Stowe on Mortimer's escape from the Tower. Fabyan writes: 'And in the beginning of August following [1323], syr Roger Mortimer of Wygmore, by meane of a sleping poyson or drinke, that he gaue vnto his kepers, as the common fame went, escaped out of the towre of London, & went vnto the queene in France' (p. 180). Stowe's account is more elaborate: 'On Lammas daye [1 August] Roger Mortimer of Wigmore, by giuing to his keepers a sleepe drinke, escaped out of the Tower, breaking through the wal and comming into ye kitchin neare adioyning to the Kings lodgings, and getting out of the toppe thereof, came to a Warde of the Tower, and so with cordes knitte ladder-wise, prepared afore hande by a friende of hys,

got to another Warde, and so with greate feare got to the *Thamis*, and with his helper and two moe of his counsell passed the riuer, and auoyding the high wayes came to the sea, and there finding a shippe, passed ouer into *Fraunce*' (p. 346).

96 See Campbell, ed., *The Mirror for Magistrates*, pp. 81–89.

97 Waith, 'Edward II: The Shadow of Action,' *T.D.R.*, 8.4 (summer 1964), 59–76.

98 Marlowe, however, complicates our largely negative response to the queen in the latter half of Act IV. Although Kent has warned us that 'she bears a face of love' to her husband while 'conspir[ing]' with Mortimer (IV.vi.13–14), her lines to Sir John of Hainault and the others of her party later in the scene, 'I rue my lord's ill fortune, but, alas, / Care of my country called me to this war' (IV.vi.64–65), are ambiguous. We cannot be quite sure whether her words here are merely politic or represent a final twinge of guilt for her actions (and therefore of lingering attachment to the king).

99 Robert Fricker, 'The Dramatic Structure of *Edward II*,' *E.S.*, 34 (1953), 212.

100 Harry Levin notes this connection; see *The Overreacher*, p. 90.

101 Levin observes that the name Lightborn is the same as that of a devil in the Chester cycle and 'is neither more nor less than an Anglicization of "Lucifer"' (*The Overreacher*, p. 101). F. N. Lees extends Levin's perception by pointing out that Lightborn is in fact 'the chief supporter' of Lucifer in the Chester plays; he also suggests that the red-hot spit that the Marlovian character employs as a murder weapon fits the diabolical origins of the character, since devils were often depicted or associated with spits. Lees also notices that the Guild plays on the fall of Lucifer were traditionally acted by the Tanners, the craft with which Marlowe's family had long been connected; see Charlton–Waller, eds., *Edward II*, rev. F. N. Lees, pp. 221–222. It might be added that Lightborn's name seems ironically chosen to personify the hideous method of assassination employed, for the murderer (in a sense different from Lucifer's) becomes a literal 'bearer of light': his fiery spit, an illumination of sorts, is the instrument of death, and, in a further play on the character's name, Marlowe stages Lightborn's entrance to his victim by introducing a lantern or torch, so that Edward cries out in terror, 'Who's there? What light is that? Wherefore comes thou?' (V.v.41).

102 Fricker, contending that the 'structural unit' of the play 'is neither the act nor the scene, but what may be called the scenic section' (p. 214), analyses Marlowe's design in terms of musical patterns and analogies. Since Fricker based his valuable study on a division of the play significantly different from that of the present edition, this conclusion is understandable. My own act and scene divisions, indebted mainly to the Broughton edition of 1818 (see my discussion of the text above), make Fricker's contention less tenable; for much of what he perceives about the rhythms and layout of *Edward II* agrees with my own account of its structure. For example, Fricker's notion of the action as consisting 'of three successive waves and counterwaves which differ from one another only by their growing size' (p. 214)—that is, by the successive undulations of the lines of Edward and Mortimer as protagonist and

antagonist—does little violence to the five-act division for which I have been arguing.

103 Shakespeare coined the phrase in *3 Henry VI* where it serves as York's epithet for Margaret of Anjou (I.iv.111). Thomas Gray reapplied it to Queen Isabella in line 57 of his Pindaric ode,'The Bard' (1757), and the sobriquet has stuck to Edward II's spouse ever since. Bertolt Brecht picked it up in his adaptation of Marlowe's play; see Brecht's *Leben Eduards des Zweiten von England* (Potdsam, 1924), pp. 61, 89; also Brecht, *Edward II: A Chronicle Play*, trans. Eric Bentley (New York, 1966), pp. 46, 69.

104 Bevington, *From Mankind to Marlowe: Growth of Structure in the Popular Drama of Tudor England* (Cambridge, Mass., 1962), p. 244.

105 See Deats, 'Edward II: A Study in Androgyny,' pp. 30–41. Levin (*The Overreacher*, p. 94) cites a passage from Drayton's *Piers Gaveston* (1593) that illustrates the popular conception of Edward II's homoeroticism and that implies the dominance of the favourite over the king in more than one sense; in Drayton's poem, Gaveston, speaking of Edward, says, 'I waxt his winges, and taught him art to flye, / Who on his back might beare me through the skye' (ll. 281–282). Deats points out, however, that Marlowe complicates the image of Edward as the passive, or feminine, figure in the sexual relationship by giving to Gaveston some of the attributes of the 'Femme Fatale' and by allowing Lancaster to demean him as the 'Greekish strumpet' (p. 38). Bruce R. Smith also discusses the complexity of sexual role-playing in the play; see *Homosexual Desire in Shakespeare's England: A Cultrual Poetics* (Chicago, 1991), pp. 189–223.

106 Warton, *The History of English Poetry* (London, 1774–81), III, 438; Lamb, *Specimens* (1808), in Lucas, ed., *Works*, IV, 24.

107 See Drake, *Shakspeare and His Times* (London, 1817), II, 247; Broughton, ed., *Edward II*, p. v; Hunt, *Imagination and Fancy* (London, 1844), p. 141; F. W. Hawkins, *The Life of Edmund Kean* (London, 1869), II, 40; A. C. Swinburne, 'The Three Stages of Shakespeare,' *Fortnightly Review*, N.S. 17, 23 (1 May 1875), 629.

108 James Broughton, 'Life and Writings of Christopher Marlowe,' *Gentlemen's Magazine*, 100 (1830), 593.

109 Ward, *A History of English Dramatic Literature to the Death of Queen Anne* (London, 1875), I, 196–199; Ellis, ed., *Christopher Marlowe* (London, 1887), p. xlii.

110 See Hudson, *Shakespeare: His Life, Art, and Characters* (Boston, Mass., 1872), I, 115; Dyce, *Works of Marlowe* (1865 ed.), p. xxiv; Bradley, 'Christopher Marlowe,' in T. H. Ward, ed., *The English Poets: Selections with Critical Introductions by Various Writers*, 3rd ed. (London, 1881), I, 413.

111 Hazlitt, *Lectures on the Dramatic Literature of the Age of Elizabeth* (1820), in P. P. Howe, ed., *The Complete Works of William Hazlitt* (London, 1930–34), VI, 211.

112 Dowden, 'Christopher Marlowe,' *Fortnightly Review*, N.S. 7, 13 (1 January 1870), 74.

113 Saintsbury, *A History of Elizabethan Literature* (London, 1887), p. 77; Lowell, *The Old English Dramatists* (London, 1892), p. 40.

114 Ward, *History*, I, 197; Symonds, *Shakspere's Predecessors in the English*

Drama, 2nd ed. (London, 1900), p. 485; Bradley, 'Christopher Marlowe,' p. 417.

115 Hawkins, *Life of Edmund Kean*, II, 40; unsigned review of Bullen's *Works of Christopher Marlowe*, *The Nation* [New York], 40 (21 May 1885), 424.

116 For a psychoanalytic reading of Marlowe's canon in which the homosexual component figures pervasively, see Constance Brown Kuriyama, *Hammer or Anvil: Psychological Patterns in Christopher Marlowe's Plays* (New Brunswick, N.J., 1980).

117 E. M. W. Tillyard, *Shakespeare's History Plays* (London, 1944), pp. 106–109.

118 Leech, 'Marlowe's *Edward II*: Power and Suffering,' p. 187; Maxwell, 'The Plays of Christopher Marlowe,' in Boris Ford, ed., *The Age of Shakespeare: Volume 2 of the Pelican Guide to English Literature*, 3rd ed. (Harmondsworth, 1960), p. 175; Steane, *Marlowe: A Critical Study* (Cambridge, 1965), pp. 122–123; Sanders, *The Dramatist and the Received Idea: Studies in the Plays of Marlowe & Shakespeare* (Cambridge, 1968), p. 126; Wickham, *Shakespeare's Dramatic Heritage*, pp. 165–166; Clemen, 'Shakespeare and Marlowe,' pp. 130–131. Muriel Bradbrook, like Sanders, finds that *Edward II* is disappointing both dramatically and poetically, but calls it 'merely a history' because of its failure to present a 'central feeling or theme' (*Themes and Conventions of Elizabethan Tragedy* [Cambridge, 1935], p. 161).

119 Bevington, *Tudor Drama and Politics: A Critical Approach to Topical Meaning* (Cambridge, Mass., 1968), p. 218. Like Bevington and Kocher, Michael Manheim notices the unstable shifting of political sympathies in the play, but, with Sanders, considers these to represent mainly confusion rather than subtlety on Marlowe's part; see *The Weak King Dilemma in the Shakespearean History Play* (Syracuse, 1973), pp. 36–53.

120 Leech, 'Marlowe's *Edward II*: Power and Suffering,' p. 195.

121 Kocher, *Christopher Marlowe: A Study of his Thought, Learning, and Character* (Chapel Hill, N.C., 1946), p. 207; Poirier, *Christopher Marlowe* (London, 1951), p. 173.

122 Voss, '*Edward II*: Marlowe's Historical Tragedy,' *E.S.*, 63 (1982), 530.

123 Ribner, *The English History Play in the Age of Shakespeare*, rev. ed. (New York, 1965), p. 124. M. M. Reese agrees: 'Marlowe was chiefly interested in the character of the King, but while the political significance of the play is only intermittent, it is not casual. Edward is a king, his failings are the failings of a ruler, and the crisis of his reign is political; Marlowe recognises that the sins of the man cannot be separated from the sins of his government' (*The Cease of Majesty: A Study of Shakespeare's History Plays* [London, 1961], pp. 80–81).

124 Ribner, *The English History Play*, pp. 126–129.

125 Cole, *Suffering and Evil in the Plays of Christopher Marlowe* (Princeton, 1962), pp. 184–185.

126 U. M. Ellis-Fermor, *Christopher Marlowe* (London, 1927), pp. 113, 117; see also Brodwin, '*Edward II*: Marlowe's Culminating Treatment of Love,' *E.L.H.*, 31 (1964), 139–155. Citing an article by Chalfont Robinson in the *American Journal of Insanity* (January 1910), Ellis-Fermor notes that 'The historical Edward II revealed all the characteristics—most of them naturally unlovable—of a degenerate' (p. 116).

127 Praz, 'Christopher Marlowe,' *English Studies*, 13 (1931), 218; Empson, 'Two Proper Crimes,' *The Nation* [New York], 163, no. 16 (19 October 1946), 444–445.

128 Masinton, *Christopher Marlowe's Tragic Vision: A Study in Damnation* (Athens, Ohio, 1972), pp. 90–94; Godshalk, *The Marlovian World Picture* (The Hague, 1974), pp. 67–69.

129 Kuriyama, *Hammer or Anvil*, pp. 201, 189, 194, 203. Noting the historical parallel between Edward II and James I (whose homosexuality and predilection for male favourites sometimes caused them to be compared during the latter's reign), Kuriyama suggests that Marlowe 'may well have heard rumors of James's early affair with [Esmé Stuart, Duke of] Lennox' and perhaps even that he may 'have been attracted to the reign of Edward partly because of its resemblance to the contemporary reign of James' in Scotland (p. 209). It might be added that the revival of *Edward II* at the Red Bull after James had assumed the English throne could well have been influenced by the same parallel. For further discussion of the popular comparison of James I to Edward II, see Charles R. Forker, 'Sexuality and Eroticism on the Renaissance Stage,' *South Central Review*, 7.4 (1990), 1–22.

130 Weil, *Christopher Marlowe: Merlin's Prophet* (Cambridge, 1977), pp. 147, 162; Greenblatt, 'Marlowe and Renaissance Self-Fashioning,' in Alvin Kernan, ed., *Two Renaissance Mythmakers: Christopher Marlowe and Ben Jonson* (Baltimore, 1977), p. 52.

131 Boyette, 'Wanton Humour and Wanton Poets: Homosexuality in Marlowe's *Edward II*,' *Tulane Studies in English*, 22 (1977), 48–49; Cunningham, 'Renaissance Execution and Marlovian Elocution: The Drama of Death,' *P.M.L.A.*, 105.2 (1990), 218. The notion of *Edward II* as Marlowe's strategically coded protest against homophobia is now fairly widespread. Simon Shepherd in *Marlowe and the Politics of Elizabethan Theatre* (Brighton, 1986) absorbs the question of deviant sexuality into the larger patterns of gendered language and the construction of manliness by which, he supposes, the hegemonic Elizabethan state maintained its power and control. Jennifer Brady writes that 'The re-enactment of Edward's sin in his murder, a murder Mortimer orders, approves and vicariously participates in, marks the crime as a phobic, sadistic denigration of homosexual love'; see 'Fear and Loathing in Marlowe's *Edward II*,' in Carole Levin and Karen Robertson, eds., *Sexuality and Politics in Renaissance Drama*, Studies in Renaissance Literature, Vol. 10 (Lewiston, N.Y., 1991), p. 177. Thomas Cartelli argues that 'Marlowe carnivalizes Edward's and Gaveston's deviations from orthodox social and political behavior. By making the king himself and his base-born favorite the agents of antiauthoritarian misrule, he establishes a provocative alliance between royalty and presumption, united in an erotically charged assault on the constraints imposed on both by an aggressive peerage and an entrenched church'; see 'King Edward's Body,' in *Marlowe, Shakespeare, and the Economy of Theatrical Experience* (Philadelphia, 1991), p. 129. In the most forbiddingly theorized discussion to date, Gregory W. Bredbeck (*Sodomy and Interpretation: Marlowe to Milton* [Ithaca, N.Y., 1991]), treats the play 'as an extended exposition (and hence a demystification and undercutting) of how to inscribe sexual difference onto the tabula rasa of amorphous power' (p. 60). For Bred-

beck, *Edward II* 'foregrounds the interrelatedness of fleshly action and material power' (p. 72), thus dramatizing and enforcing the principle that 'sodomy does not create disorder; rather, disorder demands sodomy' (p. 77).

132 Huebert, 'Tobacco and Boys and Marlowe,' *Sewanee Review*, 92.2 (1984), 209, 212.

133 Summers, 'Sex, Politics, and Self-Realization in *Edward II*,' in Kenneth Friedenreich, Roma Gill, and Constance B. Kuriyama, eds., *'A Poet & a Filthy Play-maker': New Essays on Christopher Marlowe* (New York, 1988), pp. 223–224, 228, 236.

134 Smith, *Homosexual Desire*, pp. 211, 216–217, 221–222.

135 Malcolm Kelsall, *Christopher Marlowe* (Leiden, 1981), p. 47.

136 Clifford Leech speaks of the boy king as 'a stern and just judge' and reminds us 'how reverently his name is invoked in *Richard II*' (*Christopher Marlowe: Poet for the Stage* [New York, 1986], p. 24. Kelsall (*Christopher Marlowe*, pp. 66–69) and Michael Hattaway (*Elizabethan Popular Theatre: Plays in Performance* [London, 1982], p. 159) are much less confident about final justice and political order at the end of the tragedy.

137 Leech, *Christopher Marlowe: Poet for the Stage*, pp. 143–144.

138 Mahood, *Poetry and Humanism* (London, 1950), p. 85.

139 See Chambers, *Elizabethan Stage*, III, 425. Allusions in Henslowe's *Diary* to 'Mortymer' and 'the Spencers' (ed. Foakes and Rickert, pp. 106, 107, 184, 205) are almost certainly not to Marlowe's tragedy.

140 See Bentley, *Jacobean and Caroline Stage*, I, 174; VI, 218; also George Fullmer Reynolds, *The Staging of Elizabethan Plays At the Red Bull Theater, 1605–1625* (New York, 1940), p. 7; also note 129 above.

141 See Hakim, 'Marlowe on the English Stage,' pp. 108, 111–112.

142 C. F. Tucker Brooke quotes a nameless spectator's reaction to the 1903 production: 'The Wonder is not so much that [the play] should have held spellbound an audience, some of whom, perhaps many of whom, were not educated in dramatic literature, as that it should all these years have been neglected of managers'; see 'The Reputation of Christopher Marlowe,' *Connecticut Academy of Arts and Sciences Transactions*, 25 (1922), 407.

143 Quoted in Hakim, 'Marlowe on the English Stage,' p. 134.

144 Speaight, *William Poel and the Elizabethan Revival* (London, 1954), p. 179.

145 See Hakim, 'Marlowe on the English Stage,' pp. 131–135. Hakim's examination of Poel's promptbook reveals extensive cutting of a kind that toned down the political as well as the sexual content of Marlowe's original.

146 Anonymous review in *The Pilot* (15 August 1903), quoted in C. B. Purdom, *Harley Granville Barker: Man of the Theatre, Dramatist and Scholar* (London, 1955), p. 17.

147 Dan H. Lawrence, ed., *Bernard Shaw: Collected Letters, 1898–1910* (New York, 1972), p. 361.

148 Quoted in Geckle, *Text and Performance*, p. 80. Geckle quotes several reviews including one from *The Stage* (4 May 1905).

149 Ibid., p. 80.

150 Ibid., p. 80.

151 Quoted in T. C. Kemp and J. C. Trewin, *The Stratford Festival: A History of the Stratford Memorial Theatre* (Birmingham, 1953), p. 72.

152 See Bakeless, *Tragicall History*, II, 27.

153 Agate, 'Edward the Second,' *The Contemporary Theatre, 1923* (25 November 1923); rpt. in Agate, *Brief Chronicles: A Survey of the Plays of Shakespeare and the Elizabethans in Actual Performance* (London, 1943), pp. 136–138. See also Ivor Brown, 'Two Platform Plays,' *Saturday Review*, 136 (24 November 1923), 566–567.

154 Bakeless, II, 27; see also 'Great English Play in Prague,' *Manchester Guardian* (15 February 1922), p. 5.

155 See Ulrich Weisstein, 'The First Version of Brecht/Feuchtwanger's *Leben Eduards des Zweiten von England* and Its Relation to the Standard Text,' *J.E.G.P.*, 69 (1970), 196 n. 13.

156 Translated excerpts from Herbert Jhering's review of the Munich performance were printed in the programme of the National Theatre's 1968 revival of the Brecht play; see John Bowen, 'The Brecht *Edward II*,' *Plays and Players*, 15 (July 1968), 14.

157 Louise J. Laboulle, 'A Note on Bertolt Brecht's Adaptation of Marlowe's *Edward II*,' *M.L.N.*, 54 (1959), 214.

158 For the 1956 London performance, see Hakim, 'Marlowe on the English Stage,' p. 254; for the East Berlin production, see Otis L. Guernsey Jr, ed., *The Best Plays of 1974–1975* (New York, 1975), p. 123.

159 See Eric Bentley, trans., *Bertolt Brecht: Edward II, A Chronicle Play* (New York, 1966), p. 100; also reviews in the *Times* (1 May 1968), p. 8; the *Guardian* (1 May 1968), p. 6; and *Plays and Players*, 15 (July 1968), 14–17, 70.

160 See the review in the *Toronto Globe and Mail* (23 March 1971), p. 17. The English translation used was that of Jean Benedetti; see John Willett and Ralph Manheim, eds., *Bertolt Brecht: Collected Plays*, I (London, 1970), 179–268.

161 See reviews of these productions by David Zane Mairowitz (*Plays and Players*, 23 [October 1975], 26–27) and by Barbara Schulman (*Plays and Players*, no. 343 [April 1982], 33–34).

162 See Otis L. Guernsey Jr, ed., *The Best Plays of 1982–1983* (New York, 1983), p. 418.

163 *Spectator*, 136 (13 March 1926), 482.

164 See 'The Holywell Players,' *Times* (3 April 1928), p. 14; also 'Christ Church Play,' *Times* (10 February 1933), p. 10.

165 Bakeless, II, 27.

166 See Frank M. Caldiero, 'Marlowe's *Edward II*: A Performance in America,' *N.&Q.*, 186 (1944), 159.

167 See George Freedley, 'City College Puts on *Edward II*,' *New York Morning Telegraph* (1 May 1948), p. 2; see also Otis L. Guernsey Jr, ed., *The Best Plays of 1975–1976* (New York, 1976), p. 324.

168 *Times* (4 December 1951), p. 8, and Greenwald, *Directions by Indirections* (Newark, 1985), p. 25 and note; see also Simon Raven's favourable notice in the *Cambridge Review*, 73 (19 January 1952), 220–222.

169 For the Oxford University Dramatic Society production, see Anthony Hartley, 'What's Wrong with Edinburgh?,' *Spectator* (3 September 1954), p. 276; also Norman Marshall, *The Producer and the Play*, 2nd ed.

(London, 1962), p. 219. For the three Planchon productions, see Yvette Daoust, *Roger Planchon: Director and Playwright* (Cambridge: Cambridge University Press, 1981), pp. 74–81, and also the *Times* (8 August 1960), p. 5. Marshall briefly discusses the Planchon versions (*The Producer and the Play*, pp. 291–292).

170 See *Times* (17 January 1955), p. 5.

171 See also *Plays and Players*, 3 (May 1956), 22–23.

172 See 'Summer Plays at Ludlow,' *Times* (10 July 1956), p. 14; also J. C. Trewin, 'The World of the Theatre,' *Illustrated London News*, 229 (28 July 1956), 156.

173 For the ANTA production, directed by Edward G. Greer, see a review in the *New York Times* (12 February 1958), which praises it as an 'intelligent airing' of Marlowe's play and claims that it had 'never before [been] performed by a professional troupe in New York' (p. 32). Otis L. Guernsey Jr (without informative detail) mentions an Equity Library Theatre performance during the same season; see *The Best Plays of 1975–1976* (New York, 1976), p. 324. This, however, probably represents a confusion with Kidd's ANTA production since no evidence of a second New York performance in 1957–58 has been found; see Garrison P. Sherwood's 'Off Broadway,' in Guernsey, *The Best Plays of 1957–1958* (New York, 1958), p. 56, which lists a production of *Edward II* in an ambiguous context that could easily have led Guernsey to suppose (mistakenly) that all the plays mentioned were Equity Library productions.

174 See Leech, 'Marlowe's *Edward II*: Power and Suffering,' pp. 181–196. Other laudatory comments on this production can be found in an interview with Toby Robertson conducted by John Russell Brown; see 'Directing *Edward II*,' *T.D.R.*, 8 (summer 1964), 174–183. See also the reviews quoted by Geckle, *Text and Performance*, pp. 81–84; also the *Times* (12 August 1958), p. 10, and (26 August 1958), p. 11.

175 See the reviews in *Punch*, 247 (8 July 1964), 65, and the *Times* (2 July 1964), p. 16; other reviews are cited by Geckle, *Text and Performance*, pp. 98–99.

176 For the Bristol Old Vic production, see Wickham, '*Edward II*,' *New Theatre*, 5 (April–June 1964), 20–21; also Wickham, '*Exeunt to the Cave*: Notes on the Staging of Marlowe's Plays,' *T.D.R.*, 8.4 (summer 1964), 184–194. For the Harvard reading, see Lloyd Schwartz, 'Marlowe Readings at the Loeb,' *Harvard Drama Review*, I.5 (20 March 1964), unpaginated, and the *Harvard Crimson* (6 March 1964), p. 2 (Professor Schwartz obligingly sent me a copy of his hard-to-obtain article). For the London Marlowe Society production, see H. G. M., 'The Marlowe Society Presents *Edward II*,' *Theatre World* (London), 60 (April 1964), 34; *Times* (5 March 1964), p. 5; *Illustrated London News* (14 March 1964), p. 405. For the Manchester University performance, see 'More Age of Shakespeare Productions,' *Stage and Television Today* (14 May 1964), p. 15; also Pistotnik, 'Marlowe in Performance,' p. 366.

177 For the Mountview Theatre Club production, see Hakim, 'Marlowe on the English Stage,' p. 357; for the Birmingham Repertory production, see notices in the *Birmingham Post* (27 April 1966), p. 7, and *Stage and Television Today* (12 May 1966), p. 16.

178 See W. Granger Blair, 'Shakespeareans to Be in Spy Film,' *New York Times* (11 February 1966), p. 36; also James Robert Parish and Michael R. Pitts, *The Great Spy Pictures* (Metuchen, N.J., 1974), pp. 137–138.

179 For the University of Toronto production see reviews in the *Toronto Globe and Mail* (21 January 1967), p. 14, and the *Toronto Daily Star* (26 January 1967), p. 22. For the Theatre Toronto production see reviews in the *Toronto Telegram* (10 January 1969, p. 42; 13 January 1969, p. 41) and the *Toronto Daily Star* (10 January 1969), p. 22. See also the *New York Times* (19 January 1969), sec. 2, p. 30.

180 Geckle, *Text and Performance*, pp. 84–98; see also Michael Billington's interview with McKellen in the *Illustrated London News* (17 January 1970), pp. 22–23.

181 Nevertheless, McKellen's flamboyantly homosexual characterization of Edward II elicited a protest from the Edinburgh City Councillors, who objected to such a performance being staged in the place where the General Assembly of the traditionally Calvinist Church of Scotland annually meets. The most vocal of the antagonists was John Kidd, who pronounced the open kissing of Edward and Gaveston 'shocking' and 'filthy'; see the *Daily Telegraph* (30 August 1969), quoted in Pistotnik, 'Marlowe in Performance,' p. 193.

182 The king and his party wore 1960s 'mod' clothing suggestive of youthful rebellion (tight trousers, wide leather belts, shirts unbuttoned in front, and neck jewellery) while the barons were dressed in outfits that vaguely reminded one of armour or chain mail.

183 See Otis L. Guernsey Jr, ed., *The Best Plays of 1970–1971* (New York, 1971), p. 48; I am indebted to Mr Feidner, who kindly sent me photographs and a programme from his production.

184 See Dick Brukenfeld, 'His Kingdom for a Touch of Warmth,' *Village Voice* (29 October 1970), p. 56.

185 See also Otis L. Guernsey Jr, ed., *The Best Plays of 1974–1975* (New York, 1975), p. 386.

186 Gill, *New Yorker*, 51 (3 November 1975), 121; see also the review by Stanley Kauffmann in the *New Republic*, 173 (6 December 1975), 14.

187 See the Corpus Christi Association *Letter* (1977), p. 99.

188 For the Oxford productions, see Hakim, 'Marlowe on the English Stage,' p. 357, and Pistotnik, 'Marlowe in Performance,' p. 366. The quotation comes from the Brasenose College magazine, the *Brazen Nose* (1981), p. 246.

189 See the review by Kenn Stitt in *Stage and Television Today* (15 March 1984), p. 25.

190 This information is based on a personal letter from Mr Moar; the quoted words are from the Clare College *Annual* (1985), p. 33.

191 For the Equity Showcase production, see the *Toronto Globe and Mail* (16 January 1987), p. D12.

192 See the review by Michael Ratcliffe in the *Observer* (26 October 1986), p. 23.

193 See the review by Roger Holdsworth in *R.O.R.D.*, 29 (1986–87), 61–63.

194 See *Plays and Players*, no. 399 (December 1986), 26.

195 Holdsworth, *R.O.R.D.*, p. 62.

196 Beale had earlier taken the part of Kent in an unspecified student production in which 'Tony Slattery played Edward II brilliantly'; see Beale's comments in an article by Carl Miller in *RSC Magazine*, no. 1 (1990), pp. 22–23.

197 See also reviews in the *Financial Times* (12 July 1990), p. 17; and in the *Marlowe Society of America Newsletter*, 10.2 (fall 1990), 3.

198 See Malcolm Johnson, '*Edward* gets royal treatment from Yale Rep,' *The Hartford Courant* (21 March 1992), p. D6; also Alvin Klein, '*Edward the Second* at Yale Rep,' *New York Times* (5 April 1992), p. 21.

199 See Derek Jarman, *Queer Edward II* (London: British Film Institute, 1991), dedication page. See also reviews by Hugh Davenport in the *Weekly Telegraph* (27 October 1991), p. 27; by Christopher Edwards in the *Spectator*, 267 (19 October 1991), 48–49; and by Stephen Holden in the *New York Times* (20 March 1992), p. C16.

THE TROUBLESOME REIGN
AND LAMENTABLE DEATH
OF EDWARD THE SECOND,
KING OF ENGLAND,
WITH THE TRAGICAL FALL
OF PROUD MORTIMER

Title. THE TROUBLESOME REIGN . . . MORTIMER] *Q (title page);*
The troublesome raigne . . . *Mortimer:* And also the life and death of *Peirs*
Gaueston, the great Earle of Cornewall, *and mighty* fauorite of king *Edward* the
second *Q2 (title page), Q3–4 (subst.).*

The troublesome

raigne and lamentable death of
Edward *the second*, *King of*
England : with the tragicall
. *fall of proud* Mortimer:

As it was sundrie times publiquely acted
in the honourable citie of London, *by the*
right honourable the Earle of Pem-
brooke his seruants.

Written by Chri. Marlow *Gent.*

Imprinted at London for *William Iones*,
dwelling neere Holbourne conduit, at the
signe of the Gunne. 1594.

1594 (A 1 recto) Cassel
Reproduced from Greg's edition

[DRAMATIS PERSONAE

KING EDWARD THE SECOND

PRINCE EDWARD, *his son, afterwards* KING EDWARD THE THIRD

Edmund, Earl of KENT, *brother of* King Edward the Second

PIERCE OF GAVESTON, Earl of Cornwall

Guy, Earl of WARWICK

Thomas, Earl of LANCASTER

Aymer de Valence, Earl of PEMBROKE

Edmund Fitzalan, Earl of ARUNDEL

Henry, Earl of LEICESTER

SIR THOMAS BERKELEY (*spelled* 'Bartley' *in* Q)

MORTIMER SENIOR (Roger Mortimer of Chirke)

MORTIMER JUNIOR (Roger Mortimer of Wigmore), *nephew of*
  Mortimer Senior, *afterwards Lord Protector over* Edward the Third

SPENCER SENIOR (Hugh le Despenser), Earl of Winchester

SPENCER JUNIOR (Hugh le Despenser), Earl of Wiltshire, *later*
  Earl of Gloucester, *son of* Spencer Senior

The Archbishop of CANTERBURY ('Bishop' of Canterbury *in* Q;
  Walter Reynolds)

The Bishop of COVENTRY (Walter Langton)

The Bishop of WINCHESTER (John Stratford)

ROBERT BALDOCK, *a clerk, attendant on* Lady Margaret de Clare

HENRY DE BEAUMONT, *a follower of the king*

SIR WILLIAM TRUSSEL

SIR THOMAS GURNEY (Gournay) ⎱
SIR JOHN MATREVIS (Maltravers) ⎰ *henchmen of* Mortimer Junior

LIGHTBORN, *a murderer*

SIR JOHN OF HAINAULT, *brother of the* Marquis of Hainault

LEVUNE, *a Frenchman*

RICE AP HOWELL

The ABBOT (of Neath)

JAMES, *one of* Pembroke's *men*

Three Poor Men

A Chaplain

The Clerk of the crown

A Guard

DRAMATIS PERSONAE] This ed., based on Merchant; first listed, in incomplete form, in Dodsley[1]; not in Q1–4.

A Post from Scotland
A Post from France
The Mayor of Bristol
A Messenger
A Horse-Boy
A Herald
A Mower
The King's Champion

QUEEN ISABELLA, *wife of* Edward the Second, *daughter (and now sister) of the* King of France (Philip IV; Charles IV)
LADY MARGARET DE CLARE, *daughter of the* Earl of Gloucester, *niece of* King Edward the Second, *betrothed to* Gaveston

Lords, Ladies in Waiting, Soldiers, Attendants, Monks, Servants

The Scene: *England, France.*]

Act I

Enter GAVESTON *reading on a letter that was brought him
from the king.*

Gaveston. 'My father is deceased; come, Gaveston,
  And share the kingdom with thy dearest friend.'
  Ah, words that make me surfeit with delight!
  What greater bliss can hap to Gaveston
  Than live and be the favourite of a king?   5
  Sweet prince, I come. These, these thy amorous lines
  Might have enforced me to have swum from France,
  And, like Leander, gasped upon the sand,
  So thou wouldst smile and take me in thy arms.
  The sight of London to my exiled eyes   10
  Is as Elysium to a new-come soul;
  Not that I love the city or the men,
  But that it harbours him I hold so dear—

Head-title omitted] *Q2–4;* The troublesome raigne and la- / *mentable death of*
Edward *the* / second, king of England: with the / *tragicall fall of proud*
Mortimer. *Q.* (Zürich copy)   *Heading.* Act I, Scene i] *Broughton; not in*
Q.   0.1. *on*] *Q; of Q2MS.*   6. These, these] *Q1–4;* these *Q2MS.*   9.
thy] *Q;* thine *Q2MS., Q2–4.*

---

4. *hap to*] befall, happen to.
7. *France*] Edward I exiled Gaveston to his home in Ponthieu, Gascony
(territory controlled by England)—according to Holinshed, 'least the prince,
who delighted much in his companie, might by his evill and wanton counsell
fall to evill and naughtie rule' (p. 313).
8. *Leander*] Gaveston's allusion to the mythological lover who swam the
Hellespont nightly to visit Hero at Sestos and was ultimately drowned
quickly establishes the erotic nature of his relationship to Edward and
ironically foreshadows his own death. In his poem on the subject Marlowe
calls Hero 'Venus' nun' (I, 45). Marlowe's section of *Hero and Leander*
(completed by Chapman) stops well short of the tragic conclusion; but cf. 'By
this, Leander being near the land, / Cast down his weary feet, and felt the
sand. / Breathless albeit he were, he rested not . . .'(II, 227–229).
11. *Elysium*] in classical Greece the name for heaven.

The king, upon whose bosom let me die,
And with the world be still at enmity.   15
What need the arctic people love star-light
To whom the sun shines both by day and night?
Farewell base stooping to the lordly peers;
My knee shall bow to none but to the king.
As for the multitude, that are but sparks   20
Raked up in embers of their poverty,
Tanti! I'll fan first on the wind
That glanceth at my lips and flieth away.
But how now, what are these?

---

14. die] *Q;* lie *Scott.*   19. knee] *Q1–3;* knees *Q4.*   20. As] *Q;* Its
Q2MS.   21. Raked] *Q* (Rakt); bakt *Q2MS.*   22. *Tanti*] *Q;* tantum
Q2MS.   22. fan] *Q1–4* (fanne); fawn *Oxberry;* faune *Brooke.*

---

14. *die*] swoon (probably with a pun on 'ejaculate'); Deats believes that the
verb implies Gaveston's ' "male" posture' or dominant role in his homosexual
relationship with Edward ('Study in Androgyny', p. 38). Scott's emendation
lie is unnecessary as well as unimaginative.

16–17. *What . . . night?*] i.e., since there is no sunset in the Arctic during
summer, starlight is irrelevant; Gaveston implies that he has no need of
inferior favours, those of the peers (cf. ll. 18–19), because he basks in the
light of the king (traditionally associated with the sun).

18. *base*] Briggs compares *R2,* III.iii.180, where the word also mingles the
two senses of 'low' and 'ignoble.'

20–21 *sparks . . . embers*] alluding to the practice of keeping fires from
going out overnight by covering them with ashes and then raking the embers
together in the morning to enkindle flame. Merchant notes that Marlowe
extends the imagery of light (starlight, sun, sparks, embers) in order to
suggest a relationship between the principal source of light in the heavens
(analogous to the king) and lesser degrees among men.

22. *Tanti!*] So much for that! (probably Marlowe's or perhaps the compositor's spelling of Italian 'Tant' è'); spoken with contempt. Perhaps an
early suggestion of Gaveston's foreign affectations (cf. I.i.54, I.iv.412).

fan . . . on] either (1) 'fawn . . . on' or (2) 'fan . . . on', i.e., drive air upon,
cool. *Fanne* (uncorrected in all the quartos) may be a misprint for *faune* (or,
less likely, an alternative spelling of *fan,* a dialectal form of *fawn* [O.E.D.
1.9]). But since *fawne* occurs at I.iv.15 and I.iv.145, the meaning may be to
'cause a current of air to cool the wind' (cf. 'as one that beateth the air' [1
Cor. 9:26, the Epistle for Septuagesima Sunday in the Book of Common
Prayer]). Gill thinks that Marlowe 'is here continuing the metaphor of sparks
and coals' that 'needed to be fanned (or blown with bellows) into life.'
Whichever word is intended, the basic meaning is a gesture of futility.

Enter three Poor Men.

Poor Men. Such as desire your worship's service.   25
Gaveston. What canst thou do?
1 Poor Man. I can ride.
Gaveston. But I have no horses. What art thou?
2 Poor Man. A traveller.
Gaveston. Let me see; thou wouldst do well to wait at my   30
          trencher and tell me lies at dinner time, and, as I like
          your discoursing, I'll have you. And what art thou?
3 Poor Man. A soldier that hath served against the Scot.
Gaveston. Why, there are hospitals for such as you.
          I have no war, and therefore, sir, be gone.   35
3 Poor Man. Farewell, and perish by a soldier's hand,
                                              [*Offers to leave.*]
          That wouldst reward them with an hospital.
Gaveston. [*Aside*] Ay, ay. These words of his move me as
          much
          As if a goose should play the porcupine,

---

25. Such] *Q; Poor men, such Kirschbaum.*   28. horses] *Q;* horse *Q2–4.*
30–32. Let . . . thou?] *Merchant (as prose);* Let . . . well / To . . . time, /
And . . . you. / And . . . thou? *Q.*   31. dinner time] *Q;* dinner *Q2MS.*
36. *3 Poor Man*] *Oxberry (subst.);* Sold. *Q.*   36.1. *Offers . . . leave*] *Bowers
(subst.);* not in *Q.*   38. *Aside*] *Dodsley*[1] *(following line 42);* not in *Q.*   39.
porcupine] *Q2–4;* Porpintine *Q.*

24.1. The appearance of the three poor men initiates a small 'morality,'
exhibiting Gaveston's hubris and foreshadowing his fall. Marlowe employs a
related technique later with the Mower (IV.vii.45.1).
    25. *Such . . . service*] Kirschbaum's attempt to make this line a pentameter
by adding two words from the preceding stage direction seems unnecessary.
    31. *trencher*] plate (hence one's place at table).
    lies] i.e., travellers' tales.
    33. *against the Scot*] Holinshed devotes much attention to England's wars
with Scotland in the reigns of Edward I and Edward II; see Introduction,
pp. 46–47. Edward I died while engaged in such a campaign.
    34. *hospitals*] homes for maimed soldiers as well as the destitute and
aged poor; Charlton–Waller point out that 'they frequently housed very
unsavoury characters'; cf. *H5*, II.i.75–78, where prostitutes are mentioned as
frequenting 'the spital.'
    36. *perish . . . hand*] The curse, of course, is prophetic.
    36.1 *Offers*] Intends, makes as if. Cf. *Massacre at Paris*, xxi.122.
    39. *porcupine*] The superstition that the porcupine (or 'porpintine') could
shoot its quills goes back to Pliny; Charlton–Waller cite Holland's translation

And dart her plumes, thinking to pierce my breast;   40
But yet it is no pain to speak men fair.
I'll flatter these and make them live in hope.
[*To them*] You know that I came lately out of France,
And yet I have not viewed my lord the king.
If I speed well, I'll entertain you all.   45
Poor Men. We thank your worship.
Gaveston. I have some business; leave me to myself.
Poor Men. We will wait here about the court.   *Exeunt.*
Gaveston. Do. These are not men for me;
I must have wanton poets, pleasant wits,   50
Musicians that, with touching of a string,
May draw the pliant king which way I please.
Music and poetry is his delight;
Therefore I'll have Italian masques by night,

---

40. dart] *Q;* eate *Q2MS.*   42. these] *Q;* them *Q2MS.*   43. *To them*]
Oliphant (subst.); not in Q.   46, 48. *Poor Men*] *Ribner; Omnes Q.*   48.
We] *Q;* I *Q2MS.*   48. *Exeunt*] *Q; exit 3 Q2MS.*   53. is] *Q;* are *Q2MS.,*
Dodsley[1].

(VIII, xxxv), also Ascham (*Toxophilus*, ed. Edward Arber [Westminster,
1902], p. 31).

41. *speak men fair*] Deats points out that this idiom appears six other times
in the play (I.iv.63, I.iv.183, I.iv.336, II.ii.228, II.iv.28, V.i.91) and was
proverbially associated with flattery or hypocrisy ('Study in Androgyny,'
p. 32 n. 8).

45. *speed well*] succeed in rising, prosper.
entertain] take into service; cf. II.ii.240.

50. *wanton poets*] those whose appeal is amorous or lascivious; Briggs
compares *R2*, 'lascivious metres' (II.i.19). The entire speech is an imaginative
construct based upon Holinshed's description of Edward's 'disordered
maners' that included 'iesting, plaieng, banketing' (p. 318; see Appendix B,
no. 5).

53–54. *delight . . . night*] Levin notices this 'casual couplet' as suggestively
'bracket[ing]' 'sound and spectacle' (*Overreacher*, p. 92).

54. *Italian masques*] Anachronistically, Gaveston imagines sixteenth-century
rather than medieval entertainment. Bruce Smith notes that Leicester's
pageant for Queen Elizabeth at Kenilworth Castle, Gascoigne's *Princelye*
Pleasures (1575), featured retainers of the earl 'decked out as nymphs and
satyrs' and a 'boy dressed up as Diana'; he also compares Suetonius's
salacious life of Tiberius, translated by Holland, 1606 (p. 99): the emperor
'devised in the woods also and groves here and there, certaine places for
lecherie and venerous Acts: wherein he had within caves and holow rockes

Sweet speeches, comedies, and pleasing shows;   55
And in the day, when he shall walk abroad,
Like sylvan nymphs my pages shall be clad,
My men, like satyrs grazing on the lawns,
Shall with their goat-feet dance an antic hay.
Sometime a lovely boy in Dian's shape,   60
With hair that gilds the water as it glides,
Crownets of pearl about his naked arms,
And in his sportful hands an olive tree
To hide those parts which men delight to see,
Shall bathe him in a spring; and there, hard by,   65
One like Actaeon, peeping through the grove,
Shall by the angry goddess be transformed,
And, running in the likeness of an hart,
By yelping hounds pulled down, and seem to die.

---

57. sylvan] *Q2MS*. (Syluan); *Siluian Q1–4*.   58. grazing] *Q;* gasing
Q2MS.   59. goat-feet] *Q* (Goate feete); Goates feete *Q2MS*.   59. an] *Q;*
the *Q2–4*.   64. which] *Q;* as *Q2MS*.   65. hard by] *Q;* by *Q2MS*.   69.
and] *Q;* shall *Dodsley*[1].

---

youthes of both sexes standing at receit readie prostitute, in habit of *Paniskes*
and *Nymphes*' (*Homosexual Desire*, p. 212).
    58. *grazing*] i.e., moving over the lawns as though tending grazing cattle.
    59. *antic hay*] quaint country dance with interweaving lines like an old-
fashioned ('antic,' 'antique') reel. *Antic* also carries overtones of grotesquerie.
    60. *Dian's shape*] Diana's costume; see note on l. 54 above.
    62. *Crownets*] coronets, i.e., bracelets. Richard Barnfield borrows the
entire line in his 'Complaint of Daphnis for the Love of Ganimede' (l. 104),
the first eclogue in *The Affectionate Shepheard* (1594); see George Klawitter,
ed., *Richard Barnfield: The Complete Poems* (Selinsgrove, 1990), p. 82.
    66. *Actaeon*] the mythological hunter, familiar from Ovid's *Metamorphoses*
(III, 155ff.), who happened upon Diana bathing and was punished by being
turned into a stag, whom she then hunted down with his own dogs. Sunesen
was the first of several commentators to notice the symbolic and ironic
portent of the Actaeon story in its present homoerotic context, Gaveston
himself being represented emblematically by the transvestite Diana (the
'lovely boy') who teasingly attracts Edward (the royally descended Actaeon)
and who then renders him politically helpless by becoming the object of his
amorous obsession with the result that the king is ultimately pursued and
killed by the outraged nobles (the 'yelping hounds'); Sunesen points out that
Marlowe also employed the Actaeon fable for the symbolic punishment of
Benvolio in *Doctor Faustus* (xii.50–53). See 'Marlowe and the Dumb Show,'
pp. 245–247; also Deats, 'Myth and Metamorphosis,' pp. 310–311.

Such things as these best please his majesty,   70
My lord. Here comes the king and the nobles
From the parliament. I'll stand aside.

[*Walks apart.*]

Enter [EDWARD] *the* King, [*the* Earl *of*] LANCASTER, MORTIMER
SENIOR, MORTIMER JUNIOR, EDMUND Earl *of* KENT, GUY Earl *of*
WARWICK, [*and others*].

Edward. Lancaster.
Lancaster. My lord?
Gaveston. [*Aside*] That Earl of Lancaster do I abhor.   75
Edward. Will you not grant me this? [*Aside*] In spite of them
        I'll have my will; and these two Mortimers
        That cross me thus shall know I am displeased.
Mortimer Senior. If you love us, my lord, hate Gaveston.
Gaveston. [*Aside*] That villain Mortimer! I'll be his death.   80
Mortimer Junior. Mine uncle here, this earl, and I myself

70–71. majesty, / My lord. Here comes] *Brooke (subst.)*; maiestie. / My lord,
heere comes *Q1–2*; Maiesty, / My Lord, here comes *Q3–4*; majesty. / Here
comes *Dodsley*[1]; majesty. / My Lord here comes [comes;] *Dodsley*[2]; majesty. /
But soft [soft;] here come *Broughton, Broughton MS.;* majesty. / By'r lord!
here comes *Robinson;* majesty. / Here comes my lord *Dyce*[1]; majesty, / My
lord. / Here comes *Oliphant;* majesty. / My lord! Here comes *Charlton–
Waller.*   71–72. Here . . . aside.] *McLaughlin (as prose);* Here . . . nobles /
From . . . aside. *Q;* Here comes my lord / The king . . . parliament. / I'll
stand aside. *Fleay.*   72.1. Walks apart] *Dyce*[1] *(subst.) (Retires); not in Q.*
72.4. *and others*] *Broughton (subst.) (and other Nobles); &c. Q.*   75. Aside]
Scott; not in Q.   76. Aside] *Dyce*[1]*; not in Q.*   80. Aside] *Scott; not in Q.*

70–71. *his . . . lord.*] A much bedeviled passage punctuationally (see
collations above). Brooke's emendation, removing the full stop at the end of
l. 70 and placing 'My lord' in apposition with 'his majesty,' seems more
natural than the other solutions proposed. Substitution of a full stop for a
comma is a fairly common printer's error. Charlton–Waller's interpretation
of 'My lord' as an ejaculation would seem to have no parallel in Elizabethan
stage idiom.

71. *comes*] Quasi-singular verbs with plural subjects are common in Elizabethan usage; see Abbott 333.

72.3. EDMUND *Earl of* KENT] an anachronism; in 1307 the historical
Kent was only six years old.

75. *Earl of Lancaster*] As the queen's uncle, Lancaster had a personal as
well as political reason for detesting Gaveston.

81. *Mine . . . earl*] i.e., Mortimer Senior and Lancaster. Marlowe freely
alters history here. In Holinshed (p. 320) and Stowe (p. 314) the earls who

Were sworn to your father at his death
That he should ne'er return into the realm;
And know, my lord, ere I will break my oath,
This sword of mine that should offend your foes   85
Shall sleep within the scabbard at thy need,
And underneath thy banners march who will,
For Mortimer will hang his armour up.

Gaveston. [Aside] Mort Dieu!

Edward. Well, Mortimer, I'll make thee rue these words.   90
Beseems it thee to contradict thy king?
Frownst thou thereat, aspiring Lancaster?
The sword shall plane the furrows of thy brows
And hew these knees that now are grown so stiff.
I will have Gaveston, and you shall know   95
What danger 'tis to stand against your king.

Gaveston. [Aside] Well done, Ned.

Lancaster. My lord, why do you thus incense your peers,
That naturally would love and honour you
But for that base and obscure Gaveston?   100
Four earldoms have I besides Lancaster—

---

89. *Aside*] *Scott; not in Q.*   93. plane] *Q;* plaine *Q2–4.*   97. *Aside*] *Scott; not in Q.*   99–100. you / But . . . Gaveston?] *Scott;* you: / But . . . *Gaueston, Q1–4;* you? / But . . . Gaveston, *Dodsley[1].*

---

were said to have sworn to Edward I to oppose Gaveston's return were Lincoln, Warwick, and Pembroke. Holinshed also says that Thomas of Lancaster, who married Lincoln's daughter, was bound by his father-in-law on his deathbed not to readmit Gaveston to England (see Appendix B, no. 6). The Mortimers were not involved in either of these oaths; see Introduction, pp. 52–53.

85–86. *sword . . . sleep*] a familiar figure; cf. *H5*, I.ii.22.

87. *march who will*] i.e., let whoever wishes march.

89. Mort Dieu!] God's death! (obviously suggesting Gaveston's French background); also perhaps a punning allusion to the false etymology of Mortimer's name since the final *t* in '*Mort*' would be voiced (see II.iii.22–23 and note).

92. *aspiring Lancaster*] Tancock adduces *3H6*, V.vi.61; see Introduction, p. 26.

100. *base and obscure*] See Introduction, p. 51–52.

101. *Four earldoms*] In 1311 Thomas of Lancaster inherited the earldoms of Lincoln and Salisbury from his father-in-law, Henry Lacy; he had already become Earl of Lancaster, Leicester, and Derby on the death of his father, Edmund, brother of Edward I (see Holinshed, p. 331; Appendix B, no. 7).

Derby, Salisbury, Lincoln, Leicester;
These will I sell to give my soldiers pay
Ere Gaveston shall stay within the realm.
Therefore if he be come, expel him straight.   105
Kent. Barons and earls, your pride hath made me mute,
But now I'll speak—and to the proof, I hope:
I do remember, in my father's days,
Lord Percy of the north, being highly moved,
Braved Mowbery in presence of the king,   110
For which, had not his highness loved him well,
He should have lost his head; but with his look
The undaunted spirit of Percy was appeased,
And Mowbery and he were reconciled.
Yet dare you brave the king unto his face?   115
Brother, revenge it; and let these their heads
Preach upon poles for trespass of their tongues.
Warwick. O, our heads!
Edward. Ay, yours; and therefore I would wish you
        grant—
Warwick. Bridle thy anger, gentle Mortimer.   120
Mortimer Junior. I cannot nor I will not; I must speak.
Cousin, our hands, I hope, shall fence our heads,
And strike off his that makes you threaten us.

---

106. *Kent.*] *Q1–3 (Edm.); Ed. Q4; Edw. Dodsley*[1].   109. Percy] *Q*
(Percie), Q3–4; Peirce Q2.   110, 114. Mowbery] *Q (Mowberie), Q2*
(Moubery); Moubray Q3–4, Mowbray Dyce[1].   117. Preach] *Q;* Perch
Dodsley[1].

---

103. *These . . . pay*] By intending to pay soldiers under his command
directly with his own funds, Lancaster threatens to destroy their official
loyalty to the king. Historically, Lancaster controlled his own private army.

107. *to the proof*] irrefutably.

108. *I do remember*] An incident invented by Marlowe. Lunt suggests that
it may have been based on the quarrel involving Mowbray that Shakespeare
later used for the opening scenes of *R2*.

117. *Preach upon poles*] cf. III.i.20; see Introduction, p. 56. Marlowe
might also have remembered *2H6*, IV.vii.124, where the heads of Lord Say
and Sir John Cromer are carried on poles.

118. *our heads*] with the emphasis on 'our' (cf. 'yours' in l. 119).

122. *Cousin*] The younger Mortimer was only distantly related to Edward
II through his mother, a kinswoman of the king's mother.

fence] defend.

123. *his*] i.e., Gaveston's (foreshadowing the favourite's death).

Come uncle, let us leave the brainsick king,
And henceforth parley with our naked swords.   125
Mortimer Senior. Welshry hath men enough to save our heads.
Warwick. [*Sarcastically*] All Warwickshire will love him for
    my sake.
Lancaster. [*With like irony*] And northward Gaveston hath
    many friends.
    Adieu, my lord, and either change your mind,
    Or look to see the throne where you should sit   130
    To float in blood, and at thy wanton head
    The glozing head of thy base minion thrown.
                                        Exeunt Nobles [*except* KENT].
Edward. I cannot brook these haughty menaces;
    Am I a king and must be overruled?
    Brother, display my ensigns in the field.   135

---

125. parley] *Q2–3* (parlie), *Dodsley*[1] (parly); parle *Q.*   126. Welshry] *Gill*
(*see commentary note*); Wilshire *Q1–2*; Wiltshire *Q3–4*.   127. *Sarcastically*]
Oliphant; not in Q.   127. love] *Q*; leave *Dyce*[1].   128. With . . . irony]
Oliphant (subst.); not in Q.   *128. Gaveston] Q*; Lancaster *Broughton,
Oxberry.*   132.1. Nobles] *Q3* (nobels), *Q4*; Nobiles *Q1–2*.   132.1. *except*
KENT] *Dyce*[1] *(subst.); not in Q.*

---

126. *Welshry*] the population of Wales. Since Lord Mortimer of Chirke
held his greatest power in Wales during Edward II's reign, Q's 'Wilshire'
makes little sense. Roma Gill ('Mortimer's Men,' *N.&Q.*, N.S. 27 [1980],
159) argues convincingly that the compositor must have misread 'Welshrye—
or even, perhaps Welshire.' The Mortimers had no connections in Wiltshire.

131. *wanton*] reckless, undisciplined (probably with overtones of libidinous-
ness); see l. 50 above.

132. *glozing*] flattering (a pejorative variant of 'glossing', i.e., explaining
away, speaking smoothly).

base minion] See note on l. 18 above. 'Minion' (a derivative of French
mignon = darling boy) becomes a term of homophobic contempt in the
mouths of the barons; but Edward himself applies it non-pejoratively to
Gaveston at I.iv.30. Levin points out that the word occurs nine times in the
play and significantly 'charges [its] atmosphere' (*Overreacher*, pp. 92–93).
Smith discusses the politico-sexual implications of the epithet in Renaissance
history and culture (*Homosexual Desire*, pp. 211–213).

134. *must*] Cf. *R2*, III.iii.143–145, where the king indignantly reiterates
the word 'must' in a similar context. When Elizabeth I was fatally ill in
1602–03, her secretary Robert Cecil said to her, 'Madame, to content the
people you must go to bed,' to which her scornful reply was, 'Little man,
little man, the word *must* is not to be used to princes' (see Jenkins, *Elizabeth
the Great*, p. 323). See also Introduction, p. 36.

I'll bandy with the barons and the earls,
And either die or live with Gaveston.

Gaveston. [*Coming forward*] I can no longer keep me from my
    lord.

[*Kneels.*]

Edward. What, Gaveston! Welcome! Kiss not my hand;
    Embrace me, Gaveston, as I do thee.   140
    Why shouldst thou kneel? Knowest thou not who I am?
    Thy friend, thy self, another Gaveston!
    Not Hylas was more mourned of Hercules
    Than thou hast been of me since thy exile.

Gaveston. And since I went from hence, no soul in hell   145
    Hath felt more torment than poor Gaveston.

Edward. I know it. [*To* KENT] Brother, welcome home my
    friend.
    [*To* GAVESTON] Now let the treacherous Mortimers
    conspire,
    And that high-minded Earl of Lancaster.
    I have my wish in that I joy thy sight,   150
    And sooner shall the sea o'erwhelm my land

---

138. *Coming forward*] Broughton (subst.); *not in* Q.   138.1. *Kneels*] Oliphant
(*subst.*); *not in* Q.   141. Why...am?] Dyce¹ (*one line*); Why...kneele, /
Knowest...am? Q.   141. *Knowest*] Q1–3; Know'st Q4.   143. *of*] Q;
for Q2; for of Q3–4; by Oxberry.   147. *To* KENT] Merchant; *not in* Q.
148. *To* GAVESTON] Merchant; *not in* Q.   151. o'erwhelm] Q (orewhelme),
Q4; ouerwhelme Q2–3.

---

136. *bandy*] exchange blows (a metaphor from tennis).

140. *Embrace*] Cf. the similar embracement of Spencer Junior at III.i.177;
see Introduction, pp. 52, 71.

141. *kneel*] See Introduction, pp. 65–66.

142. *thy self, another Gaveston*] A proverbial idea; cf. *Jew of Malta*: 'my
second self' (III.iv.15) and *R3*: 'My other self' (II.ii.151); see Tilley F696.

143. *Hylas*] the handsome youth beloved of Hercules whom the latter took
with him when the Argonauts set off in quest of the Golden Fleece and who
was drowned by water nymphs as he was drawing water from a well. The
nymphs, having fallen in love with him, kidnapped him to their watery
domain. Hercules frantically searched for the boy and was grief-stricken by
his loss. Drayton uses the same analogy for similar homoerotic purposes in
Peirs Gaveston, ll. 1027–1032 (*Works*, I, 187).

149. *high-minded*] proud, arrogant (cf. *1H6*, I.v.12).

150. This line, identically worded, appears also in *Arden of Faversham*,
xiv.335.

Than bear the ship that shall transport thee hence.
I here create thee Lord High Chamberlain,
Chief Secretary to the state and me,
Earl of Cornwall, King and Lord of Man.   155
Gaveston. My lord, these titles far exceed my worth.
Kent. Brother, the least of these may well suffice
    For one of greater birth than Gaveston.
Edward. Cease, brother, for I cannot brook these words.
    [*To* GAVESTON] Thy worth, sweet friend, is far above my
        gifts;   160
    Therefore to equal it, receive my heart.
    If for these dignities thou be envied,
    I'll give thee more; for but to honour thee
    Is Edward pleased with kingly regiment.
    Fear'st thou thy person? Thou shalt have a guard.   165
    Wants thou gold? Go to my treasury.
    Wouldst thou be loved and feared? Receive my seal.
    Save or condemn, and in our name command
    Whatso thy mind affects or fancy likes.
Gaveston. It shall suffice me to enjoy your love,   170
    Which whiles I have, I think myself as great

---

153. thee] *Q, Q3–4;* the *Q2.*   160. *To* GAVESTON] *Merchant; not in Q.*
166. Wants] *Q;* Want'st *Dodsley*[1]*;* Wantest *Broughton, Oxberry.*

153–155. Based on Holinshed (p. 318); see Appendix B, no. 5.
155. *King . . . Man*] The rulers of the Isle of Man traditionally held certain sovereign rights and were sometimes referred to as kings although they did not formally hold a royal title and were responsible from the thirteenth century onwards to the crowns of either Scotland or England. Tancock quotes the *Chronicon Angliae,* which speaks of William of Montacute (in 1344) as 'rex Manniae.' Kirschbaum, probably correctly, sees 'a sexual pun' in the phrase (p. 75).
159. *brook*] endure.
161. *to equal . . . heart*] Briggs cites Kyd, *Soliman and Perseda:* 'To equall it: receiue my hart to boote' (I.ii.40).
162. *envied*] accented on the final syllable.
164. *regiment*] royal authority, rule (cf. *1 Tamburlaine,* I.i.117); see also III.ii.87, V.i.26.
165. *Fear'st*] Fearest for.
166. *Wants*] Do you need (Wantest).
167. *seal*] presumably the Great Seal of the realm, which would give Gaveston power and authority equal to the king's.

As Caesar riding in the Roman street
With captive kings at his triumphant car.

Enter the Bishop *of* COVENTRY.

Edward. Whither goes my lord of Coventry so fast?
Coventry. To celebrate your father's exequies.   175
     But is that wicked Gaveston returned?
Edward. Ay, priest, and lives to be revenged on thee
     That wert the only cause of his exile.
Gaveston. 'Tis true; and but for reverence of these robes
     Thou shouldst not plod one foot beyond this place.   180
Coventry. I did no more than I was bound to do,
     And Gaveston, unless thou be reclaimed,
     As then I did incense the parliament,
     So will I now, and thou shalt back to France.
Gaveston. Saving your reverence, you must pardon me.   185
                                    [*Manhandles* COVENTRY.]
Edward. Throw off his golden mitre, rend his stole
     And in the channel christen him anew.
Kent. Ah brother, lay not violent hands on him,
     For he'll complain unto the see of Rome.

---

174. Whither] *Q4;* Whether *Q1–3 (and often throughout).*   185.1. *Man-*
handles COVENTRY] *Dodsley*[3] *(subst.) ('"lays violent hands" upon the bishop');*
not in Q.

172–173. *Caesar . . . car*] Briggs quotes Peele, *Edward I*: 'Not Caesar
leading through the streetes of Rome, / The captive kings of conquered
nations, / Was in his princely triumphes honoured more . . .' (i; ll. 91–93);
cf. also *1H6*: 'We with our stately presence glorify, / Like captives bound
to a triumphant car' (I.i.21–22). Marlowe would also have remembered *2
Tamburlaine* (IV.iii) in which captive kings had actually been shown drawing
the conqueror's chariot. Given the violent death in store for him (well known
to Elizabethans), Gaveston's comparison of himself to Julius Caesar is loaded
with irony; he obviously forgets the assassination in which the ambitious
Roman's career culminated.

174–199. Based upon Holinshed, p. 318; see Appendix B, no. 5.

175. *exequies*] funeral rites.

178. *only cause . . . exile*] See Introduction, p. 55.

182. *reclaimed*] subdued, tamed.

185. *Saving your reverence*] A standard apologetic phrase used by inferiors
to superiors; Gaveston, of course, employs it in mockery.

187. *channel*] open street sewer, gutter (cf. IV.iv.12, V.iii.27) See Introduction, p. 55.

Gaveston. Let him complain unto the see of hell;   190
    I'll be revenged on him for my exile.
Edward. [*To* GAVESTON] No, spare his life, but seize upon his
    goods.
    Be thou lord bishop and receive his rents,
    And make him serve thee as thy chaplain.
    I give him thee; here, use him as thou wilt.   195
Gaveston. He shall to prison, and there die in bolts.
Edward. Ay, to the Tower, the Fleet, or where thou wilt.
Coventry. For this offence be thou accurst of God.
Edward. Who's there?   [*Calls attendants offstage.*]
              Convey this priest to the Tower.
Coventry.   True, true!
                             [*Exit guarded.*]
Edward. But in the meantime, Gaveston, away,   200
    And take possession of his house and goods.
    Come, follow me, and thou shalt have my guard
    To see it done and bring thee safe again.
Gaveston. What should a priest do with so fair a house?
    A prison may beseem his holiness.   205
                               [*Exeunt.*]

---

192. *To* GAVESTON] *This ed.; not in Q.*   199. *Calls . . . offstage*] *Kirschbaum (subst.); not in Q.*   199. to] *Q;* unto *Collier MS. (conj.).*   199. True, true] *Q;* Do, do *Dodsley¹;* Prut, prut *Dyce¹ (conj.);* Tut, tut *Collier MS. (conj.).* 199.1 *Exit guarded*] *Oliphant (subst.); not in Q.*   200. meantime] *Bullen;* meane time *Q.*   205. may] *Q1–2;* may best *Q3–4.*   205.1. *Exeunt*] *Dodsley¹; not in Q.*

---

196. *bolts*] fetters, leg irons.
197. *the Fleet*] the London prison, increasingly used for debtors in Marlowe's day but in medieval times less specialized. Marlowe follows history in sending the bishop to the Tower (l. 199), the place usually reserved for political prisoners. Holinshed mentions no prison in particular; Fabyan specifies 'the towre of London' (p. 166).
198. *accurst*] ecclesiastically anathematized, excommunicated.
199. *True, true!*] Spoken sarcastically in a punning reference to Edward's 'Convey' (the vulgar word for 'steal') in the preceding speech; cf. *R2:* '*Bolingbroke:* Go, some of you, convey him to the Tower. / *King Richard:* O, good! Convey? Conveyers are you all' (IV.i.317–318).
203. *again*] i.e., back again.
205. i.e., because of its Spartan or ascetic conditions a prison ironically may suit the priest's call to holiness. The remark would probably appeal to the popular anticlericalism of much of Marlowe's audience.

[SCENE ii]

Enter both the MORTIMERS [*on one side*], WARWICK *and* LANCASTER
[*on the other*].

Warwick. 'Tis true, the bishop is in the Tower,
    And goods and body given to Gaveston.
Lancaster. What! Will they tyrannize upon the Church?
    Ah, wicked king! accursèd Gaveston!
    This ground which is corrupted with their steps   5
    Shall be their timeless sepulchre, or mine.
Mortimer Junior. Well, let that peevish Frenchman guard him
      sure;
    Unless his breast be sword-proof he shall die.
Mortimer Senior. How now, why droops the Earl of
      Lancaster?
Mortimer Junior. Wherefore is Guy of Warwick discontent?   10
Lancaster. That villain Gaveston is made an earl.
Mortimer Senior. An earl!
Warwick. Ay, and besides Lord Chamberlain of the realm,

Heading. Scene ii] *Broughton; not in Q.*   0.1–2. *on one side . . . on the other*]
Oxberry; not in Q.

---

2. *goods and body*] see I.i.192–194.
   3. *tyrannize . . . Church*] Lancaster's outrage at the treatment of the Bishop
of Coventry may be intended to reflect the speaker's notable religiosity.
Holinshed reports that the earl 'honored men of religion' and after his
execution was considered by some to be 'a saint' and 'a martyr' to whom
'miracles' were attributed and at whose tomb superstitious devotions had to
be prevented (pp. 331–332). But see Introduction, p. 56.
   5. *corrupted*] Marlowe echoes Holinshed's word here and later (I.iv.150,
II.v.10, V.ii.2): 'he [Edward] was suddenlie so corrupted' (p. 319); 'if the
corrupter [Gaveston] . . . were once banished' (p. 319).
   6. *timeless*] untimely, early (cf. *2 Tamburlaine*, V.iii.252), possibly with a
pun on the meaning of 'eternal.'
   7. *peevish*] a derogatory term encompassing a range of meanings: (1)
foolish, silly, (2) spiteful, mischievous, and (3) perverse, headstrong; the
modern meaning ('irritable') is not particularly relevant.
   Frenchman] Stowe says that Gaveston was 'a straunger borne' (p. 326); as a
Gascon, he was of course technically a subject of Edward II.
   him] himself (reflexive).
   11. *villain*] rascal (with overtones of the older form 'villein,' a person
of ungentlemanly or uncouth origins); cf. I.ii.25, 30, I.iv.7, 14. See also
Introduction, pp. 51–52.

And Secretary too, and Lord of Man.
Mortimer Senior. We may not, nor we will not suffer this.   15
Mortimer Junior. Why post we not from hence to levy men?
Lancaster. 'My lord of Cornwall' now at every word;
    And happy is the man whom he vouchsafes,
    For vailing of his bonnet, one good look.
    Thus, arm in arm, the king and he doth march—   20
    Nay more, the guard upon his lordship waits,
    And all the court begins to flatter him.
Warwick. Thus leaning on the shoulder of the king,
    He nods, and scorns, and smiles at those that pass.
Mortimer Senior. Doth no man take exceptions at the slave?   25
Lancaster. All stomach him, but none dare speak a word.
Mortimer Junior. Ah, that bewrays their baseness, Lancaster.
    Were all the earls and barons of my mind,
    We'ld hale him from the bosom of the king,
    And at the court gate hang the peasant up,   30
    Who, swol'n with venom of ambitious pride,
    Will be the ruin of the realm and us.

Enter the [Arch]bishop *of* CANTERBURY [*talking to a* Chaplain].

---

29. We'ld] *Greg (conj.)* (Weeld); Weele *Q1–4, Dodsley*[1] (We'll); We'd
Broughton.   32.1 Archbishop] *Dodsley*[2]; Bishop *Q.*   32.1 *talking* ...
Chaplain] *Merchant (subst.); and a Messenger Broughton; not in Q.*

---

18. *happy is the man*] Holinshed describes Gaveston's arrogance in considerable detail (pp. 319–321); see Appendix B, nos. 8, 12, 13.

19. *vailing*] removing (literally 'lowering' in a gesture of respect or homage);
cf. *Jew of Malta,* II.ii.11.

24. *scorns*] Gaveston coined insulting nicknames for his prominent enemies
(Holinshed, p. 321); see Appendix B, no. 13.

25. *take exceptions at*] object to; cf. II.i.47.

26. *stomach*] resent, feel anger toward; cf. II.ii.259. The stomach was
supposed to secrete choler, the bodily humour associated with anger.

27. *bewrays*] betrays, reveals (an older form originally distinct from 'betray'
and later confounded with it); cf. I.ii.34.

30. *peasant*] i.e., upstart, parvenu; see note on I.ii.11. Cf. I.iv.6, 14.

32.1. *CANTERBURY*] Two different Archbishops of Canterbury held office
during Edward II's reign: (1) Robert Winchelsea, who was exiled by Edward
I for opposing the crown, was restored to office by Edward II in the new
reign, and continued to oppose the king's interests until his death in 1313;
and (2) Walter Reynolds, Edward II's former tutor, who curried favour with
the king and took his part as long as it was politically expedient but who later

Warwick. Here comes my lord of Canterbury's grace.
Lancaster. His countenance bewrays he is displeased.
Canterbury. [*To* Chaplain] First were his sacred garments
    rent and torn;   35
    Then laid they violent hands upon him, next
    Himself imprisoned and his goods asseized;
    This certify the Pope. Away, take horse!
                                [*Exit* Chaplain.]
Lancaster. My lord, will you take arms against the king?
Canterbury. What need I? God himself is up in arms   40
    When violence is offered to the Church.
Mortimer Junior. Then will you join with us that be his peers
    To banish or behead that Gaveston?
Canterbury. What else, my lords? for it concerns me near;
    The bishopric of Coventry is his.   45

            Enter [ISABELLA] *the* Queen.

Mortimer Junior. Madam, whither walks your majesty so fast?
Isabella. Unto the forest, gentle Mortimer,
    To live in grief and baleful discontent;

---

35. *To* Chaplain] *This ed.; not in Q.*   36. him, next] *Dodsley*[1] (*subst.*); him
next, *Q1–4.*   37. asseized] *Dodsley*[1] (asseiz'd); asceasd *Q.*   38.1 *Exit*
Chaplain] *This ed.; Exit Messenger Broughton; not in Q.*   46, 54. whither]
Q4; whether *Q1–3.*

(after the successful invasion) declared in favour of the new regime under
Mortimer and the queen and crowned Edward III in 1327. Marlowe conflates
the two prelates into a single character but (because of the requirements of
the action) with greater emphasis on the second.

37. *asseized*] confiscated, legally possessed (according to the *O.E.D.* a
nonce word, a unique form of 'seized').

38. *certify*] inform (literally 'make certain'); cf. II.vi.18, IV.i.7.

42. *his peers*] i.e., the king's peers (the antecedent being in l. 39).

45.1. *Queen*] Historically Isabella was only about sixteen at this time; see
Introduction, p. 47.

47. *forest*] wilds, wilderness. Isabella speaks figuratively of the desolation to which her husband's infidelity has brought her; no actual forest is
signified.

gentle Mortimer] Jonson echoes Isabella's phrase here together with 'sweet
Mortimer' (l. 80 below) in his unfinished *Mortimer His Fall* (ll. 47, 55; *H.&*
S., Works, VII, 61–62).

48. *baleful*] sorrowful, wretched (an obsolete sense).

For now my lord the king regards me not,
But dotes upon the love of Gaveston.   50
He claps his cheeks and hangs about his neck,
Smiles in his face and whispers in his ears,
And when I come, he frowns, as who should say
'Go whither thou wilt, seeing I have Gaveston'.
Mortimer Senior. Is it not strange that he is thus bewitched?   55
Mortimer Junior. Madam, return unto the court again.
That sly inveigling Frenchman we'll exile,
Or lose our lives; and yet, ere that day come,
The king shall lose his crown—for we have power,
And courage too, to be revenged at full.   60
Canterbury. But yet lift not your swords against the king.
Lancaster. No, but we'll lift Gaveston from hence.
Warwick. And war must be the means, or he'll stay still.
Isabella. Then let him stay; for rather than my lord
Shall be oppressed by civil mutinies,   65
I will endure a melancholy life,
And let him frolic with his minion.
Canterbury. My lords, to ease all this, but hear me speak:
We and the rest that are his counsellors
Will meet, and with a general consent   70
Confirm his banishment with our hands and seals.

---

49. now my lord the king] *Q;* now, my lord, the king *Oxberry.*   61. *Can-terbury*] *Q (Bish.); Q. Isab. Ellis.*   62. we'll] *Q* (weele); we will *Collier MS., Dyce²*.   62. Gaveston] *Q;* that Gaveston *Broughton, Broughton MS.*   65. by] *Q;* with *Q2–4.*

---

51. *claps*] pats (affectionately).
55. *bewitched*] in the figurative sense of 'infatuated, enchanted, fixated.' But Stowe (p. 327) reports that Gaveston may actually have used diabolical power over Edward; see Introduction, pp. 42, 126 n. 82, and Appendix B, no. 47.
57. *inveigling*] (1) beguiling, deceiving; (2) seducing.
60. *to . . . at full*] Cf. *Woodstock*: 'I'll be revenged at full' (I.i.69).
63. *still*] for ever, always.
67. *frolic*] gambol, sport, play (occasionally, as here, with sexual over-tones); cf. I.iv.73, II.ii.62, II.iii.17.
68. *but*] only.
71. *Confirm his banishment*] Historically (see Holinshed, p. 319), the Arch-bishop of Canterbury (Robert Winchelsea), since he was not in England at the time, did not participate in the initial plan to have Gaveston banished;

Lancaster. What we confirm the king will frustrate.
Mortimer Junior. Then may we lawfully revolt from him.
Warwick. But say, my lord, where shall this meeting be?
Canterbury. At the New Temple.   75
Mortimer Junior. Content.
Canterbury. And in the meantime I'll entreat you all
    To cross to Lambeth, and there stay with me.
Lancaster. Come then, let's away.
Mortimer Junior.   Madam, farewell.
Isabella. Farewell, sweet Mortimer; and, for my sake,   80
    Forbear to levy arms against the king.
Mortimer Junior. Ay, if words will serve; if not, I must.
                                    [Exeunt severally.]

---

77. *Canterbury*] *Dodsley²; not in Q1–4, where lines 77–78 continue as part of Mortimer Junior's speech from line 76.*   77. meantime] *Bullen;* meane time Q.   82. Ay] Q (I); Ah *Dodsley².*   82.1. *Exeunt severally*] *Gill¹ (subst.);* Exeunt *Dodsley¹; not in Q.*

---

but he willingly ratified the decision on his return. See note on l. 32.1 above; also Appendix B, nos. 3, 10.

    75. *New Temple*] So-called, as Charlton–Waller explain, 'to distinguish it from the "old" Temple in Holborn.' Before their suppression in 1308 by Edward II (see Introduction, pp. 49–50), the Knights Templar occupied quarters (the New Temple) on grounds that later came to be known as the Inns of Court. Important noblemen, as members of the brotherhood, sometimes held parliaments and councils of state there. After the Templars were outlawed, Hugh Spencer the younger was one of several men of importance who profited by the confiscation of their property.

    77. *Canterbury*] Because of the reference to Lambeth at l. 78 (see following note), editors universally follow Dodsley's emendation, reassigning this speech to Canterbury.

    78. *Lambeth*] the official residence of Archbishops of Canterbury (since 1197) on the south bank of the Thames; as Charlton–Waller note, this reference establishes the location of the scene as being either London or Westminster.

    80. *sweet Mortimer*] an early suggestion of intimacy between Isabella and Mortimer; see Introduction, pp. 53–54; also note on l. 47 above.

    82. *if words will serve*] Briggs compares *2H6*: '*Edward.* Ay, noble father, if our words will serve. / *Richard.* And if words will not, then our weapons shall' (v.i.139–140).

[SCENE iii]

Enter GAVESTON *and* [EDMUND] *the* Earl *of* KENT.

Gaveston. Edmund, the mighty prince of Lancaster,
    That hath more earldoms than an ass can bear,
    And both the Mortimers, two goodly men,
    With Guy of Warwick, that redoubted knight,
    Are gone towards Lambeth. There let them remain.   5
                                      Exeunt.

[SCENE iv]

Enter Nobles [LANCASTER, WARWICK, PEMBROKE, MORTIMER SENIOR,
MORTIMER JUNIOR, *and the* Archbishop *of* CANTERBURY, *attended*].

Lancaster. Here is the form of Gaveston's exile;
    May it please your lordship to subscribe your name.
Canterbury. Give me the paper.

Scene iii   *Heading.* Scene iii] *Broughton; not in* Q.   0.1. *Enter . . .*
KENT.] Q; *Enter Gaveston. Oxberry.*   5. Lambeth] Q; London *Cunningham.*
5. There . . . remain.] Q; *Kent.* There . . . remain. *Ellis.*   Scene iv
Heading. Scene iv] *Broughton; not in* Q.   0.1, 93.1. Nobles] *Q3–4;* Nobiles
Q1–2.   0.2. Archbishop *of* CANTERBURY] *Robinson; not in* Q.   0.2. *at-*
tended] *Dyce*[1] *(subst.); not in* Q.

    1.iii. This scene, because of its brevity, has provoked considerable negative
commentary—either as exemplifying Marlowe's poor dramatic technique or
some corruption in textual transmission. Charlton–Waller defend it appropriately as an instance of characterization 'in concentrated miniature':
'Gaveston's superb insouciance and his arrogant self-assurance are revealed in
the gay contemptuousness of all the epithets he here applies to the nobles.'
Marlowe sharpens the irony of the favourite's incipient fall by inserting this
momentary exhibition of over-confidence between the barons' plan for his
exile in the previous scene and their return with the legal instrument for his
removal in the following one.
    2. *more earldoms*] See note on 1.i.101.
    4. *redoubted*] feared, dreaded (spoken sarcastically; cf. 'goodly' in l. 3).
    5. *Lambeth*] cf. 1.ii.78. Gaveston has apparently heard about the meeting
of the nobles arranged in the preceding scene and affects to dismiss it without
a care. Ellis's unauthoritative assignment to Kent of 'There let them remain,'
adopted from Karl Elze (*Notes on Elizabethan Dramatists* [Halle, 1889], p.
113) so that the secondary character will not have to remain silent, robs
Gaveston of a touch of the 'superb insouciance' noticed by Charlton–Waller
(see note on 1.iii above).
    1.iv.1. *form*] document.

Lancaster. Quick, quick, my lord; I long to write my name.

               [CANTERBURY *and the others after him subscribe.*]

Warwick. But I long more to see him banished hence.   5

Mortimer Junior. The name of Mortimer shall fright the king,

    Unless he be declined from that base peasant.

       Enter [EDWARD] *the* King, *and* GAVESTON [*and* KENT.

       EDWARD *seats* GAVESTON *beside him on the throne*].

Edward. What, are you moved that Gaveston sits here?

    It is our pleasure; we will have it so.

Lancaster. Your grace doth well to place him by your side,   10

    For nowhere else the new earl is so safe.

Mortimer Senior. What man of noble birth can brook this

      sight?

    Quam male conveniunt!

    See what a scornful look the peasant casts.

Pembroke. Can kingly lions fawn on creeping ants?   15

Warwick. Ignoble vassal, that like Phaethon

    Aspir'st unto the guidance of the sun.

---

4. Quick . . . name.] *Dyce*[1] *(one line);* Quick . . . lorde, / I . . . name. *Q.*
4.1. CANTERBURY . . . *subscribe*] *Dyce*[1] *(subst.);* not in *Q.*   7.1. *and* KENT]
Dyce[1]; *not in Q.*   7.2. EDWARD *seats* . . . *throne*] *Kirschbaum; not in Q.*   12,
34, 83, 232. *Mortimer Senior*] *Q; Y. Mor. Wagner.*

---

    7. *declined*] turned away, separated; cf. I.iv.115. Charlton–Waller com-
pare *Ham.,* I.v.51.

    7.2. *throne*] probably carried onstage. Glynne Wickham points out that the
technology of lowering the throne from the 'heavens' (apparently first used
by Henslowe at the Rose) had not yet been invented; see '*Exeunt to the Cave*:
Notes on the Staging of Marlowe's Plays,' *T.D.R.,* 8.4 (summer 1964), 192.

    8. *sits here*] Gaveston's seat beside the king (where the queen would nor-
mally sit) is both emblematic and shocking; it signifies that Edward has made
his lover politically equal with himself. Compare the earlier offer to give
Gaveston the freedom of the royal 'seal' (I.i.167).

    13. 'How badly they [i.e., Edward and Gaveston] suit each other!' (based
on Ovid's *Metamorphoses*: 'Non bene conveniunt, nec in una sede morantur, /
maiestas et amor' [II, 846–847]—'Majesty and love do not go well together,
nor tarry long in the same dwelling place'). Cf. *Massacre at Paris,* xiv.16–17.

    16. *Phaethon*] the son of Phoebus Apollo, the sun-god, who presump-
tuously asked his father to let him drive the chariot of the sun, lost control of
the horses, was struck by a bolt of lightning, and plummeted disastrously to
earth; cf. *1 Tamburlaine,* IV.ii.49–50. The story appears in Ovid's *Metamorphoses,* I, 755ff. Shakespeare may have recalled Marlowe's allusion in *R2,*
III.iii.178–179. The sun–king analogy implied here was conventional.

Mortimer Junior. Their downfall is at hand, their forces down.
　　We will not thus be faced and over-peered.
Edward. Lay hands on that traitor Mortimer!   20
Mortimer Senior. Lay hands on that traitor Gaveston!
　　　　　　　　　　　　　　[They draw their swords.]
Kent. Is this the duty that you owe your king?
Warwick. We know our duties; let him know his peers.
　　　　　　　　　　　　　　[They seize GAVESTON.]
Edward. Whither will you bear him? Stay, or ye shall die.
Mortimer Senior. We are no traitors; therefore threaten not.   25
Gaveston. No, threaten not, my lord, but pay them home.
　　Were I a king—
Mortimer Junior. Thou villain, wherefore talks thou of a king,
　　That hardly art a gentleman by birth?
Edward. Were he a peasant, being my minion,   30
　　I'll make the proudest of you stoop to him.
Lancaster. My lord, you may not thus disparage us.
　　Away, I say, with hateful Gaveston.
Mortimer Senior. And with the Earl of Kent that favours him.
　　　　　　　　　[Exeunt KENT *and* GAVESTON *guarded.]*
Edward. Nay, then lay violent hands upon your king.   35

---

19. over-peered] *Dodsley*[1] (over-peer'd); ouerpeerd *Q.*   21. *Mortimer
Senior] Q; Y. Mor. Pinkerton.*   21.1. *They draw . . . swords] Gill*[1]; *not in
Q.*   23.1. *They seize* GAVESTON] *Gill*[1]; *(after line 21) Spencer, Kirschbaum
(subst.) (Attendants hold Gaveston); not in Q.*   24, 144. Whither] *Q4;*
Whether *Q1-3.*   28. Thou villain,] *Q;* Thou, villain! *Broughton;* Thou,
villain? *Oliphant.*   29. That] *Q;* Thou *Tancock.*   34.1. *Exeunt . . .
guarded] Broughton (subst.) (Kent and Gaveston are borne off), Dyce*[1] *(subst.)
(Attendants remove Gaveston and Kent); not in Q.*

---

19. *faced*] outfaced, bullied.
　over-peered] (1) looked down upon (2) out-peered (from the sense 'peer of
the realm').
　27. *Were I a king*–] indicating Gaveston's presumption. Briggs notes
that Greene, Richard II's favourite, makes a similar comment in a similar
context in the anonymous *Woodstock*; addressing the king, he offers, 'Were I
as you, my lord–' (i.iii.193).
　28. *villain*] see note on I.ii.11.
　30. *minion*] here without derogatory meaning; see note on I.i.132.
　32. *disparage*] degrade, treat without respect. Charlton–Waller explain
that the term originally meant 'to degrade by marrying to one of inferior
rank.'

Here, Mortimer, sit thou in Edward's throne;
Warwick and Lancaster, wear you my crown.
Was ever king thus overruled as I?
Lancaster. Learn then to rule us better and the realm.
Mortimer Junior. What we have done, our heart-blood shall
    maintain.   40
Warwick. Think you that we can brook this upstart pride?
Edward. Anger and wrathful fury stops my speech.
Canterbury. Why are you moved? Be patient, my lord,
    And see what we your counsellors have done.
                [*Gives* EDWARD *the document of* GAVESTON'S *exile.*]
Mortimer Junior. My lords, now let us all be resolute,   45
    And either have our wills or lose our lives.
Edward. Meet you for this, proud overdaring peers?
    Ere my sweet Gaveston shall part from me,
    This isle shall fleet upon the ocean
    And wander to the unfrequented Inde.   50
Canterbury. You know that I am legate to the Pope;
    On your allegiance to the see of Rome,
    Subscribe as we have done to his exile.

---

40. What . . . maintain.] *Broughton (one line);* What . . . done, / our . . .
maintaine. *Q1–3 (two lines?);* What . . . done, / Our . . . maintaine. *Q4.*
44.1. Gives . . . exile] *Kirschbaum (subst.); not in Q.*   47. overdaring] *Q;*
overbearing *Bullen.*   49. fleet] *Q;* float *Broughton.*

---

36. *sit . . . throne*] in ironic contrast to Gaveston's action at I.iv.7.1–2.
Marlowe may have been influenced by the scene in *3H6* where Richard,
Duke of York, assumes the throne in Henry VI's presence: 'look where the
sturdy rebel sits, / Even in the chair of state. Belike he means . . . To aspire
unto the crown and reign as king' (I.i.50–54).

37. *wear you my crown*] Briggs compares *Massacre at Paris*: 'Guise, wear
our crown, and be thou King of France' (xix.55).

41. *upstart*] cf. III.i.165, III.ii.21; see Introduction, pp. 51–52.

42. Cf. *1 Troublesome Reign*: 'Her passions stop the organ of her voyce'
(x; l. 1155).

49. *fleet*] drift, float (cf. IV.vii.105; also *1 Tamburlaine*, III.iii.156; *2 Tamburlaine*, I.i.40).

50. *Inde*] India (from the French form, and more common until after
Milton than the Latin 'India'). The word could signify either the continent of
India or the East Indies.

51. *legate*] As Tancock explains, the archbishop was not in fact the Pope's
official legate, although he served as his representative in England.

Mortimer Junior. [*To* CANTERBURY] Curse him if he refuse,
    and then may we
    Depose him and elect another king.   55
Edward. Ay, there it goes; but yet I will not yield.
    Curse me. Depose me. Do the worst you can.
Lancaster. Then linger not, my lord, but do it straight.
Canterbury. Remember how the bishop was abused;
    Either banish him that was the cause thereof,   60
    Or I will presently discharge these lords
    Of duty and allegiance due to thee.
Edward. [*Aside*] It boots me not to threat; I must speak
    fair.
    The legate of the Pope will be obeyed.
    [*To* CANTERBURY] My lord, you shall be Chancellor of the
    realm;   65
    Thou, Lancaster, High Admiral of our fleet.
    Young Mortimer and his uncle shall be earls,
    And you, Lord Warwick, President of the North,
    [*To* PEMBROKE] And thou of Wales. If this content you
    not,
    Make several kingdoms of this monarchy,   70
    And share it equally amongst you all,
    So I may have some nook or corner left

---

54. *To* CANTERBURY] *This ed.; not in* Q.   61. lords] *Q, Q3–4;* Lord *Q2.*
63. *Aside*] *Dodsley¹; not in* Q.   65. *To* CANTERBURY] *Kirschbaum (subst.);*
not in Q.   65. you] *Q1–2;* ye *Q3–4.*   69. *To* PEMBROKE] *Oliphant; not in*
Q.

---

54. *Curse*] excommunicate (cf. I.i.198). See note on I.iv.61–62.

61. *presently*] at once, immediately; cf. I.iv.90, v.ii.46, v.vi.53.

61–62. *discharge . . . allegiance*] Pope Pius V in 1570 had issued a bull of
excommunication against Elizabeth, freeing her subjects 'from their oath and
all manner of duty, fidelity and obedience' (see Jenkins, *Elizabeth the Great*,
p. 157).

63. *boots*] avails.

65. *Chancellor*] This and the other appointments made here are fictional.

68. *President of the North*] As Gill explains, quoting John Cowell, *The
Interpreter* (1607), 'President . . . is used in Common law for the kings Lieute-
nent in any Province or function; as President of Wales, of York, of Barwick.'

70. *several kingdoms*] Elizabeth had a particular horror of divided kingdoms
as is reflected in such plays as Sackville and Norton's *Gorboduc* and Shakespeare's *1H4* and *Lr*.

To frolic with my dearest Gaveston.

Canterbury. Nothing shall alter us; we are resolved.

Lancaster. Come, come, subscribe.   75

Mortimer Junior. Why should you love him whom the world
        hates so?

Edward. Because he loves me more than all the world.
    Ah, none but rude and savage-minded men
    Would seek the ruin of my Gaveston.
    You that be noble born should pity him.   80

Warwick. You that are princely born should shake him off.
    For shame subscribe, and let the lown depart.

Mortimer Senior. Urge him, my lord.

Canterbury. Are you content to banish him the realm?

Edward. I see I must, and therefore am content;   85
    Instead of ink, I'll write it with my tears.

                                                    [*Subscribes.*]

Mortimer Junior. The king is lovesick for his minion.

Edward. 'Tis done, and now accursèd hand fall off.

Lancaster. Give it me; I'll have it published in the streets.

Mortimer Junior. I'll see him presently dispatched away.   90

Canterbury. Now is my heart at ease.

Warwick.   And so is mine.

Pembroke. This will be good news to the common sort.

---

76. Why . . . so?] *Broughton (one line);* Why . . . him, / whome . . . so? *Q1–3*
(two lines?); Why . . . him, / Whom . . . so? *Q4.*   80. be] *Q1–2;* are *Q3–4.*
82. lown] *Q* (lowne); loon *Broughton.*   86.1. Subscribes] *Dyce¹; not in Q.*

---

73. *frolic*] see note on I.ii.67.

77. A probable echo of Kyd, *Spanish Tragedy*: 'On whom I doted more
than all the world, / Because she lov'd me more than all the world' (II.vi.5–6).

78. *rude*] uncivilized, barbarous.

80. *You . . . born*] Here Edward would appear to confirm the truth of the
barons' continual references to Gaveston's low birth.

82. *lown*] peasant, low-born fellow. Charlton–Waller cite *Per.*: 'both lord
and lown' (IV.vi.17).

86. *write . . . tears*] Cf. *R2*: 'with rainy eyes / Write sorrow on the bosom of
the earth' (III.ii.146–147).

88. *hand fall off*] Tancock cites the famous story of Archbishop Cranmer,
who at his execution allowed the hand which had signed his recantation to
burn first; a vivid account appears in Foxe's *Acts and Monuments*.

90. *presently*] See note on l. 61 above.

Mortimer Senior. Be it or no, he shall not linger here.

                Exeunt Nobles [*and all except* EDWARD].

Edward. How fast they run to banish him I love.

    They would not stir, were it to do me good.   95

    Why should a king be subject to a priest?

    Proud Rome, that hatchest such imperial grooms,

    For these thy superstitious taper-lights,

    Wherewith thy antichristian churches blaze,

    I'll fire thy crazèd buildings and enforce   100

    The papal towers to kiss the lowly ground,

    With slaughtered priests make Tiber's channel swell,

    And banks raised higher with their sepulchres.

    As for the peers that back the clergy thus,

    If I be king, not one of them shall live.   105

93.1. Nobles] *Q3–4*; *Nobiles Q1–2*.   93.1. *and all . . .* EDWARD] Broughton (*subst.*) (*Exeunt Nobles and Archbishop*); *not in Q*.   102. make] *Dodsley¹*; may *Q1–4*.   103. raised] *Q1–4*; raise *Dodsley¹*; rise *Scott*.

---

96. Cf. *1 Troublesome Reign*: 'so I scorne to be subject to the greatest Prelate in the world' (v; ll. 478–479).

97. *Proud Rome*] Commentators usually note that this anti-papistical outburst is more characteristic of Elizabethan popular feeling than of medieval sentiment; it even seems somewhat out of character for the speaker and may, as Irving Ribner suggests, reflect Marlowe's own religio-political attitude ('Marlowe's *Edward II* and the Tudor History Play,' *E.L.H.*, 22 [1955], 252). This likelihood is somewhat strengthened by a garbled version of ll. 100–101 in a similarly anti-papal speech of *Massacre at Paris*: 'I'll fire his crazed buildings, and incense / The papal towers to kiss the holy earth' (xxiv. 62–63).

grooms] servants.

99. *antichristian*] i.e., because loyal to the Pope, often regarded as the Antichrist by Protestant extremists and partisans.

100. *crazèd*] shattered, ruined; or perhaps 'crazed (i.e., cracked) by fire' in a proleptic sense.

102. *make*] Modern editors are divided as to whether to emend here. Some retain Q's 'may' by inserting a full stop at the end of the previous line and by understanding what follows as Edward's passive wish for the filling of the Tiber with slaughtered priests. I accept Dodsley's alteration ('make'), adopted by many editors (including Tucker Brooke and Bowers), as more consistent with the violence of Edward's anti-Catholic threats. The speaker has already threatened to fire churches and topple papal edifices; *making* the river rise by filling it with the corpses of priests and raising its banks with their sepulchres continues both the violence and syntax of the preceding lines more naturally.

Enter GAVESTON.

Gaveston. My lord, I hear it whispered everywhere
    That I am banished and must fly the land.
Edward. 'Tis true, sweet Gaveston. O were it false!
    The legate of the Pope will have it so,
    And thou must hence, or I shall be deposed.   110
    But I will reign to be revenged of them,
    And therefore, sweet friend, take it patiently.
    Live where thou wilt—I'll send thee gold enough.
    And long thou shalt not stay; or if thou dost,
    I'll come to thee. My love shall ne'er decline.   115
Gaveston. Is all my hope turned to this hell of grief?
Edward. Rend not my heart with thy too-piercing words.
    Thou from this land, I from my self am banished.
Gaveston. To go from hence grieves not poor Gaveston,
    But to forsake you, in whose gracious looks   120
    The blessedness of Gaveston remains,
    For nowhere else seeks he felicity.
Edward. And only this torments my wretched soul
    That, whether I will or no, thou must depart.
    Be governor of Ireland in my stead,   125
    And there abide till fortune call thee home.
    Here, take my picture, and let me wear thine;
                 [They exchange miniature portraits.]
    O might I keep thee here, as I do this,
    Happy were I. But now most miserable!
Gaveston. 'Tis something to be pitied of a king.   130
Edward. Thou shalt not hence; I'll hide thee, Gaveston.
Gaveston. I shall be found, and then 'twill grieve me more.

---

108. false!] *Dodsley*[1]; false, *Q1–4*.   111. of] *Q; on Dodsley*[1].   117. too-
piercing] *Q* (too piercing); to piercing *Q2*; to-piercing *Wagner (conj.).*
127.1. *They exchange . . . portraits*] *Dyce*[1] *(subst.); not in Q.*

---

   111. *revenged of*] revenged upon.
   113. *I'll send thee gold*] Based on Holinshed, pp. 319–320; see Appendix
B, no. 10.
   115. Cf. the parting of Suffolk and Queen Margaret in *2H6*, III.ii; see
Introduction, pp. 33–34.
   116. *this hell of grief*] Cf. *Arden of Faversham*: 'this hell of grief' (xviii.12).
   125. *governor of Ireland*] Based on Holinshed, p. 320; see Appendix B, no.
10.

Edward. Kind words and mutual talk makes our grief greater;
    Therefore, with dumb embracement, let us part—
    Stay, Gaveston, I cannot leave thee thus.   135
Gaveston. For every look my lord drops down a tear;
    Seeing I must go, do not renew my sorrow.
Edward. The time is little that thou hast to stay,
    And therefore give me leave to look my fill.
    But come, sweet friend, I'll bear thee on thy way.   140
Gaveston. The peers will frown.
Edward. I pass not for their anger. Come, let's go.
    O that we might as well return as go.

Enter QUEEN ISABELLA.

Isabella. Whither goes my lord?
Edward. Fawn not on me, French strumpet; get thee gone.   145
Isabella. On whom but on my husband should I fawn?
Gaveston. On Mortimer; with whom, ungentle queen—
    I say no more; judge you the rest, my lord.
Isabella. In saying this, thou wrongst me, Gaveston.
    Is't not enough that thou corrupts my lord,   150
    And art a bawd to his affections,
    But thou must call mine honour thus in question?
Gaveston. I mean not so; your grace must pardon me.
Edward. Thou art too familiar with that Mortimer,
    And by thy means is Gaveston exiled;   155
    But I would wish thee reconcile the lords,
    Or thou shalt ne'er be reconciled to me.

---

136. lord drops] *Q1–4;* lord, drops *Oxberry;* love drops *Dodsley*[1].   143.1.
Enter . . . ISABELLA] *Broughton (subst.); Enter Edmund and Queen Isabell Q.*

---

134. *dumb*] silent.
136. *my lord drops*] Oxberry's inserted comma makes 'look' rather than 'lord' the subject of 'drops.' The unemended text makes better sense: each of Gaveston's looks causes Edward to drop a tear.
140. *bear*] accompany.
142. *pass*] care; cf. v.i.77. Charlton–Waller cite *1 Tamburlaine*: 'I pass not for his threats' (i.i.109).
147. *On Mortimer*] see Introduction, pp. 53–54.
150. *corrupts*] see note on i.ii.5.
151. *bawd to his affections*] pander to his desires (or lustful passions); for 'affections' in this sense, cf. Spenser, *Faerie Queene*, ii.iv.34.

Isabella. Your highness knows it lies not in my power.

Edward. Away then; touch me not. Come, Gaveston.

Isabella. [*To* GAVESTON] Villain, 'tis thou that robb'st me of
    my lord.   160

Gaveston. Madam, 'tis you that rob me of my lord.

Edward. Speak not unto her; let her droop and pine.

Isabella. Wherein, my lord, have I deserved these words?
    Witness the tears that Isabella sheds,
    Witness this heart, that sighing for thee breaks,   165
    How dear my lord is to poor Isabel.

Edward. And witness heaven how dear thou art to me.
    There weep; for till my Gaveston be repealed,
    Assure thyself thou com'st not in my sight.

                            Exeunt EDWARD *and* GAVESTON.

Isabella. O miserable and distressèd queen!   170
    Would, when I left sweet France and was embarked,
    That charming Circe, walking on the waves,
    Had changed my shape, or at the marriage-day
    The cup of Hymen had been full of poison,
    Or with those arms that twined about my neck   175
    I had been stifled, and not lived to see
    The king my lord thus to abandon me.

---

160. *To* GAVESTON] *This ed.; not in* Q.   172. Circe] *Broughton, Oxberry;*
Circes *Q1–4.*   173. at] *Q1–2;* that *Q3–4.*

---

168. *repealed*] recalled from banishment (from Fr. *rappeler*).

172. *charming Circe*] the mythological enchantress who by her charms changed some of Odysseus's men into swine. Marlowe's allusion is to Ovid, *Metamorphoses*, XIV, 48ff., a passage in which Circe is described skimming along the surface of the sea as she sets out to transform Scylla into a monster by poisoning her bathing pool; but the image of Hymen, the god of marriage, is superimposed upon that of Circe through the idea of the poisoned cup in l. 174. Gareth Roberts in 'Three Notes on Uses of Circe by Spenser, Marlowe and Milton' (*N.&Q.*, N.S. 25 [1978], 433–435) points out the unconscious irony in Isabella's wish to be transformed or poisoned, for in addition to the destruction of her marriage, she later becomes a figure of lust in the play. Scylla was often interpreted as an innocent (a virgin) who became the monstrous type of lasciviousness. Isabella's despairing wish for metamorphosis may also support Marlowe's homosexual theme by suggesting the queen's desire to become male—the better to compete with her rival Gaveston.

174. *Hymen*] See preceding note.

175. *those arms*] i.e., Edward's arms (when the king had embraced Isabella at their wedding).

Like frantic Juno will I fill the earth
With ghastly murmur of my sighs and cries,
For never doted Jove on Ganymede   180
So much as he on cursèd Gaveston.
But that will more exasperate his wrath;
I must entreat him, I must speak him fair,
And be a means to call home Gaveston.
And yet he'll ever dote on Gaveston,   185
And so am I for ever miserable.

Enter the Nobles [LANCASTER, WARWICK, PEMBROKE, MORTIMER
   SENIOR, *and* MORTIMER JUNIOR] *to* [ISABELLA] *the* Queen.

Lancaster. Look where the sister of the King of France
    Sits wringing of her hands and beats her breast.
Warwick. The king, I fear, hath ill entreated her.
Pembroke. Hard is the heart that injures such a saint.   190
Mortimer Junior. I know 'tis 'long of Gaveston she weeps.
Mortimer Senior. Why? He is gone.
Mortimer Junior.   Madam, how fares your grace?

182–185. But . . . Gaveston] *Q; not in Oxberry.*   187. sister] *Q;* daughter
Dodsley[3] *(conj.).*   189. ill entreated] *Q* (ill intreated); ill-treated *Dodsley*[2]*;*
sore ill-treated *Broughton.*   190. injures] *Q* (iniures), *Q3–4;* iniuries *Q2;*
injuries *Fleay.*

---

178. *frantic Juno*] based on Ovid, *Metamorphoses*, X, 155–161; when
Jupiter chose Ganymede on account of his beauty to be his cup-bearer, Juno
became frenzied with jealousy. Marlowe had already used the homoeroticism
of the Jupiter–Ganymede relationship (including Juno's resentment of it)
for the opening scene of *Dido.* The comparison of Ganymede to Gaveston
in ll. 180–181 underscores the homosexuality of the king's passion, for a
'Ganymede' was the standard term in Marlowe's age for the younger partner
in a love affair between males. Drayton calls Gaveston 'King *Edwards Ganemed*'
(*Peirs Gaveston*, l. 1269).
  179. *ghastly*] horrifying, ghostlike.
  184. *be a means*] Isabella's intercession in behalf of Gaveston is Marlowe's
invention; see Introduction, pp. 53–54.
  189. *ill entreated*] ill used, treated badly; cf. *Jew of Malta*: 'Entreat them
well, as we have used thee' (v.ii.17); also *Ovid's Elegies*: 'ill she is entreated'
(III.ii.22). A secondary meaning, 'harshly enjoined' (in anticipation of ll.
200–201), is also possible.
  191. *'long of*] on account of, because of ('along of'); a dialectal expression
common in London and southern England. Cf. *Cym.*: 'and long of her it was
/ That we met here so strangely' (V.v.273–274).

Isabella. Ah, Mortimer, now breaks the king's hate forth,
 And he confesseth that he loves me not.
Mortimer Junior. Cry quittance, madam, then; and love not
  him.   195
Isabella. No, rather will I die a thousand deaths.
 And yet I love in vain; he'll ne'er love me.
Lancaster. Fear ye not, madam; now his minion's gone,
 His wanton humour will be quickly left.
Isabella. O never, Lancaster! I am enjoined   200
 To sue unto you all for his repeal.
 This wills my lord; and this must I perform,
 Or else be banished from his highess' presence.
Lancaster. For his repeal! Madam, he comes not back,
 Unless the sea cast up his shipwreck body.   205
Warwick. And to behold so sweet a sight as that
 There's none here but would run his horse to death.
Mortimer Junior. But madam, would you have us call him
  home?
Isabella. Ay, Mortimer, for till he be restored,
 The angry king hath banished me the court;   210
 And therefore, as thou lovest and tend'rest me,
 Be thou my advocate unto these peers.
Mortimer Junior. What, would ye have me plead for Gaveston?
Mortimer Senior. Plead for him he that will, I am resolved.
Lancaster. And so am I, my lord; dissuade the queen. 215

---

205. shipwreck] *This ed.;* shipwrack *Q;* shipwrackt *Q2–4;* shipwreck'd
Dodsley[1]. 211. lovest] *Q1–3;* lov'st *Q4.* 211. tend'rest] *Q* (tendrest);
tender'st *Dodsley*[1]; tenderest *Merchant.* 213. ye] *Q;* you *Q2–4.* 214. he
that] *Q;* that *Q2–4.*

---

195. *Cry quittance*] (1) get even with him (cry quits) and (2) quit him, leave
him. *Quittance* is a legal term for release from an obligation.

199. *wanton humour*] amorous mood (deriving from the tradition that
human dispositions were caused by bodily fluids or humours).

201. *repeal*] see note on I.iv.168.

205. *shipwreck*] Briggs cites *Hero and Leander:* 'shipwrack treasure' (II,
164), a parallel instance of the noun used adjectivally.

207. *none . . . would*] i.e., none here who would not.

211. *tend'rest*] care for; cf. *Ham.:* 'Tender yourself more dearly' (I.iii.108).

213. *ye*] probably a plural form (in which case Mortimer addresses the
other nobles rather than the queen). But note Q2's 'correction' to 'you'; 'ye'
was sometimes used in the singular (see Abbott 236).

Isabella. O Lancaster, let him dissuade the king,
　　For 'tis against my will he should return.
Warwick. Then speak not for him; let the peasant go.
Isabella. 'Tis for myself I speak, and not for him.
Pembroke. No speaking will prevail, and therefore cease.　　220
Mortimer Junior. Fair queen, forbear to angle for the fish
　　Which, being caught, strikes him that takes it dead—
　　I mean that vile torpedo, Gaveston,
　　That now, I hope, floats on the Irish seas.
Isabella. Sweet Mortimer, sit down by me a while,　　225
　　And I will tell thee reasons of such weight
　　As thou wilt soon subscribe to his repeal.
Mortimer Junior. It is impossible; but speak your mind.
Isabella. Then thus—but none shall hear it but ourselves.
　　　　　　　　　[*Draws* MORTIMER JUNIOR *to a seat apart.*]
Lancaster. My lords, albeit the queen win Mortimer,　　230
　　Will you be resolute and hold with me?
Mortimer Senior. Not I, against my nephew.
Pembroke. Fear not; the queen's words cannot alter him.
Warwick. No? Do but mark how earnestly she pleads.
Lancaster. And see how coldly his looks make denial.　　235
Warwick. She smiles! Now, for my life, his mind is changed.
Lancaster. I'll rather lose his friendship, I, than grant.
Mortimer Junior. [*Coming forward*] Well, of necessity, it must
　　be so.
　　My lords, that I abhor base Gaveston
　　I hope your honours make no question;　　240

229.1. *Draws . . . apart*] Broughton (subst.); not in Q.　　234. No? Do]
Scott; No, doe *Q1-4*.　　237. I] *Q*; ay *Dodsley*[1].　　238. *Coming forward*]
Broughton (subst.); not in Q.

---

216. *him*] i.e., Mortimer Senior.

223. *torpedo*] cramp-fish or electric ray (a flat fish that can administer
electrical shocks to any creature that touches it). Pliny describes it in his
Natural History (Holland, trans., IX, 42; p. 261). Charlton–Waller quote a
passage from Sylvester's translation of Du Bartas (originally published in
1605) that greatly exaggerates the poisonous (or numbing) effects of the
torpedo; see *Divine Weeks* (Fifth Day of the First Week, ll. 235–266), I, 238.

224. *floats*] i.e., sails (with perhaps the secondary meaning, 'floats like a
drowned corpse'); cf. I.iv.252, and also Sir Thomas Browne, *Pseudodoxia
Epidemica*: 'persons drowned arise and float the ninth day' (IV.vi), II, 288.

237. *grant*] assent.

And therefore, though I plead for his repeal,
'Tis not for his sake, but for our avail—
Nay, for the realm's behoof and for the king's.
Lancaster. Fie Mortimer, dishonour not thyself!
Can this be true, 'twas good to banish him?   245
And is this true, to call him home again?
Such reasons make white black and dark night day.
Mortimer Junior. My lord of Lancaster, mark the respect.
Lancaster. In no respect can contraries be true.
Isabella. Yet, good my lord, hear what he can allege.   250
Warwick. All that he speaks is nothing. We are resolved.
Mortimer Junior. Do you not wish that Gaveston were dead?
Pembroke. I would he were.
Mortimer Junior. Why then, my lord, give me but leave to
     speak.
Mortimer Senior. But nephew, do not play the sophister.   255
Mortimer Junior. This which I urge is of a burning zeal
To mend the king and do our country good.
Know you not Gaveston hath store of gold,
Which may in Ireland purchase him such friends
As he will front the mightiest of us all?   260
And whereas he shall live and be beloved,
'Tis hard for us to work his overthrow.
Warwick. Mark you but that, my lord of Lancaster.

---

245. 'twas] *Q;* was't *Wagner (conj.).*   246. true] *Q;* good *Broughton, Neilson*
(conj.).   260. front] *Q;* 'front *Broughton.*

---

242. *avail*] advantage.
243. *behoof*] welfare, benefit.
246. *true*] correct, right (i.e., true to, or consistent with, the statement in
the preceding line); Broughton's 'good' is unnecessary.
248. *respect*] special circumstance or consideration.
250. *allege*] offer as a reason (an obsolete use).
255. *play the sophister*] a proverbial phrase meaning 'beguile by means of
specious or misleading arguments.' Stowe refers to 'the great deceyte of
Sophisters' (p. 357) in connection with the ambiguous letter used to instruct
the murderers of Edward II.
258. *store of gold*] based on Holinshed, p. 320 (see Appendix B, no. 10).
260. *front*] confront defiantly; cf. *T.N.*: 'front her, board her, woo her,
assail her' (1.iii.55–56).
261. *whereas*] while.

Mortimer Junior. But were he here, detested as he is,
    How easily might some base slave be suborned   265
    To greet his lordship with a poniard,
    And none so much as blame the murderer,
    But rather praise him for that brave attempt,
    And in the chronicle enroll his name
    For purging of the realm of such a plague.   270
Pembroke. He saith true.
Lancaster. Ay, but how chance this was not done before?
Mortimer Junior. Because, my lords, it was not thought upon.
    Nay more, when he shall know it lies in us
    To banish him, and then to call him home,   275
    'Twill make him vail the topflag of his pride
    And fear to offend the meanest nobleman.
Mortimer Senior. But how if he do not, nephew?
Mortimer Junior. Then may we with some colour rise in arms,
    For howsoever we have borne it out,   280
    'Tis treason to be up against the king.
    So shall we have the people of our side,
    Which, for his father's sake, lean to the king
    But cannot brook a night-grown mushroom—
    Such a one as my lord of Cornwall is—   285
    Should bear us down of the nobility;
    And when the commons and the nobles join,

---

267. murderer] *Q1–2* (murtherer); murther *Q3–4.*   282. of] *Q1–2;* on
Q3–4.   284. mushroom] *Dodsley*[1]*;* mushrump *Q1–4.*

---

265. *suborned*] procured by secret collusion.

272. *how chance*] how chances it; cf. *Jew of Malta*: 'How chance you came
not with those other ships . . . ?' (1.i.89).

276. *vail*] lower (see note on 1.ii.19). Cf. Lodge, *Wounds of Civil War*,
1.i.179.

279. *colour*] pretext, excuse; see Introduction, pp. 28–29.

282. *of our side*] i.e., on our side (common because both 'on' and 'of' were
frequently reduced to the same sound—'o' or 'a').

284. *night-grown mushroom*] The mushroom, because it commonly springs
up overnight, became proverbial as a metaphor for the political climber or
socially ambitious upstart; see Tilly M1319. Cf. Chapman, *Bussy D'Ambois*:
'great D'Ambois / (Fortune's proud mushroom shot up in the night)' (III.i.97
–98).

'Tis not the king can buckler Gaveston;
We'll pull him from the strongest hold he hath.
My lords, if to perform this I be slack,   290
Think me as base a groom as Gaveston.
Lancaster. On that condition Lancaster will grant.
Pembroke. And so will Pembroke.
Warwick.   And I.
Mortimer Senior.   And I.
Mortimer Junior. In this I count me highly gratified,
And Mortimer will rest at your command.   295
Isabella. And when this favour Isabel forgets,
Then let her live abandoned and forlorn.
But see, in happy time, my lord the king,
Having brought the Earl of Cornwall on his way,
Is new returned. This news will glad him much,   300

---

293. *Pembroke.* And . . . Pembroke. *Warwick.* And I.] *Ellis; War.* And so
will *Penbrooke* and I. *Q; War.* And so will I and Pembroke. *Broughton.*
293. And so . . . And I . . . And I.] *Tancock (one line);* And so . . . and
I. / *Mor. se.* And I. *Q.*   300. new] *Q1–2;* news *Q3–4 (misprint);* now
Broughton, Bowers (conj.).

---

288. *buckler*] shield (somewhat unusual as a verb, but cf. *2H6*, III.ii.216;
3H6, III.iii.99).

289. *hold*] stronghold, keep (with a possible pun on 'bodily embrace'); cf.
II.iv.4.

291. *groom*] slave; cf. l. 97 above.

293. I accept Ellis's emendation dividing this line among three speakers
(rather than Q's two) as being both more natural and more dramatic. Q has
Warwick assenting on Pembroke's behalf as well as on his own in a decision
of the utmost political importance, as though he totally dominated or over-
awed his fellow peer; but nothing else in the text supports such an unequal
relationship. If the manuscript was crowded or unclear at this point, the
compositor might have been confused by a speech prefix that duplicated the
proper name in the words that immediately follow it, not realizing that
Pembroke speaks of himself in the third person. This situation could have
led him to conflate Pembroke's speech with Warwick's. The parallel in
Woodstock, regardless of whether this play preceded or followed *Edward II*,
provides additional support for Ellis's arrangment: '*York and Lancaster*: On
these conditions, brother, we agree. / *Arundel.* And I. *Surrey.* And I' (I.i.191–
192).

296–297. *And when . . . forlorn*] Appropriately Briggs cites Kyd, *Soliman
and Perseda*: 'My gratious Lord, when Erastus doth forget this fauor, / Then
let him liue abandoned and forlorne' (IV.i.198–199).

299. *brought*] i.e., accompanied.

Yet not so much as me; I love him more
Than he can Gaveston. Would he loved me
But half so much, then were I treble blessed.

Enter KING EDWARD *mourning,* [*attended, with* BEAUMONT *and the*
Clerk *of the crown*].

Edward. He's gone, and for his absence thus I mourn.
Did never sorrow go so near my heart   305
As doth the want of my sweet Gaveston;
And could my crown's revénue bring him back,
I would freely give it to his enemies
And think I gained, having bought so dear a friend.
Isabella. Hark how he harps upon his minion.   310
Edward. My heart is as an anvil unto sorrow,
Which beats upon it like the Cyclops' hammers,
And with the noise turns up my giddy brain
And makes me frantic for my Gaveston.

302. loved] *Q* (lou'd); love *Bullen.*   303.1. *attended ...* BEAUMONT]
*Oliphant (subst.; Oliphant, however, identifies Beaumont with the clerk of the
crown), Kirschbaum (subst.); not in Q.*   303.1–2. *and the* Clerk *of the crown*]
This ed.; not in Q.

───

303.1–2. BEAUMONT ... *crown*] I adopt Oliphant's stage direction, since it
seems less abrupt to have Beaumont enter here with the king than to delay
his entrance (as Dyce and subsequent editors do) until l. 369—only seconds
before his required exit. Most editors (including Oliphant), however, assume
that 'clerk of the crown' (l. 368) refers to Beaumont. The *O.E.D.* defines
'clerk of the crown' as 'an officer ... who issues writs of summons to peers in
the House of Lords,' but Marlowe's meaning would seem to be more general,
i.e., a servant of the royal household in charge of drawing up official
documents and communications. Henry de Beaumont was a nobleman
(Holinshed refers to him in connection with the Scottish wars as 'the lord
Henrie Beaumont, a man of high valiancie and noble courage' [p. 323]); it is
unlikely that Edward would address such a person as a mere legal functionary
or secretarial official (before the Reformation and even after it 'clerk' usually
implied a cleric), especially since a moment later he calls him by his family
name ('Beaumont'). To assume that separate characters are involved in the
action of recalling Gaveston—one to draft the necessary document (the
clerk), the other to see that its contents are speedily executed (Beaumont)—is
more logical and makes better dramatic sense.
311–312. *My ... it*] Perhaps an echo of *Fair Em* (1589–91): 'The anvil
whereupon my heart doth beat' (iv.2).
312. *Cyclops' hammers*] In Virgil the Cyclops help Vulcan at his forges
beneath Mount Etna, supposedly making thunderbolts for Jupiter; cf.
Georgics (IV, 170ff.) and *Aeneid* (VIII, 418ff.).

Ah, had some bloodless Fury rose from hell,   315
And with my kingly sceptre struck me dead
When I was forced to leave my Gaveston!
Lancaster. *Diablo!* What passions call you these?
Isabella. My gracious lord, I come to bring you news.
Edward. That you have parlied with your Mortimer.   320
Isabella. That Gaveston, my lord, shall be repealed.
Edward. Repealed? The news is too sweet to be true.
Isabella. But will you love me if you find it so?
Edward. If it be so, what will not Edward do?
Isabella. For Gaveston, but not for Isabel.   325
Edward. For thee, fair queen, if thou lov'st Gaveston;
    I'll hang a golden tongue about thy neck,
    Seeing thou hast pleaded with so good success.

                                               [*Embraces her.*]
Isabella. No other jewels hang about my neck
    Than these, my lord; nor let me have more wealth   330

---

316. struck] *Dodsley*[1]; stroke *Q1–3*; strooke *Q4*.   320. parlied] *Dodsley*[1]
(parly'd), *Broughton*; parled *Q1–4*; parley'd *Robinson*.   326. lov'st]
Dodsley[1]; louest *Q*.   327. thy] *Q1–2*; my *Q3–4*.   328.1. *Embraces her*]
Kirschbaum (subst.); not in Q.

---

315. *had . . . rose*] i.e., if only . . . had risen.

bloodless Fury] The Furies, who lived in Tartarus (the classical hell), were
the dreaded instruments of vengeance and punishment for crimes. Edward
probably imagines his Fury as 'bloodless' because of the association with
pallor and death.

318. Diablo] the devil (a Spanish expletive).

319. *My . . . news*] As Briggs notes, Marlowe uses a variant of this line at
II.ii.140.

320. *parlied*] Q's 'parled' (apparently disyllabic and common in the period)
is little more than a variant spelling of 'parlied.'

321. *Gaveston . . . repealed*] Cf. Holinshed, p. 320 (Appendix B, no. 11).

327. *golden tongue*] Some evidence suggests that metal images of tongues
were used in jewellery of the period; Charlton-Waller cite *The Account of the
Lord High Treasurer of Scotland* (1488–92): 'a grete serpent toung set with
gold, perle and precious stanes' (I, 81).

328. *pleaded . . . success*] Cf. *2 Troublesome Reign*: 'to plead with good
successe' (ii; l. 257). *Success* means result, consequence; the word could be
used for either a positive or negative outcome.

330. *these*] i.e., Edward's arms. It is not quite clear whether Isabella
initiates or receives the embrace here, although both actions could occur
simultaneously.

Than I may fetch from this rich treasury.

[*They kiss.*]

O how a kiss revives poor Isabel!

Edward. Once more receive my hand, and let this be
A second marriage 'twixt thyself and me.

Isabella. And may it prove more happy than the first.   335
My gentle lord, bespeak these nobles fair
That wait attendance for a gracious look
And on their knees salute your majesty.

[*Nobles kneel.*]

Edward. Courageous Lancaster, embrace thy king,
And as gross vapours perish by the sun,   340
Even so let hatred with thy sovereign's smile:
Live thou with me as my companion.

Lancaster. This salutation overjoys my heart.

Edward. Warwick shall be my chiefest counsellor:
These silver hairs will more adorn my court   345
Than gaudy silks or rich embroidery.
Chide me, sweet Warwick, if I go astray.

Warwick. Slay me, my lord, when I offend your grace.

---

331. treasury] *Q* (treasurie); treasure *Dodsley*[1].   331.1. *They kiss.*] *This
ed.; Kisses him. Broughton; not in Q.*   338.1. Nobles *kneel*] *Kirschbaum;
not in Q.*   341. sovereign's] *Q3–4* (soueraignes); soueraigne *Q1–2*.
346. embroidery] *Dodsley*[1]*; imbrotherie Q.*

334. *second marriage*] For reasons of dramatic economy as well as of characterization Marlowe omits Edward's official marriage to Isabella, which
occurred in 1308 *after* the recall of Gaveston and the imprisonment of the
Bishop of Coventry (Holinshed, pp. 318–319). See Introduction, p. 47; also
Appendix B, nos. 2, 3.

336. *bespeak . . . fair*] speak to . . . kindly.

340. *gross*] thick, heavy.

342. *as my companion*] Holinshed reports that Edward and Lancaster quar-
relled and then had a brief reconciliation at the time of the latter's doing
homage for the earldom of Lincoln (p. 320); but the falling out had nothing
to do with Gaveston.

344. *chiefest counsellor*] Double or pleonastic comparatives and superlatives
were common in Elizabethan English (see Abbott 11). This honour and the
others that Edward confers in the scene are unhistorical.

348. *Slay me*] Warwick speaks with unconscious irony, for Edward will
indeed 'slay' Warwick for 'offending' him later in the action (III.ii).

Edward. In solemn triumphs and in public shows
  Pembroke shall bear the sword before the king.   350
Pembroke. And with this sword Pembroke will fight for you.
Edward. But wherefore walks young Mortimer aside?
  Be thou commander of our royal fleet,
  Or if that lofty office like thee not,
  I make thee here Lord Marshal of the realm.   355
Mortimer Junior. My lord, I'll marshal so your enemies
  As England shall be quiet and you safe.
Edward. And as for you, Lord Mortimer of Chirke,
  Whose great achievements in our foreign war
  Deserves no common place nor mean reward,   360
  Be you the general of the levied troops
  That now are ready to assail the Scots.
Mortimer Senior. In this your grace hath highly honoured me,
  For with my nature war doth best agree.
Isabella. Now is the King of England rich and strong,   365
  Having the love of his renownèd peers.
Edward. Ay, Isabel, ne'er was my heart so light.
  Clerk of the crown, direct our warrant forth
  For Gaveston to Ireland; Beaumont, fly

---

356. so] *Q1–2;* all *Q3–4.*   360. Deserves] *Q;* Deserve *Dodsley*[1].
367. light.] *Q* (light,); light— / *Enter Beaumont. Broughton.*   369. Ireland;]
Q; Ireland! *Enter Beaumont with warrant. Dyce*[2].

---

350. *bear the sword*] As a symbol of their power the sword of state is
carried in procession before English monarchs.

354. *like*] please (a common impersonal use of the verb).

358. *Chirke*] The elder Mortimer's estate was on the border between
Shropshire and Wales; the younger Mortimer (of Wigmore) held property on
the border between Herefordshire and Wales (see II.ii.195). Both were so-
called Marcher lords.

361. *Be you the general*] Marlowe invents this appointment, probably for
reasons of dramatic economy (i.e., to eliminate the senior Mortimer from the
action after this scene); Briggs suggests that Marlowe may have got the idea
from the much later involvement of the younger Mortimer (not distinguished
from his uncle in the relevant passage in Holinshed [pp. 322–323]) in a
campaign against the Scots in Ireland (1315). After his exit at I.iv.423,
Mortimer the elder does not reappear onstage. Marlowe omits his historical
imprisonment and death in the Tower.

368–369. *Clerk . . . Beaumont*] See note on ll. 303.1–2 above.

As fast as Iris or Jove's Mercury.   370
Beaumont. It shall be done, my gracious lord.
                              [*Exit, with* Clerk.]
Edward. [*To* MORTIMER JUNIOR] Lord Mortimer, we leave
    you to your charge.
Now let us in and feast it royally.
Against our friend the Earl of Cornwall comes
We'll have a general tilt and tournament,   375
And then his marriage shall be solemnized;
For wot you not that I have made him sure
Unto our cousin, the Earl of Gloucester's heir?
Lancaster. Such news we hear, my lord.
Edward. That day, if not for him, yet for my sake,   380
Who in the triumph will be challenger,
Spare for no cost; we will requite your love.

371.1. *Exit . . . Clerk*] *Kirschbaum (subst.) (Exeunt Beaumont and attendant),
Bowers (subst.) (Exeunt Clarke and Beamont); Exit. Broughton; not in Q.*
372. *To* MORTIMER JUNIOR] *This ed.; not in Q.*   377. wot] *Q;* wote *Q2–3;*
wrote *Q4.*   378. our] *Q;* your *Broughton.*   381. the triumph] *Q1–2;*
triumph *Q3–4.*

370. *Iris . . . Mercury*] Iris (the rainbow) was messenger of the gods, associated particularly with Juno (cf. Virgil, *Aeneid*, V, 606); Mercury, traditionally depicted as wearing winged sandals, was Jupiter's (Jove's) messenger.
  373. *feast it royally*] Holinshed mentions Edward's penchant for 'banketing' (p. 318); see Appendix B, no. 5.
  374. *Against*] in preparation for the time when.
  Earl of Cornwall] i.e., Gaveston.
  375. *tilt and tournament*] This mention of a chivalric tournament in which
the king himself will 'be challenger' (l. 381) just prior to Gaveston's marriage
skilfully prepares the ground for the poignancy of Edward's reminiscence of
the similar event in France before his own marriage at v.v.67–69; see
Introduction, pp. 27–28, 62.
  377. *wot*] know; cf. II.v.58, IV.vii.27.
  made him sure] i.e., betrothed (in a legally binding contract); cf. *Jew of
Malta*: 'so cast about / That ye be both made sure' (II.iii.237–238). See
Introduction, p. 63.
  378. *cousin*] i.e., niece. Margaret de Clare, the second of three daughters,
was not technically the heir to her brother's title nor to his entire estates; see
Introduction, p. 51.
  381. *triumph*] i.e., the 'general tilt and tournament' of l. 375 (cf. *R2*:
'jousts and triumphs' [v.ii.52]); ordinarily the word signified a triumphal
procession involving allegorical carpentry such as figured in the annual Lord
Mayors' pageants.

Warwick. In this, or aught, your highness shall command us.
Edward. Thanks, gentle Warwick; come, let's in and revel.
                                        Exeunt. [*The* MORTIMERS *remain.*]
Mortimer Senior. Nephew, I must to Scotland; thou stay'st
    here.   385
    Leave now to oppose thyself against the king;
    Thou seest by nature he is mild and calm,
    And seeing his mind so dotes on Gaveston,
    Let him without controlment have his will.
    The mightiest kings have had their minions: 390
    Great Alexander loved Hephestion;
    The conquering Hercules for Hylas wept;
    And for Patroclus stern Achilles drooped.

---

383. aught, your] *Q1–2* (ought, your); ought your *Q3–4;* aught your
*Dodsley*¹.   384.1. *The* MORTIMERS *remain*] *Merchant; Manent Mortimers Q.*
385. stay'st] *Dodsley*¹*;* staiest *Q;* stay's *Broughton.*   391. Hephestion]
*Dodsley*¹*; Ephestion Q.*   392. Hercules] *Dodsley*² (Herc'les); Hector *Q1–4.*
392. for] *Q1–3;* did for *Q4;* for his *Dodsley*¹.   392. wept] *Q1–3;* weepe
Q4.

---

384. *revel*] This word sometimes connoted specifically theatrical shows
('revels').

390. *minions*] See note on I.i.132. The catalogue of classical precedents for
homoerotic love introduced at this point is an obvious display on Marlowe's
part of fashionable Renaissance humanism.

391. *Alexander . . . Hephestion*] Alexander the Great (356–323 B.C.),
comparing himself to Achilles, considered Hephestion, the most intimate of
his companions, his Patroclus; see note on l. 393 below. Arrian in his life of
Alexander recounts the tradition that at Hephestion's funeral the king 'flung
himself on the body of his friend and lay there nearly all day long in tears,
and refused to be parted from him until he was dragged away by force';
see Flavius Arrianus, *The Life of Alexander the Great*, trans. Aubrey de
Sélincourt (London, 1970), p. 240. The modern biographer, Arthur Weigall,
describes the friendship as containing 'all the spirtual and mental, if not the
physical, elements of a youthful romance'; see *Alexander the Great* (New
York, 1933), p. 147.

392. *Hercules . . . Hylas*] See note on I.i.143; all editors accept Dodsley's
substitution of 'Hercules' for Q's 'Hector' (which makes no sense).

393. *Patroclus . . . Achilles*] Patroclus's death at the hands of Hector grieved
Achilles so much that he abandoned his sullen passivity and helped the
Greeks capture Troy; Homer (in epic detail) describes the funeral with its
famous games held in honour of the slain warrior (*Iliad*, XXIII). In Shakespeare's *Tro.*, Thersites alludes to the supposedly homosexual nature of the
attachment by referring scurrilously to Patroclus as Achilles' 'masculine
whore' (v.i.17).

And not kings only, but the wisest men:
The Roman Tully loved Octavius,   395
Grave Socrates, wild Alcibiades.
Then let his grace, whose youth is flexible
And promiseth as much as we can wish,
Freely enjoy that vain light-headed earl,
For riper years will wean him from such toys.   400
Mortimer Junior. Uncle, his wanton humour grieves not me,
But this I scorn—that one so basely born
Should by his sovereign's favour grow so pert
And riot it with the treasure of the realm
While soldiers mutiny for want of pay.   405
He wears a lord's revénue on his back,
And, Midas-like, he jets it in the court

---

395. Octavius] *Q3–4; Octauis Q1–2.*   404. riot it] *Q;* riot *Dodsley*[1].
404. the treasure] *Q;* treasure *Gill*[1].   404–405. realm . . . pay.] *Q3*
(realme, . . . pay.); realme, . . . paie, *Q1–2;* realm . . . pay, *Dodsley*[1].

---

395. *Roman Tully . . . Octavius*] Briggs notes that the mention of this pair
in the context of the other male couplings is inapposite. Cicero (106–43 B.C.)
was not personally close to Octavius Caesar (later the first Roman emperor),
and, as Lunt points out, after the murder of Julius Caesar, Cicero was assassinated in the proscriptions of the triumvirate with Octavius's (reluctant?)
consent. But Cicero did expediently express loyalty to Octavius, who called
the famous orator 'father' and pretended to take his advice.

396. *Socrates . . . Alcibiades*] Socrates loved and tried to nurture the young
Alcibiades, an aristocratic youth of great beauty but inclined to insolence,
irresponsibility, and self-indulgence. Plutarch speaks of the relationship:
Alcibiades 'had . . . an image of love graven in his heart, or rather (as Plato
saith) a mutual love, to wit, a holy and honest affection towards Socrates';
see 'The Life of Alcibiades' in Sir Thomas North, trans., *Plutarch's Lives*
(London, 1898), II, 244. As Gill points out, Alcibiades 'was in some measure
responsible for Socrates' death' inasmuch as 'their close friendship gave
grounds to the charge of corrupting youth on which Socrates was condemned.'

400. *toys*] amorous trifling; cf. *Dido*: 'Foolish is love, a toy' (IV.v.26).

402. *basely born*] See Introduction, pp. 51–52.

404. Based on both Holinshed, p. 320, and Stowe; see Appendix B, nos.
12, 47.

406. Probably an echo of *2H6*, I.iii.80; see Introduction, p. 24. The idea,
however, was proverbial (Tilley L452). Extravagance of dress was much
satirized in Marlowe's age.

407. *Midas-like*] i.e., as if all golden, clad in cloth of gold; the god
Dionysus gave Midas the gift of turning anything he touched into gold; cf.
Ovid, *Metamorphoses*, XI, 92ff. Gill compares Drayton, *Peirs Gaveston*: 'Now
like to *Mydas* all I touch is gould' (l. 631).

jets it] struts; Briggs compares Kyd, *Soliman and Perseda*: 'he will iet as if it
were a Goose on a greene' (I.iii.214).

With base outlandish cullions at his heels,
Whose proud fantastic liveries make such show
As if that Proteus, god of shapes, appeared.   410
I have not seen a dapper jack so brisk;
He wears a short Italian hooded cloak
Larded with pearl, and in his Tuscan cap
A jewel of more value than the crown.
Whiles other walk below, the king and he   415
From out a window laugh at such as we,
And flout our train and jest at our attire.
Uncle, 'tis this that makes me impatient.

Mortimer Senior. But nephew, now you see the king is
          changed.

Mortimer Junior. Then so am I, and live to do him service;   420
          But whiles I have a sword, a hand, a heart,

---

409. make] *Q1–3;* makes *Q4.*   415. Whiles other] *Q1–2;* Whiles others
Q3–4; While others *Dodsley*[1].   417. jest] *Q;* jet *Scott.*   418. that makes]
Q1–4; makes *Cunningham;* make *Oliphant.*   418. impatient] *Q1–4;* so
impatient *Broughton.*

---

408. *outlandish*] foreign (the original sense of the word). Gaveston, a
Gascon, had French servants; as Briggs notes, Stowe writes of Edward II
keeping Christmas at York, 'where Pierce of Gauaston was present with his
Outlandish men' (*Annals.* ed. 1592, p. 324).

cullions] low fellows (originally 'testicles'); cf. *2H6*: 'Away, base cullions'
(I.iii.40).

410. *Proteus*] a sea god who changed into countless different shapes; cf.
Ovid, *Metamorphoses*, VIII, 730–737.

411. *dapper jack*] smartly dressed fellow (here used depreciatively).
brisk] spruce.

412. *Italian hooded cloak*] Deats argues that Gaveston's Italian fashions
would help to convey both the character's Machiavellian politics and his
homosexuality since the Italians of the Renaissance were notorious for sexual
deviance ('Study in Androgyny,' p. 39 n. 21). Much is made in *Woodstock* of
the political and moral contrast between the foppish foreign attire of Richard
II's new favourites and the plain, sober, English dress of the established
nobility. Gill cites Dekker's attack on 'Apishness' in his *Seven Deadly Sinnes
of London* (1606), which contains a disparaging allusion to an Elizabethan
dandy who affects foreign fashions as 'the *Gaueston of the Time*' (p. 31).

413. *Larded*] encrusted, decorated.

415. *other*] i.e., others. Briggs cites Marlowe's translation, *Ovid's Elegies*:
'Be thou as bold as other' (I.vi.12).

417. *flout*] mock.
train] attendants.

I will not yield to any such upstart.
You know my mind. Come, uncle, let's away.

Exeunt.

---

422. *upstart*] cf. l. 41 above.

Act II

Enter SPENCER [JUNIOR] *and* BALDOCK.

Baldock. Spencer,
    Seeing that our lord th' Earl of Gloucester's dead,
    Which of the nobles dost thou mean to serve?
Spencer Junior. Not Mortimer, nor any of his side,
    Because the king and he are enemies.   5
    Baldock, learn this of me: a factious lord
    Shall hardly do himself good, much less us;
    But he that hath the favour of a king
    May with one word advance us while we live.
    The liberal Earl of Cornwall is the man   10
    On whose good fortune Spencer's hope depends.
Baldock. What, mean you then to be his follower?
Spencer Junior. No, his companion; for he loves me well

Heading. Act II, Scene i] *Broughton; not in Q.*   1–2. Spencer, / Seeing . . .
dead] *Dyce*[1]; *one line in Q.*   3. dost] *Q, Q4;* doest *Q2–3.*

---

2. *Earl of Gloucester*] Gilbert de Clare, ninth Earl of Gloucester, was killed
at Bannockburn (1314) *after* rather than before Gaveston's execution (1312);
it is possible, however, that Marlowe was thinking of the eighth earl (Gilbert
de Clare senior), who died in 1295 (see l. 46 and note below; also Lady
Margaret de Clare's reference to Baldock and Spencer as 'my father's servants' at
II.ii.239). Baldock and Spencer Junior were never dependent upon either
nobleman; for Baldock's political prominence in the reign (he became Lord
Chancellor) and his connection with the Spencers, see Holinshed, p. 332
(Appendix B, no. 14). Marlowe probably got the idea for the younger
Spencer's relationship to Gloucester and to Gaveston (Spencer speaks of
becoming Gaveston's 'companion' in l. 13 below) from the fact that both
Gaveston and Spencer married sisters of Gilbert de Clare junior; see Intro-
duction, pp. 50–51.

6. *factious*] given to political partisanship, seditious.

10–11. In history Spencer Junior was opposed to Gaveston, not his
partisan; after Gaveston's execution the nobles nominated him to be Chamberlain, the post Gaveston had previously held. See Introduction, p. 51; also
Holinshed, p. 321 (Appendix B, no. 20).

13. *companion*] See note on l. 2 above.

And would have once preferred me to the king.
Baldock. But he is banished; there's small hope of him.   15
Spencer Junior. Ay, for a while; but Baldock, mark the end:
   A friend of mine told me in secrecy
   That he's repealed and sent for back again;
   And even now a post came from the court
   With letters to our lady from the king,   20
   And as she read, she smiled, which makes me think
   It is about her lover, Gaveston.
Baldock. 'Tis like enough, for since he was exiled,
   She neither walks abroad nor comes in sight.
   But I had thought the match had been broke off   25
   And that his banishment had changed her mind.
Spencer Junior. Our lady's first love is not wavering;
   My life for thine, she will have Gaveston.
Baldock. Then hope I by her means to be preferred,
   Having read unto her since she was a child.   30
Spencer Junior. Then, Baldock, you must cast the scholar off
   And learn to court it like a gentleman.
   'Tis not a black coat and a little band,
   A velvet-caped cloak, faced before with serge,

---

34. cloak] *Q;* coat *Oliphant.*

---

14. *preferred*] recommended.

20. *our lady*] i.e., Margaret de Clare (in Marlowe betrothed rather than married to Gaveston). According to Holinshed (p. 318; see Appendix B, no. 9), the marriage 'was solemnized' in 1307, the first year of the reign and before the favourite's exile.

30. *Having read unto her*] Marlowe conceives of Baldock (who historically was a cleric and doctor of Oxford) as Lady Margaret's tutor and perhaps also the family's private chaplain (cf. the reference to his 'saying a long grace' in l. 37 below). The portrait is obviously anachronistic, being that of a sixteenth-century academic.

32. *court it*] i.e., behave like a courtier.

33. *black coat . . . little band*] the traditionally modest (and menial) dress of the scholar as caricatured in such portraits as Overbury's 'A Meere Scholler' ('a silly fellow in black') and Earle's 'A down-right scholar' ('He has been used to . . . dark clothes, and his eyes dazzle at a sattin suit'); see W. J. Paylor, ed., *The Overburian Characters* (Oxford, 1936), pp. 33–34, and Israel Gollancz, ed., *Microcosmographie* (London, 1899), pp. 32–34. Spencer implies a contrast between the small strip of cloth worn around the neck (the 'little band') and the more ostentatious ruff of the courtier. Note the implied ridicule of puritanism and its association with hypocrisy; cf. l. 45 below).

34. *serge*] a cheap, homely material used to reinforce the more costly

And smelling to a nosegay all the day,   35
Or holding of a napkin in your hand,
Or saying a long grace at a table's end,
Or making low legs to a nobleman,
Or looking downward with your eyelids close,
And saying 'truly, an't may please your honour,'   40
Can get you any favour with great men.
You must be proud, bold, pleasant, resolute—
And now and then stab, as occasion serves.

Baldock. Spencer, thou knowest I hate such formal toys,
And use them but of mere hypocrisy.   45
Mine old lord, whiles he lived, was so precise
That he would take exceptions at my buttons,
And, being like pins' heads, blame me for the bigness,
Which made me curate-like in mine attire,
Though inwardly licentious enough,   50

---

44. knowest] *Q1–3;* know'st *Q4.*   44. formal] *Q1–2; not in Q3–4.*
45. of] *Q1–3;* as *Q4.*   48. pins'] *Dodsley²;* pins *Q;* pin's *Ellis.*

---

velvet. Tancock notes that Earle in his character of a 'A young raw preacher'
mentions nearly identical details of attire: 'his narrow velvet cape, and serge
facing' (*Microcosmographie,* p. 8).

35. *smelling to a nosegay*] an effeminate affectation of delicacy; also a
precaution against taking ill in time of plague.

37. *at a table's end*] i.e., at the bottom end of a long table (and therefore
low on the scale of social precedence).

38. *making low legs*] making low obeisances with the leg thrust forward.

39. *eyelids close*] eyelids nearly closed (in modesty); cf. *Hero and Leander:*
'vailing her eyelids close' (I, 159).

40. *an't*] if it.

42. *pleasant*] jocular, witty (often with a touch of irreverence or disre-
spect); cf. *H5:* 'We are glad the Dauphin is so pleasant with us' (I.ii.259).

44. *formal toys*] prim behaviour.

46. *old*] former; cf. Marlowe, *Lucan's First Book:* 'that late deeds would
dim / Old triumphs' (ll. 121–122). The ninth Earl of Gloucester was only
twenty-three at the time of his death; his father, the eighth earl, died at the
age of fifty-two. See note on l. 2 above.

precise] puritanically punctilious (the Puritans were often disparagingly
referred to as 'precisians'); cf. *Jew of Malta:* 'be thou so precise / As they
may think it done of holiness' (I.ii.284–285).

47. *take exceptions at*] See note on I.ii.25.

50. *licentious*] loose, unrestrained (probably with overtones of lasciviousa-
ness). The metre requires all four syllables to be prounounced (li-cen-ti-
ous).

And apt for any kind of villainy.
I am none of these common pedants, I,
That cannot speak without '*propterea quod.*'
Spencer Junior. But one of those that saith '*quandoquidem*'
And hath a special gift to form a verb.   55
Baldock. Leave off this jesting—here my lady comes.

[*They draw aside.*]

Enter the LADY [MARGARET DE CLARE].

Lady Margaret. The grief for his exile was not so much
As is the joy of his returning home.
This letter came from my sweet Gaveston.

[*Reads a letter.*]

What needst thou, love, thus to excuse thyself?   60
I know thou couldst not come and visit me.
'I will not long be from thee, though I die';

---

52. pedants] *Q2–4;* pendants *Q.*   54. *quandoquidem*] *Q1–3;* quando quidem
Q4.   56.1. *They draw aside*] *Hampden; not in Q.*   59.1. *Reads a letter*]
Dodsley[1] *(subst.) (after line 61); not in Q.*

---

53. propterea quod] because, for this reason. Since university students
were supposed to converse in Latin, their speech mannerisms could become a
natural focus of satire.

54. quandoquidem] This term means essentially the same thing as '*propterea
quod*' above, but a joke of some sort is apparently intended, perhaps derived
from Marlowe's student days at Cambridge. A nice or fashionable distinction
between the two usages (now lost) seems to be implied, possibly, as Briggs
explains, because '*propterea quod*' is more cumbrous and is associated with
prose rather than with the elegance of verse.

55. *form a verb*] The meaning of this phrase has been much debated:
Tancock believes that it is a translation of Quintilian's '*verba formare*' (1.12.9)
—'to pronounce correctly' and, by extension, 'to put a thing neatly,' 'to say
the right thing'; Ribner glosses 'to use language eloquently'; Charlton–
Waller think it may signify 'to twist and combine speech to serve any
purpose' as in coining a new verb; Millar Maclure in his manuscript notes,
basing his observation on Lewis and Short's Latin *Dictionary* (*verbum*, II, B),
points out that the phrase 'can mean to make a deceitful or silly remark' and
thinks some indecency may be involved; Lees (in his revision of Charlton–
Waller, p. 226) suggests the meaning, 'conjugate' a verb, with the additional
implication of proper pronunciation of the Latin. This latter explanation is
plausible and probably the simplest.

62. *die*] Perhaps with a quibble on the sexual meaning; cf. 1.i.14.

This argues the entire love of my lord.
'When I forsake thee, death seize on my heart';
But rest thee here where Gaveston shall sleep.   65
                         [*Puts the letter into her bosom.*]
Now to the letter of my lord the king.
                              [*Reads another letter.*]
He wills me to repair unto the court
And meet my Gaveston. Why do I stay,
Seeing that he talks thus of my marriage-day?
Who's there? Baldock,   70
             [BALDOCK *and* SPENCER JUNIOR *come forward.*]
See that my coach be ready; I must hence.
Baldock. It shall be done, madam.
Lady Margaret. And meet me at the park pale presently.
                                    Exit [BALDOCK].
Spencer, stay you and bear me company,
For I have joyful news to tell thee of;   75
My lord of Cornwall is a-coming over
And will be at the court as soon as we.
Spencer Junior. I knew the king would have him home again.
Lady Margaret. If all things sort out as I hope they will,
Thy service, Spencer, shall be thought upon.   80
Spencer Junior. I humbly thank your ladyship.
Lady Margaret. Come, lead the way; I long till I am there.
                                        [*Exeunt.*]

---

65. rest thee] *Q*; thee *Q2*; stay thee *Q3–4.*   65.1. *Puts . . . bosom*]
Broughton MS., *Dyce*[1]; *not in Q.*   66.1. *Reads . . . letter*] *Gill*[1] *(subst.); not
in Q.*   70. Who's there? Baldock,] *Oliphant;* Whose there, *Balduck? Q;*
Who's there? Baldock! *Dyce*[1].   70.1. BALDOCK . . . *forward*] *Hampden
(subst.); not in Q.*   73. park pale] *Q*; park-pail *Dodsley*[1].   73.1. *Exit*
BALDOCK] *Dyce*[1]; *Exit Q (after line 72).*   82.1. *Exeunt*] *Dodsley*[1]; *not in Q.*

---

69. *marriage-day*] See note on l. 20 above.
71. *coach*] An anachronism; according to Stowe, the first coach in England
was made in 1555 for the Earl of Rutland (C. L. Kingsford, ed., *A Survey of
London* [Oxford, 1908], II, 282).
73. *park pale*] fence or paling at the edge of the estate's park.
presently] See note on I.iv.90.

[SCENE ii]

Enter EDWARD, [ISABELLA] *the* Queen, LANCASTER, MORTIMER
[JUNIOR], WARWICK, PEMBROKE, KENT, Attendants.

Edward. The wind is good; I wonder why he stays.
   I fear me he is wracked upon the sea.
Isabella. Look, Lancaster, how passionate he is,
   And still his mind runs on his minion.
Lancaster. My lord—   5
Edward. How now, what news? Is Gaveston arrived?
Mortimer Junior. Nothing but Gaveston! What means your
    grace?
   You have matters of more weight to think upon;
   The King of France sets foot in Normandy.
Edward. A trifle! We'll expel him when we please.   10
   But tell me, Mortimer, what's thy device

Heading. Scene ii] *Broughton; not in* Q.   2. wracked] Q (wrackt); wreck'd
Dodsley².

---

   1. *The wind is good*] Edward awaits Gaveston near Tynemouth Castle (cf.
l. 51 below). If we imagine Gaveston as returning from Ireland (the place of
his first banishment in Edward II's reign), the geography is anomalous; but
Marlowe conflates the second banishment (to Flanders) with the first. In
Holinshed (p. 320; see Appendix B, no. 11) the king meets his friend at
Chester; Tynemouth is mentioned only in passing as a place where Gaveston
later enjoys temporary royal protection in his attempt to evade the hostile
nobles (p. 321; see Appendix B, no. 17). See also note on II.iii.16.
   3. *passionate*] emotional, excited.
   4. *his mind . . . minion*] Cf. *Massacre at Paris*: 'His mind, you see, runs on
his minions' (xiv.45).
   9. *King . . . Normandy*] Cf. III.i.63–64. Marlowe invents this invasion; see
Introduction, p. 48.
   11. *device*] an emblematic painting or 'impresa' on a shield, usually with a
motto. David Bevington and James Shapiro assume that the decorated shields
described in this scene are present and visible to the speaker as well as to the
audience; see '"What are kings, when Regiment is gone?": The Decay
of Ceremony in *Edward II*,' in Kenneth Friedenreich, Roma Gill, and
Constance B. Kuriyama, eds., '*A Poet and a filthy Play-maker*': *New Essays
on Christopher Marlowe* (New York, 1988), pp. 269–271. This is possible
(note the word 'display' in l. 33), but perhaps the shields are only being
invoked mentally as though intended for a future occasion—'the stately
triumph' mentioned in l. 12 (cf. 'not worth the telling' in l. 13). Would
Mortimer and Lancaster be carrying tournament shields on the occasion of
Gaveston's debarkation?

   Against the stately triumph we decreed?
Mortimer Junior. A homely one, my lord, not worth the
      telling.
Edward. Prithee let me know it.
Mortimer Junior. But seeing you are so desirous, thus it is: 15
   A lofty cedar tree fair flourishing,
   On whose top branches kingly eagles perch,
   And by the bark a canker creeps me up
   And gets unto the highest bough of all;
   The motto: *Æque tandem.*   20
Edward. And what is yours, my lord of Lancaster?
Lancaster. My lord, mine's more obscure than Mortimer's:
   Pliny reports there is a flying fish
   Which all the other fishes deadly hate,
   And therefore, being pursued, it takes the air;   25
   No sooner is it up, but there's a fowl
   That seizeth it; this fish, my lord, I bear;

---

14. Prithee] *Q* (Prethee); Prey thee *Q2–4;* Pray thee *Dodsley*[1].   19. unto]
Q; into *Cunningham.*   23. is a] *Q, Q3–4;* is *Q2.*

---

   12. *triumph*] see note on I.iv.381.
   18. *canker*] canker-worm, a caterpillar that attacks plants.
   creeps me up] i.e., creeps up. Abbott (220) explains the redundant *me* in
such constructions as a survival of the reflexive use of the verb—a means by
which the speaker calls attention to himself as in the expression, 'mark me.'
   20. *Æque tandem*] equal finally (or 'equal in height'); i.e., the canker-
worm (Gaveston) climbs to the height of the 'kingly eagles' (the highest
peers) and so becomes their equal in prestige and power. The emblem
implies of course that Gaveston will destroy the 'lofty cedar' (King Edward;
cf. l. 38) on which the welfare of everyone depends.
   23. *Pliny reports*] Editors point out that Pliny the Elder gives no such
description in his *Natural History* as here alleged, although the mistake is
understandable because he was famous for reporting such curiosities. As
Tancock suggests, Marlowe probably misattributes an account of flying fish
given in an account of Sir John Hawkins's *Second Voyage* (1565), later
printed in Richard Hakluyt's *Principal Navigations* (1589): 'Of these [flying
fish] we sawe comming out of Guinea, a hundredth in a companie, which
being chased by the Giltheads, otherwise called the Bonitoes [i.e., the tunny-
fish], doe to avoyde them the better take their flight out of the water, but yet
are they not able to flie farre . . . [;] when they can flye no further, [they] fall
into the water. . . . There is a sea foule also that chaseth this flying fish as wel
as the Bonito; for as the flying fish taketh her flight, so doth this foule pursue
to take her . . .' (p. 542). It is also possible that Lancaster has forgotten the
source of the report and mentions Pliny to add verisimilitude.

The motto this: *Undique mors est.*
Edward. Proud Mortimer! Ungentle Lancaster!
   Is this the love you bear your sovereign?   30
   Is this the fruit your reconcilement bears?
   Can you in words make show of amity
   And in your shields display your rancorous minds?
   What call you this but private libelling
   Against the Earl of Cornwall and my brother?   35
Isabella. Sweet husband be content; they all love you.
Edward. They love me not that hate my Gaveston.
   I am that cedar (shake me not too much!)
   And you the eagles; soar ye ne'er so high,
   I have the jesses that will pull you down,   40
   And *Æque tandem* shall that canker cry
   Unto the proudest peer of Britainy.
   Though thou compar'st him to a flying fish,
   And threat'nest death whether he rise or fall,
   'Tis not the hugest monster of the sea   45
   Nor foulest harpy that shall swallow him.

---

29. *Edward.*] *Q* (*Edw.*); *Kent. Dyce*[1].   39. ye] *Q1–3;* you *Q4.*
40. jesses] *Broughton* (gesses); gresses *Q1–4.*   40. you] *Q;* ye *Pinkerton.*
43. compar'st] *Q* (comparst); comparest *Scott.*   44. threat'nest] *Q2–4*
(threatnest); threatenest *Q;* threaten'st *Dyce*[1].

---

28. Undique mors est] On all sides there is death.

29. *Edward*] Dyce's assignment of this speech to Kent was based on a misunderstanding of the word 'brother' in l. 35; see note below.

31. *Is . . . bears?*] Cf. *Arden of Faversham:* 'Is this the fruit thy reconcilement buds?' (I.i.186).

35. *my brother*] i.e., Gaveston (a term of endearment). Stowe notes that King Edward wished that Gaveston could 'succeede him in the Kyngdome, calling him brother' (p. 327); see Appendix B, no. 47.

40. *jesses*] short thongs or straps attached to the legs of a trained falcon.

42. *Britainy*] i.e., England. But as Charlton–Waller explain, in the sixteenth century the word often referred to England and Scotland together (as in Shakespeare), probably because a union of the two crowns was already in prospect. Great Britain signified the entire island and was distinguished from lesser Britain (modern Brittany).

46. *foulest harpy*] In mythology the Harpies were loathsome, voracious, vulture-like females who snatched food and befouled banquet tables; they plagued the blind Phineus, a ruler in eastern Thrace, who entertained the Argonauts.

Mortimer Junior. [*To* Nobles] If in his absence thus he favours
    him,
    What will he do whenas he shall be present?
Lancaster. That shall we see; look where his lordship comes.

Enter GAVESTON.

Edward. My Gaveston!   50
    Welcome to Tynemouth, welcome to thy friend.
    Thy absence made me droop and pine away,
    For as the lovers of fair Danaë,
    When she was locked up in a brazen tower,
    Desired her more and waxed outrageous,   55
    So did it sure with me; and now thy sight
    Is sweeter far than was thy parting hence
    Bitter and irksome to my sobbing heart.
Gaveston. Sweet lord and king, your speech preventeth mine,
    Yet have I words left to express my joy: 60
    The shepherd nipped with biting winter's rage

---

47. *To* Nobles] *Oliphant (subst.); not in* Q.   48. whenas] *Oxberry;* when as
Q.   50–51. My Gaveston . . . friend.] *Dyce*[1]*; one line in* Q.   51, 220.
Tynemouth] Q *(Tinmouth, Tinmoth);* Chester *Broughton.*   56. sure] *Q1–3;*
fare *Q4.*   61. shepherd] *Q4* (Shepheard); sheepeherd *Q1–3.*

---

53. *Danaë*] a Greek heroine locked up in a brazen tower by her father
Acrisius, who was trying to forestall a prediction that her child should kill
him. Jupiter, however, impregnated Danaë in the form of a golden shower
(cf. III.ii.83), and the resulting son (Perseus) fulfilled the prophecy. Inasmuch as Renaissance moralists tended to interpret the myth as illustrating
the corrupting effects of wealth upon chastity, Edward's allusion projects a
certain unconscious irony. Danaë had no lovers in the tower apart from
Jupiter, but Marlowe may have been thinking of other episodes in which she
was involved: she had been seduced by her uncle Proteus and, according to
some traditions, was later forced into a liaison (or even marriage) with
Polydectes, King of Seriphos. Gill suggests that 'lovers' in the same line,
although uncorrected in all the quartos, may be a compositorial error for
'lover.'
    55. *outrageous*] immoderate, unrestrained; cf. v.i.19.
    59. *preventeth*] anticipates.
    61. Although images of the chilliness of the shepherd's calling are com-
mon, Marlowe may have recalled the molehill reverie of Shakespeare's Henry
VI, who speaks of the 'shepherd, blowing of his nails' (*3H6,* II.v.3). For the
relationship of this play and this scene to *Edward II,* see Introduction,
pp. 31–32.

Frolics not more to see the painted spring
Than I do to behold your majesty.
Edward. Will none of you salute my Gaveston?
Lancaster. Salute him? Yes! Welcome, Lord Chamberlain.   65
Mortimer Junior. Welcome is the good Earl of Cornwall.
Warwick. Welcome, Lord Governor of the Isle of Man.
Pembroke. Welcome, Master Secretary.
Kent. Brother, do you hear them?
Edward. Still will these earls and barons use me thus!   70
Gaveston. My lord, I cannot brook these injuries.
Isabella. [*Aside*] Ay me, poor soul, when these begin to jar.
Edward. Return it to their throats; I'll be thy warrant.
Gaveston. Base leaden earls that glory in your birth,
    Go sit at home and eat your tenants' beef,   75
    And come not here to scoff at Gaveston,
    Whose mounting thoughts did never creep so low
    As to bestow a look on such as you.
Lancaster. Yet I disdain not to do this for you.

                                            [*Draws his sword.*]

---

68. Master Secretary] *Q* (maister secretarie); Mas. Sec't'ry *Fleay.*   70.
thus!] *Cunningham* (thus.); thus? *Q1–4.*   72. Aside] *Dyce*[1]; *not in Q.*
72. Ay] *Q* (Aye); Ah *Dodsley*[1].   79.1. Draws his sword] *Broughton (subst.);
not in Q.*

---

62. *painted*] adorned with flowers (a translation, as Tancock explains, of
the common classical phrase 'prata picta'—flowery meadows).

68. *Secretary*] official sharer of the king's secrets (the root meaning of the
term).

72. *jar*] wrangle.

73. *Return . . . throats*] i.e., make them eat their own words.

74. *Base leaden earls*] spurious nobles (like coin of alloy rather than of true
metal). Gaveston implies that, although they take refuge in aristocratic birth,
they possess no genuine nobility. Probably 'leaden' also suggests dullness of
personality, lack of imagination.

75. *eat . . . beef*] The English, especially from the perspective of Frenchmen such as Gaveston, were fabled eaters of beef: cf. *H5*, in which the
Constable of France credits the English soldiers with 'leaving their wits with
their wives' and eating 'great meals of beef . . . like wolves' (III.vii.147–150);
also *Edward III* (1590?), in which the French king speaks disparagingly of
the English fondness for 'chines of beefe' (III.iii.159).

77. *mounting thoughts*] Gaveston's overweening pride is confirmed by
several passages in Holinshed; see especially p. 320 (Appendix B, nos. 12,
13).

Edward. Treason, treason! Where's the traitor?   80
Pembroke. [*Pointing to* GAVESTON] Here, here!
Edward. Convey hence Gaveston; they'll murder him.
Gaveston. [*To* LANCASTER] The life of thee shall salve this foul
    disgrace.
Mortimer Junior. Villain, thy life, unless I miss mine aim.
                                        [*Wounds* GAVESTON.]
Isabella. Ah furious Mortimer, what hast thou done?   85
Mortimer Junior. No more than I would answer were he slain.
                              [*Exit* GAVESTON *with* Attendants.]
Edward. Yes, more than thou canst answer though he live.
    Dear shall you both aby this riotous deed.
    Out of my presence! Come not near the court.
Mortimer Junior. I'll not be barred the court for Gaveston.   90
Lancaster. We'll hale him by the ears unto the block.

---

81. *Pointing to* GAVESTON] *Kirschbaum (subst.); not in* Q.   81. here!] *Dyce²;*
here King *Q1–4.*   81–82. Here, here! / *Edward.* Convey . . . him.] *Dyce²;*
Heere . . . King: conuey . . . him. *Q1–4 (one line), Brereton (as an aside);*
Here . . . king: / Convey . . . him. *Robinson;* Here . . . king! / *Edw.* Con-
vey . . . him. *Dyce¹.*   82. *Edward.*] *Dyce¹; not in* Q.   83. *To* LANCASTER]
Kirschbaum; not in Q.   84.1. *Wounds* GAVESTON.] *Dyce¹; Wounds Gav. who
is borne off. Broughton; Offers to stab him. Robinson; not in* Q.   86.1.
Exit . . . Attendants] Dyce¹; not in Q.   88. aby] *Q (abie);* abide *Q2–4.*

81–82. *here . . . Convey*] A textual crux to which the emendation in Dyce's
second edition seems the best solution; see Greg's discussion of the problem
summarized in the Introduction, pp. 9–10.
84.1. The wounding is Marlowe's invention, based probably on Holinshed's
account of the meeting: 'Herevpon to reteine amitie, as was thought on both
sides, Peers by consent of the lords was restored home againe (the king
meeting him at Chester) to his great comfort and reioising for the time,
although the malice of the lords was such, that such ioy lasted not long' (p.
320).
86. *answer*] answer for.
88. *both*] i.e., Mortimer and Lancaster (who had also drawn his sword
against Gaveston).
    aby] pay the penalty for. In its common Elizabethan spelling ('abie') the
word got confused with 'abide' (cf. Q2–4), probably, as Charlton–Waller
suggest, because of the implied notion of abiding, i.e., waiting for, punishment.
91. An obvious foreshadowing of Gaveston's death in II.vi. Although
Marlowe follows Holinshed in making Warwick's treachery the immediate
cause of the favourite's execution, he probably remembered the chronicler's
statement at a later point that 'the erle of Lancaster was the cheefe occasioner
of his death' (p. 331).

Edward. Look to your own heads; his is sure enough.
Warwick. Look to your own crown, if you back him thus.
Kent. Warwick, these words do ill beseem thy years.
Edward. Nay all of them conspire to cross me thus;   95
    But if I live, I'll tread upon their heads
    That think with high looks thus to tread me down.
    Come Edmund, let's away and levy men;
    'Tis war that must abate these barons' pride.
          Exit [EDWARD] *the* King [*with* QUEEN ISABELLA *and* KENT].
Warwick. Let's to our castles, for the king is moved.   100
Mortimer Junior. Moved may he be and perish in his wrath.
Lancaster. [*To* MORTIMER JUNIOR] Cousin, it is no dealing
    with him now;
    He means to make us stoop by force of arms,
    And therefore let us jointly here protest
    To prosecute that Gaveston to the death.   105
Mortimer Junior. By heaven, the abject villain shall not live.
Warwick. I'll have his blood or die in seeking it.
Pembroke. The like oath Pembroke takes.
Lancaster.   And so doth Lancaster.
    Now send our heralds to defy the king
    And make the people swear to put him down.   110

          Enter a Post.

Mortimer Junior. Letters? From whence?
Post. From Scotland, my lord.

---

92. your own] *Q;* your *Cunningham.*   92. his] *Q;* his own *Wagner.*
99.1. *with* QUEEN ISABELLA *and* KENT] *Dyce*[1] *(subst.); and Kent Oxberry; not
in Q.*   102. *To* MORTIMER JUNIOR] *This ed.; not in Q.*   105. prosecute]
Q; persecute *Ellis.*   110.1. Post] *Q; Messenger Broughton, Oxberry.*
111. Letters?] *Ribner;* Letters, *Q;* Letters! *Dodsley*[1].   112. Post] *Oliphant;*
Messen. *Q1–4.*

---

92. *sure*] safe, secure.
94. *ill . . . years*] i.e., because Warwick, being a senior peer (he died in
1315), should possess more wisdom; see Introduction, p. 52.
100. *moved*] angry.
102. *Cousin*] close friend or associate (as in ll. 113, 120, and 126 below;
and in *R3*, II.i.65, where the title character so addresses Buckingham); the
word was loosely used for several kinds of relationship (see note on I.iv.378).
    it is], i.e., there is.
104. *protest*] swear, vow.
109. *defy*] renounce allegiance to (the root sense of the word).

Lancaster. Why how now, cousin, how fares all our friends?
Mortimer Junior. [*Reading letter*] My uncle's taken prisoner by
    the Scots.
Lancaster. We'll have him ransomed, man; be of good cheer.   115
Mortimer Junior. They rate his ransom at five thousand
      pound.
    Who should defray the money but the king,
    Seeing he is taken prisoner in his wars?
    I'll to the king.
Lancaster. Do cousin, and I'll bear thee company.   120
Warwick. Meantime, my lord of Pembroke and myself
    Will to Newcastle here and gather head.
Mortimer Junior. About it then, and we will follow you.
Lancaster. Be resolute and full of secrecy.
Warwick. I warrant you.   125
        [*Exeunt all but* MORTIMER JUNIOR *and* LANCASTER.]
Mortimer Junior. Cousin, an if he will not ransom him,
    I'll thunder such a peal into his ears
    As never subject did unto his king.
Lancaster. Content, I'll bear my part. [*Calling*] Holla! Who's
    there?

            [*Enter* Guard.]

Mortimer Junior. Ay, marry, such a guard as this doth well.   130
Lancaster. Lead on the way.
Guard. Whither will your lordships?

---

113. fares] *Q*; fare *Dodsley*².   114. *Reading letter*] *Ribner* (*subst.*) (*after line 112*); *not in Q.*   125.1. *Exeunt* . . . LANCASTER.] *Briggs; Exit with Pembroke. Dyce*¹; *not in Q.*   126. an] *Broughton* (an'); *and Q.*   129. *Calling*] *Oliphant; not in Q.*   129. Holla] *Q;* Holloa *Cunningham.*   129.1. *Enter Guard*] *Broughton; not in Q.*   132. lordships] *Q;* lordship *Oxberry.*

---

114. Marlowe invents this incident; see Introduction, p. 47, and note on
I.iv.361. Tancock points out the resemblance of this episode to Holinshed's
account of Edmund Mortimer in the reign of Henry IV and to Shakespeare's
dramatization of it in *1H4*, I.iii.77–119.

  122. *Newcastle*] Cf. Holinshed, p. 321 (Appendix B, no. 17).

  gather head] muster troops, raise an army; cf. *Massacre at Paris*, xi.25.

  126. *an if*] if; cf. II.i.40. The double conditional particle was common (see
Abbott 103).

  130. *marry*] an exclamation supposedly derived from the name of Our
Lady.

Mortimer Junior. Whither else but to the king?
Guard. His highness is disposed to be alone.
Lancaster. Why, so he may, but we will speak to him.   135
Guard. You may not in, my lord.
Mortimer Junior. May we not?

[*Enter* KING EDWARD *and* KENT.]

Edward. How now, what noise is this?
    Who have we there? Is't you?

                                        [*Offers to go back.*]
Mortimer Junior. Nay, stay my lord; I come to bring you
        news: 140
    Mine uncle's taken prisoner by the Scots.
Edward. Then ransom him.
Lancaster. 'Twas in your wars; you should ransom him.
Mortimer Junior. And you shall ransom him, or else—
Kent. What, Mortimer, you will not threaten him?   145
Edward. Quiet yourself; you shall have the broad seal
    To gather for him thoroughout the realm.
Lancaster. Your minion Gaveston hath taught you this.
Mortimer Junior. My lord, the family of the Mortimers
    Are not so poor but, would they sell their land,   150 ·
    Would levy men enough to anger you.
    We never beg, but use such prayers as these.

                                        [*Grasps his sword.*]

137.1. *Enter . . .* KENT] *Broughton; not in Q.*   138–139. *How . . . you?*] *Q;*
How now, / What . . . you? *Dyce¹.*   139.1. *Offers . . . back*] *Bowers; Going*
Robinson; not in Q.   143. 'Twas] *Q;* It was *Wagner (conj.), Fleay.*
143. wars; you] *Q* (wars, you); wars, and you *Broughton.*   147. thorough-
out] *Q;* throughout *Q2–4.*   151. Would] *Q1–2;* 'Twoul'd *Q3–4, Dyce¹;*
Could *Dodsley¹.*   152.1. *Grasps his sword.*] *Charlton–Waller (subst.),*
Ribner; Striking his sword. Briggs; not in Q.

---

136. *in*] i.e., go in (a common ellipsis).
146. *broad seal*] a brief or letters patent under the Great Seal (as Tancock
and Charlton–Waller explain) which authorized a person to collect alms for a
special purpose and which exempted that person from the penalties to which
beggars were otherwise liable. The king is demeaning Mortimer by granting
him the right to beg (cf. l. 152 below), thereby implying that he is impov-
erished. See also notes on I.i.167 and V.ii.37.
147. *thoroughout*] Pronounced trisyllabically.

Edward. Shall I still be haunted thus?

Mortimer Junior. Nay, now you are here alone, I'll speak my
    mind.

Lancaster. And so will I, and then, my lord, farewell.   155

Mortimer Junior. The idle triumphs, masques, lascivious
    shows,

    And prodigal gifts bestowed on Gaveston

    Have drawn thy treasure dry and made thee weak;

    The murmuring commons overstretchèd hath.

Lancaster. Look for rebellion, look to be deposed.   160

    Thy garrisons are beaten out of France,

    And, lame and poor, lie groaning at the gates;

    The wild O'Neil, with swarms of Irish kerns,

    Lives uncontrolled within the English pale;

---

153. haunted] *Q;* taunted *Oxberry.*   158. treasure] *Q1–2;* treasurie *Q3–4.*
159. hath] *Q;* break *Dodsley*[1], *Neilson (conj.).*

---

153. *haunted*] pursued, followed importunately or obtrusively.

156. Based loosely on Holinshed, p. 318; see notes on 1.i.50, 54.

158. *treasure*] treasury.

159. The syntax is elliptical here; the meaning is: [this ruinous expense]
has overburdened the common people who complain [presumably because of
heavy taxation]. Briggs notes the striking similarity of this attack upon
Edward to that upon Gloucester in *2H6*, 1.iii.122–137; cf. especially Cardinal
Winchester's words, 'The commons hast thou rack'd' (l. 128). Cf. also
Woodstock: 'the murmuring Commons' rage' (1.iii.256).

161. The disasters summed up in Lancaster's speech are too unspecific
and unchronological to be based on any single passage or group of passages in
Holinshed. Charlton–Waller, however, cite one example from the chronicle
that may have been influential—a passage describing how in 1322 both the
Scots and the French took military advantage of King Edward's weakness
during his war with the barons (Holinshed, p. 332); see Appendix B, no. 16.

163–164. These lines are echoed in *The Contention*; see Introduction, p.
35. Marlowe's sources make no mention of O'Neil.

163. *Irish kerns*] Irish foot-soldiers lightly armed—usually with a sword
and shield, with a bow and sheaf of barbed arrows, or with darts. The word
occurs in Holinshed; in his Introduction to Holinshed's *Irish Historie* Stany-
hurst calls them 'a shower of hell, because they are taken for no better than
for rakehels, or the diuels black gard' (p. 45). Barnaby Riche in his *A New
Description of Ireland* (1610) says they are 'the very drosse and scum of the
Countrey . . . the verie *Hags of Hell*, fit for nothing but for the gallows' (p.
37).

164. *English pale*] the small area surrounding Dublin that was considered
relatively safe for English imigrants because it could be better controlled.

Unto the walls of York the Scots made road   165
And unresisted drave away rich spoils.
Mortimer Junior. The haughty Dane commands the narrow
    seas,
While in the harbour ride thy ships unrigged.
Lancaster. What foreign prince sends thee ambassadors?
Mortimer Junior. Who loves thee but a sort of flatterers?   170
Lancaster. Thy gentle queen, sole sister to Valois,
    Complains that thou hast left her all forlorn.
Mortimer Junior. Thy court is naked, being bereft of those
    That makes a king seem glorious to the world—
    I mean the peers whom thou shouldst dearly love;   175
    Libels are cast against thee in the street,
    Ballads and rhymes made of thy overthrow.
Lancaster. The northern borderers, seeing their houses burnt,
    Their wives and children slain, run up and down
    Cursing the name of thee and Gaveston.   180

---

165. made] *Q;* make *Dodsley*[1].   166. drave] *Q1–4;* draw *Dodsley*[1]; drive
Dyce[1].   172. forlorn] *Q* (forlorne), *Q3–4;* forlone *Q2 (misprint?).*
174. makes] *Q1–4;* make *Dodsley*[2].   176. against] *Q3–4;* again *Q1–2*
(againe).   176. street] *Q1–4;* streets *Gill*[1].   178. northern] *Dodsley*[2];
Northren *Q.*   178. borderers] *Q;* brothers *Dodsley*[1].   178. their] *Q2–4;*
the *Q.*

---

165. *walls of York*] Holinshed mentions no specific raid on York although
the city figures prominently in his account of Anglo-Scottish events; Stowe,
however, records that in 1318 'The Kyng being at *Yorke*, the Scottes entered
Englande, came to *Yorke*, and brent the Suburbs of the Citie . . . (p. 340).

    made road] i.e., made raid; 'road' (often used in Elizabethan English in the
sense of 'raid') was originally a variant of the Scottish or northern word
'raid.'

    166. *drave*] i.e., took.

    167. Cf. *3H6*: 'Stern Falconbridge commands the narrow seas' (I.i.239);
see Introduction, pp. 24, 30. The notion of Denmark's controlling the English
Channel ('the narrow seas') in Edward II's reign is totally unhistorical.

    170. *sort*] group, company.

    171. *Valois*] Isabella, whose three brothers were successively kings of
France, was actually of the house of Capet rather than a Valois; but Philip of
Valois, her cousin, succeeded her third brother (Charles IV) on the throne.

    176. *Libels*] defamatory leaflets, 'broadsides.'

    178. *their*] Bowers justifies the acceptance of Q2 here on grounds that the
tightly set line of Q made the shorter (but less satisfactory) word 'the'
necessary as a space-saving device.

    180. Unhistorically, Marlowe makes Gaveston bear blame for sufferings in
the north caused chiefly by the Anglo-Scottish war.

Mortimer Junior. When wert thou in the field with banner
    spread?
    But once! And then thy soldiers marched like players,
    With garish robes, not armour, and thyself,
    Bedaubed with gold, rode laughing at the rest,
    Nodding and shaking of thy spangled crest,   185
    Where women's favours hung like labels down.
Lancaster. And thereof came it that the fleering Scots,
    To England's high disgrace, have made this jig:
    'Maids of England, sore may you mourn,
    For your lemans you have lost at Bannocks bourne.   190
       With a heave and a ho.
    What weeneth the King of England,
    So soon to have won Scotland?
       With a rombelow.'

181. banner] *Q1–3;* banners *Q4.*   181–182. spread? / But once!] *Q*
(spred? / But once,); spread, / But once? *Dyce¹.*   187. thereof] *Q1–2;*
therefore *Q3–4.*

---

182. *But once*] Mortimer's charge that Edward had fought only once
before in Scotland is historically false; see Introduction, p. 46.

182–184. *marched . . . gold*] An elaboration of Holinshed's account of the
Bannockburn campaign (p. 322); see Appendix B, no. 15.

185. *crest*] helmet, armoured headpiece.

186. *women's favours*] Ladies customarily presented gloves, handkerchiefs,
or scarves to their lovers, who would sometimes wear them in battle.

labels] strips of parchment for appending official seals to documents; cf.
Rom., IV.i.57.

187. *fleering*] jeering and grinning contemptuously; cf. *Rom.,* I.v.58.

188. *jig*] mocking song, scurrilous rhyme; cf. *1 Tamburlaine:* 'jigging veins
of rhyming mother-wits' (I.i.1). *Edward III* alludes to such Scottish songs:
'their vild vnseuill skipping giggs, / Bray foorth their Conquest, and our
ouerthrow, / Euen in the barraine, bleake and fruitlesse aire' (I.ii; ll. 181–
183).

189. *Maids of England*] The jig comes from Fabyan's *Chronicle*, which
notes: 'This songe was after manie daies songe, in daunces, in the Carols of
the Maydens, and Mynstrelles of Scotlande, to the reprofe and disdayne
of Englyshe men, wyth dyuers other, whiche I ouer passe' (p. 169); see
Appendix B, no. 49. See also Introduction, pp. 46, 62.

190. *lemans*] sweethearts.

Bannocks bourne] i.e., the disastrous battle of Bannockburn, fought in
1314 after Gaveston's death in the marshy terrain or bog (bourne = rivulet,
spring) near the Bannock, a stream in Stirlingshire.

192. *weeneth*] hopes.

194. *rombelow*] a meaningless refrain, like 'With a heave and a ho,' that
originally was part of a song for rowers.

Mortimer Junior. Wigmore shall fly, to set my uncle free.   195
Lancaster. And when 'tis gone, our swords shall purchase
    more.
        If ye be moved, revenge it as you can;
        Look next to see us with our ensigns spread.
                        Exeunt Nobles [LANCASTER *and* MORTIMER JUNIOR].
Edward. My swelling heart for very anger breaks!
        How oft have I been baited by these peers   200
        And dare not be revenged, for their power is great?
        Yet, shall the crowing of these cockerels
        Affright a lion? Edward, unfold thy paws
        And let their lives' blood slake thy fury's hunger.
        If I be cruel and grow tyrannous,   205
        Now let them thank themselves and rue too late.
Kent. My lord, I see your love to Gaveston
        Will be the ruin of the realm and you,
        For now the wrathful nobles threaten wars;
        And therefore, brother, banish him for ever.   210
Edward. Art thou an enemy to my Gaveston?
Kent. Ay, and it grieves me that I favoured him.
Edward. Traitor, be gone; whine thou with Mortimer.

---

197. ye] *Q1–3;* you *Q4.*   197. as] *Q1–3;* if *Q4.*   198.1. Nobles] *Q3–4;*
Nobiles Q1–2.   198.1. *Exeunt* . . . MORTIMER JUNIOR] *Dyce*¹ *(subst.) (Exit
with Y. Mortimer); not in Q.*   199. for] *Q1–3;* with *Q4.*   204. lives']
Q1–4 (liues); life's *Pendry–Maxwell.*

---

195. *Wigmore shall fly*] i.e., Mortimer Junior's estate in Herefordshire shall
be quickly sold. See note on I.iv.358.

196. *purchase*] i.e., win.

197. *moved*] cf. l. 100 above.

198. *ensigns*] banners, battle flags.

202–203. *cockerels . . . lion*] M. P. Tilley and James K. Ray point out
that the lion's fear of the cock goes back to Pliny, *Natural History* (trans.
Holland), VIII, 16 and X, 21; and Plutarch, *Morals* (ed. W. W. Goodwin),
II, 96; see 'Proverbs and Proverbial Allusions in Marlowe,' *M.L.N.*, 50
(1935), 352–354. Cf. Chapman, *Bussy D'Ambois*: 'Why here's the Lion,
scared with the throat of a dunghill cock' (I.ii.149–150).

203. *unfold thy paws*] See note on V.i.11–12. Briggs cites *1 Tamburlaine*:
'princely lions when they rouse themselves, / Stretching their paws and
threat'ning herds of beasts' (I.ii.52–53). See also Introduction, p. 37.

207–208. *Gaveston . . . realm*] Marlowe (without historical warrant) prepares the ground early for Kent's later defection to the rebels; see note on
II.iii.1 and Introduction, p. 48. Edward's rejection of his brother in the
following exchange is also the dramatist's invention.

Kent. So will I, rather than with Gaveston.

Edward. Out of my sight and trouble me no more.   215

Kent. No marvel though thou scorn thy noble peers,
    When I thy brother am rejected thus.

Edward. Away!

                               Exit [KENT].

Poor Gaveston, that hast no friend but me—
Do what they can, we'll live in Tynemouth here.   220
And, so I walk with him about the walls,
What care I though the earls begirt us round?
Here comes she that's cause of all these jars.

Enter [ISABELLA] *the* Queen, *three* Ladies [MARGARET DE CLARE *and*
Ladies in Waiting], BALDOCK, *and* SPENCER [JUNIOR, *and* GAVESTON].

Isabella. My lord, 'tis thought the earls are up in arms.

Edward. Ay, and 'tis likewise thought you favour 'hem.   225

Isabella. Thus do you still suspect me without cause.

Lady Margaret. Sweet uncle, speak more kindly to the queen.

Gaveston. [*Aside to* EDWARD] My lord, dissemble with her,
    speak her fair.

Edward. Pardon me, sweet, I forgot myself.

Isabella. Your pardon is quickly got of Isabel.   230

---

216. though] *Q;* that *Dodsley*[1].   218–219. Away! . . . me] *Dyce*[1]; *one line in
Q.*   218.1. *Exit* KENT] *Dyce*[1]; *Exit Q (after line 217).*   219. that] *Q;* thou
Keltie.   219. me—] *Q (subst.)* (me,); me. *Kirschbaum.*   223.1. *three*
Ladies] *Dodsley*[2]; *Ladies 3 Q; the Lady Broughton.*   223.1–2. *Enter . . .*
SPENCER.] *Q; (no heading; continuation of II.ii) Broughton, Robinson;* Scene iii
[*new heading*]. *Enter . . . Spencer. Wagner.*   223.2. *and* GAVESTON] *Oxberry
(subst.); not in Q.*   225. 'hem] *Greg (conj.)* (hem); him *Q1–4, Charlton–
Waller;* them *Dodsley*[1]; 'em *Dyce*[1].   228. *Aside to* EDWARD] *Briggs (subst.);
not in Q.*   229. forgot] *Q;* had forgot *Robinson.*

---

223. *cause . . . jars*] Cf. *1 Troublesome Reign* (ii; l. 516).

225. *'hem*] i.e., them. Although Charlton–Waller and Gill defend Q's
'him' (as referring to Mortimer; cf. the queen's response at l. 226 and
I.iv.147), many editors accept Greg's conjectural emendation as more natural.
Edward's jealousy might indeed seem to justify the retention of 'him,' but
a direct reference to Mortimer, who is not mentioned anywhere in the
immediate context, would probably be awkward for an actor to make clear to
the audience.

228. *dissemble with her*] Gaveston's advice to his lover here interestingly
balances Mortimer's similar counsel to Isabella later in the action (V.ii.73).

Edward. The younger Mortimer is grown so brave
     That to my face he threatens civil wars.
Gaveston. Why do you not commit him to the Tower?
Edward. I dare not, for the people love him well.
Gaveston. Why then we'll have him privily made away.   235
Edward. Would Lancaster and he had both caroused
     A bowl of poison to each other's health.
     But let them go, and tell me what are these.
                    [*Indicates* BALDOCK *and* SPENCER JUNIOR.]
Lady Margaret. Two of my father's servants whilst he lived.
     May't please your grace to entertain them now.   240
Edward. [*To* BALDOCK] Tell me, where wast thou born? What
     is thine arms?
Baldock. My name is Baldock, and my gentry
     I fetched from Oxford, not from heraldry.
Edward. The fitter art thou, Baldock, for my turn.
     Wait on me, and I'll see thou shalt not want.   245

238.1. *Indicates . . .* SPENCER JUNIOR.] *This ed.; Baldock and Younger Spencer bow deeply. Kirschbaum; not in Q.*   241. *To* BALDOCK] *This ed.; not in Q.*
241. Tell . . . arms?] *Dyce*[1] *(one line);* Tell . . . borne? / What . . . armes? *Q.*
243. fetched] *Q* (fetcht); fetch *Q2–4.*

---

231. *brave*] defiant, presumptuous (cf. I.i.110).
232. *threatens civil wars*] cf. *1 Tamburlaine*: 'threaten civil war' (I.i.148).
234. Cf. *Woodstock*: 'I dare not, Greene, for . . . he's so well beloved' (IV.i.80–82); Shakespeare's Claudius also uses the same excuse for not disposing of Hamlet more directly (*Ham.*, IV.vii.16–24).
235. *privily made away*] secretly killed (a favourite idiom in Marlowe; cf. II.v.68, III.ii.45, IV.ii.52, V.v.21); cf. also *Jew of Malta*: 'I must make this villain away' (IV.iii.30). Ironically, Gaveston's suggestion balances Mortimer's earlier plan (apparently originating with the queen) to recall Gaveston from exile so that he can be murdered (I.iv.265–270); see Deats's discussion of this parallel ('Study in Androgyny,' p. 36).
238. *let them go*] i.e., enough talk of them.
239. *my father's servants*] See note on II.i.2.
240. *entertain*] See note on I.i.45.
241. *arms*] i.e., coat of arms.
243. *Oxford*] Robert Baldock did indeed hold a doctorate from Oxford but became more noted for his political role as an ally of the Spencers (he was appointed Chancellor in 1322) than for scholarship or erudition. Charlton–Waller suggest that Marlowe may have associated him with a more learned man (Rafe Baldocke, Bishop of London) who wrote a work on the history of England and whom Holinshed lists as a distinguished scholar at the end of his account of Edward II's reign (p. 342). A university education did in fact entitle a man to the status of 'gentry' (l. 242) and to be addressed as Esquire.

Baldock. I humbly thank your majesty.

Edward. Knowest thou him, Gaveston? [*Points to* SPENCER JUNIOR.]

Gaveston.   Ay, my lord.

　　His name is Spencer; he is well allied.

　　For my sake let him wait upon your grace.

　　Scarce shall you find a man of more desert.   250

Edward. Then, Spencer, wait upon me; for his sake

　　I'll grace thee with a higher style ere long.

Spencer Junior. No greater titles happen unto me

　　Than to be favoured of your majesty.

Edward. [*To* LADY MARGARET] Cousin, this day shall be your

　　　　marriage feast;   255

　　And Gaveston, think that I love thee well

　　To wed thee to our niece, the only heir

　　Unto the Earl of Gloucester late deceased.

Gaveston. I know, my lord, many will stomach me,

　　But I respect neither their love nor hate.   260

Edward. The headstrong barons shall not limit me;

　　He that I list to favour shall be great.

　　Come, let's away; and when the marriage ends,

　　Have at the rebels and their complices.

　　　　　　　　　　　　　　　　　　　　　　　　Exeunt.

247–248. Knowest . . . allied.] *Dyce*[1] *(subst.);* Knowest . . . Gaueston? / I . . .
alied, *Q.* 247. *Points to* SPENCER JUNIOR] *Oliphant (subst.); not in Q.*
251. me; for his sake] *Q1–2* (me, for his sake); me for his sake, *Q3–4;* me,
for his sake *Broughton* (sake;), *Oxberry.* 255. *To* LADY MARGARET] *This ed.;*
not in Q. 264.1. *Exeunt.*] *Broughton; Exeunt omnes. Q.*

---

248. *well allied*] of good family.

252. *higher style*] i.e., title of nobility.

255. *Cousin*] niece. Edward's sister, Joan of Acre, had married the eighth
Earl of Gloucester.

257. *only heir*] Historically, Margaret de Clare was co-heir to the Gloucester
estates with her two sisters (one of whom was to marry the younger Spencer)
—but only after the death of her brother, the ninth Earl of Gloucester, at
Bannockburn. See Introduction, p. 51.

259. *stomach*] See note on I.ii.26.

260. *respect*] care for, pay attention to.

262. *list*] choose; cf. v.iv.66.

263. *marriage ends*] See note on II.i.20.

264. *complices*] confederates, allies.

[SCENE iii]

Enter LANCASTER, MORTIMER [JUNIOR], WARWICK, PEMBROKE,
KENT [*and others*].

Kent. My lords, of love to this our native land
 I come to join with you and leave the king,
 And in your quarrel and the realm's behoof
 Will be the first that shall adventure life.
Lancaster. I fear me you are sent of policy   5
 To undermine us with a show of love.
Warwick. He is your brother; therefore have we cause
 To cast the worst and doubt of your revolt.
Kent. Mine honour shall be hostage of my truth;
 If that will not suffice, farewell my lords.   10
Mortimer Junior. Stay, Edmund; never was Plantagenet
 False of his word, and therefore trust we thee.
      [LANCASTER *and* KENT *converse apart.*]
Pembroke. But what's the reason you should leave him now?
Kent. I have informed the Earl of Lancaster.
Lancaster. And it sufficeth. Now, my lords, know this, 15

Heading. Scene iii] *Robinson;* Act III, Scene i *Broughton;* Scene iv *Wagner; not
in Q.* 0.2. *and others*] *Dyce*[1]; *and forces Broughton; not in Q.* 9. shall be]
Q1–3 (shalbe); should be *Q4.* 12.1. LANCASTER . . . *apart*] *Oliphant; not in
Q.*

---

 1. *My lords*] Neither the motive nor the timing of Kent's defection has any
basis in Marlowe's sources; see Introduction, p. 48.
 3. *realm's behoof*] cf. I.iv.243.
 4. *adventure life*] i.e., risk my life.
 5. *policy*] craft, political deception; cf. II.v.94. The word in this pejorative
Machiavellian sense was a favourite of Marlowe, appearing fourteen times in
The Jew of Malta.
 7. *brother*] Kent (Edmund of Woodstock, 1301–30) was actually Edward
II's half brother, being the son of Edward I and his second wife, Margaret of
France.
 8. *cast*] forecast, anticipate.
 doubt of] suspect. Briggs notes that Warwick's distrust of Kent because he
sides politically with his brother's enemies recalls a later Warwick's comment
about trusting Clarence, the disloyal brother of Edward IV, in *3H6*, IV.ii.7–
11.

> That Gaveston is secretly arrived,
> And here in Tynemouth frolics with the king.
> Let us with these our followers scale the walls
> And suddenly surprise them unawares.
> *Mortimer Junior.* I'll give the onset.
> *Warwick.*　　　　　　　　　　And I'll follow thee.　　　　　20
> *Mortimer Junior.* This tattered ensign of my ancestors,
> Which swept the desert shore of that dead sea
> Whereof we got the name of Mortimer,
> Will I advance upon these castle walls;
> Drums strike alarum, raise them from their sport,　　25
> And ring aloud the knell of Gaveston.
> *Lancaster.* None be so hardy as to touch the king,
> But neither spare you Gaveston nor his friends.

> > > > > > > > > > > *Exeunt.*

---

17. Tynemouth] *Q* (*Tinmoth*); Teignmouth *Broughton*. 21. tattered] *Dodsley*[1]; tottered *Q*. 24. these] *Brooke* (thes), *Greg* (*conj.*); this *Q1–4*. 24. castle] *Q* (castell); castle's *Dodsley*[1]. 25. raise] *Q*; rouse *Collier MS.* (*conj.*). 27. to touch] *Q, Q4;* touch *Q2–3.*

---

16. Gaveston's return from Ireland (as is evident in II.ii) was certainly not secret, for the nobles had agreed to it (I.iv.292–295). Marlowe seems to be thinking here of Gaveston's later and more surreptitous return from Flanders, which, according to Holinshed (pp. 320–321), was brought about by the king alone ('he eftsoones reuoked him home') without consulting the peers. Edward and Gaveston were briefly together at Tynemouth after the second recall. The inconsistency here results from the conflation of the two exiles; see Appendix B, no. 13, and Introduction, p. 51. See also note on II.ii.1.

17. *frolics*] cf. I.ii.67.

18. *scale the walls*] In Holinshed (p. 321) the nobles besiege the castle at Scarborough, not Tynemouth. Again Marlowe is compressing events.

21. *tattered*] Dodsley merely modernizes; Q's 'tottered' is a variant spelling of 'tattered.' Cf. *Jew of Malta*: 'a shaggy tottered staring slave' (IV.iii.6).

23. *the name of Mortimer*] Marlowe gives a popular but mistaken etymology of the name (the same derivation appears in Drayton's *Mortimeriados* [ll. 2708–2709; *Works*, I, 386] and in his *Heroical Epistles* ['Mortimer to Queen Isabel,' ll. 83–84]; *Works*, II, 170); see note on I.i.89. The family was not connected with crusading in the vicinity of the Dead Sea (*Mortuum Mare* in Latin) but was named after its place of origin—Mortemer, a village in Normandy. The Latin for the Norman settlement as written in documents (*de Mortuo Mari*) probably gave rise to the error.

[SCENE iv]

[*Alarums.*] *Enter*, [*at opposite doors*, EDWARD] *the* King *and*
SPENCER [JUNIOR].

Edward. O tell me, Spencer, where is Gaveston?
Spencer. I fear me he is slain, my gracious lord.
Edward. No, here he comes! Now let them spoil and kill.

[*Enter*] *to them* GAVESTON [*and others*: QUEEN ISABELLA,
LADY MARGARET DE CLARE, Lords].

Fly, fly, my lords; the earls have got the hold.
Take shipping and away to Scarborough;   5
Spencer and I will post away by land.
Gaveston. O stay, my lord; they will not injure you.
Edward. I will not trust them, Gaveston. Away!
Gaveston. Farewell, my lord.
Edward. [*To* LADY MARGARET] Lady, farewell.   10
Lady Margaret. Farewell, sweet uncle, till we meet again.
Edward. Farewell, sweet Gaveston, and farewell, niece.
Isabella. No farewell to poor Isabel, thy queen?
Edward. Yes, yes—for Mortimer your lover's sake.

Heading. Scene iv] *Robinson;* [Act III,] *Scene ii Broughton; Scene v Wagner;
not in Q.*   0.1. *Alarums*] *Broughton; not in Q.*   0.1–2. *Enter . . .* SPENCER
JUNIOR] *Dyce*[1] *(subst.) (Enter, severally, . . . Spencer); Enter the king and
Spencer, to them Gaueston, &c. Q.*   0.1. *at opposite doors*] *Bowers (subst.) (at
several doors); not in Q.*   3.1 *Enter . . .* GAVESTON] *Ribner; to them Gaueston
Q (before line 1); Enter Gaveston. Broughton (after line 2).*   3.1. *and others*]
Broughton (before line 1); &c. Q (before line 1).   3.1–2. QUEEN ISABELLA . . .
Lords] *Dyce*[1] *(subst.) (Enter . . . Isabella, King Edward, Niece . . . and Nobles);
not in Q.*   10. *To* LADY MARGARET] *This ed.; not in Q.*

---

4. *hold*] keep, fortress; cf. I.iv.289 and 2 *Tamburlaine:* 'And soldiers . . .
the hold is yours!' (III.iv.63).
5–6. Marlowe echoes Holinshed's wording: Edward, 'leauing the queene
behind him, tooke shipping' (p. 321). Again he telescopes the action: according to Holinshed, Edward and Gaveston fled together by sea to Scarborough,
where Gaveston was ultimately captured; their parting occurred at Scarborough from which place the king rode overland 'towards Warwike' (p.
321). He then learned of his friend's apprehension at the hands of the nobles.
Marlowe follows Holinshed, however, in having Edward's separation from
the queen occur at Tynemouth; see Appendix B, no. 17.
14. *for . . . sake*] See Introduction, pp. 53–54.

Isabella. Heavens can witness I love none but you.   15
                              Exeunt [all except ISABELLA].
From my embracements thus he breaks away;
O that mine arms could close this isle about,
That I might pull him to me where I would,
Or that these tears that drizzle from mine eyes
Had power to mollify his stony heart   20
That, when I had him, we might never part.

Enter the Barons [LANCASTER, WARWICK, MORTIMER JUNIOR].
Alarums [within].

Lancaster. I wonder how he scaped.
Mortimer Junior.   Who's this? The queen!
Isabella. Ay, Mortimer, the miserable queen,
Whose pining heart her inward sighs have blasted,
And body with continual mourning wasted;   25
These hands are tired with haling of my lord
From Gaveston, from wicked Gaveston—
And all in vain, for when I speak him fair,
He turns away and smiles upon his minion.
Mortimer Junior. Cease to lament, and tell us where's the
        king.   30
Isabella. What would you with the king? Is't him you seek?

15.1. *Exeunt* . . . ISABELLA] *Dodsley*[2] *(subst., after line 14) (Exeunt omnes, praeter* Isabella), *Broughton (subst.),* Oxberry; *Exeunt omnes, manet Isabella Q.*   21.1–2. Barons. *Alarums] Dodsley*[1]; *Barons alarums Q; Barons alarums (= Barons' alarums) Briggs.*   21.1. Barons] *Q (Barons);* Nobles *Broughton.*   21.1. LANCASTER . . . MORTIMER JUNIOR] *Dyce*[1] *(subst.) (Lancaster . . . Mortimer, and others); not in Q.*   21.2. *within] Dyce*[1]*; not in Q.*

17–18. Briggs compares Dido's similar frustration at the departure of Aeneas: 'O that I had a charm to keep the winds / Within the closure of a golden ball, / Or that the Tyrrhene sea were in mine arms, / That he might suffer shipwreck on my breast . . .' (*Dido,* IV.iv.99–102).

21.1. Nearly all editors follow Dodsley, inserting a full stop or comma after 'Barons'; Briggs (somewhat unconvincingly) argues that 'Barons' is a plural possessive modifying 'alarums' with the meaning 'Barons' attacks.' But 'alarums' almost always signifies the trumpets and drums of battle on the Elizabethan stage.

22. *I . . . scaped*] Briggs cites Verity's notice of the parallel to the opening of *3H6*: 'I wonder how the King escap'd our hands' (I.i.1); see also II.v.1.

26. *haling*] dragging; cf. II.ii.91.

Lancaster. No, madam, but that cursèd Gaveston.
　　Far be it from the thought of Lancaster
　　To offer violence to his sovereign.
　　We would but rid the realm of Gaveston;　　　　　　35
　　Tell us where he remains, and he shall die.
Isabella. He's gone by water unto Scarborough:
　　Pursue him quickly and he cannot scape;
　　The king hath left him, and his train is small.
Warwick. Forslow no time; sweet Lancaster, let's march.　　40
Mortimer Junior. How comes it that the king and he is parted?
Isabel. That this your army, going several ways,
　　Might be of lesser force, and with the power
　　That he intendeth presently to raise
　　Be easily suppressed; and therefore be gone.　　　　45
Mortimer Junior. Here in the river rides a Flemish hoy;
　　Let's all aboard and follow him amain.
Lancaster. The wind that bears him hence will fill our sails.
　　Come, come aboard; 'tis but an hour's sailing.
Mortimer Junior. Madam, stay you within this castle here.　　50
Isabella. No, Mortimer, I'll to my lord the king.
Mortimer Junior. Nay, rather sail with us to Scarborough.
Isabella. You know the king is so suspicious,
　　As if he hear I have but talked with you,
　　Mine honour will be called in question,　　　　　　55
　　And therefore, gentle Mortimer, be gone.

---

32. cursèd] *Q* (cursed); curs'd *Dodsley*[1].   41. is] *Q;* are *Dodsley*[1].
42. this] *Q;* thus *Dodsley*[1].   45. and therefore] *Q1–3;* therefore *Q4*.

---

38. *Pursue him quickly*] Isabella's revelation of Gaveston's place of refuge to his enemies, an action in keeping with her earlier strategy of having him recalled to be assassinated (I.iv.229, 264–270), is Marlowe's invention; see Introduction, pp. 54, 70.

40. *Forslow no time*] waste no time by delay; cf. *3H6*: 'Forslow no longer, make we hence amain' (II.iii.56).

46. *Flemish hoy*] small fishing vessel or sloop of a type used by the Flemings in the North Sea.

47. *amain*] with full force, speedily; cf. III.ii.96, v.ii.66.

52. *sail with us*] Marlowe invents this detail; Holinshed says nothing about Mortimer's attempt to persuade the queen to join him in pursuit of Gaveston.

Mortimer Junior. Madam, I cannot stay to answer you,
 But think of Mortimer as he deserves.
                    [*Exeunt* LANCASTER, WARWICK, *and* MORTIMER JUNIOR.]
Isabella. So well hast thou deserved, sweet Mortimer,
 As Isabel could live with thee for ever.   60
 In vain I look for love at Edward's hand,
 Whose eyes are fixed on none but Gaveston.
 Yet once more I'll importune him with prayers;
 If he be strange and not regard my words,
 My son and I will over into France,   65
 And to the king, my brother, there complain
 How Gaveston hath robbed me of his love.
 But yet I hope my sorrows will have end
 And Gaveston this blessèd day be slain.   [*Exit.*]

[SCENE v]

Enter GAVESTON, *pursued.*

Gaveston. Yet, lusty lords, I have escaped your hands,
 Your threats, your 'larums, and your hot pursuits,
 And though divorcèd from King Edward's eyes,
 Yet liveth Pierce of Gaveston unsurprised,

58.1. *Exeunt* . . . MORTIMER JUNIOR] *Robinson (subst.) (Exeunt Barons); not in*
Q.   63. prayers] Q (praiers); *prayer Q2–4.*   69. *Exit] Robinson; Exeunt*
Q.   *Heading. Scene* v] *Robinson (misprinted* 'Scene iv'); [Act III,] *Scene* iii
Broughton; Scene vi *Wagner; not in* Q.   2. 'larums] Q (larums); alarms
Dodsley[1].   4. Pierce] Q; Piers *Broughton.*

59–60. Marlowe obviously prepares the ground here for Isabella's adultery;
see Introduction, p. 54.
   64. *strange*] stand-offish, unresponsive.
   65. See Introduction, pp. 48, 64.
   66. *my brother*] i.e., Charles IV. Historically, Isabella's visit to Paris had
nothing to do with Gaveston, nor was it motivated by sexual jealousy; see
Introduction. pp. 48–49, 54.
   II.v.0.1. For Holinshed's account of the following episode, see Appendix
B, no. 18.
   1. *escaped your hands*] See note on II.iv.22.
   4. *Gaveston*] here pronounced as a disyllable ('Gav-ston').

Breathing, in hope (*malgrado* all your beards   5
That muster rebels thus against your king)
To see his royal sovereign once again.

Enter the Nobles [LANCASTER, WARWICK, PEMBROKE, MORTIMER
JUNIOR, Soldiers, JAMES, Horse-Boy, *and* Servants *of* PEMBROKE].

Warwick. Upon him soldiers! Take away his weapons.
Mortimer Junior. Thou proud disturber of thy country's
          peace,
     Corrupter of thy king, cause of these broils,   10
     Base flatterer, yield! And were it not for shame,
     Shame and dishonour to a soldier's name,
     Upon my weapon's point here shouldst thou fall,
     And welter in thy gore.
Lancaster.   Monster of men,
     That, like the Greekish strumpet, trained to arms   15
     And bloody wars so many valiant knights,

5. your] *Q, Q3–4;* you *Q2 (misprint?).*   6. king] *Q;* kind *Dodsley³.*   7.
see] *Q, Q3–4;* these *Q2 (misprint?).*   7.2. Soldiers . . . PEMBROKE] *Dyce¹*
(subst.) (Soldiers, James and other Attendants of Pembroke); with forces Brough-
ton; not in Q.   14. And . . . men,] *Tancock (one line);* And . . . goare /
Monster . . . men *Q.*   14–16. Monster . . . knights,] *Dyce¹;* Monster . . .
strumpet / Traind . . . warres, / So . . . knights, *Q.*   15. trained] *Q* (traind);
Traineth *Scott;* Trainest *Broughton.*   15–16. to arms / And bloody wars] *Q*
(to armes and bloudie warres); to arms *Broughton.*

5. malgrado] in spite of (cf. Fr. *maugré*); a fairly common expression, but
here possibly another means of emphasizing Gaveston's taste for Italian
fashions and attitudes. Gill suggests that Marlowe chose the Italian form for
metrical reasons.
     your beards] Gaveston seems to be scorning the long beards of the English
peers in contrast to his own fashionably cropped or clean-shaven face; long
beards were out of style by Marlowe's time.
     9. Cf. *1 Troublesome Reign*: 'Proud, and disturber of thy Countreyes
peace' (vii; l. 1059); also Peele, *Edward I*: 'the proude disturber of our state'
(v; l. 831); also *Massacre at Paris*: 'the proud disturbers of the faith' (xvi.3).
     10. *Corrupter*] See note on I.ii.5.
     broils] quarrels.
     15. *Greekish strumpet*] Helen of Troy. Deats points out that Lancaster's
association of Gaveston with the notorious cause of the Trojan war implies
also a parallel between Edward II and Paris, 'the passion-driven sybarite
whose fatal amour led to the desolation of his country'; see 'Myth and
Metamorphosis,' p. 308. Cf. also *Doctor Faustus*: 'Was this the face that
launch'd a thousand ships / And burnt the topless towers of Ilium?' (xviii.99–

    Look for no other fortune, wretch, than death;
    King Edward is not here to buckler thee.
Warwick. Lancaster, why talkst thou to the slave?
    Go, soldiers, take him hence; for, by my sword,   20
    His head shall off. Gaveston, short warning
    Shall serve thy turn; it is our country's cause
    That here severely we will execute
    Upon thy person: hang him at a bough!
Gaveston. My lord—
Warwick.   Soldiers, have him away.   25
    But for thou wert the favourite of a king,
    Thou shalt have so much honour at our hands.
                        [Gestures to indicate beheading.]
Gaveston. I thank you all, my lords; then I perceive
    That heading is one, and hanging is the other,
    And death is all.   30

               Enter Earl *of* ARUNDEL.

Lancaster. How now, my lord of Arundel?
Arundel. My lords, King Edward greets you all by me.

---

18. King] *Q2–4;* Kind *Q.*   20–22. Go . . . cause] *Dyce¹;* Go . . . hence, /
For . . . off: / *Gaueston* . . . turne: / It . . . cause *Q.*   23. severely] *Dodsley¹;*
seuerelie *Q.*   24. at] *Q;* upon *Dodsley¹;* on *Broughton.*   25. lord] *Q;* lords
Dodsley¹.   27.1. Gestures . . . beheading] *Kirschbaum (subst.) (Warwick uses
hands to imitate head-chopping); not in Q.*

---

100); see Introduction, pp. 39–40. But Lancaster's conception of Helen is
closer to the unglamorous portrait in Shakespeare's *Tro.* ('For every false
drop in her bawdy veins / A Grecian's life hath sunk' [IV.i.71–72]) than to
that in *Doctor Faustus.*

   trained] enticed (through guile), ensnared.

   18. *King Edward*] Charlton–Waller defend Q's 'kind' as a sarcastic epithet
for Edward; most editors, however, accept the 'correction' of Q2 as more
natural. Bowers observes that Marlowe 'had no tendency to employ' *kind* in
such contexts.

   buckler cf. I.iv.288.

   26–27. i.e., because he has been elevated to noble rank, Gaveston will be
granted the privilege of death by beheading—the execution of a gentleman.
Common felons were hanged.

   29–30. *That . . . all*] Gaveston comments bitterly on the technical distinction between the two forms of execution since both mean death.

Warwick. Arundel, say your message.

Arundel.   His majesty,
    Hearing that you had taken Gaveston,
    Entreateth you by me, yet but he may   35
    See him before he dies; for why, he says,
    And sends you word, he knows that die he shall;
    And if you gratify his grace so far,
    He will be mindful of the courtesy.

Warwick. How now?

Gaveston.   [*Aside*] Renownèd Edward, how thy name   40
    Revives poor Gaveston!

Warwick.   No, it needeth not,
    Arundel; we will gratify the king
    In other matters; he must pardon us in this.
    Soldiers, away with him.

Gaveston.   [*Sarcastically*] Why, my lord of Warwick,
    Will not these delays beget my hopes?   45
    I know it, lords, it is this life you aim at;
    Yet grant King Edward this.

Mortimer Junior.   Shalt thou appoint
    What we shall grant? Soldiers, away with him!
    [*To* ARUNDEL] Thus we'll gratify the king:

33–34. Arundel . . . Gaveston] *Bullen; Arundell . . . message. / His . . .*
maiesty *Q.*   34. that you] *Q;* you *Dyce²* (*conj.*), *Cunningham.*   35. yet
but] *Q;* but that *Dodsley¹.*   40. *Aside*] *This ed.; not in Q.*   40. Renownèd]
Q3–4 (Renowned); Renowmed *Q1–2;* Renown'd *Dodsley¹.*   44. Sarcas-
tically] *Kirschbaum; not in Q.*   44. Why, my lord] *Q* (Why my Lord);
Why? My lord *Fleay.*   45. Will . . . hopes?] *Q;* Will these delays beget me
any hopes? *Dodsley¹;* Will now these short delays beget my hopes? *Dyce¹;*
Will not that these delays beget my hopes. *Fleay (conj.).*   45. hopes?] *Q;*
hopes. *Oliphant.*   47–48. Yet . . . him!] *Dyce¹ (subst.);* Yet . . . this. / *Mor.
iu.* Shalt . . . graunt? / Souldiers . . . him: *Q.*   49. *To* ARUNDEL] *This ed.; not
in Q.*   49. Thus we'll] *Q* (Thus weele); Thus we will *Cunningham;* Thus far
we will *Fleay (conj.).*

---

35. *yet but*] that.

36. *for why*] because.

40–41. *Renownèd . . . Gaveston*] Note the genuine devotion to the king
implied by this private exclamation.

44–45. *Why . . . hopes?*] Although metrically rough, these lines require no
emendation. As Tancock notes, Gaveston speaks sarcastically to Warwick,
then addresses the others without irony in the lines that follow. As Merchant
observes, 'Gaveston's private form of irony greatly strengthens the character.'

We'll send his head by thee; let him bestow   50
His tears on that, for that is all he gets
Of Gaveston, or else his senseless trunk.

Lancaster. Not so, my lord, lest he bestow more cost
In burying him than he hath ever earned.

Arundel. My lords, it is his majesty's request,   55
And in the honour of a king he swears
He will but talk with him and send him back.

Warwick. When, can you tell? Arundel, no; we wot
He that the care of realm remits,
And drives his nobles to these exigents   60
For Gaveston, will, if he seize him once,
Violate any promise to possess him.

---

53. lord] *Q;* lords *Dodsley².*   56. in] *Q;* on *Dodsley¹.*   58–59. When . . .
remits] *Q;* When . . . no, / We . . . remits *Bowers.*   58. no; we wot] *Dodsley¹*
(*subst.*) (no; we wot,); no, we wot, *Q;* no, we wot. *Broughton.*   59. that]
Q1–2; that hath *Q3–4.*   59. realm] *Q* (realme); his realm *Dodsley¹; kingly*
realm *Fleay (conj.).*   59. realm remits] *Q* (realme remits); Realme-remits
Q3–4.   61. seize] *Q* (zease); seaze *Q2–4;* sees *Cunningham.*

50–51. *let . . . that*] The image of Edward weeping over the head of his
decapitated lover recalls Queen Margaret's similar grief over the head of
Suffolk in *2H6,* IV.iv.1–7; also see Introduction, pp. 33–34.

53–54. *lest . . . him*] Edward in fact gave Gaveston an elaborate funeral at
Langley two years after his death and with royal funds 'financed masses for
[his] soul all over England'; see Harold F. Hutchison, *Edward II* (New York,
1971), p. 90. Marlowe's known sources, however, make no mention of
Gaveston's burial arrangements.

57. *talk with him*] Bakeless (*Tragicall History,* II, 15) points out the echo of
Holinshed here: at his capture Gaveston set 'no other condition, but that he
might come to the kings presence to talke with him' (p. 321).

58. *wot*] See note on I.iv.377.

59. *remits*] abandons, gives up.

60. *exigents*] crises, emergencies.

61. *seize*] *Q's* 'zease' may reasonably be interpreted as a compositorial
misreading of 'sees.' Many editors, following Cunningham, prefer this solution, doubtless on the ground that the king (through Arundel) has specifically
asked to 'see' Gaveston at l. 36 above; cf. also l. 76 below. But there is no
need to emend. 'Seize,' if we imagine it to convey Edward's emotional
rapacity or sexual possessiveness, presents a more forceful and graphic image;
nor does the word necessarily weaken 'possess' in the following line if we
understand the latter in the sense of 'hold tenaciously' or 'keep.' 'Possess'
may even contain the secondary meaning of 'have sexual relations with'; cf.
Kyd, *Spanish Tragedy:* 'In secret I possess'd a worthy dame' (I.i.10).

Arundel. Then if you will not trust his grace in keep,
    My lords, I will be pledge for his return.
Mortimer Junior. It is honourable in thee to offer this,   65
    But for we know thou art a noble gentleman,
    We will not wrong thee so,
    To make away a true man for a thief.
Gaveston. How meanst thou, Mortimer? That is over-base!
Mortimer Junior. Away, base groom, robber of kings' renown.   70
    Question with thy companions and thy mates.
Pembroke. My lord Mortimer, and you my lords each one,
    To gratify the king's request therein,
    Touching the sending of this Gaveston,
    Because his majesty so earnestly   75
    Desires to see the man before his death,
    I will upon mine honour undertake
    To carry him and bring him back again,
    Provided this, that you, my lord of Arundel,
    Will join with me.
Warwick.   Pembroke, what wilt thou do?   80
    Cause yet more bloodshed? Is it not enough
    That we have taken him, but must we now
    Leave him on 'had I wist' and let him go?
Pembroke. My lords, I will not over-woo your honours,
    But if you dare trust Pembroke with the prisoner,   85
    Upon mine oath I will return him back.

---

63. grace in keep] *Q;* grace *Dodsley*[1].   67–68. We . . . thief.] *Q;* We . . .
away / A true . . . thief. *Oliphant.*   70. kings'] *Broughton;* kings *Q;* king's
Dodsley[1].   70. renown] *Q2–4* (renowne); renowme *Q.*   71. thy mates]
Q; mates *Q2–4.*   77. mine] *Q1–2;* my *Q3–4.*   81. Is it] *Q;* it is
Dodsley[1].

---

63. *in keep*] in custody. Briggs compares *Shr.*: 'For in Baptista's keep my
treasure is' (I.ii.116).

64. *be pledge*] i.e., stake my own life.

68. *make away*] See note on II.ii.235.

thief] Mortimer's epithet, perhaps, for Gaveston's profiteering as custodian
'of the kings iewels and treasure' (Holinshed, p. 320) as well as for his
robbing the king of his good name ('renown,' l. 70).

70. *groom*] Cf. I.iv.291.

71. *Question*] argue, wrangle.

83. *'had I wist'*] had I but known. A common exclamation of those who
repent too late and an allusion to the proverb 'Beware of Had I wist' (Tilley
H8–10).

Arundel. My lord of Lancaster, what say you in this?
Lancaster. Why I say, let him go on Pembroke's word.
Pembroke. And you, lord Mortimer?
Mortimer Junior. How say you, my lord of Warwick?   90
Warwick. Nay, do your pleasures; I know how 'twill prove.
Pembroke. Then give him me.
Gaveston.   Sweet sovereign, yet I come
    To see thee ere I die.
Warwick.   [*Aside*] Yet not perhaps,
    If Warwick's wit and policy prevail.
Mortimer Junior. My lord of Pembroke, we deliver him you;   95
    Return him on your honour. Sound away!
                    Exeunt [MORTIMER JUNIOR, LANCASTER, WARWICK].
            [PEMBROKE, ARUNDEL, GAVESTON, *and* PEMBROKE'S Men
        (*including* Horse-Boy), *four* Soldiers (*including* JAMES) *remain*].
Pembroke. [*To* ARUNDEL] My lord, you shall go with me;
    My house is not far hence—out of the way
    A little—but our men shall go along.
    We that have pretty wenches to our wives,   100
    Sir, must not come so near and balk their lips.

---

91. Nay . . . prove.] *Dyce*[1] (*one line*); Nay . . . pleasures, / I . . . prooue. *Q*.
93. *Aside*] *Broughton; not in Q.*   93. Yet not] *Q;* Not yet *Dodsley*[1].   96.
honour. Sound away!] *Q (subst.)* (honor, sound away.); honour, sound.—
Away. *Broughton.*   96.2–3. PEMBROKE . . . *remain*.] *Broughton (subst.);*
Manent Penbrooke, Mat. Gauest. & Penbrookes men, foure souldiers. Q.
96.2. ARUNDEL] *Broughton; Mat. Q1–4.*   96.3. *including* Horse-Boy] *This
ed.; not in Q.*   96.3. *including* JAMES] *Dyce*[1] *(subst.); not in Q.*   97. *To*
ARUNDEL] *This ed.; not in Q.*   97. My lord] *Q;* My Lord of Arundel *Dyce*[1]
(conj.), Cunningham; M' lord of Arundel *Fleay.*   101. and *Q;* to *Q2–4.*

---

92. *Sweet sovereign*] Cf. ll. 40–41 above and note.
94. *policy*] See note on II.iii.5. The theatrical Machiavellianism here attributed to Warwick has no true basis in Marlowe's sources.
96.2–3. For Q's confusion of Matrevis ('*Mat.*') with Arundel here and
later in the play, see Introduction, pp. 8–9.
97. Dyce's emendation to fill out the metre of the line is unnecessary; in
this play Marlowe sometimes introduces such irregularities for variety and to
achieve an effect of informal or mundane speech.
98. *My . . . hence*] As Bakeless (*Tragicall History*, II, 16) notices, another
verbal borrowing from Holinshed: Pembroke 'left [Gaveston] there in safe
keeping with his seruants, whilest he for one night went to visit his wife,
lieng not farre from thence' (p. 321).
100–101. As Charlton–Waller point out, this comment is an imaginative
development from Holinshed (see preceding note). Again Marlowe mingles
sexual and personal concerns with politics—and again with tragic consequences.

Arundel. 'Tis very kindly spoke, my lord of Pembroke;
    Your honour hath an adamant of power
    To draw a prince.
Pembroke.   So, my lord. Come hither, James.
    I do commit this Gaveston to thee;   105
    Be thou this night his keeper. In the morning
    We will discharge thee of thy charge; be gone.
Gaveston. Unhappy Gaveston, whither goest thou now?
    Exit [GAVESTON] *with* Servants *of* PEMBROKE [*including* JAMES].
Horse-Boy. [*To* ARUNDEL] My lord, we'll quickly be at
    Cobham.
                    Exeunt [PEMBROKE *and* ARUNDEL, *attended*].

---

102. *Arundel*] Broughton; *Mat. Q1–4.*   108. whither] *Dodsley*[1]*; whether
Q.*   108.1. *Exit* GAVESTON.] *Q (Exit.); Exit Pembroke. Fleay.*   108.1.
with Servants *of* PEMBROKE] *Robinson (subst.); cum seruis Pen. Q.*   108.1.
including JAMES] *Dyce*[1] *(subst.); not in Q.*   109. *Horse-Boy.*] *Q; Pembroke.
Gill*[1]*; 1st Servant. Broughton.*   109. *To* ARUNDEL] *This ed.; not in Q.*
109.1. *Exeunt . . . attended.*] *Bowers; Exeunt ambo. Q; Exeunt Arundel,
Pembroke, and First Servant. Broughton; Exeunt. Oxberry.*

---

103. *adamant*] magnet, loadstone.
108. *Unhappy*] unlucky, unfortunate.
108.1. Since Q's stage direction here is somewhat unclear, editors have
interpreted the grouped exits at the end of this scene in various ways (see
textual notes above). If the '*Exit*' following Gaveston's last speech applies to
Pembroke and his men (as Fleay believed), Gaveston is left onstage for a
moment with only the Horse-Boy as his guard. It seems more reasonable
to assume that '*Exit*' refers to Gaveston, who is then conducted offstage
by Pembroke's men including James (the previously designated keeper of
the prisoner). This then leaves Pembroke and Arundel to depart together
('*Exeunt ambo*') a moment later. Bowers's addition of '*attended*' takes care of
the left-over Horse-Boy, who has just reassured Arundel (Pembroke's guest)
that the distance yet to be traversed to Pembroke's house will be covered
quickly. But all the exits occur so rapidly that the precise grouping of the
actors and the order of their departure become relatively unimportant. In
performance on the characteristically deep Elizabethan stage the effect would
be very like a processional massed exit.
109. *Cobham*] a village near Gravesend in Kent far removed from the
region of Gaveston's capture, or, alternatively, an identically named village in
Surrey. Marlowe ignores geographical logic here. Gill thinks 'Cobham' may
be a mistake for 'Dedington' (Holinshed, p. 321), which 'fits the rhythm as
well as the facts.'

[SCENE vi]

Enter GAVESTON *mourning, and the* Earl *of* PEMBROKE'S Men
[*four* Soldiers *including* JAMES].

Gaveston. O treacherous Warwick, thus to wrong thy friend!
James. I see it is your life these arms pursue.
Gaveston. Weaponless must I fall and die in bands.
    O, must this day be period of my life,
    Centre of all my bliss? An ye be men,   5
    Speed to the king.

                        Enter WARWICK *and his company.*

Warwick.   My lord of Pembroke's men,
    Strive you no longer; I will have that Gaveston.

Heading. Scene vi] *Fleay, Bowers; (no heading; continuation of III.iii) Brough-*
ton; Act III, Scene i Robinson; not in Q.   0.1. *Enter* GAVESTON] Q; *not in*
Broughton; Alarum. Enter Warwick and his men pursuing Gaveston. Exeunt.
Enter Gaveston Kirschbaum.   0.2. *four* Soldiers *including* JAMES] *Bowers*
(subst.); not in Q.   2, 8. *James*] Q (*Iames; Iam.*); *Second Servant Broughton.*
5. *all my*] *Q1–2; my Q3–4.*   5. *An*] *Broughton* (an'); *And* Q.   6. *Enter*
. . . company.] Q; *Enter Warwick, with Soldiers. Broughton (before line 1).*

   II.vi. This brief scene takes place somewhere near Deddington, a village in
Oxfordshire; see note on II.v.109.
   2. *arms*] i.e., soldiers (a synecdoche).
   3. *bands*] bonds (i.e., dishonourably without being able to fight); cf. *3H6*:
'die in bands for this unmanly deed' (1.i.186).
   4–5. *O . . . bliss*] i.e., (as Tancock explains) must this day (centre of all
my bliss because I was appointed to see Edward today) ironically mark the
end of my life? Gaveston compares his anticipated reunion with the king
to the middle of the earth—the fixed centre of the universe according to
the Ptolemaic cosmology. McLaughlin interprets the meaning differently:
'Centre' signifies the middle of the earth but represents the lowest point to
which one may sink; according to this reading, Gaveston laments that in one
day he falls from the expected bliss of seeing the king to the lowest possible
hell of deprivation ('centre'). Gill, citing *Ham.* (II.ii.157–159) and *Tro.*
(IV.ii.104–106), notices that the idea of the centre in the present context
includes both depth and magnetism. Levin points out that Gaveston echoes
his earlier use of the word 'bliss' (1.i.4) to describe his relationship with
Edward and that Edward will later echo the present speech (IV.vii.61–62)
when he himself is captured (*Overreacher*, pp. 89–90). See also Introduction,
p. 75.
   5. *An*] if (often spelled 'and' as in Q).
   7. *Strive*] struggle (here physically); Pembroke's men obviously attempt to
prevent the kidnapping of Gaveston.

James. Your lordship doth dishonour to yourself
   And wrong our lord, your honourable friend.
Warwick. No, James, it is my country's cause I follow.   10
   [*To his* Men] Go, take the villain; soldiers, come away,
   We'll make quick work. [*To* JAMES] Commend me to your
       master
   My friend, and tell him that I watched it well.
   [*To* GAVESTON] Come, let thy shadow parley with King
       Edward.
Gaveston. Treacherous earl! Shall I not see the king?   15
Warwick. The King of Heaven perhaps, no other king.
   Away!

               Exeunt WARWICK *and his* Men, *with* GAVESTON.
                           [JAMES *remains with the others.*]
James. Come, fellows, it booted not for us to strive.
   We will in haste go certify our lord.

                                                        Exeunt.

---

9. wrong] *Q;* wrongs *Oliphant.*   11. *To his* Men] *This ed.; not in Q.*   12.
To JAMES] *This ed.; not in Q.*   12. master] *Q2, Q4;* maister *Q, Q3.*   14.
To GAVESTON] *This ed.; not in Q.*   15. I not] *Q;* not I *Q2–4.*   17.2. JAMES
. . . *with the others.*] *Merchant; Manet Iames cum caeteris. Q; Manent Iames cum
caeteris. Q2–4.*   18. *James.* Come] *Dodsley*[1]*;* Come *Q1–4; Second Servant.*
Come *Broughton.*   18. booted] *Q1–2;* booteth *Q3–4;* boots *Broughton.*
18. for us] *Q* (for vs); us *Broughton.*   19.1. *Exeunt*] *Q1–2; not in Q3–4.*

---

   13. *friend*] Warwick apparently speaks ironically, picking up James's
earlier reference to Pembroke as his 'honourable friend' (l. 9).
   watched it well] i.e., kept careful guard (over Gaveston). Again Warwick's
tone is ironic.
   14. *shadow*] ghost; cf. *R3:* 'A shadow like an angel, with bright hair /
Dabbled in blood' (I.iv.53–54).
   16. *King of Heaven*] cf. *R3,* I.ii.105; *R2,* III.iii.101. See also Introduction,
n. 58.
   18. *booted not*] was of no avail; cf. v.vi.90.
   19. *certify*] See note on I.II.38.

Act III

Enter KING EDWARD *and* SPENCER [JUNIOR, *and* BALDOCK],
with drums and fifes.

Edward. I long to hear an answer from the barons
    Touching my friend, my dearest Gaveston.
    Ah Spencer, not the riches of my realm
    Can ransom him; ah, he is marked to die.
    I know the malice of the younger Mortimer;   5
    Warwick, I know, is rough, and Lancaster
    Inexorable; and I shall never see
    My lovely Pierce, my Gaveston, again.
    The barons overbear me with their pride.
Spencer Junior. Were I King Edward, England's sovereign,   10
    Son to the lovely Eleanor of Spain,
    Great Edward Longshanks' issue, would I bear
    These braves, this rage, and suffer uncontrolled
    These barons thus to beard me in my land,

Heading. Act III, Scene i] *Fleay, Bowers;* [Act III,] *Scene iv Broughton; Scene
ii Robinson.*   0.1. *and Baldock*] *Dyce*[1] *(subst.) (Baldock, Noblemen of the
king's side, and Soldiers); not in Q.*   8. Pierce, my] *Q;* Pierce of *Q2–4;* Piers
of *Broughton.*   12. Edward] *Q, Q3–4;* Edvvards *Q2.*   12. Longshanks' *Q
(Longshankes);* Longshank's *Broughton.*

III.i. The action of this scene compresses events that occurred over a
period of thirteen years.

   11. *Eleanor of Spain*] i.e., Eleanor of Castile, Edward I's first queen.

   12. *Longshanks*] the nickname Edward I acquired among his contemporaries because of his long legs. It was picked up by chroniclers such as
Fabyan, who quotes a Scottish rhyme: 'What wenys kyng Edwarde, with his
longe shankes / To haue wonne Berwike . . . ' (p. 139); cf. Peele, *Edward I:*
'Longshankes your king' (i; l. 34). As Merchant notes, 'Edward I was the
type of the noble king of chivalry; his son and grandson in Marlowe's play
are related to his regal qualities, in contrast and comparison.'

   13. *braves*] insults, acts of bravado; cf. III.ii.41.

   14. *beard*] daringly affront (literally pluck by the beard, perhaps glancing
at the proverbial idea [Tilley H165] of bearding the lion, a traditional emblem of royalty); cf. Kyd, *Spanish Tragedy:* 'So hares may pull dead lions by

In mine own realm? My lord, pardon my speech.   15
Did you retain your father's magnanimity,
Did you regard the honour of your name,
You would not suffer thus your majesty
Be counterbuffed of your nobility.
Strike off their heads, and let them preach on poles;   20
No doubt such lessons they will teach the rest,
As by their preachments they will profit much
And learn obedience to their lawful king.
Edward. Yea, gentle Spencer, we have been too mild,
Too kind to them, but now have drawn our sword,   25
And if they send me not my Gaveston,
We'll steel it on their crest and poll their tops.
Baldock. This haught resolve becomes your majesty,
Not to be tied to their affection
As though your highness were a schoolboy still,   30
And must be awed and governed like a child.

---

20. preach] *Q;* perch *Dodsley*[1].   27. crest] *Q1–4;* crests *Broughton.*   27.
poll] *Dodsley*[1]*;* powle *Q1–4;* pole *Fleay.*

---

the beard' (I.ii.172); also *Jn:* 'Whose valor plucks dead lions by the beard'
(II.i.138). Erasmus, who drew upon classical sources, gave the saying cur-
rency in his *Adagia;* see Philip Edwards's note on the Kyd passage (*Spanish
Tragedy,* p. 15).

16. *magnanimity*] courage appropriate to noble rank. Tancock notes that
'The word is used rather of the haughty courage of a man superior to all
control, than in the modern sense of one who exercises a lofty spirit of
forgiveness.' Cf. *3H6:* 'Infuse his breast with magnanimity / And make him,
naked, foil a man at arms' (v.iv.41–42).

18. *suffer*] allow, permit.

19. *counterbuffed of*] beaten back by, opposed; Charlton–Waller cite
Nashe, *Have With You to Safron Walden:* 'to counterbuffe and beate backe all
those ouerthwart blowes' (*Works,* III, 28).

20. *preach on poles*] See note on I.i.117.

22. *preachments*] sermons (as here, often pejorative).

24. *too mild*] perhaps suggested by the phrase 'clemencie and patience' in
Holinshed (p. 328); see Introduction, p. 42, and v.i.122–123.

27. *steel it*] use steel, i.e., sharpen the sword.

poll their tops] decapitate them (a figure from lopping off the tops of trees to
make their foliage more dense, i.e., to make them pollards). But Edward
also puns on 'poles' in l. 20 above.

28. *haught*] lofty (from Fr. *haut*—an old form of 'haughty').

29. *their affection*] i.e., whatever they should desire (affect).

30–31. *schoolboy . . . child*] See Introduction, pp. 24, 37. Cf. also *Woodstock:* 'To awe ye like a child' (II.i.12).

Enter HUGH SPENCER [SENIOR,] *an old man, father to the young*
SPENCER [JUNIOR], *with his truncheon, and* Soldiers.

Spencer Senior. Long live my sovereign, the noble Edward,
    In peace triumphant, fortunate in wars.
Edward. Welcome old man; com'st thou in Edward's aid?
    Then tell thy prince, of whence and what thou art.   35
Spencer Senior. Lo, with a band of bowman and of pikes,
    Brown bills and targeteers, four hundred strong,
    Sworn to defend King Edward's royal right,
    I come in person to your majesty—
    Spencer, the father of Hugh Spencer there,   40
    Bound to your highness everlastingly
    For favours done in him unto us all.
Edward. Thy father, Spencer?
Spencer Junior.   True, an it like your grace,
    That pours in lieu of all your goodness shown
    His life, my lord, before your princely feet.   45
Edward. Welcome ten thousand times, old man, again;

32, 36. *Spencer Senior*] Dodsley[1]; *Spen. pa. Q1–4.*   34. com'st] *Q* (comst);
comest *Merchant.*   35. thy] *Q;* the *Q2–4.*   42. favours] *Q* (fauors);
fauour *Q2–4.*   43. *Spencer Junior*] Dodsley[1]; *Spen. filius Q.*   43. an it]
Dyce[1]; and it *Q;* an't *Broughton.*

32–33. F. N. Lees, the reviser of Charlton–Waller, compares Peele,
Descensus Astraeae (1591): 'Long may she live, long may she governe us, / In
peace triumphant, fortunate in warres' (ll. 38–39; *Minor Works,* I, 215).
Spencer Senior, as an old man, might be expected to speak prophetically like
Gaunt in *R2*; as Merchant observes, his characterization of Edward here
therefore produces 'a peculiar irony'.

    37. *Brown bills*] bronzed halberds (to prevent their rusting) as contrasted
with black (ordinary iron) halberds, i.e., long staves that combined the pike
with the battle-axe at their heads. Bills were essentially infantry weapons.

    targeteers] foot soldiers armed with targets (shields).

    40. *Spencer, the father*] This delayed introduction of Spencer Senior to the
king is Marlowe's invention; the elder Spencer, unlike his son, supported
Gaveston against the hostile barons as early as 1308, and Edward had known
both Spencers for some time. Holinshed implies the early knowledge of the
junior favourite (who later changed loyalties) when he notes that the king
'bare no good will' to the younger Spencer 'at the first' (p. 321). See
Introduction, p. 51.

    43. *an*] See note on II.vi.5.

    44. *in lieu of*] i.e., in recompense for.

[*To* SPENCER JUNIOR] Spencer, this love, this kindness to
   thy king,
Argues thy noble mind and disposition.
Spencer, I here create thee Earl of Wiltshire,
And daily will enrich thee with our favour   50
That, as the sunshine, shall reflect o'er thee.
Beside, the more to manifest our love,
Because we hear Lord Bruce doth sell his land,
And that the Mortimers are in hand withal,
Thou shalt have crowns of us t'outbid the barons;   55
And, Spencer, spare them not, but lay it on.
Soldiers, a largesse, and thrice welcome all.
Spencer Junior. My lord, here comes the queen.

    Enter [ISABELLA] *the* Queen *and* [PRINCE EDWARD] *her son,*
              and LEVUNE, *a Frenchman.*

Edward.   Madam, what news?

---

47. *To* SPENCER JUNIOR] *This ed.; not in Q.*   49. Wiltshire] *Dodsley*[1]*;*
Wilshire *Q.*   52. Beside] *Q;* Besides *Dodsley*[1].   55. t'outbid] *Q1–2;* to
outbid *Q3–4.*   56. but lay] *Q;* lay *Q2–4;* no, lay *Wagner.*   57. largesse]
Q (largis); large *Dodsley*[1].   58. comes] *Q, Q3–4;* come *Q2.*   58.2.
LEVUNE] *Q2 (Levune), Dodsley*[1]*;* Lewne *Q, Q3–4; Lejeune Broughton.*

---

49. i.e., Spencer Junior. But historically this earldom was never conferred
on any member of the medieval family. In 1322, according to Holinshed (p.
332), Spencer Senior was created Earl of Winchester (cf. III.ii.61); Tancock
speculates that since in Marlowe's time the eldest son of the Marquess of
Winchester bore the style Earl of Wiltshire (as is still the case), the dramatist
intentionally antedated the connection between the two titles.

53. *Lord . . . land*] This incident (1321) is based on Holinshed (p. 325); see
Appendix B, no. 22. The improvident nobleman, whom Holinshed calls 'lord
William de Bruce' and whose land became part of Spencer Junior's burgeon-
ing estates in Wales, was historically called William de Braose.

54. *in hand*] i.e., in process. Marlowe apparently echoes the phrase from
the same chronicle passage referred to in the previous note: '[Spencer Junior]
went awaie with the purchase, to the great displeasure of the other lords that
had beene in hand to buie it' (Holinshed, p. 325).

58.1. PRINCE EDWARD] The prince appears here for the first time
and, as usual, in the company of the queen; see Introduction, p. 71. As
Briggs points out, Holinshed (except for an early mention of the boy's birth)
gives the prince no attention until his mother, with whose politics on the
continent he is closely associated, enters the narrative.

58.2. LEVUNE] A character invented by Marlowe; see Introduction, p. 48.
Gill notes that the spelling in Q ('*Lewne*') is not a compositor's error but
rather the result of a shortage in the type font.

Isabella. News of dishonour, lord, and discontent:
    Our friend Levune, faithful and full of trust,   60
    Informeth us by letters and by words
    That Lord Valois our brother, King of France,
    Because your highness hath been slack in homage,
    Hath seizèd Normandy into his hands;
    These be the letters, this the messenger.   65
Edward. Welcome Levune; [*to* ISABELLA] tush Sib, if this be
    all,   .
    Valois and I will soon be friends again.
    But to my Gaveston—shall I never see,
    Never behold thee now? Madam, in this matter
    We will employ you and your little son;   70
    You shall go parley with the King of France.
    Boy, see you bear you bravely to the king
    And do your message with a majesty.
Prince Edward. Commit not to my youth things of more
    weight
    Than fits a prince so young as I to bear.   75

60, 66. Levune] *Dodsley*[1]; *Lewne Q, Q4; Levvne Q2-3; Lejeune Broughton.*
62. Lord Valois] *Q (Valoyes);* Valois *Dodsley*[1].   66. *to* ISABELLA] *This ed.;*
not in Q.   69. now] *Q;* more *Dodsley*[1], *Collier MS.*   75. Than] *Q* (Then);
That *Cunningham.*

---

62. *Lord Valois*] i.e., Charles IV; see note on II.ii.171.
64. *seizèd Normandy*] It was not Normandy but certain towns in Aquitaine
that were in question. Holinshed reports that 'the French king made processe
against the king of England, and seized into his hands diuerse townes and
castels in Aquitaine, alledging that he did it for the contumacie shewed by
the king of England, in refusing to come to doo his homage...' (p. 334).
The dispute with France began in 1322, a decade after the execution of
Gaveston, who, as far as his lover in the play knows, is still alive. See
Introduction, p. 48.
66. *Sib*] literally kinswoman (cf. sibling), but here wife. Lunt notes
that 'Sib' might perhaps be taken as 'an endearing contraction of Isabella.'
Edward speaks with breezy informality.
70. Prince Edward was thirteen in 1325 at the time of this embassy. The
king's use of 'your' (rather than the more usual 'my'; cf. IV.iii.71) reinforces
the impression of Isabella's domination of the prince and suggests a certain
distance between the boy and his father. Marlowe combines the historically
separate journeys of the queen and Prince Edward, who followed her to the
French court. See Holinshed, p. 336 (Appendix B, no. 25); see also Introduction, pp. 48, 64.

And fear not, lord and father; heaven's great beams
On Atlas' shoulder shall not lie more safe
Than shall your charge committed to my trust.
Isabella. Ah boy, this towardness makes thy mother fear
Thou art not marked to many days on earth.   80
Edward. Madam, we will that you with speed be shipped,
And this our son. Levune shall follow you
With all the haste we can dispatch him hence.
Choose of our lords to bear you company,
And go in peace; leave us in wars at home.   85
Isabella. Unnatural wars, where subjects brave their king—
God end them once. My lord, I take my leave
To make my preparation for France.

[*Exit* ISABELLA *and* PRINCE EDWARD.]

Enter LORD ARUNDEL.

Edward. What, Lord Arundel, dost thou come alone?
Arundel. Yea, my good lord, for Gaveston is dead.   90
Edward. Ah traitors, have they put my friend to death?
Tell me, Arundel, died he ere thou cam'st,
Or didst thou see my friend to take his death?
Arundel. Neither, my lord, for as he was surprised,
Begirt with weapons and with enemies round,   95

---

82. Levune] *Dodsley*[2]; *Lewne Q; Lewen Q2–4; Lejeune Broughton.*   88.1.
Exit . . . PRINCE EDWARD] *Dyce*[1]   *(subst.); not in Q.*   88.2. ARUNDEL]
Broughton; Matre. Q1–3; Matreuis Q4.   89, 92. Arundel] *Broughton; Matre.*
Q1–4.   90, 94, 103, 115. Arundel] *Broughton; Mat., Matr. Q1–4.*   90.
Yea] *Q1–2;* Yes *Q3–4.*   92. cam'st] *Q* (camst); camest *Scott.*

---

77. *Atlas' shoulder*] In classical mythology Atlas was a Titan (a giant)
condemned by Zeus to support the sky on his shoulders; he was commonly
depicted kneeling under the burden. Merchant suggests that the prince's
precocious bravado is the 'first sign of a regality which links him with his
grandfather, Edward Longshanks.'

79. *towardness*] readiness, aptitude. For the probable influence of *R3* upon
this speech, see Introduction, p. 25. Lunt cites the proverb, 'The good die
young'; cf. Tilley G251, L384.

81–82. *with . . . son*] See note on l. 70 above.

85. *wars at home*] i.e., civil wars with the rebellious nobles.

87. *once*] once for all.

88.2. LORD ARUNDEL] See Introduction, pp. 8–9.

94. *surprised*] captured.

I did your highness' message to them all,
Demanding him of them—entreating rather—
And said, upon the honour of my name,
That I would undertake to carry him
Unto your highness, and to bring him back.   100
Edward. And tell me, would the rebels deny me that?
Spencer Junior. Proud recreants!
Edward.   Yea Spencer, traitors all.
Arundel. I found them at the first inexorable;
    The Earl of Warwick would not bide the hearing,
    Mortimer hardly; Pembroke and Lancaster   105
    Spake least. And when they flatly had denied,
    Refusing to receive me pledge for him,
    The Earl of Pembroke mildly thus bespake:
    'My lords, because our sovereign sends for him,
    And promiseth he shall be safe returned,   110
    I will this undertake, to have him hence
    And see him re-delivered to your hands.'
Edward. Well, and how fortunes that he came not?
Spencer Junior. Some treason or some villainy was cause.
Arundel. The Earl of Warwick seized him on his way,   115
    For, being delivered unto Pembroke's men,
    Their lord rode home, thinking his prisoner safe;
    But ere he came, Warwick in ambush lay,
    And bare him to his death, and in a trench
    Strake off his head, and marched unto the camp.   120
Spencer Junior. A bloody part, flatly against law of arms.

---

104. Earl] *Q, Q3–4;* eare *Q2.*   106. Spake] *Q, Q4;* Speake *Q2–3.*   107.
me] *Q1–3;* my *Q4.*   111. will this] *Q;* will *Dodsley[1].*   113. fortunes] *Q;*
fortunes it *Dyce[1];* fortune *Oliphant.*   113. not] *Q;* not then *Fleay (conj.).*
114. cause] *Q;* the cause *Dodsley[1].*   120. Strake] *Q1–2;* Stroke *Q3–4;*
Struck *Dodsley[1].*   121. against] *Q1–3;* 'gainst *Q4.*   121. arms.] *Q;* arms.
Exit Arundel. Fleay.

---

102. *recreants*] betrayers; cf. III.ii.45.
104. *bide*] abide.
113. *fortunes*] does it happen.
119–120. *in . . . head*] Historically Gaveston was beheaded on Blacklow
Hill after some debate among the nobles; see Holinshed, p. 321 (Appendix B,
no. 19). To create greater sympathy, Marlowe purposely treats his death
more as a lynching or 'murder' (l. 125) than as an execution.
120. *Strake*] struck.

Edward. O, shall I speak, or shall I sigh and die?
Spencer Junior. My lord, refer your vengeance to the sword
    Upon these barons; hearten up your men.
    Let them not unrevenged murder your friends.   125
    Advance your standard, Edward, in the field,
    And march to fire them from their starting holes.
Edward (kneels and saith). By earth, the common mother of us
     all,
    By heaven and all the moving orbs thereof,
    By this right hand, and by my father's sword,   130
    And all the honours 'longing to my crown,
    I will have heads and lives for him—as many
    As I have manors, castles, towns, and towers.

                                          [Rises.]

    Treacherous Warwick! Traitorous Mortimer!
    If I be England's king, in lakes of gore   135
    Your headless trunks, your bodies will I trail,
    That you may drink your fill and quaff in blood,
    And stain my royal standard with the same,
    That so my bloody colours may suggest
    Remembrance of revenge immortally   140
    On your accursèd traitorous progeny—
    You villains that have slain my Gaveston.

---

125. murder] *Dodsley*[1]; murther *Q*.   128. *kneels and saith*] *Q* (*Edward kneeles, and saith*) (*centred as a stage direction*); *kneeling Dyce*[1]. 131. honours] *Q* (*honors*); honour *Wagner*.   131. 'longing] *Dodsley*[1]; longing *Q*. 133.1. *Rises*] *Dyce*[1]; *not in Q*.   140. immortally] *Q1–2* (immortallie), *Q4*; immortalitie *Q3* (*misprint?*).

---

123. *refer*] commit, assign.

   127. *fire . . . holes*] i.e., flush them from their hiding places as foxes or other quarry are smoked from their holes by means of fire; cf. *Lr*: 'fire us hence like foxes' (V.iii.23). John Palsgrave's grammar, *Lesclarcissement de la Langue Francoyse* (1530), supplies the earliest example in the *O.E.D.* of 'Stertyng hole': 'ung tapynet, lieu de refuge.'

   128. *By earth . . .*] Marlowe bases this entire speech on Holinshed's un-adorned statement that on receiving the bad news Edward II 'was woonder-fullie displeased with those lords that had thus put the said earle vnto death, making his vow that he would see his death reuenged, so that the rancour which before was kindled betwixt the king and those lords, began now to blase abroad, and spred so farre, that the king euer sought occasion how to worke them displeasure' (p. 321).

   131. *'longing*] belonging.

[*To* SPENCER JUNIOR] And in this place of honour and of
   trust,
Spencer, sweet Spencer, I adopt thee here;
And merely of our love we do create thee   145
Earl of Gloucester and Lord Chamberlain,
Despite of times, despite of enemies.
Spencer Junior. My lord, here is a messenger from the barons
   Desires access unto your majesty.
Edward. Admit him near.   150

   Enter the Herald *from the* Barons, *with his coat of arms.*

Herald. Long live King Edward, England's lawful lord.
Edward. So wish not they, I wis, that sent thee hither.
   Thou com'st from Mortimer and his complices—
   A ranker rout of rebels never was.
   Well, say thy message.   155

---

143. *To* SPENCER JUNIOR] *This ed.; not in Q.*   143. this] *Q1–4;* his *Cunningham.*   147. times] *Q;* time *Oxberry.*   148. here is] *Dodsley²;* heres is
Q1–2; heers *Q3, Q4* (heer's), *Dodsley¹* (here's).   151, 156. Herald]
Oxberry; Messen. Q.   152. I wis] *Dodsley¹;* Iwis *Q1–4.*   153. com'st] *Q*
(comst); comest *Scott.*   153. complices] *Q;* accomplices *Dodsley¹.*   154.
rout] *Q4;* route *Q;* roote *Q2–3, Dodsley¹* (root).

---

145. *merely*] simply. The word suggests that Edward's motive for honour-
ing Spencer Junior is personal attraction, not an aspect of his vengeance upon
the murderers of Gaveston.

146. Holinshed reports that 'Hugh the sonne was made high chamberleine of England, contrarie to the mind of all the noblemen' (p. 325), but
Spencer Junior was never officially Earl of Gloucester despite Holinshed's
attribution of this title to him on more than one occasion; G. E. Cokayne
(*The Complete Peerage* [London, 1910–'59]) notes that the favourite 'has been
spoken of, erroneously, by many writers as Earl of Gloucester' (V, 713),
probably because he was married to a daughter of the legitimate earl and also
because he owned extensive lands in the county. See Introduction, p. 51.

151. *England's lawful lord*] The herald's officially correct greeting underlines the irony of Edward's shaky situation, since the message he is about to
deliver amounts to an ultimatum to the king; cf. Edward's response (l. 152).

152. *I wis*] I know; the phrase derives from Middle English *ywis*
(= certainly), but was misunderstood as 'I wis' from the verb *to wit*.

153. *from Mortimer*] The historical leader of the rebel barons whom Edward was about to engage so triumphantly at Boroughbridge (1322) was
Thomas, Earl of Lancaster, not Mortimer; both the Mortimers surrendered
without resistance and were imprisoned earlier the same year. See Introduction, p. 53.

Herald. The barons up in arms by me salute
    Your highness with long life and happiness,
    And bid me say as plainer to your grace,
    That if without effusion of blood
    You will this grief have ease and remedy,   160
    That from your princely person you remove
    This Spencer [*indicating* SPENCER JUNIOR] as a putrifying
       branch
    That deads the royal vine, whose golden leaves
    Empale your princely head, your diadem,
    Whose brightness such pernicious upstarts dim;   165
    Say they—and lovingly advise your grace
    To cherish virtue and nobility,
    And have old servitors in high esteem,
    And shake off smooth dissembling flatterers.

---

160. this grief] *Q* (greefe), *Q2-3* (griefe); of this *Q4*.   162. *indicating*
SPENCER JUNIOR] *This ed.; not in Q.*   162. putrifying] *Q;* putrefying *Pendry-*
Maxwell.   163. leaves] *Q, Q3-4;* leaue *Q2 (British Library copy).*

---

158. *plainer*] complainant (an archaic legal term equivalent to plaintiff, one
who voices a grievance). Cf. *R2:* 'After our sentence plaining comes too late'
(I.iii.175).

160. i.e., will have ease *of* and remedy *for* this grief.

161–162. *you... branch*] See Holinshed, pp. 325–326 (Appendix B, nos.
21, 23). Cf. *1 Troublesome Reign:* 'Sith we have proynd the more than
needfull braunch / That did oppresse the true wel-growing stock' (xiii; ll.
1481–1482).

163. *deads*] kills (an archaic form of 'deadens'); Charlton–Waller cite
Spenser, *Tears of the Muses:* 'With whom all ioy and iolly meriment / Is also
deaded' (ll. 209–210); and Nashe, *The Unfortunate Traveller:* 'yet they were
not vtterly deaded' (*Works*, II, 275).

royal vine] The leaves that adorned the crown of Edward II and of later
kings until Henry IV were strawberry leaves, not vine leaves; see V. Wheeler-
Holohan, ed., *Boutell's Manual of Heraldry*, rev. ed. (London, 1931), p. 121.
But Marlowe's association of the vine with royalty is traditional; Cranmer in
Shakespeare's *H8* links Elizabeth at her christening with the sacred vine of
the redeemed Israel (v.v.31–53). See also v.i.47.

164. *Empale*] encircle (as with a garland); a term from heraldry.

165. *upstarts*] See notes on I.iv.41 and l. 162 above.

168. *old servitors*] i.e., retainers of long standing (as opposed to 'upstarts'
such as the Spencers). *Servitor* appears to have been used especially in
expressions of formal politesse; Gill cites *3H6:* 'My noble Queen, let former
grudges pass, / And henceforth I am thy true servitor' (III.iii.195–196).

This granted, they, their honours, and their lives   170
Are to your highness vowed and consecrate.
Spencer Junior. Ah traitors, will they still display their pride?
Edward. Away! Tarry no answer, but be gone.
     Rebels! Will they appoint their sovereign
     His sports, his pleasures, and his company?   175
     Yet ere thou go, see how I do divorce
     Spencer from me.

                                    Embraces SPENCER [JUNIOR].
                    Now get thee to thy lords,
     And tell them I will come to chastise them
     For murdering Gaveston. Hie thee, get thee gone;
     Edward with fire and sword follows at thy heels.   180

                                         [*Exit* Herald.]

     My lords, perceive you how these rebels swell?
     Soldiers, good hearts, defend your soverign's right,
     For now, even now, we march to make them stoop.
     Away!

                                              Exeunt.

---

177. *Embraces* SPENCER] *Dodsley*[1] *(subst.) (Embraces Spen.); Embrace Spencer*
Q1–4 (in right margin after lines 176, 177).   179. murdering] *Dyce*[1]; mur-
thering *Q*.   180.1. *Exit* Herald] *Dyce*[1]; *Exit Messenger. Broughton; not in*
Q.   181. lords] *Broughton;* lord *Q1–4*.

---

177. *Embraces* SPENCER] Note the deliberate parallel to the embracement
of Gaveston at I.i.140; see Introduction, p. 71. As before, the gesture seems
intended to convey an obvious eroticism, and Stowe says that Spencer Junior
'was in body very comely' (p. 332). The imperative form of the stage
direction in Q ('*Embrace*') may be further evidence that the printer's copy
had been marked up with a view to theatrical production; almost certainly,
however, the compositor was not setting (as Charlton–Waller suggest) from
'the theatre prompt copy'. See Introduction, p. 8.
     180. *Edward . . . sword*] Although Holinshed does not stress Edward's
martial prowess, he does note in summing up the reign that the king was
'strong of bodie, and healthfull, neither wanted there in him stoutnesse of
stomach' (p. 342).
     181. *lords*] Broughton's pluralization of Q's 'lord' would seem to be con-
textually desirable. As Bowers points out, 'my lord' would have to apply to
Spencer, whom Edward has just embraced as an intimate and whom (except
at IV.iii.4) he habitually addresses without such formality, or, even more
improbably, to Arundel, to whom he has not spoken directly since l. 113.
Edward is appealing to his nobles as a group just as in the following line he
appeals to his soldiers.

[SCENE ii]

Alarums, excursions, a great fight, and a retreat [sounded].
Enter [EDWARD] the King, SPENCER [SENIOR] *(the father),*
SPENCER [JUNIOR] *(the son), and the* Noblemen *of the* King's *side.*

Edward. Why do we sound retreat? Upon them, lords!
This day I shall pour vengeance with my sword
On those proud rebels that are up in arms,
And do confront and countermand their king.
Spencer Junior. I doubt it not, my lord; right will prevail.   5
Spencer Senior. 'Tis not amiss, my liege, for either part
To breathe a while; our men with sweat and dust
All choked well near, begin to faint for heat,

Heading. Scene ii] *This ed.;* [Act III,] Scene v *Broughton; (no heading; continuation of III.ii) Fleay, Ellis;* Scene iii *Robinson; (no heading; continuation of III.i) Bowers; not in Q.* 0.1. Alarums ... retreat] *Broughton (as opening stage direction of this scene); Robinson (as concluding stage direction of preceding scene); Q1–3 (printed with a space break after 'retreat'); Q4 (with a page break after 'retreat').* 0.1. sounded] *Kirschbaum; sounded, within Dyce[1]; not in Q.* 0.3. SPENCER (the son), and the Noblemen] *Q; the younger Spenser, Baldock, and Noblemen Keltie.* 5, 10, 20. Spencer Junior] *Dodsley[1]; Spen. son. Q.* 6, 22. Spencer Senior] *Dodsley[1]; Spen. fa. Q.* 7. a while] *Q; awhile Broughton, Oxberry.*

0.1–3. Tancock notes that Marlowe has radically condensed history at this point by omitting much action that occurred before the royal victory which this scene dramatizes. The dramatist 'has passed over the troubles of 1320–21; the success of the Barons, and the exile of the Despensers; the King's recovery of power; and the restoration of the favourites. In representing the outbreak of 1321–22, he condenses all into one rising and one battle, which is evidently Boroughbridge in Yorkshire, fought on March 16, 1322.' In history Edward II did not fight personally at Boroughbridge, the victory being won for him by a subordinate (Sir Andrew Harclay). See Appendix B, no. 27.

excursions] small groups of soldiers passing over the stage to suggest the confusion of battle.

1. *retreat*] Briggs points out that the king had suffered a setback in the earlier battle of Burton-on-Trent, here conflated with the battle of Boroughbridge (note the opening stage direction). The royal forces under Harclay (see preceding note) did not retreat in the latter engagement.

4. *countermand*] oppose; the modern sense of 'cancel former orders' is not operative. The *O.E.D.* lists the present instance as the earliest use of the verb in this sense.

And this retire refresheth horse and man.
Spencer Junior. Here come the rebels.   10

> *Enter the* Barons, MORTIMER [JUNIOR], LANCASTER,
> [KENT,] WARWICK, PEMBROKE, [*with others*].

Mortimer Junior. Look, Lancaster,
Yonder is Edward among his flatterers.
Lancaster. And there let him be,
Till he pay dearly for their company.
Warwick. And shall, or Warwick's sword shall smite in vain.   15
Edward. What, rebels, do you shrink and sound retreat?
Mortimer Junior. No, Edward, no; thy flatterers faint and fly.
Lancaster. Th'ad best betimes forsake them and their trains,
For they'll betray thee, traitors as they are.
Spencer Junior. Traitor on thy face, rebellious Lancaster.   20
Pembroke. Away, base upstsart; brav'st thou nobles thus?

---

9. retire] *Q;* retreat *Broughton.*   10.1. Barons] *Q;* Nobles *Broughton.*
10.2. KENT] *Gill[1]; with Kent, a silent watcher Kirschbaum; not in Q.*
10.2. *with others*] *Dyce[1] (subst.); cum caeteris Q.*   11. *Mortimer Junior*]
Broughton; Mor. Q; E Mor. Wagner, Fleay.   11–12. Look . . . flatterers.]
Bowers; Look . . . Edward / Among . . . flatterers. *Dyce[1]; one line in Q.*
12. Yonder is] *Q;* yonder's *Dodsley[1].*   12. among] *Q;* 'mong *Dodsley[1].*
12–13. among . . . be,] *Q; one line in Tancock.*   13–14. And . . . company.]
Dyce[1]; one line in Q.   18. Th'ad] *Q1–4;* They'd *Broughton;* Th'ad [=Thou
had] *Brooke;* Thou'd *Ribner.*   18. them] *Brooke, Greg (conj.);* thee *Q1–4.*
20. on] *Q;* in *Scott.*   21. brav'st] *Q* (brau'st); bravest *Scott.*

---

9. *retire*] strategic retreat; Charlton–Waller cite Milton, *Paradise Lost:*
'Discovered soon the place of her retire' (XI, 267).
18. *Th'ad*] Thou'd (contracted form of 'Thou had'); see following note.
them] Q's *thee* makes no sense, even if the preceding contraction (*Th'ad*) be
understood as 'they had,' for, as Bowers notes, this latter reading produces
an unlikely conflict between two opposite points of view—the forsaking of
the plots (from the perspective of the barons) and the forsaking of Edward
(from the king's own perspective); Brooke's emendation, suggested by Greg,
is unavoidable.
trains] intrigues, political tricks. Cf. *Jew of Malta:* 'This train he laid to
have entrapped thy life' (v.v.90).
21. *Pembroke*] Tancock notes that historically Pembroke supported the
king against the barons after the death of Gaveston. Earlier Pembroke had
sided with Warwick and Lancaster against the king but then changed alle-
giances. Marlowe gives no hint of Pembroke's political shift.
upstart] See note on I.iv.41.

Spencer Senior. A noble attempt and honourable deed
      Is it not, trow ye, to assemble aid
      And levy arms against your lawful king?
Edward. For which ere long their heads shall satisfy   25
      T'appease the wrath of their offended king.
Mortimer Junior. Then, Edward, thou wilt fight it to the last,
      And rather bathe thy sword in subjects' blood
      Than banish that pernicious company.
Edward. Ay, traitors all! Rather than thus be braved,   30
      Make England's civil towns huge heaps of stones
      And ploughs to go about our palace gates.
Warwick. A desperate and unnatural resolution.
      Alarum to the fight!
      Saint George for England and the barons' right.   35

---

23. Is it] *Q, Q3–4;* It is *Q2..*   27. wilt] *Q, Q3–4;* will *Q2.*   29. company.] *Q* (companie.); company? *Broughton.*   30. thus be] *Q;* be thus *Broughton.*   33–34. A desperate . . . fight!] *Q; one line in Oliphant.*   34. Alarum to the fight!] *Q (as part of Warwick's speech); Spencer (conj.) (as a stage direction).*   34–35. Alarum . . . right.] *Broughton;* Alarum . . . England, / And . . . right. *Q.*   35. barons'] *Scott;* Barons *Q;* baron's *Dodsley*[1].

---

23. *trow ye*] think you, believe you (here used expletively and with sarcasm). Cf. Marvell, *A Short Historical Essay Touching General Councils . . .* : 'Did not this Historian, trow you, deserve to be handled . . . ?' (A. B. Grosart, ed., *Complete Works* [Blackburn, 1875], IV, 138).

25. *satisfy*] make reparation or atonement.

31. *huge heaps of stones*] As Briggs points out, Marlowe echoes his own phrase here from his translation of Lucan: 'That rampires fallen down, huge heaps of stone / Lie in our towns, that houses are abandon'd' (ll. 25–26).

32. Briggs compares Greene, *James IV (c.* 1590): 'The plough shall furrow where the palace stood' (v.iii.7).

34. *Alarum to the fight!*] The possibility exists (cf. Spencer's conjectural emendation) that these words were meant in the printer's copy as a stage direction and that the compositor mistakenly absorbed them into Warwick's speech; for even if Broughton's relineation (which gives us the rhyme *fight/ right*) is correct, a short line is unavoidable. Such short lines, however, are far from unique in *Edward II*. Bowers argues sensibly that the rhyme produced by the relining makes it slightly more likely that the words are a shout of encouragement rather than a stage direction.

35. *Saint George for England*] An anachronism; St George was not adopted as the patron saint of England until the reign of Edward III. Cf. Drayton, *Mortimeriados*: 'Englands Red crosse upon both sides doth flye, / Saint *George* the King, saint *George* the Barrons cry' (ll. 384–385; *Works*, I, 320).

Edward. Saint George for England and King Edward's right.

> [*Exeunt severally. Alarums.*]

Enter EDWARD, [SPENCER SENIOR, SPENCER JUNIOR, BALDOCK,
LEVUNE, *and* Soldiers] *with the* Barons [KENT, WARWICK, LANCASTER,
and MORTIMER JUNIOR,] *captives.*

Edward. Now, lusty lords, now, not by chance of war
But justice of the quarrel and the cause,
Vailed is your pride. Methinks you hang the heads,
But we'll advance them, traitors! Now 'tis time   40
To be avenged on you for all your braves
And for the murder of my dearest friend,
To whom right well you knew our soul was knit,
Good Pierce of Gaveston, my sweet favourite—
Ah rebels, recreants, you made him away.   45
Kent. Brother, in regard of thee and of thy land
Did they remove that flatterer from thy throne.
Edward. So sir, you have spoke. Away, avoid our presence.

> [*Exit* KENT.]

36.1. *Exeunt severally*] *Dyce*[1] *(subst.); Exeunt Scott; not in Q.*   36.1.
Alarums] *Oxberry; Alarums and battle off-stage Merchant; not in Q.*
36.2. *Enter* EDWARD] *Fleay (no heading; continuation of III.ii);* [Act III,]
Scene vi.—*Another part of the field. Enter the King Broughton; (no heading;
continuation of III.i) Robinson; Scene iii. Enter Edward Ellis (following
Broughton and Dyce*[1] *('Another part of the field')); Scene iv. Enter Edward
Oliphant, Spencer; (no heading; continuation of III.i) Bowers.*   36.2–3.
SPENCER SENIOR . . . LEVUNE] *Gill*[1]; *the Bishop of Winchester Kirschbaum; not in
Q.*   36.3. *and* Soldiers] *Kirschbaum; not in Q.*   36.3–4. *with the* Barons
captives] *Q (subst.); Lejeune, the Spencers, Baldock, and others of his Party,
with the Nobles captives. Broughton; and his followers, with the Barons and Kent
captive. Dyce*[2].   36.3–4. KENT . . . MORTIMER JUNIOR] *Gill*[1]; *not in Q.*
39. Vailed] *Q*; *Veil'd Dodsley*[1].   42. murder] *Dodsley*[1]; *murther Q.*
44. Pierce] *Q*; *Piercy Dodsley*[1]; *Piers Broughton.*   48.1. *Exit* KENT] *Dyce*[1];
not in Q.

---

39. *Vailed*] lowered (see note on I.ii.19); possibly a reminiscence of Lodge,
Wounds of Civil War (see note on I.iv.276).
40. *advance*] a bitterly sardonic quibble on (1) promote and (2) raise higher
(since traitors' heads were often lifted up on pikes); cf. I.i.117 and III.i.20;
also l. 55 below.
41. *braves*] See note on III.i.13.
45. *recreants*] See note on III.i.102.
made him away] See note on II.ii.235.

Accursed wretches, was't in regard of us,
When we had sent our messenger to request   50
He might be spared to come to speak with us,
And Pembroke undertook for his return,
That thou, proud Warwick, watched the prisoner,
Poor Pierce, and headed him against law of arms?
For which thy head shall overlook the rest   55
As much as thou in rage outwent'st the rest!
Warwick. Tyrant, I scorn thy threats and menaces;
    'Tis but temporal that thou canst inflict.
Lancaster. The worst is death, and better die to live,
    Than live in infamy under such a king.   60
Edward. [*To* SPENCER SENIOR] Away with them, my lord of
    Winchester!
These lusty leaders, Warwick and Lancaster—
I charge you roundly, off with both their heads.
Away!

---

49. Accursed] *Q;* Accurs'd *Dodsley¹;* Accursèd *Fleay.*   50. messenger]
Q1–2; messengers *Q3–4.*   53. watched] *Q;* snatch'd *Kirschbaum.*
54. Pierce] *Q;* Piers *Broughton.*   54. against] *Q1–3;* 'gainst *Q4.*   59. to]
Q; than *Dodsley¹.*   60. Than] *Q* (Then); To *Dodsley¹.*   61. *To* SPENCER
SENIOR] *This ed.; not in Q.*   63–64. I charge . . . Away!] *Dyce¹; one line
in Q.*

---

53. *Warwick*] Again Marlowe telescopes history; Warwick had died from
illness in 1315. See Introduction, p. 52.
   watched] i.e., kept watch over.
   54. *headed*] i.e., beheaded.
   55. Marlowe may have recalled here Queen Margaret's implacable vengeance upon the Duke of York in *3H6*: 'Off with his head, and set it on York
gates, / So York may overlook the town of York' (I.iv.179–180).
   58. *temporal*] i.e., bodily punishment (as opposed to torment of the soul).
Briggs compares Peele, *Edward I*: 'It is but temporall that you can inflict' (v;
l. 880).
   59. *The worst is death*] Cf. *R2*: 'The worst is death, and death will have his
day' (III.ii.103). But the phrase may be proverbial.
   59–60. *better . . . infamy*] Proverbial (Tilley H576); cf. *Doctor Faustus*:
'We'll rather die with grief than live with shame' (xiv.25). The idea of dying
to live in eternity is very common; Charlton–Waller cite Kyd, *Cornelia*: 'But
so to die, as dying I may liue' (IV.ii.135).
   61. *my lord of Winchester*] See note on III.i.49.
   62. *Warwick*] See note on l. 53 above.
   63. *off . . . heads*] See Holinshed. p. 331 (Appendix B, no. 27).

Warwick. Farewell, vain world.
Lancaster.   Sweet Mortimer, farewell.   65
    [*Exeunt* WARWICK *and* LANCASTER, *guarded, with* SPENCER SENIOR.]
Mortimer Junior. England, unkind to thy nobility,
    Groan for this grief; behold how thou art maimed.
Edward. Go, take that haughty Mortimer to the Tower;
    There see him safe bestowed. And for the rest,
    Do speedy execution on them all;   70
    Be gone!
Mortimer Junior. What, Mortimer! Can ragged stony walls
    Immure thy virtue that aspires to heaven?
    No, Edward, England's scourge, it may not be;
    Mortimer's hope surmounts his fortune far.   75
                                        [*Exit guarded.*]
Edward. Sound drums and trumpets! March with me, my
        friends;
    Edward this day hath crowned him king anew.
                                        Exit [*attended*].

65.1. *Exeunt . . .* SPENCER SENIOR] *Gill*[1] (*subst.*); *not in* Q.   70–71. Do . . .
gone!] *Dyce*[1]; *one line in* Q.   75. his] *Q1–2*; hie [= high?] *Q3–4*.
75.1. *Exit guarded.*] *Gill*[1]; *The captive Barons are led off. Dyce*[1]; *Exit under
guard with other captive Barons. Ribner; not in* Q.   77.1. attended] *Oliphant
(subst.); not in* Q.

---

68. *Mortimer to the Tower*] See notes on III.i.153 and ll. 0.1–3 above; also
Introduction, p. 53. Holinshed is vague about the specific reasons for
Mortimer's imprisonment: he merely reports that upon the surrender of the
elder Mortimer and his adherents in 1322, the king 'shortlie after sent them
to the tower of London' (p. 329).

72. *ragged*] rugged, rough, uneven. The word was commonly applied to
stones, rocks, and the surfaces of buildings; cf. *R3*, in which the Tower is
referred to as a 'Rude ragged nurse' (IV.i.101) for the boy princes; cf. also
Edward III: 'These ragged walles no testimonie are / What is within' (I.ii; ll.
326–327).

73. *virtue*] noble power, manly inner force (with overtones of valour or
bravery; cf. L. *virtus*). For the range of meanings that shade into each other
here, compare *1 Tamburlaine* (II.v.17, IV.iv.131) and *2 Tamburlaine* (I.iii.51,
IV.i.175). The theme of aspiration (including its associations with Machiavellian *virtù*) is a Marlovian commonplace.

74. *England's scourge*] Cf. *1H6* in which Joan of Arc describes herself as
'the English scourge' (I.ii.129). The idea was common. Marlowe himself had
developed it extensively in the two parts of *Tamburlaine*; see Introduction, p.
23.

[SPENCER JUNIOR, LEVUNE, *and* BALDOCK *remain.*]
Spencer Junior. Levune, the trust that we repose in thee
　　Begets the quiet of King Edward's land;
　　Therefore be gone in haste, and with advice   80
　　Bestow that treasure on the lords of France,
　　That therewith all enchanted, like the guard
　　That suffered Jove to pass in showers of gold
　　To Danaë, all aid may be denied   ·
　　To Isabel the queen, that now in France   85
　　Makes friends, to cross the seas with her young son
　　And step into his father's regiment.
Levune. That's it these barons and the subtle queen
　　Long levelled at.
Baldock.　　　　　Yea, but Levune, thou seest
　　These barons lay their heads on blocks together;   90
　　What they intend, the hangman frustrates clean.

77.2. SPENCER JUNIOR . . . *remain.*] *Robinson (subst.); Manent Spencer filius,
Lewne & Baldock. Q.*   77.2, 78, 88, 89, 92, 96. LEVUNE] *Dyce*[1]*; Lewne Q;
Lewen Dodsley*[1]*; Lejeune Broughton; Lecune Robinson.*   82. therewith all]
Q1–3; therewithall *Q4;* therewithal *Spencer (conj.), Gill*[1].   88. it] *Q1–2,
Q4;* is *Q3 (misprint?).*   89. levelled] *Dodsley*[3] *(conj.)* (leveld), *Dyce*[1]*, Greg
(conj.);* levied *Q1–4* (leuied).

81. *Bestow that treasure*] Spencer Junior's bribing of the French through
Levune in order to vitiate the queen's attempt to enlist her brother's aid
against her husband represents a considerable simplification of the chronicle
account; negotiations with France concerning the queen's return to England
and her hostile relationship with the Spencers were more complex and
protracted than Marlowe suggests. See Holinshed, pp. 336–337 (Appendix
B, nos. 28, 31); also Introduction, pp. 48, 61.

82–84. *like . . . Danaë*] See note on II.ii.53; also Introduction, p. 72. Gill
notes: 'One interpretation of the "showers of gold" by means of which
Jupiter reached Danaë in her brazen tower is that the guards were bribed.'

87. *regiment*] See note on I.i.164.

89. *levelled at*] aimed at (originally a metaphor from shooting muskets).

90. *lay . . . together*] apparently a grim jest applying the word 'levelled'
from the previous line in a fresh sense (made level through decapitation).

91. *hangman*] i.e., executioner (the term commonly used even when the
form of death was beheading); according to Holinshed Lancaster was condemned 'to be drawne, hanged, and headed. But bicause he was the queenes
vncle, and sonne to the kings vncle, he was pardoned of all saue heading . . .'
(p. 331); for the larger historical context, see Appendix B, no. 27.

Levune. Have you no doubts, my lords; I'll clap so close
    Among the lords of France with England's gold
    That Isabel shall make her plaints in vain,
    And France shall be obdurate with her tears.   95
Spencer Junior. Then make for France amain; Levune, away!
    Proclaim King Edward's wars and victories.

                                                Exeunt.

---

92. doubts] *Q;* doubte *Q2, Q3–4* (doubt), *Dodsley*[1].   92. clap so] *Dodsley*[1];
claps *Q1–4;* creep *Oxberry.*   97.1. *Exeunt*] *Keltie; Exeunt omnes Q.*

---

    92. *clap so close*] Charlton–Waller explain: 'to strike (hands) reciprocally
in token of a bargain' in secrecy ('close'); cf. *H5:* 'and so clap hands and a
bargain' (v.ii.131); also *W.T.*: 'Ere I could make thee open thy white hand /
And clap thyself my love' (i.ii.103–104). Levune means that he will bring
the French to a certain and secret agreement concerning Isabella by means of
the bribes.

    96. *amain*] See note on ii.iv.47.

Act IV

Enter Edmund [Earl *of* KENT].

Kent. Fair blows the wind for France. Blow, gentle gale,
   Till Edmund be arrived for England's good.
   Nature, yield to my country's cause in this.
   A brother—no, a butcher of thy friends—
   Proud Edward, dost thou banish me thy presence?   5
   But I'll to France and cheer the wrongèd queen,
   And certify what Edward's looseness is.
   Unnatural king, to slaughter noblemen
   And cherish flatterers.

Heading. Act IV, Scene i] *Broughton; not in Q.*   8. noblemen] *Dyce*[1]*; noble men Q.*   9–14. And cherish . . . happily?] *Bowers;* And cherish . . . stay / Thy . . . deuice. / Holla . . . lord? / *Mortimer . . .* happilie? *Q;* And cherish . . . stay / Thy . . . night, / To . . . device. / Holla . . . lord? / Mortimer, 'tis I.— / But . . . happily? *Broughton;* And cherish . . . stay / Thy . . . night, / To . . . device! / Holla . . . there? / Is't . . . lord? / Mortimer, 'tis I. / But . . . happily? *Dyce*[1]*;* And cherish . . . stay / Thy . . . night, / To . . . there? / Is't . . . 'tis I. / But . . . happily? *Tancock.*

   1. *Fair blows the wind*] Mark Eccles (in his review of Charlton–Waller, *M.L.R.*, 30 [1935], 361) compares the opening of Drayton's 'Ballad of Agincourt': 'Faire stood the Wind for *France*' (*Works*, II, 375); cf. also *The Barons' Wars:* 'For Mortimer, that Wind most fitly blew' (*Works*, III, 33). Cf. II.ii.1, and see Introduction, p. 72. The phrase itself may be indebted to Grafton, who says that Kent (together with Mortimer, Isabella, and Prince Edward) departed for France, 'then hauyng wind at will' (p. 204). For discussion of Marlowe's use of Grafton, see Introduction, pp. 64–66.
   5. *banish me thy presence*] Kent's banishment is fictional. In the chronicle Edward II sends Kent to Guienne to defend the duchy against the French; see Holinshed, p. 332 (Appendix B, no. 29). See note on II.ii.207–208; also Introduction, p. 48.
   7. *certify*] See note on I.ii.38.
   looseness] (1) laxity, negligence, incompetence; (2) wantonness, lasciviousness. Cf. IV.iv.11.

Mortimer, I stay thy sweet escape.   10
Stand gracious gloomy night to his device.

Enter MORTIMER [JUNIOR] *disguised.*

Mortimer Junior. Holla! Who walketh there? Is't you, my
    lord?
Kent. Mortimer, 'tis I;
    But hath thy potion wrought so happily?
Mortimer Junior. It hath, my lord; the warders all asleep,   15
    I thank them, gave me leave to pass in peace.
    But hath your grace got shipping unto France?
Kent. Fear it not.

                                      Exeunt.

[SCENE ii]

Enter [ISABELLA] *the* Queen *and her son* [PRINCE EDWARD].

Isabella. Ah boy, our friends do fail us all in France.
    The lords are cruel and the king unkind.
    What shall we do?
Prince Edward.   Madam, return to England

---

10. sweet] *Q;* swift *Collier MS.*   12. Holla] *Q;* Holloa *Cunningham.*
14. thy] *Q;* my *Robinson.*   17. unto] *Q1–3* (vnto); into *Q4.*   *Heading.*
Scene ii] *Broughton; not in Q.*   3. do] *Q1–2* (doe), *Q4;* goe *Q3.*

---

10. *stay*] stay for, await.

    escape] Historically, Mortimer's escape from the Tower had no connection
with Kent; see Holinshed's account (pp. 334–335; Appendix B, no. 30).
Grafton (p. 204), however, does erroneously combine Mortimer's escape with
Kent's embarkation. See Introduction, p. 64; also notes on III.ii.68 and l. 1
above. Drayton in *The Barons' Wars* (III, stanzas 5–26; *Works*, II, 47–52)
provides a detailed narrative of Mortimer's escape.

    11. *Stand . . . device*] i.e., may the darkness of the night favourably assist
his stratagem.

    14. i.e., has your drug worked so fortunately? Holinshed is silent as to
who provided Mortimer with the sleeping potion; Lunt notes that 'he was
enabled to escape by the assistance of the Bishop of Hereford [Adam Or-
leton]' (p. xlv).

    IV.ii.1. *our . . . us*] Levune's bribing of the French has already had the
desired effect. See note on III.ii.81.

    2. *unkind*] unnatural (because he has refused to help his own sister); cf. ll.
15 and 49 below.

And please my father well, and then a fig
For all my uncle's friendship here in France.   5
I warrant you, I'll win his highness quickly;
'A loves me better than a thousand Spencers.

Isabella. Ah boy, thou art deceived at least in this,
To think that we can yet be tuned together.
No, no, we jar too far. Unkind Valois!   10
Unhappy Isabel, when France rejects!
Whither, O whither dost thou bend thy steps?

Enter SIR JOHN OF HAINAULT.

Sir John. Madam, what cheer?
Isabella.   Ah, good Sir John of Hainault,
Never so cheerless, nor so far distressed.
Sir John. I hear, sweet lady, of the king's unkindness,   15
But droop not, madam; noble minds contemn
Despair. Will your grace with me to Hainault,
And there stay time's advantage with your son?
How say you, my lord, will you go with your friends,
And shake off all our fortunes equally?   20

---

12. Whither, O whither] *Q4;* Whether, O whether *Q1–3.*   12. dost] *Q*
(doost), *Dodsley*[1]; must *Dyce*[1] *(conj.);* dar'st *Collier MS., Wagner (conj.).*
20. shake off all] *Q1–2, Q4;* shake of all *Q3;* share of all *Brooke, Greg
(conj.), Pendry–Maxwell (conj.);* share with us *Broughton, Broughton MS.
(conj.).*

---

4. *a fig*] A reference to the obscene and insulting gesture of thrusting the
thumb between two fingers and the expression 'to give a fig.'

7. *'A loves*] He loves.

10. *Valois*] See note on II.ii.171.

11. *Unhappy*] See note on II.v.108.

12.1. SIR JOHN OF HAINAULT] Younger brother of Count William of
Hainault and uncle to Philippa, the bride and future queen of Prince Edward.

15. *the king's*] i.e., Charles IV's.

16. *contemn*] despise.

17. *with me to Hainault*] In Flanders. Holinshed (p. 337) provides the
authority for the queen's alliance with Sir John; see Appendix B, no. 31.

18. *stay time's advantage*] Cf. *2 Troublesome Reign:* 'follow tymes advantage' (vii; l. 976). See note on IV.i.10.

20. i.e., cast off the hopes of French support that we both shared.
Brooke's emendation ('share of') is unnecessary; Charlton–Waller point
out that Hainault was sacrificing friendship with the French by sheltering
Isabella.

Prince Edward. So pleaseth the queen, my mother, me it
       likes.
    The King of England, nor the court of France
    Shall have me from my gracious mother's side,
    Till I be strong enough to break a staff,
    And then have at the proudest Spencer's head.   25
Sir John. Well said, my lord.
Isabella. O, my sweet heart, how do I moan thy wrongs,
    Yet triumph in the hope of thee, my joy.
    Ah sweet Sir John, even to the utmost verge
    Of Europe, or the shore of Tanaïs,   30
    Will we with thee; to Hainault—so we will.
    The marquis is a noble gentleman;
    His grace, I dare presume, will welcome me.
    But who are these?

    Enter Edmund [Earl *of* KENT] *and* MORTIMER [JUNIOR].

Kent.   Madam, long may you live
    Much happier than your friends in England do.   35
Isabella. Lord Edmund and Lord Mortimer alive!

---

23. have] *Q* (haue); heave *Broughton, Broughton MS. (conj.).*   31. thee;]
Fleay (subst.) (thee:), *McLaughlin (subst.)* (thee!), *Briggs;* thee *Q1–4.*
31. Hainault—so] *Oxberry (subst.); Henolt,* so *Q;* Hainault?—so *McLaughlin,*
Briggs (subst.); Hainault!—so *Brooke–Paradise.*

---

   21. i.e., if the plan pleases the queen, it is also pleasing to me (an archaic
impersonal contruction; see Abbott 297).

   23. *have me*] i.e., move me.

   24. *break a staff*] Technically this phrase refers to the medieval custom of
fighting duels with quarter-staves. Millar Maclure, however, may be correct
(because of the associations with chivalry) to gloss it in his manuscript notes
as 'fight with a lance'.

   25. *proudest*] exceedingly proud (the superlative used in an absolute sense;
Abbott 8).

   30. *Tanaïs*] the Latin name of the river Don, which, according to Elizabethans, marked the boundary between Europe and Asia; cf. Drayton, *Poly-
Olbion:* '*Europe* and *Asia* keep on *Tanais* either side' (XV, 349; *Works,* IV,
309).

   32. *marquis*] i.e., the Count of Hainault, brother of Sir John; Holinshed
refers to him as 'the earle of Heinault' (p. 337).

   36. *alive*] Isabella's surprise applies probably to Mortimer alone; cf. the
lines that immediately follow. Mortimer had twice been condemned to death
and twice reprieved before his escape, although the condemnations do not

Welcome to France. [*To* MORTIMER JUNIOR] The news
    was here, my lord,
That you were dead, or very near your death.
Mortimer Junior. Lady, the last was truest of the twain;
    But Mortimer, reserved for better hap,   40
    Hath shaken off the thraldom of the Tower,
    [*To* PRINCE EDWARD] And lives t'advance your standard,
        good my lord.
Prince Edward. How mean you, an the king my father lives?
    No, my lord Mortimer, not I, I trow.
Isabella. 'Not,' son! Why 'not'? I would it were no worse.   45
    But gentle lords, friendless we are in France.
Mortimer Junior. Monsieur le Grand, a noble friend of yours,
    Told us at our arrival all the news—
    How hard the nobles, how unkind the king

---

37. *To* MORTIMER JUNIOR] *This ed.; not in Q.*   42. *To* PRINCE EDWARD] *This
ed.; not in Q.*   42. t'advance] *Q1–2* (t'aduance); to aduance *Q3–4.*
43. you,] *Q1–4, Dodsley¹;* you *Cunningham, Pinkerton, Kirschbaum;* you?
Fleay, Bullen, Ellis.   43. an] *Cunningham;* and *Q1–4.*   43. lives?] *Q1–4,
Dodsley¹;* lives! *Cunningham, Wagner, Fleay.*   44. not I] *Q1–4;* not so
Broughton MS. (conj.).   45. 'Not,' son! Why 'not'?] *Kirschbaum (subst.)*
(*Not*, son? Why *not*?); Not sonne, why not? *Q;* Not, son?—why not? *Scott.*

appear in Marlowe's sources; the queen, however, has no reason at this point
to suppose that Kent has perished.

40. *better hap*] i.e., better fortune.

43. *an*] if. Q's 'and' (= 'an'?) is ambiguous, but the general sense is clear:
Prince Edward questions how he can legitimately allow his own standard to
be advanced while his father remains king. Marlowe is careful not to impugn
the political orthodoxy of the future Edward III, who at the end of the play
will determine the punishments of Mortimer Junior and Isabella for their
treasonous insurrection.

44. *not I*] Broughton's suggested emendation ('not so') is unnecessary;
the prince's words represent an abrupt ellipsis of 'I shall not advance my
standard' (see preceding note).

I trow] See note on III.ii.23. Here the expression is used intensively with
the force of 'indeed' or 'surely.'

45. *would . . . worse*] i.e., would that the prince's refusal to advance his
standard were the only impediment to our success (implying that the want of
friends is a more serious obstacle).

47. *Monsieur le Grand*] This name is aparently Marlowe's invention;
Holinshed reports that Mortimer 'was receiued [in France] by a lord of
Picardie, named monsier Iohn de Fieules, who had faire lands in England'
(p. 334).

49. *king*] i.e., of France; cf. l. 2 above.

   Hath showed himself. But, madam, right makes room   50
   Where weapons want; and though a many friends
   Are made away (as Warwick, Lancaster,
   And others of our party and faction),
   Yet have we friends, assure your grace, in England
   Would cast up caps and clap their hands for joy   55
   To see us there, appointed for our foes.
Kent. Would all were well and Edward well reclaimed,
   For England's honour, peace, and quietness.
Mortimer Junior. But by the sword, my lord, it must be
     deserved;
   The king will ne'er forsake his flatterers.   60
Sir John. My lords of England, sith the ungentle King
   Of France refuseth to give aid of arms
   To this distressèd queen his sister here,
   Go you with her to Hainault. Doubt ye not,
   We will find comfort, money, men, and friends   65
   Ere long, to bid the English king a base.

---

51. want] *Q1–4*; won't *Dodsley*[1]; wont *Oxberry*.   51. a] *Q*; so *Dodsley*[1].
53. party] *Q1–3* (partie), *Q4*, *Dodsley*[1]; part *Dyce*[1], *Fleay (conj.)*.   53.
faction] *Q*; our faction *Broughton, Broughton MS. (conj.).*   56. there,]
Dodsley[1]; there *Q*, *Q3–4*; their *Q2*.   59. deserved] *Q* (deseru'd); earn'd
Broughton, Broughton MS.   61. the] *Q1–4*; th' *Dodsley*[1].   62. France] *Q*
(Fraunce) *(Zürich copy)*; Fraunce, *Q (Cassel copy)*.   66. a base] *Q1–3*;
abase *Q4*.

---

   50. *makes room*] makes way.
   51. *want*] are wanting.
   a many] many (a common Elizabethan substantive, usually followed by the
partitive genitive 'of'; see Abbott 87).
   52. *made away*] See note on II.ii.235.
   Warwick] See note on III.ii.53.
   53. *faction*] Broughton's regularization of the metre ('our faction') is superfluous.
   56. *appointed*] made ready (i.e., armed, fitted out for battle).
   57. *reclaimed*] See note on I.i.182.
   59. *deserved*] earned. Broughton's emendation ('earn'd') has nothing but
regularization of the metre to commend it.
   61. *sith*] since.
   64. *Doubt*] Fear; cf. IV.vii.1.
   66. *bid . . . a base*] To 'bid a base' means to challenge one's opponent to
risk being taken prisoner. The phrase comes from the children's game,
prisoner's base, in which players are touched as they run from their 'base' or
'home' to that of the other side and so are captured. Briggs cites Peele,
Edward I: 'So shall I bid John Baliol bace from thee' (xii; l. 1998). Merchant
sees a pun on *abase*.

How say, young prince? What think you of the match?
Prince Edward. I think King Edward will outrun us all.
Isabella. Nay, son, not so; and you must not discourage
    Your friends that are so forward in your aid.   70
Kent. Sir John of Hainault, pardon us, I pray;
    These comforts that you give our woeful queen
    Bind us in kindness all at your command.
Isabella. Yea, gentle brother, and the God of heaven
    Prosper your happy motion, good Sir John.   75
Mortimer Junior. This noble gentleman, forward in arms,
    Was born, I see, to be our anchor-hold.
    Sir John of Hainault, be it thy renown
    That England's queen and nobles in distress
    Have been by thee restored and comforted.   80
Sir John. Madam, along, [*to* PRINCE EDWARD] and you, my
    lord, with me,
    That England's peers may Hainault's welcome see.

                                            [*Exeunt.*]

[SCENE iii]

Enter [EDWARD] *the* King, [ARUNDEL], *the two* SPENCERS
[JUNIOR *and* SENIOR], *with others.*

Edward. Thus after many threats of wrathful war,
    Triumpheth England's Edward with his friends;

---

67. How say] *Q1–4;* How say'st *Dyce¹;* Now say *Dyce¹ (conj.), Cunningham.*
67. young] *Q;* you, *Broughton, Oxberry.*   67. think you] *Q1–2* (thinke
you) *Q4;* thinke *Q3.*   67. match] *Q;* march *Dodsley¹.*   81. *To* PRINCE
EDWARD] *This ed.; not in Q.*   81. lord] *Q1–4;* lords *Dyce¹.*   82.1. Exeunt]
Dodsley¹; not in Q.   Heading. Scene iii] *Broughton; not in Q.*   0.1. ARUNDEL]
Broughton; Matr. Q1–3, Dodsley¹; Matreuis Q4.

---

67. *How say*] i.e., how say you?
   match] game (continuing the metaphor of prisoner's base from the preceding line).
   74. *brother*] i.e., brother-in-law.
   75. *motion*] proposal; Briggs cites Kyd, *Spanish Tragedy:* 'I'll make the
motion to my sovereign liege, / And work it if my counsel may prevail'
(II.iii.22–23).
   81. *lord*] Considering other confusions of singular and plural in this
text, Dyce's emendation has its attraction; but here Sir John seems to be
addressing the two individuals with whom he has become most closely
associated—Isabella and Prince Edward.

And triumph Edward with his friends uncontrolled.
[*To* SPENCER JUNIOR] My lord of Gloucester, do you hear
    the news?
Spencer Junior. What news, my lord?   5
Edward. Why man, they say there is great execution
Done through the realm. My lord of Arundel,
You have the note, have you not?
Arundel. From the lieutenant of the Tower, my lord.
Edward. I pray let us see it.
    [*He takes the note from* ARUNDEL, *then hands it to* SPENCER JUNIOR.]
                    What have we there?   10
Read it, Spencer.
                    SPENCER [JUNIOR] *reads their names.*
[*Spencer Junior.* 'The Lord William Tuchet, the Lord
William Fitzwilliam, the Lord Warren de Lisle, the Lord
Henry Bradborne, and the Lord William Chenie, barons,
with John Page, an esquire, were drawn and hanged at   15
Pomfret.

    'And then shortly after, Roger Lord Clifford, John
Lord Mowbray, and Sir Gosein d'Eevill, barons, were
drawn and hanged at York.

---

3. with his friends] *Q;* with friends *Cunningham;* henceforth *Broughton,
Broughton MS. (conj.).*   4. *To* SPENCER JUNIOR] *This ed.; not in Q.*
9. *Arundel*] *Broughton; Matr. Q1–2; Mat. Q3–4.*   10–11. I pray . . .
Spencer.] *Q (two lines); one line in Fleay.*   10. *He takes . . .* ARUNDEL]
Dyce¹; not in Q.   10. *then . . .* SPENCER JUNIOR] *Dyce¹ (subst., after line 11);
not in Q.*   12–32. *Spencer Junior.* 'The Lord William . . . and others.']
Kirschbaum (added from Holinshed); not in Q.   13. Fitzwilliam] *Merchant
(extract from Holinshed);* fitz William *Holinshed (edd. 1577, 1587), Kirschbaum.*   16. Pomfret.] *Kirschbaum (extract from Holinshed);* Pomfret afore-
saide. *Holinshed (edd. 1577, 1587).*

---

3. *triumph Edward*] i.e., may Edward triumph (optative subjunctive).
  uncontrolled] As Tancock observes, this word modifies 'Edward,' not
'friends.'
  4. *lord of Gloucester*] See note on III.i.146.
  8. *note*] official report.
  11.1–32. *reads . . . and others*] Since Q supplies no list of those executed
for Spencer to read aloud, I follow Kirschbaum by inserting in brackets the
list as given in Holinshed (p. 331) that Marlowe almost certainly had in
mind. Merchant, who stops short of adding this excerpt to his text proper,
nevertheless reprints it in a 'Note on the Text' (pp. xxvii–xxviii) and suggests that it be used in production.
  15. *drawn*] i.e., drawn on a hurdle or sledge to the place of execution.

'At Bristol in like manner were executed Sir Henry de   20
Willington and Sir Henry Montford, baronets.

'And at Gloucester, the Lord John Gifford and Sir
William Elmebridge, knight.

'And at London, the Lord Henry Teies, baron.

'At Winchelsea, Sir Thomas Culpepper, knight.   25

'At Windsor, the Lord Francis de Aldham, baron.

'And at Canterbury, the Lord Bartholomew de Badelismere and the Lord Bartholomew de Ashbornham, barons.

'Also at Cardiff, in Wales, Sir William Fleming,
knight, was executed.   30

'Divers were executed in their counties, as Sir Thomas
Mandit and others.']

Edward. Why so. They barked apace a month ago;
Now, on my life, they'll neither bark nor bite.
Now, sirs, the news from France; Gloucester, I trow   35
The lords of France love England's gold so well
As Isabella gets no aid from thence.
What now remains? Have you proclaimed, my lord,
Reward for them can bring in Mortimer?

---

20. At Bristol] *This ed. (extract from Holinshed);* And at Bristow *Holinshed
(ed. 1577);* At Bristow *Holinshed (ed. 1587), Kirschbaum.*   20. Sir Henry]
Holinshed (ed. 1587), Kirschbaum; Henry *Holinshed (ed. 1577).*   31. coun-
ties] *Kirschbaum (extract from Holinshed);* countreys *Holinshed (ed. 1577);*
countries *Holinshed (ed. 1587).*   33. Edward] *Kirschbaum; not in Q.*
33. apace] *Q2–4;* a pace *Q.*   33. a month] *Q1–2;* not long *Q3–4, Oxberry.*
37. Isabella] *Dyce¹;* Isabell *Q1–4, Dodsley¹* (Isabel).   37. gets] *Q;* will get
Broughton, Broughton MS. (conj.).   37. no] *Q;* no more *Fleay (conj.).*

27–28. *Bartholomew de Badelismere*] See Introduction, p. 55.

33. *They barked apace*] either (1) they barked rapidly like eager dogs, i.e.,
made threatening noises, or (2) they embarked swiftly (upon their treasons).
If Edward intends the second meaning here, he puns wittily on the first in
the following line.

34. *neither bark nor bite*] Alluding to the proverb 'Great barkers are no
biters,' or 'The greatest barkers are not the sorest biters' (Tilley B85–B86).

35. *I trow*] See notes on III.ii.23 and IV.ii.44.

36. *love . . . well*] See note on III.ii.81.

39. Holinshed writes, 'whosoeuer could bring the head or dead corps of
the lord Mortimer of Wigmore, should haue for his labour a thousand marks'
(p. 338). Briggs points out, however, that this proclamation was issued after
the queen and Mortimer had returned with their forces to England.

Spencer Junior. My lord, we have; and if he be in England,   40
    'A will be had ere long, I doubt it not.
Edward. If, dost thou say? Spencer, as true as death,
    He is in England's ground; our port-masters
    Are not so careless of their king's command.

Enter a Post.

    How now, what news with thee? From whence come
      these?   45
Post. Letters, my lord, and tidings forth of France
    To you, my lord of Gloucester, from Levune.
           [He gives letters to SPENCER JUNIOR.]
Edward. Read.
Spencer Junior (reads the letter). 'My duty to your honour
    premised, *et cetera*, I have, according to instructions in   50
    that behalf, dealt with the King of France his lords, and
    effected that the queen, all discontented and discom-

44.1. Post] *Q (Poaste); Messenger Broughton.*   46. Post] *Q1–4 (subst.);*
Messen. Broughton, Oxberry (subst.).   47, 60. Levune] *Dyce*[1]*; Lewne Q1–4;*
Lewen Dodsley[1]*; Lejeune Broughton; Lecune Robinson.*   47.1. *He gives . . .*
SPENCER JUNIOR] *Kirschbaum (subst.) (Gives letter to Younger Spencer); not
in Q.*   49. *Spencer Junior (reads the letter).] Q (Spencer reades the letter.)
(centred as a stage direction); Spencer reads. Broughton; reading Dyce*[1]*.*
49. *letter] Q1–2, Dodsley*[1]*; letters Q3–4, Dodsley*[2]*.*   50. premised] *Q2
(praemised), Q4, Dodsley*[1]*; promised Q; proemissed Q3.*   50. *et cetera] This
ed.; &c. Q.*   51. his] *Q; and his Broughton.*   52. effected] *Q; affected
Dodsley*[2]*.*

---

41. *'A will be had*] he will be captured.
42. *true*] certain, sure (a variant of the proverb 'as sure as death'; Tilley
D136).
44. Probably suggested by Holinshed's report that 'This escape of the lord
Mortimer greatlie troubled the king, so that immediatlie vpon the first news,
he wrote to all the shiriffes of the realme, that if he chanced to come within
their roomes, they should cause hue and crie to be raised, so as he might be
staied and arrested' (p. 334).
46. *Letters*] Historically, Walter Stapleton, Bishop of Exeter, brought
information concerning Isabella and her party to Edward II in 1326. According to Holinshed, the bishop, 'which hitherto had remained with the
queene in France, stale [stole] now from hir, and got ouer into England,
opening to the king all the counsell and whole mind of the queene' (p. 337).
50. *premised*] Q2's correction of Q ('promised'), adopted by nearly all
editors, is required by the sense: 'My duty to your honour being a premise
(i.e., of what I am about to report)'; Marlowe uses an absolute construction.

forted, is gone. Whither? If you ask, with Sir John of
Hainault, brother to the marquis, into Flanders. With
them are gone Lord Edmund and the Lord Mortimer,   55
having in their company divers of your nation, and
others; and as constant report goeth, they intend to give
King Edward battle in England sooner than he can look
for them. This is all the news of import.
                   Your honour's in all service, Levune.'   60
Edward. Ah, villains, hath that Mortimer escaped?
With him is Edmund gone associate?
And will Sir John of Hainault lead the round?
Welcome, a God's name, madam, and your son;
England shall welcome you and all your rout.   65
Gallop apace bright Phoebus through the sky,
And dusky night, in rusty iron car,
Between you both shorten the time, I pray,
That I may see that most desirèd day
When we may meet these traitors in the field.   70
Ah, nothing grieves me but my little boy
Is thus misled to countenance their ills.

---

64. a God's] *Q* (a Gods); o'God's *Broughton;* a'God's *Dyce*[1].   65. rout]
Dodsley[1]; route *Q1–4.*

---

57. *constant*] i.e., reliable.

59. *import*] importance; cf. *1H6*: 'some petty towns of no import' (1.i.91).

61. *escaped*] i.e., from England. Edward already knows about Mortimer's
escape from the Tower (cf. ll. 38–39 above).

63. *lead the round*] lead the dance.

64. *a*] in.

65. *rout*] band of followers, group (a non-pejorative use here; cf. *2 Tamburlaine*: 'See ye this rout, and know ye this same king?' [III.v.153]).

66. *Gallop apace*] For Shakespeare's indebtedness to this speech in *Rom.*,
III.ii.1–2, see Introduction, pp. 19, 73. See also note on v.i.66.

67. *night . . . car*] Briggs compares Spenser, *Faerie Queene*: 'Then to her
yron wagon she [Night] betakes' (1.v.28); also *1 Tamburlaine*: 'Let ugly
darkness with her rusty coach' (v.i.294).

71. *my little boy*] Cf. 'your little son' (III.i.70 and note). Prince Edward was
historically a year older (fourteen) at this point than in the earlier reference,
and Marlowe portrays the king, perhaps as a means of gradually increasing
sympathy towards him, as now more emotionally attached to the boy than
before.

Come, friends, to Bristol, there to make us strong;
And, winds, as equal be to bring them in
As you injurious were to bear them forth.   75

[*Exeunt.*]

[SCENE iv]

Enter [ISABELLA] *the* Queen, her son [PRINCE EDWARD],
Edmund [Earl *of* KENT], MORTIMER [JUNIOR], *and* SIR JOHN
[OF HAINAULT, *with* Soldiers].

Isabella. Now lords, our loving friends and countrymen,
Welcome to England all; with prosperous winds
Our kindest friends in Belgia have we left,
To cope with friends at home—a heavy case,

73. Bristol] *Dodsley*¹; Bristow *Q1–4*.   75.1. *Exeunt*] *Dodsley*¹; *not in Q*.
Heading. Scene iv] *Broughton; not in Q*.   0.2. Earl *of* KENT] *Broughton
(subst.)* (Kent), *Oxberry; not in Q*.   0.3. *with* Soldiers] *Kirschbaum (subst.);
not in Q*.   2. all;] *Broughton, Oxberry;* all *Q1–4;* all, *Dodsley*¹.   2. winds]
Oxberry; windes, *Q1–4, Dodsley*¹ (winds,); winds *Scott* (winds;); winds!
*Dyce*¹; winds. *Briggs.*   3. Belgia] *Q;* Belgium *Broughton.*

---

73. *Bristol*] Again Marlowe simplifies and compresses: according to Holinshed, Edward 'departed towards the marches of Wales, there to raise an
armie against the queene' (p. 338), only after Isabella's forces had established
themselves in England and the king found it strategically impossible to
defend London; stopping first at Bristol, which he left in the keeping of
Spencer Senior, 'he sailed over into Wales' with Spencer Junior, Baldock,
and Arundel (pp. 338–339). Marlowe passes over the chaotic events in
London at the time of Edward II's withdrawal from the capitol. For the
fuller context, see Appendix B, no. 32; also Introduction, p. 56.

74. *equal*] able. Marlowe represents Edward as anticipating the invasion of
Mortimer and the queen whereas, historically, they had already arrived;
see preceding note. For the structural function of the wind imagery, see
Introduction, pp. 72–73, 75.

IV.iv.2. *Welcome to England*] For Holinshed's detailed account of the
departure of Isabella's army from Hainault and arrival in England (p. 337),
see Appendix B, nos. 31, 32, 33.

3. *Belgia*] the Netherlands (from the Latin name *Gallia Belgica*).

4. *cope with*] encounter (without hostility). For this infrequent and obsolete sense of the word in the sixteenth century, Charlton–Waller cite
Shakespeare, *Luc.* (l. 99), *Ham.* (III.ii.54), and *W.T.* (IV.iv.424).

heavy case] sad state of affairs.

When force to force is knit and sword and glaive   5
In civil broils makes kin and countrymen
Slaughter themselves in others, and their sides
With their own weapons gored. But what's the help?
Misgoverned kings are cause of all this wrack;
And Edward, thou art one among them all,   10
Whose looseness hath betrayed thy land to spoil
And made the channels overflow with blood.
Of thine own people patron shouldst thou be,
But thou—
Mortimer Junior. Nay madam, if you be a warrior,
Ye must not grow so passionate in speeches.   15

---

5. glaive] *Q3-4* (glaue), *Broughton* (glave), *Oxberry*; gleaue *Q1-2*.
6. makes] *Q*; make *Q2-4*.   6. countrymen] *Q4* (countrimen), *Dodsley*[1],
Dodsley[3] (*subst.*) (country-men); country men *Q1-3*.   8. gored] *Q* (gorde);
gore *Dodsley*[1].   9. wrack] *Q1-4*; wreck *Dodsley*[1].   12. And] *Q;* Who
Robinson.   12. channels] *Q*; channell *Q2-4*, *Dodsley*[1] (channel).
12-13. blood. / Of . . . people] *Q2*, *Broughton* (*subst.*); blood, / Of . . . people
Q; blood / Of . . . people (people;); *Q3*, *Q4* (*subst.*).   13-14. Of . . .
thou—] *Dodsley*[2]; *one line in Q.*   15. Ye] *Q1-3*; You *Q4*.

---

5. *glaive*] lance; but in the sixteenth century the word came also to mean
'bill' and 'sword.'
7-8. *their . . . gored*] Briggs compares Marlowe's translation of Lucan:
'whose conquering swords their own breasts launch'd' (l. 3); cf. also the
scene in *3H6* (II.v) in which two pairs of fathers and sons emblematize the
self-destructiveness of civil war.
9. *Misgoverned kings*] Summing up the reign, Holinshed censures Edward
II for 'wanton misgouernance' (p. 342).
wrack] destruction, disaster (cf. II.ii.2). In the sixteenth and seventeenth
centuries this word got confused with and influenced by *wreck*, although the
two are etymologically separate. See note on l. 22 below.
11. *looseness*] See note on IV.i.7.
12. *channels*] See note on I.i.187.
12-13. *blood . . . patron*] Q2's punctuation clarifies that of Q, which is
ambiguous, a comma often being substituted for a full stop in Elizabethan
texts. Although some editors follow Q3, making 'Of thine own people'
modify 'blood,' this reading leaves 'patron' awkwardly and somewhat mean-
inglessly naked of a modifier.
15. *so . . . speeches*] Lunt notes the effective irony of Mortimer's interrup-
tion of the queen's 'high-flown and purposeless rhetoric' when he follows her
speech 'with his own scarcely less rhetorical speech-making.' The effect,
however, is to characterize Mortimer as a political pragmatist. For further
commentary on this exchange, see Introduction, pp. 73-74.

Lords, sith that we are by sufferance of heaven
Arrived and armèd in this prince's right,
Here for our country's cause swear we to him
All homage, fealty, and forwardness.
And for the open wrongs and injuries   20
Edward hath done to us, his queen, and land,
We come in arms to wreak it with the sword,
That England's queen in peace may repossess
Her dignities and honours, and withal
We may remove these flatterers from the king,   25
That havocs England's wealth and treasury.

---

16. Lords, sith . . . heaven] *Q (one line);* Lords, / Sith . . . heaven *Fleay.*
16. sith that] *Q;* since *Broughton;* sith *Dyce*[1] *(conj.), Cunningham.*   17.
armed] *Q2–4;* armde *Q.*   18. him] *Q (Zürich copy);* him, *(Cassel copy).*
22. wreak] *Oxberry;* wrecke *Q1–4, Dodsley*[1] [wreck]; reck *Broughton.*
22. sword] *Q2–3* (sworde), *Q4;* swords *Q.*   26. havocs] *Q1–4* (hauocks);
havock *Dodsley*[1].

---

16. *sith*] See note on IV.ii.61.
17. *this prince's*] i.e., young Prince Edward's.
19. *forwardness*] zeal, eagerness.
22. *wreak*] avenge (i.e. wreak vengeance). Oxberry's emendation is not
unreasonable; Q's 'wrecke' may be read as a variant spelling of *wreak* (see
O.E.D.). *Wreak, wreck,* and *wrack* tended to become confounded with each
other in the period; see note on l. 9 above. 'Wreck' (= destroy) suits ill with
the objective Mortimer envisions, namely that the queen 'in peace may
repossess / Her dignities and honours' (ll. 23–24). The idea of revenge may
come from Holinshed, who says that the queen sought to stir up rebellion
against Edward, 'wherby she might reuenge hir manifold iniuries' (p. 336).
   sword] Q's 'swords' (although retained by some editors) is awkwardly
unidiomatic; most (including Lunt, Kirschbaum, Gill, and Bowers) accept
the correction to the singular printed by the subsequent quartos. Bowers
thinks it likely that 'arms' (the plural earlier in the line) has 'contaminated'
the reading in Q.
   23. *repossess*] Holinshed notes that when Isabella and Prince Edward
delayed their return to England in defiance of Edward II's command, 'the
king caused to be seized into his hands, all such lands, as belonged either to
his sonne, or to his wife' (p. 337).
   26. *havocs*] i.e., creates havoc in. The *O.E.D.* cites two early uses of this
verb; see Sir Geoffrey Fenton, *Golden Epistles* (1577 ed.): 'a great Prince that
entereth into the lande of his enimie . . . to surmount and hauocke his enimie'
(p. 91); and Milton, *The Tenure of Kings and Magistrates* (1649 ed.): 'to
havock and turn upside-down whole Kingdoms of men' (p. 38). It is not
entirely clear whether 'flatterers' or 'king' is the subject of 'havocs'; see
Dodsley's emendation. Third person plural verbs ending in *s* are common in
Elizabethan English; see Abbott 333.

Sir John. Sound trumpets, my lord, and forward let us
  march;
  Edward will think we come to flatter him.
Kent. I would he never had been flattered more.
         [Trumpets sound. Exeunt.]

       [SCENE v]

[Alarums and excursions.] Enter [EDWARD] *the* King, BALDOCK,
 and SPENCER [JUNIOR] *(the son), flying about the stage.*

Spencer Junior. Fly, fly, my lord; the queen is over-strong,
  Her friends do multiply, and yours do fail.
  Shape we our course to Ireland, there to breathe.
Edward. What, was I born to fly and run away,
  And leave the Mortimers conquerors behind?   5
  Give me my horse, and let's r'enforce our troops,

29.1. *Trumpets sound]* Kirschbaum; not in Q. 29.1. *Exeunt]* Dodsley¹; not in
Q. *Heading.* Scene v] Broughton; not in Q. 0.1. *Alarums and excursions]*
Kirschbaum; not in Q. 0.2. *flying about the stage]* Q; confusedly Broughton.
1. over-strong] Q2–3 (ouerstrong), Q4; ouer strong Q. 6. and let's]
Q1–4; let's Dodsley¹; let us Fleay. 6. r'enforce] Q, Q2–4 (re'nforce);
reinforce Dodsley¹.

---

 wealth and treasury] Cf. IV.vi.52. For the possible indebtedness of this
detail to Stowe, see Introduction, p. 63.
 29. *flattered more]* Spoken with irony; Kent wishes that his brother had
never been flattered more than the hostile trumpets of his adversaries 'flatter'
him.
 IV.v.2. *Her ... multiply]* Holinshed writes, 'Immediatlie after that the
queene and hir sonne were come to land, it was woonder to see how fast the
people resorted vnto them . . .' (p. 337).
 3. *Ireland]* According to Holinshed, the king's plan, 'if there were no
remedie,' was that 'he might easilie escape ouer into Ireland, and get into
some mounteine-countrie, marish-ground, or other streict, where his enimies
should not come at him' (p. 339). See also note on IV.iii.73.
 5. *the Mortimers]* In the play Marlowe abandons the elder Mortimer as a
character after he is unhistorically captured by the Scots (see note on II.ii.
114). The historical Mortimer Senior had already died in the Tower on 3
August 1326 (see note on I.iv.361). Lunt suggests that the phrase refers to
the party supporting Mortimer Junior.
 6. *Give me my horse]* Conceivably a faint (and unconscious?) echo of the
most memorable line in *R3*: 'A horse, a horse! My kingdom for a horse!'
(V.iv.13). For Marlowe's probable indebtedness to this play, see Introduction, pp. 25–27.

And in this bed of honour die with fame.
Baldock. O no, my lord, this princely resolution
Fits not the time. Away! We are pursued.

[Exeunt.]

[SCENE vi]

[Enter] Edmund [Earl *of* KENT] *alone with a sword and target.*

Kent. This way he fled, but I am come too late.
Edward, alas, my heart relents for thee.
Proud traitor Mortimer, why dost thou chase
Thy lawful king, thy sovereign, with thy sword?
[Addressing himself] Vile wretch, and why hast thou, of all
    unkind,   5
Borne arms against thy brother and thy king?
Rain showers of vengeance on my cursèd head,
Thou God, to whom in justice it belongs
To punish this unnatural revolt.
Edward, this Mortimer aims at thy life;   10

---

7. honour] *Q* (honor) (*Zürich copy*), *Q2–4;* honors *Q* (*Cassel copy*).   9.1.
Exeunt] *Dodsley²; not in Q.   Heading.* Scene vi] *Broughton; (no heading;
continuation of IV.v) Robinson; not in Q.   0.1. Enter] Broughton, Oxberry;
not in Q.   0.1. alone with a sword and target] Q; not in Broughton.   2.
Edward,] Q (Zürich copy); Edward Q (Cassel copy).   5. Addressing himself]
This ed.; not in Q.   5. Vile] Dodsley¹; Vilde Q1–4   5. unkind] Q;
mankind Broughton.   7. my] Q; thy Cunningham.   7. head,] Dodsley¹;
head Q (Zürich copy); head. Q (Cassel copy).   8. God,] Q (Zürich copy);
God Q (Cassel copy).*

---

r'enforce] reinforce, i.e., re-encourage (ellided to accommodate the metre
and spelled to show the necessary pronunciation).
   7. *bed of honour*] Lunt compares *Tit.*: 'For two and twenty sons I never
wept, / Because they died in honor's lofty bed' (III.i.10–11).
   9. *Fits not the time*] Cf. *2 Troublesome Reign*: 'fit not the season' (ii; l. 214).
   IV.vi.0.1. *target*] shield.
   2. Tancock points out that history 'does not hint at any difference of
opinion between [Kent] and Mortimer at this time, so soon after he joined
the confederates. . . .' See also Introduction, p. 48.
   5. *unkind*] See note on IV.ii.2; also l. 9 below.
   6. *against . . . king*] A probable echo of *3H6*, v.i.85–88; see Introduction,
pp. 32–33.
   7. *vengeance . . . head*] An ironic anticipation of Kent's execution at v.iv.
105.1.

O fly him then! But, Edmund, calm this rage;
Dissemble or thou diest, for Mortimer
And Isabel do kiss while they conspire;
And yet she bears a face of love, forsooth.
Fie on that love that hatcheth death and hate.   15
Edmund, away! Bristol to Longshanks' blood
Is false; be not found single for suspect;
Proud Mortimer pries near into thy walks.

Enter [ISABELLA] *the* Queen, MORTIMER [JUNIOR], *the young* PRINCE
[EDWARD,] *and* SIR JOHN OF HAINAULT [*with* Soldiers].

Isabella. Successful battles gives the God of kings
To them that fight in right and fear his wrath.   20
Since then successfully we have prevailed,
Thanks be heaven's great architect and you.
Ere farther we proceed, my noble lords,
We here create our well belovèd son,
Of love and care unto his royal person,   25
Lord Warden of the realm; and sith the fates

16, 40, 45.1, 47. Bristol] *Dodsley²;* Bristow *Q1–4, Dodsley¹.*   16. Longshanks'] *Q* (Longshankes); Longshank's *Broughton.*   18.2. *with* Soldiers]
Kirschbaum; not in Q.   19. Successful] *Q* (Successfull), *Q4;* Succesfuls
Q2–3.   19. battles] *Q* (battells), *Brooke;* battel *Q2–3, Q4* (battell),
Dodsley² (battle).   21. successfully] *Q1–3* (succesfully); successiuely *Q4.*
22. Thanks] *Q* (Thankes); Thankt *Q2–3;* Thanked *Q4;* Thankèd *Dyce¹.*
22. heaven's] *Q* (heauens); the heaven's *Fleay (conj.).*   22. you.] *Dodsley¹;*
you, *Q1–4.*

---

12. *Dissemble*] See Introduction, pp. 74, 77.
16. *Bristol*] Again Marlowe departs from history; Holinshed (p. 339) says
that Kent led the attack on Bristol, then held by Spencer Senior, whom he
took captive on behalf of the queen; for the details, see Appendix B, no. 35.
Longshanks' blood] i.e., Edward I's son (see note on III.i.12).
17. *be . . . suspect*] i.e., be not found alone as this will lay you open to
suspicion. For *suspect* (= suspicion), cf. IV.vii.4.
19. *God of kings*] Cf. *1 Troublesome Reign:* 'Thus hath the God of Kings
with conquering arme / Dispearst the foes to true succession' (vi; ll. 1057–
1058).
22. *you*] i.e., you, my supporters. Or, possibly, the queen addresses Sir
John of Hainault, who has made the victory possible by raising troops.
25. *Of love and care*] i.e., out of love and care.
26. *Lord Warden*] Marlowe follows Holinshed (p. 339) here; see Appendix
B, no. 34.

Have made his father so infortunate,
Deal you, my lords, in this, my loving lords,
As to your wisdoms fittest seems in all.

Kent. Madam, without offence, if I may ask,   30
How will you deal with Edward in his fall?

Prince Edward. Tell me, good uncle, what Edward do you
      mean?

Kent. Nephew, your father—I dare not call him king.

Mortimer Junior. My lord of Kent, what needs these
      questions?

      'Tis not in her controlment, nor in ours;   35
      But as the realm and parliament shall please,
      So shall your brother be disposèd of.

      [*Aside to* ISABELLA] I like not this relenting mood in
      Edmund;
      Madam, 'tis good to look to him betimes.

Isabella. [*Aside to* MORTIMER JUNIOR] My lord, the Mayor of
      Bristol knows our mind?   40

Mortimer Junior. [*Aside*] Yea, madam, and they scape not
      easily

---

27. infortunate] *Q1–3;* vnfortunate *Q4.*   30–31. *Kent.* Madam . . . fall?]
Q, Q3–4; Q2 (text correct but preceded by the same two lines in error: Edm.
Madam . . . your deale . . . fall?).   34. needs] *Q* (needes); need *Broughton.*
38. *Aside to* ISABELLA] *Dodsley*[1] *(subst.); not in Q.*   40. *Aside to* MORTIMER
JUNIOR] *Oliphant (subst.); not in Q.*   40. mind?] *Briggs;* mind. *Q1–4.*
41. *Aside] Oliphant (subst.); not in Q.*   41. scape] *Q1–2, Q4;* scapt *Q3.*
41. easily] *Scott;* easilie, *Q, Dodsley*[1] (easily,); easily. *Gill*[1] *(misprint?).*

---

27. *infortunate*] a common variant of 'unfortunate' (cf. *Jn,* I.i.178; *2H6,*
IV.ix.18).

32. *what . . . mean?*] Gill notes that the prince gently reproves Kent for
failure to use his father's proper title; cf. *R2,* III.iii.7–8.

35. *controlment*] power; cf. I.iv.389.

ours] Is the increasingly overweening Mortimer perhaps already usurping
the royal plural here? His aside to Isabella makes his hypocrisy obvious, and
the later action dramatizes how quickly he establishes tyrannical power over
the captive king; see note on V.iv.101.

40. *Mayor of Bristol*] Holinshed does not actually mention the mayor,
reporting merely that Kent and his followers 'did their endeuour [of overpowering Bristol and capturing the senior Spencer] with such diligence, that
the townesmen, compounding to be saued harmlesse in bodie and goods,
deliuered the towne and castell vnto the queene, & to hir sonne the prince'
(p. 339). For the context, see Appendix B, no. 35.

That fled the field.

Isabella.   Baldock is with the king;
A goodly chancellor, is he not, my lord?

Sir John. So are the Spencers, the father and the son.

Kent. [*Aside, despairingly*] This, Edward, is the ruin of the
realm.   45

Enter RICE AP HOWELL *and the* Mayor *of* Bristol, *with* SPENCER
[SENIOR] (*the father*), [*prisoner, with* Attendants].

---

45. *Kent*] *Q1–4 (Edm.), Dodsley¹; Y. Mor. Oxberry, Dyce¹, Wagner, Tancock.*
45. *Aside, despairingly*] *Kirschbaum; To the Prince Fleay; not in Q.*   45.
This, Edward, is] *Q2–3 (subst.) (This Edward, is), Fleay; This Edward is Q,*
Q4, Dodsley¹.   45. *the realm*] *Q; thy realm Kirschbaum (conj.).*   45.1.
and the Mayor *of* Bristol] *Q; Dyce¹ prints the stage direction but suggests that*
perhaps the mayor should not appear.

---

43. *goodly chancellor*] Spoken with sarcasm, clearly. Cf. Holinshed: 'master
Robert Baldocke, a man euill beloued in the realme, was made lord chancellour of England' (p. 332) in 1322.

45. *Kent*] See textual notes for the disputed assignment and punctuation
of this speech. Oxberry, seconded independently by Dyce, reallocated this
line (given to '*Edm*' [= Edmund] in Q1–4) to Mortimer Junior in the belief
that the attitude expressed is inappropriate to the king's brother, who has
just repented his disloyalty. Tancock accepted the emendation, pointing out,
however, that earlier in the scene Kent had mentioned the necessity of
dissembling (l. 12). Briggs defends the quarto assignment on grounds that
Kent does indeed dissemble. Charlton–Waller also retain the speech for
Kent, but doubt whether an audience would recall the character's previous
statement about deception, thinking rather that spectators would prefer to
think of Edmund as a man who had deserted his brother out of noble motives
and was therefore speaking sincerely; they therefore attempt to sustain this
last interpretation by introducing commas ('This, Edward, is'). Fleay had
earlier suggested the same repunctuation but had read the speech as Kent's
aside to Prince Edward (the uncle thereby giving a lesson in politics to his
nephew). I adopt Kirschbaum's solution, retaining the commas (the second
of which in any case was introduced by Q2–3), but interpreting the speech as
a despairing apostrophe to King Edward heard only by the audience; Bowers
concurs. Charlton–Waller's assertion that 'There is no authority for the
commas in the early editions' is misleading.

45.1. RICE AP HOWELL] The *ap*, common in Welsh names, is a
patronymic (= son of). According to Holinshed, Rice ap Howell played no
part in Spencer Senior's arrest and execution (p. 339); he appears a few
paragraphs later in the narrative (p. 339) when the queen employs him in the
capture of her husband (see Appendix B, no. 34).

Mayor of Bristol] Since the mayor has no speaking part in this scene,
Dyce questioned his inclusion in Q's stage direction. Bowers speculates that
whoever marked up the manuscript in preparation for the copying out of a

Rice ap Howell. God save Queen Isabel and her princely son.
    [*Pointing to the* Mayor] Madam, the mayor and citizens of
        Bristol,
    In sign of love and duty to this presence,
    Present by me this traitor to the state—
    Spencer, the father to that wanton Spencer,   50
    That, like the lawless Catiline of Rome,
    Revelled in England's wealth and treasury.
Isabella. We thank you all.
Mortimer Junior.   Your loving care in this
    Deserveth princely favours and rewards.
    But where's the king and the other Spencer fled?   55
Rice ap Howell. Spencer the son, created Earl of Gloucester,
    Is with that smooth-tongued scholar Baldock gone,
    And shipped but late for Ireland with the king.

45.2. *prisoner, with* Attendants] *Dyce*[1]; *not in* Q.   47. *Pointing to the*
Mayor] *Kirschbaum (subst.); not in* Q.

---

promptbook might have added the mayor mistakenly because of references to
him in the adjacent dialogue. It is odd, perhaps, that neither Isabella nor
Mortimer recognizes the mayor as an individual, but the mayor's presence,
even as a mute, contributes the symbolic effect of popular approval to the
capture and imminent punishment of Spencer Senior and is therefore probably part of Marlowe's intention.

47. *mayor . . . Bristol*] See note on l. 40 above.

51. *the lawless Catiline*] Lucius Sergius Catilina (*d.* 62 B.C.), the Roman
nobleman whose famous conspiracy against the republic failed through the
opposition of Cicero and who was killed in battle. As most editors point out,
there is virtually no parallel between Catiline (who did not plunder the
Roman treasury) and the elder Spencer. Maclure (in his manuscript notes)
suspects that 'Marlowe wrote "Catiline" when he meant "Sejanus".' See note
on l. 71 below. Marlowe's use of classical allusion here is chiefly for stylistic
effect.

52. *wealth and treasury*] Marlowe repeats this phrase from IV.iv.26 (see
note above).

55. *where's*] where has (we should say 'where have').

56. *Earl of Gloucester*] See note on III.i.146.

58. *Ireland*] See note on IV.v.3. Edward and his party attempted to flee
to Ireland but failed. As Holinshed writes, 'The king with the earle of
Glocester, and the lord chancellor, taking the sea, meant to haue gone either
into the Ile of Lundaie, or else into Ireland, but being tossed with contrarie
winds for the space of a weeke togither, at length he landed in Glamorganshire' (p. 339).

Mortimer Junior. [*Aside*] Some whirlwind fetch them back, or
    sink them all!—
    They shall be started thence, I doubt it not.   60
Prince Edward. Shall I not see the king my father yet?
Kent. [*Aside*] Unhappy Edward, chased from England's
    bounds.
Sir John. Madam, what resteth? Why stand ye in a muse?
Isabella. I rue my lord's ill fortune, but, alas,
    Care of my country called me to this war.   65
Mortimer Junior. Madam, have done with care and sad
    complaint;
    Your king hath wronged your country and himself,
    And we must seek to right it as we may.
    Meanwhile, have hence this rebel to the block.
    [*To* SPENCER SENIOR, *sarcastically*] Your lordship cannot
    privilege your head!   70

---

59. *Aside*] *Robinson; not in Q.*   59. whirlwind] *Q3–4* (whirlewind),
Dodsley¹; whirle wind *Q1–2.*   60. shall be] *Q3–4;* shalbe *Q1–2.*   62.
Aside] *Dyce¹, not in Q.*   62. Unhappy] *Dodsley¹;* Vnhappies *Q1–4, Bullen*
(Unhappy's); Unhappy is *Fleay.*   63. ye] *Q1–4;* you *Dyce¹.*   69, 77.
Meanwhile] *Scott;* Meane while *Q1–4.*   70. *To* SPENCER SENIOR, *sarcas-
tically*] *Kirschbaum (subst.); not in Q.*   70. Your . . . head!] *Q; line not in
Q2–4.*

---

60. *started*] driven from hiding (a hunting term); see note on III.i.127.
61. *Shall . . . king*] Cf. II.vi.15; see Introduction, p. 74.
62. *Unhappy*] Q's 'Vnhappies' (= Unhappy is), though several editors
retain it, is somewhat unidiomatic. Bowers defends Dodsley's emendation on
the supposition that the possessive *'Englands'* later in the same line may have
contaminated the spelling of 'Vnhappie.' See note on II.v.108.
63. *resteth*] remains to be done. A common Elizabethan usage; cf. *3H6*:
'what resteth more / But that I seek occasion how to rise . . . ?' (I.ii.44).
ye] Dyce's emendation ('you'), adopted by many editors, is needless. *Ye* (=
thou) was often used as a singular; cf. *T.G.V*: *'Julia*. Will ye be gone?
Lucetta. That you may ruminate' (I.ii.49). See also note on I.iv.213.
in a muse] lost in abstraction, perplexed.
64. *I . . . fortune*] Isabella's hypocrisy at this point is probable; cf. Kent's
lines (12–15) above. But see Introduction, n. 98.
69. *to the block*] Spencer Senior 'was drawne foorth in his cote armor vnto
the common gallowes, and there hanged. His head was after cut off, and sent
to Winchester, whereof he was earle' (Holinshed, p. 339).
70. Either (1) the special prerogative granted to you in the past by the
king cannot now save your life (referring scathingly to the Spencers' former
exploitation of royal favour), or (2) your rank as a nobleman entitles you to
be spared hanging but not beheading. Since Holinshed reports that Spencer

Spencer Senior. Rebel is he that fights against his prince;
    So fought not they that fought in Edward's right.
Mortimer Junior. Take him away; he prates.

                       [Exit SPENCER SENIOR, *guarded.*]
                         You, Rice ap Howell,
    Shall do good service to her majesty,
    Being of countenance in your country here,   75
    To follow these rebellious runagates.
    We in meanwhile, madam, must take advice
    How Baldock, Spencer, and their complices
    May in their fall be followed to their end.

                                      Exeunt.

                    [SCENE vii]

    Enter the Abbot *[and]* Monks *[of Neath Abbey,* KING] EDWARD,
    SPENCER [JUNIOR], *and* BALDOCK, *[the latter three disguised].*

Abbot. Have you no doubt, my lord, have you no fear;
    As silent and as careful will we be
    To keep your royal person safe with us,

---

71. *Spencer Senior]* Broughton (*Spen. sen.*), Oxberry (*O. Spen.*); *Spen. pa.* Q.
71. *his]* Q; *the* Q2–4.   73.1. *Exit . . . guarded]* Dyce[1] (*subst.*) (*Exeunt
Attendants with E. Spenser); not in* Q.   79. *fall* Q; *flight* Collier MS.
79.1. *Exeunt.]* Scott; *Exeunt omnes.* Q.   Heading. *Scene vii]* Broughton;
Scene vi Robinson; *not in* Q.   0.1. *Monks]* Q (*Monkes*), Q3–4; *Monke* Q2.
0.1. *of Neath Abbey]* Merchant; *not in* Q.   0.2. *the latter three disguised]*
Dyce[1] (*subst.*); *disguised as monks* Bowers; *not in* Q.   2. *will we]* Q; *we will*
Q2–4.

Senior was in fact hanged (see preceding note), I suspect that the first
interpretation is the correct one.

    71. This expression of loyalty to the regime shows how inapposite is Rice
ap Howell's comparison of the elder Spencer to Catiline (IV.vi.51).

    75. *of countenance]* of recognized authority, influential, creditable. Charl-
ton–Waller cite *Ham.*: 'hath given countenance to his speech' (I.iii.114).

    76. *runagates]* runaways, vagabonds (a term of abuse that seems to have
got partly confused with *renegades* [= deserters, mutineers]); cf. *Dido*: 'And
must I rave thus for a runagate?' (V.i.265); *1 Tamburlaine*: 'Inhabited with
straggling runagates' (III.iii.57) and 'Injurious villains, thieves, runagates'
(III.iii.225).

    IV.vii.0.2. *disguised]* Cf. 'feignèd weeds' below (l. 97). Marlowe imagina-
tively constructs this entire scene from Holinshed's minimal account of Edward
II's flight and capture at Neath Abbey (p. 339); see Appendix B, no. 36.

Free from suspect and fell invasion
Of such as have your majesty in chase—   5
Yourself and those your chosen company—
As danger of this stormy time requires.
Edward. Father, thy face should harbour no deceit;
O hadst thou ever been a king, thy heart
Pierced deeply with sense of my distress,   10
Could not but take compassion of my state.
Stately and proud, in riches and in train,
Whilom I was, powerful and full of pomp;
But what is he whom rule and empery
Have not in life or death made miserable?   15
Come Spencer, come Baldock, come sit down by me;
Make trial now of that philosophy
That in our famous nurseries of arts
Thou sucked'st from Plato and from Aristotle.
Father, this life contemplative is heaven—   20

---

4. invasion] *Q* (inuasion) *(Zürich copy)*; inuasion, *Q* *(Cassel copy)*.   6.
Yourself . . . company] *Q; line not in Dodsley*[1], *Oxberry.*   6. Yourself]
Dodsley[2]; Your selfe *Q1–4*.   10. sense] *Q1–4* (sence), *Dyce*[1]; a sense
Dodsley[1].   13. was, powerful] *Q3, Dodsley*[1]; was powerful *Q1–2, Q4,
Keltie.*   14. what] *Q;* who *Wagner (conj.);* where *Wagner (conj.).*   14.
empery] *Q* (emperie); empiry *Merchant;* empire *Dodsley*[1].   16. come
Baldock] *Q1–4;* Baldock *Broughton.*   17. that philosophy] *Q1–2* (that
philosophie); philosophie *Q3;* thy Philosophie *Q4.*   19. sucked'st] *Q*
(suckedst), *Q2–4;* suck'st *Dodsley*[1]; suck'dst *Dyce*[1].

---

4. *suspect*] See note on IV.vi.17.
fell] cruel, fierce.
8. *thy . . . deceit*] Briggs cites Kyd, *Soliman and Perseda*: 'This face of thine
shuld harbour no deceit' (III.i.72); cf. 'The face is the index of the heart'
(Tilley F1). As often in Elizabethan usage, 'should' means 'would' here,
implying probability.
13. *Whilom*] Formerly, once.
14. *empery*] an earlier form of *empire*; Marlowe uses the word often.
18. *nurseries of arts*] i.e., the universities. Baldock had been educated at
Oxford; see note on II.ii.243.
19. *sucked'st*] Briggs cites the anonymous *First Part of Jeronimo* (1604):
'Hast thou worne gownes in the University, / Tost logick, suckt Philosophy . . . ?' (II.iii.7–8; *Works of Kyd*, p. 312).
20. *this life contemplative*] Referring to the standard medieval contrast
between the active and contemplative life. For the similar contemplative
motif in *3H6*, see Introduction, p. 32.

O that I might this life in quiet lead!
But we, alas, are chased; and you, my friends,
Your lives, and my dishonour they pursue.
Yet, gentle monks, for treasure, gold, nor fee,
Do you betray us and our company.   25
Monk. Your grace may sit secure, if none but we
Do wot of your abode.
Spencer Junior. Not one alive; but shrewdly I suspect
A gloomy fellow in a mead below;
'A gave a long look after us, my lord,   30
And all the land, I know, is up in arms—
Arms that pursue our lives with deadly hate.
Baldock. We were embarked for Ireland, wretched we,
With awkward winds and sore tempests driven,
To fall on shore and here to pine in fear   35
Of Mortimer and his confederates.
Edward. Mortimer! Who talks of Mortimer?

---

26. *Monk*] *Oxberry; Monks Q1–4; First Monk Broughton.*   26–27. Your . . .
abode.] *Dyce*[1]*; one line in Q.*   33. embarked] *Scott;* imbarkt *Q, Dodsley*[1]
(imbark'd).   34. sore] *Q1–3;* with sore *Q4;* surly *Dodsley*[1]*;* sorest *Broughton.*   36. confederates] *Q, Q3–4;* confiderates *Q2.*   37–38. Mortimer! . . . Mortimer,] *Q; one line in Broughton.*   37. Who talks . . .
Mortimer?] *Q; not in Broughton.*

---

25. *Do you*] i.e., do you not (the negative appearing in the 'nor' of the previous line).

27. *wot*] See note on I.iv.377.

28. *Not one alive*] i.e., not a single one of your monastery. Spencer is distinguishing between the loyal monks and the 'gloomy fellow' of the following line.

29. *gloomy*] giving out dark and sullen looks (as opposed to being himself downcast). Lunt points out that the *O.E.D.* cites this instance as the earliest recorded application of the word to a person; Marlowe, however, uses it for a god in *Dido*: 'Since gloomy Aeolus doth cease to frown' (IV.i.27). For the 'gloomy fellow' as an emblem of death, see Introduction, pp. 60, 75.

mead] meadow.

30. *long*] scrutinizing (and therefore suspicious).

33. *embarked for Ireland*] See note on IV.vi.58.

34. *awkward winds*] Jane Lee compares *The Contention*: 'nigh wrackt upon the sea, / And thrise by aukward winds driven back from Englands bounds' (ed. Farjeon, p. 702); see *New Shakspere Society's Transactions*, Ser. I, no. 4 (1875–76), 244.

sore] pronounced as a disyllable; the smoothing of the metre in Q4 and subsequent editions is superfluous.

Who wounds me with the name of Mortimer,
That bloody man? [*Kneeling*] Good father, on thy lap
Lay I this head, laden with mickle care.   40
O might I never open these eyes again,
Never again lift up this drooping head,
O never more lift up this dying heart!
Spencer Junior. Look up, my lord. Baldock, this drowsiness
Betides no good. Here even we are betrayed!   45

Enter, with Welsh hooks, RICE AP HOWELL [*and* Soldiers], *a* Mower,
and the Earl *of* LEICESTER. [*They remain temporarily upstage.*]

---

39. *Kneeling*] *Kirschbaum (subst.); not in Q.*   41. open] *Q1–2;* ope *Q3–4,*
Fleay (conj.); op'n *Fleay (conj.).*   44. *Spencer Junior*] *Q (Spen. son), Oxberry*
(Y. Spen.); Spen. sen. *Dodsley¹⁻².*   45. Here even] *Q1–4;* even here
Broughton, Oxberry.   45. Here . . . betrayed!] *Q; Oliphant (following stage
direction at line 45.1).*   45.1. RICE AP HOWELL] *Q2–4; Rice up Howell Q.*
45.1. *and* Soldiers] *This ed.; not in Q.*   45.1. Mower] *Q;* Peasant *Broughton.*   45.2. *of* LEICESTER] *Q, Q3–4;* Leicester *Q2.*   45.2. *They . . .
upstage.*] *This ed.; not in Q.*

---

40. *mickle*] much (a northern form, still used in Scotland); cf. *Dido*: 'And
wrought him mickle woe' (III.ii.41).

41–43. Cf. v.i.110. For the probable indebtedness to Grafton here, see
Introduction, p. 65. Cf. also *2 Troublesome Reign*: 'revive thy dying heart'
(vii; l. 972).

44–45. *this . . . good*] Drowsiness was traditionally considered to be an evil
omen; cf. *Arden of Faversham*: 'I am so heavy that I can scarce go. / This
drowsiness in me bodes little good' (v.16–17); and John Melton, *Astrologaster*
(1620): 'if a man be drowie, it is a signe of ill lucke' (p. 46). See also *Tit.,*
II.iii.195–197.

45.1. *Welsh hooks*] There has been vigorous debate about the nature of
these implements—whether they are (1) military partisans or pikes with cross
pieces below their blades or (2) bill-hooks, i.e., agricultural tools with hooked
ends for mowing or cutting brush. The *O.E.D.* suggests that the word bore
both senses. Charlton–Waller assume that weapons are intended, citing
several instances from the drama including Falstaff's reference to Glendower:
'he of Wales that . . . swore the devil his true liegeman upon the cross of a
Welsh hook' (*1H4*, II.iv.333–335), and Peele, *Edward I*: 'scowre the marches
with your Welshmens hookes' (ii; l. 616). Such weapons would be appropriate to the soldiers who presumably accompany Leicester, the arresting officer. Michael J. Warren, however, correctly notes that it is unusual, even
pointless, to specify military weapons in such contexts and argues, convincingly in my view, that the 'Welsh hooks' are probably farm implements
carried by the Mower and possibly others of the party; see 'Welsh Hooks in
Edward II,' *N.&Q.*, N.S. 25 (1978), 109–110. The Welsh hooks, particu-

Mower. [*To* RICE AP HOWELL, *pointing*] Upon my life, those be
    the men ye seek.
Rice ap Howell. Fellow, enough. [*To* LEICESTER] My lord,
    I pray be short;
    A fair commission warrants what we do.
Leicester. [*Aside, with irony*] The queen's commission, urged
    by Mortimer!
    What cannot gallant Mortimer with the queen?   50
    Alas, see where he sits and hopes unseen
    T'escape their hands that seek to reave his life.
    Too true it is: *quem dies vidit veniens superbum,*
    Hunc dies vidit fugiens iacentem.
    But Leicester, leave to grow so passionate.—   55

46, 116. *Mower*] Q; *Peasant Broughton.*   46. *To* RICE AP HOWELL] *This ed.;*
not in Q.   46. *pointing*] *Kirschbaum* (*subst.*); *not in* Q.   46. *those*] Q; *these*
Q2–4.   47. *To* LEICESTER] *Kirschbaum; not in* Q.   49. *Aside*] *Oliphant*
(*subst.*); *Kirschbaum* (*after line 50*); *not in* Q.   49. *with irony*] *This ed.; not in*
Q.   50. *gallant* Mortimer] Q1–2, *Dodsley*[1]; *Mortimer* Q3–4, *Dodsley*[2].
50. *with*] Q1–3; *doe with* Q4, *Broughton* (do with), *Oxberry.*   52. *T'escape*]
Q; *To 'scape Broughton; To escape Cunningham.*

---

larly if they are scythelike tools, would give visual point to the symbolism of
the 'gloomy fellow' mentioned earlier (l. 29) and add effectively to our sense
of the king's vulnerability by introducing a note of roughness—even of rustic
savagery—to the moment of his capture (cf. 'rip up this panting breast' at l.
66 below). Possibly also Marlowe recalled Fleming's moralistic interpolation
in Holinshed condemning Edward's rebellious subjects, who 'should haue
beene the pillers of the kings estate, and not the hooked engins to pull him
downe from his throne' (p. 341).

    45.2. LEICESTER] Henry, Earl of Leicester, the younger brother of
Lancaster and, like him, bitterly opposed to the Spencers; he seems, however, to have been more humane than his brother (cf. v.i.7). Later in 1330 he
was instrumental in bringing about Mortimer's fall (cf. his hostile aside at ll.
49–50 below).

    46. *Mower*] The 'gloomy fellow' of l. 29; see note on l. 45.1 above. We
may perhaps wonder how the Mower could be so certain of his identification
in an age before photography made important persons instantly familiar to
obscure subjects. The Mower's function, however, is more symbolic than
naturalistic. Death mysteriously knows each of his victims.

    52. *reave*] take away, deprive (cf. *bereave*).

    53–54. quem dies . . . iacentem] A popular quotation from Seneca's
Thyestes: 'Whom the rising sun has seen high in pride, him the setting sun
has seen laid low' (ll. 613–614). English versions appear in *Edward III* (v.i.;
ll. 2279–2280) and Jonson's *Sejanus* (v.903–904; *H.&S.*, IV, 470).

    55. *leave . . . passionate*] Leicester's sympathy for Edward here prepares us

[*Coming forward with his party*] Spencer and Baldock—by
　　no other names—
I arrest you of high treason here.
Stand not on titles, but obey th'arrest;
'Tis in the name of Isabel the queen.
[*To* KING EDWARD] My lord, why droop you thus?　　　　60
Edward. O day! The last of all my bliss on earth,
　　Centre of all misfortune. O my stars!
　　Why do you lower unkindly on a king?
　　Comes Leicester, then, in Isabella's name
　　To take my life, my company, from me?　　　　　　65
　　Here, man, rip up this panting breast of mine,
　　And take my heart in rescue of my friends!
Rice ap Howell. Away with them.
Spencer Junior.　　　　　　　　It may become thee yet
　　To let us take our farewell of his grace.

---

56. *Coming forward . . . party*] *This ed.; not in Q.*　　58. th'arrest] *Q;* the
arrest *Scott.*　　60. *To* KING EDWARD] *This ed.; not in Q.*　　63. lower] *Q*
(lowre), *Dodsley*[1] (low'r); lour *Dyce*[1].　　64. Comes Leicester, then] *Q*
(Comes Leister then); Come *Leister* then *Q2;* Came *Leister* then *Q3–4;* Come,
Leicester, then *Oxberry.*　　64. Isabella's] *Q (Isabellas);* Isabel's *Oxberry.*

---

for his later replacement by Berkeley at v.i.135–136. Holinshed reports that
when the king was in Leicester's charge at Killingworth, it was reported to
the queen that 'the erle . . . fauoured hir husband too much' (p. 341). Stowe
(*Annals*, 1592 ed.) says that 'the Earle of Leicester did take pity vppon
Edwarde his coosin' (p. 342).

56. *by no other names*] i.e., without the full recitation of their ranks and
titles (as would be customary in official documents of arrest). The omission
conveys the abridgement of their legal rights as well as contempt.

61–62. *O . . . misfortune*] An echo of Gaveston's speech; see note on
II.vi.4–5.

62–63. *O . . . king?*] Briggs cites Kyd, *Soliman and Perseda*: 'Ah heauens,
that hitherto haue smilde on me, / Why doe you vnkindly lowre on *Solyman?*'
(v.iv.82–83).

66. *rip . . . breast*] See note on l. 45.1 above. Perhaps Edward's extravagant
expression of devotion to his 'friends' was prompted by Fleming's disapprov-
ing words in Holinshed about the king's 'addict[ing] himselfe, or rather
fix[ing] his hart' upon Gaveston (p. 320); see Introduction, pp. 41–42. Cf.
also *1 Troublesome Reign*: 'O would she with her hands pull forth my heart, /
I could affoord it to appease these broyles' (iv; ll. 816–817).

68–69. *It . . . grace*] As in the case of Gaveston, Marlowe dramatizes the
genuineness of Spencer's fondness for Edward; he now has nothing to gain
by false pretence.

Abbot. [*Aside*] My heart with pity earns to see this sight;   70
    A king to bear these words and proud commands!
Edward. Spencer,
    Ah sweet Spencer, thus then must we part?
Spencer Junior. We must, my lord; so will the angry heavens.
Edward. Nay, so will hell and cruel Mortimer;   75
    The gentle heavens have not to do in this.
Baldock. My lord, it is in vain to grieve or storm.
    Here humbly of your grace we take our leaves;
    Our lots are cast. I fear me, so is thine.
Edward. In heaven we may, in earth never shall we meet.   80
    And Leicester, say, what shall become of us?
Leicester. Your majesty must go to Killingworth.
Edward. Must! 'Tis somewhat hard when kings must go.
Leicester. Here is a litter ready for your grace
    That waits your pleasure; and the day grows old.   85
Rice ap Howell. As good be gone as stay and be benighted.

---

70. *Aside*] Dyce[1]; *Neilson (for line 71 only); not in Q.*   70. earns] *Q* (earnes);
yearns *Dodsley*[1].   72–73. Spencer . . . part?] *Bowers; one line in Q.*   73.
Ah sweet] *Q* (a sweet); sweet *Dodsley*[1]; oh, sweet *Fleay.*   73. part?]
Dodsley[1]; part. *Q1–4.*   76. not] *Q;* nought *Broughton;* naught *Wagner
(conj.).*   80. never shall we] *Q;* ne'er shall we *Dodsley*[1]; we ne'er shall
Broughton.   82. Killingworth] *Q, Q3–4;* Killingwoth *Q2;* Kenilworth
Broughton.   84. litter] *Q;* letter *Keltie (misprint?).*   87. in] *Q1–2;* on *Q3–4.*

---

70. *earns*] grieves bitterly (a variant of *yearns*); cf. *H5*: 'my manly heart
doth earn' (II.iii.3).

74. *will*] command, determine.

79. *I . . . thine*] An obvious but effective touch of tragic foreshadowing.

81. *us*] Edward clings to the royal plural; as Leicester's reply makes clear,
'us' does not refer to the king and his friends.

82. *Killingworth*] An alternative form of 'Kenilworth'; for the spelling in
Holinshed, see Introduction, p. 41.

83. *Must*] Cf. 1.i.134; see also Introduction, p. 36.

86. *As good . . . benighted*] A somewhat puzzling statement since, obviously, the night will come in either case. Rice ap Howell presumably implies
that it is preferable to set out before dark and thus cover part of the distance
before nightfall than to lose time by remaining at Neath until morning. 'As
good . . . as' appears to be an understated way of saying 'Better . . . than.'

87. *Lay me in a hearse*] Another tragic foreshadowing; the play ends with
Edward's 'hearse' (v.vi.97) in procession.

Edward. A litter hast thou? Lay me in a hearse,
　　And to the gates of hell convey me hence;
　　Let Pluto's bells ring out my fatal knell
　　And hags howl for my death at Charon's shore,   90
　　For friends hath Edward none but these, and these,
　　And these must die under a tyrant's sword.
Rice ap Howell. My lord, be going; care not for these,
　　For we shall see them shorter by the heads.
Edward. Well, that shall be shall be; part we must.   95
　　Sweet Spencer, gentle Baldock, part we must.
　　Hence feignèd weeds, unfeignèd are my woes!
　　　　　　　　　　　　　　　　[*He throws off his disguise.*]
　　Father, farewell. Leicester, thou stay'st for me,

---

91. Edward] *Q;* hapless Edward *Dyce*[1] *(conj.), Cunningham.*   91. these,
and these] *Q;* these [these;] and these *Dodsley*[1-2]*;* these, *Dyce*[1-2]*, Cunningham*
(these;).   92. And these must] *Q;* Must *Dodsley*[1].   95. that] *Q;* what
Dodsley[1]*;* that that *Fleay (conj.).*   95. shall be, shall be] *Q4, Dodsley*[1]*;*
shalbe, shalbe *Q1-3;* which must be, shall be *Broughton.*   97.1. *He . . .
disguise*] *Dyce*[1] *(subst.); not in Q.*

---

89. *Pluto's bells*] Briggs cites Peele, *Battle of Alcazar*: 'The bels of Pluto
ring revenge amaine . . . ' (I.i; l. 168). The idea of bells in hell (like the
howling 'hags' of the following line) is medieval, not classical.

90. *Charon*] the boatman of the classical underworld who ferried the dead
across the river Styx.

91–92. *these, and these, / And these*] In the first of these lines, Edward
distinguishes between two sets of friends: (1) the monks of Neath, and (2)
Spencer and Baldock (or vice versa). Finally he refers to the second pair
again, those who must die by the tyrant Mortimer. In performance, the
speaker's gestures would make the references unambiguous.

94. *shorter by the heads*] A fairly common witicism for beheading. Cf.
Edward I (ii; l. 608) and *R2* (III.iii.13–14).

95. *that shall be shall be*] i.e., what shall be shall be (an Italian proverb); cf.
Doctor Faustus: 'What doctrine call you this? *Che serà, serà:* / What will be,
shall be!' (I.i.46–47).

97. *feignèd weeds*] false clothes (i.e., Edward's monkish disguise). Verity
noted Marlowe's probable indebtedness to Peele's *Edward I*, in which the
king is disguised in 'friar's weeds' in order to discover his wife's infidelity:
'Unhappie King, dishonored in thy stocke, / Hence faigned weedes, un-
faigned is my griefe' (xxiii; ll. 2518–2519). In Peele's context the disguise is
essential to the plot, whereas in Marlowe it is inessential and, apart from this
reference, is never mentioned. For the priority of Peele's play to *Edward II*,
see Charlton–Waller, pp. 8–10; also Introduction, p. 15.

And go I must. Life, farewell, with my friends!

       Exeunt [KING] EDWARD *and* LEICESTER.

Spencer Junior. O is he gone? Is noble Edward gone?   100
  Parted from hence, never to see us more?
  Rend, sphere of heaven, and fire, forsake thy orb,
  Earth, melt to air; gone is my sovereign,
  Gone, gone alas, never to make return.
Baldock. Spencer, I see our souls are fleeted hence;   105
  We are deprived the sunshine of our life.
  Make for a new life, man; throw up thy eyes,
  And heart and hand to heaven's immortal throne,
  Pay nature's debt with cheerful countenance.
  Reduce we all our lessons unto this: 110

99.1. LEICESTER] *Q; Lancaster Q2–4.* 102. Rend] *Dodsley[1]; Rent Q.*
105. fleeted] *Q; fleeting Q2–4.* 108. hand] *Q; hands Cunningham.*

---

99. *Life... friends*] Edward means that his friendship for Baldock and Spencer is so fundamental to his existence that to lose the first is also to forfeit the second. Briggs compares the parting of Queen Margaret from Suffolk in *2H6*: 'Yet now farewell, and farewell life with thee!' (III.ii.356).

99.1. *LEICESTER*] The 'correction' ('*Lancaster*') in Q2–4 is not an error; Henry, Earl of Leicester, the younger brother of the Lancaster who was executed in III.ii, eventually assumed his brother's title (see note on l. 45.2 above). I retain Q's reading since obviously it prevents confusion.

100. Cf. Elinor's parting from her husband in *The Contention*: 'Then is he gone, is noble Gloster gone...?' (ed. Farjeon, p. 694). For the relation between this play and *Edward II*, see Introduction, pp. 35–36. Briggs cites a more distant parallel in Kyd, *Spanish Tragedy*, II.v.42.

102. *Rend*] tear apart (Q's 'Rent' is simply an Elizabethan spelling of the same word). Lunt notes that the apocalyptic imagery of this speech 'is reminiscent of Faustus' final, fearful agony'; cf. especially *Doctor Faustus*, xix.134–190.

fire, forsake thy orb] Some astronomers held that there was a sphere or orb of fire (*coelum igneum*), an addition to the traditional Aristotelian description of the universe; Mephistophilis denies its existence in *Doctor Faustus*, vi.62–63.

103–104. *gone... return*] See note on ll. 68–69 above; also Introduction, pp. 75, 81.

105. *fleeted*] See note on I.iv.49. Cf. *2 Troublesome Reign*: 'My soule doth fleete, worlds vanities farewell' (v; l. 667).

106. *sunshine of our life*] Identification of the king with the sun was a standard Elizabethan analogy; cf. *R2*, III.iii.62–64.

To die, sweet Spencer, therefore live we all;
Spencer, all live to die, and rise to fall.

Rice ap Howell. Come, come, keep these preachments till
you come to the place appointed. You, and such as you
are, have made wise work in England. [*Sardonically*] Will   115
your lordships away?

Mower. [*To* RICE AP HOWELL] Your worship, I trust, will
remember me?

Rice ap Howell. Remember thee, fellow? What else? Follow
me to the town.

[*Exeunt.*]

113–120. Come . . . town.] *Broughton (as prose)*; Come . . . appointed /
You . . . England. / Will . . . away? / *Mower.* Your . . . me? / *Rice.* Remember . . . else, / Follow . . . towne. *Q1–4, Dodsley[1]*; Come . . . England (*as
prose*). Will . . . away? / *Mower.* Your . . . me? / *Rice.* Remember . . . else? /
Follow . . . town. *Cunningham*; Come . . . come / To . . . are, / Have . . . away?
/ *Mow.* Your . . . me? / *Rice.* Remember thee? / Fellow . . . town. *Fleay.*
115. *Sardonically*] *This ed.; Ironically Kirschbaum; not in Q.*   116. your
lordships] *Q;* you *Fleay.*   117. *To* RICE AP HOWELL] *This ed.; not in Q.*
117. worship] *Q;* Lordship *Q2–4.*   118.1. *Exeunt*] *Dodsley[2]; not in Q.*

111–112. A religious cliché, but appropriate to Baldock's clerical station;
cf. Lancaster's similar words in a similar context (III.ii.59–60).

114. *place appointed*] i.e., the gallows (or scaffold) where the condemned
characteristically made moralistic speeches to spectators.

115. *wise work*] Spoken, of course, with sarcasm.

117. *remember*] i.e., with remuneration.

118. *What else?*] Of course (i.e., 'what else would I do but remember
you?'); cf. V.iv.22, V.v.25.

Act V

Enter [EDWARD] *the* King, LEICESTER, *with a* Bishop
[*of* WINCHESTER] *for the crown,* [*and* TRUSSEL].

Leicester. Be patient, good my lord, cease to lament.

Heading. Act V, Scene i] *Robinson;* [Act IV,] Scene viii *Broughton; not in*
Q.   0.1. *a* Bishop] *Q; Bishops Oxberry.*   0.2. *of* WINCHESTER] *Dodsley²;*
Hereford Briggs; not in Q.   0.2. *and* TRUSSEL] *Dyce¹; and Attendants Brough-*
ton; and Attendant Oxberry; not in Q.

0.1–2. *Bishop* of WINCHESTER] Most editors accept this designation of
the unspecified bishop originally added by Dodsley² (1780); '*for the crown*'
(i.e., for the purpose of transporting the crown to London). Briggs dissents,
believing that the bishop must be Hereford (Adam Orleton)—a conclusion
based on his assumption, mistaken in my view, that Winchester later learns
of Edward's abdication by letter (see v.ii.22–36 in the present edition and the
commentary on this crux in the Introduction, pp. 10–11, where it is suggested
that the bishop's presence in this scene may have been an afterthought—
either by Marlowe himself or by a reviser). Holinshed (pp. 340–341) says
that several bishops (Winchester and Lincoln first, then Hereford later) were
among those sent to Killingworth to urge Edward to abdicate; but he
associates the first two bishops rather than Hereford with Leicester, as
Leicester and the bishop in the present episode are associated (see Appendix
B, no. 37). Probably Marlowe, who greatly simplifies the politics of Edward's
resignation, originally had no particular bishop in mind for the retrieval of
the crown but decided on Winchester for reasons of stage economy. Since the
queen addresses Winchester by name in the following scene when he delivers
the crown physically (v.ii.27), it must also be Winchester who participates in
the action at this point.

0.2. TRUSSEL] Perhaps here Marlowe followed Fabyan, who actually
mentions that 'the Procuratour of that Parlement [i.e., modern 'Proctor'
or Speaker of the House of Commons], syr wyllyam Trussel' was among
'certayne solempne messangers [who] were sent vnto the kinge, to the Castell
of Kenelworth' (p. 185). Holinshed does not include Trussel in the group
who approached Edward in his prison, but does report immediately after the
monarch's agreement to abdicate that 'On the same daie sir William Trussell
procurator for the whole parlement did renounce the old king in name of the
whole parlement' (p. 341). For Trussel's presence in this scene, see note on
the speech prefix at l. 84 below.

Imagine Killingworth Castle were your court,
And that you lay for pleasure here a space,
Not of compulsion or necessity.
Edward. Leicester, if gentle words might comfort me,   5
Thy speeches long ago had eased my sorrows,
For kind and loving hast thou always been.
The griefs of private men are soon allayed,
But not of kings. The forest deer, being struck,
Runs to an herb that closeth up the wounds;   10
But when the imperial lion's flesh is gored,
He rends and tears it with his wrathful paw,
And highly scorning that the lowly earth
Should drink his blood, mounts up into the air.
And so it fares with me, whose dauntless mind   15
The ambitious Mortimer would seek to curb,
And that unnatural queen, false Isabel,

---

2. Killingworth] *Q;* Kenilworth *Broughton.*   13. And highly] *Dodsley*[1];
Highly *Q1–4.*   14. into] *Q;* to *Q2–4.*

2–4. A proverbial sentiment; McLaughlin compares *R2*: 'All places that
the eye of heaven visits / Are to a wise man ports and happy havens. / Teach
thy necessity to reason thus: / There is no virtue like necessity' (I.iii.275–
278); see also Tilley M426.

3. *lay*] resided (the preterite subjunctive of *lie*).

7. See note on IV.vii.55.

9–10. *The . . . herb*] The superstition that the herb dittany (or dictamnum)
had the power to cure wounded deer or other animals in their natural habitat
is ancient, appearing in Aristotle, Cicero, and Virgil; cf. also Lyly, *Euphues*:
'the Harte beeing pearced with the darte, runneth out of hande to the hearbe
Dictanum, and is healed' (*Complete Works*, ed. R. W. Bond [Oxford, 1902], I,
208).

11–12. See note on II.ii.203. Analogies between the king and the lion
were commonplace; cf. II.ii.203–204 and Fleming's addition to Holinshed:
'the anger and displeasure of the king is as the roring of a lion, and his
reuenge ineuitable' (p. 331). For the likely indebtedness of *R2* (v.i.29–31) to
this passage, see Introduction, p. 37.

14. *mounts . . . air*] Cf. *3H6*, v.vi.61–62, and see note on I.i.92. Christopher Brennan ('Notes on the Text of Marlowe,' *Beiblatt zur Anglia*, 16
[1905], 209) proposes to emend the phrase to '[it (= blood)] mounts up,' thus
construing the meaning as even more parallel to the passage in *3H6*. Q,
however, makes good sense as it stands: the lion mounts up when threatened,
not its blood, and Lunt alleges that in fact 'a lion at its last gasp does spring
up in the air and then fall down dead.'

That thus hath pent and mewed me in a prison;
For such outrageous passions cloy my soul,
As with the wings of rancour and disdain   20
Full often am I soaring up to heaven
To plain me to the gods against them both.
But when I call to mind I am a king,
Methinks I should revenge me of the wrongs
That Mortimer and Isabel have done.   25
But what are kings when regiment is gone
But perfect shadows in a sunshine day?
My nobles rule, I bear the name of king;
I wear the crown, but am controlled by them,
By Mortimer, and my unconstant queen,   30
Who spots my nuptial bed with infamy
Whilst I am lodged within this cave of care,
Where sorrow at my elbow still attends
To company my heart with sad laments,
That bleeds within me for this strange exchange.   35
But tell me, must I now resign my crown
To make usurping Mortimer a king?
Winchester. Your grace mistakes; it is for England's good

---

19. cloy] *Q* (cloye), *Dodsley²;* claw *Dodsley¹.*   21. often] *Q;* oft *Q2–4.*
24. Methinks] *Dodsley¹;* Me thinkes *Q1–4.*   24. the] *Q;* my *Q2–4.*   30.
unconstant] *Q1–4;* inconstant *Broughton.*   38, 90, 95. Winchester] *Dodsley²;*
Bish. *Q.*

---

18. *pent*] i.e., penned (like a farm animal).
   mewed] caged (like a falcon). Lunt explains that *mew* derives from L.
mutare (= to change); the word at first signified moulting (the changing of
feathers) and was later applied to the enclosures where the birds were kept
for this purpose.
   20–21. Edward extends the metaphor from falconry in l. 18 above.
   22. *plain me*] complain; see note on III.i.158.
   26. *regiment*] See note on I.i.164.
   27. *perfect...day*] Michael Hattaway suggests that Edward puns here
on 'shadows' in the sense of actors (*Elizabethan Popular Theatre: Plays in
Performance* [London, 1982], p. 141); cf. *M.N.D:* 'If we shadows have
offended...' (v.i.419). For the sunshine–shadow motif, see Introduction,
pp. 30, 40–41, 76.
   30. *unconstant*] unfaithful, inconstant.
   34. *company*] keep company with, accompany; cf. *Cym.:* 'The soldier that
did company these three' (v.v.410).

And princely Edward's right we crave the crown.

Edward. No, 'tis for Mortimer, not Edward's head,   40
For he's a lamb, encompassèd by wolves,
Which in a moment will abridge his life.
But if proud Mortimer do wear this crown,
Heavens turn it to a blaze of quenchless fire,
Or, like the snaky wreath of Tisiphon,   45
Engirt the temples of his hateful head;
So shall not England's vine be perishèd,
But Edward's name survive though Edward dies.

Leicester. My lord, why waste you thus the time away?
They stay your answer; will you yield your crown?   50

---

44. Heavens] *Q;* Heav'ns *Dodsley*[1]; Heaven *Broughton;* Heav'n *Oxberry.*
47. vine] *Oxberry;* Vines *Q1–4.*   48. survive] *Q4* (suruiue), *Dodsley*[1–2];
suruiues *Q1–2;* suruies *Q3.*

---

39. *princely . . . right*] Holinshed says that the bishops of Winchester and
Lincoln, 'hauing secret conference with the king, . . . sought to frame his
mind, so as he might be contented to resigne the crowne to his sonne,
bearing him in hand, that if he refused so to doo, the people in respect of the
euill will which they had conceiued against him, would not faile but proceed
to the election of some other that should happilie not touch him in linage' (p.
340).

41. *lamb . . . wolves*] Cf. *1H6,* I.v.30; *3H6,* I.i.240–242, I.iv.5; and *R3,*
IV.iv.22–23. Such imagery, however, deriving as it does from classical
precedent, is conventional.

44. *a . . . fire*] Cf. *Dido:* 'In whose stern faces shin'd the quenchless fire'
(II.i.186), and *2 Tamburlaine:* 'The devils there in chains of quenchless
flame . . .' (II.iii.24); also *Luc.:* 'balls of quenchless fire' (l. 1554). Marlowe
draws upon the classical legend of Glauce (also called Creusa), whom Medea
hated because she became the rival for whom Jason divorced her; in revenge
Medea gave Glauce a golden crown that suddenly emitted consuming flames
and attached itself irremovably to her head (Euripides, *Medea,* ll. 1186–
1194). Chettle used the burning crown in the plot of his revenge play, *The
Tragedy of Hoffman (c.* 1602).

45. *Tisiphon*] Tisiphone, one of the Furies (associated with vengeance for
crimes), whose locks were writhing snakes (cf. Virgil, *Aeneid,* VI, 571). See
also *Arden of Faversham:* 'arms, / That like the snakes of black Tisiphone /
Sting me with their embracings' (xiv.143–145).

47. *England's vine*] There seem to have been no vineyards in medieval and
Renaissance England. Oxberry's emendation ('vine') correctly recognizes the
emblematic vine of royal lineage; see note on III.i.163.

48. *survive*] Q4's reading (followed by Dodsley and others), although it can
claim no authority, makes Marlowe's syntax much clearer: 'survive' is a
subjunctive form implying futurity and is parallel to 'be perishèd' (l. 47).

50. *stay*] await.

Edward. Ah Leicester, weigh how hardly I can brook
 To lose my crown and kingdom without cause,
 To give ambitious Mortimer my right,
 That like a mountain overwhelms my bliss,
 In which extreme my mind here murdered is.   55
 But what the heavens appoint I must obey.
 Here, take my crown—the life of Edward too.

             [Takes off crown.]

 Two kings in England cannot reign at once.
 But stay awhile; let me be king till night,
 That I may gaze upon this glittering crown;   60
 So shall my eyes receive their last content,
 My head, the latest honour due to it,
 And jointly both yield up their wishèd right.
 Continue ever thou celestial sun;
 Let never silent night possess this clime.   65
 Stand still you watches of the element;
 All times and seasons rest you at a stay,
 That Edward may be still fair England's king.
 But day's bright beams doth vanish fast away,

---

51. weigh] *Q3* (waigh), *Q4;* way *Q1–2*. 55. extreme] *Q1–2* (extreame);
extreams *Q3–4*. 55. murdered] *Dyce¹;* murthered *Q*. 56. what] *Q;* that
Q2–4. 57.1. *Takes off crown*] *Dyce¹ (subst.); not in Q*. 59. awhile] *Q4;* a
while *Q1–3*. 59. be king] *Q, Q3–4;* King *Q2*. 69. beams] *Q* (beames);
beame *Q2–4*.

---

52. *without cause*] Edward's failure of self-knowledge here is notable,
especially considering Holinshed's statement that 'he knew that he was fallen
into this miserie through his owne offenses' (p. 340); see Introduction,
pp. 59, 62.

58. Cf. *1H4*: 'Nor can one England brook a double reign / Of Harry Percy
and the Prince of Wales' (v.iv.66–67).

63. *wishèd right*] i.e., desired right.

64. *celestial sun*] See notes on IV.vii.106 and l. 27 above.

66. Cf. *Doctor Faustus*: 'Stand still, you ever-moving spheres of heaven'
(xix.136); also *Ovid's Elegies*, I.xiii.40, associated with and partly quoted
from Ovid's Latin in the same context. The 'watches of the element' are the
planets of the sky; for *element* (= sky), cf. *H5*, IV.i.102. The entire line marks
an effective ironic contrast to Edward's earlier utterance at IV.iii.66.

69. *beams doth*] Such apparent failures of aggreement between subject and
verb are common in Elizabethan usage; *doth* was sometimes taken as a plural
form (Abbott 332).

And needs I must resign my wishèd crown.   70
Inhuman creatures, nursed with tiger's milk,
Why gape you for your sovereign's overthrow—
My diadem, I mean, and guiltless life?
See, monsters, see, I'll wear my crown again.

                                        [*Puts on crown.*]
What, fear you not the fury of your king?   75
But hapless Edward, thou art fondly led.
They pass not for thy frowns as late they did,
But seek to make a new-elected king,
Which fills my mind with strange despairing thoughts,
Which thoughts are martyrèd with endless torments;   80
And in this torment comfort find I none
But that I feel the crown upon my head;
And therefore let me wear it yet a while.

Trussel. My lord, the parliament must have present news,

74.1. *Puts on crown*] Robinson *(subst.); not in Q.*   78. seek] *Q4* (seeke);
seekes *Q1–3.*   80. martyrèd] *Q* (martyred); martyr'd *Dodsley*[1].   83. a
while] *Q1–4;* awhile *Broughton, Oxberry.*   84, 124. *Trussel*] *Dyce*[1] *(Trus.);*
Tru. Q1–4; Trusty *Dodsley*[1]; Bishop of Winchester *Broughton, Oxberry (subst.).*
84. parliament] *Q2–4;* parlement *Q.*

---

70. *wishèd crown*] See note on l. 63 above.

71. *tiger's milk*] Cf. l. 116 below. For the possible influence of *3H6* on this
imagery, see Introduction, p. 31. Cf. also *Dido*: 'And tigers of Hyrcania gave
thee suck' (v.i.159).

73. *guiltless life*] Marlowe deliberately departs from his sources here (see
note on l. 52 above). Cf. also Fabyan, who speaks of Edward's 'greate remors
of conscience' (p. 174) and of his taking 'greate repentaunce of hys former
life' (p. 185); Grafton echoes Fabyan's 'great remorse of conscience' (p. 200).
Stowe says that Edward shed tears, confessing that he 'was very sorie that hee
hadde behaued hymselfe so euill towards the people of his Kyngdome' (p.
350).

76. *fondly*] foolishly.

77. *pass*] See note on I.iv.142.

78. *new-elected king*] Based on Holinshed; see note on l. 39 above. Cf. *2
Troublesome Reign*: 'their new elected King' (ii; l. 189).

79–80. *strange . . . martyrèd*] Cf. the personified 'thoughts' of the extended
conceit in *R2*: 'A generation of still-breeding thoughts; / And these same
thoughts people this little world, / In humours like the people of this world, /
For no thought is contented' (v.v.8–11).

82. *feel the crown*] Cf. *1 Troublesome Reign*: 'then he may feele the crowne'
(xiii; l. 1663).

84. *Trussel*] Doubt has existed as to the validity of this speech prefix
because the only textual authority for the character in the entire drama

And therefore say, will you resign or no?   85

The King *rageth.*

Edward. I'll not resign, but whilst I live, be king!

Traitors, be gone, and join you with Mortimer.

Elect, conspire, install, do what you will;

Their blood and yours shall seal these treacheries.

Winchester. This answer we'll return, and so farewell.   90

[WINCHESTER *and* TRUSSEL *offer to leave.*]

85.1. *The* King *rageth*] *Q1–4; not in Broughton.*   86. but] *Q1–2;* not *Q3–4.*   86. live, be king] *Dodsley*[1]; liue, *Q1–4;* live! *Cunningham;* live— *Kirschbaum;* live *Merchant;* live, I'll live *Brereton, Charlton–Waller.*   87. and join] *Q1–4;* join *Cunningham.*   90.1. WINCHESTER . . . *leave*] *Dyce*[1] *(subst.) (Going with Trussel); not in Q.*

---

consists of Q's '*Tru.*' here and at l. 124 below; Trussel is nowhere named in the stage directions nor in the dialogue. Dodsley believed that '*Tru.*' stood for a character named Trusty; both Broughton and Oxberry assigned the lines in question to the Bishop of Winchester. Although Greg queries the allocation, Dyce's designation ('*Trus.*' for Trussel) involves fewer problems than the other solutions proposed and has the warrant of being mentioned in connection with Edward's resignation by Fabyan, Grafton, and Holinshed. See note on l. 0.2 above.

85.1. Eugene M. Waith notes that this stage direction 'makes . . . an interesting association with Herod, the archetypal rager [of the mystery cycles], whose greatest fury was also provoked by the frustration of his plans. In the Coventry Shearmen and Tailors' play is the direction, "*Here Erode ragis in the pagond and in the strete also*"' ('*Edward II*: The Shadow of Action,' *T.D.R.*, 8.4 [summer 1964], 73–74). Waith also mentions Hamlet's reference to thespian raging as typified by the biblical tyrant: 'tear[ing] a passion to tatters,' which 'out-Herods Herod' (*Ham.*, III.ii.9–14). It is worth noting that in the 1592 edition of Stowe (perhaps too late for Marlowe), Edward when he is asked to abdicate is described as being so 'distraught of his wittes' that he 'sodainely swowned' (*Annals*, p. 341).

86. *whilst . . . king*] A major crux. The line in Q lacks a metrical foot as well as being incomplete in sense. Charlton–Waller defend J. Le Gay Brereton's emendation ('whilst I live, I'll live'; 'Marlowe: Some Textual Notes,' *M.L.R.*, 6 [1911], 95) on grounds that 'the omission of a second *live* is more easily explicable than the omission of anything else'; but the redundancy thus produced is dramatically flat and unMarlovian in its impotence. Kirschbaum's solution, to make Edward break off in mid-sentence by adding a dash ('live—'), has much to commend it, but still leaves the speaker's meaning obscure. Merchant's removal of the comma ('whilst I live / Traitors be gone') strains the syntax and is unidiomatic. I accept Dodsley's emendation (like Bowers and most other editors) as making the best sense of the passage metrically and substantively, for at this point Edward *is* clearly refusing to resign.

Leicester. [*Aside to* EDWARD] Call them again, my lord, and
    speak them fair,
    For if they go, the prince shall lose his right.
Edward. Call thou them back; I have no power to speak.
Leicester. [*To* WINCHESTER] My lord, the king is willing to
    resign.
Winchester. If he be not, let him choose—   95
Edward. O would I might! But heavens and earth conspire
    To make me miserable. Here, receive my crown.
    Receive it? No, these innocent hands of mine
    Shall not be guilty of so foul a crime.
    He of you all that most desires my blood   100
    And will be called the murderer of a king,
    Take it. What, are you moved? Pity you me?
    Then send for unrelenting Mortimer
    And Isabel, whose eyes, being turned to steel,
    Will sooner sparkle fire than shed a tear.   105
    Yet stay, for rather than I will look on them,
    Here, here!

                          [*He resigns the crown.*]
            Now, sweet God of heaven,
    Make me despise this transitory pomp,

---

91. *Aside to* EDWARD] *Oliphant (subst.); not in Q.*   94. *to* WINCHESTER] *This ed.; not in Q.*   95. choose—] *Merchant;* choose. *Q.*   96. heavens] *Q;* heav'n *Dodsley*[1]; heaven *Scott.*   101. murderer] *Broughton;* murtherer *Q.* 104. being] *Q2–4;* beene *Q,* Gill[1] (been).   107. *He resigns the crown*] *Broughton (subst.), Merchant; not in Q.*

---

91. *Call them again*] For the probable imitation of *R3* at this point, see Introduction, n. 61.
98. *these innocent hands*] See notes on ll. 52 and 73 above.
99. *so foul a crime*] In *R2* Shakespeare embroiders this idea of the king's involvement in the crime of deposition by the use of his own hands: cf. especially 'With mine own hands I give away my crown' (IV.i.209); 'one heinous article, / Containing the deposing of a king' (IV.i.234–235); 'I find myself a traitor with the rest; / For I have given here my soul's consent / T' undeck the pompous body of a king' (IV.i.249–251).
101. *murderer of a king*] No suggestion of murdering the king has yet been broached; like Richard II in Shakespeare's play, Edward II partly invites his violent death by anticipating it.
104–105. For Isabella's implacability in relation to the sources, see Introduction, p. 43.

And sit for aye enthronizèd in heaven.
Come, death, and with thy fingers close my eyes,   110
Or, if I live, let me forget myself.
Winchester. My lord—
Edward. Call me not lord! Away, out of my sight!
Ah, pardon me; grief makes me lunatic.
Let not that Mortimer protect my son.   115
More safety is there in a tiger's jaws

---

109. enthronizèd] *Q* (inthronized), *Scott;* inthroniz'd *Dodsley*¹, *Oxberry* (enthroniz'd). 111. myself] *Q4;* my selfe *Q1–3.* 112. Winchester.] *Robinson; Leicester. (Lei.) Broughton; Enter Bartley* [i.e., Berkeley]. / *Bartley. Q1–4.* 113–114. Call . . . lunatic.] *Broughton;* Call . . . lorde, / Away . . . me, / Greefe . . . lunatick, *Q1–4.* 116. is there] *Q;* there is *Q2–4.*

109. *for aye*] for ever.

enthronizèd] An archaic variant of *enthroned*; cf. Peele, *Edward I*: 'in her royall seate inthronized' (i; l. 244). Holinshed uses the word (p. 343) in connection with the coronation of Edward III.

110. *Come, death*] Cf. *Rom.*: 'Come, death, and welcome!' (III.v.24). Grafton could have influenced this line; cf. IV.vii.41–43 and note.

111. *let me forget myself*] Briggs compares *R2*: 'Or that I could forget what I have been, / Or not remember what I must be now!' (III.iii.138–139).

112. *Winchester*] Q places Berkeley's entrance (too early, it would seem) just before this speech and then assigns the brief 'My lord' to him. The compositor undoubtedly thought that the speech and the entrance belonged together, probably because he took '*B.*' (a possible abbreviation for *Bishop*) as referring to 'Bartley' (i.e., Berkeley). It has been obvious to most editors that Berkeley does not enter until l. 127.1. Broughton properly delayed the entrance but gave 'My lord' to Leicester; Brereton, however, in the article already mentioned (see note on l. 86 above) defended Q, arguing that Berkeley does indeed enter at the point specified, salutes the king, but is then kept waiting to be recognized. Nearly all editors, following Robinson, reassign the speech to the Bishop of Winchester and rearrange the text to make Berkeley's entrance the occasion for Leicester's announcement, 'Another post' at l. 128. For further discussion of the staging and the printer's copy, see Introduction, p. 10.

113. *Call me not lord!*] Again Briggs compares *R2*: '*Northumberland.* My lord— / *King Richard.* No lord of thine, thou haught insulting man, / Nor no man's lord' (IV.i.254–256).

114. *grief makes me lunatic*] Cf. l. 85.1 (and note) above.

115. *protect*] i.e., be Lord Protector (or regent) over; cf. V.ii.12, V.ii.88, V.iv.54, V.iv.62. This is an anachronism; no such title existed in the reign of Edward II, the earliest recorded use in the *O.E.D.* being 1427. Marlowe probably picked up the word from Shakespeare's first historical tetralogy, where it appears repeatedly; see also Introduction, pp. 24, 26–27.

116. *tiger's jaws*] See note on l. 71 above.

Than his embracements. Bear this to the queen,
Wet with my tears and dried again with sighs.

                           [Gives a handkerchief.]

If with the sight thereof she be not moved,
Return it back and dip it in my blood.   120
Commend me to my son, and bid him rule
Better than I. Yet how have I transgressed
Unless it be with too much clemency?

Trussel. And thus most humbly do we take our leave.

        [Exeunt WINCHESTER *and* TRUSSEL *with the crown.]*

Edward. Farewell. I know the next news that they bring   125
Will be my death, and welcome shall it be;
To wretched men death is felicity.

           [Enter BERKELEY *to* LEICESTER *with a letter.]*

---

117. Than] *Q2–4* (Then); This *Q (misprint).*   117. embracements] *Q*
(imbrasements), *Dodsley*[1–2]; embracement *Dodsley*[3].   118.1. *Gives a hand-
kerchief*] *Dyce*[1]; *not in Q.*   124.1. *Exeunt . . .* WINCHESTER *and* TRUSSEL]
Dyce[1]; *Exit Bishop of Winchester and Attendants.* Broughton; *not in Q.*
124.1. *with the crown*] *Dyce*[1]; *not in Q.*   125. Farewell . . . bring] *Q*;
Farewell. / I know . . . bring *Keltie.*   127.1. *Enter* BERKELEY *. . . letter.*]
Bowers (subst.); Enter Berkley. Broughton; *Enter Berkeley, who gives a paper to
Leicester. Dyce*[1]; *not in Q1–4, Dodsley*[1–2], *Scott, Oxberry, all of which place
Berkeley's entrance after line 111 (see note at line 112).*

---

117. *Bear . . . queen*] The sending of the handkerchief is Marlowe's invention.

118. Shakespeare elaborates the same conceit in *Ven.*: 'she with her tears /
Doth quench the maiden burning of his cheeks. / Then with her windy sighs
and golden hairs / To fan and blow them dry again she seeks' (ll. 49–52).

120. *dip it in my blood*] See Introduction, p. 31.

123. *too much clemency*] Briggs suggests that Edward glances ruefully at his
earlier sparing of Mortimer (III.ii.68). Fleming refers to Edward's 'clemencie'
(Holinshed, p. 328) in connection with his leniency toward Lancaster; see
Introduction, p. 42. Holinshed also notes that the king sought support from
the Welsh 'bicause he had euer vsed them gentlie, and shewed no rigor
towards them for their riotous misgouernance' (p. 339). The idea of too much
clemency as a weakness in rulers was commonplace; cf. Dekker, *Whore of
Babylon*: 'All mercy in a Prince, makes vile the state, / All justice makes euen
cowards desperate' (IV.ii.22–23). Dekker's lines are based on Seneca's well-
known essay, *De Clementia*, I.ii.2.

124. *Trussel*] See note on l. 84 above.

126. *welcome shall it be*] See note on l. 110 above.

127.1. Enter *BERKELEY*] See note on l. 112 above. For Holinshed's
account (p. 341) of the following action, see Appendix B, no. 37.

Leicester. Another post. What news brings he?
Edward. Such news as I expect. Come, Berkeley, come,
    And tell thy message to my naked breast.   130
Berkeley. My lord, think not a thought so villainous
    Can harbour in a man of noble birth.
    To do your highness service and devoir
    And save you from your foes, Berkeley would die.
Leicester. [*Reading letter*] My lord, the council of the queen
    commands   135
    That I resign my charge.
Edward. And who must keep me now? [*To* BERKELEY] Must
    you, my lord?
Berkeley. Ay, my most gracious lord, so 'tis decreed.
Edward. [*Taking the letter*] By Mortimer, whose name is
    written here.
    Well may I rend his name that rends my heart!   140
                            [*Tears the paper.*]
    This poor revenge hath something eased my mind.
    So may his limbs be torn, as is this paper!

129, 134, 144, 151. Berkeley] *Broughton* (Berkley); *Bartley Q.*   131, 138,
144, 148, 151. *Berkeley*] *Broughton (Berk.); Bart., Bartley Q.*   135. *Reading
letter*] *Gill*[1]; *not in Q.*   135. of] *Q1–2;* and *Q3* (&), *Q4.*   135. com-
mands] *Q* (commaunds); command *Scott.*   137. *to* BERKELEY] *This ed.; not
in Q.*   139. *Taking the letter*] *Dyce*[1] *(subst.); Showing the order to Edward
Oxberry (after Berkeley's speech at line 138); not in Q.*   140. rend] *Dodsley*[1];
rent *Q1–4.*   140.1 *Tears the paper*] *Broughton; not in Q.*

---

130. *to my naked breast*] Charlton–Waller interpret these words literally,
assuming that Edward 'offers his naked breast as to a murderer's dagger.' Cf.
also his 'rip up this panting breast' (IV.vii.66) when he was threatened at
Neath.

133. *devoir*] duty.

136. *resign my charge*] See note on IV.vii.55.

141. *This poor revenge*] The symbolism and histrionic impotence of Edward's
tearing up Mortimer's letter may be compared to Richard II's similar gesture
of shattering the mirror (*R2*, IV.i.289). Both occur immediately after the
protagonist has been compelled to resign the crown, both are responses to
frustration, and both are essentially self-destructive; both, too, represent
imaginative fictions for which Holinshed or other sources offer no historical
basis.

142. *So . . . torn*] Perhaps Edward is thinking of the traditional punishment
for high treason—being quartered or cut into four pieces after being hanged
and disembowelled. If this analogy is intended, Edward probably tears the
letter twice across, thus quartering it. In fact Mortimer seems to have been

Hear me, immortal Jove, and grant it too.
Berkeley. Your grace must hence with me to Berkeley
    straight.
Edward. Whither you will; all places are alike,   145
    And every earth is fit for burial.
Leicester. [*To* BERKELEY] Favour him, my lord, as much as
    lieth in you.
Berkeley. Even so betide my soul as I use him.
Edward. Mine enemy hath pitied my estate,
    And that's the cause that I am now removed.   150
Berkeley. And thinks your grace that Berkeley will be cruel?
Edward. I know not; but of this am I assured,
    That death ends all, and I can die but once.
    Leicester, farewell.
Leicester. Not yet, my lord; I'll bear you on your way.   155
                                       Exeunt.

[SCENE ii]

Enter MORTIMER [JUNIOR] *and* QUEEN ISABELLA.

Mortimer Junior. Fair Isabel, now have we our desire.

---

143. immortal] *Q1–2, Q4;* immorrall *Q3.*   145. Whither] *Q2–4;* Whether
Q.   147. *to* BERKELEY] *This ed.; not in Q.*   149. Mine] *Q1–2;* My *Q3–4.*
155.1. *Exeunt.*] *Broughton;* Exeunt omnes. *Q.*   Heading. Scene ii] *Robinson;*
Act V, Scene i *Broughton; not in Q.*

---

spared such butchery; Holinshed reports that he was 'drawne and hanged, at
the common place of execution . . . His bodie remained two daies and two
nights on the gallowes, and after taken downe was deliuered to the friers
minors, who buried him in their church . . . with great pompe and funerall
exequies' (p. 349). Grafton, however, says that Mortimer was beheaded and
then 'quartered' (p. 223); see Introduction, p. 65.

   143. *Jove*] The Lord Chamberlain's ruling against blasphemy and profan-
ity on the stage often led to this and other substitutions for 'God' in
theatre dialogue. Marlowe, however, is anything but consistent in the practice; cf. v.ii.98.

   147. *Favour him*] See note on IV.vii.55.

   148. *so betide my soul*] let my soul be so treated.

   149. *Mine . . . estate*] 'Estate' means 'condition.' In the light of the terrible
and almost legendary fate in store for Edward, this line is heavy with
dramatic irony. Whether the speaker himself intends irony, however, is less
clear.

   153. *I . . . once*] Proverbial (Tilley M219); cf. *2H4*: 'A man can die but
once. We owe God a death' (III.II.235–236).

The proud corrupters of the light-brained king
Have done their homage to the lofty gallows,
And he himself lies in captivity.
Be ruled by me, and we will rule the realm.   5
In any case, take heed of childish fear,
For now we hold an old wolf by the ears,
That, if he slip, will seize upon us both,
And gripe the sorer, being griped himself.
Think therefore, madam, that imports us much   10
To erect your son with all the speed we may,
And that I be Protector over him,
For our behoof will bear the greater sway

---

7. ears] *Q1–2* (eares); eare *Q3–4*.   9. gripe] *Q1–4;* grip *Fleay*.   9.
griped] *Dyce*^{1–2} (grip'd); gript *Q1–4*, *Spencer* (gripp'd), *Baskervill* (gripped).
10. that] *Q1–4;* it *Dodsley*¹*;* that it *Keltie;* that't *Fleay*.   10. us] *Q3–4* (vs);
as *Q1–2*.   11. To erect] *Q1–4;* T'erect *Fleay;* To elect *Broughton, Oxberry*.
11. with all] *Q4;* withall *Q1–3*.   13. behoof] *Q;* behoof [behoof;] *Scott*.
13. will] *Q1–2;* twill *Q3–4, Dodsley*² ('twill).

---

2. *corrupters*] See note on I.ii.5.
light-brained king] Cf. Holinshed's statement that Edward was 'of a good
and courteous nature, though not of most pregnant wit' (p. 342); Holinshed
also characterizes the king as 'of nature giuen to lightnesse' (p. 318).
    3. *lofty gallows*] According to Holinshed, the younger Spencer was 'hanged
on a paire of gallowes of fiftie foot in heigth' (p. 339).
    5. *Be ruled by me*] See Introduction, pp. 28, 43.
    7. *hold . . . ears*] A proverbial expression (Tilley W603); cf. Webster, *The
White Devil*, V.i.154–155.
    9. *gripe the sorer*] clutch more painfully (as an ainimal seizes its prey); cf.
V.iii.57; also *1 Tamburlaine*: 'With greedy talons gripe my bleeding heart'
(II.vii.49).
    griped] Dyce's emendation of Q's 'gript' preserves the rhetorical repetition
of 'gripe' obviously intended (see previous note). *Grip* and *gripe*, originally
separate, tended to fall together in the period.
    10. *that . . . much*] i.e., that it is very important for us. Q3's 'us' (correct-
ing Q's 'as') is syntactically necessary and can be supported palaeographically
as the compositor's misreading of *a* for *u*. The grammar is elliptical, 'it'
being clearly implied; the various emendations of Dodsley, Keltie, and Fleay
are therefore unnecessary.
    11. *erect*] set up, establish.
    12. *Protector*] See note on V.i.115.
    13. *behoof*] advantage; cf. I.iv.243, II.iii.3.

Whenas a king's name shall be underwrit.
Isabella. Sweet Mortimer, the life of Isabel,   15
Be thou persuaded that I love thee well,
And therefore, so the prince my son be safe,
Whom I esteem as dear as these mine eyes,
Conclude against his father what thou wilt,
And I myself will willingly subscribe.   20
Mortimer Junior. First would I hear news that he were
deposed,
And then let me alone to handle him.

Enter Messenger [*and then the* Bishop *of* WINCHESTER
with the crown].

Letters! From whence?
Messenger.   From Killingworth, my lord.
Isabella. How fares my lord the king?
Messenger. In health, madam, but full of pensiveness.   25

---

14. Whenas] *Oxberry;* When as *Q1–4;* When that *Broughton.*   14. under-
writ] *Broughton, Dyce*[1] (under-writ); vnder writ *Q1–4.*   21. news] *Q1–4*
(newes); the news *Scott.*   21. that he] *Q;* he *Q2–4.*   22. alone to] *Q;*
alone *Merchant (misprint?).*   22.1. *Enter* Messenger] *Q; Enter Messenger and
Winchester Scott.*   22.1–2. *and then . . . crown*] *Bowers; Enter Winchester
with the crown (after line 26) Robinson; not in Q.*   23. Letters] *Dyce*[1]*; Mor.
iu.* [*speech prefix*] Letters *Q1–4.*   23. Letters! From whence?] *Dodsley*[1]*;*
Letters, from whence? *Q, Q4;* Letters from whence? *Q2–3;* Letters. From
whence? *McLaughlin.*   23, 31, 59, 118. Killingworth] *Q;* Kenilworth
Broughton.

---

14. *Whenas*] when; cf. v.vi.83.

18. *as dear . . . eyes*] Proverbial (Dent, *Shakespeare's Proverbial Language,*
E249.1); cf. *Lr,* I.i.56.

22. *let me alone*] i.e., leave it to me; cf. l. 37 below. The *Mirror for
Magistrates* and Grafton's chronicle are the sources that ascribe principal
responsibility for Edward's murder to Mortimer; see Introduction, pp. 63–
64.

22.1. Enter . . . WINCHESTER] The awkward staging here—the apparent arrival of the Messenger and the Bishop at the same moment for a similar
purpose—presents a crux (see textual notes above). I follow Scott modified
by Bowers. For the problematic entrance and exit of Winchester in this
scene, neither of them specified in Q, see Introduction, pp. 10–11; see also
note on v.i.0.1–2.

25. *pensiveness*] melancholy, heaviness of heart, sorrow. Cf. *Dido:* 'dying
pensiveness' (IV.ii.44).

Isabella. Alas, poor soul, would I could ease his grief.

    [*Acknowledging the arrival of the crown*] Thanks, gentle
        Winchester. [*To the* Messenger] Sirrah, be gone.

                                      [*Exit* Messenger.]

Winchester. [*Presenting the document of abdication*] The king
        hath willingly resigned his crown.

Isabella. O happy news! Send for the prince, my son.

Winchester. Further, ere this letter was sealed, Lord Berkeley
        came,   30
        So that he now is gone from Killingworth,
        And we have heard that Edmund laid a plot
        To set his brother free; no more but so.

---

26. grief.] *Q* (greefe,); grief! / *Winchester presents papers. Scott;* grief. / *Enter
Bishop of Winchester Dodsley*[3] *(conj.);* grief! / *Enter Winchester with the crown.
Robinson;* grief! / *Enter the Bishop of Winchester. He bows deeply. Kirschbaum.*
27. *Acknowledging . . . crown*] *This ed.; not in Q.*   27. *To the* Messenger]
Robinson; not in Q.   27.1. *Exit* Messenger] *Dodsley*[1]*; not in Q.*   28.
Presenting . . . abdication] *This ed.; not in Q.*   30. *Winchester. Further*] *Q*
*(Bish. Further); B. of Win. (pointing to letter in Queen's hand) Further Kirsch-
baum.*   30. ere] *Dodsley*[1]*; or Q1–4.*   30. this letter] *Q;* this *Dyce*[1] *(conj.),
Cunningham.*   30, 34, 40, 47, 60. Berkeley] *Dodsley*[2]*; Bartley Q.*   33. but
so.] *Q;* but so. *Exit. Broughton.*

---

26. *would . . . grief*] For Fleming's stress on Isabella's hypocrisy (Holinshed,
p. 341), see Introduction, pp. 42–43; see also Appendix B, no. 38. See also
note on l. 70 below.

30. *this letter*] The content of this letter (obviously one of those delivered
by the Messenger at l. 23 above) is never actually read out or announced
onstage; but Winchester, who already knows the burden of the written
message and was apparently at Killingworth when it was dispatched, makes
this unnecessary by anticipating its news in his speech. See note on l. 22.1
above.

31. *he now is gone*] i.e., the king has been removed from Killingworth
Castle (apparently to Berkeley Castle).

32. *Edmund laid a plot*] Marlowe radically compresses Holinshed, who
reports that Kent actually attempted to rescue his brother twice—once in
1327 (p. 341), and again in 1329 after the king's death in the false belief that
Edward had survived (p. 348); see Appendix B, nos. 38, 43. See also
Introduction, p. 57.

33. *no more but so*] i.e., in short, without more ado (a common Elizabethan
expression); cf. *Jew of Malta*: 'No more but so: it must and shall be done'
(IV.i.128).

The lord of Berkeley is so pitiful
As Leicester that had charge of him before.   35
Isabella. Then let some other be his guardian.

[*Exit* WINCHESTER.]

Mortimer Junior. Let me alone—here is the privy seal.
Who's there? [*To* Attendants *within*] Call hither Gurney
and Matrevis.
To dash the heavy-headed Edmund's drift,
Berkeley shall be discharged, the king removed,   40
And none but we shall know where he lieth.
Isabella. But Mortimer, as long as he survives,
What safety rests for us, or for my son?

---

34. The lord] *Q; Mort. jun.* [*speech prefix*] The lord *Broughton.*   34. is so]
Q; is as *Broughton, Oxberry;* is *Scott.*   36.1. *Exit* WINCHESTER] *Bowers*
(*subst.*); *Dyce*[1] (*after line 37*); *not in Q.*   37. privy seal] *Q* (priuie seale);
privy seal! (*Points to himself*). *Kirschbaum.*   38. *To* Attendants *within*]
Dyce[1]; *not in Q.*   41. And none . . . lieth] *Q;* And where he lieth none but
we shall know *Fleay.*   41. lieth] *Q;* doth lie *Broughton.*

---

34. *so pitiful*] as pitiful. Elizabethans frequently used *so* before *as* in
constructions where modern English uses *as . . . as* (Abbott 275). Holinshed
notes: 'But forsomuch as the lord Berkley vsed him [i.e., Edward] more
courteouslie than his aduersaries wished him to doo, he was discharged of
that office . . .' (p. 341).

36.1. See note on l. 22.1 above.

37. *Let me alone*] See note l. 22 above.

privy seal] The official seal of royal power, second in importance to the
Great Seal, that Mortimer will use to authorize the letter he will direct
Matrevis to draft (see l. 46 below) for his signature. The use of the privy seal
(introduced early in the thirteenth century) became so important that the
office of Keeper of the Privy Seal evolved in the later Middle Ages into one of
the most powerful positions of state in the kingdom. See also notes on I.i.167
and II.ii.146.

38. *Gurney and Matrevis*] Holinshed refers to these men as 'sir Thomas
Gourney' and 'the lord Matreuers' (p. 341); Marlowe deprives them of titles
and treats them as hired thugs. It is clear from the metre that the second
figure must be pronounced Matrévis.

39. *dash*] quell, destroy. Charlton–Waller explain that in the sixteenth
century the term was regularly used to describe the rejection of a bill in
Parliament; it survives today only in the phrase 'to dash one's hopes.'

heavy-headed] i.e., stupid, dull.

drift] plot, stratagem.

40–41. *king . . . he lieth*] Marlowe follows Holinshed and Stowe closely
here; see Appendix B, no. 38.

43. *rests*] See note on IV.vi.63.

Mortimer Junior. Speak, shall he presently be dispatched and
    die?
Isabella. I would he were, so it were not by my means.   45

     Enter MATREVIS *and* GURNEY. [MORTIMER JUNIOR *confers
      with them apart.*]

Mortimer Junior. Enough. Matrevis, write a letter presently
    Unto the lord of Berkeley from ourself
    That he resign the king to thee and Gurney;
    And when 'tis done, we will subscribe our name.
Matrevis. It shall be done, my lord.

                                  [*He writes.*]
Mortimer Junior.   Gurney.
Gurney.   My lord?   50
Mortimer Junior. As thou intendest to rise by Mortimer,
    Who now makes Fortune's wheel turn as he please,
    Seek all the means thou canst to make him droop,
    And neither give him kind word nor good look.
Gurney. I warrant you, my lord.   55
Mortimer Junior. And this above the rest, because we hear
    That Edmund casts to work his liberty,

45.1–2. MORTIMER JUNIOR . . . *apart*] *This ed.; not in* Q.   46. Enough . . .
presently] Q (*one line*); Enough. / Matrevis . . . presently *Fleay (subst.).*   47.
ourself] *Dodsley*[1]; our selfe Q1–4, Merchant (our self).   50. He writes]
Dyce[1] *(subst.); not in* Q.

---

45. See Introduction, p. 43.
46. *presently*] See note on I.iv.90.
48. *resign*] reassign, turn over.
52. *makes . . . please*] Briggs cites *1 Tamburlaine*: 'I hold the Fates bound
fast in iron chains, / And with my hand turn Fortune's wheel about' (I.ii.
173–174); also 'Your love hath Fortune so at his command / That she shall
stay, and turn her wheel no more' (v.i.374–375). See also Introduction, pp.
25–26. Don Cameron Allen discusses the concept of fortune in Marlowe, relating it to Giovanni Pontano's idea of the *fortunati*—men who, like Tamburlaine,
rely on no code of conduct but merely follow their impulses to carry them to
their highest goals; see 'Renaissance Remedies for Fortune: Marlowe and the
Fortunati,' *S.P.*, 38 (1941), 188–197. Allen suggests that since Marlowe uses
the word *fortune* twenty-nine times in the two parts of *Tamburlaine* and only
eight times in *Edward II*, he greatly tempered and modified this essentially
amoral concept in the later plays.
53–54. *make . . . look*] It is Stowe among the chroniclers who particularly
stresses the psychological tormenting of Edward II; see note on l. 64 below.
57. *casts*] designs, plans.

Remove him still from place to place by night,
Till at the last he come to Killingworth,
And then from thence to Berkeley back again;   60
And by the way to make him fret the more,
Speak curstly to him; and in any case
Let no man comfort him if he chance to weep,
But amplify his grief with bitter words.

Matrevis. Fear not, my lord, we'll do as you command.   65
Mortimer Junior. So now away; post thitherwards amain.
Isabella. Whither goes this letter? To my lord the king?
Commend me humbly to his majesty,
And tell him that I labour all in vain
To ease his grief and work his liberty.   70
And bear him this, as witness of my love.

                                     [*Gives a jewel.*]

Matrevis. I will, madam.

                         Exeunt MATREVIS *and* GURNEY.
            [QUEEN ISABELLA *and* MORTIMER JUNIOR *remain.*]

---

59. Till] *Q2–4; And Q.*   59. he] *Q*; be *Kirschbaum.*   66. thitherwards]
Dodsley[1]; thither wards *Q1–4.*   71.1. *Gives a jewel.*] *Kirschbaum; Gives a
ring. Broughton, Oxberry; Gives some token. Gill*[1].   72.2. ISABELLA . . .
remain.] *Robinson (subst.) (Exeunt all but Isabel and Mortimer.); Manent Isabell
and Mortimer. Q.*

---

58. *from . . . night*] See note on ll. 40–41 above. Stowe reports that Edward's
keepers 'brought him out by nighte from *Kenilworth*' and 'in a certaine darke
night . . . conueyed him . . . to *Berkeley*' (p. 355).

61. *by the way*] i.e., along the way.

62. *curstly*] harshly, malignantly.

64. Stowe says, for instance, 'Euerye worde [Edward] spake was contraried
by them [i.e., Gurney and Matrevis], giuing out moste slaunderously, that he
was madde' (p. 355).

66. *amain*] See note on II.iv.47.

70. *ease his grief*] Cf l. 26 and note above. Isabella echoes her earlier phrase
as though she had rehearsed the lie.

71. *bear him this*] The imaginative Broughton undoubtedly understood this
line correctly (see textual note on l. 71.1). Isabella probably sends a jewel
(perhaps a ring) here—very likely the same jewel that Edward later offers to
Lightborn at v.v.83. Such an interpretation adds significant irony and pathos
to the recipient's final suffering, during which, incidentally, Edward also
reminisces about his early courtship of Isabella in France (v.v.67–69).
Holinshed, however, says that the queen sent her husband 'courteous and
louing letters with apparell and other such things' (p. 341).

Enter the young PRINCE [EDWARD], *and* [Edmund] *the* Earl *of* KENT
talking with him.

Mortimer Junior. [*Aside to* ISABELLA] Finely dissembled; do so
    still, sweet queen.
Here comes the young prince with the Earl of Kent.
Isabella. [*Aside to* MORTIMER JUNIOR] Something he whispers
    in his childish ears.   75
Mortimer Junior. [*Aside*] If he have such access unto the
    prince,
Our plots and stratagems will soon be dashed.
Isabella. [*Aside*] Use Edmund friendly, as if all were well.
Mortimer Junior. [*To* KENT] How fares my honourable lord of
    Kent?
Kent. In health, sweet Mortimer. [*To* ISABELLA] How fares
    your grace?   80
Isabella. Well—if my lord your brother were enlarged.
Kent. I hear of late he hath deposed himself.
Isabella. The more my grief.
Mortimer Junior. And mine.
Kent. [*Aside*] Ah, they do dissemble.   85
Isabella. Sweet son, come hither; I must talk with thee.
Mortimer Junior. [*To* KENT] Thou, being his uncle and the
    next of blood,
Do look to be Protector over the prince.

72.3–4. *Enter . . . with him.*] *Q; (after line 73) Keltie; (after line 74) Fraser–*
Rabkin; (after line 78) Dyce[1–2].   73. *Aside to* ISABELLA] *Baskervill (subst.);*
not in Q.   75. *Aside to* MORTIMER JUNIOR] *Oliphant (subst.), Baskervill; not*
in Q.   75. Something] *Dodsley*[1]; *Some thing Q1–4.*   76. *Aside*] *Oliphant*
(subst.), Baskervill; not in Q.   78. *Aside*] *Oliphant (subst.), Baskervill; not in*
Q.   79. *To* KENT] *This ed.; not in Q.*   80. *To* ISABELLA] *This ed.; not in*
Q.   83–85. The more . . . dissemble.] *Q (as prose?); one line in Tancock.*
85. *Aside*] *Dodsley*[1]; *not in Q.*   87. *to* KENT] *This ed.; not in Q.*   87.
Thou] *Q;* You *Q2–4.*

---

   73. *Finely . . . still*] See note on II.ii.228. For Fleming's description of the
dissembling (Holinshed, p. 341), see Introduction, p. 43.
   77. *dashed*] See note on l. 39 above.
   81. *enlarged*] set at liberty. Merchant thinks that the queen puns ironically
on the sense of 'released from life' (i.e., dead).
   82. *deposed himself*] i.e., agreed to abdicate.
   85. *dissemble*] Cf. l. 73 above.
   88. *Protector*] See note on v.i.115.

Kent. Not I, my lord; who should protect the son
　　But she that gave him life—I mean the queen?　　　　　90
Prince Edward. Mother, persuade me not to wear the crown.
　　Let him be king; I am too young to reign.
Isabella. But be content, seeing it his highness' pleasure.
Prince Edward. Let me but see him first, and then I will.
Kent. Ay, do, sweet nephew.　　　　　　　　　　　　　95
Isabella. Brother, you know it is impossible.
Prince Edward. Why, is he dead?
Isabella. No, God forbid.
Kent. I would those words proceeded from your heart.
Mortimer Junior. Inconstant Edmund, dost thou favour him　　100
　　That wast a cause of his imprisonment?
Kent. The more cause have I now to make amends.

---

93. it] *Q1–2;* it is *Q3–4;* 'tis *Dyce*[1].　97–98. Why...dead? / No...
forbid.] *Q (as prose); one line in Tancock.*　100. dost] *Q (doost), Dodsley*[1]*;*
doest *Q2–4;* does *Pendry–Maxwell.*　101. a] *Q1–4;* the *Neilson.*

89–90. *who ... queen*] Officially, Isabella was regent for the young Edward
III. Holinshed refers to 'queene Isabell, and such other as were appointed
gouernours to the yoong king' (p. 341).

91. *persuade me not*] The prince's reluctance is based on Holinshed (p.
340); see Appendix B, no. 37.

92. *him*] i.e., Edward II; cf. 'Let me but see him' two lines below.

93. *seeing ... pleasure*] i.e., inasmuch as it *is* Edward II's wish that the
prince be crowned (elliptical construction).

97. *Why, is he dead?*] An effective touch of tragic foreboding.

100–101. *Edmund ... cause*] 'That' is governed by 'Edmund,' not by
'him,' as is shown by the second person singular of the verb ('wast'); for the
separation of a relative pronoun from its antecedent and for the substitution
of *that* for *who*, see Abbott 262. Mortimer claims that Kent had earlier
agreed to his brother's imprisonment, which Kent in response surprisingly
acknowledges—with apparent inconsistency for dramatic purposes since
Kent's defection from the rebel party had preceded the king's capture (cf. his
soliloquy at the opening of IV.vi). Possibly Marlowe intends us to imagine
that Kent reluctantly (perhaps for reasons of self-protection; cf. IV.vi.12)
went along with Mortimer and the queen on the decision to incarcerate
Edward. But the appearance of contradiction probably results from the
compression of history. Holinshed says that Kent was involved in the capture
of the elder Spencer at Bristol (p. 339) and is silent about his change of heart
until he mentions Kent's secret plotting to free his brother from Berkeley
Castle (p. 341).

Mortimer Junior. I tell thee 'tis not meet that one so false
    Should come about the person of a prince.
    [*To* PRINCE EDWARD] My lord, he hath betrayed the king,
        his brother,   105
    And therefore trust him not.
Prince Edward. But he repents and sorrows for it now.
Isabella. Come son, and go with this gentle lord and me.
Prince Edward. With you I will, but not with Mortimer.
Mortimer Junior. Why youngling, 'sdain'st thou so of
    Mortimer?   110
    Then I will carry thee by force away.
Prince Edward. Help, uncle Kent, Mortimer will wrong me.
    [MORTIMER JUNIOR *grasps* PRINCE EDWARD; KENT *tries to intervene.*]
Isabella. Brother Edmund, strive not; we are his friends.
    Isabel is nearer than the Earl of Kent.
Kent. Sister, Edward is my charge; redeem him.   115

---

103. I tell thee] *Q; (Aside to Q. Isab.)* I tell thee *Dyce²; (To the queen)* I tell
thee *Briggs (not as an aside).*   105. *To* PRINCE EDWARD] *Oliphant; not in
Q.*   110. 'sdain'st] *Robinson;* s'dainst *Q1–4, Dodsley²* ('s'dainst), *Merchant*
('s'dainst); dain'st *Dodsley¹;* disdain'st *Scott.*   112.1. MORTIMER . . . *inter-
vene*] *Kirschbaum; not in Q.*

103–104. Dyce (see textual note) assumed that these lines, spoken obviously to the queen, should be inaudible to the others onstage; Briggs's
interpretation, however, is undoubtedly correct: 'Surely Mortimer would not
have laid the emphasis that he does upon "false" and "prince," had the
words been intended solely for the queen's ears. Addressed to her, but not
as an aside, the speech is perfectly natural and lends vividness to the
dialogue. . . .' Cf. Kyd, *Soliman and Perseda:* 'It is not meete that one so base
as thou / Shouldst come about the person of a King' (I.v.71–72).

105. *betrayed*] i.e., because he had deserted the king's cause for that of
Mortimer and the queen after the execution of Warwick and Lancaster and
after his own banishment (cf. IV.i.5–11).

108. *this gentle lord*] i.e., Mortimer. Note the suggestion of endearment in
'gentle'; cf. I.ii.47, II.iv.59–60.

110. *youngling*] novice (here a term of contempt).
'sdain'st] A contracted form of *disdainest.*

114. *nearer*] i.e., nearer in blood, more closely related (as a mother is in
comparison to an uncle). Kent, the prince's uncle, was the half brother of
Edward II. The prince's grandmother was Eleanor of Castile, Edward I's first
wife.

115. *charge*] responsibility.
redeem him] give him back to me.

Isabella. [*Leaving*] Edward is my son, and I will keep him.
Kent. [*To* ISABELLA] Mortimer shall know that he hath
     wronged me.
     [*Aside*] Hence will I haste to Killingworth Castle
     And rescue agèd Edward from his foes,
     To be revenged on Mortimer and thee.   120
          Exeunt [*on one side* QUEEN ISABELLA, PRINCE EDWARD, *and*
                    MORTIMER JUNIOR; *on the other* KENT].

[SCENE iii]

Enter MATREVIS *and* GURNEY *with* [EDWARD] *the* King
                [*and* Soldiers].

Matrevis. My lord, be not pensive; we are your friends.

---

116. *Leaving*] *Bowers* (*subst.*) (*Is going off*); *not in Q.*   117. *To* ISABELLA]
This ed.; not in Q.   117. wronged] *Q* (wrongde), *Dodsley*[1] (wrong'd);
wrongèd] *Dyce*[1].   118. *Aside*] *Robinson; not in Q.*   120.1–2. *Exeunt . . .*
KENT.] *Dyce*[1]; *Exeunt omnes. Q1–4.*   *Heading.* Scene iii] *Robinson;* Scene ii
Broughton; not in Q.   0.2. *and* Soldiers] *Scott* (*subst.*); *not in Q.*

---

118. *Killingworth Castle*] From a reader's point of view references to the
location of Edward's prisons in Act V are somewhat confusing. At l. 31
Winchester reports that Edward (in Berkeley's charge) has departed from
Killingworth, the inference being that he is currently being kept at Berkeley
Castle; later Mortimer, in his strategy to frustrate Kent's attempt at rescue,
orders Matrevis to keep Edward on the move 'Till at the last he come to
Killingworth, / And then from thence to Berkeley back again' (ll. 59–60).
Now Kent intends to rescue his brother at Killingworth (how he knows the
correct location is hazy), but in the following scene after the shaving episode
Edward and his keepers are just arriving at Killingworth (v.iii.48; cf. also
v.iv.82). Finally Edward is murdered at Berkeley Castle from the 'dungeon'
(v.v.37) of which he emerges to face Lightborn, although there is no actual
mention of the castle's name at this point. In performance, of course, a mere
impression of geographical movement is all that is required so that the strict
logic and historical sequence of minor details can be safely ignored.
   119. *rescue agèd Edward*] Edward II was only forty-three at the time of his
murder, but the adjective clearly suggests premature ageing as the result of
suffering; cf. 'old wolf' (l. 7 above) and 'old Edward' (v.iii.23). Stowe refers
several times to 'the olde king' (e.g., p. 357) in order to distinguish Edward
II from Edward III. In the play the youth of the successor to the throne helps
to emphasize the protagonist's age through contrast. The intended rescue
here seems to be based mainly on Holinshed's account (p. 348) of Kent's
second attempt; see note on l. 32 above.
   120. *thee*] i.e., Queen Isabella.
   v.iii.1. *pensive*] See note on v.ii.25.

Men are ordained to live in misery;
Therefore come; dalliance dangereth our lives.
Edward. Friends, whither must unhappy Edward go?
  Will hateful Mortimer appoint no rest?   5
  Must I be vexèd like the nightly bird
  Whose sight is loathsome to all wingèd fowls?
  When will the fury of his mind assuage?
  When will his heart be satisfied with blood?
  If mine will serve, unbowel straight this breast,   10
  And give my heart to Isabel and him;
  It is the chiefest mark they level at.
Gurney. Not so, my liege; the queen hath given this charge
  To keep your grace in safety.
  Your passions make your dolours to increase.   15
Edward. This usage makes my misery increase.
  But can my air of life continue long
  When all my senses are annoyed with stench?
  Within a dungeon England's king is kept,
  Where I am starved for want of sustenance.   20

---

4. Friends,] *Q;* Friends! *Broughton.*   14. To] *Q;* Only to *Dyce*[1-2] *(conj.),*
Cunningham.   15. to increase] *Q1–3;* increase *Q4.*   20. starved] *Dodsley*[1]
(starv'd); steru'd *Q.*

---

2. A commonplace; cf. 'No man is happy before his death' (Tilley M333).

3. *dalliance dangereth*] delay endangers.

4. *unhappy*] See note on II.v.108.

6. *vexèd . . . bird*] i.e., tormented as the owl (a nocturnal bird, traditionally an omen of death) torments its prey; for the idea that the owl is especially 'loathsome to all wingèd fowls' (l. 7), Charlton–Waller cite *The Owl and the Nightingale,* (ed. J. H. G. Grattan and G. F. H. Sykes [London, 1945], p. 3), ll. 61ff.

8. *assuage*] be assuaged, be appeased.

10. *unbowel . . . breast*] Cf. 'rip up this panting breast' (IV.vii.66 and note).

12. *level*] See note on III.ii.89.

17. *air of life*] i.e., breath of life (a translation of L. *aura vitae*); cf. *2 Tamburlaine*: 'Hath sucked the measure of that vital air / That feeds the body' (II.iv.44–45).

18. *annoyed with stench*] This detail comes from Holinshed; see Introduction, pp. 58–59.

19. *Within a dungeon*] For effect Marlowe anticipates the conditions of the murder scene (see notes on V.ii.118, V.v.25, V.v.40.1); Edward is still in transit to the stinking dungeon.

20. *starved . . . sustenance*] Stowe writes, 'neyther when he was hungry would they giue him suche meate as liked him, but suche as he lothed' (p. 355).

My daily diet is heart-breaking sobs,
That almost rends the closet of my heart.
Thus lives old Edward, not relieved by any,
And so must die, though pitièd by many.
O water, gentle friends, to cool my thirst   25
And clear my body from foul excrements.
Matrevis. Here's channel water, as our charge is given;
Sit down, for we'll be barbers to your grace.
Edward. [*Struggling*] Traitors, away! What, will you murder
    me,
Or choke your sovereign with puddle water?   30
Gurney. No, but wash your face and shave away your beard,
Lest you be known and so be rescuèd.
Matrevis. Why strive you thus? Your labour is in vain.
Edward. The wren may strive against the lion's strength,
But all in vain; so vainly do I strive   35

---

22. rends] *This ed.;* rents *Q1–4;* rend *Dodsley*¹⁻²; rent *Dyce*¹⁻². 29.
Struggling] *Oliphant; not in* Q. 29. murder] *Dodsley*¹; murther *Q1–4.*
34–35. strength, / But . . . vain;] *Charlton–Waller (subst.), Ribner;* strength. /
But . . . vain, *Q1–3;* strength, / But . . . vaine, *Q4.*

---

21. *heart-breaking sobs*] This detail may represent a displacement of Stowe's
account of how the king at the humiliation of being shaved (cf. ll. 27–36
below) 'beganne to weepe and to shed teares plentifullye' (p. 356); see
Introduction, pp. 62–63.
  22. *rends*] See note on IV.vii.102.
  23. *old Edward*] See note on V.ii.119.
  24. *pitièd by many*] Holinshed, describing the attempt to rescue Edward
on the part of Kent and 'diuerse of the nobilitie,' observes that 'it often
happeneth, when men be in miserie, some will euer pitie their state' (p. 341).
  26. *foul excrements*] This is Marlowe's invention; see Introduction, pp.
58–59. *Excrements* has its modern meaning here, but Maclure (in his manuscript notes), refining upon Gill, suggests that Edward's keepers out of
cruelty deliberately misunderstand the word in the archaic sense of 'hair'; cf.
L.L.L: 'dally with my excrement, with my mustachio' (V.i.100–101).
  27. *channel water*] See note on I.i.187; cf. 'puddle water' (l. 30) below.
  28. *we'll . . . grace*] The shaving episode comes from Stowe (see Appendix
B, no. 48; also note on l. 21 above); Holinshed, however, relates a parallel
incident concerning the Abbot of Bury St Edmunds (see Introduction, pp.
56–57; also Appendix B, no. 39). Bakeless (*Tragicall History,* II, 8–9,
22–23) suggests that Marlowe may have consulted the *Chronicle* of Thomas
de la Moor (or More), which contains the same story in Latin.
  34–35. *The . . . vain*] A proverbial idea with many variations; cf. 'He
never thrives who with his master strives' (Tilley M716).

To seek for mercy at a tyrant's hand.
    They wash him with puddle water, and shave his beard away.
Immortal powers, that knows the painful cares
That waits upon my poor distressèd soul,
O level all your looks upon these daring men,
That wrongs their liege and sovereign, England's king.   40
O Gaveston, it is for thee that I am wronged;
For me, both thou and both the Spencers died,
And for your sakes a thousand wrongs I'll take.
The Spencers' ghosts, wherever they remain,
Wish well to mine; then tush, for them I'll die.   45
Matrevis. 'Twixt theirs and yours shall be no enmity.
    Come, come away. [*To* Soldiers] Now put the torches
      out;
    We'll enter in by darkness to Killingworth.

          Enter Edmund [Earl *of* KENT].

Gurney. How now, who comes there?
Matrevis. Guard the king sure; it is the Earl of Kent.   50
Edward. O gentle brother, help to rescue me.

36.1. *They . . . away*] *Q; (after line 33) Broughton.*   37. knows] *Q;* know
Dodsley[1].   38. waits] *Q;* wait *Dodsley*[1].   40. wrongs] *Q;* wrong *Dodsley*[1].
41. O Gaveston] *Q;* Oh! Gaveston *Broughton.*   44. wherever] *Dodsley*[1]*;*
where euer *Q1–4.*   45. tush] *Q;* hush *Kirschbaum.*   47. *To* Soldiers] *This
ed.; not in Q.*   48. Killingworth] *Q;* Kenilworth *Broughton.*   50. Kent.]
Q; Kent. / *Enter Soldiers. Fleay.*   51. O gentle] *Q;* O, gentle *Dodsley*[1]*;* Oh!
gentle *Broughton.*

    37–40. Marlowe apparently echoes Lodge, *Wounds of Civil War* (1586–
89): 'Immortal powers that know the painful cares / That weight upon my
poor distressed heart, / O bend your brows and level all your looks / Of
dreadful awe upon these daring men' (IV.ii.87–90).
    39. *level*] See note on III.ii.89.
    41–42. *Gaveston . . . Spencers*] Although the chronicles casually note
the parallel between Gaveston and the Spencers, Marlowe sharpens and
centralizes it; see Introduction, pp. 51–52.
    46. i.e., implying that Edward will soon join his favourites in death.
Matrevis speaks with malicious irony.
    48. *by darkness*] Holinshed reports that Edward, to prevent his being
recognized, was always moved 'in the night season' (p. 341).
    48.1. According to Holinshed, Edward was actually dead when Kent
attempted in 1329 to rescue him; see Appendix B, no. 43. See also notes on
V.ii.32, V.ii.118, V.ii.119.

Matrevis. Keep them asunder; thrust in the king.
Kent. Soldiers, let me but talk to him one word.
Gurney. Lay hands upon the earl for this assault.
Kent. Lay down your weapons; traitors, yield the king!   55
                          [Soldiers *seize* KENT.]
Matrevis. Edmund, yield thou thyself or thou shalt die.
Kent. Base villains, wherefore do you gripe me thus?
Gurney. Bind him, and so convey him to the court.
Kent. Where is the court but here? Here is the king,
        And I will visit him. Why stay you me?   60
Matrevis. The court is where Lord Mortimer remains.
        Thither shall your honour go; and so farewell.
                Exeunt MATREVIS *and* GURNEY *with* [EDWARD] *the* King.
                [Edmund Earl of KENT *and the* Soldiers *remain.*]
Kent. O, miserable is that commonweal, where lords
        Keep courts and kings are locked in prison!
Soldier. Wherefore stay we? On, sirs, to the court.   65

---

54. this] *Q;* his *Q2–4.*   55. weapons; traitors,] *Spencer (subst.), Merchant;*
weapons, traitors *Q1–4;* weapons, traitors! *Dyce¹⁻², Charlton–Waller (subst.)*
(weapons, traitors;); weapons, traitors, *Dodsley¹⁻².*   55.1 Soldiers *seize*
KENT] *Oliphant (subst.), Kirschbaum (subst.) (Soldiers hold Kent) (after line 54);*
not in *Q.*   56. thou thyself] *Dodsley¹;* thou thy self *Q;* thyself *Gill¹.*
62.2. Edmund . . . remain.] *Robinson (subst.); Manent Edmund and the*
souldiers. Q.   63–64. O, miserable . . . prison!] *Q (subst.);* Oh, miserable . . . common-weal, / Where . . . prison! *Dyce¹.*   64. prison!] *Q;* prison!
/ Enter soldiers. *Merchant.*   65. Soldier.] *Broughton (subst.) (First Soldier),*
Dyce¹⁻²; Sould. Q1–4, Dodsley¹ (Sol.); Soldiers. Dodsley².

---

57. *gripe*] See note on v.ii.9. Marlowe invents this incident. Historically,
Kent was not arrested in the action of attempting to rescue Edward but was
later charged with treason when incriminating letters concerning the affair
implicated him (Holinshed, p. 348). It is not clear that Edmund himself was
ever physically involved in the rescue mission. See Appendix B, nos. 38, 43.
    61. *Lord Mortimer*] As heir to his father's barony, the younger Mortimer
was already entitled to be so addressed (cf. I.iv.372, II.v.72, II.v.89, IV.ii.36,
IV.iii.55); but in view of Marlowe's radical compression of events in the play,
Matrevis's treasonable reference to a usurper as the source of all power
probably reflects the creation of Mortimer as Earl of March in 1328 (Holinshed,
p. 347) just as Kent's arrest is similarly antedated.
    63. *commonweal*] commonwealth, body politic.

Kent. Ay, lead me whither you will, even to my death,
　　Seeing that my brother cannot be released.

　　　　　　　　　　　　　　　　　　　　　　Exeunt.

　　　　　　　　　　　[SCENE iv]

　　　　　Enter MORTIMER [JUNIOR] *alone.*

Mortimer Junior. The king must die, or Mortimer goes down;
　　The commons now begin to pity him.
　　Yet he that is the cause of Edward's death
　　Is sure to pay for it when his son is of age,
　　And therefore will I do it cunningly.　　　　　　　　　　5
　　This letter, written by a friend of ours,
　　Contains his death, yet bids them save his life.

　　　　　　　　　　　　　　　　　　　　　　[*He reads.*]

　　'*Edwardum occidere nolite timere, bonum est*;
　　Fear not to kill the king, 'tis good he die.'
　　But read it thus, and that's another sense:　　　　　　　10
　　'*Edwardum occidere nolite, timere bonum est*;
　　Kill not the king, 'tis good to fear the worst.'

---

66. whither] *Q4;* whether *Q1–3;* where *Broughton;* whi'er *Fleay.*　　67.1
Exeunt.] *Scott; Exeunt omnes. Q; Exeunt Soldiers with Kent. Broughton.*
Heading. Scene iv] *Robinson;* Scene iii *Broughton; not in Q.*　　7.1. *He reads*]
Dyce[1] *(subst.); not in Q.*　　8. *nolite timere, bonum*] *Pendry–Maxwell; nolite*
timere bonum Q1–4 (no punctuation); nolite, timere bonum Dodsley[1].　　10.
another] *Q2–4;* an other *Q.*　　11. *nolite, timere*] *Broughton; nolite timere*
Q1–4 (no punctuation).

---

　　4. *his son*] i.e., the young Edward III.
　　6. *This letter*] Holinshed attributes the 'sophisticall' letter (p. 341) to Adam
Orleton, Bishop of Hereford; see Appendix B, no. 40. See also Introduction,
p. 58, and note on v.vi.43.
　　8–12. Q leaves the Latin unpunctuated to preserve the visual ambiguity
of the riddle; with a view to the actor, who must convey the alternative
meanings to an audience solely through inflection, I follow the punctuation of
Pendry–Maxwell first, and then of Broughton. Marlowe's own translation of
the Latin, designed for dramatic presentation, marks a distinct improvement
upon both Holinshed (p. 341; see Appendix B, no. 40) and Stowe (p. 357);.
G. C. Moore Smith gives historical precedents for the same kind of quibbling
command (*T.L.S.*, 9 August 1928, p. 581); Hilda Johnstone points out that
Marlowe's incident, based mainly on Holinshed, comes ultimately from the
chronicle of Geoffrey le Baker, who wrote in the reign of Edward III (*T.L.S.*,
16 August 1928, p. 593).

Unpointed as it is, thus shall it go,
That, being dead, if it chance to be found,
Matrevis and the rest may bear the blame,   15
And we be quit that caused it to be done.
Within this room is locked the messenger
That shall convey it and perform the rest.
And by a secret token that he bears,
Shall he be murdered when the deed is done.   20
[*Calling*] Lightborn, come forth.

[*Enter* LIGHTBORN.]

                              Art thou as resolute as
    thou wast?
Lightborn. What else, my lord? And far more resolute.
Mortimer Junior. And hast thou cast how to accomplish it?
Lightborn. Ay, ay, and none shall know which way he died.
Mortimer Junior. But at his looks, Lightborn, thou wilt relent.   25
Lightborn. Relent? Ha, ha! I use much to relent.
Mortimer Junior. Well, do it bravely, and be secret.

---

21. *Calling*] Oliphant; not in Q.   21. Lightborn . . . wast?] Q (one line);
Lightborn, come forth; / Art . . . wast? Broughton; Lightborn, / Come . . .
wast? Fleay (subst.), Brooke.   21. *Enter* LIGHTBORN] Dodsley²; not in Q.
21. as resolute] Q; so resolute Q2–4.

  Double meanings, usually comic, that arise because of mistaken or absent
pointing are not uncommon in Renaissance drama; Tancock cites Udall's
Ralph Roister Doister (III.iv.36–70 and III.v.49–83), in which a love letter
bears humorously contrary senses, and *M.N.D* (v.i.108–117), where the
prologue to *Pyramus and Thisbe* creates similar mirth. Tancock also compares
the famous ambiguous prophecy of the oracle of Apollo to Pyrrhus: 'Aio te
Aeacida Romanos vincere posse' ('O son of Aeacus, my prediction is / That
you the Roman army will defeat'; attributed to Ennius by Cicero in *De
Divinatione*, II.lvi.116; ed. W. A. Falconer [London, 1923], pp. 500–502).
  14. *being dead*] i.e., Edward being dead.
  if . . . found] See note on v.vi.43.
  16. *quit*] exculpated, cleared of blame.
  21. *Lightborn*] See Introduction, n. 101.
  22. *What else*] See note on IV.vii.118.
  23. *cast*] See note on v.ii.57.
  26. *Relent? Ha, ha!*] For the probable indebtedness to *R3* here, see Introduction, n. 66.
  27. *bravely*] with swagger or panache, showily, splendidly (spoken, of
course, with grim irony). Cf. l. 36 below and v.v.115; also 'finely handled'
(v.v.39).

Lightborn. You shall not need to give instructions;
　　'Tis not the first time I have killed a man.
　　I learned in Naples how to poison flowers,　　　　　　　30
　　To strangle with a lawn thrust through the throat,
　　To pierce the windpipe with a needle's point,
　　Or whilst one is asleep, to take a quill
　　And blow a little powder in his ears.
　　Or open his mouth and pour quicksilver down.　　　　　35
　　But yet I have a braver way than these.
Mortimer Junior. What's that?
Lightborn. Nay, you shall pardon me; none shall know my
　　　　tricks.
Mortimer Junior. I care not how it is, so it be not spied.
　　Deliver this to Gurney and Matrevis.　　　　　　　　40
　　　　　　　　　　　　　　　　　[He gives the letter.]
　　At every ten miles' end thou hast a horse.

---

31. through] *Q1-2, Dodsley*[1-2] (thro'); down *Q3-4* (downe), *Dyce*[1-2].
40.1. *He . . . letter*] *Dyce*[1] (*subst.*); *not in Q.*　　41. miles'] *Q* (miles), *Q4*; mile *Q2-3*.

---

30. *I . . . Naples*] Lightborn's catalogue of murderous skills belongs to the popular stereotype of Machiavellian villainy; cf. Barabas and Ithimore in *The Jew of Malta*: 'I learned in Florence how to kiss my hand . . .' (II.iii.23); 'I walk abroad o' nights, / And kill sick people groaning under walls; / Sometimes I go about and poison wells . . .' (II.iii.176–178); 'And in the night-time secretly would I steal / To travellers' chambers, and there cut their throats; / Once at Jerusalem, where the pilgrims kneeled, / I strowèd powder on the marble stones, / And therewithal their knees would rankle so . . .' (II.iii.208–212). Cf. also Aaron in *Tit.*, v.i.98–144, and Gloucester in *3H6*, III.ii.182–193.

31. *lawn*] linen thread.

34. *powder in his ears*] Commentators note the similarity to Claudius's murder of his brother: 'thy uncle stole, / With juice of cursed hebona in a vial, / And in the porches of my ears did pour / The leprous distillment' (*Ham.*, I.v.62–65).

35. *pour quicksilver down*] Cf. *Ham.*: 'swift as quicksilver it courses through / The natural gates and alleys of the body' (I.v.67–68); Dalton and Mary Jean Gross suggest that Marlowe's passage (see preceding note) may have served Shakespeare as a source for the account of old Hamlet's poisoning ('Shakespeare, Eustachio, Marlowe, and *Hamlet*,' *N.&Q.*, N.S. 31 [June 1984], 199–200).

36. *braver*] See note on l. 27 above.

39. *spied*] i.e., seen and reported.

42. *Take this*] Referring to the 'secret token' (l. 19), not, as Dyce thought, to money.

[*Giving a token*] Take this. Away, and never see me more.
Lightborn. No?
Mortimer Junior. No, unless thou bring me news of Edward's
    death.
Lightborn. That will I quickly do. Farewell, my lord.   45
                                              [*Exit.*]
Mortimer Junior. The prince I rule, the queen do I command,
    And with a lowly congé to the ground
    The proudest lords salute me as I pass;
    I seal, I cancel, I do what I will.
    Feared am I more than loved; let me be feared,   50
    And when I frown, make all the court look pale.
    I view the prince with Aristarchus' eyes,
    Whose looks were as a breeching to a boy.
    They thrust upon me the protectorship
    And sue to me for that that I desire.   55
    While at the council table, grave enough,

---

42. *Giving a token*] *Gill*[1] (*subst.*), *Pendry–Maxwell; Giving money Dyce*[1]
(*subst.*).   43. No?] *Broughton;* No. *Q, Dodsley*[1-2] (No!).   44. No . . .
death.] *Q* (*one line*); No; / Unless . . . death.] *Fleay.*   45.1. Exit.] *Dodsley*[2];
not in Q.   52. Aristarchus'] *Q2–4* (Aristarchus); Aristorchus *Q.*   55.
that that] *Q;* that which *Dodsley*[1-2].

---

never see me more] David Bevington observes that Mortimer 'with a slip of
the tongue . . . almost gives away his own plan for the assassin's subsequent
death' (*From Mankind to Marlowe: Growth of Structure in the Popular Drama
of Tudor England* [Cambridge, Mass., 1962], p. 242).

46. Cf. *1H6*, V.v.107–108; see Introduction, p. 28.

47. *congé*] bow.

49. *seal*] See notes on I.i.167, II.ii.146, V.ii.37.

50. An idea from Machiavelli's *The Prince*, well known and much condemned in Marlowe's lifetime, although the book had to wait until 1640 for
an English translation. In Chapter XVII Machiavelli concludes: 'because
hardly can [love and fear] subsist both together, it is much safer to be feard,
than to be lov'd' (trans. Edward Dacres [London, 1640], p. 130). Briggs
compares Cicero, *De Officiis*, I.xxviii.97: 'oderint dum metuant' ('let them
hate if only they fear'; trans. Walter Miller [London, 1913], pp. 98–99).

52. *Aristarchus*] Charlton–Waller note: 'the most famous of all gram-
marians and schoolmasters of antiquity,' who became a byword for severity.
He lived at Alexandria in the second century B.C.

53. *breeching*] whipping, birching.

54. See note on V.i.115. For the probable indebtedness to *R3*, see Introduction, pp. 26–27.

And not unlike a bashful Puritan,
First I complain of imbecility,
Saying it is *onus quam gravissimum*,
Till being interrupted by my friends,   60
Suscepi that *provinciam*, as they term it,
And to conclude, I am Protector now.
Now is all sure; the queen and Mortimer
Shall rule the realm, the king, and none rule us.
Mine enemies will I plague, my friends advance,   65
And what I list command who dare control?
Maior sum quam cui possit fortuna nocere.

---

57. Puritan] *Q3* (puretaine), *Q4* (Puritaine), *Dodsley*[1] (puritan); paretaine *Q1–2*.   64. rule us] *Q;* rules us *Q2–4*.   66. command who] *Dyce*[1–2]; commaund, who *Q1–4;* command [*semi-colon*] who [command; who] *Dodsley*[2].

---

57. *bashful Puritan*] hypocritically modest precisian (an obvious anachronism reflecting the typical ridicule of religious nonconformists on the Elizabethan stage and elsewhere). Cf. Webster's character of *A Button-maker of Amsterdame*: 'Hee winkes when he praies, and thinkes he knowes the way so well to heaven, that he can finde it blindefold. . . . his devotion is *Obstinacy*, the onely solace of his heart, *Contradiction*, and his maine end *Hypocrisie*' (*Works*, IV, 33).

58. *imbecility*] infirmity, weakness of health (not implying mental incompetence); cf. *Tro.*: 'Strength should be lord of imbecility' (I.iii.114).

59. onus quam gravissimum] a very heavy burden (in anticipation of '*suscepi provinciam*'—'I have undertaken the office'—at l. 61 below). Both phrases are legal Latin and derive from the language used for the installation of Roman governors.

61. Suscepi *that* provinciam] See preceding note.

63–64. *the . . . realm*] Marlowe modifies Holinshed at this point; see Appendix B, no. 41. According to the chronicler, Mortimer was not among the 'twelue of the greatest lords within the realme' who were chosen to 'haue the rule and gouernment till [Edward III] came to more perfect yeares,' although shortly afterwards 'the queene, and the lord Roger Mortimer tooke the whole rule so into their hands, that both the king and his said councellors were gouerened onelie by them in all matters both high and low' (p. 343).

66. *list*] desire to.

67. 'I am too great for Fortune to harm me' (a quotation from Ovid, *Metamorphoses*, VI, 195; trans. F. J. Miller [London 1921], I, 300–301); cf. v.ii.52. In Ovid the speaker is Niobe, a mythic example of hubris who unwittingly invites the punishment of having her children slaughtered and of being turned into a rock from which water flows.

68. *coronation day*] According to Holinshed, Edward III 'was crowned at Westminster on the day of the Purification of our ladie' (p. 343), i.e., Candlemas 1327, by Walter Reynolds, Archbishop of Canterbury.

And that this be the coronation day,
It pleaseth me, and Isabel the queen.

                               [Trumpets sound within.]
The trumpets sound; I must go take my place.   70

      Enter the young King [EDWARD III, *the* Arch]bishop
  [*of* CANTERBURY], Champion, Nobles, [*and*] QUEEN [ISABELLA].

Canterbury. Long live King Edward, by the grace of God,
  King of England and Lord of Ireland.
Champion. If any Christian, Heathen, Turk, or Jew
  Dares but affirm that Edward's not true king,
  And will avouch his saying with the sword,   75
  I am the Champion that will combat him.
Mortimer Junior. None comes. Sound trumpets.

                                  [Trumpets sound.]
King Edward III.   Champion, here's to thee.
       [Drinks a toast and gives Champion *the goblet.*]
Isabella. Lord Mortimer, now take him to your charge.

69.1. *Trumpets sound within*] *Dyce*[1] *(subst.); not in* Q.   70.1–2. *Enter* . . .
QUEEN] *Q; Enter* . . . Queen [*continuation of Scene iv*] *Robinson; Scene v* [*new
heading followed by group entrance*] *Oliphant.*   70.1. Archbishop *of* CANTER-
BURY] *Dyce*[1–2]*, Cunningham (subst.)* [*Archbishop*]*; Bishop* Q1–4*; Bishop of
Canterbury Merchant; Bishop of Winchester Broughton; Bishops Oxberry.*
71. Canterbury] *Dyce*[1] *(subst.); Bish.* Q*; B. of Win. Broughton.*   74. Dares]
Q1–4*; Dare Oxberry.*   77.1. *Trumpets sound*] *Dyce*[1] *(subst.); not in* Q.
77, 80, 88, 91, 94, 106, 111. King Edward III] *Dyce*[1] *(subst.); King* Q.
77.1. *Drinks . . . goblet.*] *Charlton–Waller (conj.), Spencer (conj.), Lunt
(subst.), Gill*[1]*; Drinks. Pendry–Maxwell; Gives a purse. Dyce*[1–2].

70.2. Champion] Lunt notes: 'The Coronation procession enters, including
the King's Champion, an ancient officer who at the time of the coronation
rode armed into Westminster Hall, and with a proclamation made by a herald
threw down his gauntlet, and challenged any who disputed the King's right
to the throne to single combat. After the challenge the King drank to the
Champion out of a silver-gilt cup which he then handed to the Champion
as his fee [see l. 77 and stage direction below]. The ceremony has been
discontinued since the coronation of George IV.' Lunt objects to the inconsistency of young Edward's participation in this custom since the boy had
earlier objected to assuming the crown without his father's personal authorization (v.ii.91–94); Edward II, however, has by now officially abdicated in
favour of his son, and in any case Marlowe makes it abundantly clear (cf. his
powerlessness to save Kent in the action that directly follows and especially
Kent's charge at l. 85) that the youthful successor is still being manipulated
by his mother and Mortimer.

Enter Soldiers *with* [Edmund,] *the* Earl *of* KENT, prisoner.

Mortimer Junior. What traitor have we there with blades and
 bills?
Soldier. Edmund, the Earl of Kent.
King Edward III.   What hath he done?   80
Soldier. 'A would have taken the king away perforce,
 As we were bringing him to Killingworth.
Mortimer Junior. Did you attempt his rescue, Edmund?
 Speak.
Kent. Mortimer, I did; he is our king,
 And thou compell'st this prince to wear the crown.   85
Mortimer Junior. Strike off his head! He shall have martial
 law.
Kent. Strike off my head? Base traitor, I defy thee.
King Edward III. [*To* MORTIMER JUNIOR] My lord, he is my
 uncle and shall live.
Mortimer Junior. My lord, he is your enemy and shall die.
Kent. Stay, villains.   90
King Edward III. Sweet mother, if I cannot pardon him,
 Entreat my Lord Protector for his life.
Isabella. Son, be content; I dare not speak a word.
King Edward III. Nor I, and yet methinks I should
 command;
 But, seeing I cannot, I'll entreat for him.   95
 [*To* MORTIMER JUNIOR] My lord, if you will let my uncle
 live,

80, 81. *Soldier*] *Broughton (subst.) (First Soldier), Dyce*[1–2]*; Sould. Q, Dodsley*[1]
(Sol.). 82. Killingworth] *Q;* Kenilworth *Broughton.* 83. Edmund?
Speak] *Dodsley*[2]*;* Edmund speake? *Q;* Edmund, speak?*Dodsley*[1]*.* 85.
compell'st] *Q2* (compel'st), *Q4;* compelst *Q, Q3.* 88. *To* MORTIMER
JUNIOR] *This ed.; not in Q.* 94. methinks] *Dodsley*[1]*;* me thinkes *Q.* 96.
To MORTIMER JUNIOR] *This ed.; not in Q.*

---

79. *What traitor*] See notes on v.ii.32, v.ii.119, v.iii.57.
blades and bills] swords and halberds.
86. *shall have*] will get.
martial law] This detail is unhistorical; Holinshed (p. 348) reports that
Kent was tried and convicted by the peers in Parliament; see Appendix B,
no. 43. Marlowe may intend a parallel with the summary 'justice' meted out
to Gaveston.
96. *let my uncle live*] For the similarity to *R3*, see Introduction, p. 25.

I will requite it when I come to age.

Mortimer Junior. 'Tis for your highness' good and for the
 realm's.

 [*To* Soldiers] How often shall I bid you bear him hence?

Kent. [*To* MORTIMER JUNIOR] Art thou king? Must I die at thy
 command?   100

Mortimer Junior. At our command. Once more, away with
 him.

Kent. [*Struggling*] Let me but stay and speak; I will not go.
 Either my brother or his son is king,
 And none of both them thirst for Edmund's blood.
 And therefore, soldiers, whither will you hale me? 105
      They hale Edmund [Earl *of* KENT] *away,*
        and carry him to be beheaded.

King Edward III. [*To* ISABELLA] What safety may I look for at
 his hands,
 If that my uncle shall be murdered thus?

Isabella. Fear not, sweet boy, I'll guard thee from thy foes.
 Had Edmund lived, he would have sought thy death.
 Come son, we'll ride a-hunting in the park.   110

King Edward III. And shall my uncle Edmund ride with us?

---

99. *To* Soldiers] *Broughton (subst.); not in Q.* 100. *To* MORTIMER JUNIOR]
This ed.; not in Q. 100. king] *Q1–2; a* king *Q3–4.* 102. *Struggling*]
Kirschbaum (subst.); not in Q. 104. none of both them] *Q2, Q4;* none of
both, then *Q, Q3, Kirschbaum (subst.)* (none of both then); neither of them
Scott. 105. whither] *Q4;* whether *Q1–3.* 105.1–2. *They* hale . . .
beheaded.] *Q; Edmund is borne off. Broughton.* 106. *To* ISABELLA] *This ed.;
Points to Mortimer. Kirschbaum; not in Q.* 107. murdered] *Dodsley¹;*
murthered *Q.*

---

101. *our command*] Marlowe achieves a subtly ironic effect here: 'our'
refers ostensibly to the queen and himself, the *de facto* guardians of the king,
but the phrase also conveys the suggestion that Mortimer has arrogantly
usurped the royal plural; see note on IV.vi.35.

104. *none of both them*] i.e., neither of them. This phrase, which is awkward and sounds unidiomatic, clearly gave the early printers trouble: Q2
corrected Q's 'both, then' to 'both them'; then Q3 reintroduced the original
error, which Q4 in turn had to recorrect. The problem appears to be the
puzzling and unnecessary 'them,' perhaps introduced to fill out the metre.

106. *his hands*] i.e., Mortimer's.

111. Briggs, taking this speech at face value, wonders how a boy of
fourteen could 'ask this childish question'; but surely Edward speaks with
precocious irony, not naively.

Isabella. He is a traitor; think not on him. Come.

Exeunt.

[SCENE v]

Enter MATREVIS and GURNEY.

Matrevis. Gurney, I wonder the king dies not,
    Being in a vault up to the knees in water,
    To which the channels of the castle run,
    From whence a damp continually ariseth
    That were enough to poison any man,   5
    Much more a king brought up so tenderly.
Gurney. And so do I, Matrevis. Yesternight
    I opened but the door to throw him meat,
    And I was almost stifled with the savour.
Matrevis. He hath a body able to endure   10
    More than we can inflict, and therefore now
    Let us assail his mind another while.
Gurney. Send for him out thence, and I will anger him.

112.1. *Exeunt.*] *Broughton; Exeunt omnes. Q.*   *Heading.* Scene v] *Robinson;*
Scene iv *Broughton;* Scene vi *Oliphant; not in Q.*   3. castle] *Q1–2* (castell);
Bastell *Q3–4 (misprint?).*   3. run] *Q1–3* (runne); runs *Q4.*   11. inflict]
Q4; enflict *Q1–3.*

---

2. Marlowe imaginatively augments the physical and psychological sufferings of the captive Edward II as given in Holinshed (p. 341); see Appendix
B, no. 44, and Introduction, pp. 58–59.

5. *enough . . . man*] Probably based on Holinshed's statement that Edward,
'bearing it out stronglie, as a man of a tough nature, continued still in life, so
as it seemed he was verie like to escape that danger [of being overcome with
the stench of carrion], as he had by purging either vp or downe auoided the
force of such poison as had beene ministred to him sundrie times before, of
purpose so to rid him' (p. 341). Fabyan says that Edward 'was fayre of
bodye, and greate of strength' (p. 164).

10. *a . . . endure*] Edward's endurance becomes a dramatic and redeeming
evidence of his innate regality. Merchant compares the 'sifting' of the Old
Man in *Doctor Faustus*: Faustus asks Mephistophilis to afflict the 'aged
man . . . With greatest torment that our hell affords,' to which the reply is,
'His faith is great; I cannot touch his soul; / But what I may afflict his body
with / I will attempt, which is but little worth' (xviii.84–89). See preceding
note.

Matrevis. But stay, who's this?

          Enter LIGHTBORN [*bearing a letter*].

Lightborn.   My Lord Protector greets you.
                        [*Gives the letter.*]
Gurney. What's here? I know not how to conster it.   15
Matrevis. Gurney, it was left unpointed for the nonce:
    [*Reading*] '*Edwardum occidere nolite timere*—';
    That's his meaning.
Lightborn. Know you this token?
                        [*Shows the token*].
         I must have the king.
Matrevis. Ay, stay a while; thou shalt have answer straight.   20
    [*Aside to* GURNEY] This villain's sent to make away the
      king.
Gurney. [*Aside*] I thought as much.
Matrevis.   [*Aside*] And when the murder's done,
    See how he must be handled for his labour.
    Pereat iste! Let him have the king.
    [*To* LIGHTBORN] What else? Here is the keys; this is the
      lake.   25

---

14. *bearing a letter*] Merchant; not in Q.   14.1. *Gives the letter*] Dyce[1]
(subst.); *Giving a paper* Scott.   15. conster] Q; construe Q2–4.   17.
Reading] This ed.; not in Q.   19. *Shows the token*] Gill[2]; *Gives token* Dyce[1];
not in Q.   20. a while] Q1–4; awhile Broughton.   21. *Aside to* GURNEY]
Bullen (subst.); not in Q.   22. Aside . . . Aside] Bullen; not in Q.   25. *To*
LIGHTBORN] This ed.; (after line 25) Merchant; not in Q.   25. Here is] Q1–2
(heere is); heer's Q3, Q4 (here's); here are Merchant.   25. keys] Q1–4; key
Broughton.   25. lake] Q1–4; lock Collier MS., Bullen (conj.), Ellis.

15. *conster*] translate (a variant of *construe*); cf. *Shr.*, III.i.30.
16. *for the nonce*] for this particular occasion, i.e. on purpose; cf. *Ham.*:
'I'll have prepar'd him / A chalice for the nonce' (IV.vii.159–160).
21. *make away*] See note on II.ii.235.
24. Pereat iste!] Let him perish. The order for Lightborn's murder has
been written in Latin so that the victim cannot read it.
25. *What else?*] See note on IV.vii.118. Since Lightborn uses it twice (cf.
v.iv.22), this expression, perhaps accompanied by a recognizable gesture,
may be an individualizing trait or habit of speech.
lake] dungeon, underground pit; cf. *2 Tamburlaine*: 'And travel headlong
to the lake of hell' (III.v.24). Briggs, who has carefully investigated this word
('On the Meaning of the Word "Lake" in Marlowe's *Edward II*,' *M.L.N.*, 39

Do as you are commanded by my lord.

Lightborn. I know what I must do. Get you away.

Yet be not far off; I shall need your help.

See that in the next room I have a fire,

And get me a spit, and let it be red hot.   30

Matrevis. Very well.

Gurney. Need you anything besides?

Lightborn. What else? A table and a featherbed.

---

30. spit] *Q, Q3–4;* spet *Q2.*   33. What else? A table] *Q* (What else, a table), *Dyce*$^{1-2}$; A table *Dodsley*$^{1-2}$.

[1924], 437–438), shows that it derives from L. *lacus* (= den, cave, or pit, among other meanings) and appears in numerous medieval and Renaissance works. H. W. Crundell suggests that 'lake' may reflect the biblical account of the prophet Jeremiah's incarceration in the mire of a disused cistern (Jeremiah 38:6); see 'The Death of Edward II in Marlowe's Play,' *N.&Q.*, 179 (1940), 207. The attempt to emend to 'lock' because of the proximity of 'keys' (see textual note) or the retention of 'lake' with the meaning of *moat* (even though 'the moat' is mentioned later at l. 117 as the place where Lightborn's corpse is disposed of) are misguided.

30. *spit*] Dyce, Briggs, Charlton–Waller, and others have assumed that because Q fails to mention the spit (explicit in the sources) in either dialogue or stage directions during the staging of the murder, Marlowe omitted it from the action. This seems most unlikely. From the perspective of modern theatrical practice, Q's stage directions are deficient in numerous places. Moreover, the sensational method of Edward's death was notorious, and Elizabethan audiences, who were anything but squeamish, would have expected to see it represented even if (as Merchant supposes) the actual penetration was shielded from full view 'behind the arras of a stage pavilion or "inner stage".' The spitting is symbolically important to the homosexual theme of the entire drama, and Lightborn's name (with its diabolical and visual associations) even seems to evoke the spit. If the playwright had intended not to show it, there would be little reason for having the murderer mention his weapon during his preparations, thereby setting up a disappointing anticlimax.

33. *A . . . featherbed*] Marlowe's sources differ slightly on the implements used for Edward II's murder. Holinshed writes that the murderers held the king down 'with heauie featherbeds or a table (as some write)' so that the spit could be inserted, their motive being to conceal the 'appearance of any wound or hurt' (p. 341); see Appendix B, no. 44 for the full account. Stowe says, 'they came running in vppon him, as he laye in his bedde, with greate heauye featherbeddes, as much in weyghte as xv menne coulde beare, wherwyth they oppressed and smothered hym, into whom also they thrust a plummers yron, being made redde hotte, vp into his bowels, throughe a certaine instrumente like to the end of a Trumpet, or glister pipe, put in hys fundiment, burning thereby his inward partes' (pp. 357–358). Grafton

Gurney. That's all?

Lightborn. Ay, ay; so, when I call you, bring it in.   35

Matrevis. Fear not you that.

Gurney. Here's a light to go into the dungeon.

> [*He gives a light, then exit with* MATREVIS.]

Lightborn. So now, must I about this gear; ne'er was there any

    So finely handled as this king shall be.

> [*Opens the dungeon.*]

---

36. you] *Q;* thou *Q2–4.*   36–37. Fear . . . that. / Here's . . . dungeon.] *Q;*
Fear . . . that. / Here is . . . light / To go . . . dungeon. *Fleay.*   37–37.1.
dungeon. / *He gives* . . . MATREVIS.] *Dyce² (subst.);* dungeon. *Q1–4;* dungeon.
/ *Exeunt separately. Broughton;* dungeon. / *Exit with Matrevis. Dyce¹.*   38.
Lightborn. So now] *Q; Light.* So now [*continuation of Scene v*] *Robinson;* Scene
v [*new heading*]. / *Enter Lightborn.* / *Light.* So, now *Broughton.*   38. So
now . . . any] *Q (one line);* So now, / Must . . . any *Dyce²;* So, / Now . . . any
Bowers.   39. shall be] *Q4;* shalbe *Q1–3.*   39.1. *Opens the dungeon*]
Oliphant; not in Q.

---

reports that the murderers 'layde a great Table vpon his belly, and with
strength of men at all the foure corners pressed it downe vpon his body,
wherewith the king awooke and beyng sore afrayde of death turned hys
bodye, so that then he laye grouelyng. Then these murderers tooke a horne
and thrust it vp into his fundement as farre as they might, and then tooke a
hote burnying Spit, and put it thorough the horne into his body, and in
the ende kylled and vilye murdered him' (p. 218). Fabyan omits details
altogether, relating only that 'the said Edward by the meanes of sir Roger
Mortimer was miserably slayne' (p. 194). Marlowe appears to synthesize
these accounts, using both the table and the featherbed—the first to hold the
king in place, the other to cushion his body from tell-tale bruises (see ll.
111–112 below). Then the lethal spit is inserted.

It is also worth noting that Holinshed reports a similar use of featherbeds
in his account of the murder of Thomas of Woodstock, Duke of Gloucester,
in Richard II's reign; here Thomas Mowbray, the king's agent, 'caused his
seruants to cast featherbeds vpon [Gloucester], and so smoother him to death'
(p. 489). For the parallel to the smothering of Duke Humphrey in *The
Contention* and the possible indebtedness to Marlowe, see Introduction,
pp. 35–36.

35. *it*] i.e., all of it (the table, the featherbed, and the spit).

37. *a light*] Marlowe may intend an ironic connection to Lightborn's name
(cf. l. 41 below); see note on v.iv.21.

38. *So now*] Dyce, imagining that Lightborn draws aside a curtain to
reveal the king (see stage direction at l. 40.1 and note), unnecessarily marks a
fresh scene at this point.

gear] business, job. Purvis Boyette, citing Marlowe's use of the word *gear*
in *Ovid's Elegies* (I.vi.36), where it refers to 'sexual organs,' thinks 'a sexual
pun' is involved here; see 'Wanton Humour and Wanton Poets: Homosexuality in Marlowe's *Edward II,*' *Tulane Studies in English*, 22 (1977), 47.

Foh! Here's a place indeed with all my heart.   40

[EDWARD *comes up from below, or is discovered.*]

Edward. Who's there? What light is that? Wherefore comes
    thou?
Lightborn. To comfort you and bring you joyful news.
Edward. Small comfort finds poor Edward in thy looks.
    Villain, I know thou com'st to murder me.
Lightborn. To murder you, my most gracious lord?   45
    Far is it from my heart to do you harm.
    The queen sent me to see how you were used,
    For she relents at this your misery.
    And what eyes can refrain from shedding tears

40.1. EDWARD ... *discovered.*] *Bowers* (subst.); *Enters. Oxberry* (after line 41);
Opens the dungeon, where the deposed King is seen standing in mire. Oliphant
(after line 39); *Draws curtain before rear stage. Brooke–Paradise* (after line 39),
Kirschbaum (subst.); *Discovers King Edward II. Spencer; not in Q.*   41.
comes] *Q*; com'st *Q2–4*; comest *Merchant.*   44. com'st] *Q* (comst), *Q2–4*;
comest *Merchant.*   44, 45, 86, 97. murder] *Dodsley*[1]; murther *Q*.

40.1. *Q*'s staging here is unclear. Given the use of the word 'lake' earlier in
the scene (see note on l. 25 above) and also 'dungeon' (ll. 37, 55), it is logical
to suppose that a trapdoor is used and that the king emerges from below. This
action would accord fittingly with the hellish symbolism of Edward's
confinement and suffering. Glynne Wickham, however, argues that the
theatres for which Marlowe wrote made use of 'removable trestle-stages' and
were too early for use of the trap to have been practicable; he concludes: 'the
fact must be faced that in none of Marlowe's plays do any stage-directions
exist authorizing us to assume the existence of a stage-trap at floor level'
('*Exeunt to the Cave*: Notes on the Staging of Marlowe's Plays,' *T.D.R.*, 8.4
[summer 1964], 188–189). Dyce's notion of Edward's being discovered
behind a curtain (see previous note) may therefore be correct. Lunt also
thinks that 'the Inner Stage ... represents Edward's dungeon.' Marlowe
clearly departs from Holinshed, where Edward is lodged 'in a chamber ouer a
foule filthie dungeon' (p. 341) rather than in one. Perhaps alternative stagings
were used in Marlowe's age depending on the venue.
    41. *Wherefore comes thou?*] The situation here is suggestively like the
murders of Henry VI and Clarence in Shakespeare's first tetralogy. Cf. *3H6*:
'*King Henry.* But wherefore dost thou come? Is 't for my life? / *Gloucester.*
Think'st thou I am an executioner? / *King Henry.* A persecutor, I am sure,
thou art' (v.vi.29–31); *R3*: '*Clarence.* In God's name what art thou? / *First
Murderer.* A man, as you are. . . .*Clarence.* How darkly and how deadly dost
thou speak! / Your eyes do meance me. Why look you pale? / Who sent you
hither? Wherefore do you come?' (I.iv.165–174).
    48. *relents*] softens, becomes tender.

To see a king in this most piteous state?   50
Edward. Weepst thou already? List awhile to me,
  And then thy heart, were it as Gurney's is,
  Or as Matrevis', hewn from the Caucasus,
  Yet will it melt ere I have done my tale.
  This dungeon where they keep me is the sink   55
  Wherein the filth of all the castle falls.
Lightborn. O villains!
Edward. And there in mire and puddle have I stood
  This ten days' space; and lest that I should sleep,
  One plays continually upon a drum.   60
  They give me bread and water, being a king,
  So that for want of sleep and sustenance
  My mind's distempered, and my body's numbed,
  And whether I have limbs or no I know not.
  O, would my blood dropped out from every vein,   65
  As doth this water from my tattered robes.
  Tell Isabel, the queen, I looked not thus
  When for her sake I ran at tilt in France
  And there unhorsed the Duke of Cleremont.
Lightborn. O speak no more, my lord; this breaks my heart.   70
                           [*A bed is thrust out or brought onstage.*]

---

51. awhile] *Q4;* a while *Q1–3.*   59. days'] *Broughton;* dayes *Q1–4,*
Dodsley[1–2] (days); day' *Robinson.*   65. dropped] *Q* (dropt); drop *Dodsley*[1].
66. tattered] *Q1–3, Dodsley*[1] (tatter'd); tottered *Q4.*   69. Cleremont] *Q;*
Claremont *Keltie.*   70.1. *A bed . . . onstage.*] *This ed.;* Claps hands, and a
servant brings in a feather-bed. Kirschbaum; not in Q.

---

50. This line underscores Marlowe's point that the desecration of royalty
is an important aspect of the tragedy.
  51. *List*] Listen.
  53. *Caucasus*] The mountain range bordering Asia (between the Black and
Caspian seas) proverbially noted for its barren rocks and rugged impen-
etrability.
  62–63. *for . . . numbed*] Briggs compares Bajazeth in *1 Tamburlaine*: 'My
empty stomach, full of idle heat, / Draws bloody humours from my feeble
parts, / Preserving life by hasting cruel death. / My veins are pale, my sinews
hard and dry, / My joints be numbed; unless I eat, I die' (IV.iv.96–99).
  67–68. For the indebtedness to *2H6* and perhaps also Fabyan, see
Introduction, pp. 27–28, 62. Levin remarks of this speech, 'It is a far cry
of triumph, more theatrical than chivalric; but Shakespeare must have borne
it in mind when Othello, on the verge of suicide, remembered his victory
over the Turk at Aleppo' (*Overreacher*, p. 96).

Lie on this bed and rest yourself awhile.
Edward. These looks of thine can harbour nought but death.
I see my tragedy written in thy brows.
Yet stay a while; forbear thy bloody hand,
And let me see the stroke before it comes,   75
That even then when I shall lose my life,
My mind may be more steadfast on my God.
Lightborn. What means your highness to mistrust me thus?
Edward. What means thou to dissemble with me thus?
Lightborn. These hands were never stained with innocent
blood,   80
Nor shall they now be tainted with a king's.
Edward. Forgive my thought for having such a thought.

---

71. yourself] *Dodsley*[1–2]; your selfe *Q1–4*.   71. awhile] *Scott;* a while
Q1–4.   74. a while] *Q1–4;* awhile *Broughton*.   76. even] *Dodsley*[1]; and
euen *Q1–4*.   79. means] *Q* (meanes), *Q3–4;* mean'st *Q2*.   82. my
thought] *Q;* me then *Broughton;* my fau't *Fleay*.   83.1. *Gives a jewel*]
Dyce[1] *(subst.); not in Q.*

---

71. *Lie on this bed*] Despite Briggs, Charlton–Waller, and Lunt, all of
whom assume that Lightborn offers Edward the featherbed mentioned earlier
at l. 33, this must be a different bed altogether. As is clear from the chronicle
accounts (see note on l. 33 above), the function of the featherbed, a soft and
flexible tick usually containing goose down, is to *cover* Edward's body for
the purpose of immobilizing and buffering it from the bruises that would
otherwise be inflicted by the upturned table; the chronicles also mention the
featherbed as a means of smothering the king. The bed introduced here,
presumably one of greater rigidity, is necessary for the victim to lie and fall
asleep upon.

73. *tragedy . . . brows*] Cf. *1 Tamburlaine*: 'characters graven in thy brows'
(I.ii.168). 'Tragedy' here obviously implies death but also embodies the
medieval concept of fall from high estate as in the *Mirror for Magistrates*.

76–77. *when . . . God*] This is unimpeachable religious orthodoxy for
Elizabethans. The Great Litany in the Book of Common Prayer contains the
petition: 'from battle, murder, and from sudden death, Good Lord deliver
us.'

82. *my thought*] As early as Broughton's edition, this phrase has puzzled
editors. Fleay emended to 'fau't' (i.e., fault), apparently in the belief that the
use of 'thought' twice in the line is unacceptably tautologous; Briggs cites
3H6: 'O montrous fault, to harbour such a thought!' (III.ii.164). It is possible
that the compositor allowed the second 'thought' to contaminate 'fault' in the
manuscript, but the line as it stands in Q makes reasonable sense if we think
of the speaker's thought in the generic sense as generating the particular
thought (or suspicion) that murder is in the offing.

One jewel have I left; receive thou this.

[*Gives a jewel.*]

Still fear I, and I know not what's the cause,
But every joint shakes as I give it thee.   85
O, if thou harbour'st murder in thy heart,
Let this gift change thy mind and save thy soul.
Know that I am a king. O, at that name,
I feel a hell of grief. Where is my crown?
Gone, gone! And do I remain alive?   90
Lightborn. You're overwatched, my lord. Lie down and rest.
Edward. But that grief keeps me waking, I should sleep;
For not these ten days have these eyes' lids closed.
Now as I speak they fall, and yet with fear
Open again. O wherefore sits thou here?   95

[*Lies on the bed.*]

Lightborn. If you mistrust me, I'll be gone, my lord.
Edward. No, no, for if thou mean'st to murder me,
Thou wilt return again, and therefore stay.

[EDWARD *falls asleep.*]

Lightborn. [*Aside*] He sleeps.
Edward. [*Waking*] O let me not die! Yet stay, O stay a while.   100
Lightborn. How now, my lord?

---

86. harbour'st] *Q1–3* (harborst), *Q4;* harbourest *Ellis.*   90. remain alive]
Q1–2 (remaine aliue); *Q3–4, Dodsley²* (remain); still remain alive *Dodsley¹;*
yet remain *Broughton.*   93. eyes' lids] *Q* (eyes lids), *Q2–3;* eye lids *Q4,*
Dodsley¹⁻² (eye-lids).   95. sits] *Q1–4;* sit'st *Dodsley¹, Broughton* (sitt'st).
95.1. Lies . . . bed] *Kirschbaum; not in Q.*   97. mean'st] *Q1–4* (meanst);
meanest *Merchant.*   98.1. EDWARD *falls asleep*] *Oxberry (subst.) (Lies down),*
Dyce² (subst.) (Sleeps); not in Q.   99. Aside] *Merchant; not in Q.*   100.
Waking] *Dyce²; not in Q.*   100. O let . . . while.] *Q (one line);* Oh! / Let . . .
while! *Fleay.*   100. die! Yet] *Q* (die, yet), *Q2–3, Dodsley¹⁻²* (subst.) (die;
yet); dye yet, *Q4, Broughton* (die yet;); die [die;] *Morpurgo.*   100. stay, O
stay] *Q1–3;* O stay *Q4;* stay *McLaughlin;* stay yet, O stay *Morpurgo.*   100.
a while] *Q1–4;* awhile *Broughton.*

---

83. *One jewel*] See note on v.ii.71.
89–90. *Where . . . alive?*] Edward's point, of course, is that losing the
crown ordinarily coincides with death; cf. the ritual statement, 'The king is
dead; long live the king.'
91. *You're overwatched*] i.e., you are exhausted from lack of sleep (cf. l. 93
below).
92. *But that*] Except that.
grief] anxiety, distress, mental suffering (not sorrow in the usual modern
sense).

Edward. Something still buzzeth in mine ears
       And tells me if I sleep I never wake.
       This fear is that which makes me tremble thus;
       And therefore tell me, wherefore art thou come?   105
Lightborn. To rid thee of thy life. Matrevis, come!

                    [*Enter* MATREVIS.]

Edward. I am too weak and feeble to resist.
       Assist me, sweet God, and receive my soul.
Lightborn. Run for the table.

                                        [*Exit* MATREVIS.]

       [*Re-enter* MATREVIS *with* GURNEY, *bringing the table,
                     a featherbed, and spit.*]

Edward. O spare me! Or dispatch me in a trice!   110
Lightborn. So, lay the table down, and stamp on it,
       But not too hard, lest that you bruise his body.
       [*Using the table and featherbed to hold him down, they murder*
              EDWARD, *who screams as the spit penetrates him.*]
Matrevis. I fear me that this cry will raise the town,

106.1. *Enter* MATREVIS.] *Gill[1]*; *Enter Gurney and Matrevis. Scott; not in Q.*
109.1. *Exit* MATREVIS] *Oliphant; not in Q.*   109.2–3. *Re-enter . . . spit*] *Gill[1]*
(subst.) (Matrevis fetches in Gurney with table and spit); Matrevis brings in a
table. Thomas, Oliphant; not in Q.   112.1–2. *Using . . . him*] *Gill[1]* (*subst.*)
(They assault Edward, who screams and dies); They murder him. Scott; not in Q.

---

102. Briggs compares *Doctor Faustus*: 'O, something soundeth in mine
ears, / "Abjure this magic . . ."' (v.7–8); 'Who buzzeth in mine ears I am a
spirit?' (vi.14).

109. *table*] Marlowe's emphasis on the table (cf. ll. 111–112 below) suggests the influence of Grafton's chronicle; see note on l. 33 above, and
Introduction, pp. 64–65.

113. *this . . . town*] Edward's piercing scream became legendary. Holinshed
writes, 'His crie did mooue manie within the castell and towne of Berkley to
compassion, plainelie hearing him vtter a wailefull noise, as the tormentors
were about to murther him, so that diuerse being awakened therewith (as
they themselues confessed) praied heartilie to God to receiue his soule, when
they vnderstood by his crie what the matter ment' (p. 341). Peele in *The
Honour of the Garter* (1593) may have remembered Marlowe's scene when he
referred to Edward II's 'tragicke cry' which 'even now me thinkes I heare, /
When gracelesse wretches murthered him by night.' Peele, like Marlowe,
attributes chief responsibility to 'that cruell Mortimer / That plotted Edwards
death' (ll. 220–224; *Minor Works*, I, 253).

And therefore let us take horse and away.

Lightborn. Tell me, sirs, was it not bravely done?   115

Gurney. Excellent well. Take this for thy reward.

> *Then* GURNEY *stabs* LIGHTBORN, [*who dies*].

Come, let us cast the body in the moat,

And bear the king's to Mortimer, our lord.

Away!

> *Exeunt* [*with the bodies*].

[SCENE vi]

Enter MORTIMER [JUNIOR] *and* MATREVIS [*at different doors*].

Mortimer Junior. Is't done, Matrevis, and the murderer dead?

Matrevis. Ay, my good lord; I would it were undone.

Mortimer Junior. Matrevis, if thou now growest penitent

    I'll be thy ghostly father; therefore choose

    Whether thou wilt be secret in this   5

    Or else die by the hand of Mortimer.

---

115. sirs] *Q;* first *Merchant (misprint?).*   115. it] *Q, Q3–4;* is *Q2 (misprint for* 'this'?); this *Fleay (conj.).*   116.1. who dies] *Dyce²; not in Q.*   118–119. And . . . lord. / Away!] *Broughton; one line in Q.*   119.1. Exeunt.] *Scott; Exeunt omnes. Q.*   119.1. with the bodies] *Dyce¹; not in Q.*   Heading. Scene vi] *Broughton;* Scene vii *Oliphant; not in Q.*   0.1. at different doors] *Bowers; not in Q.*   1. murderer] *Dodsley¹⁻²;* murtherer *Q1–4.*   3. now growest] *Q1–2;* growest *Q3–4;* now grow'st *Broughton.*

---

115. *bravely*] See note on v.iv.27.

117. *moat*] See note on l. 25 above.

118. *bear . . . Mortimer*] Marlowe of course knew nothing of the romantic story, contained in a letter to Edward III by one Manuele de Fieschi (a Genoese priest), that Edward II escaped from Berkeley Castle in disguise and after many travels in Ireland and on the continent became a religious recluse in northern Italy. For details see G. P. Cuttino and Thomas W. Lyman, 'Where is Edward II?', *Speculum*, 53 (1978), 522–544.

v.vi.4. *ghostly father*] priest (spiritual father). Mortimer is threatening Matrevis with death since it was a common function of priests to hear confessions of the dying and to ready their souls for heaven by administration of holy communion. 'To be one's priest' therefore became a grim euphemism for killing, for easing one into the afterlife; cf. Kyd, *Spanish Tragedy*: 'Who first lays hand on me, I'll be his priest' (III.iv.37). The phrase is proverbial (Tilley P587), but Marlowe may also intend a pun on 'ghostly' (i.e., I'll help turn you into a ghost). There is also probably a glancing allusion to the mandatory secrecy of crimes revealed in sacramental confession (cf. l. 5).

Matrevis. Gurney, my lord, is fled, and will, I fear,
    Betray us both; therefore let me fly.
Mortimer Junior. Fly to the savages.
Matrevis. I humbly thank your honour.   10
                                                    [Exit.]

Mortimer Junior. As for myself, I stand as Jove's huge tree,
    And others are but shrubs compared to me.
    All tremble at my name, and I fear none;
    Let's see who dare impeach me for his death.

             Enter [ISABELLA] *the* Queen.

Isabella. Ah, Mortimer, the king my son hath news   15
    His father's dead, and we have murdered him.
Mortimer Junior. What if he have? The king is yet a child.
Isabella. Ay, ay, but he tears his hair and wrings his hands,
    And vows to be revenged upon us both.
    Into the council chamber he is gone   20
    To crave the aid and succour of his peers.
    Ay me, see where he comes, and they with him.
    Now, Mortimer, begins our tragedy.

10.1. *Exit.*] *Scott; not in Q.*   11. myself] *Dodsley*[1]*; my selfe Q1–4.*   15.
Ah] *Q* (A), *Dodsley*[1-2]*; Ah! Broughton; Oh Oxberry.*   18. Ay, ay] *Q1–4*
(I, I), *Dodsley*[1-2]*; Aye Broughton, Oxberry* (Ay).   22. Ay] *Q* (Aye); Ah
Dodsley[1-2].   23.1. *and* Attendants] *Broughton; not in Q.*

    9. *to the savages*] i.e., beyond civilization. On the fates of Matrevis and
Gurney Marlowe departs from his sources. According to Holinshed, 'The
queene, [Orleton], and others . . . outlawed and banished . . . Matreuers,
and . . . Gourney, who flieng vnto [Marseilles], three yeares after being
knowne, taken, and brought toward England was beheaded on the sea, least
he should accuse the chiefe dooers. . . . Iohn Matreuers, repenting himselfe,
laie long hidden in Germanie, and in the end died penitentlie' (pp. 341–342)
See Appendix B, no. 45.
    11. *Jove's huge tree*] the oak (traditionally sacred to Jove because of its
Olympian size and strength); cf. *A.Y.L:* 'It may well be call'd Jove's tree,
when it drops forth such fruit [i.e., an acorn]' (III.ii.233). In the hierarchy of
trees, the oak was king.
    16. *we . . . him*] Among the several charges against Mortimer at his trial in
1330, the first was 'that he had procured Edward of Carnaruan the kings
father to be murthered in most heinous and tyrannous maner' (Holinshed, p.
349).
    18–19. *tears . . . revenged*] This is Marlowe's invention.
    23. *tragedy*] fall; see note on V.v.73.

Enter the King [EDWARD III] *with the* Lords [*and* Attendants].

First Lord. Fear not, my lord; know that you are a king.

King Edward III. [*To* MORTIMER JUNIOR] Villain!

Mortimer Junior.   How now, my lord?   25

King Edward III. Think not that I am frighted with thy
    words.

    My father's murdered through thy treachery,

    And thou shalt die; and on his mournful hearse

    Thy hateful and accursèd head shall lie

    To witness to the world that by thy means   30

    His kingly body was too soon interred.

Isabella. Weep not, sweet son.

King Edward III. Forbid not me to weep; he was my father;

    And had you loved him half so well as I,

    You could not bear his death thus patiently.   35

    But you, I fear, conspired with Mortimer.

First Lord. [*To* MORTIMER JUNIOR] Why speak you not unto
    my lord the king?

Mortimer Junior. Because I think it scorn to be accused.

---

24. *First Lord.*] *Broughton; Lords. Q1–4.*   25. *To* MORTIMER JUNIOR] *This
ed.; not in Q.*   25. How] *Q, Q3–4;* Ho *Q2.*   37. *First Lord.*] *Broughton;
Lords. Q1–4; Second Lord. Gill¹.*   37. *To* MORTIMER JUNIOR] *This ed.; not
in Q.*   38. think it] *Collier MS., Dyce² (conj.), Wagner (conj.), Ellis;* thinke
Q1–4.   38. be] *Q;* be so *Scott.*   39. dare] *Q;* dares *Q2–4.*

---

28. *thou shalt die*] Marlowe radically compresses history here; see Introduction, p. 45. For Holinshed's account of Mortimer's capture, trial, and
execution, see Appendix B, no. 46.

29. *accursèd head*] Of all Marlowe's sources, Grafton is the only one to
report that Mortimer was beheaded in addition to being quartered; according
to Holinshed, Stowe, and Fabyan, he was hanged. See Introduction, p. 65;
also Appendix B, nos. 46, 50.

32. *Weep not, sweet son*] Briggs compares *Lust's Dominion*: '*Queen Mother.
Sweet sonne. Philip.* Sweet mother: oh! how I now do shame / To lay on one
so foul so fair a name: / Had you been a true mother, a true wife, / This King
had not so soon been robb'd of life' (I.ii.106–109). This play (*c.* 1600),
ascribed by modern scholars to Dekker, Haughton, and Day, carried the
words 'Written by *Christofer Marloe*, Gent.' on its title page when first
published in 1657.

38. *think it scorn*] I accept Dyce's emendation (inserting 'it') as much for
idiomatic as for metrical reasons. Marlowe regularly uses this construction
but in no parallel instance omits the indefinite pronoun; cf. 'think it loss' (*I*

Who is the man dare say I murdered him?

King Edward III. Traitor, in me my loving father speaks   40
And plainly saith, 'twas thou that murd'redst him.

Mortimer Junior. But hath your grace no other proof than
this?

King Edward III. Yes, if this be the hand of Mortimer.

[*Shows a letter.*]

Mortimer Junior. [*Aside to* ISABELLA] False Gurney hath
betrayed me and himself.

Isabella. [*Aside*] I feared as much; murder cannot be hid.   45

Mortimer Junior. 'Tis my hand; what gather you by this?

King Edward III. That thither thou didst send a murderer.

Mortimer Junior. What murderer? Bring forth the man I sent.

King Edward III. Ah, Mortimer, thou knowest that he is
slain;
And so shalt thou be too. [*To* Attendants] Why stays he
here?   50
Bring him unto a hurdle, drag him forth;

---

41. murd'redst] *Q* (murdredst), *Q3*; murdrest *Q2*, *Dodsley*[1-3] (murd'rest);
murtheredst *Q4*, *World's Classics* (murther'dst); murdered *Scott*, *Broughton*
(murder'd); murderest *Oxberry*; murderèdest *Dyce*[1]; murder'dst *Dyce*[2].
42. But hath] *Q*; (*To the Queen*) But hath *Broughton*.   43.1. *Shows a letter.*]
Dodsley[3] (conj.), *Dyce*[1]; Shows token. *Gill*[1]; not in *Q*.   44. *Aside to* ISABELLA]
Dyce[1]; not in *Q*.   45. *Aside*] *Cunningham*; not in *Q*.   45. murder] *Dods-*
ley[1]; murther *Q*.   47, 48. murderer] *Dodsley*[1]; murtherer *Q1-4*.   49.
Ah] *Q* (A), *Dyce*[1-2]; Ay *Dodsley*[1-2], *Broughton* (Aye).   49. knowest] *Q1-3*;
know'st *Q4*.   50. *To* Attendants] *This ed.; not in Q.*

Tamburlaine, I.ii.215), 'think it good' (*1 Tamburlaine,* II.iv.10), 'think it
requisite' (*2 Tamburlaine,* III.i.71), 'think it good' (*Massacre at Paris,* i.19),
'think it shame' (*Ovid's Elegies,* II, xvii, 1).

40. *in . . . speaks*] As Merchant notes, 'Marlowe carefully withholds this
final show of authority in the young prince until, at this point, at the death of
his father, he is king in legal fact.'

43. *the hand of Mortimer*] As Tancock pointed out, Marlowe is inconsistent
here; Mortimer (in soliloquy) has already said that the incriminating letter
was 'written by a friend of ours' (v.iv.6 and note).

44. *False . . . me*] A departure from Holinshed; see note on l. 9 above.

45. *murder cannot be hid*] Proverbial (Tilley M1315); cf. Kyd, *Spanish
Tragedy*: 'The heavens are just, murder cannot be hid' (II.v.57).

51. *hurdle*] a frame or sledge on which condemned criminals were drawn to
execution.

Hang him, I say, and set his quarters up!
But bring his head back presently to me.
Isabella. For my sake, sweet son, pity Mortimer.
Mortimer Junior. Madam, entreat not; I will rather die   55
 Than sue for life unto a paltry boy.
King Edward III. Hence with the traitor, with the murderer!
Mortimer Junior. Base Fortune, now I see that in thy wheel
 There is a point to which, when men aspire,
 They tumble headlong down. That point I touched,   60
 And, seeing there was no place to mount up higher,
 Why should I grieve at my declining fall?
 Farewell, fair queen; weep not for Mortimer,
 That scorns the world, and, as a traveller,
 Goes to discover countries yet unknown.   65
King Edward III. What! Suffer you the traitor to delay?
    [*Exit* MORTIMER JUNIOR *with* FIRST LORD, *attended.*]
Isabella. As thou receivèd'st thy life from me,
 Spill not the blood of gentle Mortimer.
King Edward III. This argues that you spilt my father's
  blood,
 Else would you not entreat for Mortimer.   70
Isabella. I spill his blood? No!
King Edward III. Ay, madam, you; for so the rumour runs.

---

54. For . . . son] *Q* (For my sake sweete sonne); Sweet son, for my sake *Broughton.*   66.1. *Exit . . . attended.*] *Dyce*[1] (*subst.*), *Bowers; Mortimer borne off. Scott (after line 70); Exit Mortimer guarded. Oxberry; Young Mortimer is taken away by Second Lord and some Attendants. Oliphant; not in Q.*   67. receivèd'st] *Q1–3* (receiuedst); receiv'd'st *Q4* (receiud'st), *Broughton;* receivèdest *Dyce*[1–2]; receivest *Thomas;* receiv'dst *Pendry–Maxwell.*   71. blood? No!] *Q1–2* (bloud? no.), *Dodsley*[1–2]; bloud? *Q3–4.*

52–53. *set . . . back*] Hanging, drawing, and quartering constituted the official punishment for treason in medieval and Renaissance England, although for certain noblemen (as in the case of Marlowe's contemporary, Essex) the gruesome penalty was sometimes commuted to simple beheading. But Marlowe undoubtedly found these details in Grafton; see notes on v.i.142 and l. 29 above.

 presently] See note on I.iv.90.

 58. *Base Fortune*] See note on v.ii.52.

 64–65. *traveller . . . unknown*] Cf. *Ham.*, III.i.80–81; see Introduction, p. 19.

Isabella. That rumour is untrue; for loving thee
    Is this report raised on poor Isabel.
King Edward III. I do not think her so unnatural.   75
Second Lord. My lord, I fear me it will prove too true.
King Edward III. Mother, you are suspected for his death,
    And therefore we commit you to the Tower
    Till further trial may be made thereof;
    If you be guilty, though I be your son,   80
    Think not to find me slack or pitiful.
Isabella. Nay, to my death, for too long have I lived
    Whenas my son thinks to abridge my days.
King Edward III. Away with her. Her words enforce these
    tears,
    And I shall pity her if she speak again.   85
        [SECOND LORD, *attended, arrests* ISABELLA.]
Isabella. Shall I not mourn for my belovèd lord,
    And with the rest accompany him to his grave?

---

76. *Second Lord*] *Dyce*[1-2]; *Lords. Q1–4; Lord. Robinson; First Lord. Brough-*
ton, Oxberry; Third Lord. Gill[1].   79. may be] *Q1–2;* be *Q3–4.*   83.
Whenas] *Oxberry;* When as *Q;* When that *Broughton.*   85.1. SECOND
LORD . . . ISABELLA] *This ed.; not in Q.*   87. his] *Q1–2;* the *Q3–4.*

73–74. *for . . . Isabel*] The queen tries to imply that the rumour of her
complicity in the murder arises because she (with Mortimer's help) has been
solicitous for her son's throne.

78. *to the Tower*] Isabella was not imprisoned in the Tower but rather
placed under house arrest at Castle Rising in Norfolk. Holinshed says that in
a 'parlement holden at Westminster, the king tooke into his hand, by aduise
of the states there assembled, all the possessions, lands and reuenues that
belonged to the queene his mother, she hauing assigned to hir a thousand
pounds by yeare, for the maintenance of hir estate, being appointed to
remaine in a certeine place, and not to go elsewhere abroad: yet the king to
comfort hir, would lightlie euerie yeare once come to visit hir' (p. 349).

79. *trial*] enquiry, investigation.

82. Echoed in *The Contention*; see Introduction, n. 70; cf. also *Arden of
Faversham*: 'But bear me hence, for I have lived too long' (xviii.35); and *2
Troublesome Reign*: 'he rather livd too long' (viii; l. 1065).

83. *Whenas*] See note on v.ii.14.

abridge my days] Cf. *1 Tamburlaine*: 'Now, Bajazeth, abridge thy baneful
days' (v.i.286).

86. *my belovèd lord*] Isabella undoubtedly wishes to be understood here as
referring to her husband Edward II; but given her adulterous attachment
throughout much of the later action, the audience would perhaps discern a
covert and ironic reference to Mortimer.

Second Lord. Thus, madam, 'tis the king's will you shall
    hence.
Isabella. He hath forgotten me; [*to* Attendants] stay, I am his
    mother.
Second Lord. That boots not; therefore, gentle madam, go.   90
Isabella. Then come, sweet death, and rid me of this grief.
                [*Exit* ISABELLA *with* SECOND LORD, *attended.*]

    [*Re-enter* FIRST LORD *with the head of* MORTIMER JUNIOR.]

First Lord. My lord, here is the head of Mortimer.
King Edward III. Go fetch my father's hearse, where it shall
    lie,
And bring my funeral robes.
                        [*Exeunt* Attendants.]
               Accursèd head!
Could I have ruled thee then, as I do now,   95
Thou hadst not hatched this monstrous treachery.
Here comes the hearse;

    [*Re-enter* Attendants *with the hearse and funeral robes.*]

---

88. *Second Lord*] *Dyce*[1-2]; *Lords. Q1–4; Lord. Robinson; First Lord. Brough-
ton, Oxberry.*   88. Thus] *Q1–4; Nay Broughton; Tush Dyce*[2] *(conj.).*
89. *to* Attendants] *This ed.; not in Q.*   90. *Second Lord*] *Dyce*[1-2]; *Lords.
Q1–4; Lord. Robinson; First Lord. Broughton, Oxberry; Third Lord. Gill*[1].
91.1. *Exit . . . attended.*] *Dyce*[1] *(subst.) (Exit Second Lord and some of the
Attendants), Ribner; Exeunt Queen and Lords. Scott; Exit guarded. Broughton;
Exit with First Lord. Oliphant; Exit with Attendants. Briggs; not in Q.*   91.2.
Re-enter . . . MORTIMER JUNIOR] *Dyce*[1] *(subst.); Enter a Soldier with the head of
Mortimer Jun. Broughton; Re-enter Second Lord. Oxberry; Re-enter a Lord, with
the head of Mortimer. Robinson; Enter Lords with the head of Mortimer. Spencer;
not in Q.*   92. *First Lord*] *Broughton; Lords. Q1–4; Second Lord. Oxberry;
Lord. Cunningham.*   94. *Exeunt* Attendants.] *Dyce*[1]; *Exit Attendant. Gill*[1]
Exit Lord. Gill[2]; *not in Q.*   97.1. *Re-enter . . . robes.*] *Dyce*[1]; *not in Q.*

---

90. *boots*] See note on II.vi.18.

91. *come, sweet death*] Cf. Kyd, *Soliman and Perseda*: 'Come therefore,
gentle death, and ease my griefe' (I.iv.126); also *Rom.*: 'Come, death, and
welcome!' (III.v.24); and *Ven.*: 'sweet Death' (l. 997).

94. *Accursèd head*] The repetition of this phrase (cf. v.vi.29) helps to
establish the severed head of Mortimer as an icon of retributive justice in the
play; cf. also l. 99 below. Kent applies a variant of the same phrase to his
own head at IV.vi.7.

97. *help . . . lords*] Tancock compares *R2*: 'Lords, I protest, my soul is full
of woe. . . .Come mourn with me for what I do lament' (v.vi.44–46).

help me to mourn, my lords.
Sweet father, here unto thy murdered ghost,
I offer up this wicked traitor's head,
And let these tears, distilling from mine eyes,   100
Be witness of my grief and innocency.

[*Exeunt.*]

FINIS

Imprinted at London for William Jones, and are to be
sold at his shop, near unto Holborn Conduit. 1594.

101. innocency] *Q* (innocencie), *Dyce*[1-2]; innocence *Dodsley*[1-2].   101.1.
Exeunt.] *Scott; Exeunt omnes. Gill*[1]; *not in Q.*   101.2. FINIS] *Q; not in
Dodsley*[1-2].   101.3-4. *Colophon.* Imprinted . . . 1594.] *Hampden;* Imprinted at London for *William* / Ihones, *and are to be solde at his* / shop, neere
vnto Houlburne / *Conduit. 1594. Q, Brooke, Briggs; not in Q2-4.*

───

100. *distilling*] melting, falling slowly; cf. Greene, *Alphonsus, King of
Aragon*: 'the salt-brine teares / Distilling downe poore *Faustas* withered
cheekes' (v.iii; ll. 1722-1723).

APPENDIX A
Broughton and Oxberry collations excluded from the textual notes

Act I, Scene i

5 favourite] Q (fauorit); fav'rite Broughton.
10 my] Q; mine Broughton.
23 glanceth] Q (glaunceth); glances Broughton.
23 flieth] Q; flies Broughton.
25 Poor Men] Q; 1st Poor Man Broughton.
33 Scot] Q; Scots Broughton.
35 be gone] Q; begone Broughton.
49 men] Q; the men Broughton.
71 comes] Q; come Broughton, Oxberry.
75 do I] Q; I do Broughton.
94 these] Q; those Broughton.
124 the] Q; this Broughton.
139 Kiss] Q; nay, kiss Broughton.
148 treacherous] Q; traitorous Broughton.

151 my] Q; the Broughton.
155 Earl] Q (Earle); The earl Broughton.
162 be envied] Q; should'st be envied Broughton; envied be Oxberry.
169 Whatso] Q (What so); Whate'er Broughton.
171 whiles] Q; while Broughton.
172 street] Q; streets Broughton.
179 these] Q; those Broughton.
192 No] Q; Well Broughton.
196 bolts] Q (boults); bonds Broughton.
197 the Fleet] Q (the fleete); Fleet Broughton.
204 a house] Q; an house Broughton.

Act I, Scene ii

20 doth] Q; do Broughton.
25 exceptions] Q; exception Broughton.
27, 34 bewrays] Q; betrays Broughton.

51 cheeks] Q (cheekes); cheek Oxberry.

Act I, Scene iii

5 towards] Q; tow'rds Broughton.

Act I, Scene iv

2 May it]; May't Broughton.
17 unto] Q (vnto); to Broughton.
20, 21 on] Q; upon Broughton.
36 in] Q; on Oxberry.
38 thus] Q; so Broughton.
41 upstart] Q; upstart's Broughton.

42 stops] Q; stop Broughton.
43 my lord] Q; good my lord Broughton.
62 due to] Q; to Broughton.
80 noble] Q1-4; nobly Broughton.
133 makes] Q; make Broughton.

142 pass] *Q* (passe); care *Broughton*.
147 with *Q;* on *Oxberry*.
153 mean] *Q* (meane); meant
      Broughton.
154 Thou art] *Q;* Thou'rt
      Broughton.
161 you] *Q;* thou *Oxberry*.
161 rob] *Q;* robb'st *Oxberry*.
168 repealed] *Q;* recalled *Broughton*.
180 doted Jove] *Q;* Jove doated
      Broughton.
182–185 But . . . Gaveston] *Q; not
      in Oxberry*.
194 confesseth] *Q;* confesses
      Broughton.
201, 204, 227, 241 repeal] *Q;* recal
      Broughton.
211 tend'rest] *Q* (tendrest);
      honourest *Broughton*.
225 a while] *Q;* awhile *Broughton,
      Oxberry*.
227, 260, 357 As] *Q;* That
      Broughton.
249 be true] *Q;* agree *Broughton*.
251 We are] *Q;* we're *Broughton*.

265 easily] *Q* (easilie); easy
      Broughton.
268 that] *Q;* the *Broughton*.
271 saith] *Q;* sayeth *Broughton*.
273 lords] *Q;* lord *Broughton*.
277 to offend] *Q;* t'offend
      Broughton.
282 shall we] *Q;* we shall *Oxberry*.
283 Which] *Q;* Who *Broughton*.
286 us down] *Q;* down us
      Broughton.
299 brought] *Q;* ta'en *Broughton*.
303 treble] *Q;* trebly *Broughton*.
308 I would] *Q;* I'd *Broughton*.
321, 322 repealed] *Q;* recalled
      Broughton.
351 Pembroke will] *Q;* will
      Pembroke *Broughton*.
359 war] *Q* (warre); wars *Broughton*.
360 nor] *Q;* or *Broughton*.
386 to oppose] *Q;* t'oppose
      Broughton.

Act II, Scene i

2 that our] *Q;* our *Broughton*.
18 repealed] *Q* (repeald); recalled
      Broughton.
30 she] *Q;* I *Broughton*.
39 downward] *Q* (downeward);
      downwards *Broughton*.

47 exceptions] *Q;* exception
      Broughton.
48 the] *Q;* their *Broughton*.
52 these] *Q;* those *Broughton*.
61 know] *Q;* knew *Broughton*.

Act II, Scene ii

15 But seeing you are] *Q;* Well,
      since you're *Broughton*.
20, 41 Æque] *Q;* Œque *Broughton*.
60 words left] *Q;* words *Oxberry*.
86 were] *Q;* where *Broughton*
      (*misprint?*).
116 pound] *Q;* pounds *Broughton,
      Oxberry*.
147 gather] *Q;* gather gold
      Broughton.
154 you are] *Q1–4;* you're *Oxberry*.
188 jig] *Q* (Iig); ligge *Oxberry*.
189 Maids] *Q; Maidens Broughton*.

190 bourne] *Q* (borne); burn
      Broughton.
201 for their] *Q;* their *Broughton*.
201 power is] *Q;* power's so
      Broughton.
207 to] *Q;* for *Oxberry*.
216 scorn] *Q;* scorn'st *Broughton*.
219 hast] *Q;* has *Oxberry*.
230 pardon is] *Q;* pardon's
      Broughton.
239 whilst] *Q;* while *Broughton*.
241 thine arms] *Q;* thy name and
      arms *Broughton*.

247 Knowest] *Q;* Know'st *Broughton.*

253 titles] *Q;* title *Broughton.*

Act II, Scene iii

2 with you] *Q;* you *Broughton.*
2 leave] *Q* (leaue); to leave *Broughton.*

3 and] *Q;* for *Broughton.*
12 of] *Q;* to *Broughton.*

Act II, Scene iv

15 Heavens] *Q;* Heaven *Broughton, Oxberry.*

54 As] *Q;* That *Broughton.*

Act II, Scene v

15 Greekish] *Q;* Grecian *Broughton.*
25 have] *Q;* heave *Broughton.*
26 favourite] *Q* (fauorit); fav'rite *Broughton.*
40 name] *Q;* gracious name *Broughton.*
41 No] *Q;* Nay *Broughton.*
46 know it] *Q;* know, my *Broughton.*

65 It is] *Q;* 'Tis *Broughton.*
72 My lord] *Q;* Lord *Broughton.*
87 in] *Q;* to *Broughton.*
95 him you] *Q;* him *Broughton;* him to you *Oxberry.*
100 to] *Q;* for *Broughton.*
107 be gone] *Q* (be gon); begone *Broughton.*

Act II, Scene vi

3 bands] *Q;* bonds *Broughton.*
7 have that] *Q;* have *Broughton.*

17 Away] *Q; not in Broughton.*

Act III, Scene i

21 teach the rest] *Q;* profit much *Oxberry.*
22 As . . . much] *Q; line not in Oxberry.*
22 As by their preachments] *Q;* That by their preaching *Broughton.*
25 have] *Q;* we've *Broughton.*
33 wars] *Q* (warres); war *Broughton.*
43 True] *Q;* The same *Broughton.*
55 the] *Q;* those *Broughton.*
62 brother] *Q;* dear brother *Broughton.*
69 thee] *Q;* him *Broughton.*
69 this matter] *Q;* this *Broughton.*

75 fits] *Q;* suits *Oxberry.*
75 a prince so young] *Q;* so young a prince *Broughton.*
81 you] *Q;* thou *Broughton.*
89 Lord] *Q;* my lord *Broughton.*
91 Ah] *Q;* Oh *Broughton.*
92 Tell] *Q;* But tell *Broughton.*
103 at the first] *Q;* at first *Oxberry.*
145 of] *Q;* out of *Oxberry.*
156 arms] *Q;* arm *Oxberry.*
159 blood] *Q;* more blood *Broughton.*
173 Tarry] *Q;* wait for *Broughton.*
183 even] *Q* (euen); e'en *Broughton.*
183 stoop] *Q;* stop *Oxberry.*

Act III, Scene ii

37 now, not] *Q;* not *Oxberry.*
37 chance] *Q;* the chance *Oxberry.*
40 advance] *Q;* exalt *Broughton.*
43 knew] *Q;* know *Broughton.*
56 thou in rage] *Q1–4;* thou
   Oxberry.
71 Be gone] *Q* (be gon); Begone
   Broughton.

72 ragged] *Q;* rugged *Broughton.*
79 King] *Q;* Kind *Broughton.*
92 lords] *Q;* lord *Broughton.*
95 with] *Q;* 'gainst *Broughton.*

Act IV, Scene i

1 gale] *Q;* gales *Broughton.*
4 thy] *Q;* his *Broughton.*

5 thou] *Q;* thy *Broughton*
  (misprint?).

Act IV, Scene ii

21 So pleaseth] *Q;* If't please
   Broughton.
44 not I] *Q;* not so *Broughton.*

69 and you] *Q;* you *Broughton.*
69 discourage] *Q;* thus discourage
   Broughton.

Act IV, Scene iii

10 there] *Q;* here *Broughton.*
11.1 *their*] *Q;* the *Broughton.*
37 As] *Q;* That *Broughton.*
39 can] *Q;* that *Broughton.*
43 in] *Q;* on *Broughton.*
45 come] *Q;* comes *Oxberry.*

50 instructions] *Q;* my instructions
   Broughton.
67 dusky] *Q1–3* (duskie), *Q4;*
   dusty *Oxberry.*
70 these] *Q;* those *Broughton,*
   Oxberry.

Act IV, Scene iv

10 among] *Q;* amongst *Broughton.*
13 shouldst thou] *Q;* thou
   should'st *Broughton.*

25 these] *Q1–4;* those *Broughton,*
   Oxberry.
27 my lord] *Q;* then *Broughton.*

Act IV, Scene v

7 this] *Q;* the *Broughton.*

Act IV, Scene vi

18 into] *Q;* unto *Broughton.*
26 sith] *Q;* since *Broughton.*
40 Mayor] *Q* (Maior); may'r
   Broughton.

55 the other] *Q;* t'other *Broughton.*
69 have] *Q;* heave *Broughton.*

Act IV, Scene vii

6 those] *Q;* these *Broughton.*
32 lives] *Q* (liues); life *Broughton.*
34 tempests] *Q;* tempest *Oxberry.*
57 arrest] *Q;* do arrest *Broughton,*
   Oxberry.

77 in vain] *Q;* vain *Broughton.*
83 somewhat] *Q* (somwhat);
   something *Broughton.*
91 friends] *Q;* friend *Oxberry.*
107 thy] *Q;* thine *Broughton.*

Act V, Scene i

4 of] *Q;* for *Oxberry.*
7 hast thou always] *Q;* always
   hast thou *Broughton.*
20 As] *Q1–4;* That *Broughton.*
21 soaring] *Q;* for soaring
   Broughton.
32 Whilst] *Q;* While *Broughton.*
35 strange] *Q;* sad *Broughton.*
36 my] *Q;* the *Broughton.*
39 crave] *Q;* claim *Broughton.*
41 by] *Q;* with *Broughton.*
51 Ah Leicester] *Q* (Ah Leister);
   Oh! Leicester *Broughton.*

62 due] *Q1–3* (dew), *Q4;* done
   Broughton.
77 pass] *Q;* care *Broughton.*
81 this torment] *Q;* these torments
   Broughton.
114 Ah] *Q* (ah); Oh *Broughton.*
116 jaws] *Q1–4;* paws *Broughton.*
134 Berkeley would] *Q* (*Bartley*
   would); would Berkley
   Broughton.
152 am I] *Q;* I am *Broughton.*

Act V, Scene ii

44 dispatched and die] *Q;*
   dispatched *Broughton.*
85 they] *Q;* how they *Broughton.*

108 and go] *Q;* go *Broughton.*
115 redeem] *Q;* release *Broughton.*

Act V, Scene iii

1 pensive] *Q;* so pensive
   Broughton.
1 we are] *Q;* we're *Broughton.*
3 dangereth] *Q;* endangereth
   Broughton.
13 this] *Q;* us *Broughton.*
39 O level] *Q;* Level *Broughton.*

39 all your] *Q;* your *Broughton.*
41 that I am] *Q;* I'm *Broughton.*
48 to] *Q;* into *Broughton.*
49 there] *Q;* here *Broughton,*
   Oxberry.
66 even] *Q;* e'en *Broughton.*

Act V, Scene iv

4 for it] *Q;* for't *Broughton.*
22 And] *Q* (and); nay *Broughton.*
39 so it] *Q;* so't *Broughton.*
44 bring] *Q;* bring'st *Broughton.*
46 do I] *Q;* I do *Broughton.*
63 is all] *Q1–4;* all is *Broughton.*

64 the king] *Q;* and king
   Broughton.
65 Mine] *Q;* My *Oxberry.*
81 taken] *Q;* ta'en *Broughton.*
85 this] *Q;* the *Broughton.*

Act V, Scene v

13 I will] *Q1–4;* I'll *Broughton.*
16 it was] *Q;* 'twas *Broughton.*
29 See that] *Q;* See *Broughton.*
29 room] *Q;* room that *Broughton.*
30 And get] *Q;* Get *Broughton.*
37 light to go] *Q;* light; go
   Oxberry.
53 the Caucasus] *Q;* Caucasus
   Broughton.

92 grief keeps] *Q* (greefe keepes);
   thou keep'st *Oxberry.*
100 O let] *Q;* Let *Broughton.*
103 never] *Q;* ne'er shall *Broughton.*
104 is that] *Q;* it is *Broughton.*
112 that you] *Q;* thou *Oxberry.*
118 king's] *Q;* news *Broughton.*

Act V, Scene vi

5 secret] *Q;* secret still *Broughton.*
8 fly] *Q;* fly too *Broughton.*
26 frighted] *Q;* frightened *Oxberry.*
33 not me] *Q1–4;* me not
   Broughton.

46 'Tis] *Q1–4* (Tis); It is
   Broughton.
98 ghost] *Q;* head *Oxberry.*
99 head] *Q;* ghost *Oxberry.*

APPENDIX B
Longer extracts from Marlowe's sources

I FROM RAPHAEL HOLINSHED, THE THIRD VOLUME OF
CHRONICLES, BEGINNING AT DUKE
WILLIAM . . . COMMONLIE CALLED THE
CONQUEROR . . . (1587)

Background material

1305

[1] In the three and thirtith yeare of his reigne, king Edward [I] put
his sonne prince Edward in prison, bicause that he had riotouslie
broken the parke of Walter Langton bishop of Chester; and bicause
the prince had doone this deed by the procurement of a lewd and
wanton person, one Peers Gauaston, an esquire of Gascoine, the king
banished him the realme, least the prince, who delighted much in
his companie, might by his euill and wanton counsell fall to euill and
naughtie rule.

(*p. 313*)

1307

[2] . . . this cardinall [Petrus Hispanus] being at Carleill, and hauing
made a sermon in praise of peace, vpon the conclusion of marriage
betwixt the prince of Wales and the French kings daughter, in the
end he reuested himselfe and the other bishops which were present,
and then with candels light, and causing the bels to be roong, they
accursed in terrible wise Robert Bruce the vsurper of the crowne of
Scotland, with all his partakers, aiders and mainteiners. . . . He [i.e.,
Edward I] sent his sonne Edward [from Scotland] into England,
that vpon knowledge had what the French king did touching the
agreement, he might accordinglie proceed in the marriage to be
made with his daughter.

After the prince was departed from the campe, his father king
Edward was taken with sore sickenesse, yet he remooued from
Carleill, where the same sickness first tooke him, vnto Burrough
vpon Sand, and there the daie after being the seuenth daie of Iulie,
he ended his life, after he had reigned 34 yeares, six moneths and
one and twentie daies. . . .

But now to conclude with this noble prince king Edward the first, he was sure not onelie valiant but also politike, labouring to bring this diuided Ile, into one entier monarchie, which he went verie neere to haue atchiued, for whereas he was fullie bent to make a conquest of Scotland, in like case as he had alreadie doone of Wales, if he had liued any longer time to haue dispatched Robert le Bruce, that onelie stood in his waie, it was verie likelie that he should haue found none other to haue raised banner against him about the quarrell or title to the claime of that realme.

(*pp. 316–317*)

1308

[3] About the two and twentith of Ianuarie, the king sailed ouer into France, and at Bullongne in Picardie on the foure and twentith day of Ianuarie, he did homage to the French king for his lands of Gascoine and Pontieu, and on the morrow after, maried Isabell the French kings daughter, and on the seauenth of Februarie he returned with hir into England, and comming to London, was ioifullie receiued of the citizens, and on the fiue and twentith daie of Februarie, being Shrouesundaie in the leape yeare, they were solemnlie crowned by the bishop of Winchester, bicause that Robert [Winchelsea] the archbishop of Canturburie was not as then within the realme. . . .

(*pp. 318–319*)

1312

[4] This yeare, the thirteenth of Nouember, the kings eldest sonne named Edward (which succeeded his father in the kingdome by the name of Edward the third) was borne at Windsore.

(*p. 321*)

Act I, Scene i

1307

[5] Edward, the second of that name, the sonne of Edward the first, borne at Carnaruan in Wales, began his reigne ouer England the seauenth day of Iulie, in the yeare of our Lord 1307. . . . His fathers corpse was conueied from Burgh vpon Sands, vnto the abbeie of Waltham, there to remaine, till things were readie for the buriall, which was appointed at Westminster.

Within three daies after, when the lord treasurer Walter de

Langton bishop of Couentrie and Lichfield (thorough whose complaint Peers de Gaueston had been banished the land) was going
towards Westminster, to make preparation for the same buriall, he
was vpon commandement from the new king arrested, committed to
prison, and after deliuered to the hands of the said Peers, being then
returned againe into the realme, who sent him from castell to castell
as a prisoner. His lands and tenements were seized to the kings vse,
but his mooueables were giuen to the foresaid Peers. . . .

But now concerning the demeanour of this new king, whose
disordered maners brought himselfe and manie others vnto destruction; we find that in the beginning of his gouernement, though he
was of nature giuen to lightnesse, yet being restreined with the
prudent aduertisements of certeine of his councellors, to the end he
might shew some likelihood of good proofe, he counterfeited a kind
of grauitie, vertue and modestie; but yet he could not throughlie be
so bridled, but that foorthwith he began to plaie diuers wanton and
light parts, at the first indeed not outragiouslie, but by little and
little, and that couertlie. For hauing reuoked againe into England his
old mate the said Peers de Gaueston, he receiued him into most high
fauour, creating him earle of Cornewall, and lord of Man, his
principall secretarie, and lord chamberlaine of the realme, through
whose companie and societie he was suddenlie so corrupted, that he
burst out into most heinous vices; for then vsing the said Peers as a
procurer of his disordred dooings, he began to haue his nobles in no
regard, to set nothing by their instructions, and to take small heed
vnto the good gouernement of the commonwealth, so that within a
while, he gaue himselfe to wantonnes, passing his time in voluptuous
pleasure, and riotous excesse: and to helpe them forward in that
kind of life, the foresaid Peers, who (as it may be thought, he had
sworne to make the king to forget himselfe, and the state, to the
which he was called) furnished his court with companies of iesters,
ruffians, flattering parasites, musicians, and other vile and naughtie
ribalds, that the king might spend both daies and nights in iesting,
plaieng, banketing, and in such other filthie and dishonorable exercises: and moreouer, desirous to aduance those that were like to
him selfe, he procured for them honorable offices, all which notable
preferments and dignities, sith they were ill bestowed, were rather to
be accounted dishonorable than otherwise, both to the giuer and the
receiuer. . . .

                                                        (*p. 318*)

Act I, Scene i

1311

[6] Lieng on his death bed, he [i.e., the Earl of Lincoln] requested (as was reported) Thomas earle of Lancaster, who had married his daughter, that in any wise he should stand with the other lords in defense of the commonwelth, and to mainteine his quarrell against the earle of Cornewall, which request earle Thomas faithfullie accomplished: for by the pursute of him, and of the earle of Warwike cheefelie, the said earle of Cornewall was at length taken and beheaded (as after shall appeare). Some write that king Edward the first vpon his death-bed, charged the earles of Lincolne, Warwike, and Penbroke, to foresee that the foresaid Peers returned not againe into England, least by his euill example he might induce his sonne the prince to lewdnesse, as before he had alreadie doone.

(*p. 320*)

Act I, Scene i

1322

[7] In this sort came the mightie earle of Lancaster to his end, being the greatest peere in the realme, and one of the mightiest earles in christendome: for when he began to leauie warre against the king, he was possessed of fiue earledomes, Lancaster, Lincolne, Salisburie, Leicester, and Derbie, beside other seigniories, lands, and possessions, great to his aduancement in honor and puissance.

(*p. 331*)

Act I, Scene ii

1308

[8] The malice which the lords had conceiued against the earle of Cornewall still increased, the more indeed through the high bearing of him, being now aduanced to honour. For being a goodlie gentleman and a stout, he would not once yeeld an inch to any of them which worthilie procured him great enuie amongst the cheefest peeres of all the realme, as sir Henrie Lacie earle of Lincolne, sir Guie earle of Warwicke, and sir Aimer de Valence earle of Penbroke, the earles of Glocester, Hereford, Arundell, and others, which vpon such wrath and displeasure as they had conceiued against him, thought it not conuenient to suffer the same any longer, in hope that the kings mind might happilie be altered into a better purpose, being not altogither conuerted into a venemous disposition, but so that it

might be cured, if the corrupter thereof were once banished from
him.

(p. 319)

Act I, Scene iv

1307

[9] Moreouer, at the same parlement, a marriage was concluded
betwixt the earle of Cornewall Peers de Gaueston, and the daughter
of Gilbert de Clare earle of Glocester, which he had by his wife the
countesse Ioane de Acres the kings sister, which marriage was
solemnized on All hallowes day next insuing.

(p. 318)

Act I, Scene iv

1308

[10] Herevpon they assembled togither in the parlement time, at the
new temple, on saturdaie next before the feast of saint Dunstan, and
there ordeined that the said Peers should abiure the realme, and
depart the same on the morrow after the Natiuitie of saint Iohn
Baptist at the furthest, and not to returne into the same againe at
any time then after to come. To this ordinance the king (although
against his will) bicause he saw himselfe and the realme in danger,
gaue his consent. . . . The archbishop of Canturburie [i.e., Robert
Winchelsea], being latelie returned from Rome, where he had
remained in exile in the late deceassed kings daies for a certeine
time, did pronounce the said Peers accursed, if he taried within the
realme longer than the appointed time, and likewise all those that
should aid, helpe, or mainteine him, as also if he should at any time
hereafter returne againe into the land. To conclude, this matter
was so followed, that at length he was constreined to withdraw
himselfe to Bristow, and so by sea as a banished man to saile into
Ireland.

The king being sore offended herewith, as he that fauoured the
earle more than that he could be without his companie, threatned
the lords to be reuenged for this displeasure, and ceassed not to
send into Ireland vnto Peers, comforting him both with freendlie
messages, and rich presents, and as it were to shew that he meant to
reteine him still in his fauour, he made him ruler of Ireland as his
deputie there.

(pp. 319–320)

Act I, Scene iv

1309

[11] The lords perceiuing the kings affection, and that the treasure was spent as lauishlie as before, thought with themselues that it might be that the king would both amend his passed trade of life, and that Peers being restored home, would rather aduise him thereto, than follow his old maners, considering that it might be well perceiued, that if he continued in the incouraging of the king to lewdnesse, as in times past he had doone, he could not thinke but that the lords would be readie to correct him, as by proofe he had now tried their meanings to be no lesse. Herevpon to reteine amitie, as was thought on both sides, Peers by consent of the lords was restored home againe (the king meeting him at Chester) to his great comfort and reioising for the time, although the malice of the lords was such, that such ioy lasted not long. . . .

(*p. 320*)

Act I, Scene iv

1310

[12] The king this yeare fearing the enuie of the lords against Peers de Gaueston, placed him for his more safetie in Bambourgh castell, bearing the prelats and lords in hand, that he had committed him there to prison for their pleasures.

. . . The king indeed was lewdlie led, for after that the earle of Cornewall was returned into England, he shewed himselfe no changeling (as writers doo affirme) but through support of the kings fauour, bare himselfe so high in his doings, which were without all good order, that he seemed to disdaine all the peeres & barons of the realme. Also after the old sort he prouoked the king to all naughtie rule and riotous demeanour, and hauing the custodie of the kings iewels and treasure, he tooke out of the iewell-house a table, & a paire of trestels of gold, which he deliuered vnto a merchant called Aimerie de Friscobald, commanding him to conueie them ouer the sea into Gascoine. This table was iudged of the common people, to belong sometime vnto king Arthur, and therefore men grudged the more that the same should thus be sent out of the realme.

(*p. 320*)

Act I, Scene iv

1311

[13] The lords perceiuing the mischeefe that dailie followed and increased by that naughtie man (as they tooke it) the earle of

Cornewall, assembled at Lincolne, and there tooke counsell togither,
and concluded eftsoones to banish him out of the realme, and so
therevpon shortlie after, about Christmasse (as some write) or rather,
as other haue, within the quindene of saint Michaell, he was exiled
into Flanders, sore against the kings will and pleasure, who made
such account of him, that (as appeared) he could not be quiet in
mind without his companie, & therefore about Candlemasse he
eftsoones reuoked him home.

But he being nothing at all amended of those his euill manners,
rather demeaned himselfe woorse than before he had doone, namelie
towards the lords, against whom vsing reprochfull speech, he called
the earle of Glocester bastard, the earle of Lincolne latlie deceased
bursten bellie, the earle of Warwike the blacke hound of Arderne,
and the earle of Lancaster churle.

(*pp. 320–321*)

Act II, Scene i

1322

[**14**] At this time also master Robert Baldocke, a man euill beloued
in the realme, was made lord chancellour of England. This Robert
Baldocke, and one Simon Reding were great fauourers of the Spensers, and so likewise was the earle of Arundell, whereby it may be
thought, that the Spensers did helpe to aduance them into the kings
fauour, so that they bare no small rule in the realme, during the
time that the same Spensers continued in prosperitie, which for the
terme of fiue yeares after that the foresaid barons (as before is
expressed) were brought to confusion [i.e., after Boroughbridge],
did woonderfullie increase, and the queene for that she gaue good
and faithfull counsell, was nothing regarded, but by the Spensers
meanes cleerelie worne out of the kings fauour.

(*p. 332*)

Act II, Scene ii

1314

[**15**] In this meane time, Robert Bruce recouered the most part of all
Scotland, winning out of the Englishmens hands such castels as they
held within Scotland, chasing all the souldiers which laie there in
garrison, out of the countrie, and subduing such of the Scots as held
on the English part.

King Edward to be reuenged herof, with a mightie armie brauelie
furnished, and gorgiouslie apparelled, more seemelie for a triumph,
than meet to incounter with the cruell enimie in the field, entred

Scotland, in purpose speciallie to rescue the castell of Sterling, as then besieged by the Scotishmen. But at his approching neere to the same, Robert Bruce was readie with his power to giue him battell. In the which king Edward nothing doubtfull of losse, had so vnwiselie ordered his people, and confounded their ranks, that euen at the first ioining, they were not onelie beaten downe and ouerthrowne, by those that coped with them at hand, but also were wounded with shot a farre off, by those their enimies which stood behind to succour their fellowes when need required, so that in the end the Englishmen fled to saue their liues, and were chased and slaine by the Scots in great number.

(*p. 322*)

Act II, Scene ii

1322

[**16**] Here is to be noted, that during the time whilest the ciuill warre was in hand betwixt king Edward and his barons, the Scots and Frenchmen were not idle, for the Scots wasted & destroied the countrie of the bishoprike of Durham . . . & the Frenchmen made roades & incursions into the borders of Guien, alledging that they did it vpon good and sufficient occasion, for that king Edward had not doone his homage vnto the king of France, as he ought to haue doone, for the duchie of Aquitaine, and the countie of Pontieu. But the true occasion that mooued them to attempt the warres at that present, was for that they were in hope to recouer all the lands which the king of England held within France, cleerelie out of his hands, for so much as they vnterstood the discord betwixt him and his barons, and how infortunatlie he had sped against the Scots, by reason whereof they iudged the time to serue most fitlie now for their purpose.

(*p. 332*)

Act II, Scenes iii and iv

1312

[**17**] Such lords and other more that were thus abused at this earle of Cornewals hands, determined to be reuenged vpon him, and to dispatch the realme of such a wicked person: and therevpon assembling their powers togither, came towards Newcastell, whither the king from Yorke was remooued, and now hearing of their approch, he got him to Tinmouth, where the queene laie, and vnderstanding there that Newcastell was taken by the lords, he

leauing the queene behind him, tooke shipping, and sailed from thence with his dearelie belooued familiar the earle of Cornewall, vnto Scarbourgh, where he left him in the castell, and rode himselfe towards Warwike.

(p. 321)

Act II, Scene v

1312

[18] The lords hearing where the earle of Cornewall was, made thither [i.e., to Scarborough] with all speed, and besieging the castell, at length constreined their enimie to yeeld himselfe into their hands, requiring no other condition, but that he might come to the kings presence to talke with him.

The king hearing that his best belooued familiar was thus apprehended, sent to the lords, requiring them to spare his life, and that he might be brought to his presence, promising withall that he would see them fullie satisfied in all their requests against him. Wherevpon the earle of Penbroke persuaded with the barons to grant to the kings desire, vntertaking vpon forfeiture of all that he had, to bring him to the king and backe againe to them, in such state and condition as he receiued him. When the barons had consented to his motion, he tooke the earle of Cornewall with him to bring him where the king laie, and comming to Dedington, left him there in safe keeping with his seruants, whilest he for one night went to visit his wife, lieng not farre from thence.

(p. 321)

Act II, Scene vi

1312

[19] The same night it chanced, that Guie erle of Warwike came to the verie place where the erle of Cornewall was left, and taking him from his keepers, brought him vnto Warwike, where incontinentlie it was thought best to put him to death, but that some doubting the kings displeasure, aduised the residue to staie; and so they did, till at length an ancient graue man amongst them exhorted them to vse the occasion now offered, and not to let slip the meane to deliuer the realme of such a dangerous person, that had wrought so much mischeefe, and might turne them all to such perill, as afterwards they should not be able to auoid, nor find shift how to remedie it. And thus persuaded by his words, they caused him streitwaies to be

brought foorth to a place called Blackelow, otherwise named by most writers, Gauerslie heath, where he had his head smitten from his shoulders, the twentith day of Iune being tuesdaie. A iust reward for so scornefull and contemptuous a merchant, as in respect of himselfe (bicause he was in the princes fauour) esteemed the Nobles of the land as men of such inferioritie, as that in comparison of him they deserued no little iot or mite of honour. But lo the vice of ambition, accompanied with a rable of other outrages, euen a reprochfull end, with an euerlasting marke of infamie, which he pulled by violent meanes on himselfe with the cords of his owne lewdnesse, and could not escape this fatall fall. . . .

(*p. 321*)

Act III, Scene i

1312

[20] When the king had knowledge hereof, he was woonderfullie displeased with those lords that had thus put the said earle vnto death, making his vow that he would see his death reuenged, so that the rancour which before was kindled betwixt the king and those lords, began now to blase abroad, and spred so farre, that the king euer sought occasion how to worke them displeasure. . . . King Edward now after that the foresaid Piers Gaueston the earle of Cornewall was dead, nothing reformed his maners, but as one that detested the counsell and admonition of his Nobles, chose such to be about him, and to be of his priuie councell, which were knowne to be men of corrupt and most wicked liuing (as the writers of that age report) amongst these were two of the Spensers, Hugh the father, and Hugh the sonne, which were notable instruments to bring him vnto the liking of all kind of naughtie and euill rule.

By the counsell therefore of these Spensers, he was wholie lead and gouerned: wherewith manie were much offended . . . for suerlie . . . the lords wrested him too much, and beyond the bounds of reason, causing him to receiue to be about him whome it pleased them to appoint. For the yoonger Spenser, who in place of the earle of Cornwall was ordeined to be his chamberleine, it was knowne to them well inough, that the king bare no good will at all to him at the first, though afterwards through the prudent policie, and diligent industrie of the man, he quicklie crept into his fauour, and that further than those that preferred him could have wished.

(*p. 321*)

Act III, Scene i

1319

[21] Thus all the kings exploits by one means or other quailed, and came but to euill successe, so that the English nation began to grow in contempt by the infortunate gouernment of the prince, the which as one out of the right waie, rashlie and with no good aduisement ordered his dooings, which thing so greeued the noblemen of the realme, that they studied day and night by what means they might procure him to looke better to his office and dutie, which they iudged might well be brought to passe, his nature being not altogither euill, if they might find shift to remooue from him the two Spensers, Hugh the father, and Hugh the sonne, who were gotten into such fauour with him, that they onelie did all things, and without them nothing was doone, so that they were now had in as great hatred and indignation . . . both of the lords and commons, as euer in times past was Peers de Gaueston the late earle of Cornwall. But the lords minded not so much the destruction of these Spensers, but that the king ment as much their aduancement, so that Hugh the sonne was made high chamberleine of England, contrarie to the mind of all the noblemen, by reason whereof he bare himselfe so hautie and proud, that no lord within the land might gainsaie that which in his conceit seemed good.

(p. 325)

Act III, Scene i

1321

[22] . . . the lord William de Bruce that in the marches of Wales enioied diuerse faire possessions to him descended from his ancestors, but through want of good gouernement was run behind hand, offered to sell a certeine portion of his lands called Gowers land lieng in the marches there, vnto diuerse noble men that had their lands adioining to the same, as to the earle of Hereford, and to the two lords Mortimers, the vncle & nephue, albeit the lord Mowbraie that had maried the onelie daughter and heire of the lord Bruce, thought verelie in the end to haue had it, as due to his wife by right of inheritance. But at length (as vnhap would) Hugh Spenser the yoonger lord chamberleine, coueting that land (bicause it laie neere on each side to other lands that he had in those parts) found such means through the kings furtherance and helpe, that he went awaie

with the purchase, to the great displeasure of the other lords that
had beene in hand to buie it.

(*p. 325*)

Act III, Scene i

1321

[23] [Frustrated in their armed quarrels with the Spencers, the
barons, banding together, marched] towards the parlement that was
summoned to be holden at London. . . . At their comming to S.
Albons, they sent the bishops of London, Salisburie, Elie, Hereford,
and Chichester, to the king with their humble suit in outward
apperance, though in effect and verie deed more presumptuous than
was requisite. Their cheefe request was that it might please his
highnesse to put from him the Spensers, whose counsell they knew
to be greatlie against his honour, and hereof not to faile if he
tendered the quiet of his realme.

(*p. 326*)

Act III, Scene i

1321

[24] . . . the said Spensers counselled the king to foreiudge sir Hugh
Audlie, sonne to the lord Hugh Audlie [and brother-in-law of the
deceased ninth Earl of Gloucester], and to take into his hands his
castels and possessions. They compassed also to haue atteinted the
lord Roger Damorie [another brother-in-law of Gloucester], that
thereby they might haue enioed the whole earledome of Glocester.

(*p. 327*)

Act III, Scene i

1325

[25] Finallie it was thought good, that the queene shuld go ouer to
hir brother the French king [i.e., Charles IV], to confirme that
treatie of peace vpon some reasonable conditions. She willinglie
tooke vpon hir the charge, and so with the lord Iohn Crumwell, &
other foure knights, without any other great traine, taking sea, she
landed in France, where of the king hir brother she was ioifullie
receiued, and finallie she being the mediatrix, it was finallie ac-
corded, that the K. of England should giue to his eldest sonne [i.e.,
Prince Edward] the duchie of Aquitaine, and the countie of Pontieu,
and that the French king receiuing homage of him for the same, he
should restore into his hands the said countie, and the lands in

Guien, for the which they were at variance, and for those countries
which had beene forraied and spoiled, the earle of Aniou should
fullie see him satisfied, as right did require.

Upon the couenants the French king wrote his letters patents into
England, and other letters also of safe conduct, as well for the sonne
as for the king himselfe, if it should please him to come ouer
himselfe in person. Upon which choise great deliberation was had,
. . . diuerse thinking it best that the king should go ouer himselfe:
but the earle of Winchester and his sonne the lord chamberleine
[i.e., the Spencers], that neither durst go ouer themselues with the
king, nor abide at home in his absence, gaue contrarie counsell, and
at length preuailed so, that it was fullie determined that the kings
eldest sonne Edward should go ouer, which turned to their destruction, as it appeared afterward.

(p. 336)

Act III, Scene ii

1321–22

[26] The earle of Hereford, the lord Roger Mortimer of Cherke, &
the lord Roger Mortimer of Wigmore, entring the marches of Wales,
came to Glocester, and tooke that citie. . . . The Welshmen with
their capteine. . . tooke the castels in Wales, which were kept by the
people of the lord Mortimer the elder. They tooke also the castels of
Mole, Chirke, and Olono, the keepers whereof [including both the
Mortimers] comming vnto the king to Shrewsburie submitted
themselues to him, who shortlie after sent them to the tower of
London.

(pp. 328–329)

Act III, Scene ii

1322

[27] [Edward II] sent afore him certeine bands to Burton vpon
Trent, where he ment to haue lodged: but the earles of Lancaster
and Hereford . . . and many other, being gotten thither before, kept
the bridge, and assailing the kings people which he had thus sent
before, some of them they slue, and some they wounded, so defending the bridge, that none could passe, and by reason that the waters,
and speciallie the riuer of Trent through abundance of raine that was
latelie fallen, were raised, there was no meane to passe by the foords,
wherevpon the king was constreined to staie the space of three daies,
in which meane time, the earles and their complices fortified the

bridge at Burton, with barriers and such like defenses, after the maner of warre, but the king at length vpon deliberate aduise taken how to passe the riuer, ordeined, that the earle of Surrie with certeine armed men, should go ouer by a bridge that was three miles distant from Burton, that he might come vpon the backes of the enimies, as they were fighting with those that should assaile them afront. . . .

. . . But the earles of Lancaster and Hereford, with other in their companie that fled from the discomfiture at Burton, lost manie men and horsses in their flieng away, by reason of such pursuit as was made after them. Diuerse of them that had taken part with the lords against the king, came now and submitted themselues vnto him. . . . [Much weakened, the forces of Lancaster and Hereford] came to Borough bridge, where sir Andrew de Herkley . . . had forlaid the passage, and there. . . , he setting vpon the barons, in the end discomfited them, and chased their people.

In this fight was slaine the earle of Hereford . . . and diuerse others. And there were taken Thomas earle of Lancaster . . . [as well as many others of noble and gentlemanly rank]. . . . Upon the one and twentith of March, came sir Andrew de Harkley vnto Pomfret, bringing with him the earle of Lancaster and other prisoners. The king was come thither a few daies before, and had the castell yeelded to him by the constable, that not manie daies past was appointed to the keeping thereof by the earle, which earle now being brought thither captiue, was mocked, scorned, and in derision called king Arthur.

On the morrow . . . , he was brought before these noble men [Kent, Pembroke, Arundel, Spencer Senior] . . . and others . . . before whome he was arreigned of high treason. . . . [The] said earle of Lancaster was therevpon adiudged to die, according to the law in such cases prouided, that is, to be drawne, hanged, and headed. But bicause he was the queenes vncle, and sonne to the kings vncle, he was pardoned of all saue heading, and so accordinglie therevnto suffered at Pomfret the two and twentith of March.

Thus the king seemed to be reuenged of the displeasure doone to him by the earle of Lancaster, for the beheading of Peers de Gaueston earle of Cornewall, whom he so deerelie loued, and bicause the earle of Lancaster was the cheefe occasioner of his death, the king neuer loued him entirelie after. So that here is verified the censure of the scripture expressed by the wisedome of Salomon, that the anger and displeasure of the king is as the roring of a lion, and his reuenge ineuitable. Wherefore it is an hie point of discretion in such as are mightie, to take heed how they giue edge vnto the wrath of their souereigne, which if it be not by submission made blunt, the burthen of the smart insuing will lie heauie vpon the offendor, euen to his vtter vndooing, and losse (perhaps) of life.

(pp. 329–331)

Act III, Scene ii

1325–26

[28] King Edward not a little offended with king Charles, by whose meanes he knew that the woman [i.e., Queen Isabella] thus lingered abroad, he procured pope Iohn to write his letters vnto the French king, admonishing him to send home his sister and hir sonne vnto hir husband. But when this nothing auailed, a proclamation was made in the moneth of December . . . that if the queene and hir sonne entred not the land by the octaues of the Epiphanie next insuing in peaceable wise, they should be taken for enimies to the realme and crowne of England. Here authors varie, for some write, that vpon knowledge had of this proclamation, the queene determined to returne into England foorthwith, that she might be reconciled to hir husband.

Others write, and that more truelie, how she being highlie displeased, both with the Spensers and the king hir husband, that suffered himselfe to be misled by their counsels, did appoint indeed to returne into England, not to be reconciled, but to stir the people to some rebellion, wherby she might reuenge hir manifold iniuries. Which (as the proofe of the thing shewed) seemeth to be most true, for she being a wise woman, & considering that sith the Spensers had excluded, put out, and remooued all good men, from and besides the kings councell, and placed in their roomes such of their clients, seruants and freends as pleased them, she might well thinke that there was small hope to be had in hir husband, who heard no man but the said Spensers, which she knew hated hir deadlie. Wherevpon, after that the tearme prefixed in the proclamation was expired, the king caused to be seized into his hands, all such lands, as belonged either to his sonne, or to his wife.

About the same time, one sir Robert Walkfare . . . got ouer to the queene into France, and so the number of them that ran out of the realme vnto hir dailie increased. . . . Diuerse other . . . fled out of the realme vnto the queene, and vnto hir sonne the earle of Chester [i.e., Prince Edward]. But in the meane time, Walter Stapleton bishop of

Excester, which hitherto had remained with the queene in France, stale now from hir, and got ouer into England, opening to the king all the counsell and whole mind of the queene: which thing turned first of all vnto his owne destruction, as shall after appeare. . . .

The king of England stood not onelie in doubt of the Frenchmen, but more of his owne people that remained in France, least they thorough helpe of the French should inuade the land, and therefore he commanded the hauens and ports to be suerlie watched, lest some sudden inuasion might happilie be attempted, for it was well vnderstood, that the queene meant not to returne, till she might bring with hir the lord Mortimer, and the other banished men, who in no wise could obteine anie fauour at the kings hands, so long as the Spensers bare rule. . . .

King Edward vnderstanding all the queenes drift, at length sought the French kings fauour, and did so much by letters and promise of bribes with him and his councell, that queene Isabell was destitute in manner of all helpe there . . . .

(*pp. 336–337*)

Act IV, Scene i

1322

[29] King Edward being thus beset with two mischiefes [i.e., threats from Scotland and France] both at one time, thought good first to prouide remedie against the neerer danger, which by the Scots was still at hand, and therefore he meant to go against them himselfe, and to send his brother Edmund earle of Kent into Guien, to defend that countrie from the Frenchmen.

(*p. 332*)

Act IV, Scenes i, ii, and iii

1323

[30] . . . the lord Roger Mortimer of Wigmor, guing his keepers a drinke that brought them into a sound and heauie sleepe, escaped out of the tower of London where he was prisoner. This escape of the lord Mortimer greatlie troubled the king, so that immediatlie vpon the first news, he wrote to all the shiriffes of the realme, that if he chanced to come within their roomes, they should cause hue and crie to be raised, so as he might be staied and arrested, but he made such shift, that he got ouer into France, where he was receiued by a lord of Picardie . . . who had faire lands in England, and therefore the king wrote to him, reprouing him of vnthankfulnesse, con-

sidering he had beene euer readie to pleasure him, and to aduance
his profits and commodities, and yet notwithstanding he did succour
the said lord Mortimer, and other rebels that were fled out of his
realme.

(*pp. 334–335*)

Act IV, Scenes ii and iii

1326

[31] [Having been refused assistance by the French because of
Edward II's bribes, Queen Isabella] was glad to withdraw into
Heinault, by the comfort of Iohn the lord Beaumont, the earle of
Heinault his brother, who being then in the court of France, and
lamenting queene Isabels case, imagined with himselfe of some
marriage that might be had betwixt the yoong prince of Wales, and
some of the daughters of his brother the earle of Heinault, and
therevpon required hir to go into Heinault, and he would be glad to
attend hir. She gladlie consenting hereto, went thither with him,
where she was most ioifullie receiued with hir sonne, and all other of
hir traine.

The Spensers (some write) procured hir banishment out of France,
and that she was aduised by the earle of Arthois cheefelie to repaire
into Heinault. Also I find, that the Spensers deliuered fiue barrels of
siluer, the summe amounting vnto fiue thousand marks, vnto one
Arnold of Spaine a broker, appointing him to conueie it ouer into
France, to bestowe it vpon such freends as they had there of the
French kings counsell, by whose means the king of France did
banish his sister out of his relme. . . . Neuertheless, certeine it is,
that . . . sir Iohn de Heinault . . . was appointed with certeine bands
of men of arms . . . to passe ouer with the said queene and hir sonne
into England, and so therevpon began to make his purueiance for
that iournie, which thing when it came to the knowledge of king
Edward and the Spensers, they caused musters to be taken through
the realme, and ordeined beacons to be set vp, kept and watched
. . . to warne the countries adioining to assemble and resist them.

But queene Isabell and hir sonne, with such others as were with
hir in Heinault, staied not their iournie for doubt of all their aduersaries prouision, but immediatlie . . . they tooke the sea, namelie
the queene, hir sonne, Edmund of Wodstoke earle of Kent, sir Iohn
de Heinault aforesaid, and the lord Roger Mortimer of Wigmore, a
man of good experience in the warres, and diuerse others, hauing
with them a small companie of Englishmen . . . to the number of

2757 armed men, the which sailing foorth towards England, landed at length in Suffolke, at an hauen called Orwell besides Harwich, the 25 daie of September. . . .

[After Isabella and her forces had landed, Edward II abandoned his capitol and went to Wales] to raise an armie against the queene. Before his departure from London, he set foorth a proclamation, that euerie man vnder paine of forfeiting of life & goods, should resist them that were thus landed, assaile, and kill them, the queene, his sonne Edward, and his brother the earle of Kent onelie excepted; and whosoeuer could bring the head or dead corps of the lord Mortimer of Wigmore, should haue for his labour a thousand marks.

(*pp. 337–338*)

Act IV, Scene iv

1326

[**32**] At the time of the queenes landing he [i.e., King Edward] was at London, and being sore amazed with the newes, he required aid of the Londoners. They answered, that they would doo all the honour they might vnto the king, the queene, and to their sonne the lawfull heire of the land: but as for strangers & traitors to the realme, they would keepe them out of their gates, and resist them with all their forces: but to go foorth of the citie further than that they might returne before sunne-setting, they refused. . . .

The king not greatlie liking of this answer, fortified the tower, and leauing within it his yoonger son Iohn of Eltham, and the wife of the lord chamberleine Hugh Spenser the yoonger that was his neece, he [departed London to raise an army in Wales]. . . . The queenes proclamations . . . willed all men to hope for peace, the Spensers publike enimies of the realme, and the lord chancellor Robert Baldocke, with their assistants onlie excepted, through whose meanes the present trouble was happened to the realme. And . . . who so euer could bring to the queene the head of Hugh Spenser the yoonger, should haue two thousand pounds of the queenes gift.

The king at his departure from London, left maister Walter Stapleton the bishop of Excester behind him, to haue the rule of the citie of London. Then shortlie after, the queene with hir son, making towards London, wrote a letter to the maior, and the citizens, requiring to haue assistance for the putting downe of the Spensers. . . . To this letter no answer at the first was made, wherefore an other was sent. . . . This letter being directed to the maior and communaltie of London, conteining in effect, that the cause of their landing and entring into the realme at that time, was onelie for the honor of the king and wealth of the realme, meaning hurt to no maner of person, but to the Spensers, was fastened vpon the crosse in Cheape. . . . Diuerse copies of the same letter were set vp, and fastened vpon windowes and doores in other places of the citie, and one of the same copies was tacked vpon the lord maiors gates.

After which letter thus published in the citie, a great number of artificers, and other that loued not to sit in rest vpon such occasion of discord offered, . . . assembled in great numbers, & with weapon in hand came to the lord maior of the citie, whom they knew to fauour the kings part, & therefore they forced him through feare of some iniurious violence, to receiue an oth to stand to their ordinance, which was to put to death all those that were aduersaries to the queene, or had by any meanes procured the hinderance of the cities liberties, vnder pretext of which oth they ran and tooke one of the citizens, called Iohn Marshall, who bicause he was verie familiar with the earle of Glocester [i.e., Spencer Junior], and therefore suspected to haue accused the citizens, they stroke off his head, and spoiled all his goods.

On the same day, . . . continuing their rage, they ran to the house of the bishop of Excester, Walter de Stapleton, and setting fire on the gates, they entred and spoiled him of all his plate, iewels, monie and goods. And as it chanced . . . , the bishop being at the same time returning from the fields, would not seeme to shrinke . . . ; but sitting on horssebacke, [he] came to the north doore of S. Paule, where forthwith the furious people laid violent hands on him, threw him downe, and drew him most outragiouslie into Cheapeside, where they proclamed him an open traitor, a seducer of the king, and a destroier of their liberties. . . . [Having stripped him of his garments,] they shore his head from his shoulders, and to the like death they put two of his seruants. . . . The bishops head was set on a pole for a spectacle, that the remembrance of his death, and the cause thereof might continue. . . . The morrow after that they had thus beheaded the bishop of Excester, they tooke by chance sir Iohn Weston constable of the tower, and from him they tooke the keies of the same tower, and so entering the tower, they set all the prisoners at libertie, and in like case all those that were imprisoned in maner through the land were permitted to go at large, and all the banished men and outlawes were likewise restored home.

The Londoners hauing the tower thus at their commandement, remooued all the officers therein placed by the king, and put other in their roomes, in the name of the lord Iohn de Eltham the kings son, whom they named warden of the citie and land. And yet they ceassed not to commit manie robberies & other outragious & most insolent parts.

(p. 338)

Act IV, Scene v

1326

[33] Immediatlie after that the queene and hir sonne were come to land, it was woonder to see how fast the people resorted vnto them; and first of all, the earle Marshall, in whose lands she first came on shore, repaired vnto hir, so did the earle of Leicester, and diuerse barons & knights of those parts, with all the prelats in manner of the land . . . the which being ioined with the queene, made a great armie. The archbishop of Canturburie and others aided hir with monie.

(pp. 337–338)

Act IV, Scenes v and vi

1326

[34] Againe, he [i.e., Edward II] drew the rather into that part [i.e., Wales], that if there were no remedie, he might easilie escape ouer into Ireland, and get into some mounteine-countrie, marish-ground, or other streict, where his enimies should not come at him. . . .

The king with the earle of Glocester [i.e., Spencer Junior], and the lord chancellor [i.e., Baldock], taking the sea, meant to haue gone either into the Ile of Lundaie, or else into Ireland, but being tossed with contrarie winds for the space of a weeke togither, at length he landed in Glamorganshire, and got him to the abbeie and castell of Neith, there secretlie remaining vpon trust of the Welshmens promises. . . .

But now touching the king, whilest he was thus abroad, and no man wist where he was become, proclamations were made in the queenes armie dailie, in the which he was summoned to returne, and to take the rule of the relme into his hands, if he would be conformable to the minds of his true liege men; but when he appeared not, the lords of the land assembled in councell at Hereford, whither the queene was come from Bristow, and there was the lord Edward prince of Wales and duke of Aquitaine made warden of England, by common decree, vnto whome all men, as to the lord

warden of the realme, made fealtie, in receiuing an oth of allegiance
to be faithfull and loiall to him. . . .

The queene remained about a moneths space at Hereford, and in
the meane while sent the lord Henrie erle of Leicester, and the lord
William la Zouch, and one Rice ap Howell, that was latelie deliuered
out of the tower where he was prisoner, into Wales, to see if they
might find means to apprehend the king by helpe of their acquaint-
ance in those parts, all three of them hauing lands thereabouts,
where it was knowne the king for the more part kept.

(*p. 339*)

Act IV, Scene vi

1326

[35] . . . the queene accompanied with a great power . . . went
straight vnto Glocester, and sent before hir vnto Bristow the earle of
Kent, the kings brother, sir Iohn of Hennegew, with other, to
take the earle of Winchester [i.e., Spencer Senior]. They did their
endeuour with such diligence, that the townesmen, compounding to
be saued harmlesse in bodie and goods, deliuered the towne and
castell vnto the queene, & to hir sonne the prince. . . .

From Glocester she passed by Berkley, and restored the castell of
Berkley (which the earle of Glocester, Hugh Spenser the yoonger
had held) vnto the lord Thomas Berkley . . . togither with all the
appurtenances to the honor of Berkley belonging. From thence she
went to Bristow, and the morrow after hir thither comming, being
the euen of the apostles Simon and Iude, through the instant calling
vpon of the people, the earle of Winchester was drawne foorth in his
cote armor vnto the common gallows, and there hanged. His head
was after cut off, and sent to Winchester, whereof he was earle.

(*p. 339*)

Act IV, Scene vii

1326–27

[36] They [i.e., Leicester and his party] vsed such diligence in that
charge, that finallie with large gifts bestowed on the Welshmen, they
came to vnderstand where the king was, and so on the day of saint
Edmund the archbishop, being the sixteenth of Nouember, they
tooke him in the monasterie of Neith . . . togither with Hugh
Spenser the sonne called earle of Glocester, the lord chancellour
Robert de Baldocke, and Simon de Reading the kings marshall, not
caring for other the kings seruants, whome they suffered to escape.

The king was deliuered to the earle of Leicester, who conueied him by Monmouth and Leadburie, to Killingworth castle, where he remained the whole winter. The earle of Glocester, the lord chancellor, and Simon de Reading, were brought to Hereford, and there presented to the queene, where on the foure & twentith of Nouember, the said earle was drawne and hanged on a paire of gallowes of fiftie foot in heigth. Then was his head striken off, his bowels taken out of his bodie and burnt, and his bodie diuided in quarters. His head was sent to London, and set vpon the bridge with other, & his quarters were sent to foure seuerall parts of the realme, and there pight vpon poles, to be seene of the people. He was drawne in his owne cote armour, about the which there were letters embrodered plaine to be read, conteining a parcell of the 52 psalme. . . . The common fame went, that after this Hugh Spenser the sonne was taken, he would receiue no sustenance, wherefore he was the sooner put to death, or else had he beene conueied to London, there to haue suffered. Iohn earle of Arundell was taken on S. Hughs day. . . . [He and others] were put to death at Hereford, by procurement of the lord Mortimer of Wigmore . . . for what he willed the same was doone, and without him the queene in all matters did nothing.

The chancellour Robert de Baldocke being committed to the custodie of Adam de Torleton bishop of Hereford, remained at Hereford in safe keeping till Candlemasse next, and then the bishop being at London, appointed him to be brought vp, where not without the bishops consent (as was thought) he was taken out of his house by violence, and laid in Newgate, where shortlie after through inward sorow and extreame greefe of mind he ended his life.

(*pp. 339–340*)

Act V, Scene i

1326–27

[37] . . . the king in the meane while remain[ed] . . . at Killingworth, in a kind of honorable estate, although he was prisoner. After Christmasse, the queene with hir son and such lords as were then with them, remooued to London, where at their comming thither, which was before the feast of the Epiphanie, they were receiued with great ioy, triumph, and large gifts, and so brought to Westminster, where the morrow after the same feast, the parlement which before hand had beene summoned began, in which it was concluded and fullie agreed by all the states (for none durst speake to the contrarie)

that for diuerse articles which were put vp against the king, he was not worthie longer to reigne, and therefore should be deposed, and withall they willed to haue his sonne Edward duke of Aquitaine to reigne in his place. This ordinance was openlie pronounced in the great hall at Westminster by one of the lords, . . . to the which all the people consented. The archbishop of Canturburie [i.e., Walter Reynolds] taking his theame, *Vox populi, vox Dei*, made a sermon, exhorting the people to praie to God to bestow of his grace vpon the new king. And so when the sermon was ended, euerie man departed to his lodging. But the duke of Aquitaine, when he perceiued that his mother tooke the matter heauilie in appearance, for that hir husband should be thus depriued of the crowne, he protested that he would neuer take it on him, without his fathers consent, and so therevpon it was concluded, that certeine solemne messengers should go to Killingworth to mooue the king to make resignation of his crowne and title of the kingdome vnto his sonne.

There were sent on this message (as some write) three or (as other haue) two bishops, two earles, two abbats, two or . . . foure barons, and for euerie countie, citie, and burrough, and likewise for the cinque ports, certeine knights and burgesses. . . . The bishops of Winchester and Lincolne went before, and comming to Killingworth, associated with them the earle of Leicester, of some called the earle of Lancaster, that had the king in keeping. And hauing secret conference with the king, they sought to frame his mind, so as he might be contented to resigne the crowne to his sonne, bearing him in hand, that if he refused so to doo, the people in respect of the euill will which they had conceiued against him, would not faile but proceed to the election of some other that should happilie not touch him in linage. And sith this was the onlie meane to bring the land in quiet, they willed him to consider how much he was bound in conscience to take that waie that should be so beneficiall to the whole realme.

The king being sore troubled to heare such displeasant newes, was brought into a maruelous agonie: but in the end, for the quiet of the realme and doubt of further danger to himselfe, he determined to follow their aduise, and so when the other commissioners were come, and that the bishop of Hereford had declared the cause wherefore they were sent, the king in presence of them all, notwithstanding his outward countenance discouered how much it inwardlie grieued him; yet after he was come to himselfe, he answered that he knew that he was fallen into this miserie through his owne offenses, and therefore he was contented patientlie to suffer it, but yet it could not (he said) but greeue him, that he had in such wise runne into the hatred of all his people: notwithstanding he gaue the lords most heartie thanks, that they had so forgotten their receiued iniuries, and ceassed not to beare so much good will towards his sonne Edward, as to wish that he might reigne ouer them. Therefore to satisfie them, sith otherwise it might not be, he vtterlie renounced his right to the kingdome, and to the whole administration thereof. And lastlie he besought the lords now in his miserie to forgiue him such offenses as he had committed against them. Ah lamentable ruine from roialtie to miserable calamitie, procured by them cheefelie that should haue beene the pillers of the kings estate, and not the hooked engins to pull him downe from his throne! . . .

The ambassadours with this answer returning to London, declared the same vnto all the states, . . . whervpon great ioy was made of all men, to consider that they might now by course of law proceed to the choosing of a new king. And so thervpon the nine and twentith day of Ianuarie in session of parlement then at Westminster assembled, was the third king Edward, sonne to king Edward the second, chosen and elected king of England, by the authoritie of the same parlement, first . . . confirmed by his fathers resignation. . . . On the same daie sir William Trusell procurator for the whole parlement did renounce the old king in name of the whole parlement, with all homages and fealties due to him. . . .

[After] he was deposed of his kinglie honour and title, he remained for a time at Killingworth, in custodie of the earle of Leicester. But within a while the queene was informed by the bishop of Hereford, (whose hatred towards him had no end) that the erle of Leicester fauoured hir husband too much, and more than stood with the suertie of hir sonnes state, wherevpon he was appointed to the keeping of two other lords, Thomas Berkley, and Iohn Matreuers, who receiuing him of the earle of Leicester the third of Aprill, conueied him from Killingworth vnto the castell of Berkley, situate not farre off from the riuer of Seuerne, almost the midwaie betwixt Glocester and Bristow.

(*pp. 340–341*)

Act V, Scenes ii and iii

1327

[38] But forsomuch as the lord Berkley vsed him more courteouslie than his aduersaries wished him to doo, he was discharged of that

office, and sir Thomas Gourney appointed in his stead, who togither with the lord Matreuers conueied him secretlie (for feare least he should be taken from them by force) from one strong place to another . . . still remoouing with him in the night season, till at length they thought it should not be knowne whither they had conueied him. And so at length they brought him backe againe in secret maner vnto the castell of Berkley, where whilest he remained (as some write) the queene would send vnto him courteous and louing letters with apparell and other such things, but she would not once come neere to visit him, bearing him in hand that she durst not, for feare of the peoples displeasure, who hated him so extreamelie. Howbeit, she with the rest of hir confederats had (no doubt) laid the plot of their deuise for his dispatch, though by painted words she pretended a kind of remorse to him in this his distresse, & would seeme to be faultlesse in the sight of the world. . . .

But as he continued in prison, closelie kept, so that none of his freends might haue accesse vnto him, as in such cases it often happeneth, when men be in miserie, some will euer pitie their state, there were diuerse of the nobilitie (of whome the earle of Kent was cheefe) began to deuise means by secret conference had togither, how they might restore him to libertie, discommending greatlie both queene Isabell, and such other as were appointed gouernours to the yoong king, for his fathers streict imprisonment. The queene and other the gouernours vnderstanding this conspiracie of the earle of Kent, and of his brother, durst not yet in that new and greene world go about to punish it, but rather thought good to take awaie from them the occasion of accomplishing their purpose. And herevpon the queene and the bishop of Hereford wrote sharpe letters vnto his keepers, blaming them greatlie, for that they dealt so gentlie with him, and kept him no streictlier, but suffered him to haue such libertie, that he aduertised some of his freends abroad how and in what manner he was vsed. . . .

(*p. 341*)

Act V, Scene iii

1327

[39] . . . for diuerse of the former offendors [i.e., riotous inhabitants of the monastic town of Bury St. Edmunds in Suffolk], bearing grudge towards the abbat for breaking promise with them at London, did confederat themselues togither, and priuilie in the night comm-

ing to the manour of Chennington where the abbat then did lie,
burst open the gates, and entring by force, first bound all his
seruants, and after they had robbed the house, they tooke the abbat,
and shauing him, secretlie conueied him to London, and there
remoouing him from street to street vnknowne, had him ouer the
Thames into Kent, and at length transported him ouer vnto Dist
in Brabant, where they kept him for a time in much penurie,
thraldome and miserie, vntill at length the matter being vnderstood,
they were all excommunicate, first by the archbishop, & after by
the pope. At the last, his freends hauing knowledge where he was,
they found means to deliuer him out of the hands of those theeues,
and finallie brought him home with procession, and so he was
restored to his house againe.

(p. 346)

Act V, Scene iv

1327

[**40**] . . . the bishop of Hereford [i.e., Adam Orleton] vnder a sophisticall forme of words signified to them [i.e., Edward's keepers] by
his letters, that they should dispatch him out of the waie, the tenor
whereof wrapped in obscuritie ran thus:

Edwardum occidere nolite timere bonum est:
To kill Edward will not to feare it is good.

Which riddle or doubtfull kind of speech, as it might be taken in
two contrarie senses, onelie by placing the point in orthographie
called *Coma*, they construed in the worse sense, putting the *Comma*
after *Timere*. . . .

(p. 341)

Act IV, Scene iv

(1327)

[**41**] Edward the third of that name, the sonne of Edward the
second, and of Isabell the onelie daughter of Philip le Beau, & sister
to Charles the [fourth] king of France, began his reigne as king of
England, his father yet liuing, the 25 daie of Ianuarie . . . in the
yeare of our lord 1327. . . . He was crowned at Westminster on the
day of the Purification of our ladie next insuing, by the hands of
Walter [Reynolds] the archbishop of Canturburie.

And bicause he was but fourteen yeares of age, so that to gouerne

of himselfe he was not sufficient, it was decreed that twelue of the
greatest lords within the realme should haue the rule and gouernment till he came to more perfect yeares. The names of which lords
were as followeth. The archbishop of Canturburie, the archbishop of
Yorke, the bishops of Winchester and of Hereford, Henrie earle of
Lancaster, Thomas Brotherton earle marshall, Edmund of Woodstoke earle of Kent, Iohn earle of Warren, the lord Thomas Wake,
the lord Henrie Percie, the lord Oliuer de Ingham, & the lord Iohn
Ros. These were sworne of the kings councell, and charged with
the gouernement as they would make answer. But this ordinance
continued not long: for the queene, and the lord Roger Mortimer
tooke the whole rule so into their hands, that both the king and his
said councellors were gouerned onelie by them in all matters both
high and low. Neuerthelesse, although they had taken the regiment
vpon them, yet could they not foresee the tumults and vprores that
presentlie vpon the yoong kings inthronizing did insue: but needs it
must come to passe that is left written where children weare the
crowne, & beare the scepter in hand,

Vae pueri terrae saepissime sunt ibi guerrae.
[Woe to the land ruled by a child; there most often wars occur.]

(*pp.* 343)

Act V, Scene iv

1328

[42] After the quindene of saint Michaell, king Edward [III] held a
parlement at Salisburie, in which the lord Roger Mortimer was
created earle of March, the lord Iohn of Eltham the kings brother
was made earle of Cornwall, and the lord Iames Butler of Ireland
earle of Ormond. . . . But the earle of March tooke the most part of
the rule of all things perteining either to the king or realme into his
owne hands: so that the whole gouernment rested in a manner
betwixt the queene mother and him. The other of the councell that
were first appointed, were in manner displaced; for they bare no rule
to speake of at all, which caused no small grudge to arise against the
queene and the said earle of March, who mainteined such ports, and
kept among them such retinue of seruants, that their prouision was
woonderfull, which they caused to be taken vp, namelie for the
queene, at the kings price, to the sore oppression of the people,
which tooke it displesantlie inough.

(*pp.* 347–348)

Act V, Scene iv

1329–30

[43] The king [i.e., Edward III] about the beginning, or (as other saie) about the middle of Lent, held a parlement at Winchester, during the which, Edmund of Woodstoke earle of Kent the kings vncle was arrested the morrow after saint Gregories day, and being arreigned vpon certeine confessions and letters found about him, he was found giltie of treason. There were diuerse in trouble about the same matter, for the earle vpon his open confession before sundrie lords of the realme, declared that not onelie by commandement from the pope, but also by the setting on of diuerse nobles of this land (whome he named) he was persuaded to indeuour himselfe by all waies and meanes possible how to deliuer his brother king Edward the second out of prison, and to restore him to the crowne, whome one Thomas Dunhed, a frier of the order of preachers in London, affirmed for certeine to be aliue, hauing (as he himself said) called vp a spirit to vnderstand the truth thereof, and so what by counsell of the said frier, and of three other friers of the same order, he had purposed to worke some meane how to deliuer him, and to restore him againe to the kingdome. Among the letters that were found about him, disclosing a great part of his practise, some there were, which he had written and directed vnto his brother the said king Edward, as by some writers it should appeare.

The bishop of London and certeine other great personages, whome he had accused, were permitted to go at libertie, vnder suerties taken for their good demeanour and foorth comming. But Robert de Touton, and the frier that had raised the spirit for to know whether the kings father were liuing or not, were committed to prison, wherein the frier remained till he died. The earle himselfe was had out of the castell gate at Winchester, and there lost his head the 19 day of March, chiefelie (as was thought) thorough the malice of the queene mother, and of the earle of March [i.e., Mortimer]: whose pride and high presumption the said earle of Kent might not well abide. His death was the lesse lamented, bicause of the presumptuous gouernement of his seruants and retinue, which he kept about him, for that they riding abroad, would take vp things at their pleasure, not paieng nor agreeing with the partie to whome such things belonged; in so much that by their meanes, who ought to haue doone their vttermost for the inlargement of his honour, he grew in greater obloquie and reproch: a fowle fault in seruants so to abuse their lords names to their priuat profit, to whome they cannot be too trustie. But such are to be warned, that by the same wherin they offend, they shall be punished, euen with seruants faithlesse to plague their vntrustinesse. . . .

(*p. 348*)

Act V, Scene v

1327

[44] . . . and so presuming of this commandement as they tooke it from the bishop [of Hereford], they [i.e., Edward II's keepers] lodged the miserable prisoner in a chamber ouer a foule filthie dungeon, full of dead carrion, trusting so to make an end of him, with the abhominable stinch thereof: but he bearing it out stronglie, as a man of a tough nature, continued still in life, so as it seemed he was verie like to escape that danger, as he had by purging either vp or downe auoided the force of such poison as had beene ministred to him sundrie times before, of purpose so to rid him.

Wherevpon when they sawe that such practises would not serue their turne, they came suddenlie one night into the chamber where he laie in bed fast asleepe, and with heauie featherbeds or a table (as some write) being cast vpon him, they kept him down and withall put into his fundament an horne, and through the same they thrust vp into his bodie an hot spit, or (as other haue) through the pipe of a trumpet a plumbers instrument of iron made verie hot, the which passing vp into his intrailes, and being rolled to and fro, burnt the same, but so as no appearance of any wound or hurt outwardlie might be once perceiued. His crie did mooue manie within the castell and towne of Berkley to compassion, plainelie hearing him vtter a wailefull noise, as the tormentors were about to murther him, so that diuerse being awakened therewith (as they themselues confessed) praied heartilie to God to receiue his soule, when they vnderstood by his crie what the matter ment.

. . . Thus was king Edward murthered, in the yeare 1327, on the 22 of September. The fame went that by this Edward the second, after his death manie miracles were wrought. So that the like opinion of him was conceiued as before had beene of earle Thomas of Lancaster, namelie amongst the common people. He was knowne to be of a good and courteous nature, though not of most pregnant wit.

And albeit in his youth he fell into certeine light crimes, and after by the companie and counsell of euill men, was induced vnto more heinous vices, yet was it thought that he purged the same by repentance, and patientlie suffered manie reproofes, and finallie

death it selfe (as before ye haue heard) after a most cruell maner. He
had suerlie good cause to repent his former trade of liuing, for by his
vndiscreet and wanton misgouernance, there were headed and put to
death during his reigne (by iudgement of law) to the number of 28
barons and knights, ouer and beside such as were slaine in Scotland
by his infortunate conduct.

All these mischeefes and manie more happened not onlie to him,
but also to the whole state of the realme, in that he wanted iudgement and prudent discretion to make choise of sage and discreet
councellors, receiuing those into his fauour, that abused the same
to their priuate gaine and aduantage, not respecting the aduancement of the common-wealth, so they themselues might atteine to
riches and honour, for which they onelie sought, in somuch that by
their couetous rapine, spoile, and immoderate ambition, the hearts
of the common people & nobilitie were quite estranged from the
dutifull loue and obedience which they ought to haue shewed to
their souereigne, going about by force to wrest him to follow their
wils, and to seeke the destruction of them whome he commonlie
fauoured, wherein suerlie they were worthie of blame, and to tast (as
manie of them did) the deserued punishment for their disobedient
and disloiall demeanors. For it was not the waie which they tooke to
helpe the disfigured state of the common-wealth, but rather the
readie meane to ouerthrow all, as if Gods goodnesse had not beene
the greater it must needs haue come to passe, as to those that shall
well consider the pitifull tragedie of this kings time it may well
appeare.

(pp. 341–342)

Act V, Scene vi

1327

[45] The queene, the bishop [of Hereford], and others, that their
tyrannie might be hid, outlawed and banished the lord Matreuers,
and Thomas Gourney, who flieng vnto Marcels [i.e., Marseilles],
three yeares after being knowne, taken, and brought toward England
was beheaded on the sea, least he should accuse the chiefe dooers, as
the bishop and other. Iohn Matreuers, repenting himselfe, laie long
hidden in Germanie, and in the end died penitentlie.

(pp. 341–342)

Act V, Scene vi

1330

[46] Also in a parlement holden at Notingham about saint Lukes tide, sir Roger Mortimer the earle of March was apprehended the seuenteenth day of October within the castell of Notingham, where the king with the two queenes, his mother and his wife, and diuerse other were as then lodged. And though the keies of the castell were dailie and nightlie in the custodie of the said earle of March, and that his power was such, as it was doubted how he might be arrested (for he had, as some writers affirme, at that present in retinue nine score knights, besides esquiers, gentlemen and yeomen) yet at length by the kings helpe, the lord William Montacute . . . and diuerse other, which had accused the said earle of March for the murther of king Edward the second, found means by intelligence had with sir William de Eland constable of the castell of Notingham, to take the said earle of March with his sonne the lord Roger or Geffrey Mortimer, and sir Simon Bereford, with other.

. . . From Notingham he [i.e., Mortimer] was sent vp to London with his sonne . . . , sir Simon Bereford, and the other prisoners, where they were committed to prison in the tower. Shortlie after was a parlement called at Westminster, cheefelie (as was thought) for reformation of things disordered through the misgouernance of the earle of March. But whosoeuer was glad or sorie for the trouble of the said earle, suerlie the queene mother tooke it most heauilie aboue all other, as she that loued him more (as the fame went) than stood well with hir honour. For as some write, she was found to be with child by him. They kept as it were house togither, for the earle to haue his prouision the better cheape, laid his penie with hirs, so that hir takers serued him as well as they did hir both of vittels & cariages. Of which misvsage (all regard to honour and estimation neglected) euerie subiect spake shame. For their manner of dealing, tending to such euill purposes as they continuallie thought vpon, could not be secret from the eies of the people. And their offense heerein was so much the more heinous, bicause they were persons of an extraordinarie degree, and were the more narrowlie marked of the multitude or common people. . . . But now in this parlement holden at Westminster he was attainted of high treason expressed in fiue articles, as in effect followeth.

1. First, he was charged that he had procured Edward of Carnaruan the kings father to be murthered in most heinous and tyrannous maner within the castell of Berklie. . . .

These articles with other being prooued against him, he was
adiudged by authoritie of the parlement to suffer death, and according therevnto, vpon saint Andrewes eeuen next insuing, he was at
London drawne and hanged, at the common place of execution,
called in those daies The elmes, & now Tiborne, as in some bookes
we find. His bodie remained two daies and two nights on the
gallowes, and after taken downe was deliuered to the friers minors,
who buried him in their church the morrow after he was deliuered to
them, with great pompe and funerall exequies, although afterwards
he was taken vp and carried vnto Wigmore, whereof he was lord. He
came not to his answer in iudgement, no more than any other of the
nobilitie had doone, since the death of Thomas earle of Lancaster.

. . . In this parlement holden at Westminster, the king tooke into
his hand, by aduise of the states there assembled, all the possessions,
lands and reuenues that belonged to the queeene his mother, she
hauing assigned to hir a thousand pounds by yeare, for the maintenance of hir estate, being appointed to remaine in a certeine place,
and not to go elsewhere abroad: yet the king to comfort hir, would
lightlie euerie yeare once come to visit hir. After that the erle of
March was executed . . . diuerse noble men that were departed the
realme, bicause they could not abide the pride and presumption of
the said earle, now returned. . . .

(pp. 348–349)

II   FROM JOHN STOWE, THE CHRONICLES OF ENGLAND
     FROM BRUTE UNTO THIS PRESENT YEARE (1580)

Act I, Scene ii, and Act II, Scene ii

1308

[47] The King gaue vnto Pierce of *Gauston* all such giftes and Jewels
as had bin giuen to him with the Crownes of hys Father, his
ancestours treasure, and many other things, affirming that if he
could, he should succeede him in the Kyngdome, calling him brother,
not granting any thing without his consent. The Lords therefore
enuying him, told the king, that the Father of this Pierce was a
Traytour to the King of *Fraunce*, and was for the same executed, &
that his mother was burned for a Witch, and that the said Pierce was
banished for consenting to his mothers witchcraft, and that hee had
now bewitched the King himselfe. They besought the Kyng to heare
therefore their petitions, whiche shoulde be both for his owne

Honoure and for the wealth of his people. . . . [The nobles presented four petitions in all.]

Fourthly, that he would obserue the oth he made before his Father, as of the reuoking of Peter Gauaston [i.e., of not calling him home] . . . and that all that was amisse shoulde be amended. . . .

(*p. 327*)

Act V, Scenes ii and iii

1327

[48] Isabel the Queene being perswaded that the Earle of *Leicester* too muche fauoured the olde King hyr husbande, through the subtile deuise of hyr scholemaster Adam Tarleton Bishop of *Hereforde*, appointed that Thomas Gornay, and Iohn Maltrauers Knightes, hauing receyued him [i.e., Edward II] into theyr custody, shoulde carrie him about whether they would, so that none of hys well willers shoulde haue accesse vnto him, or vnderstand where he made any long abode. These brought him out by nighte from *Kenilworth*, and first he is brought to the Castell of *Corfe*, then to *Bristow*, where for a season he was kept shut vp close in the Castel, vntil suche time as it was vnderstoode of by certaine Burgesses of the same Towne, who for the deliueraunce of the said Edward, conueyed themselues ouer Sea: whose determination beeing knowne to his keepers, in a certaine darke night they conueyed him thence to *Berkeley*. These tormentours forced him to ride bareheaded: when he woulde sleepe they would not suffer hym: neyther when he was hungry would they giue him suche meate as liked him, but suche as he lothed. Euerye worde he spake was contraried by them, giuing out moste slaunderously, that he was madde. And to conclude, in all matters that they coulde imagine, they were contrarie to hys wyll, that eyther by colde or watchyng or vnholesome meates, or melancholy or other infirmitie, he myght languishe and dye. But contrariwise, thys man being of a good disposition, by nature, stoute to suffer, and patiente throughe Gods grace to abyde griefes, hee endured all the wicked deuises of hys enymies. For as touching poysons whiche were ministred to him, by the benefit of nature he dispatched them away. These Champions (as I sayd) bring the olde king towardes *Barkeley*, being guarded with a rabble of Helhoundes, along by the graunges belonging to the Castell of *Bristow*, where that wicked man Gerney making a crown of Hey, put it on hys heade, and the souldiours that were aboute him mocked him, saying, Tprut, auaunt sir King, making a kinde of noise with theyr mouthes, as though they had

farted. These doubting to meete some of hys friendes, bent theyr iourney ouer the Parish grounds, lying by the riuer of *Seuerne*. Moreouer diuising by all meanes to disfigure him that hee mighte not be knowen, they determined to shaue as well the heare off hys heade as also off his bearde, wherefore comming by a little Water whiche ranne in a ditche, they commaunded him to alighte from his horsse to be shauen: to whome being set on a Molehill, a Barbour came with a Bason of colde Water taken out of the ditch, to whom Edwarde sayd, shall I haue no warme water? the Barber answered, this wyll serue: quoth Edward, will ye or nil yee I will haue warme water: and that he might keepe his promise, he beganne to weepe and to shed teares plentifullye (as it was reported by William Byshop, to sir Thomas de la More knight).

(pp. 355–356)

III   FROM ROBERT FABYAN, THE CHRONICLE OF
FABIAN . . . CONTINUED . . . TO THENDE OF QUEEN MARY,
VOL. II (1559)

Act II, Scene ii

1314

[49] In the vii. yeare [of Edward II's reign], for to oppresse the malyce of the Scottes, the kyng assembled a greate power, & by water entred the realme of Scotland, and destroyed suche vilages & townes as lay or stode in his way. Wherof hearyng Roberte Bruce, with the power of Scotland, coasted toward the English men, and vpon the day of the Natiuite of Sayncte Ihon the Baptist, met with kyng Edward and his hoost at a place called Estryuelin, neare vnto a fresh riuer that then was called Bannockisbourne, where betwene the Englysh and the Scottes that daye, was foughten a cruell battayle. But in the ende the Englysh men were constrayned to forsake the fielde.

Than the Scottes chased so egerli the English men, that many of them were drowned in the fore named riuer, & many a noble man of England, that day was slayne in that battayle, as sir Gilbert de Clare erle of Glouceter . . . with other lordes and barons to the number . . . of xlii. and of knightes & baronettes to ye number of lxvii, ouer xxii. men of name which that day of the Scottes were taken prysoners. And the kynge hym selfe from that battayle scaped wyth great daunger, and so wyth a few of his host, that with him escaped came vnto Berwike, and there rested him a season. Than the Scottes enflamed with pryde, in derision of the Englishmen, made this rime as foloweth.

> Maydens of Englande sore may ye morne
> For your lemmans ye haue loste at Bannockysborne.
> VVyth heue a lowe.
> VVhat weneth the king of England
> So soone to haue wone Scotland,
> VVyth rumbylowe.

This songe was after manie daies songe, in daunces, in the Carols of the Maydens, and Mynstrelles of Scotlande, to the reprofe and disdayne of Englyshe men, wyth dyuers other, whiche I ouer passe. And whan kynge Edwarde, had a season taried in Barwike, and set that towne in surety, as he than might, he returned wyth small honour into England, and came secretly to Westminster, vpon the day of Saynct Magne, or the nynetene daye of August.

(sigs. ppi^v–ppii; pp. 168 [misprinted 167]–169)

IV   FROM RICHARD GRAFTON, THE CHRONICLE AT
LARGE AND MEERE HISTORY OF THE AFFAYRES OF
ENGLANDE, VOL. II (1569)

Act V, Scene vi

1330

[50] In this time the king [Edward III] helde his high Court of Parliament at London . . . duryng which tyme the king caused Sir Roger Mortymer Erle of Marche to be apprehended at Nottyngham, and brought to London. And before the Lordes and nobles were expressed and declared in wrytyng, the wickednesse and offences of the sayde Mortymer. Then the king demaunded of his counsaile what should be done with him: And all the Lords by one assent gaue iudgement and sayd, he hath deserued to die the same death that Sir Hugh Spencer the sonne dyed. And after thys iudgement there was no sparyng, respite or delaye could be graunted: but incontinent, he was drawen on a hardell thorough London, and then set on a Ladder, and hys members cut from him, and cast into the fyre, and hys heart also, because he had conspired treason, and then quartered, and his quarters sent to foure of the best Cities of the realme, and his head set vpon London Bridge. . . .

. . . he was charged and condempned for sundry articles . . .

1 First, that Sir Edwarde of Carnaruan, which was King Edward

the second, was by his meanes, by most tyrannous death murthered in the Castel of Barkeley. . . .

5 The fift, that he had impropered vnto him diuers wards, belonging vnto the king, to his great gayne, and the kinges great hurte: and that he was more secret with Queene Isabell the kings mother, then was to Gods pleasure or the kings honour.

(*p. 223*)

V FROM [THOMAS CHURCHYARD], 'HOVV THE TWO ROGERS, SURNAMED MORTIMERS, FOR THEIR SUNDRYE VYCES, ENDED THEIRE LYUES VNFORTUNATELYE . . .' (THE LAST PART OF THE MIROUR FOR MAGISTRATES, 1578)

[51] Not he that was in Edwardes dayes the third,
 Whom Fortune brought from boote to extreme bale,
 With loue of whom, the Queene so much was stird,
 As for his sake from honour she did scale,
 And whilest Fortune, blew on this pleasaunt gale,
 Heauing him high on her tirumphall Arch,
 By meane of her hee was made Earle of March.

Whence pryde out sprang, as doth appeare by manye,
 Whom soden hap, aduaunceth in excesse,
 Among thousandes, scarse shal you fynde anye,
 Which in high wealth that humor can suppresse,
 As in this earle, playne proofe did wel expresse:
 For whereas hee too loftye was before,
 His new degree hath made him now much more.

For now alone he ruleth as him lust,
 Respecting none saue only the Queene mother,
 Which moued malice to foulder out the rust,
 Which deepe in hate, before did lye and smother.
 The Peeres, the People, as wel the one as other.
 Against him made so haynous a complaint,
 That for a traytour, they did the Earle attaynt.

Than al such crimes as hidden lay before,
 They skower a fresh, and somwhat to them adde,
 For hydden hate hath eloquence in store,
 Whan Fortune biddes small faultes to make more bad,
 Fyue haynous crymes against him soone were had,
 Causing the king to yeld vnto the Scot,
 Townes that his father, but late afore had got.

And therewithall the Charter called Ragman,
Yeuen to the Scots for brybes and priuie gayne,
That by his meanes sir Edward of Carnaruan
In Berckley Castel, most cruelly was slayne:
That with his princes mother he had layne,
And last of all by pyllage at his pleasure,
Had spoyld the kyng and commons of their treasure.

For these thynges lo, which erst were out of mynde,
Dampned he was, and hanged at the last,
In whom dame Fortune fully shewed her kynde,
For whome she heaues, she hurleth downe as fast:
If men to come, would learne by other past,
My coosins fall might cause them set asyde,
High clymim [i.e., climbing], brybing, adultery and pryde.

(sigs. B2^v–B3)

Glossarial Index to the Commentary

364

where's, IV.vi.55
Whilom, IV.vii.13
Wigmore, II.ii.195
will (*vb.*), IV.vii.74
will, march who, I.i.87
wis, I, III.i.152
wise work, IV.vii.115
wished, V.i.63, V.i.70
wist, had I, II.v.83
women's favours, II.ii.186

wot, I.iv.377, II.v.58, IV.vii.27
wrack, IV.iv.9
wreak, IV.iv.22
wrought, IV.i.14

ye (*sing.*), IV.vi.63
ye (*pl.*?), I.iv.213
yet but, II.v.35
youngling, V.ii.110